A TREATISE ON BESSEL FUNCTIONS AND THEIR APPLICATIONS TO PHYSICS

MACMILLAN AND CO., Limited
LONDON · BOMBAY · CALCUTTA · MADRAS
MELBOURNE

THE MACMILLAN COMPANY
NEW YORK · BOSTON · CHICAGO
DALLAS · ATLANTA · SAN FRANCISCO

THE MACMILLAN COMPANY
OF CANADA, LIMITED
TORONTO

A TREATISE ON

BESSEL FUNCTIONS

AND

THEIR APPLICATIONS TO PHYSICS

BY

ANDREW GRAY, F.R.S.

PROFESSOR OF NATURAL PHILOSOPHY IN THE UNIVERSITY OF GLASGOW

AND

G. B. MATHEWS, F.R.S.

SOMETIME FELLOW OF ST. JOHN'S COLLEGE, CAMBRIDGE

SECOND EDITION PREPARED BY

A. GRAY

AND

T. M. MACROBERT, D.Sc.

PROFESSOR OF MATHEMATICS IN THE UNIVERSITY OF GLASGOW

"And as for the *Mixt* Mathematikes I may onely make this prediction, that there cannot faile to bee more kindes of them, as Nature growes furder disclosed."—BACON

MACMILLAN AND CO., LIMITED

ST. MARTIN'S STREET, LONDON

1931

First Edition 1895;
Second Edition 1922.
Reprinted 1931.

PRINTED IN GREAT BRITAIN

PREFACE TO THE FIRST EDITION

THIS book has been written in view of the great and growing importance of the Bessel functions in almost every branch of mathematical physics; and its principal object is to supply in a convenient form so much of the theory of the functions as is necessary for their practical application, and to illustrate their use by a selection of physical problems, worked out in some detail.

Some readers may be inclined to think that the earlier chapters contain a needless amount of tedious analysis; but it must be remembered that the properties of the Bessel functions are not without an interest of their own on purely mathematical grounds, and that they afford excellent illustrations of the more recent theory of differential equations, and of the theory of a complex variable. And even from the purely physical point of view it is impossible to say that an analytical formula is useless for practical purposes; it may be so *now*, but experience has repeatedly shown that the most abstract analysis may unexpectedly prove to be of the highest importance in mathematical physics. As a matter of fact it will be found that little, if any, of the analytical theory included in the present work has failed to be of some use or other in the later chapters; and we are so far from thinking that anything superfluous has been inserted, that we could almost wish that space would have allowed of a more extended treatment, especially in the chapters on the complex theory and on definite integrals.

With regard to that part of the book which deals with physical applications, our aim has been to avoid, on the one hand, waste of time and space in the discussion of trivialities, and, on the other, any pretension of writing an elaborate physical treatise. We have endeavoured to choose problems of real importance which naturally require the use of the Bessel functions, and to treat them in considerable detail, so as to bring out clearly the direct physical significance of the analysis employed. One result of this course has been that the chapter on diffraction is proportionately rather long; but we hope that this section may attract more general attention in this country to the valuable and interesting results contained in Lommel's memoirs, from which the substance of that chapter is mainly derived.

It is with much pleasure that we acknowledge the help and encouragement we have received while composing this treatise. We are indebted to Lord Kelvin and Professor J. J. Thomson for permission to make free use of their researches on fluid motion and electrical oscillations respectively; to Professor A. Lodge for copies of the British Association tables from which our tables IV., V., VI., have been extracted; and to the Berlin Academy of Sciences and Dr. Meissel for permission to reprint the tables of J_0 and J_1 which appeared in the *Abhandlungen* for 1888. Dr. Meissel has also very generously placed at our disposal the materials for Tables II. and III., the former in manuscript; and Professor J. McMahon has very kindly communicated to us his formulæ for the roots of $J_n(x)=0$ and other transcendental equations. Our thanks are also especially due to Mr. G. A. Gibson, M.A., for his care in reading the proof sheets. Finally we wish to acknowledge our sense of the accuracy with which the text has been set up in type by the workmen of the Cambridge University Press.

The bibliographical list must not be regarded as anything but a list of treatises and memoirs which have been consulted during the composition of this work.

PREFACE TO THE SECOND EDITION

The aims which were kept in view in the preparation of this treatise are set forth in the foregoing preface, and have been adhered to in the present edition. But while the plan of the book has not been altered, a large number of changes will be apparent to readers who are already acquainted with it. Ill-health has very unfortunately prevented Professor G. B. Mathews from continuing his collaboration, but happily the help of Dr. T. M. MacRobert, author of *Functions of a Complex Variable*, has been secured for the complete revision to which it was decided the whole work should be subjected. With his assistance the whole of the earlier and more analytical chapters have been in great part rewritten, and without it the idea of recasting these chapters, and consequently of the production of a second edition, would probably have had to be abandoned.

It is unnecessary to specify here all the changes which have been made, but attention may be directed to one or two. To each of the first seven chapters Dr. MacRobert has appended a collection of examples. These examples serve a double purpose. They provide material by which the student may test his grip of the subject and confirm his appreciation of its theorems, and also, while stating a large variety of results, and in many cases indicating how these results are obtained, they obviate the tedious analysis which would have been necessary to set them forth in the text.

Our use of the symbol K_n, in the sense explained in Chapter III., differs from that of some other writers, but has special advantages in applications, as we think will be seen from Chapters XI. and XII., and elsewhere. The K_n of Whittaker and Watson's *Modern Analysis* must be divided by $\cos n\pi$ to be reduced to our value of the symbol. It is to be remembered that this difference makes the recurrence formulae of K_n (p. 22) differ from those of I_n.

The symbol $G_n(x)$ (see p. 23) is used in this edition in the sense assigned to it in Dr. Dougall's papers. In the first edition it stood for the real part of $G_n(x)$ as now defined. This is referred to as RG_n.

The discussion of Asymptotic Expansions in Chapter V. is new, and contains what it is hoped is a more satisfactory treatment than that of the chapter on Semi-convergent Expansions in the first edition. The method of Stokes, which cannot be said to be demonstrative in the strict sense, but which has a certain illustrative force for physicists, is given later.

Sir George Greenhill has recently called attention to the importance of the function $F_n(x)$ [Chapter III.], and urged that it should be more extensively used in analysis. But the literature of Bessel Functions has become so great, and such a wealth of results is stored up in the notation now generally adopted, that, in this new edition of a book the plan of which was fixed, we have felt ourselves unable to devote more space to the F functions than that represented by the references in Chapters III., V., VII. and XVI.

To Professor Gibson we are indebted in all parts of the analytical discussion. He has read with care the whole of the proofs, and made many valuable suggestions. But the responsibility for error rests with the authors, with whom must now be associated Dr. T. M. MacRobert as stated in the title-page.

We have to thank the workmen and officials of the Glasgow University Press for the care with which they have set up the book and attended to all matters of typography.

ANDREW GRAY.

THE UNIVERSITY,
GLASGOW, *January*, 1922.

CONTENTS

CHAPTER I

INTRODUCTORY

CHAPTER II

SOLUTION OF THE DIFFERENTIAL EQUATION

CHAPTER III

OTHER BESSEL FUNCTIONS AND RELATED FUNCTIONS

CHAPTER IV

FUNCTIONS OF INTEGRAL ORDER. EXPANSIONS IN SERIES OF BESSEL FUNCTIONS

CHAPTER V

DEFINITE INTEGRAL EXPRESSIONS FOR THE BESSEL FUNCTIONS. ASYMPTOTIC EXPANSIONS

CHAPTER VI

DEFINITE INTEGRALS INVOLVING BESSEL FUNCTIONS

CHAPTER VII

THE ZEROS OF THE BESSEL FUNCTIONS

CHAPTER VIII

FOURIER-BESSEL EXPANSIONS AND INTEGRALS

CHAPTER IX

RELATIONS BETWEEN BESSEL FUNCTIONS AND LEGENDRE FUNCTIONS. GREEN'S FUNCTION

NOTE ON THE ASYMPTOTIC EXPANSIONS.

The following extensions of the theorems on asymptotic expansions in Chapter V. were arrived at too late for insertion in the text.

If z is real and positive, formula v. (30) can be written

$$K_n(z)=\sqrt{\left(\frac{\pi}{2z}\right)}\frac{1}{\Gamma(n+\frac{1}{2})}e^{-z}\int_0^\infty e^{-\zeta}\zeta^{n-\frac{1}{2}}\left(1+\frac{\zeta}{2z}\right)^{n-\frac{1}{2}}d\zeta, \tag{1}$$

$(R(n+\frac{1}{2})>0)$, where the path of integration is a straight line which makes an angle ψ with the ξ-axis, provided only that $-\pi/2<\operatorname{amp}\psi<\pi/2$. Since the functions on both sides of (1) are holomorphic for

$$\psi-\pi<\operatorname{amp}z<\psi+\pi,\ z\neq 0,$$

it follows that the equation is valid in that region.

Now expand $(1+\zeta/2z)^{n-\frac{1}{2}}$ by the binomial theorem, expressing the remainder in the form given on page 55. Equation (9) of App. I. can be written

$$\Gamma(z)=\int_0^\infty e^{-\zeta}\zeta^{z-1}\,d\zeta, \tag{2}$$

taken over the same path as the integral in (1), provided that $R(z)>0$. Hence, applying (2) to the terms of the expansion, we obtain the formula v. (50), where

$$R_s=\frac{1}{s\,!\,\Gamma(n+\frac{1}{2}-s)(2z)^s}\int_0^\infty e^{-\zeta}\zeta^{n-\frac{1}{2}+s}\,d\zeta\int_0^1 s(1-t)^{s-1}\left(1+\frac{\zeta t}{2z}\right)^{n-\frac{1}{2}-s}dt.$$

Here write $\zeta=\lambda e^{i\psi}$, so that

$$|R_s| \leqq \left|\frac{1}{s!\,\Gamma(n+\frac{1}{2}-s)(2z)^s}\right| \int_0^\infty e^{-\lambda\cos\psi}|(\lambda e^{i\psi})^{n-\frac{1}{2}+s}|\,d\lambda$$
$$\times \int_0^1 s(1-t)^{s-1}\left|\left(1+\frac{\zeta t}{2z}\right)^{n-\frac{1}{2}-s}\right| dt,$$

and as on page 56 it can be shown that $|R_s| \leqq C|z^s|^{-1}$, where C is a constant.

Accordingly the asymptotic expansion of $K_n(z)$ is valid for

$$-3\pi/2 < \operatorname{amp} z < 3\pi/2.$$

It follows that v. (52) is valid for $-\pi < \operatorname{amp} z < 2\pi$,
v. (53) for $-\pi < \operatorname{amp} z < \pi$,
v. (54) for $0 < \operatorname{amp} z < 2\pi$,
v. (55) for $-3\pi/2 < \operatorname{amp} z < \pi/2$,
and v. (56) for $-\pi/2 < \operatorname{amp} z < 3\pi/2$.

The theorems of Chapter V., § 4, are obvious corollaries of these theorems.

CHAPTER I.

INTRODUCTORY.

BESSEL Functions, like so many others, first presented themselves in connexion with physical investigations; it may be well, therefore, before entering upon a discussion of their properties, to give a brief account of the three independent problems which led to their introduction into analysis.

§ 1. **Bernoulli's Problem.** The first of these is the problem of the small oscillations of a uniform heavy flexible chain, fixed at the upper end, and free at the lower, when it is slightly disturbed, in a vertical plane, from its position of stable equilibrium. It is assumed that each element of the string may be regarded as oscillating in a horizontal straight line. Then, if m is the mass of the chain per unit of length, l the length of the chain, y the horizontal displacement, at time t, of an element of the chain whose distance from the point of suspension is x, and if T, $T+dT$ are the pulling forces at the ends of the element, we find, by resolving horizontally,

$$m\,dx\frac{d^2y}{dt^2}=\frac{d}{dx}\left(T\frac{dy}{dx}\right)dx,$$

or

$$m\frac{d^2y}{dt^2}=\frac{d}{dx}\left(T\frac{dy}{dx}\right).$$

Now, to the degree of approximation we are adopting,

$$T=mg(l-x);$$

and hence

$$\frac{d^2y}{dt^2}=g(l-x)\frac{d^2y}{dx^2}-g\frac{dy}{dx}.$$

If we write z for $(l-x)$, and consider a mode of vibration for which $y=ue^{nti}$, u being a function of z, we shall have

$$z\frac{d^2u}{dz^2}+\frac{du}{dz}+\frac{n^2}{g}u=0.$$

Let us put $\kappa^2 = n^2/g$, and assume a solution of the form

$$u = a_0 + a_1 z + a_2 z^2 + \ldots = \Sigma a_r z^r;$$

then
$$z(2a_2 + 3 \,.\, 2a_3 z + \ldots + (r+1) r a_{r+1} z^{r-1} + \ldots)$$
$$+ (a_1 + 2a_2 z + \ldots + (r+1) a_{r+1} z^r + \ldots)$$
$$+ \kappa^2 (a_0 + a_1 z + \ldots + a_r z^r + \ldots) = 0,$$

and therefore
$$a_1 + \kappa^2 a_0 = 0,$$
$$4a_2 + \kappa^2 a_1 = 0,$$
$$\ldots\ldots\ldots\ldots\ldots\ldots$$
$$(r+1)^2 a_{r+1} + \kappa^2 a_r = 0;$$

so that
$$u = a_0 \left(1 - \kappa^2 z + \frac{\kappa^4 z^2}{2^2} - \frac{\kappa^6 z^3}{2^2 \,.\, 3^2} + \frac{\kappa^8 z^4}{2^2 \,.\, 3^2 \,.\, 4^2} - \ldots\right)$$
$$= a_0 F_0(\kappa^2 z),$$
say.

The series $F_0(\kappa^2 z)$, as will be seen presently, is a special case of a Bessel function; it is absolutely convergent for all values of κ and z.

The fact that the upper end of the chain is fixed is expressed by the condition
$$F_0(\kappa^2 l) = 0,$$
which, when l is given, is a transcendental equation to find κ, or, which comes to the same thing, n. In other words, the equation $F_0(\kappa^2 l) = 0$ expresses the influence of the physical data upon the periods of the normal vibrations of the type considered. It will be shown analytically hereafter that the equation $F_0(\kappa^2 l) = 0$ has always an infinite number of real roots; so that there will be an infinite number of possible normal vibrations. This may be thought intuitively evident, on account of the perfect flexibility of the chain; but arguments of this kind, however specious, are always untrustworthy, and in fact do not prove anything at all.

This discussion of the oscillations of a uniform chain is due to Daniel Bernoulli (*Comment. Academ. Scientiarum imper. Petropol.* t. VI. 1732). In 1781 the problem was taken up by Euler (*Acta Academ. Scientiarum imp. Petropol.*), who showed that

$$y = F_0(u) = 1 - \frac{u}{1} + \frac{u^2}{2^2} - \frac{u^3}{2^2 \,.\, 3^2} + \ldots \qquad (1)$$

is a solution of the differential equation

$$u \frac{d^2 y}{du^2} + \frac{dy}{du} + y = 0.$$

This is a particular case of the equation

$$u\frac{d^2y}{du^2}+(n+1)\frac{dy}{du}+y=0, \tag{2}$$

which can easily be transformed into Bessel's equation. Sir George Greenhill, in an article recently published in the *Philosophical Magazine* (vol. XXXVIII., 1919), has claimed that there are certain advantages in employing the solutions of this equation in place of the Bessel Functions in the theory of cylindrical harmonics. [See also III. § 5.]

A function which satisfies Laplace's Equation

$$\nabla^2 V \equiv \frac{\partial^2 V}{\partial x^2}+\frac{\partial^2 V}{\partial y^2}+\frac{\partial^2 V}{\partial z^2}=0$$

is called a Harmonic Function. If the function is homogeneous in x, y, and z, it is called a Spherical Harmonic. For the definition of Cylindrical Harmonics, see § 4.

§ 2. **Fourier's Problem.** The next appearance of a Bessel Function was in 1822, in Fourier's *Théorie Analytique de la Chaleur* (Chap. VI.), in connexion with the motion of heat in a solid cylinder.

It is supposed that a circular cylinder of infinite length is heated in such a way that the temperature at any point within it depends only upon the distance of that point from the axis of the cylinder. The cylinder is then placed in a medium which is kept at zero temperature; and it is required to find the distribution of the temperature in the cylinder after the lapse of a time t.

Let v be the temperature, at time t, at a distance x from the axis: then v is a function of x and t. Take a portion of the cylinder of unit length, and consider that part of it which is bounded by cylindrical surfaces, coaxial with the given cylinder, and of radii x, $x+dx$. If K is the conductivity of the cylinder, the excess of the amount of heat which enters the part considered above that which leaves it in the interval $(t, t+dt)$ is

$$\left\{-K\frac{\partial v}{\partial x}\cdot 2\pi x+K\left(2\pi x\frac{\partial v}{\partial x}+\frac{\partial}{\partial x}\left(2\pi x\frac{\partial v}{\partial x}\right)dx\right)\right\}dt,$$

or, say,

$$dH=2\pi K\left(x\frac{\partial^2 v}{\partial x^2}+\frac{\partial v}{\partial x}\right)dx\,dt.$$

The volume of the part is $2\pi x\,dx$, so that if D is the density and C the specific heat, the rise of temperature is $dv = \frac{\partial v}{\partial t} dt$, where

$$CD \,.\, 2\pi x \, dx \frac{\partial v}{\partial t} dt = dH.$$

Hence, by comparison of the two values of dH,

$$CD \frac{\partial v}{\partial t} = K\left(\frac{\partial^2 v}{\partial x^2} + \frac{1}{x}\frac{\partial v}{\partial x}\right).$$

Fourier writes k for K/CD, and assumes $v = ue^{-nt}$, u being a function of x only; this leads to the differential equation

$$\frac{d^2u}{dx^2} + \frac{1}{x}\frac{du}{dx} + \frac{n}{k} u = 0;$$

and now, if we put $\frac{n}{k} = g$, we find that there is a solution,

$$u = A\left(1 - \frac{gx^2}{2^2} + \frac{g^2x^4}{2^2 \,.\, 4^2} - \frac{g^3x^6}{2^2 \,.\, 4^2 \,.\, 6^2} + \ldots\right) = AJ_0(\sqrt{g}x),$$

which is substantially the same function as that obtained by Bernoulli, except that we have $\frac{1}{4}gx^2$ instead of $\kappa^2 z$.

The boundary condition leads to a transcendental equation to find g; but this is not the place to consider the problem in detail.

It may be noted that, in connection with his treatment of this problem, Fourier * was led into an investigation of the zeros of the function $F_0(\theta)$.

§ 3. **Bessel's Problem.** Bessel (*Berlin Abh.*, 1824) was originally led to the discovery of the functions which bear his name by the investigation of a problem connected with elliptic motion, which may be described as follows.

Let P be a point on an ellipse, of which AA' is the major axis, S a focus, and C the centre. Draw the ordinate NPQ meeting the auxiliary circle in Q, and join CQ, SP, SQ.

Then, in the language of astronomy, the *eccentric anomaly* of P is the number of radians in the angle ACQ, or, which is the same thing, it is ϕ, where

$$\phi = \pi \,.\, \frac{\text{area of sector } ACQ}{\text{area of semicircle } AQA'}.$$

* *Théorie Analytique de la Chaleur*, VI.

It is found convenient to introduce a quantity called the *mean anomaly*, defined by the relation

$$\mu = \pi \cdot \frac{\text{area of elliptic sector } ASP}{\text{area of semi-ellipse } APA'}.$$

(By Kepler's second law of planetary motion, μ is proportional to the time of passage from A to P, supposing that S is the centre of attraction.)

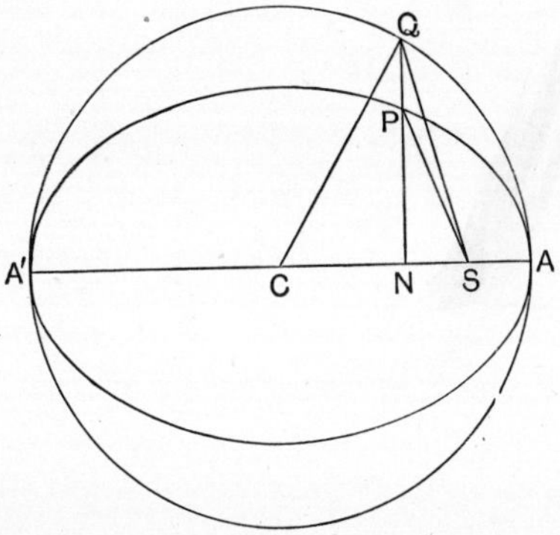

FIG. 1.

Now, by orthogonal projection,

$$\begin{aligned} \text{area of } ASP : \text{area of } APA' &= \text{area of } ASQ : \text{area of } AQA' \\ &= (ACQ - CSQ) : AQA' \\ &= (\tfrac{1}{2}a^2\phi - \tfrac{1}{2}ea^2 \sin \phi) : \tfrac{1}{2}\pi a^2 \\ &= (\phi - e \sin \phi) : \pi, \end{aligned}$$

where e is the eccentricity. Hence μ, e, ϕ are connected by the relation

$$\mu = \phi - e \sin \phi. \tag{3}$$

Moreover, if μ and ϕ vary while e remains constant, $\phi - \mu$ is a periodic function of μ, which vanishes at A and A'; that is, when μ is a multiple of π. We may therefore assume

$$\phi - \mu = \sum_1^\infty A_r \sin r\mu, \tag{4}$$

and the coefficients A_r are functions of e which have to be determined. This is the problem referred to above.

Differentiating (4) with respect to μ, we have

$$\Sigma r A_r \cos r\mu = \frac{d\phi}{d\mu} - 1,$$

and therefore, multiplying by $\cos r\mu$ and integrating,

$$\tfrac{1}{2}\pi r A_r = \int_0^\pi \left(\frac{d\phi}{d\mu} - 1\right) \cos r\mu \, d\mu$$

$$= \int_0^\pi \frac{d\phi}{d\mu} \cos r\mu \, d\mu.$$

Now $\phi = 0$ when $\mu = 0$, and $\phi = \pi$ when $\mu = \pi$; so that, by changing the independent variable from μ to ϕ, we obtain

$$\tfrac{1}{2}\pi r A_r = \int_0^\pi \cos r\mu \, d\phi$$

$$= \int_0^\pi \cos r(\phi - e \sin \phi) d\phi,$$

and

$$A_r = \frac{2}{r\pi} \int_0^\pi \cos r(\phi - e \sin \phi) d\phi, \qquad (5)$$

which is Bessel's expression for A_r as a definite integral. The function A_r can be expressed in a series of positive powers of e, and the expansion may, in fact, be obtained directly from the integral. We shall not, however, follow up the investigation here, but merely show that A_r satisfies a linear differential equation which is analogous to those of Bernoulli and Fourier.

Write x for e, and put

$$u = \frac{\pi r}{2} A_r = \int_0^\pi \cos r(\phi - x \sin \phi) \, d\phi;$$

then, after partial integration of $\frac{du}{dx}$ with respect to ϕ, we find that

$$\frac{d^2u}{dx^2} + \frac{1}{x}\frac{du}{dx} = -r^2 \int_0^\pi \cos r(\phi - x \sin \phi) \, d\phi$$

$$+ \frac{r^2}{x} \int_0^\pi \cos \phi \cos r(\phi - x \sin \phi) d\phi$$

$$= -r^2 u - \frac{r^2}{x^2} \int_0^\pi \{(1 - x \cos \phi) - 1\} \cos r(\phi - x \sin \phi) \, d\phi$$

$$= -r^2 u - \frac{r}{x^2} \Big[\sin r(\phi - x \sin \phi) \Big]_0^\pi + \frac{r^2}{x^2} u$$

$$= -\left(r^2 - \frac{r^2}{x^2}\right) u;$$

or finally,

$$\frac{d^2u}{dx^2} + \frac{1}{x}\frac{du}{dx} + r^2\left(1 - \frac{1}{x^2}\right) u = 0.$$

If we put $rx = z$, this becomes

$$\frac{d^2u}{dz^2} + \frac{1}{z}\frac{du}{dz} + \left(1 - \frac{r^2}{z^2}\right) u = 0, \qquad (6)$$

and this is what is now considered to be the standard form of Bessel's equation.

If in Fourier's equation

$$\frac{d^2u}{dx^2}+\frac{1}{x}\frac{du}{dx}+\frac{nu}{k}=0$$

we put

$$x\sqrt{\left(\frac{n}{k}\right)}=z,$$

the transformed equation is

$$\frac{d^2u}{dz^2}+\frac{1}{z}\frac{du}{dz}+u=0,$$

which is a special case of Bessel's standard form with $r=0$.

The differential equation is, for many reasons, the most convenient foundation upon which to base the theory of the functions; we shall therefore define a Bessel function to be a solution of the differential equation

$$\frac{d^2u}{dx^2}+\frac{1}{x}\frac{du}{dx}+\left(1-\frac{n^2}{x^2}\right)u=0. \tag{7}$$

§ 4. **Laplace's Equation.** One of the most natural ways in which the Bessel functions present themselves is in connection with the theory of the potential. If cylindrical coordinates ρ, ϕ, z are employed, where

$$x=\rho\cos\phi,\quad y=\rho\sin\phi,$$

then Laplace's equation $\nabla^2 V=0$, which must be satisfied by a potential function V, becomes

$$\frac{\partial^2 V}{\partial\rho^2}+\frac{1}{\rho}\frac{\partial V}{\partial\rho}+\frac{1}{\rho^2}\frac{\partial^2 V}{\partial\phi^2}+\frac{\partial^2 V}{\partial z^2}=0. \tag{8}$$

Now assume that $V=R\Phi Z$, where R, Φ, Z are respectively functions of ρ, ϕ and z alone; then if (8) be divided by $R\Phi Z/\rho^2$, it becomes

$$\frac{\rho}{R}\frac{d}{d\rho}\left(\rho\frac{dR}{d\rho}\right)+\frac{1}{\Phi}\frac{d^2\Phi}{d\phi^2}+\frac{\rho^2}{Z}\frac{d^2Z}{dz^2}=0.$$

Again, assume that $\dfrac{d^2\Phi}{d\phi^2}\Big/\Phi=-n^2$ and $\dfrac{d^2Z}{dz^2}\Big/Z=\kappa^2$; thus R satisfies

$$\rho\frac{d}{d\rho}\left(\rho\frac{dR}{d\rho}\right)+(\kappa^2\rho^2-n^2)R=0, \tag{9}$$

while $\Phi=e^{\pm in\phi}$ and $Z=e^{\pm\kappa z}$.

But if the substitution $v=\kappa\rho$ be applied to (9), it becomes

$$\frac{d^2R}{dv^2}+\frac{1}{v}\frac{dR}{dv}+\left(1-\frac{n^2}{v^2}\right)R=0, \tag{10}$$

which is Bessel's equation (7).

Accordingly, a solution of Laplace's equation is

$$V=R_n(\kappa\rho)e^{\pm in\phi}e^{\pm\kappa z}, \tag{11}$$

where $R_n(v)$ is a solution of Bessel's equation. This solution may also be put in the form

$$V=R_n(\kappa\rho)\,{\sin \atop \cos}(n\phi)e^{\pm\kappa z}. \tag{12}$$

A function of this kind is known as a Cylindrical Harmonic. If $n=0$, the Harmonic is symmetrical about the z-axis. On the Continent the solutions of Bessel's equation are called Cylinder Functions.

CHAPTER II.

SOLUTION OF THE DIFFERENTIAL EQUATION.

§1. **Solution by the Method of Frobenius.** If the operator $x\dfrac{d}{dx}$ be denoted by ϑ, Bessel's Differential Equation

$$x^2\frac{d^2y}{dx^2}+x\frac{dy}{dx}+(x^2-n^2)y=0 \qquad (1)$$

may be written

$$\vartheta^2 y+(x^2-n^2)y=0. \qquad (2)$$

In accordance with the theory of linear differential equations, two linearly independent solutions of this equation, in the form of series of ascending powers of x, can be found. To obtain these solutions put

$$\begin{aligned} y&=x^r(c_0+c_1x+c_2x^2+\dots)\\ &=\sum_{s=0}^{\infty}c_sx^{r+s}\end{aligned}$$

in the left-hand side of (2); then, since $\vartheta x^m=mx^m$,

$$\begin{aligned}\vartheta^2y+(x^2-n^2)y&=\sum_{s=0}^{\infty}\{(r+s)^2+(x^2-n^2)\}c_sx^{r+s}\\ &=\sum_{s=0}^{\infty}d_sx^{r+s}, \qquad (3)\end{aligned}$$

where

$$d_0=c_0(r^2-n^2),\quad d_1=c_1\{(r+1)^2-n^2\},$$
$$d_s=\{(r+s)^2-n^2\}c_s+c_{s-2},\quad (s=2, 3, 4, \dots).$$

If the quantities $d_0, d_1, d_2, d_3, \dots$, all vanish, the differential equation will be *formally* satisfied by this expression for y; if, moreover, the series Σc_sx^{r+s} is convergent, it will define a function which is a solution of the differential equation.

As c_0 is the coefficient of the first term in the expansion, it obviously cannot be zero; thus the equation $d_0=0$ must give

$$r^2-n^2=0.$$

This equation is called the *Indicial Equation*; from it are obtained two values $\pm n$ of the index r. If one of these values is substituted for r in $d_1=0$, $d_2=0$, $d_3=0, \ldots$, then from these equations the corresponding values of $c_1, c_2, c_3, \ldots$ can be obtained.

In general neither value of r will make $(r+1)^2-n^2$ vanish*; consequently the equation $d_1=0$ gives $c_1=0$. From the equations $d_3=0$, $d_5=0, \ldots$, it follows that the c's with odd suffixes must all be zero.

Let $r=n$; then

$$d_s=s(2n+s)c_s+c_{s-2}=0, \quad (s=2, 4, 6, \ldots).$$

Hence
$$c_2=-\frac{c_0}{2(2n+2)},$$

$$c_4=-\frac{c_2}{4(2n+4)}=\frac{c_0}{2.4.(2n+2)(2n+4)},$$

and so on. A formal solution $y=y_1$ is thus obtained, where

$$y_1 \equiv c_0 x^n\left\{1-\frac{x^2}{2(2n+2)}+\frac{x^4}{2.4(2n+2)(2n+4)}-\ldots\right\}$$

$$=c_0 \sum_{s=0}^{\infty} \frac{(-1)^s x^{n+2s}}{2.4 \ldots (2s)(2n+2)(2n+4)\ldots(2n+2s)}. \tag{4}$$

In the same way $r=-n$ gives the formal solution

$$y=y_2 \equiv c_0 x^{-n}\left\{1+\frac{x^2}{2(2n-2)}+\frac{x^4}{2.4(2n-2)(2n-4)}+\ldots\right\}, \tag{5}$$

which, as might be anticipated, only differs from y_1 by the change of n into $-n$.

If n is any real or complex quantity, not an integer, the series for y_1 and y_2 are both absolutely convergent for all values of x; each series, in fact, ultimately behaves like

$$1-\frac{x^2}{2^2}+\frac{x^4}{2^2.4^2}-\frac{x^6}{2^2.4^2.6^2}+\ldots,$$

the rapid convergence of which is obvious.

The ratio of y_1 to y_2 is not constant; hence (with the same reservation) the general solution of the differential equation is

$$y=Ay_1+By_2,$$

A and B being arbitrary constants.

* An exception occurs when $n=\frac{1}{2}$, $r=-\frac{1}{2}$; but this does not require separate discussion, since in this case the coefficients of c_0 and c_1 are the distinct solutions corresponding to $n=\frac{1}{2}$, $r=\mp\frac{1}{2}$. The only peculiarity is that $r=-\frac{1}{2}$ leads to both of these solutions.

If $n=0$, the solutions y_1 and y_2 are identical; if n is a positive integer y_2 does not exist, on account of the coefficients in the series not remaining finite. Similarly when n is a negative integer y_2 is a solution, but y_1 does not exist.

In each of these cases, therefore, it is necessary to discover a second solution; and since n appears only in the form of a square in the differential equation, it will be sufficient to suppose that n is zero or a positive integer.

Case I. In the first place let $n=0$, and assume that

$$d_1=d_2=d_3=d_4=d_5=\ldots=0;$$

then

$$c_1=c_3=c_5=c_7=\ldots=0,$$

and

$$c_{2s}=\frac{(-1)^s c_0}{(r+2)^2(r+4)^2\ldots(r+2s)^2}, \quad (s=1, 2, 3, \ldots).$$

Thus equation (3) reduces to

$$\vartheta^2 y+x^2 y=c_0 r^2 x^r, \tag{6}$$

of which

$$y=c_0 x^r\left\{1-\frac{x^2}{(r+2)^2}+\frac{x^4}{(r+2)^2(r+4)^2}-\ldots\right\} \tag{7}$$

is a solution.

If equation (6) is differentiated with regard to r, it becomes

$$\vartheta^2\left(\frac{\partial y}{\partial r}\right)+x^2\frac{\partial y}{\partial r}=c_0(2r+r^2\log x)x^r,$$

so that $\frac{\partial y}{\partial r}$ is a solution of

$$\vartheta^2 y+x^2 y=c_0 r x^r(2+r\log x). \tag{8}$$

Now, in (6) and (8), let $r=0$; then both equations reduce to

$$\vartheta^2 y+x^2 y=0, \tag{9}$$

of which two solutions are

$$y_1=(y)_{r=0}=c_0\left(1-\frac{x^2}{2^2}+\frac{x^4}{2^2\,.\,4^2}-\ldots\right) \tag{10}$$

and

$$y_2=\left(\frac{\partial y}{\partial r}\right)_{r=0}. \tag{10'}$$

When r is not a negative integer the series (7) for y can be differentiated with regard to r, and the resulting series is absolutely convergent. Since y is of the form $x^r\phi(x, r)$,

$$\frac{\partial y}{\partial r}=\phi(x, r)x^r\log x+x^r\frac{\partial}{\partial r}\phi(x, r);$$

hence

$$\frac{\partial y}{\partial r}=y\log x+c_0x^r\left\{\frac{x^2}{(r+2)^2}\frac{2}{r+2}-\frac{x^4}{(r+2)^2(r+4)^2}\left(\frac{2}{r+2}+\frac{2}{r+4}\right)+\dots\right.$$

$$\left.+\frac{(-1)^{s-1}x^{2s}}{(r+2)^2(r+4)^2\dots(r+2s)^2}\left(\frac{2}{r+2}+\frac{2}{r+4}+\dots+\frac{2}{r+2s}\right)+\dots\right\}.$$

Therefore

$$y_2=\left(\frac{\partial y}{\partial r}\right)_{r=0}=y_1\log x+c_0\left\{\frac{x^2}{2^2}\frac{1}{1}-\frac{x^4}{2^2.4^2}\left(\frac{1}{1}+\frac{1}{2}\right)+\dots\right.$$

$$\left.+\frac{(-1)^{s-1}x^{2s}}{2^2.4^2\dots(2s)^2}\left(\frac{1}{1}+\frac{1}{2}+\dots+\frac{1}{s}\right)+\dots\right\} \quad (11)$$

Thus y_1 and y_2 are independent solutions of (9).

Case II. Let n be a positive non-zero integer; assume that $c_0=c(r+n)$ and that

$$d_1=d_2=d_3=\dots=0.$$

Then equation (3) reduces to

$$\vartheta^2y+(x^2-n^2)y=c(r+n)(r^2-n^2)x^r, \quad (12)$$

of which

$$y=c(r+n)x^r\left\{1+\sum_{s=1}^{\infty}\frac{(-1)^sx^{2s}}{\left[\begin{array}{r}(r-n+2)(r-n+4)\dots(r-n+2s)\\ \times(r+n+2)\dots(r+n+2s)\end{array}\right]}\right\}$$

is a solution: this can be written

$$y=c(r+n)x^r\left\{1+\sum_{s=1}^{n-1}\frac{(-1)^sx^{2s}}{\left[\begin{array}{r}(r-n+2)(r-n+4)\dots(r-n+2s)\\ \times(r+n+2)\dots(r+n+2s)\end{array}\right]}\right\}$$

$$+c\frac{(-1)^nx^{r+2n}}{\left[\begin{array}{r}(r-n+2)(r-n+4)\dots(r+n-2)(r+n+2)\\ \times(r+n+4)\dots(r+3n)\end{array}\right]}$$

$$\times\left\{1+\sum_{s=1}^{\infty}\frac{(-1)^sx^{2s}}{\left[\begin{array}{r}(r+n+2)\dots(r+n+2s)\\ \times(r+3n+2)\dots(r+3n+2s)\end{array}\right]}\right\}.$$

If equation (12) is differentiated with regard to r, it becomes

$$\vartheta^2\left(\frac{\partial y}{\partial r}\right)+(x^2-n^2)\frac{\partial y}{\partial r}=c(r+n)\{3r-n+(r^2-n^2)\log x\}x^r. \quad (13)$$

In equations (12) and (13) put $r=-n$; then, as in *Case I.*, it is seen that

$$y_1=(y)_{r=-n}=c\frac{(-1)^nx^n}{(-2n+2)(-2n+4)\dots(-2).2.4\dots(2n)}$$

$$\times\left\{1+\sum_{s=1}^{\infty}\frac{(-1)^sx^{2s}}{2.4\dots(2s)(2n+2)(2n+4)\dots(2n+2s)}\right\} \quad (14)$$

and
$$y_2=\left(\frac{\partial y}{\partial r}\right)_{r=-n}$$
are solutions of Bessel's Equation.

Now

$$\frac{\partial y}{\partial r}=y\log x+c(r+n)x^r$$
$$\times\frac{\partial}{\partial r}\left\{1+\sum_{s=1}^{n-1}\frac{(-1)^s x^{2s}}{\left[\begin{array}{l}(r-n+2)\dots(r-n+2s)\\ \qquad\times(r+n+2)\dots(r+n+2s)\end{array}\right]}\right\}$$
$$+cx^r\left\{1+\sum_{s=1}^{n-1}\frac{(-1)^s x^{2s}}{\left[\begin{array}{l}(r-n+2)\dots(r-n+2s)\\ \qquad\times(r+n+2)\dots(r+n+2s)\end{array}\right]}\right\}$$
$$+c\frac{(-1)^n x^{r+2n}}{(r-n+2)\dots(r+n-2)(r+n+2)\dots(r+3n)}$$
$$\times\left[\sum_{p=1}^{n-1}\frac{-1}{r-n+2p}+\sum_{p=1}^{n}\frac{-1}{r+n+2p}\right.$$
$$+\sum_{s=1}^{\infty}\frac{(-1)^s x^{2s}}{(r+n+2)\dots(r+n+2s)(r+3n+2)\dots(r+3n+2s)}$$
$$\times\left\{\sum_{p=1}^{n-1}\frac{-1}{r-n+2p}+\sum_{p=1}^{n}\frac{-1}{r+n+2p}\right.$$
$$\left.\left.+\sum_{p=1}^{s}\frac{-1}{r+n+2p}+\sum_{p=1}^{s}\frac{-1}{r+3n+2p}\right\}\right].$$

Accordingly, if $r=-n$,

$$y_2=y_1\log x+cx^{-n}\left\{1+\sum_{s=1}^{n-1}\frac{x^{2s}}{2.4\dots(2s)(2n-2)(2n-4)\dots(2n-2s)}\right\}$$
$$+\frac{c}{2}\frac{x^n}{2.4\dots(2n).2.4\dots(2n-2)}$$
$$\times\left[\frac{1}{n}+\sum_{s=1}^{\infty}\frac{(-1)^s x^{2s}}{2.4\dots(2s)(2n+2)(2n+4)\dots(2n+2s)}\right.$$
$$\left.\times\left\{\sum_{p=1}^{s}\frac{1}{p}+\sum_{p=0}^{s}\frac{1}{n+p}\right\}\right]. \qquad (15)$$

The characteristic properties of the integral y_2 are that it is the sum of $y_1\log x$ and a convergent series, proceeding by ascending powers of x, in which only a limited number of negative powers of x occur. It tends to infinity as x tends to zero after the manner of x^{-n}; for any other value of x it is finite, but not uniform, on account of the logarithm which it involves.

The general solution of the differential equation is

$$Ay_1+By_2,$$

A and B being arbitrary constants.

§ 2. **Definition of the Bessel Function $J_n(x)$.** It is found convenient, when n is a positive integer, to give to the constant c_0 in equation (4) the value $1/(2^n . n!)$; y_1 is then denoted by $J_n(x)$, so that

$$J_n(x)=\frac{x^n}{2^n . n!}\left\{1-\frac{x^2}{2(2n+2)}+\frac{x^4}{2 . 4(2n+2)(2n+4)}-\dots\right\}.$$

In order to extend the definition to the case in which n is not a positive integer, Gauss's function $\Pi(n)$ * is employed instead of $n!$, with which it is identical when n is a positive integer; then

$$J_n(x)=\frac{x^n}{2^n\Pi(n)}\left\{1-\frac{x^2}{2(2n+2)}+\frac{x^4}{2 . 4(2n+2)(2n+4)}-\dots\right\}$$
$$=\sum_{s=0}^{\infty}\frac{(-1)^s}{\Pi(s)\Pi(n+s)}\left(\frac{x}{2}\right)^{n+2s}. \qquad (16)$$

$J_n(x)$ is known as the *Bessel Function of the first kind of order* n: it is a solution of Bessel's Equation for all values of n which are not negative integers. Accordingly, if n is not an integer, $J_n(x)$ and $J_{-n}(x)$ are two linearly independent solutions of the equation. If n is zero, these two solutions are identical. If n is a positive integer,

$$J_{-n}(x)=\sum_{s=0}^{\infty}\frac{(-1)^s}{\Pi(s)\Pi(-n+s)}\left(\frac{x}{2}\right)^{-n+2s}.$$

Now the factor $1/\Pi(-n+s)$ is zero for $s=0, 1, 2, \dots, (n-1)$, and is finite for all the other values of s. Hence

$$J_{-n}(x)=\sum_{s=0}^{\infty}\frac{(-1)^{n+s}}{\Pi(n+s)\Pi(s)}\left(\frac{x}{2}\right)^{n+2s}$$
$$=(-1)^nJ_n(x). \qquad (17)$$

Thus $J_{-n}(x)$ is always a solution of Bessel's Equation, but when n is an integer it is merely a constant multiple of $J_n(x)$.

§ 3. **Definition of Neumann's Bessel Function $Y_n(x)$.**† When n is a positive integer, let the arbitrary constant c in equations (14) and (15) have the value $-2^{n-1}(n-1)!$; then $y_1=J_n(x)$, and

$$y_2=J_n(x)\log x-\frac{1}{2}\sum_{s=0}^{n-1}\frac{(n-s-1)!}{s!}\left(\frac{x}{2}\right)^{-n+2s}$$
$$-\frac{1}{2}\left[\frac{1}{n!}\left(\frac{x}{2}\right)^n\frac{1}{n}+\sum_{s=1}^{\infty}\frac{(-1)^s}{s!(n+s)!}\left(\frac{x}{2}\right)^{n+2s}\left\{\sum_{p=1}^{s}\frac{1}{p}+\sum_{p=0}^{s}\frac{1}{n+p}\right\}\right].$$

* Cf. App. I.

† Karl Neumann, *Theorie der Bessel'schen Funktionen* (Leipzig, 1867), p. 41.

Now from y_2 subtract the function $\frac{1}{2}\left(\frac{1}{1}+\frac{1}{2}+\ldots+\frac{1}{n-1}\right)J_n(x)$; then the difference, which is also an integral of the equation, is denoted by $Y_n(x)$. Thus

$$Y_n(x)=J_n(x)\log x-\frac{1}{2}\sum_{s=0}^{n-1}\frac{(n-s-1)!}{s!}\left(\frac{x}{2}\right)^{-n+2s}$$

$$-\frac{1}{2}\sum_{s=0}^{\infty}\frac{(-1)^s}{s!(n+s)!}\left(\frac{x}{2}\right)^{n+2s}\{\phi(s)+\phi(n+s)\}, \qquad (18)$$

where $\phi(p)=\frac{1}{1}+\frac{1}{2}+\ldots+\frac{1}{p}$, $(p=1, 2, 3, \ldots)$, and $\phi(0)=0$.

$Y_n(x)$ is called *Neumann's Bessel Function of the second kind of order n*. In particular, the Neumann's Bessel Function of the second kind of order zero is

$$Y_0(x)=J_0(x)\log x+\frac{x^2}{2^2}-\frac{x^4}{2^2.4^2}\left(1+\frac{1}{2}\right)+\frac{x^6}{2^2.4^2.6^2}\left(1+\frac{1}{2}+\frac{1}{3}\right)-\ldots .(19)$$

§ 4. **Recurrence Formulae for $J_n(x)$.** When the argument x remains the same throughout, we may write J_n instead of $J_n(x)$, and indicate differentiation with respect to x by accents; thus J'_n will denote $\frac{d}{dx}J_n(x)$, and so on.

By differentiating equation (16) it is found that

$$xJ'_n=\sum_{s=0}^{\infty}\frac{(-1)^s(n+2s)}{\Pi(s)\,\Pi(n+s)}\left(\frac{x}{2}\right)^{n+2s}$$

$$=nJ_n+x\sum_{s=1}^{\infty}\frac{(-1)^s}{\Pi(s-1)\,\Pi(n+s)}\left(\frac{x}{2}\right)^{n+2s-1}.$$

Now, in the summation, put $s=r+1$; then

$$xJ'_n=nJ_n-x\sum_{r=0}^{\infty}\frac{(-1)^r}{\Pi(r)\,\Pi(n+1+r)}\left(\frac{x}{2}\right)^{n+1+2r}$$

$$=nJ_n-xJ_{n+1}. \qquad (20)$$

Again, $$xJ'_n+nJ_n=\sum_{s=0}^{\infty}\frac{(-1)^s(2n+2s)}{\Pi(s)\,\Pi(n+s)}\left(\frac{x}{2}\right)^{n+2s}$$

$$=x\sum_{s=0}^{\infty}\frac{(-1)^s}{\Pi(s)\,\Pi(n-1+s)}\left(\frac{x}{2}\right)^{n-1+2s}$$

$$=xJ_{n-1}.$$

Therefore $$xJ'_n=-nJ_n+xJ_{n-1}. \qquad (21)$$

Let (20) and (21) be added; then

$$2J'_n = J_{n-1} - J_{n+1}. \qquad (22)$$

From (22) and (17) it follows that

$$J'_0 = -J_1. \qquad (23)$$

If (20) be multiplied by x^{-n-1}, it can be written

$$\frac{d}{dx}(x^{-n}J_n) = -x^{-n}J_{n+1}. \qquad (24)$$

Similarly, if (21) be multiplied by x^{n-1}, it reduces to

$$\frac{d}{dx}(x^n J_n) = x^n J_{n-1}. \qquad (25)$$

Again, subtract (21) from (20), and obtain

$$\frac{2n}{x} J_n = J_{n-1} + J_{n+1}. \qquad (26)$$

Formulae (20) to (26) are very important, and are continually required in applications.

Differentiation of (22) gives

$$\begin{aligned} 4J''_n &= 2J'_{n-1} - 2J'_{n+1} \\ &= (J_{n-2} - J_n) - (J_n - J_{n+2}) \\ &= J_{n-2} - 2J_n + J_{n+2}, \end{aligned}$$

and it may be proved by induction that

$$2^s J_n^{(s)} = J_{n-s} - sJ_{n-s+2} + \frac{s(s-1)}{2!} J_{n-s+4} - \ldots + (-1)^s J_{n+s}, \qquad (27)$$

the coefficients being those of the binomial theorem for the exponent s.

The corresponding formulae for Y_n can also be established in this way, but the process is rather tedious; a shorter method of obtaining them will be indicated in Chapter III.

§ 5. Expressions for $J_n(x)$ when n is half an odd integer. From the expression (16) for $J_n(x)$ it follows that

$$\begin{aligned} J_{-\frac{1}{2}} &= \frac{x^{-\frac{1}{2}}}{2^{-\frac{1}{2}}\Pi(-\frac{1}{2})} \left\{1 - \frac{x^2}{2.1} + \frac{x^4}{2.4.1.3} - \ldots\right\} \\ &= \sqrt{\left(\frac{2}{\pi x}\right)} \cos x, \end{aligned}$$

and

$$\begin{aligned} J_{\frac{1}{2}} &= \frac{x^{\frac{1}{2}}}{2^{\frac{1}{2}}\Pi(\frac{1}{2})} \left\{1 - \frac{x^2}{2.3} + \frac{x^4}{2.4.3.5} - \ldots\right\} \\ &= \sqrt{\left(\frac{2x}{\pi}\right)} \frac{\sin x}{x} = \sqrt{\left(\frac{2}{\pi x}\right)} \sin x. \end{aligned}$$

Hence, and by means of (26), the expression for $J_{k+\frac{1}{2}}$, where k is any positive or negative integer, may be calculated. The functions thus obtained are of importance in certain physical applications, so that the following short table may be useful:

$2n$	$J_n \times \sqrt{\frac{1}{2}\pi x}$
1	$\sin x$
3	$\frac{\sin x}{x} - \cos x$
5	$\left(\frac{3}{x^2}-1\right)\sin x - \frac{3}{x}\cos x$
7	$\left(\frac{15}{x^3}-\frac{6}{x}\right)\sin x - \left(\frac{15}{x^2}-1\right)\cos x$
9	$\left(\frac{105}{x^4}-\frac{45}{x^2}+1\right)\sin x - \left(\frac{105}{x^3}-\frac{10}{x}\right)\cos x$
11	$\left(\frac{945}{x^5}-\frac{420}{x^3}+\frac{15}{x}\right)\sin x - \left(\frac{945}{x^4}-\frac{105}{x^2}+1\right)\cos x$
-1	$\cos x$
-3	$-\sin x - \frac{\cos x}{x}$
-5	$\frac{3}{x}\sin x + \left(\frac{3}{x^2}-1\right)\cos x$
-7	$-\left(\frac{15}{x^2}-1\right)\sin x - \left(\frac{15}{x^3}-\frac{6}{x}\right)\cos x$
-9	$\left(\frac{105}{x^3}-\frac{10}{x}\right)\sin x + \left(\frac{105}{x^4}-\frac{45}{x^2}+1\right)\cos x$
-11	$-\left(\frac{945}{x^4}-\frac{105}{x^2}+1\right)\sin x - \left(\frac{945}{x^5}-\frac{420}{x^3}+\frac{15}{x}\right)\cos x$

EXAMPLES.

1. Prove that

$$x^2 J_n'' = (n^2 - n - x^2) J_n + x J_{n+1}.$$

2. Show that

(i) $J_2 - J_0 = 2J_0''$; (ii) $J_2 = J_0'' - x^{-1} J_0'$; (iii) $J_3 + 3J_0' + 4J_0''' = 0$.

3. Establish the expansions:

(i) $\frac{x}{2} J_{n-1} = nJ_n - (n+2)J_{n+2} + (n+4)J_{n+4} - \dots$;

(ii) $\frac{x}{2} J_n' = \frac{n}{2} J_n - (n+2)J_{n+2} + (n+4)J_{n+4} - \dots$.

4. Verify that $x^{\frac{1}{2}} J_1(2\sqrt{x})$ and $x^{\frac{1}{2}} Y_1(2\sqrt{x})$ are solutions of

$$xy'' + y = 0.$$

5. Show that the general solution of

$$x^2 y'' - 2xy' + 4(x^4 - 1)y = 0$$

is

$$A x^{\frac{3}{2}} J_{\frac{5}{4}}(x^2) + B x^{\frac{3}{2}} J_{-\frac{5}{4}}(x^2).$$

6. Show that every solution of

$$xy'' + \tfrac{1}{2} y' + \tfrac{1}{4} y = 0$$

can be put in the form

$$A x^{\frac{1}{4}} J_{-\frac{1}{2}}(\sqrt{x}) + B x^{\frac{1}{4}} J_{\frac{1}{2}}(\sqrt{x}).$$

7. Show that, if n is an odd positive integer,

$$\frac{x}{2}\{J_n + (-1)^{\frac{n-3}{2}} J_1\} = \sum_{r=1}^{\frac{n-1}{2}} (-1)^{r-1}(n - 2r + 1) J_{n-2r+1}.$$

8. Prove that

(i) $$J_m J_n = \sum_{s=0}^{\infty} \frac{(-1)^s}{\Pi(m+s)\Pi(n+s)} \frac{\Pi(m+n+2s)}{\Pi(s)\Pi(m+n+s)} \left(\frac{x}{2}\right)^{m+n+2s};$$

(ii) $$J_n(x)\cos x = \frac{(2x)^n}{\sqrt{\pi}} \sum_{s=0}^{\infty} \frac{(-1)^s \Pi(n + 2s - \frac{1}{2})}{(2s)!\, \Pi(2n + 2s)} (2x)^{2s};$$

(iii) $$J_n(x)\sin x = \frac{(2x)^n}{\sqrt{\pi}} \sum_{s=0}^{\infty} \frac{(-1)^s \Pi(n + 2s + \frac{1}{2})}{(2s+1)!\, \Pi(2n + 2s + 1)} (2x)^{2s+1}.$$

9. Prove by induction that, if k be an integer and $n = k + \frac{1}{2}$, then

$$J_n(x) = \left(\frac{2}{\pi x}\right)^{\frac{1}{2}} \{\cos(x - \tfrac{1}{2}n\pi - \tfrac{1}{4}\pi) U_n(x) + \sin(x - \tfrac{1}{2}n\pi - \tfrac{1}{4}\pi) V_n(x)\},$$

where $$U_n(x) = 1 + \sum_{s=1} \frac{(-1)^s (4n^2 - 1^2)(4n^2 - 3^2) \dots \{4n^2 - (4s-1)^2\}}{(2s)!\, 2^{6s} x^{2s}}$$

and $$V_n(x) = \sum_{s=1} \frac{(-1)^s (4n^2 - 1^2)(4n^2 - 3^2) \dots \{4n^2 - (4s-3)^2\}}{(2s-1)!\, 2^{6s-3} x^{2s-1}},$$

the summations being continued as far as the terms with the vanishing factors in the numerators.

10. If $R(n) > -1$, show that

$$\text{(i)} \int_0^x x^{n+1} J_n(x)\,dx = x^{n+1} J_{n+1}(x) ;$$

$$\text{(ii)} \int_0^x x^{-n} J_{n+1}(x)\,dx = \frac{1}{2^n \Pi(n)} - x^{-n} J_n(x).$$

11. Show that $$AJ_n(x)\int^x \frac{dx}{xJ_n^2(x)} + BJ_n(x)$$

is the complete solution of Bessel's Equation.

12. Show that, if $R(n) > -1$,

$$\int_0^x x\{J_n(x)\}^2 dx = \tfrac{1}{2}x^2\{J_n^2 + J_{n+1}^2\} - nxJ_n J_{n+1}.$$

[Multiply Bessel's equation by $J_n'(x)$ and integrate.]

CHAPTER III.

OTHER BESSEL FUNCTIONS AND RELATED FUNCTIONS.

§1. **The Function $I_n(t)$.** The substitution $x = it$, where $i = \surd(-1)$, transforms Bessel's Equation into

$$t^2 \frac{d^2y}{dt^2} + t\frac{dy}{dt} - (n^2 + t^2)y = 0. \tag{1}$$

One solution of this equation is

$$J_n(it) = i^n \frac{t^n}{2^n \Pi(n)} \left\{1 + \frac{t^2}{2(2n+2)} + \frac{t^4}{2.4(2n+2)(2n+4)} + \dots\right\};$$

it is usual, however, to take instead of this the function

$$I_n(t) = i^{-n} J_n(it) = \sum_{s=0}^{\infty} \frac{1}{\Pi(s)\Pi(n+s)} \left(\frac{t}{2}\right)^{n+2s}, \tag{2}$$

which is known as the *modified Bessel Function of the first kind.* If n is a positive integer, it follows from II. (17) that

$$\begin{aligned} I_{-n}(t) = i^n J_{-n}(it) &= i^n \times (-1)^n J_n(it) \\ &= i^{-n} J_n(it) \\ &= I_n(t). \end{aligned} \tag{3}$$

Similarly it can be deduced from equations (20) to (27) of Chapter II. that

$$tI'_n = nI_n + tI_{n+1}, \tag{4}$$

$$tI'_n = -nI_n + tI_{n-1}, \tag{5}$$

$$2I'_n = I_{n-1} + I_{n+1}, \tag{6}$$

$$I'_0 = I_1, \tag{7}$$

$$\frac{d}{dt}(t^{-n} I_n) = t^{-n} I_{n+1}, \tag{8}$$

$$\frac{d}{dt}(t^n I_n) = t^n I_{n-1}, \tag{9}$$

$$\frac{2n}{t} I_n = I_{n-1} - I_{n+1}, \tag{10}$$

$$2^s \frac{d^s}{dt^s} I_n = I_{n-s} + sI_{n-s+2} + \frac{s(s-1)}{2!} I_{n-s+4} + \dots + I_{n+s}. \tag{11}$$

§ 2. **The Function $K_n(t)$.** If n is not an integer, $I_{-n}(t)$ is an independent solution of (1), while, if n is an integer, a second solution is $Y_n(it)$. It is found more useful, however, to take as the second solution the function $K_n(t)$ defined by the equation

$$K_n(t)=\frac{\pi}{2\sin n\pi}\{I_{-n}(t)-I_n(t)\}, \tag{12}$$

when n is not an integer. This function, which is a solution of the differential equation, is known as the *modified Bessel Function of the second kind.* It possesses the property, useful in certain physical applications, of having a zero at infinity on the positive real axis. A proof of this will be given in Chapter V.

When n tends to any integral value, the numerator and denominator of the right-hand side of (12) both tend to zero. The function $K_n(t)$ is then defined as the limit of the ratio. Now, from (2),

$$\frac{\partial}{\partial n}I_n(t)=I_n(t)\log\left(\frac{t}{2}\right)-\prod_{s=0}^{\infty}\frac{1}{\Pi(s)\Pi(n+s)}\left(\frac{t}{2}\right)^{n+2s}\psi(n+s),$$

where $\psi(x)=\dfrac{d}{dx}\log\Pi(x)$, (cf. App. I.).

Again, since $\Pi(-n+s)\Pi(n-s-1)=\pi/\sin(n-s)\pi$,

$$I_{-n}(t)=\sum_{s=0}^{p-1}\frac{1}{\Pi(s)}\left(\frac{t}{2}\right)^{-n+2s}\Pi(n-s-1)\frac{\sin(n-s)\pi}{\pi}$$
$$+\sum_{s=p}^{\infty}\frac{1}{\Pi(s)\Pi(-n+s)}\left(\frac{t}{2}\right)^{-n+2s},$$

so that

$$\frac{\partial}{\partial n}I_{-n}(t)=-I_{-n}(t)\log\left(\frac{t}{2}\right)$$
$$+\sum_{s=0}^{p-1}\left(\frac{t}{2}\right)^{-n+2s}\frac{\Pi'(n-s-1)\sin(n-s)\pi+\Pi(n-s-1)\pi\cos(n-s)\pi}{\pi\,.\,\Pi(s)}$$
$$+\sum_{s=p}^{\infty}\frac{1}{\Pi(s)\Pi(-n+s)}\left(\frac{t}{2}\right)^{-n+2s}\psi(-n+s).$$

Now let n be a positive integer, and take $p=n$; then

$$\frac{\partial}{\partial n}I_{-n}(t)=-I_{-n}(t)\log\left(\frac{t}{2}\right)+(-1)^n\sum_{s=0}^{n-1}\frac{(-1)^s\Pi(n-s-1)}{\Pi(s)}\left(\frac{t}{2}\right)^{-n+2s}$$
$$+\sum_{s=0}^{\infty}\frac{1}{\Pi(n+s)\Pi(s)}\psi(s)\left(\frac{t}{2}\right)^{n+2s}.$$

Accordingly, if n is a positive integer,

$$K_n(t)=\frac{\frac{\partial}{\partial n}\{I_{-n}(t)-I_n(t)\}}{2\cos n\pi}$$

$$=(-1)^{n+1}I_n(t)\log\left(\frac{t}{2}\right)+\frac{1}{2}\sum_{s=0}^{n-1}\frac{(-1)^s(n-s-1)!}{s!}\left(\frac{t}{2}\right)^{-n+2s}$$

$$+(-1)^n\frac{1}{2}\sum_{s=1}^{\infty}\frac{1}{s!(n+s)!}\left(\frac{t}{2}\right)^{n+2s}\{\psi(s)+\psi(n+s)\}. \quad (13)$$

In particular, since, when r is a positive integer,

$$\psi(r)=\phi(r)-\gamma,$$

where $\phi(r)=1+\frac{1}{2}+\frac{1}{3}+\ldots+\frac{1}{r}$, (cf. App. I.),

$$K_0(t)=-I_0(t)\left\{\log\left(\frac{t}{2}\right)+\gamma\right\}+\sum_{s=1}^{\infty}\frac{1}{(s!)^2}\left(\frac{t}{2}\right)^{2s}\phi(s). \quad (14)$$

An obvious deduction from (12) is the formula

$$K_{-n}=K_n. \quad (15)$$

If $-n$ be substituted for n in (5), it becomes

$$tI'_{-n}=nI_{-n}+tI_{-n-1};$$

from this equation subtract (4), and multiply by $\pi/(2\sin n\pi)$; then

$$tK'_n=nK_n-tK_{n+1}. \quad (16)$$

Here write $-n$ for n, and apply (15); thus

$$tK'_n=-nK_n-tK_{n-1}. \quad (17)$$

From (16) and (17) it follows that

$$2K'_n=-(K_{n+1}+K_{n-1}), \quad (18)$$

$$K'_0=-K_1, \quad (19)$$

$$\frac{d}{dt}(t^{-n}K_n)=-t^{-n}K_{n+1}, \quad (20)$$

$$\frac{d}{dt}(t^nK_n)=-t^nK_{n-1}, \quad (21)$$

$$\frac{2n}{t}K_n=K_{n+1}-K_{n-1}, \quad (22)$$

$$(-2)^s\frac{d^s}{dt^s}K_n=K_{n-s}+sK_{n-s+2}+\frac{s(s-1)}{2!}K_{n-s+4}+\ldots+K_{n+s}. \quad (23)$$

§ 3. **The Bessel Function** $G_n(x)$*. This function is defined by means of the equations

$$G_n(x)=e^{-\frac{in\pi}{2}}K_n(e^{-\frac{i\pi}{2}}x) \tag{24}$$

$$=\frac{\pi}{2\sin n\pi}\{J_{-n}(x)-e^{-in\pi}J_n(x)\}. \tag{25}$$

It satisfies Bessel's Equation, and is therefore a Bessel Function. When n is an integer, it can be shown directly, as in § 2, or deduced from (13), that

$$G_n(x)=-Y_n(x)+J_n(x)\left\{\log 2-\gamma+\frac{i\pi}{2}\right\} \tag{26}$$

$$=J_n(x)\left\{-\log\frac{x}{2}-\gamma+\frac{i\pi}{2}\right\}$$
$$+\frac{1}{2}\sum_{s=0}^{n-1}\frac{(n-s-1)!}{s!}\left(\frac{x}{2}\right)^{-n+2s}$$
$$+\frac{1}{2}\sum_{s=0}^{\infty}\frac{(-1)^s}{s!(n+s)!}\left(\frac{x}{2}\right)^{n+2s}\{\phi(s)+\phi(n+s)\}. \tag{26'}$$

The value of $\log 2-\gamma$ is, to twenty-two decimal places,

$$\log 2-\gamma = \cdot 11593\ 15156\ 58412\ 44881\ 07. \tag{27}$$

In (24) let $x=it$; then

$$K_n(t)=e^{\frac{in\pi}{2}}G_n(it). \tag{28}$$

Thus $G_n(x)$ has a zero at infinity on the positive imaginary axis. [See § 2.]

The following formulae (29)-(37) can be deduced from (15)-(23) by means of (24).

$$G_{-n}=e^{in\pi}G_n. \tag{29}$$

$$xG'_n=nG_n-xG_{n+1}. \tag{30}$$

$$xG'_n=-nG_n+xG_{n-1}. \tag{31}$$

$$2G'_n=G_{n-1}-G_{n+1}. \tag{32}$$

$$G'_0=-G_1. \tag{33}$$

$$\frac{d}{dx}(x^{-n}G_n)=-x^{-n}G_{n+1}. \tag{34}$$

$$\frac{d}{dx}(x^nG_n)=x^nG_{n-1}. \tag{35}$$

$$\frac{2n}{x}G_n=G_{n-1}+G_{n+1}. \tag{36}$$

$$2^s\frac{d^s}{dx^s}G_n=G_{n-s}-sG_{n-s+2}+\frac{s(s-1)}{2!}G_{n-s+4}-\ldots+(-1)^sG_{n+s}. \tag{37}$$

* Cf. Dr. J. Dougall, *Proc. Edin. Math. Soc.*, vol. XVIII.

The reader should note that formulae (30)-(37) for G_n are identical with (20)-(27) of Chapter II. for J_n; and indeed, with the aid of (25), the former set could be deduced from the latter.

Recurrence Formulae for $Y_n(x)$. Since $J_n(x)$ and $G_n(x)$ both satisfy the same recurrence formulae, it follows from (26) that $Y_n(x)$ also satisfies formulae (30)-(37).

Hankel's Bessel Function of the second kind. Hankel* took $Y_n(x)$ to denote a function which may, for convenience, be written $\overline{Y}_n(x)$, and which is defined [as in § 2] for all values of n by the formula

$$\overline{Y}_n = \frac{2\pi}{\sin 2n\pi} e^{in\pi} (J_n \cos n\pi - J_{-n}). \tag{38}$$

It can easily be verified that

$$\overline{Y}_n = \frac{2}{\cos n\pi} e^{in\pi} \left(-G_n + \frac{i\pi}{2} J_n \right). \tag{39}$$

Hence, if n is a positive integer,

$$\overline{Y}_n = 2\{Y_n - J_n (\log 2 - \gamma)\}. \tag{40}$$

As in the case of Y_n, it follows from (39) that $\overline{Y}_n$ satisfies the recurrence formulae (30)-(37).

§ 4. **Theorem.** *If $P(x)$ and $Q(x)$ are any solutions of Bessel's Equation, they satisfy a relation of the form*

$$P(x)\,Q'(x) - P'(x)\,Q(x) = C/x, \tag{41}$$

where C is a constant.

For, since P and Q satisfy Bessel's Equation,

$$\frac{d}{dx}(xP') = (n^2 - x^2)\frac{P}{x},$$

$$\frac{d}{dx}(xQ') = (n^2 - x^2)\frac{Q}{x},$$

Now multiply these equations by Q and P respectively, and subtract the first from the second; then

$$P\frac{d}{dx}(xQ') - Q\frac{d}{dx}(xP') = 0,$$

or

$$\frac{d}{dx}\{x(PQ' - P'Q)\} = 0.$$

Thus

$$x(PQ' - P'Q) = C,$$

so that

$$PQ' - P'Q = C/x.$$

* *Math. Ann.* I.

In particular, let J_n and J_{-n} be the two functions; then

$$\lim_{x\to 0} x\{J_n(x)\,J'_{-n}(x)-J'_n(x)\,J_{-n}(x)\}$$

$$=\frac{1}{\Pi(n)}\times\frac{-n}{\Pi(-n)}-\frac{n}{\Pi(n)}\times\frac{1}{\Pi(-n)}$$

$$=\frac{2}{\Pi(n)\,\Pi(-n-1)}=-2\frac{\sin n\pi}{\pi}.$$

Hence $$J_n(x)\,J'_{-n}(x)-J'_n(x)\,J_{-n}(x)=-2\frac{\sin n\pi}{\pi x}. \tag{42}$$

The reader can easily deduce that:

$$J_n\,J_{-n+1}+J_{-n}\,J_{n-1}=2\,\frac{\sin n\pi}{\pi x}, \tag{43}$$

$$-J_n\,J_{-n-1}-J_{-n}\,J_{n+1}=2\,\frac{\sin n\pi}{\pi x}, \tag{44}$$

$$G_n\,J'_n-G'_n\,J_n=\frac{1}{x}, \tag{45}$$

$$G_{n+1}\,J_n-G_n\,J_{n+1}=\frac{1}{x}, \tag{46}$$

$$J_n\,Y'_n-J'_n\,Y_n=\frac{1}{x}, \tag{47}$$

$$J_{n+1}\,Y_n-J_n\,Y_{n+1}=\frac{1}{x}, \tag{48}$$

$$I_n(t)\,I'_{-n}(t)-I'_n(t)\,I_{-n}(t)=-2\,\frac{\sin n\pi}{\pi t}, \tag{49}$$

$$I_n\,I_{-n+1}-I_{-n}\,I_{n-1}=-2\,\frac{\sin n\pi}{\pi t}, \tag{50}$$

$$I_n\,I_{-n-1}-I_{-n}\,I_{n+1}=-2\,\frac{\sin n\pi}{\pi t}, \tag{51}$$

$$K_n\,I'_n-K'_n\,I_n=\frac{1}{t}, \tag{52}$$

$$K_{n+1}\,I_n+K_n\,I_{n+1}=\frac{1}{t}. \tag{53}$$

§ 5. The Function $F_n(x)$.* It is sometimes found advantageous to make use of a function $F_n(x)$, which is defined by the equations

$$F_n(x)=x^{-\frac{1}{2}n}\,J_n(2\sqrt{x}) \tag{54}$$

$$=\frac{1}{\Pi(n)}\left\{1-\frac{x}{1.(n+1)}+\frac{x^2}{2!(n+1)(n+2)}-\dots\right\} \tag{55}$$

$$=\sum_{s=0}^{\infty}\frac{(-1)^s\,x^s}{\Pi(s)\,\Pi(n+s)}. \tag{56}$$

* Cf. Sir George Greenhill, *Phil. Mag.*, vol. XXXVIII.

The verification of the following formulae, which hold for all values of n, is left to the reader:

$$F'_n = -F_{n+1}; \tag{57}$$

$$\int_0^x F_n(x)\,dx = -F_{n-1}(x) + 1/\Pi(n-1); \tag{58}$$

$$xF''_n + (n+1)F'_n + F_n = 0; \tag{59}$$

$$xF_{n+2} - (n+1)F_{n+1} + F_n = 0; \tag{60}$$

$$\frac{d}{dx}(x^{n+1}F_{n+1}) = x^n F_n; \tag{61}$$

$$\frac{d^p}{dx^p}(x^{n+p}F_{n+p}) = x^n F_n. \tag{62}$$

§6. **Kelvin's Ber and Bei Functions.** If in (1) $n=0$ and $t=x\sqrt{i}$, the equation becomes

$$\frac{d^2y}{dx^2} + \frac{1}{x}\frac{dy}{dx} - iy = 0. \tag{63}$$

This equation is of importance in the theory of alternating currents. Independent solutions are $I_0(x\sqrt{i})$ and $K_0(x\sqrt{i})$.

The terms in the expansion of $I_0(x\sqrt{i})$ are alternately real and imaginary. Lord Kelvin denoted the real and imaginary parts of the expression by ber x and bei x respectively, so that

$$I_0(x\sqrt{i}) = \operatorname{ber} x + i \operatorname{bei} x, \tag{64}$$

where
$$\operatorname{ber} x = 1 - \frac{x^4}{2^2.4^2} + \frac{x^8}{2^2.4^2.6^2.8^2} - \dots \tag{65}$$

and
$$\operatorname{bei} x = \frac{x^2}{2^2} - \frac{x^6}{2^2.4^2.6^2} + \frac{x^{10}}{2^2.4^2.6^2.8^2.10^2} - \dots. \tag{66}$$

The analogous expression for $K_0(x\sqrt{i})$ is

$$K_0(x\sqrt{i}) = \operatorname{ker} x + i \operatorname{kei} x; \tag{67}$$

by comparison with (14) it can be seen that

$$\operatorname{ker} x = \operatorname{ber} x(\log 2 - \log x - \gamma) + \frac{1}{4}\pi \operatorname{bei} x$$
$$- \frac{x^4}{2^2.4^2}\left(1+\frac{1}{2}\right) + \frac{x^8}{2^2.4^2.6^2.8^2}\left(1+\frac{1}{2}+\frac{1}{3}+\frac{1}{4}\right) - \dots, \tag{68}$$

and
$$\operatorname{kei} x = \operatorname{bei} x(\log 2 - \log x - \gamma) - \frac{1}{4}\pi \operatorname{ber} x$$
$$+ \frac{x^2}{2^2} - \frac{x^6}{2^2.4^2.6^2}\left(1+\frac{1}{2}+\frac{1}{3}\right) + \dots. \tag{69}$$

The reader can easily verify that

$$\int_0^x x \operatorname{ber} x \, dx = x \operatorname{bei}' x, \tag{70}$$

$$\int_0^x x \operatorname{bei} x \, dx = -x \operatorname{ber}' x, \tag{71}$$

$$\int_0^x x \operatorname{ker} x \, dx = \quad x \operatorname{kei}' x, \tag{72}$$

$$\int_0^x x \operatorname{kei} x \, dx = -x \operatorname{ker} x. \tag{73}$$

For a detailed account of the ber, bei, ker, kei functions in their applications to the flow of alternating currents, see Gray's *Absolute Measurements in Electricity and Magnetism* (2nd edition, 1921), Chap. IX. Tables of these functions are given in the B.A. Report, 1912, and a shorter table, computed by Mr. Harold G. Savidge, is contained in Russell's *Alternating Currents*, Vol. I.

EXAMPLES.

1. Prove that:

$$\text{(i)} \quad x^2 G_n'' = (n^2 - n - x^2) G_n + x G_{n+1};$$

$$\text{(ii)} \quad t^2 I_n'' = (n^2 - n + t^2) I_n - t I_{n+1};$$

$$\text{(iii)} \quad t^2 K_n'' = (n^2 - n + t^2) K_n + t K_{n+1}.$$

2. Establish the expansions:

$$\text{(i)} \quad \frac{x}{2} G_{n-1} = n G_n - (n+2) G_{n+2} + (n+4) G_{n+4} - \dots;$$

$$\text{(ii)} \quad \frac{x}{2} G_n' = \frac{n}{2} G_n - (n+2) G_{n+2} + (n+4) G_{n+4} - \dots;$$

$$\text{(iii)} \quad \frac{t}{2} I_{n-1} = n I_n + (n+2) I_{n+2} + (n+4) I_{n+4} + \dots;$$

$$\text{(iv)} \quad \frac{t}{2} I_n' = \frac{n}{2} I_n + (n+2) I_{n+2} + (n+4) I_{n+4} + \dots;$$

$$\text{(v)} \quad \frac{t}{2} K_{n-1} = -n K_n - (n+2) K_{n+2} - (n+4) K_{n+4} - \dots;$$

$$\text{(vi)} \quad \frac{t}{2} K_n' = \frac{n}{2} K_n + (n+2) K_{n+2} + (n+4) K_{n+4} + \dots.$$

3. Verify that $x^{-n} J_n(x)$ and $x^{-n} G_n(x)$ are solutions of

$$xy'' + (2n+1)y' + xy = 0.$$

4. Show that $F_n(-x)$ and $x^{-\frac{1}{2}n} G_n(2i\sqrt{x})$ are independent solutions of

$$xy'' + (n+1)y' - y = 0.$$

5. Show that the complete solution of

$$x^{m+\frac{1}{2}} \frac{d^{2m+1}y}{dx^{2m+1}} \pm y = 0$$

is

$$y = \sum_{p=0}^{2m} c_p \{ F_{-m-\frac{1}{2}}(\alpha_p^2 x) \mp x^{m+\frac{1}{2}} F_{m+\frac{1}{2}}(\alpha_p^2 x) \},$$

where $c_0, c_1, \ldots, c_{2m}$ are arbitrary and $\alpha_0, \alpha_1, \ldots, \alpha_{2m}$ are the roots of $\alpha^{2m+1} = \pm i$.

6. Show that, if p is a positive integer,

$$\text{(i)}\quad x^{-n-p} J_{n+p}(x) = (-2)^p \frac{d^p}{d(x^2)^p} \{x^{-n} J_n(x)\};$$

$$\text{(ii)}\quad x^{n-p} J_{n-p}(x) = 2^p \frac{d^p}{d(x^2)^p} \{x^n J_n(x)\};$$

$$\text{(iii)}\quad x^{-n-p} G_{n+p}(x) = (-2)^p \frac{d^p}{d(x^2)^p} \{x^{-n} G_n(x)\};$$

$$\text{(iv)}\quad x^{n-p} G_{n-p}(x) = 2^p \frac{d^p}{d(x^2)^p} \{x^n G_n(x)\};$$

$$\text{(v)}\quad t^{-n-p} I_{n+p}(t) = 2^p \frac{d^p}{d(t^2)^p} \{t^{-n} I_n(t)\};$$

$$\text{(vi)}\quad t^{n-p} I_{n-p}(t) = 2^p \frac{d^p}{d(t^2)^p} \{t^n I_n(t)\}$$

$$\text{(vii)}\quad t^{-n-p} K_{n+p}(t) = (-2)^p \frac{d^p}{d(t^2)^p} \{t^{-n} K_n(t)\};$$

$$\text{(viii)}\quad t^{n-p} K_{n-p}(t) = (-2)^p \frac{d^p}{d(t^2)^p} \{t^n K_n(t)\}.$$

7. Show that:

$$\text{(i)}\quad G_{\frac{1}{2}}(x) = \sqrt{\left(\frac{\pi}{2x}\right)} e^{ix}; \qquad \text{(ii)}\quad G_{-\frac{1}{2}}(x) = i\sqrt{\left(\frac{\pi}{2x}\right)} e^{ix};$$

$$\text{(iii)}\quad I_{\frac{1}{2}}(t) = \sqrt{\left(\frac{2}{\pi t}\right)} \sinh t; \quad \text{(iv)}\quad I_{-\frac{1}{2}}(t) = \sqrt{\left(\frac{2}{\pi t}\right)} \cosh t;$$

$$\text{(v)}\quad K_{\frac{1}{2}}(t) = \sqrt{\left(\frac{\pi}{2t}\right)} e^{-t}; \qquad \text{(vi)}\quad K_{-\frac{1}{2}}(t) = \sqrt{\left(\frac{\pi}{2t}\right)} e^{-t}.$$

8. If n is a positive integer, show that:

$$\text{(i)}\quad x^{-n-\frac{1}{2}} J_{n+\frac{1}{2}}(x) = (-2)^n \sqrt{\left(\frac{2}{\pi}\right)} \frac{d^n}{d(x^2)^n} \left(\frac{\sin x}{x}\right)$$

$$\text{(ii)}\quad x^{-n-\frac{1}{2}} G_{n+\frac{1}{2}}(x) = (-2)^n \sqrt{\left(\frac{\pi}{2}\right)} \frac{d^n}{d(x^2)^n} \left(\frac{e^{ix}}{x}\right);$$

$$\text{(iii)}\quad t^{-n-\frac{1}{2}} I_{n+\frac{1}{2}}(t) = 2^n \sqrt{\left(\frac{2}{\pi}\right)} \frac{d^n}{d(t^2)^n} \left(\frac{\sinh t}{t}\right);$$

$$\text{(iv)}\quad t^{-n-\frac{1}{2}} K_{n+\frac{1}{2}}(t) = (-2)^n \sqrt{\left(\frac{\pi}{2}\right)} \frac{d^n}{d(t^2)^n} \left(\frac{e^{-t}}{t}\right).$$

9. If n is a positive integer, show that:

$$\text{(i)}\ x^{-n-\frac{1}{2}} J_{-n-\frac{1}{2}}(x) = 2^n \sqrt{\left(\frac{2}{\pi}\right)} \frac{d^n}{d(x^2)^n} \left(\frac{\cos x}{x}\right);$$

$$\text{(ii)}\ x^{-n-\frac{1}{2}} G_{-n-\frac{1}{2}}(x) = 2^n \sqrt{\left(\frac{\pi}{2}\right)} \frac{d^n}{d(x^2)^n} \left(\frac{e^{ix}}{x}\right);$$

$$\text{(iii)}\ t^{-n-\frac{1}{2}} I_{-n-\frac{1}{2}}(t) = 2^n \sqrt{\left(\frac{2}{\pi}\right)} \frac{d^n}{d(t^2)^n} \left(\frac{\cosh t}{t}\right);$$

$$\text{(iv)}\ t^{-n-\frac{1}{2}} K_{-n-\frac{1}{2}}(t) = (-2)^n \sqrt{\left(\frac{\pi}{2}\right)} \frac{d^n}{d(t^2)^n} \left(\frac{e^{-t}}{t}\right).$$

10. If n is a positive integer, show that:

$$\text{(i)}\ x^{-n} J_n(x) = (-2)^n \frac{d^n}{d(x^2)^n} J_0(x); \quad \text{(ii)}\ x^{-n} G_n(x) = (-2)^n \frac{d^n}{d(x^2)^n} G_0(x);$$

$$\text{(iii)}\ t^{-n} I_n(x) = 2^n \frac{d^n}{d(t^2)^n} I_0(t); \qquad \text{(iv)}\ t^{-n} K_n(t) = (-2)^n \frac{d^n}{d(t^2)^n} K_0(t).$$

11. Prove that:

$$\text{(i)}\ I_n(t) \cosh t = \frac{(2t)^n}{\sqrt{\pi}} \sum_{s=0}^{\infty} \frac{\Pi(n+2s-\frac{1}{2})}{(2s)!\,\Pi(2n+2s)} (2t)^{2s};$$

$$\text{(ii)}\ I_n(t) \sinh t = \frac{(2t)^n}{\sqrt{\pi}} \sum_{s=0}^{\infty} \frac{\Pi(n+2s+\frac{1}{2})}{(2s+1)!\,\Pi(2n+2s+1)} (2t)^{2s+1};$$

$$\text{(iii)} \qquad e^{-t} I_n(t) = \frac{t^n}{2^n \Pi(n)} \left\{ 1 - t + \frac{2n+3}{2!(2n+2)} t^2 - \frac{2n+5}{3!(2n+2)} t^3 \right.$$
$$\left. + \frac{(2n+5)(2n+7)}{4!(2n+2)(2n+4)} t^4 - \frac{(2n+7)(2n+9)}{5!(2n+2)(2n+4)} t^5 + \dots \right\}.$$

12. If n is a positive integer, show that

$$\frac{d^{2n}}{du^{2n}} \{u^n F_n(u)\} = (-1)^n F_n(u).$$

13. Show that:

$$\text{(i)}\ F_n(x+h) = F_n(x) - \frac{h}{1!} F_{n+1}(x) + \frac{h^2}{2!} F_{n+2}(x) - \dots;$$

$$\text{(ii)}\ \left(\frac{x}{x+h}\right)^{\frac{1}{2}n} J_n\{\sqrt{(x+h)}\}$$
$$= J_n(\sqrt{x}) - \frac{1}{1!}\left(\frac{h}{2\sqrt{x}}\right) J_{n+1}(\sqrt{x}) + \frac{1}{2!}\left(\frac{h}{2\sqrt{x}}\right)^2 J_{n+2}(\sqrt{x}) - \dots.$$

14. If p is a positive integer, prove that:

$$\text{(i)}\ (-1)^p x^n F_n(x) = x^{n+p} F_{n+2p}(x) - \frac{p}{1!}(n+p) x^{n+p-1} F_{n+2p-1}(x)$$
$$+ \frac{p(p-1)}{2!}(n+p)(n+p-1) x^{n+p-2} F_{n+2p-2}(x) - \dots;$$

$$\text{(ii)}\ (-1)^p J_n(x) = J_{n+2p}(x) - \frac{2p(n+p)}{1!\,x} J_{n+2p-1}(x)$$
$$+ \frac{2^2 p(p-1)(n+p)(n+p-1)}{2!\,x^2} J_{n+2p-2}(x) - \dots.$$

15. If n is zero or a positive integer, show that:

$$\text{(i)} \qquad F_{-n}(x) = (-x)^n F_n(x);$$

$$\text{(ii)} \quad \int_0^x F_{-n}(x)\,dx = -F_{-n-1}(x).$$

16. If $y = AF_n(x) + B\Gamma_n(x)$ is the complete solution of

$$x\frac{d^2y}{dx^2} + (n+1)\frac{dy}{dx} + y = 0,$$

show that $y = x^n\{AF_n(x) + B\Gamma_n(x)\}$ is the complete solution of

$$x\frac{d^2y}{dx^2} + (-n+1)\frac{dy}{dx} + y = 0.$$

17. If k is a positive integer, and if

$$P_k(u) = \sum_{s=0}^{p} \frac{(k-s)!}{s!} \frac{\Pi(n+k-s-1)}{(k-2s)!\,\Pi(n+s-1)} u^s,$$

where p is the greatest integer $<\frac{1}{2}(k+1)$, show that

$$P_{k+1}(u) = (n+k)P_k(u) + uP_{k-1}(u).$$

Hence prove by induction that

$$F_{n-1}(-u) = P_k(u)F_{n-1+k}(-u) + uP_{k-1}(u)F_{n+k}(-u).$$

CHAPTER IV.

FUNCTIONS OF INTEGRAL ORDER. EXPANSIONS IN SERIES OF BESSEL FUNCTIONS.

THROUGHOUT this chapter it will be supposed, unless the contrary is expressed, that the parameter n, which occurs in the definition of the Bessel functions, is a positive integer.

§ 1. **The Bessel Coefficients.** The expansions of the functions $\exp(\frac{1}{2}xt)$ and $\exp(-\frac{1}{2}xt^{-1})$ in ascending and descending powers of t respectively hold for all values of x and all non-zero values of t. Hence, when t is not zero, the product of these two expansions gives

$$\exp\frac{x}{2}(t-t^{-1}) = \sum_{r=0}^{\infty}\frac{x^r t^r}{2^r . r!}\sum_{s=0}^{\infty}\frac{(-1)^s x^s t^{-s}}{2^s . s!}$$
$$= \sum_{r=0}^{\infty}\sum_{s=0}^{\infty}\frac{(-1)^s x^{r+s} t^{r-s}}{2^{r+s} r!\, s!}.$$

If n is positive, the coefficient of t^n is obtained by putting $r=n+s$; it is

$$\sum_{s=0}^{\infty}\frac{(-1)^s x^{n+2s}}{2^{n+2s}(n+s)!\, s!} = J_n(x).$$

Similarly the coefficient of t^{-n} is obtained by writing $s=n+r$; it is $(-1)^n J_n(x)$ or $J_{-n}(x)$; thus, identically,

$$\exp\tfrac{1}{2}x(t-t^{-1}) = \sum_{n=-\infty}^{\infty} J_n(x)t^n. \qquad (1)$$

From this property of the Bessel Functions of integral order, they are, by analogy with the Legendre Coefficients, known as *Bessel Coefficients*.

The absolute convergence of the series on the right-hand side of (1) can easily be verified; for

$$\lim_{n\to\infty}|J_{n+1}(x)/J_n(x)| = \lim_{n\to\infty}|\tfrac{1}{2}x\Pi(n)/\Pi(n+1)|$$
$$= \lim_{n\to\infty}|x/(2n+2)|,$$

so that the series is convergent for all values of x and all non-zero values of t.

By writing ix for x and $-it$ for t in (1) it can be seen that

$$\exp \tfrac{1}{2}x(t+t^{-1}) = \sum_{n=-\infty}^{\infty} I_n(x)t^n. \tag{2}$$

If in (1) $t=e^{i\phi}$, the identity becomes

$$e^{ix\sin\phi} = J_0(x) + 2iJ_1(x)\sin\phi + 2J_2(x)\cos 2\phi + 2iJ_3(x)\sin 3\phi + 2J_4(x)\cos 4\phi + \dots. \tag{3}$$

In this equation equate the real and imaginary parts; then

$$\cos(x\sin\phi) = J_0(x) + 2J_2(x)\cos 2\phi + 2J_4(x)\cos 4\phi + \dots, \tag{4}$$

$$\sin(x\sin\phi) = 2J_1(x)\sin\phi + 2J_3(x)\sin 3\phi + 2J_5(x)\sin 5\phi + \dots. \tag{5}$$

Again, in (3), (4), and (5), change ϕ into $\pi/2-\phi$; thus

$$e^{ix\cos\phi} = J_0(x) + 2\sum_{s=1}^{\infty} i^s J_s(x)\cos(s\phi), \tag{6}$$

$$\cos(x\cos\phi) = J_0(x) - 2J_2(x)\cos 2\phi + 2J_4(x)\cos 4\phi - \dots, \tag{7}$$

$$\sin(x\cos\phi) = 2J_1(x)\cos\phi - 2J_3(x)\cos 3\phi + 2J_5(x)\cos 5\phi - \dots. \tag{8}$$

Formulae (3)-(8) are true for all values of ϕ and x.

Bessel's Integral. Multiply (4) by $\cos n\phi$ and integrate from 0 to π; then

$$\int_0^\pi \cos n\phi \cos(x\sin\phi)d\phi = \pi J_n(x), \text{ if } n \text{ is even (or zero)},$$

$$= 0, \text{ if } n \text{ is odd};$$

or, in a single formula, $\quad = \tfrac{1}{2}\pi\{1+(-1)^n\}J_n(x)$.

Similarly

$$\int_0^\pi \sin n\phi \sin(x\sin\phi)\,d\phi = \tfrac{1}{2}\pi\{1-(-1)^n\}J_n(x).$$

Hence, by addition,

$$\int_0^\pi \cos(n\phi - x\sin\phi)\,d\phi = \pi J_n(x), \tag{9}$$

where n is zero or any positive integer. This is known as *Bessel's Integral.*

The Eccentric Anomaly. It will be remembered that in Chapter I. an integral of the above form presented itself in connection with Bessel's astronomical problem; in fact, it was found that if

$$\mu = \phi - e\sin\phi,$$

then

$$\phi = \mu + \sum_{r=1}^{\infty} A_r \sin r\mu,$$

where

$$A_r = \frac{2}{r\pi}\int_0^\pi \cos r(\phi - e\sin\phi)d\phi.$$

It is now evident that A_r can be written in the form $(2/r)J_r(re)$, and that in this notation,

$$\phi = \mu + 2\{J_1(e)\sin\mu + \tfrac{1}{2}J_2(2e)\sin 2\mu + \tfrac{1}{3}J_3(3e)\sin 3\mu + \ldots\}. \quad (10)$$

§ 2. **Expansion of x^n in terms of Bessel Functions.** The case in which n is zero or a positive integer will be considered first. It is known that

$$2\cos n\phi = (2\cos\phi)^n - \frac{n}{1}(2\cos\phi)^{n-2} + \frac{n(n-3)}{2!}(2\cos\phi)^{n-4} - \ldots$$
$$+(-1)^s\frac{n(n-s-1)(n-s-2)\ldots(n-2s+1)}{s!}(2\cos\phi)^{n-2s} + \ldots. \quad (11)$$

Now let this expansion be applied to identities (7) and (8), and let the left-hand expressions be expanded according to powers of $x\cos\phi$: then, when the coefficients of $(\cos\phi)^n$ are equated it is found that

$$x^n = 2^n n!\{J_n + (n+2)J_{n+2} + \frac{(n+4)(n+1)}{2!}J_{n+4} + \ldots\}$$
$$= 2^n \sum_{s=0}^{\infty} \frac{(n+2s)(n+s-1)!}{s!} J_{n+2s} (n = 0, 1, 2, \ldots). \quad (12)$$

The first three cases are

$$1 = J_0 + 2J_2 + 2J_4 + \ldots + 2J_{2s} + \ldots,$$
$$x = 2J_1 + 6J_3 + 10J_5 + \ldots + 2(2s+1)J_{2s+1} + \ldots,$$
$$x^2 = 2(4J_2 + 16J_4 + 36J_6 + \ldots + 4s^2J_{2s} + \ldots).$$

When n is any number, this theorem can be written

$$x^n = 2^n \sum_{s=0}^{\infty} \frac{(n+2s)\Pi(n+s-1)}{s!} J_{n+2s}, \quad (13)$$

the truth of which can be established as follows.

Let S_h denote the sum

$$c_0 J_n + c_1 J_{n+2} + \ldots + c_h J_{n+2h},$$

where $c_s = (n+2s)\Pi(n+s-1)/(s!)$. Then, for all positive integral values of h,

$$2^n S_h = x^n - \frac{\Pi(n+h)x^{n+2h+2}}{h!\,2^{2h+2}} \sum_{r=0}^{\infty} \frac{(-)^r x^{2r}}{2^{2r}\Pi(n+r+2h+1)r!\,(r+h+1)}. \quad (14)$$

For, if this equality holds for a particular value of h, it follows that

$$2^n S_{h+1} = 2^n\{S_h + c_{h+1}J_{n+2h+2}\}$$
$$= x^n + \frac{\Pi(n+h)x^{n+2h+2}}{(h+1)!\,2^{2h+2}} \sum_{r=0}^{\infty} \frac{(-1)^r x^{2r}\left\{\begin{matrix}(n+2h+2)(r+h+1)\\ -(h+1)(n+r+2h+2)\end{matrix}\right\}}{2^{2r}\Pi(n+r+2h+2)r!\,(r+h+1)}$$
$$= x^n - \frac{\Pi(n+h+1)x^{n+2h+4}}{(h+1)!\,2^{2h+4}} \sum_{r=0}^{\infty} \frac{(-1)^r x^{2r}}{2^{2r}\Pi(n+r+2h+3)r!\,(r+h+2)}.$$

Thus the formula holds for $h+1$ if it holds for h; but it holds when $h=0$; hence it holds for all values of h.

Now the series on the right-hand side of (14) is convergent for all values of x and n; accordingly, by making h large enough, the value $|2^n S_h - x^n|$ can be made arbitrarily small. Therefore equation (13) holds for all values of x and n.

The absolute convergence of the series on the right-hand side of (13) can be verified in the same way as was done for the series in (1).

By writing ix for x in (13) it can be seen that

$$x^n = 2^n \sum_{s=0}^{\infty} (-1)^s \frac{(n+2s)\Pi(n+s-1)}{s!} I_{n+2s}. \tag{15}$$

Expansion of a Power Series in terms of Bessel Functions.

Consider the infinite series $\sum_{p=0}^{\infty} a_p x^{n+p}$: if for each power of x its expansion in terms of Bessel Functions is substituted, an equation is obtained of the form

$$\sum_{p=0}^{\infty} a_p x^{n+p} = \sum_{p=0}^{\infty} b_p J_{n+p}, \tag{16}$$

where

$$b_p = 2^{n+p}\Pi(n+p)\left\{a_p + \frac{1}{2^2(n+p-1)}\frac{a_{p-2}}{1!} + \frac{1}{2^4(n+p-1)(n+p-2)}\frac{a_{p-4}}{2!} + \dots\right\}, \tag{17}$$

the sum ending with a term in a_1 or a_0 according as p is odd or even.

It will now be shown that equation (16) is valid if the series $\Sigma a_p x^{n+p}$ is absolutely convergent, and that the series $\Sigma b_p J_{n+p}$ is then convergent.

The terms of (16) for which p is even will be first considered: let S_h and Σ_h denote the sums $a_0 x^n + a_2 x^{n+2} + \dots + a_{2h} x^{n+2h}$ and $b_0 J_n + b_2 J_{n+2} + \dots + b_{2h} J_{n+2h}$ respectively. Then from (14)

$$S_h = \Sigma_h + R_h,$$

where
$$R_h = \sum_{s=0}^{h} a_{2s} \frac{\Pi(n+h+s)\, x^{n+2h+2}}{(h-s)!\; 2^{2h+2-2s}} \times \sum_{r=0}^{\infty} \frac{(-1)^r x^{2r}}{2^{2r}\Pi(n+r+2h+1) r!\,(r+h-s+1)}.$$

The latter equation can be put in the form

$$R_h = \sum_{s=0}^{h} \frac{x^{n+2}}{n+2h+1}\left\{a_{2s}x^{2s}\frac{\Pi(n+h+s)x^{2(h-s)}}{\Pi(n+2h)}\right\}\frac{1}{2^{2h+2-2s}(h+1-s)}\phi_s,$$

where

$$\phi_s = 1 + \sum_{r=1}^{\infty} \frac{(-1)^r x^{2r}(h+1-s)}{2^{2r}(n+2h+2)(n+2h+3)\ldots(n+2h+1+r)r!(h+1-s+r)}.$$

Now

$$|\phi_s| < M,$$

where

$$M = 1 + \sum_{r=1}^{\infty} \frac{|x|^{2r}}{2^{2r}|(n+2h+2)\ldots(n+2h+1+r)|r!}.$$

Thus, when h is large,

$$|R_h| < \frac{|x|^{n+2}}{n+2h+1}\sum_{s=0}^{h}|a_{2s}x^{2s}| \times M.$$

But $\lim\limits_{h\to\infty} M = 1$: hence

$$\lim_{h\to\infty}|R_h| = 0.$$

Similarly it can be shown that the sum of the terms for which p is odd in $\Sigma a_p x^{n+p}$ is equal to the sum of the terms for which p is odd in $\Sigma b_p J_{n+p}$; therefore the two series are equal. Also $\Sigma b_p J_{n+p}$ is uniformly convergent for $|x| \leqq R$, where R is less than the radius of convergence of $\Sigma a_p x^{n+p}$.

*Sonine's Expansion.** For example, consider the expansion

$$x^n e^{ix\mu} \equiv \sum_{r=0}^{\infty} a_r x^{n+r} = \sum_{p=0}^{\infty} b_p J_{n+p}(x).$$

Here

$$a_r = i^r \mu^r/(r!), \text{ and}$$

$$b_p = 2^{n+p}\Pi(n+p)i^p\left\{\frac{\mu^p}{p!} - \frac{1}{2^2(n+p-1)}\frac{\mu^{p-2}}{1!(p-2)!} + \frac{1}{2^4(n+p-1)(n+p-2)}\frac{\mu^{p-4}}{2!(p-4)!} - \ldots\right\}$$

$$= 2^n\Pi(n-1).(n+p)i^p C_p^n(\mu),$$

where

$$C_p^n(\mu) = \frac{\Pi(n+p-1).(2\mu)^p}{\Pi(n-1)p!}\left\{1 - \frac{p(p-1)}{1!(n+p-1)}\frac{1}{(2\mu)^2} + \frac{p(p-1)(p-2)(p-3)}{2!(n+p-1)(n+p-2)}\frac{1}{(2\mu)^4} - \ldots\right\}$$

is the coefficient of λ^p in the expansion in ascending powers of λ of $(1-2\mu\lambda+\lambda^2)^{-n}$. Hence

$$x^n e^{ix\mu} = 2^n\Pi(n-1)\sum_{p=0}^{\infty}(n+p)C_p^n(\mu)i^p J_{n+p}(x).$$

Now, in this equation, write $-iz$ for x; the resulting identity

$$e^{\mu z} = (2/z)^n\Pi(n-1)\sum_{p=0}^{\infty}(n+p)C_p^n(\mu)I_{n+p}(z) \tag{18}$$

* Cf. *Math. Ann.* Vol. XVI.

is *Sonine's Expansion*, and holds for all values of n, μ, and z, except $n=0$, in which case it can easily be verified by means of (3) that, if $\mu=\cos\theta$,

$$e^{z\cos\theta}=I_0(z)+2\sum_{p=1}^{\infty}I_p(z)\cos p\theta. \qquad (19)$$

From Taylor's Theorem it follows that the series $\Sigma C_p^n(\mu)\lambda^p$ is absolutely convergent for $|\lambda|<R$, where R denotes the smaller of the two quantities $|\mu\pm\sqrt{(\mu^2-1)}|$, the moduli of the zeros of $1-2\mu\lambda+\lambda^2$; in particular, if $\mu=\cos\theta$, the series is absolutely convergent if $|\lambda|<1$. Now it is easy to show, by means of Stirling's Formula (App. I.), that the coefficient of $C_p^n(\mu)$ in (18) can always be made less than R^p by sufficiently increasing p. Thus (18) and (19) are absolutely convergent for all values of μ, n, and z.

§ 3. **The Addition Theorem.** From (1) we have

$$\sum_{n=-\infty}^{\infty}J_n(u+v)t^n=\exp\left\{\frac{u+v}{2}\left(t-\frac{1}{t}\right)\right\}$$

$$=\exp\left\{\frac{u}{2}\left(t-\frac{1}{t}\right)\right\}\times\exp\left\{\frac{v}{2}\left(t-\frac{1}{t}\right)\right\}$$

$$=\sum_{s=-\infty}^{\infty}J_s(u)t^s\times\sum_{r=-\infty}^{\infty}J_r(v)t^r.$$

Now let the two series on the right-hand side be multiplied together, and the coefficients of t^n equated; then

$$J_n(u+v)=\sum_{s=-\infty}^{\infty}J_s(u)J_{n-s}(v). \qquad (20)$$

Since $J_{-r}=(-1)^rJ_r$, this can be written

$$J_n(u+v)=\sum_{s=0}^{n}J_s(u)J_{n-s}(v)$$

$$+\sum_{s=1}^{\infty}(-1)^s\{J_s(u)J_{n+s}(v)+J_{n+s}(u)J_s(v)\} \qquad (21)$$

Corollary 1. $$I_n(u+v)=\sum_{s=-\infty}^{\infty}I_s(u)I_{n-s}(v)$$

$$=\sum_{s=0}^{n}I_s(u)I_{n-s}(v)$$

$$+\sum_{s=1}^{\infty}\{I_s(u)I_{n+s}(v)+I_{n+s}(u)I_s(v)\}. \qquad (22)$$

Corollary 2. $$J_n(x+iy)=\sum_{s=-\infty}^{\infty}i^{n-s}J_s(x)I_{n-s}(y) \qquad (23)$$

From this expression, by separating the terms in which $n-s$ are even and odd, the real and imaginary parts of $J_n(x+iy)$ can be obtained.

Generalisation of the Addition Theorem. We will now consider a remarkable extension due to Neumann* of the addition theorem.

From (1) $\exp\frac{x}{2}\left(kt-\frac{1}{kt}\right)=\sum_{-\infty}^{\infty} k^n J_n(x)t^n.$

But $$\frac{x}{2}\left(kt-\frac{1}{kt}\right)=\frac{kx}{2}\left(t-\frac{1}{t}\right)+\frac{x}{2}\left(k-\frac{1}{k}\right)\frac{1}{t};$$

therefore

$$\exp\frac{x}{2}\left(kt-\frac{1}{kt}\right)=\exp\frac{x}{2t}\left(k-\frac{1}{k}\right)\exp\frac{kx}{2}\left(t-\frac{1}{t}\right);$$

that is $$\sum_{-\infty}^{\infty} k^n J_n(x)t^n=e^{\frac{x}{2t}\left(k-\frac{1}{k}\right)}\sum_{-\infty}^{\infty} J_n(kx)t^n.$$

Put $x=r$, $k=e^{\theta i}$: then

$$\sum_{-\infty}^{\infty} J_n(re^{\theta i})t^n=e^{-\frac{ir\sin\theta}{t}}\sum_{-\infty}^{\infty} e^{n\theta i}J_n(r)t^n. \tag{24}$$

Now equate the coefficients of t^n; thus

$$J_n(re^{\theta i})=e^{n\theta i}J_n(r)-\frac{ir\sin\theta}{1!}e^{(n+1)\theta i}J_{n+1}(r)$$
$$+\frac{i^2r^2\sin^2\theta}{2!}e^{(n+2)\theta i}J_{n+2}(r)-\dots,$$
$$=\xi_n+i\eta_n, \tag{25}$$

where $$\xi_n=J_n(r)\cos n\theta+r\sin\theta\sin(n+1)\theta\,J_{n+1}(r)$$
$$-\frac{r^2\sin^2\theta}{2!}\cos(n+2)\theta\,J_{n+2}(r)$$
$$-\frac{r^3\sin^3\theta}{3!}\sin(n+3)\theta\,J_{n+3}(r)+\dots,$$

and $$\eta_n=J_n(r)\sin n\theta-r\sin\theta\cos(n+1)\theta\,J_{n+1}(r)$$
$$-\frac{r^2\sin^2\theta}{2!}\sin(n+2)\theta\,J_{n+2}(r)$$
$$+\frac{r^3\sin^3\theta}{3!}\cos(n+3)\theta\,J_{n+3}(r)+\dots.$$

As a special case, let $\theta=\pi/2$; thus

$$I_n(r)=J_n(r)+rJ_{n+1}(r)+\frac{r^2}{2!}J_{n+2}(r)+\frac{r^3}{3!}J_{n+3}(r)+\dots. \tag{26}$$

* Strictly speaking, Neumann only considers the case when $n=0$; but the generalisation immediately suggests itself.

Again, in (24) put r, θ, successively equal to b, β and c, γ, and multiply the results together; thus

$$\sum_{-\infty}^{\infty} J_n(be^{\beta i})\,t^n \sum_{-\infty}^{\infty} J_n(ce^{\gamma i})\,t^n$$
$$= e^{-\frac{i(b\sin\beta+c\sin\gamma)}{t}} \sum_{-\infty}^{\infty} e^{n\beta i} J_n(b)\,t^n \sum_{-\infty}^{\infty} e^{n\gamma i} J_n(c)\,t^n.$$

Now the left-hand expression is equal to

$$\sum_{-\infty}^{\infty} J_n(be^{\beta i}+ce^{\gamma i})\,t^n,$$

and if the right-hand side is expanded according to powers of t, the coefficient of t^n gives an expression for $J_n(be^{\beta i}+ce^{\gamma i})$ in the form

$$J_n(be^{\beta i}+ce^{\gamma i}) = C_0 - C_1 i(b\sin\beta+c\sin\gamma) + \frac{C_2 i^2(b\sin\beta+c\sin\gamma)^2}{2!} - \dots, \qquad (27)$$

where

$$C_0 = \sum_{s=-\infty}^{\infty} e^{s\beta i} J_s(b)\, e^{(n-s)\gamma i} J_{n-s}(c),$$

and similar expressions hold for C_1, C_2, ….

Since, however, this formula is too complicated for practical purposes, we shall only consider in detail the case when $be^{\beta i}+ce^{\gamma i}$ is a real quantity. Moreover, we shall suppose in the first instance that $n=0$.

If

$$be^{\beta i}+ce^{\gamma i}=a,$$

where a is real, then

$$a = b\cos\beta + c\cos\gamma \quad \text{and} \quad b\sin\beta + c\sin\gamma = 0;$$

so that

$$a^2 = (b\cos\beta+c\cos\gamma)^2 + (b\sin\beta+c\sin\gamma)^2$$
$$= b^2 + 2bc\cos(\beta-\gamma) + c^2.$$

Now put $\beta-\gamma=\alpha$; then the general formula (27) becomes in this special case

$$J_0(\sqrt{(b^2+2bc\cos\alpha+c^2)}) = J_0(b)J_0(c) + 2\sum_{s=1}^{\infty}(-1)^s J_s(b)J_s(c)\cos s\alpha. \quad (28)$$

If α is replaced by $\pi-\alpha$ the formula becomes

$$J_0(\sqrt{(b^2-2bc\cos\alpha+c^2)}) = J_0(b)J_0(c) + 2\sum_{s=1}^{\infty} J_s(b)J_s(c)\cos s\alpha, \quad (29)$$

which is Neumann's result already referred to.

By way of verification, put $\alpha=0$; then we are brought back to the addition formula (20).

Again, suppose $\alpha=\pi/2$; then

$$J_0(\sqrt{(b^2+c^2)}) = J_0(b)J_0(c) - 2J_2(b)J_2(c) + 2J_4(b)J_4(c) - \dots. \quad (30)$$

In particular, if $c=b$,

$$J_0(b\sqrt{2})=J_0^2(b)-2J_2^2(b)+2J_4^2(b)-\dots. \qquad (31)$$

In (28) and (29) suppose $b=c$; thus

$$J_0(2b\cos\tfrac{1}{2}a)=J_0^2(b)-2J_1^2(b)\cos a+2J_2^2(b)\cos 2a-\dots, \qquad (32)$$

$$J_0(2b\sin\tfrac{1}{2}a)=J_0^2(b)+2J_1^2(b)\cos a+2J_2^2(b)\cos 2a+\dots. \qquad (33)$$

Again, to (28) apply the operator $b\frac{\partial}{\partial b}+c\frac{\partial}{\partial c}$, and it is found that

$$\sqrt{(b^2+2bc\cos a+c^2)}\,J_1\{\sqrt{(b^2+2bc\cos a+c^2)}\}$$
$$=bJ_1(b)J_0(c)+cJ_0(b)J_1(c)$$
$$+\sum_{n=1}^{\infty}(-1)^n\left[\begin{matrix}b\{J_{n+1}(b)-J_{n-1}(b)\}J_n(c)\\+c\{J_{n+1}(c)-J_{n-1}(c)\}J_n(b)\end{matrix}\right]\cos na. \qquad (34)$$

By repeated applications of this operation the corresponding formulae for J_2, J_3, ... can also be obtained. They can also be obtained directly from (27). A still more general form of the Addition Theorem will be proved in Chapter VI. § 3.

§ 4. **Schlömilch's Expansion.** This chapter will be concluded by a proof of Schlömilch's theorem, that under certain conditions, which will have to be examined, any function $f(x)$ can be expanded in the form

$$f(x)=\tfrac{1}{2}a_0+a_1J_0(x)+a_2J_0(2x)+\dots+a_nJ_0(nx)+\dots, \qquad (35)$$

where

$$a_0=\frac{2}{\pi}\int_0^{\pi}\left\{f(0)+u\int_0^1\frac{f'(u\xi)\,d\xi}{\sqrt{(1-\xi^2)}}\right\}du, \qquad (36)$$

and

$$a_n=\frac{2}{\pi}\int_0^{\pi}u\cos nu\left\{\int_0^1\frac{f'(u\xi)\,d\xi}{\sqrt{(1-\xi^2)}}\right\}du, \quad (n=1, 2, 3, \dots). \qquad (37)$$

To prove this, we shall require the lemma

$$\int_0^{\pi/2}J_1(nu\sin\phi)\,d\phi=\frac{1-\cos nu}{nu}.$$

The lemma may be established as follows. We have

$$J_1(nu\sin\phi)=\sum_0^{\infty}\frac{(-1)^s n^{2s+1}u^{2s+1}\sin^{2s+1}\phi}{2^{2s+1}s!\,(s+1)!};$$

therefore

$$\int_0^{\pi/2}J_1(nu\sin\phi)\,d\phi=\sum_0^{\infty}\frac{(-1)^s n^{2s+1}u^{2s+1}}{2^{2s+1}s!\,(s+1)!}\int_0^{\pi/2}\sin^{2s+1}\phi\,d\phi$$
$$=\sum_0^{\infty}\frac{(-1)^s n^{2s+1}u^{2s+1}}{2^{2s+1}s!\,(s+1)!}\cdot\frac{2^s s!}{1.3.5\dots(2s+1)}$$
$$=\sum_0^{\infty}\frac{(-1)^s n^{2s+1}u^{2s+1}}{(2s+2)!}=\frac{1-\cos nu}{nu}.$$

Now assume that the expansion (35) is possible, and that the series can be differentiated term by term; then

$$f'(x) = -a_1 J_1(x) - 2a_2 J_1(2x) - \ldots - na_n J_1(nx) - \ldots.$$

Write $u \sin \phi$ for x, and integrate both sides with regard to ϕ between the limits 0 and $\pi/2$; thus

$$\int_0^{\pi/2} f'(u \sin \phi)\, d\phi = -\sum_1^\infty na_n \int_0^{\pi/2} J_1(nu \sin \phi)\, d\phi$$
$$= \sum a_n (\cos nu - 1)/u;$$

and therefore

$$u \int_0^{\pi/2} f'(u \sin \phi)\, d\phi = \sum_1^\infty a_n \cos nu - \sum_1^\infty a_n$$
$$= \sum_1^\infty a_n \cos nu + (\tfrac{1}{2}a_0 - f(0)).$$

This is a half-range Fourier series, so that

$$\tfrac{1}{2}a_0 - f(0) = \frac{1}{\pi}\int_0^\pi \left\{ u \int_0^{\pi/2} f'(u \sin \phi)\, d\phi \right\} du,$$

or, what is the same thing,

$$a_0 = \frac{2}{\pi}\int_0^\pi \left\{ f(0) + u \int_0^{\pi/2} f'(u \sin \phi)\, d\phi \right\} du,$$

and
$$a_n = \frac{2}{\pi}\int_0^\pi u \cos nu \left\{ \int_0^{\pi/2} f'(u \sin \phi)\, d\phi \right\} du,$$

where $n = 1, 2, 3, \ldots$.

The substitution $\sin \phi = \xi$ reduces these formulae to (36) and (37), which are the forms of the coefficients as given by Schlömilch. It must be observed, however, that the theorem has not yet been proved; all that has been effected is the determination of the coefficients under the assumption that the expression (35) is valid and that the result of differentiating it term by term is $f'(x)$.

In order to verify the result *a posteriori*, let the coefficients $a_0, a_1, a_2, \ldots$ have the values above assigned to them, and write

$$\psi(x) = \tfrac{1}{2}a_0 + a_1 J_0(x) + a_2 J_0(2x) + \ldots$$
$$= f(0) + \frac{2}{\pi}\int_0^\pi \left\{ \frac{1}{2} + \sum_1^\infty J_0(nx) \cos nu \right\} u\, du \int_0^1 \frac{f'(u\xi)}{\sqrt{(1-\xi^2)}}\, d\xi. \quad (38)$$

Now let a function $\phi(u)$ be taken such that $\phi(u) = \dfrac{1}{\sqrt{(x^2 - u^2)}}$

if $0<u<x$, but $\phi(u)=0$ if $x<u<\pi$; then $\phi(u)$ can be expanded in a cosine series

$$\phi(u)=\tfrac{1}{2}c_0+\sum_1^\infty c_n \cos nu.$$

Here
$$\int_0^\pi \phi(u)\,du=\tfrac{1}{2}\pi c_0;$$

but
$$\int_0^\pi \phi(u)\,du=\int_0^x \frac{du}{\sqrt{(x^2-u^2)}}+\int_x^\pi 0\,.\,du=\tfrac{1}{2}\pi,$$

so that $c_0=1$.

Also
$$\frac{\pi}{2}c_n=\int_0^\pi \phi(u)\cos nu\,du=\int_0^x \frac{\cos nu\,du}{\sqrt{(x^2-u^2)}}$$
$$=\int_0^{\frac{\pi}{2}} \cos(nx\sin\theta)\,d\theta=\frac{\pi}{2}J_0(nx),$$

by (9), and therefore $c_n=J_0(nx)$.

Thus
$$\phi(u)=\tfrac{1}{2}+\sum_1^\infty J_0(nx)\cos nu.$$

Now in (38) put $1/\sqrt{(x^2-u^2)}$ in place of the series, the upper limit being taken to be x instead of π; then

$$\psi(x)=f(0)+\frac{2}{\pi}\int_0^x \frac{u\,du}{\sqrt{(x^2-u^2)}}\int_0^1 \frac{f'(u\xi)\,d\xi}{\sqrt{(1-\xi^2)}},$$

or, if $u=r$ and $\xi=\sin\phi$,

$$\psi(x)=f(0)+\frac{2}{\pi}\int_0^x \frac{r\,dr}{\sqrt{(x^2-r^2)}}\int_0^{\frac{\pi}{2}} f'(r\sin\phi)\,d\phi.$$

In this double integral let the variables be changed to rectangular coordinates by means of the substitution, $r\cos\phi=\xi$ $r\sin\phi=\eta$. The area of integration is a quadrant of a circle of radius x, and therefore

$$\psi(x)=f(0)+\frac{2}{\pi}\int_0^x f'(\eta)\,d\eta\int_0^{\sqrt{(x^2-\eta^2)}} \frac{d\xi}{\sqrt{(x^2-\xi^2-\eta^2)}}$$
$$=f(0)+\{f(x)-f(0)\}=f(x),$$

provided that $f(x)$ is continuous between 0 and x.

Thus Schlömilch's expansion holds if $f(x)$ is continuous from 0 to x, and if $f'(x)$ exists and is continuous for $0\leqq x\leqq\pi$.

EXAMPLES.

1. Show that:

(i) $J_0(u+v) = J_0(u)J_0(v) - 2J_1(u)J_1(v) + 2J_2(u)J_2(v) - \dots;$

(ii) $J_0(u-v) = J_0(u)J_0(v) + 2J_1(u)J_1(v) + 2J_2(u)J_2(v) + \dots;$

(iii) $J_1(u+v) = J_0(u)J_1(v) + J_1(u)J_0(v) - J_1(u)J_2(v) - J_2(u)J_1(v) + \dots.$

2. Show that:

(i) $\cosh(x\sin\phi) = I_0(x) - 2I_2(x)\cos 2\phi + 2I_4(x)\cos 4\phi - \dots;$

(ii) $\sinh(x\sinh\phi) = 2I_1(x)\sin\phi - 2I_3(x)\sin 3\phi + 2I_5(x)\sin 5\phi - \dots;$

(iii) $\cosh(x\cos\phi) = I_0(x) + 2I_2(x)\cos 2\phi + 2I_4(x)\cos 4\phi + \dots;$

(iv) $\sinh(x\cos\phi) = 2I_1(x)\cos\phi + 2I_3(x)\cos 3\phi + 2I_5(x)\cos 5\phi + \dots;$

(v) $\cos(x\cosh\phi) = J_0(x) - 2J_2(x)\cosh 2\phi + 2J_4(x)\cosh 4\phi - \dots;$

(vi) $\sinh(x\cosh\phi) = 2I_1(x)\cosh\phi + 2I_3(x)\cosh 3\phi + 2I_5(x)\cosh 5\phi + \dots.$

3. Show that:

(i) $\cos x = J_0(x) - 2J_2(x) + 2J_4(x) - \dots;$

(ii) $\sin x = 2J_1(x) - 2J_3(x) + 2J_5(x) - \dots;$

(iii) $\cosh x = I_0(x) + 2I_2(x) + 2I_4(x) + \dots;$

(iv) $\sinh x = 2I_1(x) + 2I_3(x) + 2I_5(x) + \dots;$

(v) $x\cos x = 2\{J_1(x) - 3^2J_3(x) + 5^2J_5(x) - \dots\}.$

4. If $\mu = \phi - e\sin\phi$, prove that

$$\frac{\partial^2\phi}{\partial e^2} + \frac{1}{e}\frac{\partial\phi}{\partial e} + \frac{1-e^2}{e^2}\frac{\partial^2\phi}{\partial\mu^2} = 0,$$

and hence obtain Bessel's expression for ϕ in terms of μ.

5. Prove that, in the problem of elliptic motion, the radius-vector SP is given by the equations

(i) $a/r = (1 - e\cos\phi)^{-1} = 1 + 2\{J_1(e)\cos\mu + J_2(2e)\cos 2\mu + \dots\};$

(ii) $r/a = 1 + \frac{1}{2}e^2 - 2e\sum_1^\infty \frac{1}{n}J_n'(ne)\cos(n\mu).$

6. Prove that:

(i) $Y_0 = J_0\log x + 4(\frac{1}{2}J_2 - \frac{1}{4}J_4 + \frac{1}{6}J_6 - \dots);$

(ii) $$Y_1 = J_1\log x - \frac{1}{x} - \frac{1}{2}J_1 + \frac{6.3}{2.4}J_3 - \frac{2.5}{4.6}J_5 + \frac{6.7}{6.8}J_7 - \dots$$
$$+ \frac{6(4s+3)}{(4s+2)(4s+4)}J_{4s+3} - \frac{2(4s+5)}{(4s+4)(4s+6)}J_{4s+5} + \dots;$$

(iii) $$Y_2 = J_2 \log x - \left(\frac{2}{x^2} + \frac{1}{2}\right) - \frac{3}{4}J_2 + \frac{2\,.\,4}{1\,.\,3}J_4 + \frac{1\,.\,3}{2\,.\,4}J_6 + \dots$$
$$+ \frac{2s(2s+2)}{(2s-1)(2s+1)}J_{4s} + \frac{(2s-1)(2s+1)}{2s(2s+2)}J_{4s+2} + \dots;$$

(iv) $$Y_3 = J_3 \log x - 8/x^3 - 1/x - \tfrac{1}{4}J_1 - \tfrac{5}{3}J_3 + \dots$$
$$+ \frac{3(4s+1)}{2(2s-1)(2s+2)}J_{4s+1} - \frac{4s+3}{4s(2s+3)}J_{4s+3} + \dots \quad [s = 1, 2, \dots].$$

[For (i) assume $Y_0 = J_0 \log x + \Sigma c_n J_n$, substitute in the differential equation, and apply the recurrence formulae: the others can be deduced by differentiation.]

7. Prove that
$$\left(\frac{x}{2}\right)^{n-m} J_m(x) = \sum_{p=0}^{\infty} \frac{(n+2p)\Gamma(n+p)}{\Pi(m+p)} \frac{\Pi(m-n)}{p!\,\Pi(m-n-p)} J_{n+2p}(x).$$

8. If $0 \leq x \leq \pi$, show that
$$x = \frac{\pi^2}{4} - 2\left\{J_0(x) + \frac{1}{9}J_0(3x) + \frac{1}{25}J_0(5x) + \dots\right\}.$$

9. If n is an integer, show that
$$J_n(x) = \frac{1}{\pi i^{3n}}\int_0^{\pi} e^{-ix\cos\phi}\cos n\phi\, d\phi = \frac{1}{\pi i^n}\int_0^{\pi} e^{ix\cos\phi}\cos n\phi\, d\phi.$$

10. If n is a positive integer, show that

(i) $$Y_n = J_n \log x - \left(1 + \frac{1}{2} + \frac{1}{3} + \dots + \frac{1}{n}\right)J_n$$
$$- \frac{n!}{2}\sum_{s=0}^{n-1}\frac{1}{n-s}\left(\frac{2}{x}\right)^{n-s}\frac{J_s}{s!} - \sum_{s=1}^{\infty}(-1)^s\frac{n+2s}{s(n+s)}J_{n+2s};$$

Note.—This is the form in which the function Y_n was originally defined by Neumann.

(ii) $$Y_n = J_n \log x - \frac{1}{2}\left(1 + \frac{1}{2} + \frac{1}{3} + \dots + \frac{1}{n}\right)J_n$$
$$- \frac{1}{2}\sum_{s=0}^{n-1}\frac{(n-s-1)!}{s!}\left(\frac{x}{2}\right)^{-n+2s}$$
$$+ \frac{n+2}{2(n+1)}\{n+2\}J_{n+2} + \frac{n+4}{4(n+2)}\left\{\frac{n(n+1)}{2!} - 2\right\}J_{n+4}$$
$$+ \frac{n+6}{6(n+3)}\left\{\frac{n(n+1)(n+2)}{3!} + 2\right\}J_{n+6} + \dots$$
$$+ \frac{n+2s}{2s(n+s)}\left\{\frac{n(n+1)\dots(n+s-1)}{s!} + (-1)^{s-1}2\right\}J_{n+2s} + \dots.$$

11. Show that
$$J_1(2b\cos\tfrac{1}{2}a) = 2J_0(b)J_1(b)\cos(a/2) - 2J_1(b)J_2(b)\cos(3a/2)$$
$$+ 2J_2(b)J_3(b)\cos(5a/2) - \dots.$$

[In IV. (34) put $b = c$.]

12. Prove that

(i) $1 = J_0^2(x) + 2J_1^2(x) + 2J_2^2(x) + \ldots;$

(ii) $x^2 = 4\{J_1^2(x) + 4J_2^2(x) + 9J_3^2(x) + \ldots\};$

(iii) $$x^{2n} = 2^{2n}(n!)^2\{J_n^2 + \frac{2(n+1)}{1}J_{n+1}^2 + \frac{2(n+2)(2n+1)}{2!}J_{n+2}^2 + \ldots$$
$$+ \frac{2(n+s)(2n+1)(2n+2)\ldots(2n+s-1)}{s!}J_{n+s}^2 + \ldots\},$$

where n is a positive integer.

[In ex. 11 put $b = x$, expand both sides in terms of $\cos\frac{1}{2}\alpha$, and equate coefficients.]

13. Prove that

(i) $x = 2J_0J_1 + 6J_1J_2 + 10J_2J_3 + \ldots + 2(2s+1)J_sJ_{s+1} + \ldots;$

(ii) $$x^3 = 16\{J_1J_2 + 5J_2J_3 + 14J_3J_4 + \ldots$$
$$+ \frac{s(s+1)(2s+1)}{6}J_sJ_{s+1} + \ldots\};$$

(iii) $$x^{2n-1} = 2^{2n-1}n!(n-1)!\Big\{J_{n-1}J_n + (2n+1)J_nJ_{n+1}$$
$$+ \frac{(2n+3)}{2!}(2n)J_{n+1}J_{n+2} + \frac{(2n+5)}{3!}(2n)(2n+1)J_{n+2}J_{n+3} + \ldots$$
$$+ \frac{(2n+2s-1)(2n)(2n+1)(2n+2)\ldots(2n+s-2)}{s!}J_{n+s-1}J_{n+s} + \ldots\Big\},$$

where n is a positive integer.

14. If $\eta = \sqrt{(1+e^2)}\sin\xi$ be the equation of a curve referred to oblique axes, whose inclination is $\cot^{-1}e$, show that the equation referred to rectangular axes with OX and $O\Xi$ coinciding is

$$y = \sum_{n=1}^{\infty}(-1)^{n+1}\frac{2}{ne}J_n(ne)\sin nx.$$

15. Show that, if x is real,

$$|J_n(x)| < 1.$$

[Use IV. (9).]

CHAPTER V.

DEFINITE INTEGRAL EXPRESSIONS FOR THE BESSEL FUNCTIONS. ASYMPTOTIC EXPANSIONS.

In this chapter a number of definite integral and contour integral expressions for the Bessel functions will be given, and the asymptotic expansions will then be established. An account of Stokes' method of obtaining the asymptotic expansions, which might be of interest to physicists, will be found in Appendix II.

§ 1. **Bessel's Second Integral.** A definite integral expression for $J_n(x)$, which is only valid when n is a positive integer, was given in the previous chapter. To Bessel is also due a second formula,

$$J_n(x) = \frac{2}{\sqrt{\pi}\,.\,\Gamma(n+\frac{1}{2})}\left(\frac{x}{2}\right)^n \int_0^{\pi/2} \cos(x\sin\phi)(\cos\phi)^{2n}d\phi, \qquad (1)$$

which holds for $R(n)$* $> -\frac{1}{2}$.

To prove this, expand $\cos(x\sin\phi)$ in ascending powers of x; thus the integral is equal to

$$\int_0^{\pi/2} \sum_{s=0}^{\infty} \frac{(-1)^s x^{2s}(\sin\phi)^{2s}}{(2s)!}(\cos\phi)^{2n}d\phi$$

$$= \sum_{s=0}^{\infty} \frac{(-1)^s x^{2s}}{(2s)!}\,\tfrac{1}{2}B(s+\tfrac{1}{2}, n+\tfrac{1}{2}) \quad \text{(App. I. 14)}$$

$$= \sum_{s=0}^{\infty} \frac{(-1)^s x^{2s}}{(2s)!}\,\frac{\Gamma(s+\frac{1}{2})\Gamma(n+\frac{1}{2})}{2\Gamma(n+s+1)}.$$

But $$(2s)! = \frac{2^{2s}}{\sqrt{\pi}}\Pi(s-\tfrac{1}{2})\Pi(s) \quad \text{(App. I. 23)};$$

hence the right-hand side of (1) is equal to

$$\left(\frac{x}{2}\right)^n \sum_{s=0}^{\infty} \frac{(-1)^s x^{2s}}{2^{2s}\Pi(s)\Pi(n+s)} = J_n(x).$$

*If z is a complex number, $R(z)$ and $I(z)$ denote its real and imaginary parts respectively.

In (1) put $\pi/2-\phi$ for ϕ; then, if $R(n)>-\frac{1}{2}$,

$$J_n(x)=\frac{2}{\sqrt{\pi}\,.\,\Gamma(n+\frac{1}{2})}\left(\frac{x}{2}\right)^n\int_0^{\pi/2}\cos(x\cos\phi)(\sin\phi)^{2n}d\phi \tag{2}$$

$$=\frac{1}{\sqrt{\pi}\,.\,\Gamma(n+\frac{1}{2})}\left(\frac{x}{2}\right)^n\int_0^{\pi}\cos(x\cos\phi)(\sin\phi)^{2n}d\phi. \tag{3}$$

But
$$\int_0^{\pi}\sin(x\cos\phi)(\sin\phi)^{2n}d\phi=0;$$

hence
$$J_n(x)=\frac{1}{\sqrt{\pi}\,.\,\Gamma(n+\frac{1}{2})}\left(\frac{x}{2}\right)^n\int_0^{\pi}e^{\pm ix\cos\phi}(\sin\phi)^{2n}d\phi, \tag{4}$$

where $R(n)>-\frac{1}{2}$.

The following formulae, for all of which $R(n)>-\frac{1}{2}$, can easily be deduced from these:

$$J_n(x)=\frac{1}{\sqrt{\pi}\,.\,\Gamma(n+\frac{1}{2})}\left(\frac{x}{2}\right)^n\int_{-1}^{1}e^{\pm ix\xi}(1-\xi^2)^{n-\frac{1}{2}}d\xi \tag{5}$$

$$=\frac{1}{\sqrt{\pi}\,.\,\Gamma(n+\frac{1}{2})}\left(\frac{x}{2}\right)^n\int_{-1}^{1}\cos(x\xi)(1-\xi^2)^{n-\frac{1}{2}}d\xi; \tag{6}$$

$$I_n(x)=\frac{2}{\sqrt{\pi}\,.\,\Gamma(n+\frac{1}{2})}\left(\frac{x}{2}\right)^n\int_0^{\pi/2}\cosh(x\sin\phi)(\cos\phi)^{2n}d\phi \tag{7}$$

$$=\frac{2}{\sqrt{\pi}\,.\,\Gamma(n+\frac{1}{2})}\left(\frac{x}{2}\right)^n\int_0^{\pi/2}\cosh(x\cos\phi)(\sin\phi)^{2n}d\phi \tag{8}$$

$$=\frac{2}{\sqrt{\pi}\,.\,\Gamma(n+\frac{1}{2})}\left(\frac{x}{2}\right)^n\int_0^{1}\cosh(x\xi)(1-\xi^2)^{n-\frac{1}{2}}d\xi \tag{9}$$

$$=\frac{1}{\sqrt{\pi}\,.\,\Gamma(n+\frac{1}{2})}\left(\frac{x}{2}\right)^n\int_0^{\pi}e^{\pm x\cos\phi}(\sin\phi)^{2n}d\phi \tag{10}$$

$$=\frac{1}{\sqrt{\pi}\,.\,\Gamma(n+\frac{1}{2})}\left(\frac{x}{2}\right)^n\int_{-1}^{1}e^{\pm x\xi}(1-\xi^2)^{n-\frac{1}{2}}d\xi. \tag{11}$$

§2. **Contour Integral Expressions.** Laplace's linear differential equation

$$(az+a')\frac{d^2w}{dz^2}+(bz+b')\frac{dw}{dz}+(cz+c')=0 \tag{12}$$

can be solved as follows. Put $w=\int_C\phi(\zeta)e^{\zeta z}d\zeta$, where C denotes the contour of integration, and substitute in (12); then

$$\int_C\phi(\zeta)e^{\zeta z}\{(a\zeta^2+b\zeta+c)z+(a'\zeta^2+b'\zeta+c')\}d\zeta=0. \tag{13}$$

Hence, if $\phi(\zeta)$ satisfies the equation

$$(a'\zeta^2+b'\zeta+c')\phi(\zeta)=\frac{d}{d\zeta}\{(a\zeta^2+b\zeta+c)\phi(\zeta)\}, \tag{14}$$

equation (13) becomes $\int_C \frac{d}{d\zeta}\theta(\zeta)d\zeta = 0,$ (15)

where $$\theta(\zeta) = \phi(\zeta)e^{\zeta z}(a\zeta^2 + b\zeta + c).$$

Also equation (14) gives

$$\phi(\zeta) = \frac{1}{a\zeta^2 + b\zeta + c} e^{\int \frac{a'\zeta^2 + b'\zeta + c'}{a\zeta^2 + b\zeta + c} d\zeta}. \qquad (16)$$

Thus $\int_C \phi(\zeta)e^{\zeta z}d\zeta$ is a solution of (12), provided that C is chosen so that $\theta(\zeta)$ regains its initial value at the final point of C.

Solution of Bessel's Equation. In Bessel's Equation

$$z^2 w'' + z w' + (z^2 - n^2)w = 0$$

put $w = z^n W$; it reduces to

$$zW'' + (2n+1)W' + zW = 0.$$

This is a particular case of Laplace's equation; therefore

$$\phi(\zeta) = \frac{1}{\zeta^2+1} e^{\int \frac{(2n+1)\zeta}{\zeta^2+1} d\zeta} = (\zeta^2+1)^{n-\frac{1}{2}},$$

$$W = \int_C e^{\zeta z}(\zeta^2+1)^{n-\frac{1}{2}} d\zeta,$$

and $$\theta(\zeta) = e^{\zeta z}(\zeta^2+1)^{n+\frac{1}{2}}.$$

Hence, if ζ is replaced by $i\zeta$, it results that

$$w = z^n \int_C e^{iz\zeta}(\zeta^2 - 1)^{n-\frac{1}{2}} d\zeta \qquad (17)$$

is a solution of Bessel's Equation, provided that $e^{iz\zeta}(\zeta^2-1)^{n+\frac{1}{2}}$ regains its initial value at the final point of C.

Expression for $J_n(z)$. Consider the integral

$$w = \int^{(-1+, +1-)} e^{iz\zeta}(\zeta^2 - 1)^{n-\frac{1}{2}} d\zeta, \qquad (18)$$

where the initial point is the origin and the contour (Fig. 2)

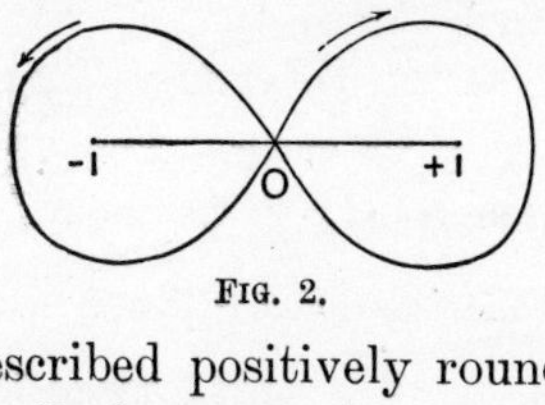

FIG. 2.

consists of a loop described positively round the point -1 followed by a loop described negatively round the point $+1$. Let the initial amplitudes of $(\zeta+1)$ and $(\zeta-1)$ be -2π and π respectively. The effect of the first loop is to increase the amplitude of $(\zeta+1)$ by 2π, while the second loop decreases the amplitude of $(\zeta-1)$ by 2π. The amplitudes of $(\zeta+1)$ and $(\zeta-1)$ are both zero at the point where ζ crosses the ξ-axis to the right of $\zeta=1$, and the final and initial amplitudes of (ζ^2-1) are equal. Thus, at the final point, $e^{iz\zeta}(\zeta^2-1)^{n+\frac{1}{2}}$ regains its initial value, so that w is a solution of Bessel's Equation.

Now in (18) expand $e^{iz\zeta}$ in powers of z, and integrate term by term; thus

$$w=\sum_{s=0}^{\infty}\frac{(iz)^s}{s!}\int^{(-1+,\,+1-)}\zeta^s(\zeta^2-1)^{n-\frac{1}{2}}d\zeta$$

$$=\sum_{s=0}^{\infty}\frac{(iz)^{2s}}{(2s)!}\times -2i\cos(n\pi)B(n+\tfrac{1}{2},\,s+\tfrac{1}{2})\text{ (App. I. 16).}$$

But $(2s)!=2^{2s}\Gamma(s+\frac{1}{2})s!/\sqrt{\pi}$; therefore

$$w=-2i\cos(n\pi)\Gamma(n+\tfrac{1}{2})\sqrt{\pi}(2/z)^nJ_n(z).$$

Hence

$$J_n(z)=\frac{i}{2\pi}\frac{\Gamma(\frac{1}{2}-n)}{\sqrt{\pi}}\left(\frac{z}{2}\right)^n\int^{(-1+,\,+1-)}e^{iz\zeta}(\zeta^2-1)^{n-\frac{1}{2}}d\zeta. \qquad (19)$$

In this equation write iz for z; then

$$I_n(z)=\frac{i}{2\pi}\frac{\Gamma(\frac{1}{2}-n)}{\sqrt{\pi}}\left(\frac{z}{2}\right)^n\int^{(-1+,\,+1-)}e^{-z\zeta}(\zeta^2-1)^{n-\frac{1}{2}}d\zeta. \qquad (20)$$

In (19) and (20) write $-z$ for z and obtain

$$J_n(z)=\frac{i}{2\pi}\frac{\Gamma(\frac{1}{2}-n)}{\sqrt{\pi}}\left(\frac{z}{2}\right)^n\int^{(-1+,\,+1-)}e^{-iz\zeta}(\zeta^2-1)^{n-\frac{1}{2}}d\zeta, \qquad (21)$$

$$I_n(z)=\frac{i}{2\pi}\frac{\Gamma(\frac{1}{2}-n)}{\sqrt{\pi}}\left(\frac{z}{2}\right)^n\int^{(-1+,\,+1-)}e^{z\zeta}(\zeta^2-1)^{n-\frac{1}{2}}d\zeta. \qquad (22)$$

By addition of (19) and (21) and (20) and (22) it follows that

$$J_n(z)=\frac{i}{2\pi}\frac{\Gamma(\frac{1}{2}-n)}{\sqrt{\pi}}\left(\frac{z}{2}\right)^n\int^{(-1+,\,+1-)}\cos(z\zeta)(\zeta^2-1)^{n-\frac{1}{2}}d\zeta. \qquad (23)$$

$$I_n(z)=\frac{i}{2\pi}\frac{\Gamma(\frac{1}{2}-n)}{\sqrt{\pi}}\left(\frac{z}{2}\right)^n\int^{(-1+,\,+1-)}\cosh(z\zeta)(\zeta^2-1)^{n-\frac{1}{2}}d\zeta. \qquad (24)$$

Any of these formulae can be verified by expanding in powers of z and integrating term by term. From them the formulae of § 1 can be deduced when $R(n)>-\frac{1}{2}$.

Expression for $K_n(z)$. In (17) replace z by iz; thus

$$w=z^n\int_C e^{-z\zeta}(\zeta^2-1)^{n-\frac{1}{2}}d\zeta \qquad (25)$$

is a solution of Bessel's Transformed Equation

$$z^2w''+zw'-(z^2+n^2)w=0, \qquad (26)$$

provided that $\theta(\zeta) \equiv e^{-z\zeta}(\zeta^2-1)^{n+\frac{1}{2}}$ regains its initial value at the final point of C.

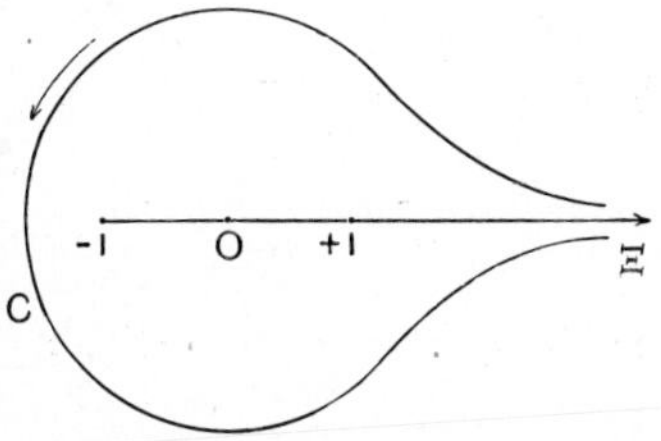

FIG. 3.

In the first place, assume that z is real and positive. Let C denote the contour of Fig. 3, with initial and final points at positive infinity on the ξ-axis, and passing positively round $\zeta=-1$: the initial value of amp(ζ^2-1) is taken to be zero, and C is drawn so that, at all points on it, $|\zeta|>1$. The integral is a solution of (26), since $\theta(\zeta)=0$ at the initial and final points.

Now in (25) expand $(\zeta^2-1)^{n-\frac{1}{2}}$ in descending powers of ζ, and integrate term by term; thus

$$w=z^n\sum_{r=0}^{\infty}(-1)^r\frac{\Pi(n-\frac{1}{2})}{\Pi(n-\frac{1}{2}-r)r!}\int_C e^{-z\zeta}\zeta^{2n-2r-1}d\zeta$$
$$=z^{-n}\sum_{r=0}^{\infty}(-1)^r\frac{\Pi(n-\frac{1}{2})z^{2r}}{\Pi(n-\frac{1}{2}-r)r!}(e^{4\pi in}-1)\Gamma(2n-2r)$$
(App. I. 8).

But $\Gamma(2n-2r)=2^{2n-2r-1}\Gamma(n-r)\Gamma(n+\frac{1}{2}-r)/\sqrt{\pi}$; hence

$$w=z^{-n}\Pi(n-\tfrac{1}{2})(e^{4\pi in}-1)\,2^{2n-1}\pi^{-\frac{1}{2}}\sum_{r=0}^{\infty}(-1)^r(z/2)^{2r}\Gamma(n-r)/r!$$
$$=(e^{4\pi in}-1)2^{n-1}\Gamma(n+\tfrac{1}{2})\pi^{-\frac{1}{2}}\Gamma(n)\Gamma(1-n)I_{-n}(z)$$
$$=i(e^{3\pi in}+e^{\pi in})\,2^n\sqrt{\pi}\,\Gamma(n+\tfrac{1}{2})I_{-n}(z). \qquad (27)$$

Now assume that $R(n+\frac{1}{2})>0$, and let C be deformed into the contour of Fig. 4; then the integrals round the small circles tend

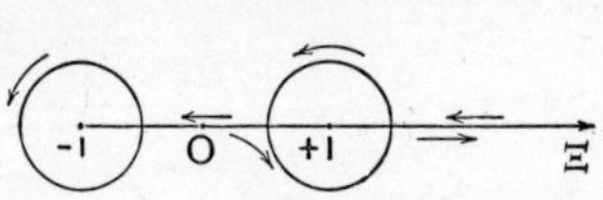

FIG. 4.

to zero with the radii of these circles. Since amp$(\zeta^2-1)=0$ initially, the value of $(\zeta^2-1)^{n-\frac{1}{2}}$ on the ξ-axis to the right of $\zeta=1$ is $(\xi^2-1)^{n-\frac{1}{2}}$; as ζ describes the small semi-circle about 1, amp$(\zeta-1)$ increases by π, so that, on the ξ-axis between 1 and -1, $(\zeta^2-1)^{n-\frac{1}{2}}$ has the value $(1-\xi^2)^{n-\frac{1}{2}}e^{i\pi(n-\frac{1}{2})}$; as ζ passes round the small circle about -1, $\text{amp}(\zeta+1)$ increases by 2π, so that the value of $(\zeta^2-1)^{n-\frac{1}{2}}$ becomes $(1-\xi^2)^{n-\frac{1}{2}}e^{3i\pi(n-\frac{1}{2})}$; similarly, after ζ has passed round the lower half of the circle round 1, the value of $(\zeta^2-1)^{n-\frac{1}{2}}$ is $(\xi^2-1)^{n-\frac{1}{2}}e^{4i\pi(n-\frac{1}{2})}$. Accordingly,

$$w=(e^{4i\pi n}-1)z^n\int_1^\infty e^{-z\xi}(\xi^2-1)^{n-\frac{1}{2}}d\xi$$

$$+i(e^{3i\pi n}+e^{i\pi n})z^n\int_{-1}^1 e^{-z\xi}(1-\xi^2)^{n-\frac{1}{2}}d\xi$$

$$=(e^{4i\pi n}-1)z^n\int_1^\infty e^{-z\xi}(\xi^2-1)^{n-\frac{1}{2}}d\xi$$

$$+i(e^{3i\pi n}+e^{i\pi n})2^n\surd\pi\,\Gamma(n+\tfrac{1}{2})I_n(z). \qquad (28)$$

It follows from (27) and (28) that

$$K_n(z)=\frac{\pi}{2\sin n\pi}\{I_{-n}(z)-I_n(z)\}$$

$$=\frac{\surd\pi}{\Gamma(n+\frac{1}{2})}\left(\frac{z}{2}\right)^n\int_1^\infty e^{-z\xi}(\xi^2-1)^{n-\frac{1}{2}}d\xi. \qquad (29)$$

Now let $\xi=\eta+1$; thus

$$K_n(z)=\frac{\surd\pi}{\Gamma(n+\frac{1}{2})}\left(\frac{z}{2}\right)^n e^{-z}\int_0^\infty e^{-z\eta}\eta^{n-\frac{1}{2}}(2+\eta)^{n-\frac{1}{2}}d\eta.$$

Again, let $\eta=\xi/z$; then

$$K_n(z)=\sqrt{\left(\frac{\pi}{2z}\right)}\frac{1}{\Gamma(n+\frac{1}{2})}e^{-z}\int_0^\infty e^{-\xi}\xi^{n-\frac{1}{2}}\left(1+\frac{\xi}{2z}\right)^{n-\frac{1}{2}}d\xi. \qquad (30)$$

Since both sides of this equation are holomorphic for $-\pi<\text{amp}\,z<\pi$, $z\neq0$, the formula holds at all points in that region, provided only that $R(n+\frac{1}{2})>0$.

Again, in (30) assume that z is real and positive, and let $z+\xi=\surd(z^2+\eta)$; then

$$K_n(z)=\sqrt{\left(\frac{\pi}{2z}\right)}\frac{1}{\Gamma(n+\frac{1}{2})}\int_0^\infty e^{-\surd(z^2+\eta)}\left(\frac{\eta}{2z}\right)^{n-\frac{1}{2}}\frac{d\eta}{2\surd(z^2+\eta)}.$$

Now it can be shown that

$$\int_0^\infty e^{-(a^2\xi^2+b^2/\xi^2)}d\xi=\frac{\surd\pi}{2a}e^{-2ab},$$

so that, when $a=\surd(z^2+\eta)$ and $b=\frac{1}{2}$,

$$\int_0^\infty e^{-\{(z^2+\eta)\xi^2+1/(4\xi^2)\}}d\xi=\frac{\surd\pi}{2\surd(z^2+\eta)}e^{-\surd(z^2+\eta)}.$$

Hence

$$K_n(z)=\frac{1}{\Gamma(n+\frac{1}{2}).(2z)^n}\int_0^\infty \eta^{n-\frac{1}{2}}d\eta\int_0^\infty e^{-\{(z^2+\eta)\xi^2+1/(4\xi^2)\}}d\xi$$

$$=\frac{1}{\Gamma(n+\frac{1}{2}).(2z)^n}\int_0^\infty e^{-\{z^2\xi^2+1/(4\xi^2)\}}d\xi\int_0^\infty e^{-\eta\xi^2}\eta^{n-\frac{1}{2}}d\eta$$

$$=\frac{1}{(2z)^n}\int_0^\infty e^{-\{z^2\xi^2+1/(4\xi^2)\}}\xi^{-2n-1}d\xi.$$

Here replace ξ^2 by $1/(2z\xi)$; thus

$$K_n(z)=\tfrac{1}{2}\int_0^\infty e^{-\frac{1}{2}z(\xi+1/\xi)}\xi^{n-1}d\xi \tag{31}$$

and

$$K_n(z)=K_{-n}(z)=\tfrac{1}{2}\int_0^\infty e^{-\frac{1}{2}z(\xi+1/\xi)}\xi^{-n-1}d\xi. \tag{32}$$

These equations are valid, provided that $R(z)>0$.

From (32) it follows that, when $R(z)$ and $R(z^2)$ are positive,

$$K_n(z)=\frac{z^n}{2}\int_0^\infty e^{-\frac{1}{2}(\xi+z^2/\xi)}\xi^{-n-1}d\xi. \tag{33}$$

In (31) let $\xi=e^t$; then

$$K_n(z)=\tfrac{1}{2}\int_{-\infty}^\infty e^{-z\cosh t}e^{nt}dt$$

$$=\int_0^\infty e^{-z\cosh t}\cosh(nt)dt, \tag{34}$$

which is valid when $R(z)>0$.

Again, let $V_n(z)$ denote the function

$$\frac{\Gamma(n+\frac{1}{2})}{\sqrt{\pi}}(2z)^n\int_0^\infty\frac{\cos\xi\,d\xi}{(\xi^2+z^2)^{n+\frac{1}{2}}},$$

where z is real and positive; then

$$V_n(z)=\frac{(2z)^n}{\sqrt{\pi}}\int_0^\infty\cos\xi\,d\xi\int_0^\infty e^{-(\xi^2+z^2)\eta}\eta^{n-\frac{1}{2}}d\eta$$

$$=\frac{(2z)^n}{\sqrt{\pi}}\int_0^\infty e^{-z^2\eta}\eta^{n-\frac{1}{2}}d\eta\int_0^\infty e^{-\xi^2\eta}\cos\xi\,d\xi.$$

But

$$\int_0^\infty e^{-a^2x^2}\cos(2bx)dx=\frac{\sqrt{\pi}}{2a}e^{-b^2/a^2};$$

hence, when $a=\sqrt{\eta}$ and $b=\frac{1}{2}$,

$$V_n(z)=\tfrac{1}{2}(2z)^n\int_0^\infty e^{-\{z^2\eta+1/(4\eta)\}}\eta^{n-1}d\eta.$$

Here replace η by $\eta/(2z)$; thus

$$V_n(z)=\tfrac{1}{2}\int_0^\infty e^{-\frac{1}{2}z(\eta+1/\eta)}\eta^{n-1}d\eta.$$

Therefore, by (31),

$$K_n(z)=\frac{\Gamma(n+\frac{1}{2})}{\sqrt{\pi}}(2z)^n\int_0^\infty\frac{\cos\xi\,d\xi}{(\xi^2+z^2)^{n+\frac{1}{2}}}. \tag{35}$$

This formula holds when $R(z)>0$ and $R(n)\geqq 0$.

Now in (35) let $\xi=z\sinh\phi$; then

$$K_n(z)=\frac{\Gamma(n+\frac{1}{2})}{\sqrt{\pi}}\left(\frac{2}{z}\right)^n\int_0^\infty\frac{\cos(z\sinh\phi)}{\cosh^{2n}\phi}d\phi, \tag{36}$$

a formula which is valid for z real and positive and $R(n)\geqq 0$.

Expression for $F_n(z)$. The function $F_n(z)$ (Ch. III. § 5) satisfies the equation

$$zw''+(n+1)w'+w=0, \tag{37}$$

which is a particular case of (12): here

$$\phi(\zeta)=\frac{1}{\zeta^2}e^{\int\{(n+1)\zeta+1\}/\zeta^2 d\zeta}=\zeta^{n-1}e^{-1/\zeta},$$

$$\theta(\zeta)=\zeta^{n+1}e^{\zeta z-1/\zeta}$$

and

$$w=\int\zeta^{n-1}e^{-1/\zeta}e^{\zeta z}d\zeta.$$

In these equations replace ζ by $1/\zeta$; then

$$w=\int_C e^{z/\zeta}e^{-\zeta}\zeta^{-n-1}d\zeta$$

is a solution of (37), provided that $e^{z/\zeta}e^{-\zeta}\zeta^{-n-1}$ has the same value at both ends of the contour.

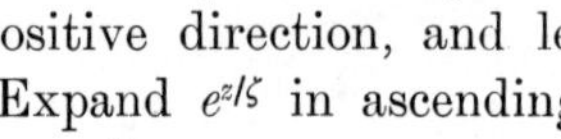

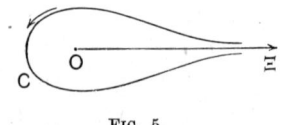

FIG. 5.

Now let C be the contour of Fig. 5, which commences and terminates at positive infinity on the ξ-axis, and passes round the origin in the positive direction, and let the initial value of amp ζ be zero. Expand $e^{z/\zeta}$ in ascending powers of z, and integrate term by term; then

$$\begin{aligned}w&=\sum_{s=0}^{\infty}\frac{z^s}{s!}\int_C e^{-\zeta}\zeta^{-n-s-1}d\zeta\\&=\sum_{s=0}^{\infty}\frac{z^s}{s!}(e^{-2\pi in}-1)\Gamma(-n-s)\quad\text{(App. I. 8)}\\&=2\pi i\,e^{-\pi in}\sum_{s=0}^{\infty}\frac{(-1)^s z^s}{s!\Pi(n+s)}.\end{aligned}$$

Therefore by III. (56),

$$\int_C e^{z/\zeta} e^{-\zeta} \zeta^{-n-1} d\zeta = 2\pi i\, e^{-\pi i n} F_n(z). \tag{38}$$

It follows, III. (54), that

$$J_n(z) = (z/2)^n F_n(z^2/4)$$

$$= \frac{1}{2\pi i} e^{\pi i n} \left(\frac{z}{2}\right)^n \int_C e^{z^2/(4\zeta)} e^{-\zeta} \zeta^{-n-1} d\zeta.$$

In this integral replace ζ by $\zeta/2$; then

$$J_n(z) = \frac{1}{2\pi i} e^{\pi i n} z^n \int_C e^{-\frac{1}{2}(\zeta - z^2/\zeta)} \zeta^{-n-1} d\zeta; \tag{39}$$

this formula can also be established by expanding $e^{\frac{1}{2}z^2/\zeta}$ in powers of z and integrating term by term.

Again, in (39) replace ζ by $\zeta e^{i\pi}$; thus

$$J_n(z) = \frac{1}{2\pi i} z^n \int_{C'} e^{\frac{1}{2}(\zeta - z^2/\zeta)} \zeta^{-n-1} d\zeta, \tag{40}$$

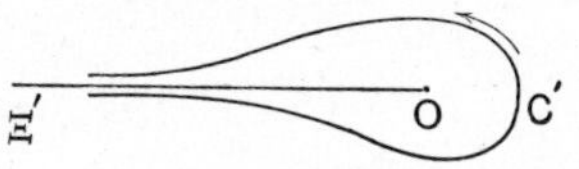

FIG. 6.

where C' is the contour of Fig. 6, commencing and terminating at negative infinity on the ξ-axis, and with $-\pi$ as initial value of amp ζ.

If $R(n) > 0$, the contour C' can be deformed into a straight line parallel to the imaginary axis at distance c from it, where c is positive; the equation is then written

$$J_n(z) = \frac{z^n}{2\pi i} \int_{c-\infty i}^{c+\infty i} e^{\frac{1}{2}(\zeta - z^2/\zeta)} \zeta^{-n-1} d\zeta. \tag{41}$$

If in (39) and (40) z is replaced by iz, it follows that

$$I_n(z) = \frac{1}{2\pi i} e^{\pi i n} z^n \int_C e^{-\frac{1}{2}(\zeta + z^2/\zeta)} \zeta^{-n-1} d\zeta \tag{42}$$

$$= \frac{1}{2\pi i} z^n \int_{C'} e^{\frac{1}{2}(\zeta + z^2/\zeta)} \zeta^{-n-1} d\zeta. \tag{43}$$

Hence, if $R(n) > 0$,

$$I_n(z) = \frac{z^n}{2\pi i} \int_{c-\infty i}^{c+\infty i} e^{\frac{1}{2}(\zeta + z^2/\zeta)} \zeta^{-n-1} d\zeta, \tag{44}$$

where c is positive.

If $R(z)>0$, replace ζ by $z\zeta$ in (39), (40), (42), and (43); then

$$J_n(z)=\frac{1}{2\pi i}e^{\pi in}\int_C e^{-\frac{1}{2}z(\zeta-1/\zeta)}\zeta^{-n-1}d\zeta \tag{45}$$

$$=\frac{1}{2\pi i}\int_{C'} e^{\frac{1}{2}z(\zeta-1/\zeta)}\zeta^{-n-1}d\zeta, \tag{46}$$

and

$$I_n(z)=\frac{1}{2\pi i}e^{\pi in}\int_C e^{-\frac{1}{2}z(\zeta+1/\zeta)}\zeta^{-n-1}d\zeta \tag{47}$$

$$=\frac{1}{2\pi i}\int_{C'} e^{\frac{1}{2}z(\zeta+1/\zeta)}\zeta^{-n-1}d\zeta. \tag{48}$$

Modification of Bessel's Integral when n is not an integer. In (46) let C' be deformed into the contour consisting of: (i) the real axis from $-\infty$ to -1; (ii) the circle $|\zeta|=1$ described positively; (iii) the real axis from -1 to $-\infty$; thus

$$J_n(z)=\frac{1}{2\pi i}(e^{-\pi in}-e^{\pi in})\int_1^\infty e^{-\frac{1}{2}z(\zeta-1/\zeta)}\zeta^{-n-1}d\zeta$$

$$+\frac{1}{2\pi}\int_{-\pi}^{\pi} e^{iz\sin\theta-in\theta}d\theta$$

$$=\frac{1}{\pi}\int_0^\pi \cos(n\theta-z\sin\theta)d\theta-\frac{\sin n\pi}{\pi}\int_0^\infty e^{-n\theta-z\sinh\theta}d\theta, \tag{49}$$

which holds when $R(z)>0$.

§ 3. **The Asymptotic Expansions.*** In this section the asymptotic expansion for $K_n(z)$ will first be found, and from it will be deduced the corresponding expansions for $G_n(z)$, $J_n(z)$, and $I_n(z)$.

A formula for the remainder in the binomial expansion is obtained as follows:

$$\int_0^1(1+zt)^{m-1}dt=\{(1+z)^m-1\}/(mz).$$

Hence
$$(1+z)^m=1+mz\int_0^1(1+zt)^{m-1}dt$$

$$=1+mz\Big[-(1-t)(1+zt)^{m-1}\Big]_0^1$$

$$+\frac{m(m-1)}{2!}z^2\int_0^1 2(1-t)(1+zt)^{m-2}dt$$

$$=1+mz+\frac{m(m-1)}{2!}z^2\Big[-(1-t)^2(1+zt)^{m-2}\Big]_0^1$$

$$+\frac{m(m-1)(m-2)}{3!}z^3\int_0^1 3(1-t)^2(1+zt)^{m-3}dt,$$

*Cf. Prof. G. A. Gibson, *Proc. Edin. Math. Soc.*, Vol. XXXVIII.

and so on; thus

$$(1+z)^m=\sum_{r=0}^{s-1}\frac{\Pi(m)}{r\,!\,\Pi(m-r)}z^r+R'_s,$$

where $$R'_s=\frac{\Pi(m)}{s\,!\,\Pi(m-s)}z^s\int_0^1 s(1-t)^{s-1}(1+zt)^{m-s}\,dt,$$

the only condition being that $(1+zt)$ must not vanish for any real value of t between 0 and 1. The numbers z and m may be real or complex, and that branch of $(1+zt)^{m-s}$ is taken which has the value 1 when $z=0$.

The above condition holds for $\left(1+\xi/(2z)\right)^{n-\frac{1}{2}}$ when ξ is real and positive and $-\pi<\operatorname{amp} z<\pi$, $z\neq 0$; thus from (30)

$$K_n(z)=\sqrt{\left(\frac{\pi}{2z}\right)}\frac{1}{\Gamma(n+\frac{1}{2})}e^{-z}$$
$$\times\left\{\sum_{r=0}^{s-1}\frac{\Gamma(n+\frac{1}{2})}{r\,!\,\Gamma(n+\frac{1}{2}-r)}\frac{1}{(2z)^r}\int_0^\infty e^{-\xi}\xi^{n-\frac{1}{2}+r}d\xi+R''_s\right\}$$
$$=\sqrt{\left(\frac{\pi}{2z}\right)}e^{-z}\left\{1+\frac{4n^2-1^2}{1!\,8z}+\frac{(4n^2-1^2)(4n^2-3^2)}{2!\,(8z)^2}+\dots\right.$$
$$\left.+\frac{(4n^2-1^2)(4n^2-3^2)\dots\{4n^2-(2s-3)^2\}}{(s-1)!\,(8z)^{s-1}}+R_s\right\}, \quad (50)$$

where

$$R_s=\frac{1}{s\,!\,\Gamma(n+\frac{1}{2}-s)(2z)^s}\int_0^\infty e^{-\xi}\xi^{n-\frac{1}{2}+s}d\xi\int_0^1 s(1-t)^{s-1}\left(1+\frac{\xi t}{2z}\right)^{n-\frac{1}{2}-s}dt.$$

The series (50), if regarded as an infinite series, is divergent. It will be shown, however, that, by making $|z|$ large enough, R_s can be made indefinitely small; so that, for large values of z a finite number of terms will give an approximate value of $K_n(z)$. An expansion of this kind, consisting of a finite number of terms and a remainder which can be made arbitrarily small by sufficiently increasing the variable, is called an *asymptotic expansion.*

Now let $z=\rho(\cos\phi+i\sin\phi)$, so that

$$1+\frac{\xi t}{2z}=1+\frac{\xi t}{2\rho}(\cos\phi-i\sin\phi).$$

Consider first the case in which $-\pi/2\leqq\phi\leqq\pi/2$; since $\cos\phi\geqq 0$,

$$\left|1+\frac{\xi t}{2z}\right|\geqq 1+\frac{\xi t}{2\rho}\cos\phi\geqq 1.$$

Choose s so large that $s+\frac{1}{2}>R(n)$; then, if $n=\alpha+i\beta$,

$$\left|\left(1+\frac{\xi t}{2z}\right)^{n-\frac{1}{2}-s}\right|=\left|1+\frac{\xi t}{2z}\right|^{\alpha-\frac{1}{2}-s}e^{-\psi\beta},$$

where ψ is the amplitude of $1+\xi t/(2z)$. But $-\pi/2 \leqq \psi \leqq \pi/2$; thus

$$\left|\left(1+\frac{\xi t}{2z}\right)^{n-\frac{1}{2}-s}\right| \leqq e^{\frac{1}{2}\pi|\beta|}.$$

Accordingly,

$$|R_s| < \left|\frac{1}{s!\Gamma(n+\frac{1}{2}-s)(2z)^s}\right| \left|\int_0^\infty e^{-\xi}\xi^{\alpha-\frac{1}{2}+s}d\xi \int_0^1 s(1-t)^{s-1}dt \times e^{\frac{1}{2}\pi|\beta|}\right.$$

$$> \left|\frac{1}{s!\Gamma(n+\frac{1}{2}-s)(2z)^s}\right| \left|\int_0^\infty e^{-\xi}\xi^{\alpha-\frac{1}{2}+s}d\xi \times e^{\frac{1}{2}\pi|\beta|}\right.$$

$$> \left|\frac{\Gamma(\alpha+\frac{1}{2}+s)}{s!\Gamma(n+\frac{1}{2}-s)}\frac{1}{(2z)^s}\right| \times e^{\frac{1}{2}\pi|\beta|}.$$

Thus, if n is real and $n > -\frac{1}{2}$, $s+\frac{1}{2} > n$, and if z is real and positive, the modulus of the remainder is less than the modulus of the succeeding term.

Again, consider the cases

$$-\pi < \phi \leqq -\pi/2, \quad \pi/2 \leqq \phi < \pi;$$

then

$$\left|1+\frac{\xi t}{2z}\right| = \sqrt{\left(1+\frac{\xi t}{\rho}\cos\phi + \frac{\xi^2 t^2}{4\rho^2}\right)}$$

$$= \sqrt{\left\{\sin^2\phi + \left(\cos\phi + \frac{\xi t}{2\rho}\right)^2\right\}}$$

$$\geqq |\sin\phi|.$$

Thus, if $s+\frac{1}{2} > R(n)$,

$$\left|\left(1+\frac{\xi t}{2z}\right)^{n-\frac{1}{2}-s}\right| < \frac{e^{\pi|\beta|}}{|\sin\phi|^{s+\frac{1}{2}-\alpha}}.$$

Accordingly, if $s+\frac{1}{2} > R(n)$ and $n=\alpha+i\beta$,

$$\left.\begin{array}{l} |R_s| < \dfrac{1}{k}\left|\dfrac{\Gamma(\alpha+\frac{1}{2}+s)}{s!\Gamma(n+\frac{1}{2}-s)}\dfrac{1}{(2z)^s}\right|, \\ \text{where } k=e^{-\frac{1}{2}\pi|\beta|} \text{ if } -\pi/2 \leqq \phi \leqq \pi/2, \\ \text{and } k=|\sin\phi|^{s+\frac{1}{2}-\alpha}e^{-\pi|\beta|} \text{ if } \begin{cases} \pi/2 \leqq \phi < \pi \\ -\pi/2 \geqq \phi > -\pi. \end{cases} \end{array}\right\} \quad (51)$$

Since $K_{-n}(z)=K_n(z)$, the expansion also holds when n is negative.

It follows that $(-\pi < \operatorname{amp} z < \pi)$

$$\operatorname*{Lim}_{z\to\infty} K_n(z) \Big/ \left\{\sqrt{\left(\frac{\pi}{2z}\right)}e^{-z}\right\} = 1,$$

so that $K_n(z)$ vanishes at infinity, provided that

$$-\pi/2 \leqq \operatorname{amp} z \leqq \pi/2.$$

Asymptotic Expansion of $G_n(z)$. Since

$$G_n(z)=e^{-\frac{1}{2}n\pi i}K_n(e^{-i\pi/2}z),$$

its asymptotic expansion is

$$G_n(z)=\sqrt{\left(\frac{\pi}{2z}\right)}e^{-\frac{n\pi i}{2}+i\left(z+\frac{\pi}{4}\right)}$$

$$\times\left[\left\{1-\frac{(4n^2-1^2)(4n^2-3^2)}{2!(8z)^2}+\frac{\left\{\begin{matrix}(4n^2-1^2)(4n^2-3^2)\\ \times(4n^2-5^2)(4n^2-7^2)\end{matrix}\right\}}{4!(8z)^4}-\ldots\right\}\right.$$

$$\left.+i\left\{\frac{(4n^2-1^2)}{1!8z}-\frac{(4n^2-1^2)(4n^2-3^2)(4n^2-5^2)}{3!(8z)^3}+\ldots\right\}\right], \quad (52)$$

where $-\pi/2<\operatorname{amp} z<3\pi/2$.

Asymptotic Expansion of $J_n(z)$. Again, since

$$J_n(ze^{i\pi})=e^{in\pi}J_n(z),$$

we can write $$\pi i J_n(z)=G_n(z)-e^{in\pi}G_n(ze^{i\pi}).$$

Thus, if $-\pi/2<\operatorname{amp} z<\pi/2$, the asymptotic expansion of $J_n(z)$ is

$$J_n(z)=\sqrt{\left(\frac{2}{\pi z}\right)}\left\{1-\frac{(4n^2-1^2)(4n^2-3^2)}{2!(8z)^2}\right.$$

$$\left.+\frac{(4n^2-1^2)(4n^2-3^2)(4n^2-5^2)(4n^2-7^2)}{4!(8z)^4}-\ldots\right\}\cos\left(z-\frac{\pi}{4}-\frac{n\pi}{2}\right)$$

$$-\sqrt{\left(\frac{2}{\pi z}\right)}\left\{\frac{(4n^2-1^2)}{1!8z}-\frac{(4n^2-1^2)(4n^2-3^2)(4n^2-5^2)}{3!(8z)^3}+\ldots\right\}$$

$$\times\sin\left(z-\frac{\pi}{4}-\frac{n\pi}{2}\right). \quad (53)$$

Also, since $J_n(z)=e^{in\pi}J_n(ze^{-i\pi})$, it follows that, when

$$\pi/2<\operatorname{amp} z<3\pi/2,$$

the expansion is

$$J_n(z)=ie^{in\pi}\sqrt{\left(\frac{2}{\pi z}\right)}\left\{1-\frac{(4n^2-1^2)(4n^2-3^2)}{2!(8z)^2}+\ldots\right\}\cos\left(z+\frac{\pi}{4}+\frac{n\pi}{2}\right)$$

$$-ie^{in\pi}\sqrt{\left(\frac{2}{\pi z}\right)}\left\{\frac{4n^2-1^2}{1!8z}-\frac{(4n^2-1^2)(4n^2-3^2)(4n^2-5^2)}{3!(8z)^3}+\ldots\right\}$$

$$\times\sin\left(z+\frac{\pi}{4}+\frac{n\pi}{2}\right). \quad (54)$$

Asymptotic Expansion of $I_n(z)$. Since

$$\pi i I_n(z)=e^{-in\pi}K_n(z)-K_n(ze^{i\pi}),$$

the asymptotic expansion of $I_n(z)$, when $-\pi < \operatorname{amp} z < 0$, can be written

$$I_n(z) = e^{-i(n+\frac{1}{2})\pi} \frac{1}{\surd(2\pi z)} e^{-z}\left\{1 + \frac{4n^2-1^2}{1!\,8z} + \frac{(4n^2-1^2)(4n^2-3^2)}{2!\,(8z)^2} + \ldots\right\}$$

$$+ \frac{1}{\surd(2\pi z)} e^{z}\left\{1 - \frac{4n^2-1^2}{1!\,8z} + \frac{(4n^2-1^2)(4n^2-3^2)}{2!\,(8z)^2} - \ldots\right\}. \qquad (55)$$

Also, since $I_n(z) = e^{in\pi} I_n(ze^{-i\pi})$, it follows that, when $0 < \operatorname{amp} z < \pi$,

$$I_n(z) = \frac{1}{\surd(2\pi z)} e^{z}\left\{1 - \frac{4n^2-1^2}{1!\,8z} + \frac{(4n^2-1^2)(4n^2-3^2)}{2!\,(8z)^2} - \ldots\right\}$$

$$+ e^{i(n+\frac{1}{2})\pi} \frac{1}{\surd(2\pi z)} e^{-z}\left\{1 + \frac{4n^2-1^2}{1!\,8z} + \frac{(4n^2-1^2)(4n^2-3^2)}{2!\,(8z)^2} + \ldots\right\}. \qquad (56)$$

Asymptotic Expansions of the Ber and Bei Functions. If $0 < \operatorname{amp} z < \pi/2$, the asymptotic expansion of $I_0(z)$ may be written

$$I_0(z) = \frac{1}{\surd(2\pi z)} e^{z}\left\{1 + \frac{1^2}{1!\,8z} + \frac{1^2.3^2}{2!\,(8z)^2} + \ldots\right\}$$

$$= \frac{1}{\surd(2\pi z)} \exp\left\{z + \log\left(1 + \frac{1}{8z} + \frac{9}{128z^2} + \frac{75}{1024z^3} + \frac{3675}{32768z^4} + \ldots\right)\right\}$$

$$= \frac{1}{\surd(2\pi z)} \exp\left(z + \frac{1}{8z} + \frac{1}{16z^2} + \frac{25}{384z^3} + \frac{13}{128z^4} + \ldots\right).$$

Hence, if x is real and positive,

$$I_0(x\surd i) = \frac{1}{\surd(2\pi x)} \exp\left(-\frac{i\pi}{8} + x\frac{1+i}{\surd 2} + \frac{1-i}{8\surd 2x} - \frac{i}{16x^2}\right.$$

$$\left. - \frac{25}{384x^3}\frac{1+i}{\surd 2} - \frac{13}{128x^4} + \ldots\right)$$

$$= \frac{e^{\beta}}{\surd(2\pi x)} (\cos\alpha + i\sin\alpha),$$

where $\alpha = \frac{x}{\surd 2} - \frac{\pi}{8} - \frac{1}{8\surd 2x} - \frac{1}{16x^2} - \frac{25}{384\surd 2x^3} + \ldots,$

and $\beta = \frac{x}{\surd 2} + \frac{1}{8\surd 2x} - \frac{25}{384\surd 2x^3} - \frac{13}{128x^4} - \ldots.$

Therefore, with these expressions for α and β,

$$\operatorname{ber} x = \frac{e^{\beta}}{\surd(2\pi x)} \cos\alpha, \quad \operatorname{bei} x = \frac{e^{\beta}}{\surd(2\pi x)} \sin\alpha. \qquad (57)$$

Similarly, the asymptotic expansion of $K_0(z)$ is

$$K_0(z) = \sqrt{\left(\frac{\pi}{2z}\right)} e^{-z}\left\{1 - \frac{1^2}{1!\,8z} + \frac{1^2.3^2}{2!\,(8z)^2} - \frac{1^2.3^2.5^2}{3!\,(8z)^3} + \ldots\right\},$$

so that, when x is real and positive,

$$\operatorname{ker} x = \sqrt{\left(\frac{\pi}{2x}\right)} e^{\delta} \cos \gamma, \quad \operatorname{kei} x = \sqrt{\left(\frac{\pi}{2x}\right)} e^{\delta} \sin \gamma, \tag{58}$$

where $$\gamma = -\frac{x}{\sqrt{2}} - \frac{\pi}{8} + \frac{1}{8\sqrt{2x}} - \frac{1}{16x^2} + \frac{25}{384\sqrt{2x^3}} - \ldots,$$

and $$\delta = -\frac{x}{\sqrt{2}} - \frac{1}{8\sqrt{2x}} + \frac{25}{384\sqrt{2x^3}} - \frac{13}{128x^4} + \ldots.$$

The expressions for γ and δ are obtained from those for α and β by changing the sign of x.

Bessel Functions for which n is half an odd integer. When n is half an odd integer, the series in (50) terminates, so that the expansion gives the exact value of $K_n(z)$. Thus the expressions for the asymptotic expansions of all the Bessel Functions terminate and give the exact values of the functions. For instance, the expressions for $J_n(x)$ in the table on page 17 can be obtained in this way.

§ **4. Asymptotic Expressions for the Bessel Functions.** It has been shown that, if $-\pi < \operatorname{amp} z < \pi$,

$$\lim_{z \to \infty} K_n(z) \bigg/ \left\{ \sqrt{\left(\frac{\pi}{2z}\right)} e^{-z} \right\} = 1.$$

That this is also true if $\operatorname{amp} z = \pm\pi$ can be proved as follows. If $R(n+\frac{1}{2}) > 0$, the formula (30),

$$K_n(z) = \sqrt{\left(\frac{\pi}{2z}\right)} \frac{1}{\Gamma(n+\frac{1}{2})} e^{-z} \int_0^{\infty} e^{-\xi} \xi^{n-\frac{1}{2}} \left(1 + \frac{\xi}{2z}\right)^{n-\frac{1}{2}} d\xi,$$

is valid for $z \neq 0$, $-\pi < \operatorname{amp} z < \pi$, since both sides of the equation are holomorphic in that region. Now let $z = xe^{i\theta}$, where x is real and positive, and let the path of integration be deformed into the contour consisting of: (i) the ξ-axis from 0 to $2x - \epsilon$; (ii) a semi-circle of centre $2x$ and radius ϵ lying above the ξ-axis; (iii) the ξ-axis from $2x + \epsilon$ to ∞. Then the integral is holomorphic in z at $z = xe^{i\pi}$. If $\theta = -\pi$, the semi-circle is taken to lie below the ξ-axis. Since $R(n+\frac{1}{2}) > 0$, the integral round the semi-circle tends to zero with ϵ.

Hence, if $z = xe^{\pm i\pi}$,

$$K_n(z) = \sqrt{\left(\frac{\pi}{2z}\right)} \frac{1}{\Gamma(n+\frac{1}{2})} e^{-z} \{I_1 + e^{\mp i\pi(n-\frac{1}{2})} I_2\},$$

where $$I_1 = \int_0^{2x} e^{-\xi} \xi^{n-\frac{1}{2}} \left(1 - \frac{\xi}{2x}\right)^{n-\frac{1}{2}} d\xi$$

and $$I_2 = \int_{2x}^{\infty} e^{-\xi} \xi^{n-\frac{1}{2}} \left(\frac{\xi}{2x} - 1\right)^{n-\frac{1}{2}} d\xi.$$

In the first place, consider the value of I_1. If $0 \leqq \xi \leqq x$, then

$$\left(1-\frac{\xi}{2x}\right)^{n-\frac{1}{2}} = 1-(n-\tfrac{1}{2})\frac{\xi}{2x}\int_0^1 \left(1-\frac{\xi t}{2x}\right)^{n-\frac{3}{2}} dt$$

$$= 1-(n-\tfrac{1}{2})\frac{\lambda\xi}{2x},$$

where
$$|\lambda| \leqq \int_0^1 \left(1-\frac{\xi t}{2x}\right)^{a-\frac{3}{2}} dt \quad (R(n)=a)$$

$$\leqq 1, \text{ if } a \geqq \tfrac{3}{2},$$

$$\leqq \frac{2\left(1-\dfrac{1}{2^{a-\frac{1}{2}}}\right)}{a-\frac{1}{2}}, \text{ if } a \leqq \tfrac{3}{2}.$$

If $a=\frac{1}{2}$ the last of these inequalities becomes

$$|\lambda| < 2 \log 2.$$

Now
$$I_1 = \int_0^x e^{-\xi}\xi^{n-\frac{1}{2}}\left(1-\frac{\xi}{2x}\right)^{n-\frac{1}{2}} d\xi + V,$$

where
$$V = \int_x^{2x} e^{-\xi}\xi^{n-\frac{1}{2}}\left(1-\frac{\xi}{2x}\right)^{n-\frac{1}{2}} d\xi.$$

But
$$|V| \leqq \int_x^{2x} e^{-\xi}\xi^{a-\frac{1}{2}}\left(1-\frac{\xi}{2x}\right)^{a-\frac{1}{2}} d\xi;$$

hence, by the First Theorem of Mean Value,

$$|V| \leqq e^{-(1+\theta)x}(1+\theta)^{a-\frac{1}{2}}x^{a-\frac{1}{2}}\int_x^{2x}\left(1-\frac{\xi}{2x}\right)^{a-\frac{1}{2}} d\xi, \quad 0<\theta<1,$$

$$\leqq e^{-(1+\theta)x}x^{a+\frac{1}{2}}\left(\frac{1+\theta}{2}\right)^{a-\frac{1}{2}}\frac{1}{a+\frac{1}{2}}$$

$$\leqq e^{-(1+\theta)x}x^{a+\frac{1}{2}}k,$$

where k is finite. Accordingly, when $x \to \infty$, this integral $\to 0$.

Again,

$$\int_0^x e^{-\xi}\xi^{n-\frac{1}{2}}\left(1-\frac{\xi}{2x}\right)^{n-\frac{1}{2}} d\xi = \int_0^x e^{-\xi}\xi^{n-\frac{1}{2}}\, d\xi - (n-\tfrac{1}{2})\frac{1}{2x}\int_0^x \lambda e^{-\xi}\xi^{n+\frac{1}{2}}\, d\xi.$$

The second term $\to 0$ when $x \to \infty$, since it is numerically not greater than

$$\frac{|n-\frac{1}{2}|}{2x}|\lambda|\int_0^x e^{-\xi}\xi^{a+\frac{1}{2}} d\xi.$$

Therefore
$$\lim_{x\to\infty} I_1 = \int_0^\infty e^{-\xi}\xi^{n-\frac{1}{2}} d\xi = \Gamma(n+\tfrac{1}{2}).$$

In the next place,

$$|I_2| \leqq \int_{2x}^\infty e^{-\xi}\xi^{a-\frac{1}{2}}\left(\frac{\xi}{2x}-1\right)^{a-\frac{1}{2}} d\xi.$$

Here put $\xi = 2x(1+\eta)$; then

$$|I_2| \leqq e^{-2x}(2x)^{\alpha+\frac{1}{2}} \int_0^\infty e^{-2x\eta}(1+\eta)^{\alpha-\frac{1}{2}}\eta^{\alpha-\frac{1}{2}}d\eta$$

$$< e^{-2x}(2x)^{\alpha+\frac{1}{2}} \int_0^\infty e^{-\eta}(1+\eta)^{\alpha-\frac{1}{2}}\eta^{\alpha-\frac{1}{2}}d\eta.$$

Hence $$\operatorname*{Lim}_{x\to\infty} I_2 = 0.$$

Accordingly, if $\operatorname{amp} z = \pm\pi$,

$$\operatorname*{Lim}_{z\to\infty} K_n(z) \Big/ \left\{\sqrt{\left(\frac{\pi}{2z}\right)} e^{-z}\right\} = 1. \tag{59}$$

Since $K_{-n}(z) = K_n(z)$, this is true for all values of n.

The corresponding theorems for the other Bessel Functions can be deduced from this. They are:

$$\operatorname*{Lim}_{z\to\infty} G_n(z) \Big/ \left\{\sqrt{\left(\frac{\pi}{2z}\right)} e^{-\frac{1}{2}n\pi i + i(z+\pi/4)}\right\} = 1, \tag{60}$$

where $-\pi/2 \leqq \operatorname{amp} z \leqq 3\pi/2$;

$$\operatorname*{Lim}_{z\to\infty} J_n(z) \Big/ \left\{\sqrt{\left(\frac{2}{\pi z}\right)} \cos(z - \pi/4 - n\pi/2)\right\} = 1, \tag{61}$$

where $-\pi/2 \leqq \operatorname{amp} z < 0$, or $0 < \operatorname{amp} z \leqq \pi/2$;

$$\operatorname*{Lim}_{z\to\infty} J_n(z) \Big/ \left\{ie^{in\pi}\sqrt{\left(\frac{2}{\pi z}\right)} \cos(z + \pi/4 + n\pi/2)\right\} = 1, \tag{62}$$

where $\pi/2 \leqq \operatorname{amp} z < \pi$, or $\pi < \operatorname{amp} z \leqq 3\pi/2$;

$$\operatorname*{Lim}_{z\to\infty} I_n(z) \Big/ \left\{\frac{1}{\sqrt{(2\pi z)}} e^z + e^{-i(n+\frac{1}{2})\pi} \frac{1}{\sqrt{(2\pi z)}} e^{-z}\right\} = 1, \tag{63}$$

where $-\pi \leqq \operatorname{amp} z < -\pi/2$, or $-\pi/2 < \operatorname{amp} z \leqq 0$;

$$\operatorname*{Lim}_{z\to\infty} I_n(z) \Big/ \left\{\frac{1}{\sqrt{(2\pi z)}} e^z + e^{i(n+\frac{1}{2})\pi} \frac{1}{\sqrt{(2\pi z)}} e^{-z}\right\} = 1, \tag{64}$$

where $0 \leqq \operatorname{amp} z < \pi/2$, or $\pi/2 < \operatorname{amp} z \leqq \pi$.

§ 5. **Asymptotic Expressions for the Bessel Functions, regarded as Functions of their Orders.** From the series for $J_n(x)$ and $I_n(x)$ it follows that

$$\operatorname*{Lim}_{n\to\infty} \left[J_n(x) \Big/ \left\{\frac{x^n}{2^n \Pi(n)}\right\}\right] = 1, \tag{65}$$

$$\operatorname*{Lim}_{n\to\infty} \left[I_n(x) \Big/ \left\{\frac{x^n}{2^n \Pi(n)}\right\}\right] = 1. \tag{66}$$

Now (App. I.) if $-\pi < \operatorname{amp} n < \pi$,

$$\operatorname*{Lim}_{n\to\infty} \left[\Pi(n) \Big/ \left\{\sqrt{(2\pi n)} \left(\frac{n}{e}\right)^n\right\}\right] = 1.$$

Hence, if x is real and positive and $n=Me^{i\alpha}$,

$$\operatorname*{Lim}_{n\to\infty}\left[|I_n(x)|\bigg/\left\{\frac{x^{M\cos\alpha}}{2^{M\cos\alpha}\surd(2\pi M)(M/e)^{M\cos\alpha}e^{-M\alpha\sin\alpha}}\right\}\right]=1,$$

or

$$\operatorname*{Lim}_{n\to\infty}\left[|I_n(x)|\bigg/\left\{\frac{1}{\surd(2\pi M)}\left(\frac{xe}{2M}\right)^{M\cos\alpha}e^{M\alpha\sin\alpha}\right\}\right]=1, \qquad (67)$$

where $-\pi<\alpha<\pi$.

Again $K_n(x)$ is even in n; if x is real and positive, $K_n(x)$ is real for n real, and therefore for n imaginary: also for the four values $n=\pm p\pm iq$ it has the same modulus.

Let $0\leqq \operatorname{amp} n<\pi/2$; then

$$\operatorname*{Lim}_{n\to\infty}\left[K_n(x)\bigg/\left\{\frac{\pi}{2\sin n\pi}I_{-n}(x)\right\}\right]=1.$$

Therefore

$$\operatorname*{Lim}_{n\to\infty}\left[K_n(x)\bigg/\left\{\frac{\Pi(n)}{2n}\left(\frac{2}{x}\right)^n\right\}\right]=1. \qquad (68)$$

Again, let $n=is$, where s is real and positive; then, since

$$\operatorname*{Lim}_{n\to\infty}\left[K_n(x)\bigg/\left\{\frac{\Pi(n)}{2n}\left(\frac{x}{2}\right)^{-n}-\frac{\Pi(-n)}{2n}\left(\frac{x}{2}\right)^n\right\}\right]=1,$$

$$\operatorname*{Lim}_{s\to\infty}\left[K_{is}(x)\bigg/\left\{\sqrt{\left(\frac{2\pi}{s}\right)}e^{-\pi s/2}\sin\left(\frac{\pi}{4}+s\log s-s-s\log\left(\frac{x}{2}\right)\right)\right\}\right]=1. \quad (69)$$

Finally, since the function

$$\phi(\lambda, a, b)\equiv J_n(\lambda a)\,G_n(\lambda b)-J_n(\lambda b)\,G_n(\lambda a)$$

is equal to

$$\frac{\pi}{2\sin n\pi}\left\{J_n(\lambda a)J_{-n}(\lambda b)-J_n(\lambda b)J_{-n}(\lambda a)\right\},$$

$$\operatorname*{Lim}_{n\to\infty}\left[\phi(\lambda, a, b)\bigg/\left\{\frac{1}{2n}\left(\left(\frac{a}{b}\right)^n-\left(\frac{b}{a}\right)^n\right)\right\}\right]=1,$$

or

$$\operatorname*{Lim}_{n\to\infty}\left[\phi(\lambda, a, b)\bigg/\left\{\frac{1}{n}\sinh\left(n\log\left(\frac{a}{b}\right)\right)\right\}\right]=1. \qquad (70)$$

EXAMPLES.

1. Prove that

(i) $$\frac{1}{\pi}\int_0^\pi \cos\{r\cos(\phi+\theta)\}\,d\phi=J_0(r);$$

(ii) $$\frac{1}{\pi}\int_0^\pi e^{ix\cos\phi}\cos(y\sin\phi)\,d\phi=J_0\{\surd(x^2+y^2)\}.$$

2. If $R(n+\frac{1}{2})>0$ and $-\pi/2<\operatorname{amp} z<3\pi/2$, show that

$$G_n(z)=\sqrt{\left(\frac{\pi}{2z}\right)}\frac{1}{\Gamma(n+\frac{1}{2})}e^{\frac{-n\pi i}{2}+i\left(z+\frac{\pi}{4}\right)}\int_0^\infty e^{-\xi}\xi^{n-\frac{1}{2}}\left(1+\frac{i\xi}{2z}\right)^{n-\frac{1}{2}}d\xi.$$

3. If $R(n+\frac{1}{2})>0$ and $-\pi/2<\operatorname{amp} z<\pi/2$, show that

$$J_n(z)=\frac{1}{\sqrt{(2\pi z)}}\frac{1}{\Gamma(n+\frac{1}{2})}\left[\begin{array}{l} e^{\frac{-n\pi i}{2}+i\left(z-\frac{\pi}{4}\right)}\int_0^\infty e^{-\xi}\xi^{n-\frac{1}{2}}\left(1+\frac{i\xi}{2z}\right)^{n-\frac{1}{2}}d\xi \\ +e^{\frac{n\pi i}{2}-i\left(z-\frac{\pi}{4}\right)}\int_0^\infty e^{-\xi}\xi^{n-\frac{1}{2}}\left(1-\frac{i\xi}{2z}\right)^{n-\frac{1}{2}}d\xi \end{array}\right].$$

4. If $R(n+\frac{1}{2})>0$ and $-\pi/2<\operatorname{amp} z<\pi/2$, show that

$$J_n(z)=\frac{2^{n+1}z^n}{\sqrt{\pi}\,.\,\Gamma(n+\frac{1}{2})}\int_0^{\pi/2} e^{-2z\cot\phi}(\cos\phi)^{n-\frac{1}{2}}(\operatorname{cosec}\phi)^{2n+1}\sin\{z-(n-\tfrac{1}{2})\phi\}\,d\phi.$$

[In 3 put $\xi=2z\cot\phi$.]

5. If $R(n+\frac{1}{2})>0$ and $-\pi/2<\operatorname{amp} z<\pi/2$, show that

$$Ae^{iz}z^n\int_0^\infty v^{n-\frac{1}{2}}(1+iv)^{n-\frac{1}{2}}e^{-2vz}dv+Be^{-iz}z^n\int_0^\infty v^{n-\frac{1}{2}}(1-iv)^{n-\frac{1}{2}}e^{-2vz}dv$$

is a solution of Bessel's equation, and determine A and B so that this may represent $J_n(z)$.

6. Show that, if $R(n+\frac{1}{2})>0$ and $-\pi/2<\operatorname{amp} z<\pi/2$,

$$K_n(z)=\frac{\sqrt{\pi}}{\Gamma(n+\frac{1}{2})}\left(\frac{z}{2}\right)^n\int_0^\infty e^{-z\cosh\phi}\sinh^{2n}\phi\,d\phi.$$

7. Show that

$$J_n(z)=\frac{1}{\pi}e^{\pm n\pi i}\left\{\int_0^\pi\cos(n\theta+z\sin\theta)\,d\theta-\sin n\pi\int_0^\infty e^{-n\theta+z\sinh\theta}d\theta\right\},$$

according as $\pi/2<\operatorname{amp} z<\pi$ or $-\pi<\operatorname{amp} z<-\pi/2$.

8. Prove that, if $n=k+\frac{1}{2}$, where k is zero or an integer,

$$J_n^2(x)+J_{-n}^2(x)$$

is a rational integral function of x^{-1}, and show that

$$J_{-\frac{1}{2}}^2+J_{\frac{1}{2}}^2=\frac{2}{\pi x};\quad J_{-\frac{3}{2}}^2+J_{\frac{3}{2}}^2=\frac{2}{\pi x}\left(1+\frac{1}{x^2}\right).$$

9. Show that $\qquad J_0(x)=\dfrac{2}{\pi}\displaystyle\int_1^\infty\frac{\sin(\xi x)\,d\xi}{\sqrt{(\xi^2-1)}}.$

[From v. (29), $G_0(x)=K_0(-ix)=\displaystyle\int_1^\infty\frac{e^{ix\xi}\,d\xi}{\sqrt{(\xi^2-1)}}$. Equate imaginary parts.]

CHAPTER VI.

DEFINITE INTEGRALS INVOLVING BESSEL FUNCTIONS.

§1. Various Integrals. Many definite integrals involving Bessel functions have been evaluated by different mathematicians, more especially by Weber, Sonine, Hankel, and Gegenbauer. In the present chapter we shall give a selection of these integrals; others will be found among the examples.

If the function
$$\frac{z^n}{bz^2+2iaz+b},$$
where n is zero or a positive integer and a and b are real and positive, be integrated round a circle in the complex plane with the origin as centre and radius unity, it will be found that
$$\int_0^{2\pi}\frac{\cos n\phi\, d\phi}{a-ib\cos\phi}=\frac{2\pi i^n}{\surd(a^2+b^2)}\left\{\frac{\surd(a^2+b^2)-a}{b}\right\}^n.$$
But, from (IV. 6),
$$J_n(x)=\frac{(-i)^n}{\pi}\int_0^{\pi}e^{ix\cos\phi}\cos n\phi\, d\phi.$$

Hence, if n is zero or a positive integer,
$$\begin{aligned}\int_0^{\infty}e^{-ax}J_n(bx)dx&=\frac{(-i)^n}{\pi}\int_0^{\infty}e^{-ax}dx\int_0^{\pi}e^{ibx\cos\phi}\cos n\phi\, d\phi\\&=\frac{(-i)^n}{\pi}\int_0^{\pi}\cos n\phi\, d\phi\int_0^{\infty}e^{-(a-ib\cos\phi)x}dx\\&=\frac{(-i)^n}{\pi}\int_0^{\pi}\frac{\cos n\phi\, d\phi}{a-ib\cos\phi}\\&=\frac{1}{\surd(a^2+b^2)}\left\{\frac{\surd(a^2+b^2)-a}{b}\right\}^n.\qquad(1)\end{aligned}$$

From (V. 61, 62) it follows that this is valid for complex values of a and b, provided that $R(a\pm ib)\geqq 0$. That value of $\surd(a^2+b^2)$ is taken which tends to a when b tends to zero. The theorem is true, even when n is not an integer, if $R(n)>-1$.

(See Ex. 14 at the end of the chapter.) If $n=0$, (1) becomes

$$\int_0^\infty e^{-ax}J_0(bx)dx=\frac{1}{\sqrt{(a^2+b^2)}}. \tag{2}$$

In (1) keep a and b real and positive, and make a tend to zero; then, if n is zero or a positive integer,

$$\int_0^\infty J_n(bx)dx=\frac{1}{b}, \tag{3}$$

and, in particular,

$$\int_0^\infty J_n(x)dx=1. \tag{4}$$

It will be proved below that (3) holds for $R(n)>-1$.

Again, in (1) write ai instead of a; then, if a and b are real and positive,

$$\int_0^\infty e^{-axi}J_n(bx)dx=\frac{1}{\sqrt{(b^2-a^2)}}\left\{\frac{\sqrt{(b^2-a^2)}-ia}{b}\right\}^n. \tag{5}$$

If $b^2>a^2$, it follows from (3) that the positive value of $\sqrt{(b^2-a^2)}$ must be taken; if $b^2<a^2$, we must put

$$\sqrt{(b^2-a^2)}=i\sqrt{(a^2-b^2)},$$

since this reduces to ia when b is zero.

From (5) we deduce Weber's results,

$$\left.\begin{aligned}\int_0^\infty J_0(bx)\cos ax\,dx&=\frac{1}{\sqrt{(b^2-a^2)}},\\ \int_0^\infty J_0(bx)\sin ax\,dx&=0,\end{aligned}\right\}b^2>a^2. \tag{6}$$

$$\left.\begin{aligned}\int_0^\infty J_0(bx)\cos ax\,dx&=0,\\ \int_0^\infty J_0(bx)\sin ax\,dx&=\frac{1}{\sqrt{(a^2-b^2)}},\end{aligned}\right\}a^2>b^2. \tag{7}$$

Another set of formulae is obtained as follows. The integral

$$I\equiv\int_0^\infty x^{m-1}J_n(ax)dx$$

is convergent if $R(m+n)>0$, $R(m)<\frac{3}{2}$, a real and positive. Formula (v. 2) gives

$$I=\frac{2}{\sqrt{\pi}\Gamma(n+\frac{1}{2})}\left(\frac{a}{2}\right)^n\int_0^\infty x^{m+n-1}dx\int_0^{\frac{\pi}{2}}\cos(ax\cos\phi)(\sin\phi)^{2n}d\phi,$$

provided that $R(n)>-\frac{1}{2}$: on changing the order of integration and applying App. I. (11) this becomes

$$\frac{2\Gamma(m+n)\cos\frac{1}{2}\pi(m+n)}{\sqrt{\pi}\Gamma(n+\frac{1}{2})\,2^n a^m}\int_0^{\frac{\pi}{2}}(\sin\phi)^{2n}(\cos\phi)^{-m-n}d\phi,$$

provided that $R(m+n)<1$; hence (App. I. 14)

$$I=\frac{\Gamma(m+n)\cos\frac{1}{2}\pi(m+n)\Gamma\left(\frac{1-m-n}{2}\right)}{\sqrt{\pi}\,2^n a^m\Gamma\left(1+\frac{n-m}{2}\right)}.$$

But $\qquad \Gamma(m+n)=\pi^{-\frac{1}{2}}2^{m+n-1}\Gamma\left(\frac{m+n}{2}\right)\Gamma\left(\frac{1+m+n}{2}\right);$

thus
$$\int_0^\infty x^{m-1}J_n(ax)dx=\frac{2^{m-1}\Gamma\left(\frac{m+n}{2}\right)}{a^m\Gamma\left(1+\frac{n-m}{2}\right)}, \tag{8}$$

where $R(m+n)>0$, $R(m)<\frac{3}{2}$, a real and positive.

Formula (3) follows from (8) when $m=1$; it is valid for $R(n)>-1$. If $m=0$, then

$$\int_0^\infty \frac{J_n(ax)}{x}dx=\frac{1}{n}, \tag{9}$$

which holds for $R(n)>0$, a real and positive.

From III. (25) it follows that

$$\int_0^\infty x^{m-1}G_n(ax)dx=\frac{2^{m-1}}{a^m}\frac{\pi}{2\sin n\pi}\left\{\frac{\Gamma\left(\frac{m-n}{2}\right)}{\Gamma\left(1-\frac{n+m}{2}\right)}-e^{-in\pi}\frac{\Gamma\left(\frac{m+n}{2}\right)}{\Gamma\left(1+\frac{n-m}{2}\right)}\right\}$$

$$=\frac{2^{m-1}}{a^m}\frac{\pi}{2\sin n\pi}\Gamma\left(\frac{m-n}{2}\right)\Gamma\left(\frac{m+n}{2}\right)$$
$$\times\frac{1}{\pi}\left\{\sin\left(\frac{m+n}{2}\right)\pi-e^{-in\pi}\sin\left(\frac{m-n}{2}\right)\pi\right\}$$

$$=\frac{2^{m-2}}{a^m}e^{i\frac{m-n}{2}\pi}\Gamma\left(\frac{m-n}{2}\right)\Gamma\left(\frac{m+n}{2}\right). \tag{10}$$

In this equation replace a by ia; thus

$$\int_0^\infty x^{m-1}K_n(ax)dx=\frac{2^{m-2}}{a^m}\Gamma\left(\frac{m+n}{2}\right)\Gamma\left(\frac{m-n}{2}\right), \tag{11}$$

which is valid for $R(m\pm n)>0$, $R(a)>0$.

We will next consider a group of integrals which have been obtained by Weber (*Crelle,* LXIX.) by means of a very ingenious analysis.

Let V be a function which is one-valued, finite and continuous, as well as its space-flux in any direction, throughout the whole of space, and which also satisfies the equation

$$\nabla^2V+m^2V=0.$$

Using polar coordinates r, θ, ϕ, and putting $\cos\theta=\mu$, this equation is

$$\frac{1}{r^2}\left\{\frac{\partial}{\partial r}\left(r^2\frac{\partial V}{\partial r}\right)+\frac{\partial}{\partial\mu}\left((1-\mu^2)\frac{\partial V}{\partial\mu}\right)+\frac{1}{1-\mu^2}\frac{\partial^2 V}{\partial\phi^2}\right\}=-m^2V.$$

Let $\omega=\int_{-1}^{+1}\int_{-\pi}^{+\pi}V\,d\mu\,d\phi$; then, observing that

$$\int_{-1}^{+1}\int_{-\pi}^{+\pi}d\mu\,d\phi\left\{\frac{\partial}{\partial\mu}\left((1-\mu^2)\frac{dV}{\partial\mu}\right)+\frac{1}{1-\mu^2}\frac{\partial^2 V}{\partial\phi^2}\right\}=0,$$

because $\frac{\partial V}{\partial\phi}$ and $\frac{\partial V}{\partial\mu}$ are one-valued, we have

$$-m^2\omega=\frac{1}{r^2}\frac{\partial}{\partial r}\left(r^2\frac{\partial\omega}{\partial r}\right),$$

or, which is the same thing,

$$\frac{\partial^2}{\partial r^2}(r\omega)+m^2r\omega=0;$$

whence $$\omega=\frac{1}{r}(A\sin mr+B\cos mr),$$

where A and B are independent of r. If ω is finite when $r=0$ we must have $B=0$, and

$$\omega=\frac{\omega_0\sin mr}{mr},$$

where ω_0 is the value of ω when $r=0$. Now from the definition of ω it is clear that, if V_0 is the value of V when $r=0$,

$$\omega_0=V_0\int_{-1}^{+1}\int_{-\pi}^{+\pi}d\mu\,d\phi=4\pi V_0,$$

and therefore $$\omega=\frac{4\pi V_0}{m}\frac{\sin mr}{r}. \qquad (12)$$

Now consider V as a function of rectangular coordinates a, b, c, and put

$$V=\Phi(a,\,b,\,c);$$

moreover let us write

$$\int_{-\infty}^{+\infty}\int_{-\infty}^{+\infty}\int_{-\infty}^{+\infty}\Phi(a,\,b,\,c)\,e^{-p^2\{(a-x)^2+(b-y)^2+(c-z)^2\}}\,da\,db\,dc=\Omega.$$

Then if we introduce polar coordinates by writing

$$a-x=r\sin\theta\cos\phi,$$
$$b-y=r\sin\theta\sin\phi,$$
$$c-z=r\cos\theta,\qquad \cos\theta=\mu,$$

we have $$\Omega=\int_0^\infty r^2e^{-p^2r^2}\,dr\int_{-1}^{+1}\int_{-\pi}^{+\pi}\Phi'\,d\mu\,d\phi,$$

where Φ' is the transformed expression for Φ.

By (12) this is

$$\Omega = \frac{4\pi}{m}\Phi_0'\int_0^\infty re^{-p^2r^2}\sin mr\,dr$$
$$=\frac{4\pi}{m}\Phi(x, y, z)\,.\,\frac{m}{4p^3}\sqrt{\pi}\,e^{-\frac{m^2}{4p^2}}.$$

Hence, finally,

$$\int_{-\infty}^{+\infty}\int_{-\infty}^{+\infty}\int_{-\infty}^{+\infty}\Phi(a, b, c)e^{-p^2\{(a-x)^2+(b-y)^2+(c-z)^2\}}\,da\,db\,dc$$
$$=\frac{\pi^{\frac{3}{2}}}{p^3}e^{-\frac{m^2}{4p^2}}\Phi(x, y, z). \quad (13)$$

Suppose now that Φ is independent of c; then, since

$$\int_{-\infty}^{+\infty}e^{-p^2(c-z)^2}dc = \int_{-\infty}^{+\infty}e^{-p^2t^2}dt = \sqrt{\pi}/p,$$

we have

$$\int_{-\infty}^{+\infty}\int_{-\infty}^{+\infty}\Phi(a, b)e^{-p^2\{(a-x)^2+(b-y)^2\}}\,da\,db = \frac{\pi}{p^2}e^{-\frac{m^2}{4p^2}}\Phi(x, y), \quad (14)$$

the equation satisfied by Φ being

$$\frac{\partial^2\Phi}{\partial a^2}+\frac{\partial^2\Phi}{\partial b^2}+m^2\Phi = 0.$$

In particular we may put

$$\Phi = J_0(mr),$$

where $r^2 = a^2+b^2$, $a = r\cos\theta$, $b = r\sin\theta$,

and suppose that $x = y = 0$;

then the formula becomes, after integration with respect to θ,

$$\int_0^\infty re^{-p^2r^2}J_0(mr)dr = \frac{1}{2p^2}e^{-\frac{m^2}{4p^2}}. \quad (15)$$

More generally, by putting

$$\Phi = J_n(mr)(A\cos n\theta + B\sin n\theta),$$
$$x = \rho\cos\beta, \quad y = \rho\sin\beta,$$

we obtain

$$e^{-p^2\rho^2}\int_0^\infty re^{-p^2r^2}J_n(mr)dr\int_{-\pi}^{+\pi}e^{2p^2\rho r\cos(\theta-\beta)}(A\cos n\theta+B\sin n\theta)\,d\theta$$
$$=\frac{\pi}{p^2}e^{-\frac{m^2}{4p^2}}J_n(m\rho)(A\cos n\beta+B\sin n\beta). \quad (16)$$

In this formula put

$$A = 1, \quad B = i, \quad \beta = \tfrac{1}{2}\pi;$$

then the integral with respect to θ is

$$\int_{-\pi}^{+\pi}e^{2p^2\rho r\sin\theta+n\theta i}d\theta = 2\int_0^\pi\cos(2ip^2\rho r\sin\theta - n\theta)\,d\theta$$
$$= 2\pi i^n I_n(2p^2\rho r).$$

$$x^2\frac{d^2v}{dx^2}+x\frac{dv}{dx}+(\mu^2x^2-n^2)v$$

hen

$$\mu^2)x+\frac{n^2-m^2}{x}\Big\}uv\,dx=\Big[\,x\Big(u$$

s obtained by multiplying (21
y, subtracting and integrating

e that $m=n$, and let $u=J_n($

$$(\lambda x)J_n(\mu x)dx=x\{\mu J_n(\lambda x)J_n'($$

The formula thus becomes, after substitution, and division of both sides by $2\pi i^n e^{-p^2\rho^2}$,

$$\int_0^\infty re^{-p^2r^2}J_n(mr)I_n(2p^2\rho r)\,dr=\frac{1}{2p^2}e^{-\frac{m^2}{4p^2}+p^2\rho^2}J_n(m\rho),$$

or, more symmetrically, putting λ for m, and μ for $2p^2\rho$,

$$\int_0^\infty re^{-p^2r^2}J_n(\lambda r)I_n(\mu r)\,dr=\frac{1}{2p^2}e^{-\frac{\lambda^2-\mu^2}{4p^2}}J_n\left(\frac{\lambda\mu}{2p^2}\right), \tag{17}$$

or again, changing μ into $i\mu$, which does not affect the convergence of the integral,

$$\int_0^\infty re^{-p^2r^2}J_n(\lambda r)J_n(\mu r)\,dr=\frac{1}{2p^2}e^{-\frac{\lambda^2+\mu^2}{4p^2}}I_n\left(\frac{\lambda\mu}{2p^2}\right). \tag{18}$$

By making μ tend to zero, we obtain the additional result

$$\int_0^\infty r^{n+1}e^{-p^2r^2}J_n(\lambda r)\,dr=\frac{\lambda^n}{(2p^2)^{n+1}}e^{-\frac{\lambda^2}{4p^2}}. \tag{19}$$

In all these formulae the real parts of p^2 and n must be positive in order to secure the convergence of the integrals.

§ 2. **Lommel Integrals.*** If u and v are solutions of the equations

$$x^2\frac{d^2u}{dx^2}+x\frac{du}{dx}+(\lambda^2x^2-m^2)u=0, \tag{20}$$

$$x^2\frac{d^2v}{dx^2}+x\frac{dv}{dx}+(\mu^2x^2-n^2)v=0 \tag{21}$$

respectively, then

$$\int_a^b\left\{(\lambda^2-\mu^2)x+\frac{n^2-m^2}{x}\right\}uv\,dx=\left[x\left(u\frac{dv}{dx}-v\frac{du}{dx}\right)\right]_a^b. \tag{22}$$

This result is obtained by multiplying (21) and (22) by v/x and u/x respectively, subtracting and integrating.

Now suppose that $m=n$, and let $u=J_n(\lambda x)$, $v=J_n(\mu x)$; thus, if $R(n)>-1$,

$$(\lambda^2-\mu^2)\int_0^x xJ_n(\lambda x)J_n(\mu x)\,dx=x\{\mu J_n(\lambda x)J_n'(\mu x)-\lambda J_n(\mu x)J_n'(\lambda x)\} \tag{23}$$

Again, let $\mu=\lambda+\epsilon$, where ϵ is small; then

$$(-2\lambda\epsilon-\epsilon^2)\int_0^x xJ_n(\lambda x)\left\{J_n(\lambda x)+\epsilon\frac{\partial}{\partial\lambda}J_n(\lambda x)+\dots\right\}dx$$
$$=\epsilon x[J_n(\lambda x)J_n'(\lambda x)+\lambda xJ_n(\lambda x)J_n''(\lambda x)-\lambda x\{J_n'(\lambda x)\}^2+\dots].$$

* *Math. Ann.* XIV.

Divide this equation by $-2\lambda\epsilon$, and make ϵ tend to zero; thus, if $R(n) > -1$,

$$\int_0^x x\{J_n(\lambda x)\}^2 dx = \frac{x^2}{2}\left[\{J'_n(\lambda x)\}^2 - J_n(\lambda x)J''_n(\lambda x) - \frac{1}{\lambda x}J_n(\lambda x)J'_n(\lambda x)\right]$$

$$= \frac{x^2}{2}\left[\{J'_n(\lambda x)\}^2 + \left(1 - \frac{n^2}{\lambda^2 x^2}\right)\{J_n(\lambda x)\}^2\right]. \qquad (24)$$

Similarly, if u and v are solutions of the equations

$$x^2 y'' + xy' - (\lambda^2 x^2 + m^2)y = 0, \qquad (25)$$

$$x^2 y'' + xy' - (\mu^2 x^2 + n^2)y = 0 \qquad (26)$$

respectively, then

$$\int_a^b \left\{(\lambda^2 - \mu^2)x + \frac{m^2 - n^2}{x}\right\} uv\, dx = -\left[x\left(u\frac{dv}{dx} - v\frac{du}{dx}\right)\right]_a^b. \qquad (27)$$

Hence, if $R(n) > -1$,

$$(\lambda^2 - \mu^2)\int_0^x xI_n(\lambda x)I_n(\mu x)dx = x\{\lambda I_n(\mu x)I'_n(\lambda x) - \mu I_n(\lambda x)I'_n(\mu x)\}, \qquad (28)$$

and

$$\int_0^x x\{I_n(\lambda x)\}^2 dx = -\frac{x^2}{2}\left[\{I'_n(\lambda x)\}^2 - I_n(\lambda x)I''_n(\lambda x) - \frac{1}{\lambda x}I_n(\lambda x)I'_n(\lambda x)\right]$$

$$= -\frac{x^2}{2}\left[\{I'_n(\lambda x)\}^2 - \left(1 + \frac{n^2}{\lambda^2 x^2}\right)\{I_n(\lambda x)\}^2\right]; \qquad (29)$$

while, if $R(\lambda + \mu) > 0$,

$$(\lambda^2 - \mu^2)\int_x^\infty xK_n(\lambda x)K_n(\mu x)dx = x\{\mu K_n(\lambda x)K'_n(\mu x) - \lambda K_n(\mu x)K'_n(\lambda x)\},$$

and (30)

$$\int_x^\infty x\{K_n(\lambda x)\}^2 dx = \frac{x^2}{2}\left[\{K'_n(\lambda x)\}^2 - K_n(\lambda x)K_n(\lambda x) - \frac{1}{\lambda x}K_n(\lambda x)K'_n(\lambda x)\right]$$

$$= \frac{x^2}{2}\left[\{K'_n(\lambda x)\}^2 - \left(1 + \frac{n^2}{\lambda^2 x^2}\right)\{K_n(\lambda x)\}^2\right]. \qquad (31)$$

Again if,

$$u = J_n(ax)G_n(\rho x) - J_n(\rho x)G_n(ax),$$
$$v = J_n(ay)G_n(\rho y) - J_n(\rho y)G_n(ay),$$

where a and b are real and positive, and if u and v are regarded as functions of ρ, then

$$\int_a^b uv\rho\, d\rho = \frac{1}{x^2 - y^2}\left\{\rho\left(u\frac{dv}{d\rho} - v\frac{du}{d\rho}\right)\right\}_{\rho=b} \qquad (32)$$

and

$$\int_a^b u^2\rho\, d\rho = -\frac{1}{2x}\left\{\rho\left(u\frac{\partial^2 u}{\partial\rho\,\partial x} - \frac{\partial u}{\partial x}\frac{\partial u}{\partial\rho}\right)\right\}_{\rho=b}. \qquad (33)$$

Similarly, if a and b are real and positive, and

$$u=I_n(ax)K_n(\rho x)-I_n(\rho x)K_n(ax),$$
$$v=I_n(ay)K_n(\rho y)-I_n(\rho y)K_n(ay),$$

$$\int_a^b uv\rho\,d\rho=-\frac{1}{x^2-y^2}\left\{\rho\left(u\frac{dv}{d\rho}-v\frac{du}{d\rho}\right)\right\}_{\rho=b}, \tag{34}$$

$$\int_a^b u^2\rho\,d\rho=\frac{1}{2x}\left\{\rho\left(u\frac{\partial^2 u}{\partial\rho\,\partial x}-\frac{\partial u}{\partial x}\frac{\partial u}{\partial\rho}\right)\right\}_{\rho=b}. \tag{35}$$

Another set of integrals is obtained from (22) by making $\lambda=\mu$; for example, let $u=J_m(\lambda x)$, $v=J_n(\lambda x)$; then, if $R(m+n)>0$,

$$\int_0^1 J_m(\lambda x)J_n(\lambda x)\frac{dx}{x}=\frac{\lambda}{m^2-n^2}\{J_n(\lambda)J_m'(\lambda)-J_m(\lambda)J_n'(\lambda)\}, \tag{36}$$

and, if $R(n)>0$.

$$\int_0^1\{J_n(\lambda x)\}^2\frac{dx}{x}=\frac{\lambda}{2n}\left\{J_n(\lambda)\frac{\partial}{\partial n}J_n'(\lambda)-J_n'(\lambda)\frac{\partial}{\partial n}J_n(\lambda)\right\} \tag{37}$$

Similarly, if $R(m+n)>0$,

$$\int_0^1 I_m(\lambda x)I_n(\lambda x)\frac{dx}{x}=\frac{\lambda}{m^2-n^2}\{I_n(\lambda)I_m'(\lambda)-I_m(\lambda)I_n'(\lambda)\}, \tag{38}$$

and, if $R(n)>0$,

$$\int_0^1\{I_n(\lambda x)\}^2\frac{dx}{x}=\frac{\lambda}{2n}\left\{I_n(\lambda)\frac{\partial}{\partial n}I_n'(\lambda)-I_n'(\lambda)\frac{\partial}{\partial n}I_n(\lambda)\right\}. \tag{39}$$

Again, if $R(\lambda)>0$, then, for all values of m and n,

$$\int_1^\infty K_m(\lambda x)K_n(\lambda x)\frac{dx}{x}=\frac{\lambda}{m^2-n^2}\left\{K_m(\lambda)K_n'(\lambda)-K_n(\lambda)K_m'(\lambda)\right\} \tag{40}$$

and $$\int_1^\infty\{K_n(\lambda x)\}^2\frac{dx}{x}=\frac{\lambda}{2n}\left\{K_n'(\lambda)\frac{\partial}{\partial n}K_n(\lambda)-K_n(\lambda)\frac{\partial}{\partial n}K_n'(\lambda)\right\}. \tag{41}$$

Finally, if a and b are real and positive, and

$$u=I_m(\lambda a)K_m(\lambda x)-I_m(\lambda x)K_m(\lambda a),$$
$$v=I_n(\lambda a)K_n(\lambda x)-I_n(\lambda x)K_n(\lambda a),$$

then $$\int_a^b uv\frac{dx}{x}=\frac{b}{m^2-n^2}\left\{v\frac{du}{dx}-u\frac{dv}{dx}\right\}_{x=b}, \tag{42}$$

and $$\int_a^b v^2\frac{dx}{x}=\frac{b}{2n}\left\{v\frac{\partial^2 v}{\partial n\,\partial x}-\frac{\partial v}{\partial n}\frac{\partial v}{\partial x}\right\}_{x=b}. \tag{43}$$

§ 3. Gegenbauer's Addition Formulae.* The addition theorems for the Bessel Functions can be established by means of integrals involving Bessel Functions.†

* *Wiener Sitzungsberichte*, Bd. 70, II. pp. 13, 14; 1874.

† Cf. Prof. H. M. Macdonald, *Proceed. London Math. Soc.*, Vol. XXXII.

Consider the transformed Bessel Equation

$$x^2y''+xy'-(n^2+x^2)y=0, \tag{44}$$

and let

$$y=\int e^{-\frac{1}{2}\left(\zeta+\frac{a^2+b^2}{\zeta}\right)} I_n\left(\frac{ab}{\zeta}\right)\frac{d\zeta}{\zeta}; \tag{45}$$

then

$$\frac{\partial y}{\partial a}=\int e^{-\frac{1}{2}\left(\zeta+\frac{a^2+b^2}{\zeta}\right)}\left\{-\frac{a}{\zeta}I_n\left(\frac{ab}{\zeta}\right)+\frac{b}{\zeta}I_n'\left(\frac{ab}{\zeta}\right)\right\}\frac{d\zeta}{\zeta}$$

and

$$\frac{\partial^2 y}{\partial a^2}=\int e^{-\frac{1}{2}\left(\zeta+\frac{a^2+b^2}{\zeta}\right)}\left\{\begin{array}{l}\frac{a^2}{\zeta^2}I_n\left(\frac{ab}{\zeta}\right)-\frac{2ab}{\zeta^2}I_n'\left(\frac{ab}{\zeta}\right)\\ -\frac{1}{\zeta}I_n\left(\frac{ab}{\zeta}\right)+\frac{b^2}{\zeta^2}I_n''\left(\frac{ab}{\zeta}\right)\end{array}\right\}\frac{d\zeta}{\zeta}.$$

Hence

$$\frac{\partial^2 y}{\partial a^2}+\frac{1}{a}\frac{\partial y}{\partial a}-\left(1+\frac{n^2}{a^2}\right)y$$

$$=\int e^{-\frac{1}{2}\left(\zeta+\frac{a^2+b^2}{\zeta}\right)}\left\{\begin{array}{l}\left(\frac{a^2}{\zeta^2}-\frac{2}{\zeta}-1-\frac{n^2}{a^2}\right)I_n\left(\frac{ab}{\zeta}\right)\\ \qquad+\left(\frac{b}{a\zeta}-2\frac{ab}{\zeta^2}\right)I_n'\left(\frac{ab}{\zeta}\right)+\frac{b^2}{\zeta^2}I_n''\left(\frac{ab}{\zeta}\right)\end{array}\right\}\frac{d\zeta}{\zeta}$$

$$=\int e^{-\frac{1}{2}\left(\zeta+\frac{a^2+b^2}{\zeta}\right)}\left\{\left(\frac{a^2+b^2}{\zeta^2}-\frac{2}{\zeta}-1\right)I_n\left(\frac{ab}{\zeta}\right)-\frac{2ab}{\zeta^2}I_n'\left(\frac{ab}{\zeta}\right)\right\}\frac{d\zeta}{\zeta}$$

$$=2\int\frac{d}{d\zeta}\left\{e^{-\frac{1}{2}\left(\zeta+\frac{a^2+b^2}{\zeta}\right)}I_n\left(\frac{ab}{\zeta}\right)\frac{1}{\zeta}\right\}d\zeta.$$

Thus y is a solution of (44) with a as independent variable instead of x, provided that

$$\theta(\zeta)\equiv e^{-\frac{1}{2}\left(\zeta+\frac{a^2+b^2}{\zeta}\right)}I_n\left(\frac{ab}{\zeta}\right)\frac{1}{\zeta} \tag{46}$$

has the same value at both ends of the contour of integration.

In the expression for y replace ζ by $-\zeta$; then one solution of (44) with a in place of x is

$$u_1=\int_C e^{\frac{1}{2}\left(\zeta+\frac{a^2+b^2}{\zeta}\right)}I_n\left(\frac{ab}{\zeta}\right)\frac{d\zeta}{\zeta}, \tag{47}$$

where C is the contour of Fig. 6, page 53.

It follows from the symmetry of u_1 with respect to a and b that

$$u_1=AI_n(a)I_n(b)+BI_n(a)I_{-n}(b)+CI_{-n}(a)I_n(b)+DI_{-n}(a)I_{-n}(b).$$

Now assume that $R(n)>0$; then, since $\lim_{b\to 0}(u_1/b^n)$ is finite, $B=D=0$; similarly $C=0$, so that

$$u_1=AI_n(a)I_n(b).$$

Again, $\lim\limits_{b\to 0} (u_1/b^n) = \dfrac{a^n}{2^n\Pi(n)}\displaystyle\int_C e^{\frac{1}{2}(\zeta+a^2/\zeta)}\zeta^{-n-1}d\zeta;$

hence, v. (43), $\dfrac{2\pi i}{2^n\Pi(n)}I_n(a) = \dfrac{A}{2^n\Pi(n)}I_n(a).$

Accordingly,
$$u_1 = 2\pi i I_n(a) I_n(b), \tag{48}$$
but both sides of the equation are holomorphic in n; hence the identity holds for all values of n.

In (48) replace a and b by ia and ib; then
$$\int_C e^{\frac{1}{2}\left(\zeta-\frac{a^2+b^2}{\zeta}\right)} I_n\left(\frac{ab}{\zeta}\right)\frac{d\zeta}{\zeta} = 2\pi i J_n(a) J_n(b). \tag{49}$$

Addition Theorem for J_n. If $R^2 = a^2+b^2-2ab\cos\theta$, then, from v. (40),
$$\begin{aligned}\frac{J_n(R)}{R^n} &= \frac{1}{2\pi i}\int_C e^{\frac{1}{2}(\zeta-R^2/\zeta)}\zeta^{-n-1}d\zeta\\ &= \frac{1}{2\pi i}\int_C e^{\frac{1}{2}\left(\zeta-\frac{a^2+b^2}{\zeta}\right)} e^{\frac{ab\cos\theta}{\zeta}}\zeta^{-n-1}d\zeta.\end{aligned} \tag{50}$$

Now, by Sonine's Expansion, IV. (18),
$$e^{(ab\cos\theta)/\zeta} = \left(\frac{2\zeta}{ab}\right)^n \Pi(n-1)\sum_{p=0}^{\infty}(n+p)C_p^n(\cos\theta) I_{n+p}\left(\frac{ab}{\zeta}\right), \tag{51}$$
except when $n=0$, in which case, IV. (19),
$$e^{(ab\cos\theta)/\zeta} = I_0\left(\frac{ab}{\zeta}\right) + 2\sum_{p=1}^{\infty} I_p\left(\frac{ab}{\zeta}\right)\cos p\theta. \tag{52}$$

Accordingly, if series (51) and (52) are substituted in (50), and term by term integration carried out by means of (49), it follows that, for $n\neq 0$,
$$\frac{J_n(R)}{R^n} = \left(\frac{2}{ab}\right)^n \Pi(n-1)\sum_{p=0}^{\infty}(n+p)C_p^n(\cos\theta) J_{n+p}(a) J_{n+p}(b), \tag{53}$$
while, if $n=0$,
$$J_0(R) = J_0(a)J_0(b) + 2\sum_{p=1}^{\infty}\cos p\theta\, J_p(a) J_p(b). \tag{54}$$

If in these equations a and b are replaced by ia and ib, they become
$$\frac{I_n(R)}{R^n} = \left(\frac{2}{ab}\right)^n \Pi(n-1)\sum_{p=0}^{\infty}(-1)^p(n+p)C_p^n(\cos\theta) I_{n+p}(a) I_{n+p}(b), \tag{55}$$
and
$$I_0(R) = I_0(a)I_0(b) + 2\sum_{p=1}^{\infty}(-1)^p\cos p\theta\, I_p(a) I_p(b). \tag{56}$$

Again, let

$$u_2=\int_0^\infty e^{-\frac{1}{2}\left(\zeta+\frac{a^2+b^2}{\zeta}\right)} I_n\left(\frac{ab}{\zeta}\right)\frac{d\zeta}{\zeta}$$
$$=AI_n(a)I_n(b)+BI_n(a)I_{-n}(b)$$
$$+CI_{-n}(a)I_n(b)+DI_{-n}(a)I_{-n}(b);$$

also let it be assumed that b is real and positive; in order that condition (46) may be satisfied $(R\{(a\pm b)^2\}$ must be positive. Let $a=\xi+i\eta$; then this condition can be written $(\xi\pm b)^2>\eta^2$, which is satisfied if (ξ, η) or a lies within the square bounded by the four lines $\xi\pm b=\pm\eta$.

By considering the value of $\lim_{a\to 0}\{u_2/a^n\}$ it is seen that $C=D=0$; also

$$\lim_{a\to 0}\{u_2/a^n\}=\frac{b^n}{2^n\Pi(n)}\int_0^\infty e^{-\frac{1}{2}(\zeta+b^2/\zeta)}\frac{d\zeta}{\zeta^{n+1}};$$

hence, IV. (33), $\dfrac{2K_n(b)}{2^n\Pi(n)}=\dfrac{1}{2^n\Pi(n)}\{AI_n(b)+BI_{-n}(b)\}.$

Accordingly, if b is real and positive, and if $|a|<b/\sqrt{2}$,

$$\int_0^\infty e^{-\frac{1}{2}\left(\zeta+\frac{a^2+b^2}{\zeta}\right)} I_n\left(\frac{ab}{\zeta}\right)\frac{d\zeta}{\zeta}=2K_n(b)I_n(a). \tag{57}$$

Addition Theorem for K_n. Now, V. (33),

$$\frac{K_n(R)}{R^n}=\frac{1}{2}\int_0^\infty e^{-\frac{1}{2}\left(\zeta+\frac{a^2+b^2-2ab\cos\theta}{\zeta}\right)}\frac{d\zeta}{\zeta^{n+1}};$$

and, since $R(a^2+b^2)>0$, it is permissible* to substitute for $e^{-2ab\cos\theta/\zeta}$ and integrate term by term, as was done in the preceding case. Accordingly, if $n\neq 0$,

$$\frac{K_n(R)}{R^n}=\left(\frac{2}{ab}\right)^n\Pi(n-1)\sum_{p=0}^\infty(n+p)C_p^n(\cos\theta)K_{n+p}(b)I_{n+p}(a). \tag{58}$$

But this series converges like $\Sigma C_p^n(\cos\theta)\left(\dfrac{a}{b}\right)^{n+p}$; therefore (Ch. IV. § 2) the theorem holds, provided that $|a|<|b|$.

Similarly, if $|a|<|b|$,

$$K_0(R)=I_0(a)K_0(b)+2\sum_{p=1}^\infty\cos p\theta\, I_p(a)K_p(b). \tag{59}$$

It is left to the reader to deduce that, if $|a|<|b|$,

$$\frac{G_n(R)}{R^n}=\left(\frac{2}{ab}\right)^n\Pi(n-1)\sum_{p=0}^\infty(n+p)C_p^n(\cos\theta)G_{n+p}(b)J_{n+p}(a), \tag{60}$$

$$G_0(R)=J_0(a)G_0(b)+2\sum_{p=1}^\infty\cos p\theta\, J_p(a)G_p(b), \tag{61}$$

* Cf. Bromwich, *Inf. Series*, § 176B.

$$\frac{Y_n(R)}{R^n}=\left(\frac{2}{ab}\right)^n \Pi(n-1)\sum_{p=0}^{\infty}(n+p)C_p^n(\cos\theta)\,Y_{n+p}(b)J_{n+p}(a), \quad (62)$$

$$Y_0(R)=J_0(a)\,Y_0(b)+2\sum_{p=1}^{\infty}\cos p\theta\,J_p(a)\,Y_p(b). \quad (63)$$

EXAMPLES.

1. Show that, for all values of a and b for which the integral exists,

$$\int_0^\infty e^{-\frac{1}{2}\left(t+\frac{a^2+b^2}{t}\right)}K_n\left(\frac{ab}{t}\right)\frac{dt}{t}=2K_n(a)\,K_n(b).$$

2. Show that, if $R^2=a^2+b^2-2ab\cos\theta$,

$$J_{\frac{1}{2}}(R)=\sqrt{\left(\frac{2\pi R}{ab}\right)}\sum_{n=0}^{\infty}(n+\tfrac{1}{2})P_n(\cos\theta)J_{n+\frac{1}{2}}(a)J_{n+\frac{1}{2}}(b),$$

and that, if $|a|<|b|$,

$$K_{\frac{1}{2}}(R)=\sqrt{\left(\frac{2\pi R}{ab}\right)}\sum_{n=0}^{\infty}(n+\tfrac{1}{2})P_n(\cos\theta)I_{n+\frac{1}{2}}(a)K_{n+\frac{1}{2}}(b).$$

3. If $u>0$, and $n=0, 1, 2, \ldots$, prove that

$$\int_0^\infty e^{-x\sinh u}J_n(x)\,dx=e^{-nu}\operatorname{sech} u.$$

4. If x is real and positive, show that

$$K_0(x)=\int_0^\infty \frac{tJ_0(tx)}{1+t^2}\,dt.$$

[From v. (35) and vi. (2) we get

$$K_0(x)=\int_0^\infty \frac{\cos\xi\,d\xi}{\sqrt{(\xi^2+x^2)}}=\int_0^\infty \cos\xi\,d\xi\int_0^\infty e^{-\xi t}J_0(tx)\,dt,$$

and then change the order of integration. For an alternative proof see Ex. 27.]

5. If $R(a\pm ib)>0$, show that

$$\int_0^\infty K_0(ax)\cos bx\,dx=\tfrac{1}{2}\pi(a^2+b^2)^{-\frac{1}{2}}.$$

[Substitute for $K_0(ax)$ from Ex. 4, and change the order of integration.]

6. Show that

$$\int_0^\infty e^{-ax}K_0(bx)\,dx=(b^2-a^2)^{-\frac{1}{2}}\tan^{-1}\frac{\sqrt{(b^2-a^2)}}{a} \quad (b>a)$$

$$=(a^2-b^2)^{-\frac{1}{2}}\tanh^{-1}\frac{\sqrt{(a^2-b^2)}}{a} \quad (b<a).$$

7. Prove that, if $R(a\pm ib)\geqq 0$,

$$\int_0^\infty K_0(ax)J_0(bx)\,dx=(a^2+b^2)^{-\frac{1}{2}}\frac{\pi}{2}F\left(\frac{1}{2},\frac{1}{2},1,\frac{b^2}{a^2+b^2}\right).$$

[Expand $J_0(bx)$ in series, and apply vi. (11) and App. I. (33).]

8. Show that, if $R(a \pm 2ib) \geqq 0$,

$$\int_0^\infty e^{-ax}\{J_0(bx)\}^2 dx = (a^2+4b^2)^{-\frac{1}{2}} F\left(\frac{1}{2}, \frac{1}{2}, 1, \frac{4b^2}{a^2+4b^2}\right).$$

[Use Ex. 8 of Ch. II.]

9. Prove that, if $R(a \pm ib) > 0$, $R(m+n) > 0$, $|a| > |b|$,

$$\int_0^\infty e^{-ax} J_n(bx) x^{m-1} dx = \frac{b^n}{2^n a^{m+n}} \frac{\Gamma(m+n)}{\Pi(n)} F\left(\frac{m+n}{2}, \frac{m+n+1}{2}, n+1, -\frac{b^2}{a^2}\right).$$

[Expand $J_n(bx)$ in series, and integrate term by term.]

10. If $R(a \pm ib) > 0$, $R(2n+1) > 0$, show that

$$\int_0^\infty e^{-ax} J_n(bx) x^n dx = \frac{1}{\sqrt{\pi}} \Gamma(n+\tfrac{1}{2})(2b)^n (a^2+b^2)^{-n-\frac{1}{2}}.$$

11. If $R(a \pm ib) > 0$, $R(2n) > 0$, show that

$$\int_0^\infty e^{-ax} J_n(bx) x^{n+1} dx = \frac{2}{\sqrt{\pi}} \Gamma(n+\tfrac{3}{2}) a (2b)^n (a^2+b^2)^{-n-\frac{3}{2}}.$$

12. If a is real and positive, and $R(n) > -1$, show that

$$\int_0^\infty J_n(ax) \log x \, dx = \frac{1}{a}\left\{\psi\left(\frac{n-1}{2}\right) + \log\left(\frac{2}{a}\right)\right\}.$$

[Differentiate VI. (8) with regard to m, and put $m=1$.]

13. Show that $$\int_0^\infty e^{1-x} F_0(x) \, dx = 1.$$

[Apply VI. (15).]

14. Prove that, if $R(a \pm ib) > 0$, $R(n) > -1$,

$$\int_0^\infty e^{-(ax)} J_n(bx) \, dx = \frac{1}{\sqrt{(a^2+b^2)}} \left\{\frac{\sqrt{(a^2+b^2)} - a}{b}\right\}^n,$$

and deduce that, if $a > 1$, $R(n) > -1$,

$$\int_0^\infty e^{-ax} I_n(x) \, dx = \frac{1}{\sqrt{(a^2-1)}} \{a - \sqrt{(a^2-1)}\}^n.$$

[In Ex. 9 put $m=1$, and apply App. I. (35).]

15. If $a > 1$, $R(n) > -1$, show that

$$\int_0^\infty e^{\pm iax} J_n(x) \, dx = i^{\pm(n+1)} \frac{1}{\sqrt{(a^2-1)}} \{a - \sqrt{(a^2-1)}\}^n.$$

Deduce that, if $a > 1$, $R(n) > -1$,

$$\int_0^\infty J_n(x) \cos ax \, dx = -\sin \tfrac{1}{2}n\pi \frac{1}{\sqrt{(a^2-1)}} \{a - \sqrt{(a^2-1)}\}^n,$$

while, if $a > 1$, $R(n) > -2$,

$$\int_0^\infty J_n(x) \sin ax \, dx = \cos \tfrac{1}{2}n\pi \frac{1}{\sqrt{(a^2-1)}} \{a - \sqrt{(a^2-1)}\}^n.$$

[Take the second integral of Ex. 14 round an infinite rectangle, with the positive real axis as one side and the positive or negative imaginary axis as another.]

16. If $-1<a<1$, $-1<R(n)<1$, show that

$$\cos\tfrac{1}{2}n\pi\int_0^\infty K_n(x)\cosh ax\,dx=\frac{\pi}{2}\frac{\cos(n\sin^{-1}a)}{\sqrt{(1-a^2)}}.$$

[Expand $\cosh ax$, and apply VI. (11) and App. I. (39).]

17. If $-1<a<1$, $-1<R(n)<1$, show that

$$i^{n-1}\cos\tfrac{1}{2}n\pi\int_0^\infty G_n(x)\cos ax\,dx=\frac{\pi}{2}\frac{\cos(n\sin^{-1}a)}{\sqrt{(1-a^2)}}.$$

18. If $-1<a<1$, $-2<R(n)<2$, show that

(i) $$\sin\tfrac{1}{2}n\pi\int_0^\infty K_n(x)\sinh ax\,dx=\frac{\pi}{2}\frac{\sin(n\sin^{-1}a)}{\sqrt{(1-a^2)}};$$

(ii) $$i^{n-2}\sin\tfrac{1}{2}n\pi\int_0^\infty G_n(x)\sin ax\,dx=\frac{\pi}{2}\frac{\sin(n\sin^{-1}a)}{\sqrt{(1-a^2)}}.$$

19. Prove that, if $-1<a<1$, $R(n)>-2$,

$$\int_0^\infty J_n(x)\sin ax\,dx=\frac{\sin(n\sin^{-1}a)}{\sqrt{(1-a^2)}}.$$

[In Ex. 18 (ii) multiply by i^{-n}, and equate imaginary parts.]

20. If $-1<a<1$, $R(n)>-1$, show that

$$\int_0^\infty J_n(x)\cos ax\,dx=\frac{\cos(n\sin^{-1}a)}{\sqrt{(1-a^2)}}.$$

21. If $-1\leqq a\leqq 1$, $-1<R(n)<1$, show that

$$\cos\tfrac{1}{2}n\pi\int_0^\infty K_n(x)\frac{\sinh ax}{x}\,dx=\frac{\pi}{2}\frac{\sin(n\sin^{-1}a)}{n}.$$

[In Ex. 16 integrate with regard to a.]

22. If $-1\leqq a\leqq 1$, $-1<R(n)<1$, show that

$$i^{n-1}\cos\tfrac{1}{2}n\pi\int_0^\infty G_n(x)\frac{\sin ax}{x}\,dx=\frac{\pi}{2}\frac{\sin(n\sin^{-1}a)}{n}.$$

Deduce that, if $-1\leqq a\leqq 1$, $R(n)>-1$,

$$\int_0^\infty J_n(x)\frac{\sin ax}{x}\,dx=\frac{\sin(n\sin^{-1}a)}{n}.$$

23. Prove that, if $-1\leqq a\leqq 1$, $R(n)>0$,

$$\int_0^\infty J_n(x)\frac{\cos ax}{x}\,dx=\frac{\cos(n\sin^{-1}a)}{n}.$$

[In Ex. 19 integrate with regard to a.]

24. If $a\geqq 1$, $R(n)>0$, show that

$$\int_0^\infty J_n(x)\frac{\cos ax}{x}\,dx=\frac{\cos\frac{1}{2}n\pi}{n}\{a-\sqrt{(a^2-1)}\}^n.$$

[Integrate the third equation of Ex. 15 with regard to a.]

25. If $a \geqq 1$, $R(n) > -1$, show that

$$\int_0^\infty J_n(x) \frac{\sin ax}{x} dx = \frac{\sin \frac{1}{2}n\pi}{n} \{a - \sqrt{(a^2-1)}\}^n.$$

26. Prove that $$\int_0^\infty Y_0(x)\, dx = \log 2 - \gamma.$$

[Integrate $G_0(z)$ round the rectangle bounded by $y=0$, $y=M$, $x = \pm M$, indented at the origin, and make $M \to \infty$.]

27. If $x > a$, show that

$$\text{(i)} \quad \int_0^\infty \frac{\sin(a\lambda) J_0(\lambda x)\, d\lambda}{k^2+\lambda^2} = \frac{\sinh ka}{k} K_0(kx),$$

$$\text{(ii)} \quad \int_0^\infty \frac{\lambda \cos(a\lambda) J_0(\lambda x)\, d\lambda}{k^2+\lambda^2} = \cosh ka\, K_0(kx).$$

[Integrate $\sin a\lambda\, G_0(\lambda x)/(k^2+\lambda^2)$ and $\lambda \cos a\lambda\, G_0(\lambda x)/(k^2+\lambda^2)$ round the contour of Ex. 26.]

28. If $a > 0$, $-a < x < a$, show that

$$\text{(i)} \quad \int_0^\infty \frac{\cos(a\lambda) J_0(\lambda x)}{k^2+\lambda^2} d\lambda = \frac{\pi}{2} \frac{e^{-ka}}{k} I_0(kx),$$

$$\text{(ii)} \quad \int_0^\infty \frac{\lambda \sin(a\lambda) J_0(\lambda x)}{k^2+\lambda^2} d\lambda = \frac{\pi}{2} e^{-ka} I_0(kx).$$

[Integrate $e^{ia\lambda} J_0(\lambda x)/(k^2+\lambda^2)$ and $\lambda e^{ia\lambda} J_0(\lambda x)/(k^2+\lambda^2)$ round the contour of Ex. 26.]

29. Prove that $$\int_0^\infty J_1(x) J_0(ax)\, dx = \begin{cases} 1 & (a^2 < 1), \\ \frac{1}{2} & (a^2 = 1), \\ 0 & (a^2 > 1). \end{cases}$$

[For $a^2 > 1$ and $a^2 < 1$ put $J_1(x) = \frac{2}{\pi}\int_0^{\pi/2} \sin(x \sin\theta) \sin\theta\, d\theta$ (IV. 9), and change the order of integration; for $a^2 = 1$ put $J_1(x) = -J_0'(x)$.]

CHAPTER VII.

THE ZEROS OF THE BESSEL FUNCTIONS.

§ 1. Theorems on the Zeros of the Bessel Functions.

Theorem I. If y is any solution of the linear differential equation

$$ay''+by'+cy=0, \qquad (1)$$

where a, b, c are holomorphic functions of x, the function y cannot have any repeated zeros except possibly for values of x which satisfy $a=0$.

For if y has a repeated zero, then $y=0$ and $y'=0$; hence, from (1), since a is not zero, y'' must be zero. Now let (1) be differentiated, and it will be seen that $y'''=0$; by proceeding in this way it can be shown that all the derivatives of y must vanish, and therefore, by Taylor's Theorem, y vanishes identically.

Thus the function $F_n(x)$ cannot have any repeated zeros except that, when n is a negative integer <-1, it has repeated zeros at $x=0$; while the Bessel Functions and the modified Bessel Functions have no repeated zeros except possibly at $x=0$.

Since the functions $J'_n(x)$ and $axJ'_n(x)+bJ_n(x)$ satisfy linear differential equations of the second order,* it follows that they also have no repeated zeros except possibly at $x=0$.

Cor. $J_n(x)$ and $J'_n(x)$ have no common zeros except possibly at $x=0$.

Note. If n is real and a is a positive real zero of $J_n(x)$, then, since $x^{-n}J_n(x)$ is an even function of x, it follows that

* These equations are

$$x^2(x^2-n^2)y''+x(x^2-3n^2)y'+\{(x^2-n^2)^2-(x^2+n^2)\}y=0,$$

and

$$x^2\{a^2(x^2-n^2)+b^2\}y''-x\{a^2(x^2+n^2)-b^2\}y'$$
$$+\{a^2(x^2-n^2)^2+2abx^2+b^2(x^2-n^2)\}y=0.$$

$-a$ is also a zero of $J_n(x)$. This is likewise true of the functions $J'_n(x)$ and $axJ'_n(x)+bJ_n(x)$.

Theorem II. Two linearly independent integrals of (1) cannot both vanish for a value of x which does not make a vanish.

This theorem, which is true for all linear differential equations, can be verified for the Bessel Functions by means of the relation

III. (41) $$PQ'-P'Q=C/x.$$

For if P and Q both vanish for a non-zero value of x, then $C=0$. But if this is so P will be a constant multiple of Q, so that P and Q will not be linearly independent.

*Theorem III.** Let the coefficients a, b, c in (1) be real and continuous functions of x in the interval (α, β), and suppose that a does not vanish in that interval; then, if y_1 and y_2 are two real independent integrals of (1), and if x_0 and x_1 are two consecutive zeros of y_1 within the interval (α, β), there is one and only one zero of y_2 within the interval (x_0, x_1).

For, let $y_2=uy_1$; then, differentiating y_2 and substituting in (1), we have

$$2au'y'_1+au''y_1+bu'y_1=0,$$

so that

$$u'=\frac{C}{y_1^2}e^{-\int_{x_0}^{x}\frac{b}{a}dx}.$$

It follows that u always varies in the same sense when x increases from x_0 to x_1 Now u is infinite for $x=x_0$ and for $x=x_1$; hence it constantly increases from $-\infty$ to $+\infty$, or else constantly decreases from $+\infty$ to $-\infty$. Thus y_2 vanishes once and only once within the interval (x_0, x_1).

For example, when n is real, between any two consecutive positive or negative zeros of $J_n(x)$ there lies one and only one zero of $Y_n(x)$.

Theorem IV. The functions $F_n(x)$ and $F_{n+1}(x)$ cannot have any common zeros, except possibly at $x=0$.

For, if they have, then, since $F'_n=-F_{n+1}$, F_n will have a double zero, which is impossible.

It follows that J_n and J_{n+1} cannot have a common zero, ex-

*Cf. Goursat's *Mathematical Analysis*, translated by Hedrick and Dunkel, Vol. II., Part II., p. 111.

cept possibly at $x=0$. This can also be shown directly by means of the formula

$$J'_n - nJ_n/x = -J_{n+1};$$

for if J_n and J_{n+1} have a common zero, J_n and J'_n will then have a common zero.

The corresponding theorems can be established for the other Bessel and modified Bessel Functions by means of the corresponding formulae.

Theorem V. If n is real, then between any two consecutive real zeros of $x^{-n}J_n$ there lies one and only one zero of $x^{-n}J_{n+1}$.

For, II. (24), $$\frac{d}{dx}\{x^{-n}J_n\} = -x^{-n}J_{n+1},$$

and therefore, since $x^{-n}J_n$ and $x^{-n}J_{n+1}$ are continuous functions, it follows from Rolle's Theorem that between each consecutive pair of real zeros of $x^{-n}J_n$ there is at least one real zero of $x^{-n}J_{n+1}$.

Similarly, since, II. (25),

$$\frac{d}{dx}\{x^{n+1}J_{n+1}\} = x^{n+1}J_n,$$

between each consecutive pair of zeros of $x^{n+1}J_{n+1}$, there is at least one zero of $x^{n+1}J_n$.

This proves the theorem except for the numerically smallest zeros $\pm\xi$ of $x^{-n}J_n$. But 0 is a zero of $x^{-n}J_{n+1}$, and if there is any other positive zero of $x^{-n}J_{n+1}$, say ξ_1, which is less than ξ, then $x^{n+1}J_n$ would have a zero between 0 and ξ_1, which contradicts the hypothesis that there are no zeros of $x^{n+1}J_n$ between 0 and ξ.

Theorem VI. If n is real and greater than -1, $J_n(x)$ cannot have any complex zeros.

For if $p+iq$ is a zero, $p-iq$ must also be a zero. Hence, if $p+iq$ and $p-iq$ are substituted for λ and μ in VI. (23), it follows that

$$\int_0^1 xJ_n\{(p+iq)x\}J_n\{(p-iq)x\}\,dx = 0.$$

But $J_n\{(p+iq)x\}$ and $J_n\{(p-iq)x\}$ are conjugate complex numbers, so that the integrand is positive; thus the integral cannot be zero, and therefore the theorem must hold.

Similarly from VI. (30) it can be deduced that if n is any real number, $K_n(x)$ cannot have a complex zero with real part positive.

Theorem VII. If n is real and greater than -1, $J_n(x)$ cannot have any purely imaginary zeros.

For if $J_n(x)$ had an imaginary zero, it would be a real zero of $I_n(x)$; but from the expansion for $I_n(x)$ it is obvious that no real value of x can make it vanish.

Theorem VIII. If n is real, $K_n(x)$ cannot be zero for any positive value of x.

This is obvious from v. (30) and III. (15).

Theorem IX. If n is real, $G_n(x)$ has no real zeros.

In the first place, let n be not an integer; then, if $G_n(x)=0$, it follows from III. (25) that

$$J_{-n}(x)-e^{-in\pi}J_n(x)=0.$$

But since n is not an integer, $e^{-in\pi}$ is complex, and therefore both $J_n(x)$ and $J_{-n}(x)$ must vanish, which contradicts Theorem II.

Again, if n is a positive integer, then from III. (26), if $G_n(x)=0$, $Y_n(x)$ and $J_n(x)$ must both be zero, which is impossible.

Corollary. If n is real, $K_n(x)$ cannot have a purely imaginary zero.

Theorem X. If n is real, $J_n(ax)G_n(bx)-J_n(bx)G_n(ax)$, where a and b are real and positive, is a uniform, even function of x, whose zeros are all real and simple.

That the function is uniform and even can be seen by expressing G_n in terms of J_n and J_{-n}. To show that it has no complex zeros, put $p+iq$ and $p-iq$ for x and y in VI. (32). Again, suppose that $x=iq$ is an imaginary zero: then

$$I_n(aq)/I_n(bq)=K_n(aq)/K_n(bq).$$

But if $n>0$, and $b>a$, it is clear from the expansion for I_n that $I_n(aq)/I_n(bq)<1$; also from v. (30) it is evident that, if $n\geqq 0$, $K_n(aq)/K_n(bq)>1$. Therefore, if $n\geqq 0$, the function cannot have an imaginary zero. But the function is an even function of n; hence it cannot have an imaginary zero if n is real. Finally, to prove that it has no repeated zeros, consider equation (33) of Chapter VI. For a repeated zero the right-hand side is zero; but the integral on the left-hand side is positive. Thus all the zeros are simple.

Theorem XI. If n is real and >-1, $J(x)$ cannot have any complex zeros.

For, if $\lambda = p+iq$ is a complex zero of $J'_n(x)$, then $\mu = p-iq$ will also be a zero; hence, from VI. (23),

$$\int_0^1 xJ_n(\lambda x)J_n(\mu x)\,dx = 0,$$

which is impossible, since $J_n(\lambda x)J_n(\mu x)$, being the product of two conjugate complex quantities, is positive.

This is also true of the function $axJ'_n(x)+bJ_n(x)$. For, if $\lambda = p+iq$, $\mu = p-iq$ are zeros, then

$$a\lambda J'_n(\lambda)+bJ_n(\lambda)=0,$$
$$a\mu J'_n(\mu)+bJ_n(\mu)=0,$$

and therefore, eliminating a and b between these equations, we have

$$\mu J_n(\lambda)J'_n(\mu) - \lambda J_n(\mu)J'_n(\lambda) = 0.$$

Thus, by VI. (23),

$$\int_0^1 xJ_n(\lambda x)J_n(\mu x)\,dx = 0,$$

which is impossible.

Theorem XII. If n is real and $\geqq 0$, $J'_n(x)$ cannot have an imaginary zero.

For if it had, then $I'_n(\lambda)$ would vanish for non-zero real values of λ: but, III. (4),

$$\lambda^{-n+1}I'_n(\lambda) = \lambda^{-n}\{nI_n(\lambda)+\lambda I_{n+1}(\lambda)\},$$

and both terms on the right-hand side are positive if λ is real and non-zero; hence $\lambda^{-n+1}I'_n(\lambda)$ does not vanish.

Similarly, if a and b are positive, and if n is real and $\geqq 0$, $axJ'_n(x)+bJ_n(x)$ has no imaginary zeros.

Theorem XIII. If n is real and >0, and if a and b are the least positive zeros of $J_n(x)$ and $J'_n(x)$ respectively, then $a>b>n$.

For, since $J'_n(x)$ is positive as x increases from 0, $J_n(b)$, the first turning value of $J_n(x)$, is a maximum. Thus $J_n(b)$ is positive, $J'_n(b)=0$, and $J''_n(b)$ is negative. But, from Bessel's equation,

$$b^2J''_n(b)+(b^2-n^2)J_n(b)=0,$$

so that $b^2>n^2$. Hence $b>n$, and therefore $a>b>n$. When $n=0$, $a>b=0$.

Theorem XIV. If n is real and $\geqq 0$, between two consecutive zeros of $J_n(x)$ there lies one and only one zero of $J'_n(x)$.

By Rolle's theorem there is certainly one such zero of $J'_n(x)$. If there be more than one, there must be at least three; but this is impossible because, for at least one of the three, b say, $J''_n(b)$ and $J_n(b)$ would be of the same sign, which, from Bessel's equation, is clearly impossible, since $b^2 > n^2$.

This theorem could also be deduced from *example* 3 at the end of the chapter. For

$$\frac{d}{dx}\left\{\frac{J'_n}{J_n}\right\} = -\frac{n}{x^2} - \sum_{s=1}^{\infty}\left\{\frac{1}{(x-\kappa_s)^2} + \frac{1}{(x+\kappa_s)^2}\right\},$$

so that J'_n/J_n decreases steadily from $+\infty$ to $-\infty$ as x increases between two consecutive zeros.

Cor. One and only one zero of $aJ'_n(x)+bJ_n(x)$ lies between two consecutive zeros of $J_n(x)$.

For J'_n/J_n takes the value $-b/a$ once and only once in the interval.

Theorem XV. If n is real and $\geqq 0$, between two consecutive positive zeros of $J_n(x)$ there lies one and only one zero of $axJ'_n(x)+bJ_n(x)$.

For, if $y = J'^2_n + \left(1-\frac{n^2}{x^2}\right)J^2_n$,

$$\frac{d}{dx}\left(\frac{xJ'_n}{J_n}\right) = -\frac{xy}{J^2_n}.$$

Hence, between any two consecutive positive zeros of J_n, say p and q, $\frac{d}{dx}\left(\frac{xJ'_n}{J_n}\right)$ is negative, since $q > p > n$. Thus the function xJ'_n/J_n decreases steadily from $+\infty$ to $-\infty$ as x increases from p to q, and therefore it takes any given value once and once only. Accordingly, the equation

$$axJ'_n(x)+bJ_n(x)=0$$

has one and only one root in the interval (p, q).

Again, $$\frac{d}{dx}(x^2y) = 2xJ^2_n,$$

so that, if x is positive, x^2y is an increasing function. But, if $n \geqq 0$, $x^2y = 0$ when $x = 0$; therefore $x^2y \geqq 0$ for $x \geqq 0$. Accordingly, if β is the smallest positive zero of $J_n(x)$, $\frac{d}{dx}\left(\frac{xJ'_n}{J_n}\right)$ is negative for $0 < x < \beta$. But $\lim_{x\to 0}\frac{xJ'_n}{J_n} = n$; hence xJ'_n/J_n decreases from n to $-\infty$ as x increases from 0 to β.

This theorem could also be deduced from *example* 3, since

$$\frac{d}{dx}\left\{\frac{xJ'_n}{J_n}\right\} = -\sum_{s=1}^{\infty}\frac{4\kappa_s^2 x}{(x^2-\kappa_s^2)^2}.$$

§ 2. The Zeros of $J_n(x)$. It will now be proved that $J_n(x)$, where n is real, has an infinite number of real zeros. The method employed is that which was given by Bessel* for the case $n=0$.

From v. (6),

$$J_n(x) = \frac{2}{\sqrt{\pi}\,\Gamma(n+\frac{1}{2})}\left(\frac{x}{2}\right)^n \int_0^1 \cos(x\xi)(1-\xi^2)^{n-\frac{1}{2}}\,d\xi.$$

In the first place, assume that $-\frac{1}{2}<n<\frac{1}{2}$. Take $x=(m+\frac{1}{2})\pi$, where m is zero or a positive integer; then, if $\eta=(2m+1)\xi$,

$$\begin{aligned} J_n(m\pi+\tfrac{1}{2}\pi) &= \frac{2}{\sqrt{\pi}\,\Gamma(n+\frac{1}{2})}\left(\frac{x}{2}\right)^n \int_0^{2m+1}\cos(\tfrac{1}{2}\pi\eta)\left\{1-\frac{\eta^2}{(2m+1)^2}\right\}^{n-\frac{1}{2}}\frac{d\eta}{2m+1} \\ &= \frac{2}{\sqrt{\pi}\,\Gamma(n+\frac{1}{2})}\left(\frac{x}{2}\right)^n \{\tfrac{1}{2}u_0-u_1+u_2-\ldots+(-1)^m u_m\}, \end{aligned}$$

where
$$\begin{aligned} u_r &= (-1)^r\int_{2r-1}^{2r+1}\cos(\tfrac{1}{2}\pi\eta)\left\{1-\frac{\eta^2}{(2m+1)^2}\right\}^{n-\frac{1}{2}}\frac{d\eta}{2m+1} \\ &= \int_{-1}^{1}\cos(\tfrac{1}{2}\pi\eta)\left\{1-\frac{(\eta+2r)^2}{(2m+1)^2}\right\}^{n-\frac{1}{2}}\frac{d\eta}{2m+1}. \end{aligned}$$

Now each u_r is positive, and, since $n<\frac{1}{2}$, $u_r<u_{r+1}$: thus $J_n(m\pi+\frac{1}{2}\pi)$ is positive or negative according as m is even or odd. Consequently, as x increases from $(r-\frac{1}{2})\pi$ to $(r+\frac{1}{2})\pi$, $J_n(x)$ changes sign, and must therefore vanish for some value of x in the interval. Moreover, from the formulae given in Chapter II. § 5, it is clear that $J_{-\frac{1}{2}}(x)$ and $J_{\frac{1}{2}}(x)$ have also an infinite number of real zeros. Thus, if $-\frac{1}{2}\leqq n\leqq\frac{1}{2}$, $J_n(x)$ has an infinite number of real positive zeros; the negative zeros are equal and opposite to the positive zeros.

From Theorem V. of the previous section it follows that the theorem holds for all real values of n.

That $J_n(x)$ has an infinite number of real zeros can also be deduced from the asymptotic expansion v. (53). For, if $x=m\pi+\frac{1}{4}\pi+\frac{1}{2}n\pi$, where m is an integer, the first term of the expansion is $\sqrt{\left(\frac{2}{\pi x}\right)}\cos m\pi$, and, for sufficiently great values

* *Berlin Abhandlungen* (1824), Art. 14.

of m, this term determines the sign of $J_n(x)$. Thus, between two large consecutive values of m, $J_n(x)$ changes sign, so that there must be at least one zero in the interval. A similar proof applies to such functions as $J'(x)$, $Y_n(x)$, and $axJ'_n(x)+bJ_n(x)$.

Since, as $x \to \infty$, $J_n(x) \Big/ \sqrt{\left(\frac{2}{\pi x}\right)} \cos(x - \frac{1}{4}\pi - \frac{1}{2}n\pi) \to 1$,

it is evident that the large positive roots of $J_n(x)$ are approximately given by

$$x = (k + \tfrac{3}{4} + \tfrac{1}{2}n)\pi,$$

where k is a large positive integer. The negative roots are numerically equal to the positive roots.

As an example of the degree of approximation, suppose that $n=0$ and $k=9$; then

$$(k+\tfrac{3}{4})\pi = 30{\cdot}6305\ldots,$$

the true value of the corresponding root being

$$30{\cdot}6346\ldots.$$

Stokes' Method of Calculating the Zeros of $J_n(x)$. The best practical method of calculating the zeros is that of Stokes,* which depends upon the asymptotic expansion for $J_n(x)$.

To fix the ideas, suppose $n=0$. Then, when x is large, we have approximately

$$J_0(x) = \sqrt{\frac{2}{\pi x}}\left\{P \cos\left(x - \frac{\pi}{4}\right) + Q \sin\left(x - \frac{\pi}{4}\right)\right\},$$

where $$P = 1 - \frac{1^2 . 3^2}{2!(8x)^2} + \frac{1^2 . 3^2 . 5^2 . 7^2}{4!(8x)^4} - \ldots$$

$$Q = \frac{1}{8x} - \frac{1^2 . 3^2 . 5^2}{3!(8x)^3} + \frac{1^2 . 3^2 . 5^2 . 7^2 . 9^2}{5!(8x)^5} - \ldots\ldots$$

Put $$P = M\cos\psi, \quad Q = M \sin\psi;$$

then $$M = \sqrt{P^2+Q^2}, \quad \psi = \tan^{-1}\frac{Q}{P}.$$

Now substitute the above expansions for P and Q, and obtain the asymptotic expansions

$$\left.\begin{aligned} M &= 1 - \frac{1}{16x^2} + \frac{53}{512x^4} - \ldots, \\ \psi &= \tan^{-1}\left(\frac{1}{8x} - \frac{33}{512x^3} + \frac{3417}{16384x^5} - \ldots\right). \end{aligned}\right\} \quad (2)$$

* *Camb. Phil. Trans.* IX. (1856), p. 182.

The value of $J_0(x)$ is (approximately)

$$\sqrt{\frac{2}{\pi x}}\, M \cos\left(x-\frac{\pi}{4}-\psi\right), \tag{3}$$

which vanishes when $x=(k-\frac{1}{4})\pi+\psi$,
k being any integer.

Write, for the moment,

$$\phi=(k-\tfrac{1}{4})\pi;$$

then we have to solve the transcendental equation

$$x=\phi+\tan^{-1}\left(\frac{1}{8x}-\frac{33}{512x^3}+\frac{3417}{16384x^5}-\dots\right)$$

on the supposition that ϕ and x are both large.

Assume $$x=\phi+\frac{a}{\phi}+\frac{b}{\phi^3}+\frac{c}{\phi^5}+\dots;$$

then, with the help of Gregory's series,

$$\phi+\frac{a}{\phi}+\frac{b}{\phi^3}+\frac{c}{\phi^5}+\dots$$
$$=\phi+\frac{1}{8}\left(\frac{1}{\phi}-\frac{a}{\phi^3}+\dots\right)-\frac{33}{512}\left(\frac{1}{\phi^3}-\dots\right)+\dots$$
$$-\frac{1}{3.512}\left(\frac{1}{\phi^3}-\dots\right)+\dots,$$

and therefore $$a=\frac{1}{8},\quad b=-\frac{31}{384},\quad \text{etc.}$$

Substituting for ϕ its value $(k-\frac{1}{4})\pi$, we have finally

$$\frac{x}{\pi}=(k-\tfrac{1}{4})+\frac{1}{2\pi^2(4k-1)}-\frac{31}{6\pi^4(4k-1)^3}+\dots,$$

or, reducing to decimals,

$$\frac{x}{\pi}=k-{\cdot}25+\frac{{\cdot}050661}{4k-1}-\frac{{\cdot}053041}{(4k-1)^3}+\frac{{\cdot}262051}{(4k-1)^5}-\dots. \tag{4}$$

The corresponding formula for the roots of $J_1(x)=0$ is

$$\frac{x}{\pi}=k+{\cdot}25-\frac{{\cdot}151982}{4k+1}+\frac{{\cdot}015399}{(4k+1)^3}-\frac{{\cdot}245270}{(4k+1)^5}+\dots. \tag{5}$$

The same method is applicable to Bessel functions of higher orders. [See Appendix III.]

The general formula for the kth root of $J_n(x)=0$ is

$$\left.\begin{aligned}x=a-\frac{m-1}{8a}-\frac{4(m-1)(7m-31)}{3(8a)^3}\\ -\frac{32(m-1)(83m^2-982m+3779)}{15(8a)^5}+\dots,\end{aligned}\right\} \tag{6}$$

where $a=\frac{1}{4}\pi(2n-1+4k)$, $m=4n^2$.

This formula is due to Prof. McMahon, and was kindly communicated to the authors by Lord Rayleigh. It has been worked out independently by Mr. W. St. B. Griffith, so that there is no reasonable doubt of its correctness. It may be remarked that Stokes gives the incorrect value ·245835 for the numerator of the last term on the right-hand side of (5); the error has somehow arisen in the reduction of $1179/(5\pi^6)$, which is the exact value, to a decimal.

The values of the roots may also be obtained by interpolation from a table of the functions, provided the tabular difference is sufficiently small.

The reader will find at the end of the book a graph of the functions $J_0(x)$ and $J_1(x)$ extending over a sufficient interval to show how they behave when x is comparatively large.

§ 3. Zeros of the Bessel Functions regarded as Functions of their Orders.* If x and n are real, $J_n(x)$ is a real function of n. In VI. (36) put $m=p+iq$ and $n=p-iq$, and it will be seen as before that $J_n(x)$ does not vanish for any complex values of n with real part positive; similarly for $I_n(x)$. Also, from VI. (40) and VI. (42), if x is real and a and b positive,

$$K_n(x) \quad \text{and} \quad I_n(ax)\,K_n(bx)-I_n(bx)\,K_n(ax)$$

do not vanish for n complex.

If x is real and n positive $J_n(x)$ cannot have any repeated zeros. For, if n were a repeated zero, $J_n(x)$ and $\frac{\partial}{\partial n}J_n(x)$ would vanish, which is impossible by VI. (37).

Again, if x is real, $J_n(x)$ cannot have an imaginary zero; for then $J_{-n}(x)$ would also vanish, so that, from III. (42), it would result that $\sin n\pi=0$, which is not the case: similarly for $I_n(x)$. Also, if x is real and $n>-1$, $I_n(x)$ has no real zeros; this follows from the infinite series for $I_n(x)$. Again, from V. (30) and III. (15) it results that, if x is positive, $K_n(x)$ has no real zeros, and, as in Theorem X., it can be shown that, if x is real and a and b positive, $I_n(ax)\,K_n(bx)-I_n(bx)\,K_n(ax)$ has no real zeros. Thus the two latter functions only vanish when n is purely imaginary, and it can be shown that they have an infinite number of such zeros. For, if not, the function $1/\{ne^{-in\pi/2}K_n(x)\}$ would vanish for n infinite, and would have

* Cf. Dr. J. Dougall, *Proc. Edin. Math. Soc.*, Vol. XVIII.

only a finite number of non-essential singularities; thus it would be a rational integral function of n, which is not the case: similarly for the other function.

EXAMPLES.

1. If n is real and positive, show that the value of the least positive zero of $J_n(x)/x^n$ tends to infinity with n.

2. If a is a positive zero of $J_0(x)$, show that

$$\sqrt{(a+\pi)}\, J_0(a+\pi) = -\int_a^{a+\pi} \frac{\sin(x-a)}{4x^{3/2}} J_0(x)\, dx.$$

Hence show that the difference between two successive zeros of $J_0(x)$ is less than π.

[Verify that

$$\sqrt{x}\sin(x-a)\, J_0'(x) + \frac{\sin(x-a)}{2\sqrt{x}} J_0(x) - \sqrt{x}\cos(x-a)\, J_0(x)$$

$$= -\int_a^x \frac{\sin(x-a)}{4x^{\frac{3}{2}}} J_0(x)\, dx,$$

and put $x = a+\pi$.]

3. If $a_1, a_2, a_3, \ldots$ are the zeros of $z^{-n}J_n(z)$ arranged in order of non-descending magnitudes of their moduli, show that

$$J_n(z) = \frac{z^n}{2^n\Pi(n)} \prod_{s=1}^{\infty} \left\{\left(1 - \frac{z}{a_s}\right) e^{\frac{z}{a_s}}\right\},$$

and deduce that, if n is real and > -1,

$$J_n(z) = \frac{z^n}{2^n\Pi(n)} \prod_{s=1}^{\infty} \left(1 - \frac{z^2}{\kappa_s^2}\right),$$

where $\kappa_1, \kappa_2, \kappa_3, \ldots$ are the positive zeros of $J_n(z)$.

[From II. (24) and V. (61), (62) we have

$$\operatorname*{Lim}_{|\zeta|\to\infty} \frac{\frac{d}{d\zeta}\{\zeta^{-n}J_n(\zeta)\}}{\zeta^{-n}J_n(\zeta)} = \operatorname*{Lim}_{|\zeta|\to\infty} \frac{J_{n+1}(\zeta)}{J_n(\zeta)} = \mp i,$$

according as $I(\zeta) \gtrless 0$; thus the integral

$$\frac{1}{2\pi i}\int \frac{\frac{d}{d\zeta}\{\zeta^{-n}J_n(\zeta)\}}{\zeta^{-n}J_n(\zeta)} \frac{d\zeta}{\zeta - z},$$

taken round a circle with the origin as centre and radius chosen so that the circle does not pass through a zero of $J_n(\zeta)$, tends to zero as the radius tends to infinity. Therefore, by the theory of residues,

$$\frac{\frac{d}{dz}\{z^{-n}J_n(z)\}}{z^{-n}J_n(z)} = \sum_{s=1}^{\infty}\left\{\frac{1}{z-\alpha_s}+\frac{1}{\alpha_s}\right\},$$

since $\Sigma\alpha_s^{-2}$ is absolutely convergent.

Hence, integrating from 0 to z, we have

$$z^{-n}J_n(z) = A\prod_{s=1}^{\infty}\left\{\left(1-\frac{z}{\alpha_s}\right)e^{\frac{z}{\alpha_s}}\right\}.$$

To determine A, take the limit when $z\to 0$.]

CHAPTER VIII.

FOURIER-BESSEL EXPANSIONS AND INTEGRALS.

§ 1. **The Fourier-Bessel Expansions.** It was proved in Chapter VI., § 2, that, if $R(n) > -1$,

$$\int_0^1 xJ_n(\lambda x)J_n(\mu x)\,dx = \frac{1}{\lambda^2-\mu^2}\{\mu J_n(\lambda)J_n'(\mu) - \lambda J_n(\mu)J_n'(\lambda)\} \quad (1)$$

and

$$\int_0^1 x\{J_n(\lambda x)\}^2\,dx = \frac{1}{2\lambda}[\lambda\{J_n'(\lambda)\}^2 - J_n(\lambda)J_n'(\lambda) - \lambda J_n(\lambda)J_n''(\lambda)] \quad (2)$$

$$= \tfrac{1}{2}[\{J_n'(\lambda)\}^2 + (1-n^2/\lambda^2)\{J_n(\lambda)\}^2]. \quad (3)$$

From (1) it follows that

$$\int_0^1 xJ_n(\lambda x)J_n(\mu x)\,dx = 0,$$

provided that $\lambda \neq \mu$, and that

$$\mu J_n(\lambda)J_n'(\mu) - \lambda J_n(\mu)J_n'(\lambda) = 0.$$

These conditions are satisfied, among other ways,

(i) if λ, μ, are different roots of $J_n(x)=0$,

(ii) if they are different roots of $J_n'(x)=0$,

(iii) if they are different roots of

$$AxJ_n'(x) + BJ_n(x) = 0,$$

where A and B are constants. [See Chapter VII. Theorem XI.]

In Chapter VII. it was shown that, if n is real and greater than -1, the zeros of $x^{-n}J_n(x)$ are real and distinct, and that similar theorems hold for $x^{-n+1}J_n'(x)$ and $x^{-n}\{AxJ_n'(x)+BJ_n(x)\}$.

To show the application of these results, we will employ the function

$$\phi = e^{-\lambda z}J_0(\lambda r)$$

to obtain the solution of a problem in the conduction of heat. Consider the solid cylinder bounded by the surfaces $r=1$, $z=0$,

$z=+\infty$, and suppose that its convex surface is surrounded by a medium of temperature zero. Then when the flow of heat has become steady, the temperature V at any point in the cylinder must satisfy the equation

$$\nabla^2 V=0,$$

and moreover, when $r=1$,

$$k\frac{\partial V}{\partial r}+hV=0,$$

where k is the conductivity of the material of the cylinder, and h is what Fourier calls the "external conductivity."

If we put $V=\phi$, the first condition is satisfied; and the second will also be satisfied, if

$$\lambda k J_0'(\lambda)+hJ_0(\lambda)=0. \tag{4}$$

Suppose, then, that λ is any positive root of this equation, and suppose, moreover, that the base of the cylinder is permanently heated so that the temperature at a distance r from the centre is $J_0(\lambda r)$. Then the temperature at any point within the cylinder is

$$V=e^{-\lambda z}J_0(\lambda r),$$

because this satisfies all the conditions of the problem.

The equation (4) has an infinite number of positive real roots λ_1, λ_2, etc., so that we can construct a more general function

$$\phi=\sum_1^\infty A_s e^{-\lambda_s z}J_0(\lambda_s r) \tag{5}$$

and this will represent the temperature of the same cylinder when subject to the same conditions, except that the temperature at any point of the base is now given by

$$\phi_0=\sum_1^\infty A_s J_0(\lambda_s r). \tag{6}$$

Now there does not appear to be any physical objection to supposing an arbitrary distribution of temperature over the base of the cylinder, provided the temperature varies continuously from point to point and is everywhere finite. In particular we may suppose the distribution symmetrical about the centre, and put

$$\phi_0=f(r),$$

where $f(r)$ is any function of r which is one-valued, finite and continuous from $r=0$ to $r=1$. The question is whether this function can be reduced, for the range considered, to the form expressed by (6).

Assuming that this is so, we can at once obtain the coefficients A_s in the form of definite integrals; for if we put

$$f(r)=\Sigma A_s J_0(\lambda_s r) \tag{7}$$

it follows by (1), (3), and (4) that

$$\int_0^1 J_0(\lambda_s r)f(r)\,r\,dr = A_s\int_0^1 J_0^2(\lambda_s r)\,r\,dr$$
$$=\frac{A_s}{2}\left(\frac{h^2}{k^2\lambda_s^2}+1\right)J_0^2(\lambda_s),$$

and therefore

$$A_s=\frac{2k^2\lambda_s^2}{(h^2+k^2\lambda_s^2)J_0^2(\lambda_s)}\int_0^1 J_0(\lambda_s r)f(r)\,r\,dr. \tag{8}$$

Whenever the transformation (7) is legitimate, the function

$$\phi=\Sigma A_s e^{-\lambda_s z}J_0(\lambda_s r) \tag{9}$$

gives the temperature at any point of the cylinder, when its convex surface, as before, is surrounded by a medium of zero temperature, and the circular base is permanently heated according to the law

$$\phi_0=f(r)=\Sigma A_s J_0(\lambda_s r);$$

the coefficients A_s being given by the formula (8).

A much more general form of potential function is obtained by putting

$$\phi=\Sigma(A\cos n\theta+B\sin n\theta)e^{-\lambda z}J_n(\lambda r), \tag{10}$$

where the summation refers to n and λ independently.

If we restrict the quantities n to integral values and take for the quantities λ the positive roots of $J_n(\lambda)=0$, we have a potential which remains unaltered when θ is changed into $\theta+2\pi$, which vanishes when $z=+\infty$, and also when $r=1$. The value when $z=0$ is

$$\phi_0=\Sigma(A\cos n\theta+B\sin n\theta)J_n(\lambda r). \tag{11}$$

The function ϕ may be interpreted as the temperature at any point in a solid cylinder when the flow of heat is steady, the convex surface maintained at a constant temperature zero, and the base of the cylinder heated according to the law expressed by (11). We are led to inquire whether an arbitrary function $f(r, \theta)$, subject only to the conditions of being finite, one-valued, and continuous over the circle $r=1$, can be reduced to the form of the right-hand member of (11).

Whenever this reduction is possible, it is easy to obtain the coefficients. Thus if, with a more complete notation, we have

$$f(r, \theta) = \Sigma\Sigma(A_{n,s} \cos n\theta + B_{n,s} \sin n\theta) J_n(\lambda_s r), \tag{12}$$

we find successively

$$\int_0^{2\pi} f(r, \theta) \cos n\theta \, d\theta = \sum_s \pi A_{n,s} J_n(\lambda_s r)$$

and $$\int_0^1 \int_0^{2\pi} f(r, \theta) \cos n\theta J_n(\lambda_s r) r \, d\theta \, dr = \pi A_{n,s} \int_0^1 J_n^2(\lambda_s r) r \, dr$$

$$= \frac{\pi}{2} J_n'^2(\lambda_s) A_{n,s}$$

by (3); so that

$$A_{n,s} = \frac{2}{\pi J_n'^2(\lambda_s)} \int_0 \int_0^{2\pi} f(r, \theta) \sin n\theta J_n(\lambda_s r) r \, d\theta \, dr;$$

and in the same way (13)

$$B_{n,s} = \frac{2}{\pi J_n'^2(\lambda_s)} \int_0^1 \int_0^{2\pi} f(r, \theta) \sin n\theta J_n(\lambda_s r) r \, d\theta \, dr.$$

Other physical problems may be constructed which suggest analytical expansions analogous to (7) and (12); some of these are given in the Miscellaneous Examples.

§ 2. Validity of the Expansions. The conditions under which these expansions are valid have been discussed by various writers,* but, as a rule, such investigations are too lengthy for reproduction here. An outline will, however, be given of a comparatively simple proof† depending on contour integration. The discussion will be confined to the expansion

$$f(r) = \sum_{s=1}^{\infty} A_s J_0(\lambda_s r), \tag{14}$$

where $\lambda_1, \lambda_2, \ldots$ are the positive zeros of $J_0(x)$; the method is also applicable to the other Fourier-Bessel expansions.

The sum of the first ν terms of the series on the right-hand side of (14) is

$$2 \int_0^1 x f(x) \sum_{s=1}^{\nu} \frac{J_0(\lambda_s x) J_0(\lambda_s r)}{\{J_0'(\lambda_s)\}^2} dx.$$

* Cf. Prof. U. Dini, *Serie di Fourier*, Vol. I., Pisa, 1880, and Prof. W. H. Young, *Proc. Lond. Math. Soc.*, Ser. 2., Vol. 18.

† Cf. Dr. T. M. MacRobert, *Proc. Edin. Math. Soc.*, Vol. 39.

Consider the integral

$$\int \frac{\zeta G_0(\zeta) J_0(\zeta x) J_0(\zeta r)}{J_0(\zeta)} d\zeta$$

taken round the contour consisting of the ξ-axis from $-M$ to M, indented at $\zeta=0$ and at the zeros of $J_0(\zeta)$, and the lines $\xi=\pm M$, $\eta=N$, where M and N are positive and M is chosen to lie between the zeros λ_ν and $\lambda_{\nu+1}$. The integrand is holomorphic within the contour, so that the value of the integral is zero.

The integral round the small semicircle at $\zeta=0$ tends to zero with the radius. Also, since, by III. (46),

$$G_0(\zeta) J_0'(\zeta) - J_0(\zeta) G_0'(\zeta) = 1/\zeta,$$

it follows that $\lambda_s G_0(\lambda_s) = 1/J_0'(\lambda_s)$; hence the sum of the integrals round the small semicircles at the zeros of $J_0(\xi)$ tends to

$$-2\pi i \sum_{s=1}^{\nu} \frac{J_0(\lambda_s x) J_0(\lambda_s r)}{\{J_0'(\lambda_s)\}^2}$$

as the radii tend to zero.

Again, along the ξ-axis, the integrand is uniform and odd apart from the term in $G_0(\zeta)$ which involves $\log \zeta$; this latter term gives rise to an integral

$$i\pi \int_0^M \xi J_0(\xi x) J_0(\xi r)\, d\xi,$$

while the remaining integrals from $-M$ to O, and from O to M cancel each other.

But, VI. (23), $\int_0^M \xi J_0(\xi x) J_0(\xi r)\, d\xi$

$$= \frac{M}{x^2 - r^2}\{-rJ_0(Mx)J_1(Mr) + xJ_0(Mr)J_1(Mx)\}.$$

In the right-hand side of this equation replace the Bessel Functions by their asymptotic expansions; then the integral has the value

$$\frac{1}{\pi\sqrt{(xr)}}\left\{\frac{\sin\{M(x-r)\}}{x-r} - \frac{\cos\{M(x+r)\}}{x+r}\right\} + \frac{P}{M},$$

where P is finite for all values of M.

Now let N tend to infinity; then, if $|x+r| < 2$, the integral along $\eta=N$ tends to zero. Also, if the Bessel Functions in the integrals along $\xi=\pm M$ be replaced by their asymptotic expansions, these integrals can be put in the form $I+Q/M$, where Q is finite and

$$I=\frac{1}{\surd(xr)}\{\sin(Mx)\times V_1+\cos(Mx)\times V_2\},$$

the functions V_1 and V_2 remaining finite for all values of M, provided that $|x+r|<2$.

It follows that, if $0\leqq r<1$, and since $0\leqq x\leqq 1$,

$$\sum_{s=1}^{\nu}\frac{J_0(\lambda_s x)J_0(\lambda_s r)}{\{J_0'(\lambda_s)\}^2}=\frac{1}{2\pi\surd(xr)}\left\{\frac{\sin\{M(x-r)\}}{x-r}-\frac{\cos\{M(x+r)\}}{x+r}\right\}$$
$$+\frac{P}{M}+\frac{1}{\surd(xr)}\sum{}^{\sin}_{\cos}(Mx)\,V_s+\frac{Q}{M}. \qquad (15)$$

Now, by the theory of Dirichlet Integrals,

$$\operatorname*{Lim}_{M\to\infty}\int_a^b\phi(x)\,{}^{\sin}_{\cos}(Mx)\,dx=0,$$

provided that, for $a\leqq x\leqq b$, $\phi(x)$ is finite and continuous, except for a finite number of finite discontinuities, and has only a finite number of maxima and minima; while, subject to the same conditions,

$$\operatorname*{Lim}_{M\to\infty}\int_a^b\phi(x)\frac{\sin\{M(x-r)\}}{x-r}dx=\frac{\pi}{2}\{\phi(r+0)+\phi(r-0)\}$$

for $a<r<b$.

Accordingly, if $f(x)$ satisfies these conditions for $0\leqq x\leqq 1$, multiply (15) by $2xf(x)$, integrate from 0 to 1, and let ν and M tend to infinity; then

$$\sum_{s=1}^{\infty}A_sJ_0(\lambda_s r)=\tfrac{1}{2}\{f(r+0)+f(r-0)\}, \qquad (16)$$

provided that $0<r<1$.

When $r=1$, $J_0(\lambda_s r)=0$, and therefore the sum of the series is zero.

When $r=0$, it can be shown that the sum of the series is $f(+0)$.

§3. **The Fourier-Bessel Integrals.** A theorem analogous to Fourier's Theorem will now be established. It may be stated as follows:

If for $p\leqq r\leqq q$, where p and q are real and positive, $\phi(r)$ is continuous, except for a finite number of finite dis-

continuities, and has only a finite number of maxima and minima, and if $R(n) > -1$, *then*

$$\left.\begin{aligned}\int_0^\infty d\lambda \int_p^q \lambda\rho\, \phi(\rho) J_n(\lambda\rho) J_n(\lambda r)\, d\rho \\ &= \tfrac{1}{2}\{\phi(r+0)+\phi(r-0)\}, \quad p<r<q, \\ &= \tfrac{1}{2}\phi(r+0), \text{ if } r=p, \\ &= \tfrac{1}{2}\phi(r-0), \text{ if } r=q, \\ &= 0, \text{ if } 0<r<p, \text{ or } r>q.\end{aligned}\right\} \quad (17)$$

If $R(n) > -1$, then, from VI. (23) and II. (20),

$$\begin{aligned}\int_0^h \lambda J_n(\lambda\rho) J_n(\lambda r)\, d\lambda &= \frac{1}{\rho^2 - r^2}\{-rhJ_n(\rho h)J_{n+1}(rh) \\ &\qquad + \rho h J_n(rh) J_{n+1}(\rho h)\} \\ &= \frac{1}{\rho^2-r^2}\frac{2}{\pi}\left\{\sqrt{\left(\frac{\rho}{r}\right)} \cos\left(rh - \tfrac{1}{4}\pi - \tfrac{1}{2}n\pi\right) \sin\left(\rho h - \tfrac{1}{4}\pi - \tfrac{1}{2}n\pi\right)\right. \\ &\qquad \left. - \sqrt{\left(\frac{r}{\rho}\right)} \cos\left(\rho h - \tfrac{1}{4}\pi - \tfrac{1}{2}n\pi\right) \sin\left(rh - \tfrac{1}{4}\pi - \tfrac{1}{2}n\pi\right)\right\} + \frac{P}{h},\end{aligned}$$

where P is finite for all values of h,

$$\begin{aligned}&= \frac{1}{\rho^2-r^2} \cdot \frac{1}{\pi}\left[\sqrt{\left(\frac{\rho}{r}\right)}\{-\cos((r+\rho)h - n\pi) + \sin((\rho - r)h)\}\right. \\ &\qquad \left. + \sqrt{\left(\frac{r}{\rho}\right)}\{\cos((\rho+r)h - n\pi) + \sin((\rho-r)h)\}\right] + \frac{P}{h}.\end{aligned}$$

Now multiply both sides of this equation by $\rho\phi(\rho)$, integrate from p to q, and take the limit when h tends to infinity; then, since p and q are positive,

$$\begin{aligned}\int_p^q \rho\phi(\rho) \int_0^\infty \lambda J_n(\lambda\rho) J_n(\lambda r)\, d\lambda\, d\rho \\ &= \tfrac{1}{2}\{\phi(r+0)+\phi(r-0)\}, \text{ if } p<r<q, \\ &= \tfrac{1}{2}\phi(r+0), \text{ if } r=p, \\ &= \tfrac{1}{2}\phi(r-0), \text{ if } r=q, \\ &= 0, \text{ if } 0<r<p, \text{ or } r>q,\end{aligned}$$

where $\phi(r)$ satisfies the conditions stated in the last section for the validity of the Dirichlet integrals.

If in addition $\phi(r)$ satisfies the condition that $\int_p^q r\phi(r)\,dr$ is absolutely convergent, the order of integration may be changed, and the theorem is proved.

CHAPTER IX.

RELATIONS BETWEEN BESSEL FUNCTIONS AND ASSOCIATED LEGENDRE FUNCTIONS. GREEN'S FUNCTION.

§1. **Bessel Functions as Limiting Cases of Associated Legendre Functions.** Employing the notation of App. I. (32), we can define the Associated Legendre Function $P_n^m(z)$ of order n and rank m, where n and m are any numbers, by means of the equation

$$P_n^m(z) = \frac{\Pi(n+m)}{2^m \Pi(m)\Pi(n-m)}(1-z^2)^{\frac{1}{2}m} \times F\left(m-n, m+n+1, m+1, \frac{1-z}{2}\right), \qquad (1)$$

where $(1-z^2)^{\frac{1}{2}m}$ has the value 1 when $z=0$.

Hence

$$\frac{1}{n^m} P_n^m\left(1-\frac{z^2}{2n^2}\right) = \frac{\Pi(n+m)z^m}{2^m\Pi(m)\Pi(n-m)n^{2m}}\left(1-\frac{z^2}{4n^2}\right)^{\frac{1}{2}m} \times F\left(m-n, m+n+1, m+1, \frac{z^2}{4n^2}\right).$$

Now* make $n \to \infty$, so that, if $\delta = 1/n$, $\delta \to 0$; then, by Stirling's Formula (App. I. 10),

$$\frac{\Pi(n+m)}{\Pi(n-m)n^{2m}} \to 1; \text{ also } \left(1-\frac{z^2}{4n^2}\right)^{\frac{1}{2}m} \to 1.$$

Further, the $(r+1)^{\text{th}}$ term of the hypergeometric series is

$$(-1)^r \frac{(1-m\delta)\{1+(m+r)\delta\}\{1-(m+1)^2\delta^2\} \{1-(m+2)^2\delta^2\}\ldots\{1-(m+r-1)^2\delta^2\}}{(m+1)(m+2)\ldots(m+r)\,.\,r!}\left(\frac{z}{2}\right)^{2r};$$

this is a continuous function of δ, and the series is uniformly convergent in δ in a region enclosing $\delta=0$; hence

$$\lim_{n\to\infty}\left[\frac{1}{n^m}P_n^m\left(1-\frac{z^2}{2n^2}\right)\right] = J_m(z). \qquad (2)$$

* Cf. Whittaker and Watson, *Analysis*, p. 361.

It follows that $$\lim_{n\to\infty}\left[\frac{1}{n^m}P_n^m\left(\cos\frac{z}{n}\right)\right]=J_m(z), \qquad (3)$$
and in particular that
$$\lim_{n\to\infty}P_n\left(\cos\frac{z}{n}\right)=J_0(z). \qquad (4)$$

§ 2. **Associated Legendre Functions as Integrals involving Bessel Functions.*** The function
$$e^{-\lambda z}J_m(\lambda\rho)\cos m\phi,$$
where z, ρ, ϕ are cylindrical coordinates, is a solution of Laplace's Equation for all values of λ; hence, if $z>0$ and $R(m+n)>-1$,
$$\cos m\phi\int_0^\infty e^{-\lambda z}J_m(\lambda\rho)\lambda^n d\lambda$$
is also a solution of Laplace's Equation.

Now, in this expression introduce the substitutions
$$z=r\cos\theta,\quad \rho=r\sin\theta,\quad \lambda r=\kappa,$$
and the integral becomes
$$r^{-n-1}\cos m\phi\int_0^\infty e^{-\kappa\cos\theta}J_m(\kappa\sin\theta)\kappa^n\,d\kappa,$$
which is a potential function expressed in terms of the polar coordinates r, θ, and ϕ.

Since r and ϕ appear only in the factors r^{-n-1} and $\cos m\phi$, it follows that
$$\int_0^\infty e^{-\kappa\cos\theta}J_m(\kappa\sin\theta)\kappa^n\,d\kappa=Ap_n^m(\mu)+Bp_n^{-m}(\mu),$$
where $\mu=\cos\theta$ and
$$p_n^m(\mu)=\Pi(n-m)P_n^m(\mu)$$
$$=\frac{\Pi(m+n)}{\Pi(m)}\left(\frac{1-\mu}{1+\mu}\right)^{\frac{1}{2}m}F\left(-n,\,n+1,\,1+m,\,\frac{1-\mu}{2}\right)$$
$$=\frac{\Pi(m+n)}{2^m\Pi(m)}(1-\mu^2)^{\frac{1}{2}m}F\left(m-n,\,m+n+1,\,m+1,\frac{1-\mu}{2}\right). \qquad (5)$$

To determine the constants A and B, suppose that $R(m)>0$; then $p_n^{-m}(\mu)$ is infinite when $\theta=0$, so that B must be zero. Again, divide by $\sin^m\theta$ and let $\theta\to 0$; thus
$$\int_0^\infty e^{-\kappa}\frac{1}{2^m\Pi(m)}\kappa^{m+n}\,d\kappa=A\,\frac{\Pi(m+n)}{2^m\Pi(m)}.$$

*Cf. Dr. John Dougall, *Proc. Edin. Math. Soc.*, Vol. XVIII.

Hence $A=1$ and

$$\int_0^\infty e^{-\lambda z} J_m(\lambda\rho)\lambda^n\, d\lambda = \frac{1}{r^{n+1}} p_n^m(\mu) \tag{6}$$

for all values of m, n, θ for which both sides of the equation retain a meaning. If $m=n=0$ this reduces to

$$\int_0^\infty e^{-\lambda z} J_0(\lambda\rho)\, d\lambda = \frac{1}{r}, \tag{7}$$

which is identical with VI. (2), since $r=\sqrt{(\rho^2+z^2)}$.

If $r=1$, then

$$\int_0^\infty e^{-\lambda\cos\theta} J_m(\lambda\sin\theta)\lambda^n\, d\lambda = p_n^m(\mu), \tag{8}$$

which holds if $-\pi/2<\theta<\pi/2$ and $R(m+n)>-1$.

In order to remove the restriction on m and n, take the integral in (6) round the contour C' of Fig. 6 (p. 53); then, if $R(z)>0$ and the initial amplitude of λ is $-\pi$,

$$\int_C e^{\lambda z} J_m(\lambda\rho)\lambda^n d\lambda = 2i\sin(m+n+1)\pi\,\frac{1}{r^{n+1}} p_n^m\left(\frac{z}{r}\right). \tag{9}$$

An integral expression for $p_n^m(\mu)$ which will be valid for $0<\theta<\pi$ can be obtained as follows

Consider the integral

$$\int_0^\infty e^{i\lambda\cos\theta} K_m(\lambda\sin\theta)\lambda^n d\lambda,$$

where $R(n\pm m)>-1$. Since $K_m(\lambda\sin\theta)=i^m G_m(i\lambda\sin\theta)$, this may be written

$$\int e^{\lambda\cos\theta} i^m G_m(\lambda\sin\theta)\lambda^n d\lambda\,.\, i^{-n-1},$$

where the path of integration is the upper half of the imaginary axis from the origin to infinity. If $0<\theta<\pi/2$, $\sin\theta$ and $\cos\theta$ are both positive, and therefore this path can be deformed into the negative real axis from 0 to $-\infty$. Hence

$$\int_0^\infty e^{i\lambda\cos\theta} K_m(\lambda\sin\theta)\lambda^n d\lambda$$

$$= \int_0^\infty e^{-\lambda\cos\theta} i^m G_m(e^{i\pi}\lambda\sin\theta)\lambda^n d\lambda\,.\, i^{n+1}$$

$$= \frac{\pi}{2\sin m\pi} i^{n+1}\int_0^\infty e^{-\lambda\cos\theta}\{i^{-m}J_{-m}(\lambda\sin\theta) - i^m J_m(\lambda\sin\theta)\}\lambda^n d\lambda$$

$$= \frac{\pi}{2\sin m\pi} i^{n+1}\{i^{-m}p_n^{-m}(\mu) - i^m p_n^m(\mu)\}. \tag{10}$$

Again,

$$\int_0^\infty e^{-i\lambda\cos\theta} K_m(\lambda\sin\theta)\lambda^n d\lambda$$

$$= \int e^{-\lambda\cos\theta} i^m G_m(\lambda\sin\theta)\lambda^n d\lambda\, i^{-n-1},$$

the latter integral being taken up the imaginary axis from the origin to infinity.

If $0<\theta<\pi/2$, this can be deformed into the positive real axis from 0 to $+\infty$; hence

$$\int_0^\infty e^{-i\lambda\cos\theta} K_m(\lambda\sin\theta)\lambda^n d\lambda$$

$$= \int_0^\infty e^{-\lambda\cos\theta} i^m G_m(\lambda\sin\theta)\lambda^n d\lambda\,.\, i^{-n-1}$$

$$= \frac{\pi}{2\sin m\pi} i^{-n-1}\{i^m p_n^{-m}(\mu) - i^{-m} p_n^m(\mu)\}. \qquad (11)$$

Now multiply (10) by i^{m-n-1} and (11) by i^{-m+n+1}, and subtract; thus

$$\int_0^\infty \sin\left\{\lambda\cos\theta + (m-n-1)\frac{\pi}{2}\right\} K_m(\lambda\sin\theta)\lambda^n d\lambda = -\frac{\pi}{2} p_n^m(\mu), \qquad (12)$$

provided that $R(n\pm m) > -1$ and $0<\theta<\pi$.

In particular, if $n=m=0$, and $r\sin\theta=\rho$, $r\cos\theta=z$, $\lambda=r\kappa$,

$$\frac{2}{\pi}\int_0^\infty \cos\kappa z\, K_0(\kappa\rho)\, d\kappa = \frac{1}{r}. \qquad (13)$$

§ 3. **Dougall's Expressions for the Green's Function.*** The Addition Theorem for the function K_0 may be written

$$K_0(\lambda R) = K_0(\lambda a) I_0(\lambda b) + 2\sum_{m=1}^{\infty} K_m(\lambda a) I_m(\lambda b)\cos m(\phi-\phi')$$

$$= 2\Sigma' K_m(\lambda a) I_m(\lambda b)\cos m(\phi-\phi'),$$

where $$R^2 = a^2 + b^2 - 2ab\cos(\phi-\phi'):$$

here a and b are taken to be real, and such that $0<b<a$.

This series may be transformed into an integral as follows.

Consider the function of m,

$$\frac{\cos m(\pi-\phi+\phi')}{\sin m\pi} K_m(\lambda a) I_m(\lambda b),$$

in which a, b, λ are taken to be real and positive, and

$$0<\phi-\phi'<2\pi.$$

Let the function be integrated with regard to m round a contour in the m-plane consisting of a large semicircle on the

* Cf. Dr. John Dougall, *Proc. Edin. Math. Soc.*, Vol. XVIII.

right of the imaginary axis described in the negative direction and the imaginary axis indented at the origin. To avoid the zeros of $\sin m\pi$ the radius of the semicircle can be taken to be half an odd integer. The integral round the semicircle tends to zero as the radius tends to infinity, while the integral round the small semicircle at the origin tends to $i\pi \times \frac{1}{\pi} K_0(\lambda a) I_0(\lambda b)$. Thus

$$\int_{-\infty}^{\infty} \frac{\cosh s(\pi - \phi + \phi')}{\sin is\pi} K_{is}(\lambda a) I_{is}(\lambda b) i \, ds$$
$$+ i K_0(\lambda a) I_0(\lambda b) = -2\pi i \times (\text{sum of the residues at points on the positive real axis})$$
$$= -2\pi i \sum_{m=1}^{\infty} \frac{1}{\pi} \cos m(\phi - \phi') K_m(\lambda a) I_m(\lambda b).$$

Accordingly,

$$\frac{2}{\pi} \int_0^{\infty} \cosh s(\pi - \phi + \phi') K_{is}(\lambda a) K_{is}(\lambda b) \, ds$$
$$= K_0(\lambda a) I_0(\lambda b) + 2 \sum_{m=1}^{\infty} \cos m(\phi - \phi') K_m(\lambda a) I_m(\lambda b)$$
$$= K_0(\lambda R). \tag{14}$$

Green's Function. In the applications of mathematics to physics a problem of frequent occurrence is the determination of a potential function which has the value zero at the boundary of a given space, and is discontinuous at only one point within the space; at this point, or pole, the difference between this function (the Green's function) and the reciprocal of the distance from the pole must tend to a definite limit as the variable point approaches the pole. The pole is taken to be the point (x', y', z'), or, in cylindrical coordinates (ρ', z', ϕ'), while the variable point is (x, y, z) or (ρ, z, ϕ). The reciprocal of the distance will be denoted by T, the Green's function by V, and

$$\sqrt{\{\rho^2 + \rho'^2 - 2\rho\rho' \cos(\phi - \phi')\}}$$

by R. Various spaces bounded by planes and cylinders will be considered, and in each case three methods of representing the Green's function will be given.

Case I. Whole of Space. The Green's function is simply T: hence, from (7),

$$V = T = \int_0^{\infty} e^{-\lambda(z-z')} J_0(\lambda R) \, d\lambda \tag{15}$$
$$= 2\int_0^{\infty} e^{-\lambda(z-z')} \{\Sigma' J_m(\lambda\rho) J_m(\lambda\rho') \cos m(\phi - \phi')\} d\lambda, \tag{16}$$

where $z > z'$ or $z = z'$, $R \neq 0$. If $z < z'$, interchange z and z'.

Again, from (13),

$$V = T = \frac{2}{\pi}\int_0^\infty \cos\lambda(z-z')K_0(\lambda R)\,d\lambda \tag{17}$$

$$= \frac{4}{\pi}\int_0^\infty \cos\lambda(z-z')\{\Sigma' K_m(\lambda\rho)I_m(\lambda\rho')\cos m(\phi-\phi')\}\,d\lambda, \tag{18}$$

where $\rho > \rho'$.

The third form is derived from (17) by means of (14): it is

$$V = \frac{4}{\pi^2}\int_0^\infty \cos\lambda(z-z')\,d\lambda\int_0^\infty \cosh s(\pi-\phi+\phi')K_{is}(\lambda\rho)K_{is}(\lambda\rho')\,ds, \tag{19}$$

where $0 < \phi - \phi' < 2\pi$.

These three solutions (16), (18) and (19) are named by Dougall the z, ρ and ϕ forms: three similar forms will be obtained in the other cases. It is advantageous to have these different forms, as each has its own region of rapid convergence.

Case II. Space bounded by two parallel planes; $z=0$ and $z=c>0$. The Green's function is obtained by adding to T a potential non-singular throughout the space, and equal to $-T$ on the boundary. If (15) be used for T, then the complementary potential must take the values

$$-\int_0^\infty e^{-\lambda(c-z')}J_0(\lambda R)\,d\lambda \text{ on } z=c$$

and

$$-\int_0^\infty e^{-\lambda z'}J_0(\lambda R)\,d\lambda \text{ on } z=0.$$

Such a potential is

$$-\int_0^\infty \left\{\frac{\sinh(\lambda z)}{\sinh(\lambda c)}e^{-\lambda(c-z')} + \frac{\sinh\lambda(c-z)}{\sinh\lambda c}e^{-\lambda z'}\right\}J_0(\lambda R)\,d\lambda.$$

To obtain V add T, which, when $z>z'$, is

$$\int_0^\infty e^{-\lambda(z-z')}J_0(\lambda R)\,d\lambda.$$

Thus $$V = 2\int_0^\infty \frac{\sinh\lambda(c-z)\sinh(\lambda z')}{\sinh(\lambda c)}J_0(\lambda R)\,d\lambda;\ z>z' \tag{20}$$

For $z<z'$, interchange z and z'.

Again, since

$$\pi i J_0(\lambda R) = G_0(\lambda R) - G_0(e^{i\pi}\lambda R),$$

this integral can be written

$$V = \frac{2}{\pi i}\int \frac{\sinh\lambda(c-z)\sinh(\lambda z')}{\sinh(\lambda c)}G_0(\lambda R)\,d\lambda,$$

provided that $R>0$, the integral being taken round a contour consisting of the real axis indented at the origin and an infinite semicircle above the real axis; hence, by the theory of residues,

$$V=\frac{4}{c}\sum_{p=1}^{\infty}\sin\left(\frac{p\pi z}{c}\right)\sin\left(\frac{p\pi z'}{c}\right)K_0\left(\frac{p\pi R}{c}\right),\quad R>0, \tag{21}$$

$$=\frac{8}{c}\sum_{p=1}^{\infty}\sin\left(\frac{p\pi z}{c}\right)\sin\left(\frac{p\pi z'}{c}\right)\sum_m{}' K_m\left(\frac{p\pi\rho}{c}\right)I_m\left(\frac{p\pi\rho'}{c}\right)\times\cos m(\phi-\phi'), \tag{22}$$

provided that $\rho>\rho'$.

Or, from (14),

$$V=\frac{8}{\pi c}\sum_{p=1}^{\infty}\sin\left(\frac{p\pi z}{c}\right)\sin\left(\frac{p\pi z'}{c}\right)\times\int_0^{\infty}\cosh s(\pi-\phi+\phi')K_{is}\left(\frac{p\pi\rho}{c}\right)K_{is}\left(\frac{p\pi\rho'}{c}\right)ds, \tag{23}$$

where $0<\phi-\phi'<2\pi$.

Case III. Space bounded externally by a cylinder, $\rho=a$. From (18) it follows that

$$V=\frac{4}{\pi}\int_0^{\infty}\cos\lambda(z-z')\left[\sum_m{}'\frac{I_m(\lambda\rho')}{I_m(\lambda a)}\{I_m(\lambda a)K_m(\lambda\rho)-I_m(\lambda\rho)K_m(\lambda a)\}\times\cos m(\phi-\phi')\right]d\lambda, \tag{24}$$

where $\rho>\rho'$.

Now change the order of summation; then

$$V=\frac{4}{\pi}\sum_m{}'\cos m(\phi-\phi')\int_0^{\infty}\cos\lambda(z-z')\frac{I_m(\lambda\rho')}{I_m(\lambda a)}\begin{Bmatrix}I_m(\lambda a)K_m(\lambda\rho)\\-I_m(\lambda\rho)K_m(\lambda a)\end{Bmatrix}d\lambda$$

$$=\frac{2}{i\pi}\sum_m{}'\cos m(\phi-\phi')\int e^{-\lambda(z-z')}\frac{J_m(\lambda\rho')}{J_m(\lambda a)}\begin{Bmatrix}J_m(\lambda a)G_m(\lambda\rho)\\-J_m(\lambda\rho)G_m(\lambda a)\end{Bmatrix}d\lambda,$$

taken round a contour consisting of the imaginary axis indented at the origin, and an infinite semicircle to the right of the imaginary axis described negatively; hence, by the theory of residues,

$$V=\frac{4}{a}\sum_m{}'\cos m(\phi-\phi')\times\sum_{s=1}^{\infty}e^{-\lambda_s(z-z')}J_m(\lambda_s\rho)J_m(\lambda_s\rho')G_m(\lambda_s a)/\{J'_m(\lambda_s a)\},$$

where λ_s is a positive zero of $J_m(\lambda a)$,

$$=\frac{4}{a^2}\sum_m{}'\cos m(\phi-\phi')\sum_{s=1}^{\infty}e^{-\lambda_s(z-z')}J_m(\lambda_s\rho)J_m(\lambda_s\rho')/\{\lambda_s(J'_m(\lambda_s a))^2\}, \tag{25}$$

since $G_m(\lambda a)J'_m(\lambda a)-J_m(\lambda a)G'_m(\lambda a)=1/(\lambda a)$. Here $z>z'$.

The third form is obtained from (24) as follows. Consider the integral

$$\int \frac{\cos m(\pi-\phi+\phi')}{\sin m\pi}\frac{I_m(\lambda\rho')}{I_m(\lambda a)}\{I_m(\lambda a)K_m(\lambda\rho)-I_m(\lambda\rho)K_m(\lambda a)\}\,dm,$$

taken round a contour in the m-plane consisting of the imaginary axis indented at the origin and an infinite semicircle to the right of the imaginary axis. It is found that

$$\int_0^\infty \frac{\cosh s(\pi-\phi+\phi')}{\sinh s\pi}\left\{\frac{I_{is}(\lambda\rho')}{I_{is}(\lambda a)}-\frac{I_{-is}(\lambda\rho')}{I_{-is}(\lambda a)}\right\}$$
$$\times\{I_{is}(\lambda a)K_{is}(\lambda\rho)-I_{is}(\lambda\rho)K_{is}(\lambda a)\}\,ds$$
$$=-2\pi i\sum_m{}' \frac{\cos m(\phi-\phi')}{\pi}\frac{I_m(\lambda\rho')}{I_m(\lambda a)}\{I_m(\lambda a)K_m(\lambda\rho)-I_m(\lambda\rho)K_m(\lambda a)\}. \tag{26}$$

Hence

$$V=\frac{4}{\pi^2}\int_0^\infty \cos\lambda(z-z')\,d\lambda$$
$$\times\int_0^\infty \cosh s(\pi-\phi+\phi')\left\{\begin{matrix}(I_{is}(\lambda a)K_{is}(\lambda\rho')-I_{is}(\lambda\rho')K_{is}(\lambda a))\\ \times(I_{is}(\lambda a)K_{is}(\lambda\rho)-I_{is}(\lambda\rho)K_{is}(\lambda a))\end{matrix}\right\}$$
$$\times\frac{ds}{I_{is}(\lambda a)I_{-is}(\lambda a)}, \tag{27}$$

where $0<\phi-\phi'<2\pi$.

Case IV. Space bounded by two axial planes, $\phi=0$ *and* $\phi=a>0$. From (19)

$$T=\frac{4}{\pi^2}\int_0^\infty \cos\lambda(z-z')\int_0^\infty \cosh s\{\pi\mp(\phi-\phi')\}K_{is}(\lambda\rho)K_{is}(\lambda\rho')\,ds\,d\lambda,$$

according as $\phi\gtrless\phi'$.

Hence to T must be added the function

$$-\frac{4}{\pi^2}\int_0^\infty \cos\lambda(z-z')\int_0^\infty\left\{\begin{matrix}\dfrac{\sinh s\phi}{\sinh sa}\cosh s(\pi-a+\phi')\\ +\dfrac{\sinh s(a-\phi)}{\sinh sa}\cosh s(\pi-\phi')\end{matrix}\right\}$$
$$\times K_{is}(\lambda\rho)K_{is}(\lambda\rho')\,ds\,d\lambda,$$

so that, if $\phi>\phi'$,

$$V=\frac{8}{\pi^2}\int_0^\infty \cos\lambda(z-z')\,d\lambda$$
$$\times\int_0^\infty \frac{\sinh s\pi}{\sinh sa}\sinh s(a-\phi)\sinh(s\phi')K_{is}(\lambda\rho)K_{is}(\lambda\rho')\,ds. \tag{28}$$

Now the second integral in this equation can be written

$$\int_0^{i\infty} \frac{\sin s\pi}{\sin s\alpha} \sin s(\alpha-\phi) \sin(s\phi') K_s(\lambda\rho) K_s(\lambda\rho')\, i\, ds$$

$$= -\frac{i\pi}{2}\int_{-i\infty}^{i\infty} \frac{\sin s(\alpha-\phi)\sin(s\phi')}{\sin(s\alpha)} K_s(\lambda\rho) I_s(\lambda\rho')\, ds$$

$= -\pi^2 \times$ (sum of the residues to the right of the imaginary axis),

provided that $\rho > \rho'$.

Thus

$$V = \frac{8}{\alpha}\int_0^\infty \cos\lambda(z-z') \times \sum_{m=1}^{\infty}\left\{\sin\left(\frac{m\pi\phi}{\alpha}\right)\sin\left(\frac{m\pi\phi'}{\alpha}\right) K_{\frac{m\pi}{\alpha}}(\lambda\rho) I_{\frac{m\pi}{\alpha}}(\lambda\rho')\right\} d\lambda, \qquad (29)$$

provided that $\rho > \rho'$. Hence

$$V = \frac{8}{\alpha}\sum_{m=1}^{\infty} \sin\left(\frac{m\pi\phi}{\alpha}\right)\sin\left(\frac{m\pi\phi'}{\alpha}\right) \times \int_0^\infty \cos\lambda(z-z')\, G_{\frac{m\pi}{\alpha}}(i\lambda\rho) J_{\frac{m\pi}{\alpha}}(i\lambda\rho')\, d\lambda.$$

This integral can be put in the form

$$\frac{1}{2i}\int_0^{i\infty} \{e^{\lambda(z-z')} + e^{-\lambda(z-z')}\} G_s(\lambda\rho) J_s(\lambda\rho')\, d\lambda,$$

where $s = m\pi/\alpha$; so that, if $z > z'$, it is equal to

$$\frac{1}{2i}\int_0^{-\infty} e^{\lambda(z-z')} G_s(\lambda\rho) J_s(\lambda\rho')\, d\lambda + \frac{1}{2i}\int_0^\infty e^{-\lambda(z-z')} G_s(\lambda\rho) J_s(\lambda\rho')\, d\lambda$$

$$= \frac{1}{2i}\int_0^\infty e^{-\lambda(z-z')} J_s(\lambda\rho')\{G_s(\lambda\rho) - e^{is\pi} G_s(\lambda\rho e^{i\pi})\}\, d\lambda$$

$$= \frac{\pi}{2}\int_0^\infty e^{-\lambda(z-z')} J_s(\lambda\rho) J_s(\lambda\rho')\, d\lambda.$$

Hence, if $z > z'$,

$$V = \frac{4\pi}{\alpha}\sum_{m=1}^{\infty} \sin\left(\frac{m\pi\phi}{\alpha}\right)\sin\left(\frac{m\pi\phi'}{\alpha}\right) \times \int_0^\infty e^{-\lambda(z-z')} J_{\frac{m\pi}{\alpha}}(\lambda\rho) J_{\frac{m\pi}{\alpha}}(\lambda\rho')\, d\lambda. \qquad (30)$$

Case V. Space bounded externally by two parallel planes and a cylinder; $z=0$, $z=c$, $\rho=a$. From (22)

$$V=\frac{8}{c}\sum_{p=1}^{\infty}\sin\left(\frac{p\pi z}{c}\right)\sin\left(\frac{p\pi z'}{c}\right)$$
$$\times\sum_{m}{}'\frac{I_m(p\pi\rho'/c)}{I_m(p\pi a/c)}\left\{I_m(p\pi a/c)K_m(p\pi\rho/c)-I_m(p\pi\rho/c)K_m(p\pi a/c)\right\}$$
$$\times\cos m(\phi-\phi'), \qquad (31)$$

provided that $\rho>\rho'$.

Again, from (25) it follows as in *Case II.* that the potential which must be added to T is

$$-\frac{4}{a^2}\sum_{m}{}'\cos m(\phi-\phi')\sum_{s=1}^{\infty}\left\{\frac{\sinh\lambda_s z}{\sinh\lambda_s c}e^{-\lambda_s(c-z')}+\frac{\sinh\lambda_s(c-z)}{\sinh\lambda_s c}e^{-\lambda z'}\right\}$$
$$\times J_m(\lambda_s\rho)J_m(\lambda_s\rho')/[\lambda_s\{J_m'(\lambda_s a)\}^2],$$

so that

$$V=\frac{8}{a^2}\sum_{m}{}'\cos m(\phi-\phi')$$
$$\times\sum_{s=1}^{\infty}\frac{\sinh\lambda_s(c-z)\sinh\lambda_s z'}{\sinh\lambda_s c}J_m(\lambda_s\rho)J_m(\lambda_s\rho')/[\lambda_s\{J'_m(\lambda_s a)\}^2], \qquad (32)$$

where $z>z'$.

Finally, from (31) and (26) it follows that

$$V=\frac{8}{\pi c}\sum_{p=1}^{\infty}\sin\left(\frac{p\pi z}{c}\right)\sin\left(\frac{p\pi z'}{c}\right)$$
$$\times\int_0^{\infty}\cosh s(\pi-\phi+\phi')f(\rho)f(\rho')\,ds/\{I_{is}(\lambda a)I_{-is}(\lambda a)\}, \qquad (33)$$

where $f(\rho)=I_{is}(\lambda a)K_{is}(\lambda\rho)-I_{is}(\lambda\rho)K_{is}(\lambda a)$ and $0<\phi-\phi'<2\pi$.

Case VI. Space bounded by two parallel planes and two axial planes; $z=0$, $z=c$, $\phi=0$, $\phi=a$. From (23), by the process employed in *Case IV.* to obtain (28), it can be deduced that, for $\phi>\phi'$,

$$V=\frac{16}{\pi c}\sum_{p=1}^{\infty}\sin\left(\frac{p\pi z}{c}\right)\sin\left(\frac{p\pi z'}{c}\right)$$
$$\times\int_0^{\infty}\frac{\sinh s\pi}{\sinh sa}\sinh s(a-\phi)\sinh(s\phi')K_{is}\left(\frac{p\pi\rho}{c}\right)K_{is}\left(\frac{p\pi\rho'}{c}\right)ds. \qquad (34)$$

From (30), by the process employed in *Case II.*, it follows that, for $z>z'$,

$$V=\frac{8\pi}{a}\sum_{m=1}^{\infty}\sin\left(\frac{m\pi\phi}{a}\right)\sin\left(\frac{m\pi\phi'}{a}\right)$$
$$\times\int_0^{\infty}\frac{\sinh\lambda(c-z)\sinh\lambda z'}{\sinh\lambda c}J_{\frac{m\pi}{a}}(\lambda\rho)J_{\frac{m\pi}{a}}(\lambda\rho')\,d\lambda. \qquad (35)$$

Finally, if the integral in (34) be evaluated as in *Case IV.*, then, for $\rho > \rho'$,

$$V = \frac{16\pi}{ca}\sum_{p=1}^{\infty}\sin\left(\frac{p\pi z}{c}\right)\sin\left(\frac{p\pi z'}{c}\right)$$
$$\times\sum_{m=1}^{\infty}\sin\left(\frac{m\pi\phi}{\alpha}\right)\sin\left(\frac{m\pi\phi'}{\alpha}\right)K_{\frac{m\pi}{\alpha}}\left(\frac{p\pi\rho}{c}\right)I_{\frac{m\pi}{\alpha}}\left(\frac{p\pi\rho'}{c}\right). \quad (36)$$

Case VII. Space bounded by two axial planes and a cylinder; $\phi = 0$, $\phi = \alpha$, $\rho = a$. From (29), if $\rho > \rho'$,

$$V = \frac{8}{\alpha}\int_0^{\infty}\cos\lambda(z-z')\,d\lambda\sum_{m=1}^{\infty}\sin\frac{m\pi\phi}{\alpha}\sin\frac{m\pi\phi'}{\alpha}$$
$$\times\left\{I_{\frac{m\pi}{\alpha}}(\lambda a)K_{\frac{m\pi}{\alpha}}(\lambda\rho) - I_{\frac{m\pi}{\alpha}}(\lambda\rho)K_{\frac{m\pi}{\alpha}}(\lambda a)\right\}I_{\frac{m\pi}{\alpha}}(\lambda\rho')/I_{\frac{m\pi}{\alpha}}(\lambda a). \quad (37)$$

From (27), as in *Case IV.*, if $\phi > \phi'$,

$$V = \frac{8}{\pi^2}\int_0^{\infty}\cos\lambda(z-z')\,d\lambda$$
$$\times\int_0^{\infty}\frac{\sinh s\pi}{\sinh s\alpha}\sinh s(\alpha-\phi)\sinh(s\phi')f(\rho)f(\rho')\frac{ds}{I_{is}(\lambda a)I_{-is}(\lambda a)}, \quad (38)$$

where $f(\rho) = I_{is}(\lambda a)K_{is}(\lambda\rho) - I_{is}(\lambda\rho)K_{is}(\lambda a)$.

Again, from (37), as in *Case III.*, if $z > z'$,

$$V = \frac{8\pi}{a^2\alpha}\sum_{m=1}^{\infty}\sin\left(\frac{m\pi\phi}{\alpha}\right)\sin\left(\frac{m\pi\phi'}{\alpha}\right)$$
$$\times\sum_{s=1}^{\infty}e^{-\lambda_s(z-z')}J_{\frac{m\pi}{\alpha}}(\lambda_s\rho)J_{\frac{m\pi}{\alpha}}(\lambda_s\rho')/[\lambda_s\{J'_{\frac{m\pi}{\alpha}}(\lambda_s a)\}^2], \quad (39)$$

where λ_s is a positive zero of $J_{\frac{m\pi}{\alpha}}(\lambda a)$.

Case VIII. Space bounded by two axial planes, two parallel planes, and a cylinder; $\phi = 0$, $\phi = \alpha$, $z = 0$, $z = c$, $\rho = a$. From (39), as in *Case II.*, if $z > z'$,

$$V = \frac{16\pi}{a^2\alpha}\sum_{m=1}^{\infty}\sin\left(\frac{m\pi\phi}{\alpha}\right)\sin\left(\frac{m\pi\phi'}{\alpha}\right)$$
$$\times\sum_{s=1}^{\infty}\frac{\sinh\lambda_s(c-z)\sinh(\lambda_s z')}{\sinh(\lambda_s c)}J_{\frac{m\pi}{\alpha}}(\lambda_s\rho)J_{\frac{m\pi}{\alpha}}(\lambda_s\rho')/[\lambda_s\{J'_{\frac{m\pi}{\alpha}}(\lambda_s a)\}^2]. \quad (40)$$

From (36), if $\rho > \rho'$,

$$V = \frac{16\pi}{c\alpha}\sum_{p=1}^{\infty}\sin\left(\frac{p\pi z}{c}\right)\sin\left(\frac{p\pi z'}{c}\right)\sum_{m=1}^{\infty}\sin\left(\frac{m\pi\phi}{\alpha}\right)\sin\left(\frac{m\pi\phi'}{\alpha}\right)$$
$$\times\{I_{\frac{m\pi}{\alpha}}(\lambda a)K_{\frac{m\pi}{\alpha}}(\lambda\rho) - I_{\frac{m\pi}{\alpha}}(\lambda\rho)K_{\frac{m\pi}{\alpha}}(\lambda a)\}I_{\frac{m\pi}{\alpha}}(\lambda\rho')/I_{\frac{m\pi}{\alpha}}(\lambda a). \quad (41)$$

From (33), if $\phi > \phi'$,

$$V = \frac{16}{\pi c} \sum_{p=1}^{\infty} \sin\left(\frac{p\pi z}{c}\right) \sin\left(\frac{p\pi z'}{c}\right)$$

$$\times \int_0^{\infty} \frac{\sinh(s\pi)}{\sinh(sa)} \sinh s(a-\phi) \sinh(s\phi') f(\rho) f(\rho')\, ds / \{I_{is}(\lambda a) I_{-is}(\lambda a)\}. \tag{42}$$

Case IX. Space bounded by two parallel planes, two axial planes, and two cylinders; $z=0$, $z=c$, $\phi=0$, $\phi=a$, $\rho=a$, $\rho=b$, $b>a$. From (36) subtract a potential which has the same values on the cylinder and vanishes on the planes. This potential is obtained by writing for $K_{\frac{m\pi}{a}}\left(\frac{p\pi\rho}{c}\right) I_{\frac{m\pi}{a}}\left(\frac{p\pi\rho'}{c}\right)$ in (36) the expression

$$K_s(\lambda b) I_s(\lambda\rho') \frac{I_s(\lambda a) K_s(\lambda\rho) - I_s(\lambda\rho) K_s(\lambda a)}{I_s(\lambda a) K_s(\lambda b) - I_s(\lambda b) K_s(\lambda a)}$$

$$+ I_s(\lambda a) K_s(\lambda\rho') \frac{I_s(\lambda\rho) K_s(\lambda b) - I_s(\lambda b) K_s(\lambda\rho)}{I_s(\lambda a) K_s(\lambda b) - I_s(\lambda b) K_s(\lambda a)},$$

where $s = m\pi/a$, $\lambda = p\pi/c$.

Thus, if $\rho > \rho'$,

$$V = \frac{16\pi}{ca} \sum_{p=1}^{\infty} \sin\left(\frac{p\pi z}{c}\right) \sin\left(\frac{p\pi z'}{c}\right) \sum_{m=1}^{\infty} \sin\left(\frac{m\pi\phi}{a}\right) \sin\left(\frac{m\pi\phi'}{a}\right) \times E_m,$$

where E_m denotes the function

$$\frac{\{I_s(\lambda a) K_s(\lambda\rho') - I_s(\lambda\rho') K_s(\lambda a)\}\{I_s(\lambda b) K_s(\lambda\rho) - I_s(\lambda\rho) K_s(\lambda b)\}}{I_s(\lambda a) K_s(\lambda b) - I_s(\lambda b) K_s(\lambda a)}, \tag{43}$$

and $s = m\pi/a$, $\lambda = p\pi/c$.

In (43) change the order of summation and assume that $z > z'$. The function

$$\frac{\sinh\lambda(c-z)\sinh(\lambda z')}{\sinh(\lambda c)}$$

$$\times \frac{\{J_s(\lambda a) G_s(\lambda\rho') - J_s(\lambda\rho') G_s(\lambda a)\}\{J_s(\lambda b) G_s(\lambda\rho) - J_s(\lambda\rho) G_s(\lambda b)\}}{J_s(\lambda a) G_s(\lambda b) - J_s(\lambda b) G_s(\lambda a)}$$

is a uniform, odd function of λ, and its integral round a large circle which does not pass through a zero of the denominator tends to zero as the radius tends to infinity. The sum of all the residues, those at the (pure imaginary) zeros of $\sinh(\lambda c)$ and those at the (real) zeros of $J_s(\lambda a) G_s(\lambda b) - J_s(\lambda b) G_s(\lambda a)$ is zero.

Hence, if $z>z'$,

$$V=-\frac{16\pi}{a}\sum_{m=1}^{\infty}\sin(s\phi)\sin(s\phi')\sum_{\lambda}\frac{\sinh\lambda(c-z)\sinh(\lambda z')}{\sinh(\lambda c)}$$
$$\times\{J_s(\lambda a)G_s(\lambda\rho')-J_s(\lambda\rho')G_s(\lambda a)\}\{J_s(\lambda b)G_s(\lambda\rho)-J_s(\lambda\rho)G_s(\lambda b)\}$$
$$\div\frac{d}{d\lambda}\{J_s(\lambda a)G_s(\lambda b)-J_s(\lambda b)G_s(\lambda a)\}, \qquad (44)$$

where the λ's are the positive zeros of

$$J_s(\lambda a)G_s(\lambda b)-J_s(\lambda b)G_s(\lambda a).$$

Similarly the ϕ form can be obtained from (43) by applying contour integration to the function

$$\frac{\sin s(\alpha-\phi)\sin(s\phi')}{\sin(s\alpha)}$$
$$\times\frac{\{I_s(\lambda a)K_s(\lambda\rho')-I_s(\lambda\rho')K_s(\lambda a)\}\{I_s(\lambda b)K_s(\lambda\rho)-I_s(\lambda\rho)K_s(\lambda b)\}}{I_s(\lambda a)K_s(\lambda b)-I_s(\lambda b)K_s(\lambda a)}.$$

It is, if $\phi>\phi'$,

$$V=-\frac{16\pi}{c}\sum_{p=1}^{\infty}\sin(\lambda z)\sin(\lambda z')\sum_{s}\frac{\sinh s(\alpha-\phi)\sinh(s\phi')}{\sinh(s\alpha)}$$
$$\times\{I_{is}(\lambda a)K_{is}(\lambda\rho')-I_{is}(\lambda\rho')K_{is}(\lambda a)\}\{I_{is}(\lambda b)K_{is}(\lambda\rho)-I_{is}(\lambda\rho)K_{is}(\lambda b)\}$$
$$\div\frac{d}{ds}\{I_{is}(\lambda a)K_{is}(\lambda b)-I_{is}(\lambda b)K_{is}(\lambda a)\}, \qquad (45)$$

where $\lambda=p\pi/c$ and the s's are the positive zeros of

$$I_{is}(\lambda a)K_{is}(\lambda b)-I_{is}(\lambda b)K_{is}(\lambda a).$$

If Spherical Harmonics are employed instead of Bessel Functions the bounding surfaces consist of spheres, cones, and axial planes; for the discussion of these cases the reader is referred to Dr. Dougall's paper.

CHAPTER X.

VIBRATIONS OF MEMBRANES.

ONE of the simplest applications of the Bessel functions occurs in the theory of the transverse vibrations of a plane circular membrane. By the term *membrane* we shall understand a thin, perfectly flexible, material lamina, of uniform density throughout; and we shall suppose that it is maintained in a state of uniform tension by means of suitable constraints applied at one or more closed boundaries, all situated in the same plane. When the membrane is slightly displaced from its position of stable equilibrium, and then left to itself, it will execute small oscillations, the nature of which we shall proceed to consider, under certain assumptions made for the purpose of simplifying the analysis.

We shall attend only to the transverse vibrations, and assume that the tension remains unaltered during the motion; moreover if $z=0$ represents the plane which contains the membrane in its undisturbed position, and if

$$z=\phi(x, y)$$

defines the form of the membrane at any instant, it will be supposed that $\partial\phi/\partial x$ and $\partial\phi/\partial y$ are so small that their squares may be neglected.

Let σ be the mass of the membrane per unit of area, and let $T\,ds$ be the tension across a straight line of length ds drawn anywhere upon the membrane; moreover let dS be an element of area, which for simplicity we may suppose bounded by lines of curvature. Then if r_1, r_2 are the principal radii of curvature, the applied force on the element is

$$T\left(\frac{1}{r_1}+\frac{1}{r_2}\right)dS,$$

and its line of action is along the normal to the element. For clearness, suppose that the element is concave to the positive direction of the axis of z: then the equation of motion is

$$\sigma\, dS \frac{\partial^2 z}{\partial t^2} = T\left(\frac{1}{r_1} + \frac{1}{r_2}\right) dS \cos\psi,$$

where ψ is the small angle which the inward-drawn normal makes with the axis of z.

Now, neglecting squares of small quantities,*

$$\frac{1}{r_1} + \frac{1}{r_2} = \frac{\partial^2 z}{\partial x^2} + \frac{\partial^2 z}{\partial y^2},$$

and

$$\cos\psi = 1;$$

hence the equation of motion becomes

$$\frac{\partial^2 z}{\partial t^2} = c^2\left(\frac{\partial^2 z}{\partial x^2} + \frac{\partial^2 z}{\partial y^2}\right) \tag{1}$$

with

$$c^2 = \frac{T}{\sigma}. \tag{2}$$

It remains to find a solution of (1) sufficiently general to satisfy the initial and boundary conditions; these are that z and $\partial z/\partial t$ may have prescribed values when $t=0$, and that $z=0$, for all values of t, at points on the fixed boundaries of the membrane.

By changing from rectangular to cylindrical coordinates the equation (1) may be transformed into

$$\frac{\partial^2 z}{\partial t^2} = c^2\left(\frac{\partial^2 z}{\partial r^2} + \frac{1}{r}\frac{\partial z}{\partial r} + \frac{1}{r^2}\frac{\partial^2 z}{\partial \theta^2}\right). \tag{3}$$

Now suppose that the membrane is circular, and bounded by the circle $r=a$; then we have to find a solution of (3) so as to satisfy the initial conditions, and such that $z=0$, when $r=a$, for all values of t.

Assume

$$z = u \cos pt, \tag{4}$$

where u is independent of t; then putting

$$\frac{p}{c} = \kappa, \tag{5}$$

u has to satisfy the equation

$$\frac{\partial^2 u}{\partial r^2} + \frac{1}{r}\frac{\partial u}{\partial r} + \frac{1}{r^2}\frac{\partial^2 u}{\partial \theta^2} + \kappa^2 u = 0; \tag{6}$$

and if we assume further that

$$u = v \cos n\theta, \tag{7}$$

* Cf. Bell, *Coordinate Geometry*, 2nd Edit., p. 337 (4).

where v is a function of r only, this will be a solution provided that

$$\frac{d^2v}{dr^2}+\frac{1}{r}\frac{dv}{dr}+\left(\kappa^2-\frac{n^2}{r^2}\right)v=0. \qquad (8)$$

It will be sufficient for our present purpose to suppose that n is a positive integer; this being so, the solution of (8) is

$$v=AJ_n(\kappa r)+BY_n(\kappa r).$$

From the conditions of the problem v must be finite when $r=0$: hence $B=0$, and we have a solution of (3) in the form

$$z=AJ_n(\kappa r)\cos n\theta\cos pt$$
$$=AJ_n(\kappa r)\cos n\theta\cos\kappa ct. \qquad (9)$$

In order that the boundary condition may be satisfied, we must have

$$J_n(\kappa a)=0, \qquad (10)$$

and this is a transcendental equation to find κ. It has been proved in Chap. VII. that this equation has an infinite number of real roots κ_1, κ_2, κ_3, etc.; to each of these corresponds a normal vibration of the type (9). The initial conditions which result in this particular type of vibration and no others are that when $t=0$,

$$z=AJ_n(\kappa r)\cos n\theta,$$
$$\frac{\partial z}{\partial t}=0.$$

By assigning to n the values 0, 1, 2, etc., and taking with each value of n the associated quantities $\kappa_1^{(n)}$, $\kappa_2^{(n)}$, $\kappa_3^{(n)}$, etc., derived from $J_n(\kappa a)=0$, we are enabled to construct the more general solution

$$z=\Sigma(A_{ns}\cos n\theta\cos\kappa_s^{(n)}ct+B_{ns}\sin n\theta\cos\kappa_s^{(n)}ct$$
$$+C_{ns}\cos n\theta\sin\kappa_s^{(n)}ct+D_{ns}\sin n\theta\sin\kappa_s^{(n)}ct)J_n(\kappa_s^{(n)}r), \qquad (11)$$

where A_{ns}, B_{ns}, C_{ns}, D_{ns} denote arbitrary constants.

If the initial configuration is defined by

$$z=f(r,\theta),$$

we must have

$$f(r,\theta)=\Sigma(A_{ns}\cos n\theta+B_{ns}\sin n\theta)J_n(\kappa_s^{(n)}r), \qquad (12)$$

and whenever $f(r,\theta)$ admits of an expansion of this form the coefficients A_{ns}, B_{ns} are determined as in Chap. VIII. in the form of definite integrals. In fact, writing κ_s, for convenience, instead of $\kappa_s^{(n)}$,

$$\left.\begin{aligned}A_{ns}&=\frac{2}{\pi a^2J_n'^2(\kappa_s a)}\int_0^{2\pi}d\theta\int_0^a f(r,\theta)\cos n\theta J_n(\kappa_s r)r\,dr,\\ B_{ns}&=\frac{2}{\pi a^2J_n'^2(\kappa_s a)}\int_0^{2\pi}d\theta\int_0^a f(r,\theta)\sin n\theta J_n(\kappa_s r)r\,dr.\end{aligned}\right\} \qquad (13)$$

Since $J_n(\kappa_s a)=0$, it follows from II. (21) that

$$J_n'(\kappa_s a)=J_{n-1}(\kappa_s a),$$

so that we may put $J_{n-1}^2(\kappa_s a)$ for $J_n'^2(\kappa_s a)$ in the expressions for A_{ns}, B_{ns}.

If the membrane starts from rest, the coefficients C_{ns}, D_{ns} are all zero. If, however, we suppose, for the sake of greater generality, that the initial motion is defined by the equation

$$\left(\frac{\partial z}{\partial t}\right)_0=\phi(r, \theta),$$

we must have

$$\phi(r, \theta)=\Sigma\kappa_s^{(n)}c(C_{ns}\cos n\theta+D_{ns}\sin n\theta)J_n(\kappa_s^{(n)}r), \tag{14}$$

from which the coefficients C_{ns}, D_{ns} may be determined.

From the nature of the case the functions $f(r, \theta)$, $\phi(r, \theta)$ are one-valued, finite, and continuous, and are periodic in θ, the period being 2π or an aliquot part of 2π; thus $f(r, \theta)$,—and in like manner $\phi(r, \theta)$,—may be expanded in the form

$$f(r, \theta)=a_0+a_1\cos\theta+a_2\cos 2\theta+\ldots$$
$$+b_1\sin\theta+b_2\sin 2\theta+\ldots,$$

the quantities a_s, b_s being functions of r. The possibility of expanding these functions in series of the form $\Sigma A_s J_n(\kappa_s r)$ has been already considered in Chap. VIII.

In order to realise more clearly the character of the solution thus obtained, let us return to the normal oscillation corresponding to

$$z=J_n(\kappa_s r)\cos n\theta\cos\kappa_s ct, \tag{15}$$

κ_s being the sth root of $J_n(\kappa_s a)=0$.

Each element of the membrane executes a simple harmonic oscillation of period

$$\frac{2\pi}{\kappa_s c}=\frac{2\pi}{\kappa_s}\sqrt{\frac{\sigma}{T}},$$

and of amplitude

$$J_n(\kappa_s r)\cos n\theta.$$

The amplitude vanishes, and the element accordingly remains at rest, if

$$J_n(\kappa_s r)=0,$$

or if

$$\cos n\theta=0.$$

The first equation is satisfied, not only when $r=a$, that is at the boundary, but also when

$$r=\frac{\kappa_1}{\kappa_s}a,\quad r=\frac{\kappa_2}{\kappa_s}a,\ \ldots\ r=\frac{\kappa_{s-1}}{\kappa_s}a;$$

consequently there exists a series of $(s-1)$ nodal circles concentric with the fixed boundary.

The second equation, $\cos n\theta = 0$, is satisfied when

$$\theta = \frac{\pi}{2n}, \quad \theta = \frac{3\pi}{2n}, \ldots \theta = \frac{(4n-1)\pi}{2n};$$

therefore there is a system of n nodal diameters dividing the membrane into $2n$ equal segments every one of which vibrates in precisely the same way. It should be observed, however, that at any particular instant two adjacent segments are in opposite phases.

The normal vibration considered is a possible form of oscillation not only for the complete circle but also for a membrane bounded by portions of the nodal circles and nodal diameters.

If we write μ_s for $\kappa_s a$, so that μ_s is the sth root of $J_n(x) = 0$, the period may be written in the form

$$\frac{2\pi a}{\mu_s}\sqrt{\left(\frac{\sigma}{T}\right)} = \frac{2}{\mu_s}\sqrt{\left(\frac{\pi M}{T}\right)}, \qquad (16)$$

where M is the mass of the whole membrane. This shows very clearly how the period is increased by increasing the mass of the membrane, or diminishing the tension to which it is subjected.

As a particular case, suppose $n = 0$, and let $\mu_1 = 2{\cdot}4048$, the smallest root of $J_0(x) = 0$; then we have the gravest mode of vibration which is symmetrical about the centre, and its frequency is

$$\frac{\mu_1}{2\sqrt{\pi}}\sqrt{\frac{T}{M}} = \sqrt{\frac{T}{M}} \times {\cdot}678389.$$

Thus, for instance, if a circular membrane 10 cm. in diameter and weighing ·006 grm. per square cm. vibrates in its gravest mode with a frequency 220, corresponding to the standard A adopted by Lord Rayleigh, the tension T is determined by

$$\sqrt{\left(\frac{T}{25\pi \times {\cdot}006}\right)} \times {\cdot}6784 = 220,$$

whence

$$T = \left(\frac{220}{{\cdot}6784}\right)^2 \times {\cdot}15\pi = 49560$$

in dynes per centimetre, approximately. In gravitational units of force this is about 50 grams per centimetre, or, roughly, 3·4 lb. per foot.

In the case of an annular membrane bounded by the circles $r=a$ and $r=b$, the normal type of vibration will generally involve both Bessel and Neumann functions. Thus if we put

$$z=A\left\{\frac{J_n(\kappa r)}{J_n(\kappa a)}-\frac{Y_n(\kappa r)}{Y_n(\kappa a)}\right\}\cos n\theta\cos\kappa ct, \tag{17}$$

this will correspond to a possible mode of vibration provided that κ is determined so as to satisfy

$$J_n(\kappa a)Y_n(\kappa b)-J_n(\kappa b)Y_n(\kappa a)=0. \tag{18}$$

It may be inferred from the asymptotic values of J_n and Y_n that this equation has an infinite number of real roots; and it seems probable that the solution

$$z=\Sigma\Sigma\{A\cos n\theta+B\sin n\theta\}\left\{\frac{J_n(\kappa r)}{J_n(\kappa a)}-\frac{Y_n(\kappa r)}{Y_n(\kappa a)}\right\}\cos\kappa ct \tag{19}$$

is sufficiently general to meet the case when the membrane starts from rest in the configuration defined by

$$z=f(r,\theta).$$

Assuming that this is so, the coefficients A, B can be expressed in the form of definite integrals by a method precisely similar to that explained in Chap. VIII. Thus if we write

$$u=\frac{J_n(\kappa r)}{J_n(\kappa a)}-\frac{Y_n(\kappa r)}{Y_n(\kappa a)},$$

it will be found that

$$\left.\begin{aligned}\int_0^{2\pi}d\theta\int_a^b f(r,\theta)\,ur\cos n\theta\,dr=LA,\\ \int_0^{2\pi}d\theta\int_a^b f(r,\theta)\,ur\sin n\theta\,dr=LB,\end{aligned}\right\} \tag{20}$$

where $$L=\pi\int_a^b u^2r\,dr=\frac{\pi b}{2\kappa}\left\{\frac{\partial u}{\partial r}\frac{\partial u}{\partial\kappa}\right\}_{r=b}, \qquad \text{VI. (33).}$$

Now $$\left(\frac{\partial u}{\partial r}\right)_{r=b}=\kappa\left\{\frac{J_n'(\kappa b)}{J_n(\kappa a)}-\frac{Y_n'(\kappa b)}{Y_n(\kappa a)}\right\}$$

$$=\kappa\frac{Y_n(\kappa b)}{Y_n(\kappa a)}\left\{\frac{J_n'(\kappa b)}{J_n(\kappa b)}-\frac{Y_n'(\kappa b)}{Y_n(\kappa b)}\right\} \text{ by (18)}$$

$$=-\frac{1}{b\,J_n(\kappa b)\,Y_n(\kappa a)} \text{ by III. (47).}$$

Similarly

$$\left(\frac{\partial u}{\partial \kappa}\right)_{r=b} = b\left\{\frac{J_n'(\kappa b)}{J_n(\kappa a)} - \frac{Y_n'(\kappa b)}{Y_n(\kappa a)}\right\} + \frac{J_n(\kappa b)}{\kappa\{J_n(\kappa a)\}^2 Y_n(\kappa a)}.$$

Hence $$L = \pi\frac{b^2}{2}\left\{\frac{J_n'(\kappa b)}{J_n(\kappa a)} - \frac{Y_n'(\kappa b)}{Y_n(\kappa a)}\right\}^2 - \frac{\pi}{2\kappa^2}\frac{1}{\{J_n(\kappa a)\, Y_n(\kappa a)\}^2}$$

$$= \pi\left[\frac{r^2}{2}\left\{\frac{J_n'(\kappa r)}{J_n(\kappa a)} - \frac{Y_n'(\kappa r)}{Y_n(\kappa a)}\right\}^2\right]_a^b. \qquad (21)$$

For a more detailed treatment of the subject of this chapter the reader is referred to Riemann's *Partielle Differential-gleichungen* and Lord Rayleigh's *Theory of Sound*.

CHAPTER XI.

HYDRODYNAMICS.

IN Chapter I. § 4 it has been shown that the expression

$$\phi=\Sigma(A\cos n\theta+B\sin n\theta)\,e^{-\lambda z}J_n(\lambda r)$$

satisfies Laplace's equation

$$\nabla^2\phi=0,$$

and some physical applications of this result have already been considered. In the theory of fluid motion ϕ may be interpreted as a velocity-potential defining a form of steady irrotational motion of an incompressible fluid, and is a proper form to assume when we have to deal with cylindrical boundaries.

We shall not stay to discuss any of the special problems thus suggested, but proceed to consider some in which the method of procedure is less obvious.

§ 1. **Stokes' Current Function for Motion in Coaxial Planes.** Let there be a mass of incompressible fluid of unit density moving in such a way that the path of each element lies in a plane containing the axis of z, and that the molecular, or, more properly, the elemental rotation is equal to ω, the axis of rotation for any element being perpendicular to the plane which contains its path.

Then,* taking cylindrical coordinates r, θ, z as usual, and denoting by u, v the component velocities along r and parallel to the axis of z respectively,

$$\frac{\partial}{\partial r}(ur)+\frac{\partial}{\partial z}(vr)=0, \tag{1}$$

and

$$\frac{\partial v}{\partial r}-\frac{\partial u}{\partial z}=2\omega. \tag{2}$$

* Cf. Lamb's *Hydrodynamics*, 3rd Edition, p. 118.

Equation (1) shows that we may put

$$ur = -\frac{\partial\psi}{\partial z}, \quad vr = \frac{\partial\psi}{\partial r}, \tag{3}$$

where ψ is Stokes' current function; thus equation (2) becomes

$$\frac{\partial}{\partial r}\left(\frac{1}{r}\frac{\partial\psi}{\partial r}\right) + \frac{\partial}{\partial z}\left(\frac{1}{r}\frac{\partial\psi}{\partial z}\right) - 2\omega = 0. \tag{4}$$

When the motion is steady, ψ is a function of r and z; and if we put

$$q^2 = u^2 + v^2,$$

so that q is the resultant velocity, and take the density to be unity, the dynamical equations may be written in the form

$$\left.\begin{aligned} \frac{\partial p}{\partial r} + \frac{\partial}{\partial r}(\tfrac{1}{2}q^2) - 2\frac{\omega}{r}\frac{\partial\psi}{\partial r} &= 0, \\ \frac{\partial p}{\partial z} + \frac{\partial}{\partial z}(\tfrac{1}{2}q^2) - 2\frac{\omega}{r}\frac{\partial\psi}{\partial z} &= 0, \end{aligned}\right\} \tag{5}$$

whence it follows that ω/r must be expressible as a function of ψ. The simplest hypothesis is

$$\omega = \zeta r, \tag{6}$$

where ζ is a constant; on this assumption, (4) becomes

$$\frac{\partial}{\partial r}\left(\frac{1}{r}\frac{\partial\psi}{\partial r}\right) + \frac{\partial}{\partial z}\left(\frac{1}{r}\frac{\partial\psi}{\partial z}\right) - 2\zeta r = 0. \tag{7}$$

Now the ordinary differential equation

$$\frac{d}{dr}\left(\frac{1}{r}\frac{d\chi}{dr}\right) - 2\zeta r = 0$$

is satisfied by

$$\chi = \tfrac{1}{4}\zeta r^4 + Ar^2 + B,$$

where A and B are arbitrary constants; and if we assume

$$\psi = \chi + \rho r \cosh nz,$$

where ρ is a function of r only, we find from (7) that

$$\frac{d^2\rho}{dr^2} + \frac{1}{r}\frac{d\rho}{dr} + \left(n^2 - \frac{1}{r^2}\right)\rho = 0,$$

the solution of which is

$$\rho = C_n J_1(nr) + D_n Y_1(nr).$$

Finally, then,

$$\psi = \tfrac{1}{4}\zeta r^4 + Ar^2 + B + r\sum_n \{C_n J_1(nr) + D_n Y_1(nr)\} \cosh nz, \tag{8}$$

where the values of n and of the other constants have to be determined so as to meet the requirements of the boundary conditions.

Suppose, for instance, that the fluid fills the finite space inclosed by the cylinders $r=a$, $r=b$ and the planes $z=\pm h$. Then the boundary conditions are

$$\frac{\partial\psi}{\partial z}=0,$$

where $r=a$ or b, for all values of z; and

$$\frac{\partial\psi}{\partial r}=0$$

when $z=\pm h$, for all values of r such that

$$a \geqq r \geqq b.$$

One way of satisfying these conditions is to make ψ constant and equal to zero at every point on the boundary. Now if we put

$$\psi=\tfrac{1}{4}\zeta(r^2-a^2)(r^2-b^2)-\zeta r\sum_n C_n\left\{\frac{J_1(nr)}{J_1(na)}-\frac{Y_1(nr)}{Y_1(na)}\right\}\frac{\cosh nz}{\cosh nh}, \quad (9)$$

this is of the right form, and vanishes for $r=a$. It vanishes when $r=b$, provided the values of n are chosen so as to satisfy

$$J_1(na)\,Y_1(nb)-J_1(nb)\,Y_1(na)=0; \quad (10)$$

and, finally, it vanishes when $z=\pm h$ if the coefficients C_n are determined so that

$$\sum_n C_n\left\{\frac{J_1(nr)}{J_1(na)}-\frac{Y_1(nr)}{Y_1(na)}\right\}=\tfrac{1}{4}(r^2-a^2)(r^2-b^2)/r \quad (11)$$

for all values of r such that

$$a \geqq r \geqq b.$$

Assuming the possibility of this expansion, we can find the coefficients in the usual way by integration.

The stream-lines are defined by

$$\psi=\text{const.},\quad \theta=\text{const.},$$

so that the outermost particles of fluid remain, throughout the motion, in contact with the containing vessel.

(The above solution was given in the Mathematical Tripos, Jan. 1884.)

§ 2. Oscillations of a Cylindrical Vortex. Some very interesting results have been obtained by Lord Kelvin (*Phil. Mag.* (5) x. (1880), p. 155; *Collected Papers,* Vol. IV.) in connection with the oscillations of a cylindrical vortex about a state of steady motion.

In Cartesian Coordinates the Eulerian equations of motion are

$$-\frac{\partial p}{\partial x}=\frac{\partial u}{\partial t}+u\frac{\partial u}{\partial x}+v\frac{\partial u}{\partial y}+w\frac{\partial u}{\partial z},$$

and two similar equations.

For cylindrical coordinates (r, θ, z), w and z remain unaltered. Let rectangular axes OP and OQ be taken in the (x, y) plane so that OP passes through the projection on that plane of the element of fluid under consideration. Then if u and v be the velocities of the element parallel to OP and OQ, these axes are turning round at the rate v/r. The accelerations of the element which are due to the rotation of the axes are

$$-\frac{v^2}{r}, \quad +\frac{uv}{r}.$$

Hence, if we put ω for v/r, the equations of motion become

$$\left.\begin{aligned}-\frac{\partial p}{\partial r}&=\frac{\partial u}{\partial t}-r\omega^2+u\frac{\partial u}{\partial r}+\omega\frac{\partial u}{\partial \theta}+w\frac{\partial u}{\partial z},\\ -\frac{\partial p}{r\,\partial \theta}&=\frac{\partial (r\omega)}{\partial t}+u\omega+u\frac{\partial (r\omega)}{\partial r}+\omega\frac{\partial (r\omega)}{\partial \theta}+w\frac{\partial (r\omega)}{\partial z},\\ -\frac{\partial p}{\partial z}&=\frac{\partial w}{\partial t}+u\frac{\partial w}{\partial r}+\omega\frac{\partial w}{\partial \theta}+w\frac{\partial w}{\partial z},\end{aligned}\right\} \qquad (12)$$

while the Cartesian equation of continuity

$$\frac{\partial u}{\partial x}+\frac{\partial v}{\partial y}+\frac{\partial w}{\partial z}=0$$

becomes

$$\frac{\partial u}{\partial r}+\frac{u}{r}+\frac{\partial (r\omega)}{r\,\partial \theta}+\frac{\partial w}{\partial z}=0. \qquad (13)$$

It is to be understood that r, θ, z are independent of t, while u, ω, w are supposed expressed as explicit functions of r, θ, z, t; and the density of the liquid is taken to be unity.

We obtain a possible state of steady motion by supposing that

$$u=0, \quad w=0, \quad \omega=q \text{ (a constant)};$$

this makes the resultant velocity

$$v=qr, \qquad (14)$$

while the pressure is

$$\pi=\int q^2r\,dr=\pi_0+\tfrac{1}{2}q^2r^2, \qquad (15)$$

π being a constant depending on the boundary conditions.

Now assume as a solution of (12) and (13)

$$\left.\begin{aligned} u&=U\cos mz\sin(nt-s\theta), & r\omega&=v+V\cos mz\cos(nt-s\theta),\\ w&=W\sin mz\sin(nt-s\theta), & p&=\pi+\Pi\cos mz\cos(nt-s\theta),\end{aligned}\right\}\qquad(16)$$

where s is a real integer, m, n are constants, and U, V, W, Π are functions of r which are small in comparison with v. Then substituting in (12) and (13) and neglecting squares and products of small quantities, we obtain the approximate equations

$$\left.\begin{aligned} -\frac{d\Pi}{dr}&=\quad(n-sq)U-2qV,\\ -\frac{s}{r}\Pi&=-(n-sq)V+2qU,\\ m\Pi&=\quad(n-sq)W,\end{aligned}\right\}\qquad(17)$$

$$\frac{\partial U}{\partial r}+\frac{U}{r}+\frac{s}{r}V+mW=0.\qquad(18)$$

From equations (17) we obtain

$$\left.\begin{aligned} U&=\frac{(n-sq)\left\{(n-sq)\dfrac{dW}{dr}-\dfrac{2sq}{r}W\right\}}{m\{4q^2-(n-sq)^2\}},\\ V&=\frac{(n-sq)\left\{2q\dfrac{dW}{dr}-\dfrac{s(n-sq)}{r}W\right\}}{m\{4q^2-(n-sq)^2\}},\end{aligned}\right\}\qquad(19)$$

and on substituting these expressions in (18) we find, after a little reduction, that

$$\frac{d^2W}{dr^2}+\frac{1}{r}\frac{dW}{dr}+\left\{\frac{m^2\{4q^2-(n-sq)^2\}}{(n-sq)^2}-\frac{s^2}{r^2}\right\}W=0.\qquad(20)$$

If the quantity $\qquad \dfrac{m^2\{4q^2-(n-sq)^2\}}{(n-sq)^2}$

is positive, let it be called κ^2; if it is negative, let it be denoted by $-\lambda^2$. Then, in the first case,

$$W=AJ_s(\kappa r)+BY_s(\kappa r),\qquad(21)$$

and, in the second case,

$$W=CI_s(\lambda r)+DK_s(\lambda r).\qquad(22)$$

The constants must be determined by appropriate initial or boundary conditions. For instance, suppose the fluid to occupy, during the steady motion, the whole interior of the cylinder $r=a$. Then in order that, in the disturbed motion, w may be everywhere small, it is necessary that $B=0$ in (21) and $D=0$ in (22).

To fix the ideas, suppose m, n, s, q *assigned*, and that

$$4q^2 > (n-sq)^2;$$

then, by (19) and (21),

$$U = \frac{A(n-sq)\left\{(n-sq)\kappa J_s'(\kappa r) - \frac{2sq}{r} J_s(\kappa r)\right\}}{m\{4q^2-(n-sq)^2\}}. \qquad (23)$$

By (16) the corresponding radial velocity is

$$u = U \cos mz \sin (nt - s\theta),$$

and if U_0 is the value of U when $r=a$, the initial velocity along the radius, for $r=a$, is

$$-U_0 \cos mz \sin s\theta.$$

Now U_0 may have any (small) constant value; supposing that this is prescribed, the constant A is determined, its value being, by (23),

$$A = \frac{\{4q^2-(n-sq)^2\}mU_0}{(n-sq)\left\{(n-sq)\kappa J_s'(\kappa a) - \frac{2sq}{a} J_s(\kappa a)\right\}}$$

$$= \frac{\kappa^2 U_0/m}{\kappa J_s'(\kappa a) - \frac{2sq}{(n-sq)a} J_s(\kappa a)}. \qquad (24)$$

Of course, the other initial component velocities and the initial pressure must be adjusted so as to be consistent with the equations (16)—(19).

There is no difficulty in realising the general nature of the disturbance represented by the equations (16); it evidently travels round the axis of the cylinder with constant angular velocity n/s.

When q is given, we can obtain a very general solution by compounding the different disturbances of the type considered which arise when we take different values of m, n, s; according to Lord Kelvin it is possible to construct in this way the solution for "any arbitrary distribution of the generative disturbance over the cylindric surface, and for any arbitrary periodic function of the time."

The general solution involves both the J and the I functions.

Another case of steady motion is that of a hollow irrotational vortex in a fixed cylindrical tube. This is obtained by putting

$$u=0, \quad w=0, \quad r^2\omega = c,$$

where c is a constant; the velocity-potential is $c\theta$, and the velocity at any point is

$$v=\frac{c}{r}. \tag{25}$$

If a is the radius of the free surface, the pressure for the undisturbed motion is

$$\pi=\pi_0+\frac{1}{2}c^2\left(\frac{1}{a^2}-\frac{1}{r^2}\right). \tag{26}$$

Putting these values of v and π in equations (16) and proceeding as before, we find for the approximate equations corresponding to (17) and (18)

$$\left.\begin{aligned} -\frac{d\Pi}{dr}&=\left(n-\frac{cs}{r^2}\right)U-\frac{2cV}{r^2},\\ -\frac{s}{r}\Pi&=-\left(n-\frac{cs}{r^2}\right)V,\\ m\Pi&=\left(n-\frac{cs}{r^2}\right)W,\end{aligned}\right\} \tag{27}$$

$$\frac{dU}{dr}+\frac{U}{r}+\frac{sV}{r}+mW=0. \tag{28}$$

Hence

$$\left.\begin{aligned} V&=\frac{s}{mr}W,\quad \Pi=\frac{1}{m}\left(n-\frac{cs}{r^2}\right)W,\\ U&=-\frac{1}{m}\frac{dW}{dr};\end{aligned}\right\} \tag{29}$$

and therefore the differential equation satisfied by W is

$$\frac{d^2W}{dr^2}+\frac{1}{r}\frac{dW}{dr}-\left(m^2+\frac{s^2}{r^2}\right)W=0.$$

Consequently

$$W=AI_s(mr)+BK_s(mr), \tag{30}$$

where A, B are arbitrary constants.

If the fixed boundary is defined by $r=b$, we must have $u=0$ when $r=b$; that is, by (16) and (29),

$$\frac{dW}{dr}=0 \quad \text{when } r=b.$$

Thus

$$W=C\left\{\frac{I_s(mr)}{I_s'(mb)}-\frac{K_s(mr)}{K_s'(mb)}\right\}. \tag{31}$$

We have still to express the condition that $p=\pi_0$ at every point on the free surface for the disturbed motion. To do this we must find a first approximation to the form of the free surface. In the steady motion, the coordinates r, z *of a particle of fluid* remain invariable and

$$\dot{\theta}=\frac{c}{r^2}, \quad \text{whence } \theta=\frac{ct}{r^2}.$$

In the disturbed motion r does not differ much from its mean value r_0, and if we take the equation

$$\dot{r}=U\cos mz\sin(nt-s\theta)$$

we obtain a first approximation by putting $\theta=\frac{ct}{r_0^2}$, giving U its mean value U_0 and neglecting the variation of z: thus

$$\dot{r}=U_0\cos mz\sin\left(n-\frac{cs}{r_0^2}\right)t,$$

and therefore

$$r=r_0-\frac{U_0}{n-\frac{cs}{r_0^2}}\cos mz\cos(nt-s\theta). \tag{32}$$

If we put $r_0=a$, and write U_a for the corresponding value of U_0, the approximate equation of the free surface is

$$r=a-\frac{U_a}{n-\frac{sc}{a^2}}\cos mz\cos(nt-s\theta). \tag{33}$$

Now, by (16) and (26),

$$p=\pi_0+\frac{1}{2}c^2\left(\frac{1}{a^2}-\frac{1}{r^2}\right)+\Pi\cos mz\cos(nt-s\theta),$$

and the condition $p=\pi_0$ gives, with the help of (33),

$$0=\frac{1}{2}c^2\left\{\frac{1}{a^2}-\frac{1}{\left[a-\frac{U_a}{n-\frac{sc}{a^2}}\cos mz\cos(nt-s\theta)\right]^2}\right\}$$
$$+\Pi\cos mz\cos(nt-s\theta);$$

that is, neglecting the squares of small quantities,

$$\Pi-\frac{c^2}{a^3}\frac{U_a}{n-\frac{sc}{a^2}}=0. \tag{34}$$

Also, by (29), $$\Pi=\frac{1}{m}\left(n-\frac{sc}{a^2}\right)W_a,$$

$$U_a=-\frac{1}{m}\left(\frac{dW}{dr}\right)_{r=a};$$

thus, with the value of W given in (31), the condition (34) becomes

$$\left(n-\frac{sc}{a^2}\right)^2\left\{\frac{I_s(ma)}{I_s'(mb)}-\frac{K_s(ma)}{K_s'(mb)}\right\} + \frac{mc^2}{a^3}\left\{\frac{I_s'(ma)}{I_s'(mb)}-\frac{K_s'(ma)}{K_s'(mb)}\right\}=0. \qquad (35)$$

This may be regarded as an equation to find n when the other quantities are given. If we write

$$\frac{c}{a^2}=q \qquad (36)$$

(the angular velocity at the free surface in the steady motion), and

$$N=-ma\left\{\frac{I_s'(ma)}{I_s'(mb)}-\frac{K_s'(ma)}{K_s'(mb)}\right\}\div\left\{\frac{I_s(ma)}{I_s'(mb)}-\frac{K_s(ma)}{K_s'(mb)}\right\}, \qquad (37)$$

the roots of the equation (35) are given by

$$n=q(s\pm\sqrt{N}). \qquad (38)$$

N is an abstract number, which is positive whenever a, b, m are real and positive and $b>a$. Thus the steady motion is stable in relation to disturbances of the type here considered. This might have been anticipated, from other considerations.

The interpretation of (38) is that corresponding to each set of values m, s there are two oscillations of the type (16), travelling with angular velocities

$$q\left(1+\frac{\sqrt{N}}{s}\right) \quad \text{and} \quad q\left(1-\frac{\sqrt{N}}{s}\right)$$

respectively about the axis of the vortex.

A special case worth noticing is when $b=\infty$. In this case we must put

$$W=AK_s(mr),$$

and (37) reduces to

$$N=-ma\frac{K_s'(ma)}{K_s(ma)}.$$

The third case considered by Lord Kelvin is that of a cylindrical core rotating like a solid body and surrounded by liquid which extends to infinity and moves irrotationally, with no slip at the interface between it and the core. Thus if a is the radius of the core, we have

$$\left.\begin{aligned} v&=qr \quad \text{when } r<a,\\ v&=\frac{qa^2}{r} \quad \text{when } r>a,\end{aligned}\right\} \qquad (39)$$

for the undisturbed motion.

For the disturbed motion we start as before with equations (16), and by precisely the same analysis we find

$$\left.\begin{aligned} W &= AJ_s(\kappa r) \quad \text{when } r<a, \\ W &= BK_s(mr) \quad \text{when } r>a, \\ \text{with} \quad \kappa^2 &= \frac{m^2\{4q^2-(n-sq)^2\}}{(n-sq)^2}. \end{aligned}\right\} \tag{40}$$

At the interface U, W and Π must have the same value on both sides. Now, by (17) and (27), it follows that the values of Π are the same when those of W agree; hence the two conditions to be satisfied are, by (23) and (29),

$$AJ_s(\kappa a) = BK_s(ma), \tag{41}$$

and

$$\frac{A(n-sq)\left\{(n-sq)\,\kappa J'_s(\kappa a) - \frac{2sq}{a} J_s(\kappa a)\right\}}{m\{4q^2-(n-sq)^2\}} = -BK'_s(ma). \tag{42}$$

Eliminating A/B, we obtain, on reduction,

$$\frac{\kappa a J'_s(\kappa a)}{J_s(\kappa a)} + \frac{\kappa^2 a K'_s(ma)}{mK_s(ma)} - \frac{2sq}{n-sq} = 0,$$

or, which is the same thing,

$$\frac{m\kappa a J'_s(\kappa a)}{J_s(\kappa a)} + \frac{\kappa^2 a K'_s(ma)}{K_s(ma)} - s\sqrt{(\kappa^2+m^2)} = 0, \tag{43}$$

a transcendental equation to find κ when the other constants are given. When κ is known, n is given by

$$n = q\left(s \pm \frac{2m}{\sqrt{(\kappa^2+m^2)}}\right).$$

For a proof that the equation (43) has an infinite number of real roots, and for a more complete discussion of the three problems in question, the reader is referred to the original paper above cited.

Since the expression for w involves the factor $\sin mz$, we may, if we like, suppose that the planes $z=0$ and $z=\pi/m$ are fixed boundaries of the fluid.

§ 3. **Wave Motion in a Cylindrical Tank.** We will now consider the irrotational wave-motion of homogeneous liquid contained in a cylindrical tank of radius a and depth h. The upper surface is supposed free, and in the plane $z=0$ when undisturbed.

The velocity-potential ϕ must satisfy the equation

$$\frac{\partial^2\phi}{\partial r^2}+\frac{1}{r}\frac{\partial\phi}{\partial r}+\frac{1}{r^2}\frac{\partial^2\phi}{\partial\theta^2}+\frac{\partial^2\phi}{\partial z^2}=0, \tag{44}$$

and also the boundary conditions

$$\left.\begin{aligned}\frac{\partial\phi}{\partial z}&=0 \quad \text{when } z=-h,\\ \frac{\partial\phi}{\partial r}&=0 \quad \text{when } r=a.\end{aligned}\right\} \tag{45}$$

These conditions are all fulfilled if we assume

$$\phi=AJ_n(\kappa r)\sin n\theta\cosh\kappa(z+h)\cos mt, \tag{46}$$

provided that κ is chosen so that

$$J_n'(\kappa a)=0. \tag{47}$$

If gravity is the only force acting, we have, as the condition for a free surface,

$$\frac{\partial^2\phi}{\partial t^2}+g\frac{\partial\phi}{\partial z}=0 \tag{48}$$

when $z=0$, neglecting small quantities of the second order; therefore

$$-m^2\cosh\kappa h+g\kappa\sinh\kappa h=0,$$

or

$$m^2=g\kappa\tanh\kappa h. \tag{49}$$

The equations (46), (47), (49) give a form of ϕ corresponding to a normal type of oscillation; when the liquid occupies the whole interior of the tank, n must be an integer in order that ϕ may be one-valued. The equation (47) has an infinite number of roots $\kappa_1^{(n)}$, $\kappa_2^{(n)}$, etc., so that for each value of n we may write, more generally,

$$\phi=\sum_s A_s J_n(\kappa_s^{(n)}r)\cosh\kappa_s^{(n)}(z+h)\cos m_s^{(n)}t\sin n\theta, \tag{50}$$

and by compounding the solutions which arise from different integral values of n we obtain an expression for ϕ which contains a doubly infinite number of terms. Moreover, instead of the single trigonometrical factor

$$A\cos mt\sin n\theta$$

in the typical term, we may put

$$(A\cos mt+B\sin mt)\sin n\theta+(C\cos mt+D\sin mt)\cos n\theta,$$

where A, B, C, D are arbitrary constants.

As a simple illustration, let us take $n=0$, and put

$$\phi=\Sigma A J_0(\kappa r)\cosh\kappa(z+h)\sin mt;$$

then if, as usual, we write η for the elevation of the free surface at any moment above the mean level,

$$\dot{\eta}=\left(\frac{\partial\phi}{\partial z}\right)_{z=0}=\Sigma\kappa A J_0(\kappa r)\sinh\kappa h\sin mt, \tag{51}$$

and since this vanishes when $t=0$, the liquid must be supposed to start from rest. Integrating (51) with regard to t, we have a possible initial form of the free surface defined by

$$\eta=-\Sigma\frac{\kappa}{m}A\sinh\kappa h J_0(\kappa r), \tag{52}$$

the summation referring to the roots of

$$J_0'(\kappa a)=0.$$

By the methods of Chap. VIII. the solution may be adapted to suit a prescribed form of initial free surface defined by the equation

$$\eta=f(r).$$

It will be observed that in (49) κh is an abstract number; and if, in the special case last considered, we put $\kappa a=\lambda$, so that λ is a root of $J_0'(\lambda)=0$, the period of the corresponding oscillation is

$$\frac{2\pi}{m}=2\pi\sqrt{\left(\frac{a}{\lambda g}\coth\frac{\lambda h}{a}\right)}.$$

A specially interesting case occurs when a rigid vertical diaphragm, whose thickness may be neglected, extends from the axis of the tank to its circumference. If the position of the diaphragm is defined by $\theta=0$, we must have, in addition to the other conditions,

$$\frac{\partial\phi}{\partial\theta}=0 \quad \text{when } \theta=0 \text{ or } 2\pi.$$

This excludes some, but not all, of the normal oscillations which are possible in the absence of the barrier; but besides those which can be retained, we have a new set which are obtained by supposing

$$n=k+\tfrac{1}{2},$$

where k is any integer. Thus in the simplest case, when $k=0$, we may put

$$\phi=AJ_{\frac{1}{2}}(\kappa r)\cos\frac{\theta}{2}\cosh\kappa(z+h)\cos mt, \tag{53}$$

or, which is the same thing,

$$\phi = A' r^{-\frac{1}{2}} \sin(\kappa r) \cos\frac{\theta}{2} \cosh\kappa(z+h) \cos mt,$$

with the conditions
$$\left.\begin{aligned} \tan\kappa a - 2\kappa a = 0, \\ m^2 = g\kappa \tanh\kappa h. \end{aligned}\right\} \qquad (54)$$

The equation $\tan x - 2x = 0$

has an infinite number of real roots, and to each of these corresponds an oscillation of the type represented by (53).

More generally, if we put

$$n = \frac{(2k+1)\pi}{2a} \quad [a < \tfrac{1}{2}\pi],$$

where k is any integer, the function

$$\phi = (A \cos mt + B \sin mt) J_n(\kappa r) \cosh\kappa(z+h) \sin n\theta,$$

with the conditions (47) and (49) as before, defines a normal type of oscillation in a tank of depth h bounded by the cylinder $r = a$ and the planes $\theta = \pm a$.

Similar considerations apply to the vibrations of a circular membrane with one radius fixed, and of a membrane in the shape of a sector of a circle (see Rayleigh's *Theory of Sound*, 2nd Ed., I. p. 322).

§ **4. Oscillations of a Rotating Liquid.** Another instructive problem, due to Lord Kelvin (*Phil. Mag.* (5) X. (1880), p. 109; *Collected Papers*, Vol. IV.), may be stated as follows.

A circular basin, containing heavy homogeneous liquid, rotates with uniform angular velocity ω about the vertical through its centre; it is required to investigate the oscillations of the liquid on the assumptions that the motion of each particle is nearly horizontal, and only deviates slightly from what it would be if the liquid and basin together rotated like a rigid body; and further that the velocity is always equal for particles in the same vertical.

The legitimacy of these assumptions is secured if we suppose that, if a is the radius of the basin, $\omega^2 a$ is small in comparison with g and that the greatest depth of the liquid is small in comparison with a. We shall suppose, for simplicity, that the mean depth is constant, and equal to h.

Let the motion be referred to horizontal rectangular axes which meet on the axis of rotation, and are rigidly connected with the basin. Then, if u, v are the component velocities, parallel to these axes, of a particle whose coordinates are x, y, the approximate equations of motion are *

$$\left.\begin{aligned}\frac{\partial u}{\partial t}-2\omega v=-\frac{1}{\rho}\frac{\partial p}{\partial x},\\ \frac{\partial v}{\partial t}+2\omega u=-\frac{1}{\rho}\frac{\partial p}{\partial y}.\end{aligned}\right\} \tag{55}$$

If $h+z$ is the depth of the liquid in the vertical through the point considered, the equation of continuity is

$$h\left(\frac{\partial u}{\partial x}+\frac{\partial v}{\partial y}\right)+\frac{\partial z}{\partial t}=0; \tag{56}$$

while the condition for a free surface leads to the equations

$$\left.\begin{aligned}\frac{\partial p}{\partial x}=g\rho\frac{\partial z}{\partial x},\\ \frac{\partial p}{\partial y}=g\rho\frac{\partial z}{\partial y}.\end{aligned}\right\} \tag{57}$$

If we eliminate p from (55) by means of (57) and change to polar coordinates, we obtain

$$\left.\begin{aligned}\frac{\partial u}{\partial t}-2\omega v+g\frac{\partial z}{\partial r}\quad=0,\\ \frac{\partial v}{\partial t}+2\omega u+g\frac{\partial z}{r\,\partial\theta}=0,\end{aligned}\right\} \tag{58}$$

where u, v now denote the component velocities along the radius vector and perpendicular to it.

The equation of continuity, in the new notation, is

$$h\left(\frac{\partial u}{\partial r}+\frac{\partial v}{r\,\partial\theta}+\frac{u}{r}\right)+\frac{\partial z}{\partial t}=0. \tag{59}$$

From the equations (58) we obtain

$$\left.\begin{aligned}\left(\frac{\partial^2}{\partial t^2}+4\omega^2\right)u=-g\frac{\partial^2 z}{\partial r\,\partial t}-2\omega g\frac{\partial z}{r\,\partial\theta},\\ \left(\frac{\partial^2}{\partial t^2}+4\omega^2\right)v=2\omega g\frac{\partial z}{\partial r}-g\frac{\partial^2 z}{r\,\partial\theta\,\partial t};\end{aligned}\right\} \tag{60}$$

hence, by operating on (59) with $\left(\frac{\partial^2}{\partial t^2}+4\omega^2\right)$ and eliminating u, v, we obtain a differential equation in z, which, after reduction, is found to be

$$\left(\frac{\partial^2}{\partial t^2}+4\omega^2\right)\frac{\partial z}{\partial t}=gh\left(\frac{\partial^2}{\partial r^2}+\frac{1}{r}\frac{\partial}{\partial r}+\frac{1}{r^2}\frac{\partial^2}{\partial\theta^2}\right)\frac{\partial z}{\partial t}. \tag{61}$$

* Cf. Lamb, *Hydrodynamics*, 3rd. Ed. p. 302.

Let us assume $z = \zeta \cos(m\theta - nt)$,

where m, n are constants, and ζ is a function of r only: then on substitution in (61) we find

$$\frac{d^2\zeta}{dr^2} + \frac{1}{r}\frac{d\zeta}{dr} + \left(\kappa^2 - \frac{m^2}{r^2}\right)\zeta = 0, \tag{62}$$

where

$$\kappa^2 = \frac{n^2 - 4\omega^2}{gh}. \tag{63}$$

The work now proceeds as in other similar cases already considered. Thus, for instance, in the simplest case, that of an open circular pond with a vertical bank, we take m to be a real integer, and put

$$z = J_m(\kappa r)\cos(m\theta - nt). \tag{64}$$

The boundary condition

$$u = 0 \quad \text{when } r = a$$

gives, by (60), for the determination of n, the equation

$$2m\omega J_m(\kappa a) - n\kappa a J'_m(\kappa a) = 0. \tag{65}$$

If ω^2 is small in comparison with gh, we have approximately

$$\kappa^2 = \frac{n^2}{gh},$$

and (65) becomes

$$2m\omega J_m\left(\frac{na}{\sqrt{(gh)}}\right) - \frac{n^2 a}{\sqrt{(gh)}} J'_m\left(\frac{na}{\sqrt{(gh)}}\right) = 0.$$

In the general case it will be found that the equations (58) and (60) are satisfied by putting

$$u = U\sin(m\theta - nt), \quad v = V\cos(m\theta - nt), \tag{66}$$

with

$$\left.\begin{aligned} U &= \frac{g}{n^2 - 4\omega^2}\left(n\frac{d\zeta}{dr} - \frac{2m\omega\zeta}{r}\right), \\ V &= \frac{g}{n^2 - 4\omega^2}\left(-2\omega\frac{d\zeta}{dr} + \frac{mn\zeta}{r}\right). \end{aligned}\right\} \tag{67}$$

By assuming for the solution of (62)

$$\zeta = AJ_m(\kappa r) + BY_m(\kappa r)$$

we obtain a value for z which may be adapted to the case of a circular pond with a circular island in the middle.

It should be remarked that the problem was suggested to Lord Kelvin by Laplace's dynamical theory of the tides: the solution is applicable to waves in a shallow lake or inland sea, if we put $\omega = \gamma \sin\lambda$, γ being the earth's angular velocity, and λ the latitude of the lake or sea, which is supposed to be of comparatively small dimensions.

§ 5. **Two-Dimensional Motion of a Viscous Liquid.** We will conclude the chapter with a brief account of the application of Bessel Functions to the two-dimensional motion of a viscous liquid. It may be shown that if we suppose the liquid to be of unit density, and that no forces act, the equations of motion are *

$$\left.\begin{aligned} \dot{u}-\frac{v^2}{r}&=-\frac{\partial p}{\partial r}+\mu\left(\nabla^2 u-\frac{u}{r^2}-\frac{2}{r^2}\frac{\partial v}{\partial \theta}\right), \\ \dot{v}+\frac{uv}{r}&=-\frac{\partial p}{r\,\partial \theta}+\mu\left(\nabla^2 v-\frac{v}{r^2}+\frac{2}{r^2}\frac{\partial u}{\partial \theta}\right), \end{aligned}\right\} \tag{68}$$

where $\nabla^2 u \equiv \frac{\partial^2 u}{\partial r^2}+\frac{1}{r}\frac{\partial u}{\partial r}+\frac{1}{r^2}\frac{\partial^2 u}{\partial \theta^2}$. The axes here rotate and the considerations of (12), § 2, apply.

If ψ is the current function,

$$u=\frac{\partial \psi}{r\,\partial \theta}, \quad v=-\frac{\partial \psi}{\partial r};$$

and if we put

$$\mu\nabla^2\psi-\frac{\partial \psi}{\partial t}=\chi, \tag{69}$$

the equations of motion may be written in the form

$$\left.\begin{aligned} \dot{u}-\frac{v^2}{r}&=-\frac{\partial p}{\partial r}+\frac{1}{r}\frac{\partial \chi}{\partial \theta}+\frac{\partial u}{\partial t}, \\ \dot{v}+\frac{uv}{r}&=-\frac{\partial p}{r\,\partial \theta}-\frac{\partial \chi}{\partial r}+\frac{\partial v}{\partial t}. \end{aligned}\right\} \tag{70}$$

If the squares and products of the velocities are neglected,

$$\dot{u}=\frac{\partial u}{\partial t}, \quad \dot{v}=\frac{\partial v}{\partial t},$$

and the equations become

$$\left.\begin{aligned} \frac{\partial p}{\partial r}-\frac{1}{r}\frac{\partial \chi}{\partial \theta}&=0, \\ \frac{\partial p}{\partial \theta}+r\frac{\partial \chi}{\partial r}&=0. \end{aligned}\right\} \tag{71}$$

Hence, eliminating p,

$$\frac{\partial}{\partial r}\left(r\frac{\partial \chi}{\partial r}\right)+\frac{1}{r}\frac{\partial^2 \chi}{\partial \theta^2}=0,$$

or, which is the same thing,

$$\nabla^2\chi=0. \tag{72}$$

* Cf. Lamb, *Hydrodynamics*, 3rd Ed. p. 585.

A comparatively simple solution can be constructed by supposing that

$$\chi = 0$$

and
$$\psi = \Psi e^{mti},$$

where Ψ is a function of r only. This leads to

$$\frac{d^2\Psi}{dr^2} + \frac{1}{r}\frac{d\Psi}{dr} - \frac{mi}{\mu}\Psi = 0,$$

so that, if $\kappa^2 = m/\mu$,

$$\Psi = AI_0(\kappa r\sqrt{i}) + BK_0(\kappa r\sqrt{i}).$$

But if ψ is finite when $r=0$, then $B=0$, and one value of Ψ is

$$\Psi = A\{\operatorname{ber}(\kappa r) + i \operatorname{bei}(\kappa r)\}.$$

We obtain a real function for ψ by putting

$$\begin{aligned} \psi &= (\alpha + \beta i)e^{mti}\{\operatorname{ber}(\kappa r) + i\operatorname{bei}(\kappa r)\} \\ &\qquad + (\alpha - \beta i)e^{-mti}\{\operatorname{ber}(\kappa r) - i\operatorname{bei}(\kappa r)\} \\ &= 2\alpha\{\cos(mt)\operatorname{ber}(\kappa r) - \sin(mt)\operatorname{bei}(\kappa r)\} \\ &\qquad - 2\beta\{\cos(mt)\operatorname{bei}(\kappa r) + \sin(mt)\operatorname{ber}(\kappa r)\}, \end{aligned} \tag{73}$$

where α, β, m are any real constants. Now suppose that the velocity is prescribed to be $a\omega \sin(mt)$ when $r=a$; then

$$a\omega \sin(mt) = -\left(\frac{\partial\psi}{\partial r}\right)_{r=a},$$

and therefore
$$\left.\begin{aligned} \alpha \operatorname{ber}'(\kappa a) - \beta \operatorname{bei}'(\kappa a) &= 0 \\ a\omega = -2\alpha\kappa \operatorname{bei}'(\kappa a) - 2\beta\kappa &\operatorname{ber}'(\kappa a). \end{aligned}\right\} \tag{74}$$
and

Hence, from (73) and (74),

$$\begin{aligned} \psi = -\frac{a\omega}{\kappa}\cos(mt)&\left\{\frac{\operatorname{ber}(\kappa r)\operatorname{bei}'(\kappa a) - \operatorname{bei}(\kappa r)\operatorname{ber}'(\kappa a)}{\operatorname{ber}'^2(\kappa a) + \operatorname{bei}'^2(\kappa a)}\right\} \\ + \frac{a\omega}{\kappa}\sin(mt)&\left\{\frac{\operatorname{ber}(\kappa r)\operatorname{ber}'(\kappa a) + \operatorname{bei}(\kappa r)\operatorname{bei}'(\kappa a)}{\operatorname{ber}'^2(\kappa a) + \operatorname{bei}'^2(\kappa a)}\right\}. \end{aligned} \tag{75}$$

The boundary condition may be realised by supposing the liquid to fill the interior of an infinite cylinder of radius a, which is constrained to move with angular velocity $\omega \sin mt$ about its axis, carrying with it the particles of liquid which are in contact with it.

(This example is taken from the paper set in the Mathematical Tripos, Wednesday afternoon, Jan. 3, 1883.)

Pendulum moving in a Viscous Fluid. A very important application of the theory is contained in Stokes' memoir "On the effect of the internal friction of fluids on the motion of pendulums" (*Camb. Phil. Trans.*, vol. IX.): for the details of the investigation the reader should consult the original paper, but we shall endeavour to give an outline of the analysis.

The practical problem is that of taking into account the viscosity of the air in considering the small oscillations, under the action of gravity, of a cylindrical pendulum. In order to simplify the analysis, we begin by supposing that we have an infinite cylinder of radius a, surrounded by viscous liquid of density ρ, also extending to infinity; and we proceed to construct a possible state of two-dimensional motion in which the cylinder moves to and fro along the initial line $\theta=0$ in such a way that its velocity V at any instant is expressed by the formula

$$V=ce^{2\nu nti}+c_0e^{-2\nu n_0ti}, \tag{76}$$

where $\nu=\mu/\rho$, μ being the coefficient of viscosity; n, n_0 are conjugate complex constants, and c, c_0 are conjugate complex constants of small absolute value.

The current function ψ must vanish at infinity, and satisfy the equation

$$\nabla^2\left(\nabla^2-\frac{1}{\nu}\frac{\partial}{\partial t}\right)\psi=0, \tag{77}$$

and, in addition, the boundary conditions

$$\frac{\partial\psi}{\partial\theta}=Va\cos\theta,\quad \frac{\partial\psi}{\partial r}=V\sin\theta, \tag{78}$$

when $r=a$.

Now if we assume

$$\psi=\left[e^{2\nu nti}\left\{\frac{A}{r}+B\chi(r)\right\}+e^{-2\nu n_0ti}\left\{\frac{A_0}{r}+B_0\chi_0(r)\right\}\right]\sin\theta \tag{79}$$

part of this expression, namely ψ_1, the sum of the first and third terms, satisfies the equation

$$\nabla^2\psi_1=0,$$

and ψ_2, the remaining part, satisfies

$$\left(\nabla^2-\frac{1}{\nu}\frac{\partial}{\partial t}\right)\psi_2=0,$$

provided the functions χ, χ_0 are chosen so that

$$\left.\begin{aligned}\frac{d^2\chi}{dr^2}+\frac{1}{r}\frac{d\chi}{dr}-\left(2in+\frac{1}{r^2}\right)\chi=0,\\ \frac{d^2\chi_0}{dr^2}+\frac{1}{r}\frac{d\chi_0}{dr}-\left(-2in_0+\frac{1}{r^2}\right)\chi_0=0.\end{aligned}\right\} \tag{80}$$

Thus, $\psi=\psi_1+\psi_2$ satisfies

$$\nabla^2\psi-\frac{1}{\nu}\frac{\partial}{\partial t}\psi_2=0. \tag{81}$$

Since ψ vanishes at infinity, and $K_1=-K_0'$, suitable solutions of equations (80) are

$$\left.\begin{aligned}\chi&=\text{ker}'(\sqrt{(2n)}r)+i\,\text{kei}'(\sqrt{(2n)}r),\\ \chi_0&=\text{ker}'(\sqrt{(2n_0)}r)-i\,\text{kei}'(\sqrt{(2n_0)}r).\end{aligned}\right\} \tag{82}$$

The boundary conditions are satisfied if

$$\frac{A}{a}+B\chi(a)=ca,$$

$$-\frac{A}{a^2}+B\chi'(a)=c;$$

whence

$$\left.\begin{aligned}A&=\frac{ca^2\{a\chi'(a)-\chi(a)\}}{\chi(a)+a\chi'(a)},\\ B&=\frac{2ca}{\chi(a)+a\chi'(a)},\end{aligned}\right\} \tag{83}$$

and A_0, B_0 are obtained from these by putting χ_0 for χ, c_0 for c, and $-i$ for i.

The equations (79), (82), (83) may be regarded as giving the motion of the fluid when the cylinder is *constrained* to move according to the law expressed by (76).

Let now Z denote the resistance to the motion of the cylinder, arising from the viscosity of the surrounding liquid, per unit length of the cylinder; then, proceeding as in Basset's *Hydrodynamics*, II. 279, 280, we have*

$$Z=a\int_0^{2\pi}(-P\cos\theta+U\sin\theta)_{r=a}\,d\theta,$$

where

$$P=-p-\tfrac{2}{3}\mu\delta+2\mu\frac{\partial u}{\partial r},$$

$$U=\mu\left(\frac{1}{r}\frac{\partial u}{\partial\theta}+\frac{\partial v}{\partial r}-\frac{v}{r}\right),$$

$$\delta=\frac{\partial u}{\partial r}+\frac{1}{r}\frac{\partial v}{\partial\theta}+\frac{u}{r}.$$

But, when $r=a$,

$$\frac{\partial u}{\partial r}=0,\quad \delta=0,\quad \frac{\partial u}{\partial\theta}=-V\sin\theta,\quad \frac{1}{r}\frac{\partial u}{\partial\theta}-\frac{v}{r}=0,$$

*Cf. Lamb, *Hydrodynamics*, 3rd Ed. p. 535, and Love, *Elasticity*, 2nd Ed. p. 56.

while, from (81),
$$\frac{\partial v}{\partial r} = -\frac{1}{\nu}\frac{\partial \psi_2}{\partial t},$$

so that
$$P = -p, \quad U = -\rho\frac{\partial \psi_2}{\partial t}.$$

Now, integrating by parts, we have

$$\int_0^{2\pi} p\cos\theta\, d\theta = -\int_0^{2\pi}\frac{\partial p}{\partial \theta}\sin\theta\, d\theta$$
$$= \rho a\int_0^{2\pi}\frac{\partial}{\partial r}\left\{\nu\nabla^2\psi - \frac{\partial \psi}{\partial t}\right\}\sin\theta\, d\theta, \text{ by (71) and (69),}$$
$$= -\rho a\int_0^{2\pi}\frac{\partial^2 \psi_1}{\partial r\,\partial t}\sin\theta\, d\theta, \text{ by (81).}$$

Hence
$$Z = -\rho a\int_0^{2\pi}\frac{\partial}{\partial t}\left(a\frac{\partial \psi_1}{\partial r} + \psi_2\right)_{r=a}\sin\theta\, d\theta$$
$$= 2\pi\rho\nu i a\left(nLe^{2\nu n t i} - n_0 L_0 e^{-2\nu n_0 t i}\right), \tag{84}$$

where
$$L = \frac{A}{a} - B\chi(a)$$
$$= \frac{ca\{a\chi'(a) - 3\chi(a)\}}{\chi(a) + a\chi'(a)}, \tag{85}$$

and L_0 is conjugate to L.

Let σ be the density of the cylinder: then the force which must act at time t upon each unit length of it, in order to maintain the prescribed motion, is

$$F = \pi\sigma a^2\frac{dV}{dt} + Z$$
$$= 2\pi i\nu a^2\left(Ne^{2\nu n t i} - N_0 e^{-2\nu n_0 t i}\right), \tag{86}$$

with
$$\left.\begin{aligned} N &= nc\left[\sigma + \frac{\rho\{a\chi'(a) - 3\chi(a)\}}{\chi(a) + a\chi'(a)}\right], \\ N_0 &= \text{the conjugate quantity.}\end{aligned}\right\} \tag{87}$$

Now let us suppose that we have a pendulum consisting of a heavy cylindrical bob suspended by a fine wire and making small oscillations in air under the action of gravity. We shall assume that when the amplitude of the oscillation is sufficiently small, and the period sufficiently great, the motion will be approximately of the same type as that which has just been worked out for an infinite cylinder; so that if ξ is the horizontal displacement of the bob at time t from its mean position, we shall have

$$\dot{\xi} = V = ce^{2\nu n t i} + c_0 e^{-2\nu n_0 t i}. \tag{88}$$

The force arising from gravity which acts upon the bob is, per unit of length, and to the first order of small quantities,

$$-\pi(\sigma-\rho)a^2 \cdot \frac{g}{l}\xi,$$

where l is the distance of the centre of mass of the pendulum from the point of suspension.

Equating this to the value of F given above, we have the conditional equation

$$2i\nu l(Ne^{2\nu nti}-N_0e^{-2\nu n_0ti})+(\sigma-\rho)g\xi=0, \qquad (89)$$

which must hold at every instant, and may therefore be differentiated with regard to the time. Doing this, and substituting for $\dot{\xi}$ its value in terms of the time, we obtain

$$\{-4n\nu^2lN+(\sigma-\rho)gc\}e^{2\nu nti}+\{-4n_0\nu^2lN_0+(\sigma-\rho)gc_0\}e^{-2\nu n_0ti}=0,$$

which is satisfied identically if we put

$$(\sigma-\rho)gc=4n\nu^2lN,$$

or, which is the same thing,

$$\frac{(\sigma-\rho)g}{l}=4\left(\sigma+\frac{a\chi'(a)-3\chi(a)}{\chi(a)+a\chi'(a)}\rho\right)\nu^2n^2. \qquad (90)$$

This, with $\chi(a)$ defined by (82) above, is an equation to find n which must be solved by approximation: since the motion is actually retarded, the proper value of n must have a positive imaginary part. As might be expected, when ρ is very small in comparison with σ,

$$4\nu^2n^2=g/l$$

approximately.

The constants c and c_0 are determined by the initial values of ξ and $\dot{\xi}$, together with the equations (88) and (89).

CHAPTER XII.

STEADY FLOW OF ELECTRICITY OR OF HEAT IN UNIFORM ISOTROPIC MEDIA.

CHAPTER VIII. above, which deals with Fourier-Bessel Expansions, contains all that is required for the application of Bessel Functions to problems regarding the distribution of potential; but it may be advisable to supplement that theoretical discussion by a few examples fully worked out. We take here a few cases of electric flow of some physical interest. Other problems with notes as to their solution in certain cases will be found in the collection of Examples at the end of the book. In the discussions in this chapter we speak of the flow as electric; but the problems solved may be regarded as problems in the theory of the steady flux of heat or incompressible fluid moving irrotationally, or even of the distribution of potential and force in an electrostatic field. The method of translation is well understood. The potential in the flux of electricity becomes the temperature in the thermal analogue, while the conductivities and strength of source (or sink) involve no change of nomenclature; the potential in the flux theory and that in the electrostatic theory coincide, the sources and sinks in the former become positive and negative charges in the latter, while specific inductive capacity takes the place of conductivity.

§ 1. **Electric Potential.** If V be the potential, then in all the problems here considered the differential equation which holds throughout the medium is

$$\frac{\partial^2 V}{\partial x^2}+\frac{\partial^2 V}{\partial y^2}+\frac{\partial^2 V}{\partial z^2}=0, \tag{1}$$

or, in cylindrical coordinates r, θ, z,

$$\frac{\partial^2 V}{\partial r^2}+\frac{1}{r}\frac{\partial V}{\partial r}+\frac{1}{r^2}\frac{\partial^2 V}{\partial \theta^2}+\frac{\partial^2 V}{\partial z^2}=0. \tag{2}$$

At the surface of separation of two media of different conductivities k_1, k_2 the condition which holds is

$$k_1 \frac{\partial V_1}{\partial n_1} + k_2 \frac{\partial V_2}{\partial n_2} = 0, \tag{3}$$

where n_1, n_2 denote normals drawn from a point of the surface into the respective media, and V_1, V_2 are the potentials in the two media infinitely near that point. If one of the media is an insulator, so that say $k_2 = 0$, the equation of condition is

$$\frac{\partial V}{\partial n} = 0. \tag{4}$$

Let us define a source or sink as a place where electricity is led into or drawn off from the medium, and consider the electricity delivered or drawn off uniformly over a small spherical electrode of perfectly conducting substance (of radius r) buried in the medium at a distance great in comparison with r from any part of the bounding surface. Let it be kept at potential V, and deliver or withdraw a total quantity S per unit of time, then since $V = \text{constant}/r$,

$$\frac{V}{S} = \frac{1}{4\pi kr}. \tag{5}$$

The quantity on the right is half the resistance between a source and a sink thus buried in the medium and kept at a difference of potential $2V$.

If the electrode is on the surface (supposed of continuous curvature) of the medium, the electrode must be considered as a hemisphere, and the resistance will be double the former amount. In this case

$$\frac{V}{S} = \frac{1}{2\pi kr}. \tag{6}$$

Where r is made infinitely small we must have rV finite, and therefore in the two cases just specified

$$\left.\begin{aligned} \text{Lt}\, rV &= \frac{S}{4\pi k}, \\ \text{Lt}\, rV &= \frac{S}{2\pi k}. \end{aligned}\right\} \tag{7}$$

Equations (1), (2), (3), and (7) are the conditions to be fulfilled in the problems which we now proceed to give examples of. Those we here choose are taken from a very instructive paper by Weber ("Ueber Bessel'sche Functionen und ihre Anwendung auf die Theorie der elektrischen Ströme," *Crelle*, Bd. 75, 1873), and are given with only some changes in notation to suit that adopted in the present treatise, and the addition of some explanatory analysis.

Potential due to Charged Circular Disk. We shall prove first the following proposition. If V be the potential due to a circular disk of radius r_1 on which there is a charge of electricity in equilibrium unaffected by the action of electricity external to the disk, then if z be taken along the axis of the disk, and the origin at the centre,

$$V=\frac{2c}{\pi}\int_0^\infty e^{\mp\lambda z}\sin(\lambda r_1)J_0(\lambda r)\frac{d\lambda}{\lambda}, \qquad (8)$$

where the upper sign is to be taken for positive values of z and the lower for negative values, and c is the potential at the disk.

In the first place this expression for V satisfies (2); if then we can prove that it reduces to a constant when $z=0$, and gives the proper value of the electric density, we shall have verified the solution. By VI. (6), (7)

$$\left.\begin{aligned}\int_0^\infty \cos(\lambda s)J_0(\lambda r)\,d\lambda &= \frac{1}{\sqrt{(r^2-s^2)}}, \quad r>s\geqq 0 \quad \text{(i)},\\ &=0, \quad 0<r<s \quad \text{(ii)}.\end{aligned}\right\} \qquad (9)$$

In case (i) integrate with respect to s from 0 to r_1, and change the order of integration; then

$$\int_0^\infty \frac{\sin(\lambda r_1)}{\lambda}J_0(\lambda r)\,d\lambda=\sin^{-1}\left(\frac{r_1}{r}\right), \quad r>r_1\geqq 0. \qquad (10)$$

Since the integral converges, this equation also holds for $r=r_1$; the value of the integral is then $\frac{1}{2}\pi$.

In case (ii) integrate with respect to s from r_2 to r_1, where $r_1\geqq r_2>r>0$; then

$$\int_0^\infty\left\{\frac{\sin(\lambda r_1)}{\lambda}-\frac{\sin(\lambda r_2)}{\lambda}\right\}J_0(\lambda r)\,d\lambda=0, \quad 0<r\leqq r_2\leqq r_1.$$

Now let $r_2=r$; then, by (10),

$$\int_0^\infty \frac{\sin(\lambda r_1)}{\lambda}J_0(\lambda r)\,d\lambda=\frac{\pi}{2}, \quad 0\leqq r<r_1.$$

Hence, finally,

$$\left.\begin{aligned}\frac{2c}{\pi}\int_0^\infty \sin(\lambda r_1)J_0(\lambda r)\frac{d\lambda}{\lambda}&=c, \text{ if } r<r_1,\\ &=\frac{2c}{\pi}\sin^{-1}\frac{r_1}{r}, \text{ if } r>r_1;\end{aligned}\right\} \qquad (11)$$

when $r_1=r$, the two results coincide.

Thus the expression

$$V=\frac{2c}{\pi}\int_0^\infty e^{\mp\lambda z}\sin(\lambda r_1)J_0(\lambda r)\frac{d\lambda}{\lambda} \qquad (12)$$

satisfies the differential equation, gives a constant potential at every point of the disk of radius r_1, and is, as well as $\partial V/\partial z$, continuous when $z=0$, for all values of r.

Lastly, to find the distribution, we have for $z=+0$

$$-\frac{1}{4\pi}\frac{\partial V}{\partial z}=\frac{c}{2\pi^2}\int_0^\infty \sin(\lambda r_1)J_0(\lambda r)\,d\lambda=\frac{c}{2\pi^2}\frac{1}{\sqrt{r_1^2-r^2}} \qquad (13)$$

by VI. (7). Or the whole density, taking the two faces of the disk together, is $c/(\pi^2\sqrt{r_1^2-r^2})$. This is a result which can be otherwise obtained. Hence the solution is completely verified.

§ 2. **Circular Disk Electrode in Unlimited Medium.** We can now convert this result into the solution of a problem in the flow of electricity. Let us suppose that the electrode supplying electricity is the disk we have just imagined, and let it be composed of perfectly conducting material, and be immersed in an unlimited medium of conductivity k. Then to a constant the potential at any point of the electrode is

$$V=\frac{2c}{\pi}\int\sin(\lambda r_1)J_0(\lambda r)\frac{d\lambda}{\lambda}. \qquad (14)$$

The sink or sinks may be supposed at a very great distance, so that they do not disturb the flow in the neighbourhood of this disk-shaped source.

The rate of flow from the disk to the medium is $-k\partial V/\partial z$ per unit of area at each point of the electrode, and is of course in the direction of the normal. At the edge by (13) the flow will be infinite if the disk is a very thin oblate ellipsoid of revolution, as it is here supposed to be; but in this, and in any actual case, the total flow from the vicinity of the edge can obviously be made as small as we please in comparison with the total flow elsewhere by increasing the radius of the disk.

The total flow from the disk to the medium is thus

$$S=-2k\int_0^{2\pi}\int_0^{r_1}\frac{\partial V}{\partial z}r\,dr\,d\phi.$$

Putting in this for $\partial V/\partial z$ its value we get

$$S=-\frac{4ck}{\pi}\int_0^{2\pi}\{\sqrt{r_1^2-r^2}\}_0^{r_1}\,d\phi$$

$$=8ckr_1.$$

Thus the amount supplied by each side of the disk per unit time is $4ckr_1$, and we have

$$c = \frac{S}{8kr_1}. \tag{15}$$

If the disk is laid on the bounding surface of a conductor the flow will take place only from one face to the conducting mass, and S has only half of its value in the other case. Then

$$c = \frac{S}{4kr_1}. \tag{16}$$

In this case the condition $\partial V/\partial n = 0$ holds all over the surface except at the disk electrode, and of course (2) holds within the conductor. At any point of the disk distant r from the centre

$$-\frac{\partial V}{\partial z} = \frac{2c}{\pi}\frac{1}{\sqrt{r_1^2 - r^2}} = \frac{S}{2\pi k r_1}\frac{1}{\sqrt{r_1^2 - r^2}}. \tag{17}$$

We can now find the resistance of the conducting mass between two such conducting electrodes, a source and a sink, placed anywhere on the surface at such a distance apart that the stream-lines from or to either of them are not in its neighbourhood disturbed by the position of the other. The whole current up to the disk by which the current enters is S, and we have seen that c is the potential of that disk. For distinction let the potentials of the source and sink disks be denoted by c_1, c_2; then if R be the resistance between them,

$$R = \frac{c_1 - c_2}{S}.$$

If the wires leading the current up to and away from the electrodes have resistances ρ_1, ρ_2, and have their farther extremities (at the generator or battery) at potentials V_1, V_2, the falls of potential along the inleading electrode, and along the outgoing are

$$V_1 - c_1 = S\rho_1, \quad c_2 - V_2 = S\rho_2,$$

so that

$$V_1 - V_2 - (c_1 - c_2) = S(\rho_1 + \rho_2),$$

and

$$R = \frac{1}{S}\{V_1 - V_2 - S(\rho_1 + \rho_2)\}. \tag{18}$$

Another expression for the resistance can be found as follows. We have seen that the potential at the source-disk is c_1, also that for conduction from one side of the disk

$$S = 4c_1 k r_1.$$

For the sink-disk the outward current in like manner is

$$S = -4c_2 k r_2.$$

Hence $$S = 2k(c_1 r_1 - c_2 r_2).$$

But also $$R = \frac{c_1 - c_2}{S} = \frac{c_1 - c_2}{2k(c_1 r_1 - c_2 r_2)},$$

and $c_1 r_1 = -c_2 r_2$, so that

$$R = \frac{r_1 + r_2}{4k r_1 r_2} = \frac{1}{4k r_1} + \frac{1}{4k r_2}. \tag{19}$$

From the latter form of the result we infer that $1/4kr_1$ is the part of the resistance due to the first disk, $1/4kr_2$ the part due to the second. This result is of great importance, for it gives a means of calculating an inferior limit to the correction to be made on the resistance of a cylindrical wire in consequence of its being joined to a large mass of metal.

§ 3. **Conductor bounded by Parallel Planes.** From this problem we can proceed to another which is identical with that of Nobili's rings solved first by Riemann. An infinite conductor is bounded by two parallel planes $z = \pm a$, and two disk electrodes are applied to these planes, so that their centres lie in the axis of z. It is required to find the potential at each point of the conductor and the resistance between the electrodes. From the distribution of potential the stream-lines can of course be found also.

The solution must fulfil the following conditions:

$$\frac{\partial^2 V}{\partial r^2} + \frac{1}{r}\frac{\partial V}{\partial r} + \frac{\partial^2 V}{\partial z^2} = 0, \quad \text{for } -a < z < +a,$$

$$\frac{\partial V}{\partial z} = 0, \quad \text{for } z = \pm a,\ r > r_1$$

$$\frac{\partial V}{\partial z} = \frac{S}{2\pi k r_1 \sqrt{r_1^2 - r^2}}, \quad \text{for } z = \pm a,\ r < r_1.$$

According to the last condition the current is supposed to flow along the axis in the direction of z decreasing.

The first condition is satisfied by assuming

$$V = \int_0^\infty \{\phi(\lambda) e^{\lambda z} + \psi(\lambda) e^{-\lambda z}\} J_0(\lambda r)\, d\lambda, \tag{20}$$

where $\phi(\lambda)$, $\psi(\lambda)$ are arbitrary functions of λ which render the integral convergent and fulfil the other necessary conditions.

Without loss of generality V may be supposed zero when $z=0$, and hence we must put $\phi(\lambda)=-\psi(\lambda)$. Thus (20) becomes

$$V=\int_0^\infty 2\phi(\lambda)\sinh(\lambda z)J_0(\lambda r)\,d\lambda. \tag{21}$$

With regard to the other two conditions, by VI. (6), (7) above,

$$\int_0^\infty \sin(\lambda r_1)J_0(\lambda r)\,d\lambda=0, \text{ when } r>r_1,$$

$$=\frac{1}{\sqrt{r_1^2-r^2}}, \text{ when } r<r_1.$$

Hence if we take

$$2\phi(\lambda)\cosh(\lambda a)\,.\,\lambda=\frac{S}{2\pi k r_1}\sin(\lambda r_1),$$

or

$$\phi(\lambda)=\frac{S}{4\pi k r_1}\frac{\sin\lambda r_1}{\cosh(\lambda a)}\frac{1}{\lambda} \tag{22}$$

both conditions will be satisfied. The solution of the problem is therefore

$$V=\frac{S}{2\pi k r_1}\int_0^\infty \frac{\sinh(\lambda z)}{\cosh(\lambda a)}\sin(\lambda r_1)J_0(\lambda r)\frac{d\lambda}{\lambda}. \tag{23}$$

From this we can easily obtain an approximation to the resistance R between the electrodes. For we have from (23)

$$c_1-c_2=\frac{S}{\pi k r_1}\int_0^\infty \tanh(\lambda a)J_0(\lambda r)\sin(\lambda r_1)\frac{d\lambda}{\lambda}$$

$$=\frac{S}{\pi k r_1}\int_0^\infty\left(1-\frac{2e^{-2\lambda a}}{1+e^{-2\lambda a}}\right)J_0(\lambda r)\sin(\lambda r_1)\frac{d\lambda}{\lambda}$$

$$=\frac{S}{2kr_1}-\int_0^\infty \frac{2e^{-2\lambda a}}{1+e^{-2\lambda a}}J_0(\lambda r)\sin(\lambda r_1)\frac{d\lambda}{\lambda}, \tag{24}$$

by (11).

If the integral in (24) be neglected when r_1 is small, we have, to a first approximation,

$$R=\frac{c_1-c_2}{S}=\frac{1}{2kr_1}.$$

This of course could have been obtained at once from (19) by simply putting $r_1=r_2$. To obtain a nearer approximation the integrand in (24) may be expanded in powers of r and r_1. If terms of the order r_1^3/a^3 and upwards be neglected, the result is

$$R=\frac{1}{2kr_1}-\frac{\log 2}{\pi k a}. \tag{25}$$

If the electrodes are extremely small we may put λr_1 for $\sin \lambda r_1$, and we obtain from (23)

$$V = \frac{S}{2\pi k}\int_0^\infty \frac{\sinh(\lambda z)}{\cosh(\lambda a)} J_0(\lambda r)\, d\lambda. \tag{26}$$

In order to obtain an expansion in infinite series for this expression, consider the integral

$$\int \frac{\sinh(\lambda z)}{\cosh(\lambda a)} G_0(\lambda r)\, d\lambda,$$

where $z < a$, $r > 0$, taken round the contour consisting of the real axis, indented at the origin, and an infinite semicircle above the real axis. The integrals round the semicircles tend to zero. Now

$$G_0(\lambda r) = -J_0(\lambda r)\log(\lambda r) + \text{an even function of } \lambda,$$

so that the integrals along the positive and negative parts of the real axis cancel each other except for a term

$$i\pi \int_0^\infty \frac{\sinh(\lambda z)}{\cosh(\lambda a)} J_0(\lambda r)\, d\lambda$$

due to $\log(\lambda r)$.

Accordingly, by Cauchy's Theorem of Residues, since $\cosh(\lambda a)$ vanishes when $\lambda a = i(n + \frac{1}{2})\pi$,

$$\int_0^\infty \frac{\sinh(\lambda z)}{\cosh(\lambda a)} J_0(\lambda r)\, d\lambda = 2\sum_{n=1}^{\infty} \frac{\sin\left(\frac{2n+1}{2a}\pi z\right)}{a \sin\left(\frac{2n+1}{2}\pi\right)} K_0\left(\frac{(2n+1)\pi r}{2a}\right).$$

Therefore

$$V = \frac{S}{\pi k a}\sum_1^\infty \sin\left(\frac{n\pi}{2}\right)\sin\left(\frac{n\pi z}{2a}\right) K_0\left(\frac{n\pi r}{2a}\right). \tag{27}$$

From the asymptotic expansion of $K_0(z)$ it follows that the series is convergent so long as $r > 0$. This solution of the problem agrees with that given by Riemann (*Werke*, p. 58, or *Pogg. Ann.* Bd. 95, March, 1855). [Identify by v. (29).]

§ 4. **Conductor bounded by Circular Cylinder and Parallel Planes.** If, the electrodes being still regarded as small, the conducting mass instead of being infinite be a circular cylinder of axis z and radius c, bounded by non-conducting matter, the problem becomes more complicated. To solve it in this case a part V' must be added to V, fulfilling the following conditions:

(i) $\dfrac{\partial^2 V'}{\partial r^2} + \dfrac{1}{r}\dfrac{\partial V'}{\partial r} + \dfrac{\partial^2 V'}{\partial z^2} = 0$, for $r < c$, $-a < z < +a$,

(ii) $$\frac{\partial V'}{\partial z} = 0, \text{ for } z = \pm a,$$

(iii) $$\frac{\partial V'}{\partial r} + \frac{\partial V}{\partial r} = 0, \text{ for } r = c, \quad -a < z < +a,$$

and V' is finite throughout the cylinder.

These conditions are fulfilled by

$$V' = \frac{S}{\pi ka} \sum_1^\infty \sin\frac{n\pi}{2} \sin\frac{n\pi z}{2a} \frac{K_1\left(\frac{n\pi c}{2a}\right)}{I_1\left(\frac{n\pi c}{2a}\right)} I_0\left(\frac{n\pi r}{2a}\right), \tag{28}$$

which is convergent for $r \leqq 2c$. Hence the total potential at any point ($r \neq 0$) is given by

$$V + V' = \frac{S}{\pi ka} \sum_1^\infty \sin\frac{n\pi}{2} \sin\frac{n\pi z}{2a}$$
$$\times \frac{K_1\left(\frac{n\pi c}{2a}\right) I_0\left(\frac{n\pi r}{2a}\right) + I_1\left(\frac{n\pi c}{2a}\right) K_0\left(\frac{n\pi r}{2a}\right)}{I_1\left(\frac{n\pi c}{2a}\right)}. \tag{29}$$

When $r = 0$, $I_0\left(\frac{n\pi r}{2a}\right) = 1$, so that the change in the resistance due to the limitation of the flow to the finite cylinder is

$$\frac{2}{\pi ka} \sum K_1\left(\frac{n\pi c}{2a}\right) \Big/ I_1\left(\frac{n\pi c}{2a}\right) = \frac{2}{ka} e^{-\frac{\pi c}{a}}$$

if $\frac{a}{c}$ be very small. Hence the resistance is approximately

$$R = \frac{1}{2kr_1} - \frac{\log 2}{\pi ka} + \frac{2}{ka} e^{-\frac{\pi c}{a}}. \tag{30}$$

§ 5. **Metal Plate and Conductor separated by Film.** We now pass to another problem also considered by Weber. A plane metal plate, which may be regarded as of infinite extent, is separated from a conductor of relatively smaller conductivity by a thin stratum of slightly conducting material. For example, this may be a film of gas separating a plane surface of metal from a conducting liquid as in cases of polarization in cells. We shall calculate the resistance for the case in which the electrode is small and is applied at a point within the conducting mass. Take the axis of z along the line through the point electrode perpendicular to the metal plate, and the origin on the surface of the conductor close to the plate. Thus the point electrode is applied at the point $z = a$, $r = 0$.

We further suppose that there is a difference of potential u between the surface of the conductor and the metal plate on the other side of the film. This will give a slope of potential through the film of amount w/δ if δ be the film thickness. If the conductivity of the film be k_1 the resistance for unit of area will be δ/k_1, and thus the flow per unit of area across the film is wk_1/δ. This must be equal to the rate at which electricity is conducted up to the surface of the conductor from within, which is $k\,\partial V/\partial z$. Thus if w be the *positive* difference between the conductor surface and the plate, the condition holds when $z=0$,

$$-h\frac{\partial V}{\partial z}+w=0,$$

where $$h=\delta k/k_1.$$

Let ρ, ρ', be the distances of any point z, r from the electrode and from its image in the surface respectively. Then the differential equation and the other conditions laid down are satisfied by

$$V=\frac{S}{4\pi k}\left(\frac{1}{\rho}-\frac{1}{\rho'}\right)+w, \qquad (31)$$

provided that w fulfils the equations

$$-h\frac{\partial V}{\partial z}+w=0$$

at the surface, and

$$\frac{\partial^2 w}{\partial r^2}+\frac{1}{r}\frac{\partial w}{\partial r}+\frac{\partial^2 w}{\partial z^2}=0, \qquad (32)$$

throughout the conductor. The first term on the right of (31) is the solution we should have had if the film had not existed, the second is the increased potential at each point in consequence of the rise in crossing the film from the plate.

A value of w which satisfies (32) is given by

$$w=\int_0^\infty e^{-\lambda z}\phi(\lambda)J_0(\lambda r)\,d\lambda, \qquad (33)$$

where $\phi(\lambda)$ is an arbitrary function of λ to be determined. Now since

$$\rho^2=(z-a)^2+r^2, \quad \rho'^2=(z+a)^2+r^2,$$

$$\frac{\partial V}{\partial z}=-\frac{S}{4\pi k}\frac{z-a}{\rho^3}+\frac{S}{4\pi k}\frac{z+a}{\rho'^3}+\frac{\partial w}{\partial z}$$

$$=\frac{S}{2\pi k}\frac{a}{(a^2+r^2)^{\frac{3}{2}}}+\frac{\partial w}{\partial z},$$

when $z=0$. Hence the surface condition becomes, having regard to (33),

$$\frac{hS}{2\pi k}\frac{a}{(a^2+r^2)^{\frac{3}{2}}}-\int_0^\infty (1+h\lambda)\phi(\lambda)J_0(\lambda r)\,d\lambda=0. \tag{34}$$

But differentiating with respect to a the equation

$$\int_0^\infty e^{-a\lambda}J_0(\lambda r)\,d\lambda=\frac{1}{(a^2+r^2)^{\frac{1}{2}}},$$

we get

$$\int_0^\infty e^{-a\lambda}J_0(\lambda r)\lambda\,d\lambda=\frac{a}{(a^2+r^2)^{\frac{3}{2}}}. \tag{35}$$

This substituted in (34) gives

$$\phi(\lambda)=\frac{hS}{2\pi k}\frac{\lambda e^{-a\lambda}}{1+h\lambda}.$$

Hence

$$w=\frac{hS}{2\pi k}\int_0^\infty e^{-\lambda(z+a)}\frac{J_0(\lambda r)\lambda\,d\lambda}{1+h\lambda}.$$

Now

$$e^{\frac{z+a}{h}}\int_{\frac{z+a}{h}}^\infty e^{-(1+h\lambda)t}\,dt=\frac{e^{-\lambda(z+a)}}{1+h\lambda},$$

so that we have

$$w=\frac{hS}{2\pi k}e^{\frac{z+a}{h}}\int_{\frac{z+a}{h}}^\infty dt\,e^{-t}\int_0^\infty e^{-h\lambda t}J_0(\lambda r)\lambda\,d\lambda$$

$$=\frac{S}{2\pi hk}e^{\frac{z+a}{h}}\int_{\frac{z+a}{h}}^\infty\frac{te^{-t}dt}{\left(t^2+\frac{r^2}{h^2}\right)^{\frac{3}{2}}},\text{ by (35)},$$

$$=\frac{S}{2\pi k\rho'}-\frac{S}{2\pi kh}e^{\frac{z+a}{h}}\int_{\frac{z+a}{h}}^\infty\frac{e^{-t}dt}{\left(t^2+\frac{r^2}{h^2}\right)^{\frac{1}{2}}} \tag{36}$$

by integration by parts. Thus we obtain for the potential at any point z, r,

$$V=\frac{S}{4\pi k}\left(\frac{1}{\rho}+\frac{1}{\rho'}\right)-\frac{S}{2\pi kh}e^{\frac{z+a}{h}}\int_{\frac{z+a}{h}}^\infty\frac{e^{-t}dt}{\left(t^2+\frac{r^2}{h^2}\right)^{\frac{1}{2}}}.$$

Take a new variable ζ given by

$$ht=\zeta+z+a,$$

and the solution becomes

$$V=\frac{S}{4\pi k}\left(\frac{1}{\rho}+\frac{1}{\rho'}\right)-\frac{S}{2\pi kh}\int_0^\infty\frac{e^{-\frac{\zeta}{h}}d\zeta}{\sqrt{(\zeta+z+a)^2+r^2}} \tag{37}$$

The meaning of this solution is that the introduction of the non-conducting film renders the distribution of potential that which would exist for the same total flow S, were there a combination of two equal positive sources of strength $S/(4\pi k)$, at the electrode and its image, with a linear source extending along the axis of z from the image to $-\infty$, and of intensity

$$-\frac{S}{2\pi kh}e^{-\frac{\zeta}{h}}$$

per unit of length, at distance ζ from the point $-(z+a)$.

If the conducting mass be of small thickness, then nearly enough $\rho=\rho'=r$, and $z+a=a$. Thus we obtain

$$V=\frac{S}{2\pi k}\left\{\frac{1}{r}-\int_0^\infty\frac{e^{-t}dt}{\sqrt{h^2t^2+r^2}}\right\} \tag{38}$$

if, as we suppose, $(z+a)/h$ may be neglected.

If h/r be small we can expand $(h^2t^2+r^2)^{-\frac{1}{2}}$ in ascending powers of t by the binomial theorem and integrate term by term. We thus get

$$\int_0^\infty\frac{e^{-t}dt}{\sqrt{h^2t^2+r^2}}=\frac{1}{r}\int_0^\infty e^{-t}\Sigma(-1)^n\frac{1.3\ldots(2n-1)}{2.4\ldots2n}\left(\frac{h}{r}\right)^{2n}t^{2n}dt$$

$$=\frac{1}{r}\Sigma(-1)^n\{1.3\ldots(2n-1)\}^2\left(\frac{h}{r}\right)^{2n}, \tag{39}$$

by which the value of the integral may be calculated if r be not too small. Hence if r be very great,

$$V=\frac{S}{2\pi k}\frac{h^2}{r^3},$$

or the potential at a great distance from the electrode varies inversely as the cube of the distance.

Conductor bounded by Parallel Planes. We may solve similarly the problem in which the conducting mass is bounded by two parallel infinite planes, the metal plate $z=0$, and the plane $z=a$, and the source is a disk electrode of radius r_1, with its centre on the axis of z, applied to the latter. As before, a feebly conducting film is supposed to exist between the metal plate and the conducting substance.

We simply add a quantity w, as before, to the distribution of potential which could have existed if there had been no film.

Thus, by the solution for the infinite stratum with disk electrode worked out in § 3, we have

$$V=\frac{S}{2\pi k r_1}\int_0^\infty \frac{\sinh \lambda z}{\cosh \lambda a}\sin(\lambda r_1)J_0(\lambda r)\frac{d\lambda}{\lambda}+w. \qquad (40)$$

The potential w must fulfil the conditions

$$\frac{\partial w}{\partial z}=0, \text{ for } z=a$$

(since the flow from the source-electrode is supposed unaffected by w),

$$h\frac{\partial V}{\partial z}-w=0, \text{ for } z=0,$$

besides of course the differential equation for points within the medium.

The first condition is satisfied if we take

$$w=\int_0^\infty 2\cosh\lambda(z-a)\phi(\lambda)J_0(\lambda r)\,d\lambda.$$

Also when $z=0$,

$$\begin{aligned} h\frac{\partial V}{\partial z}-w &= \frac{Sh}{2\pi k r_1}\int_0^\infty \frac{\sin(\lambda r_1)}{\cosh(\lambda a)}J_0(\lambda r)\,d\lambda \\ &\quad -2h\int_0^\infty \sinh(\lambda a)\lambda\phi(\lambda)J_0(\lambda r)\,d\lambda \\ &\quad -2\int_0^\infty \cosh(\lambda a)\phi(\lambda)J_0(\lambda r)\,d\lambda \\ &=0. \end{aligned}$$

Hence $\phi(\lambda)=\dfrac{Sh}{4\pi k r_1}\,\dfrac{\sin(\lambda r_1)}{\cosh(\lambda a)\{\cosh(\lambda a)+h\lambda\sinh(\lambda a)\}}$,

and

$$w=\frac{Sh}{2\pi k r_1}\int_0^\infty \frac{\cosh\lambda(z-a)\sin(\lambda r_1)J_0(\lambda r)\,d\lambda}{\cosh(\lambda a)\{\cosh(\lambda a)+h\lambda\sinh(\lambda a)\}}, \qquad (41)$$

so that

$$V=\frac{S}{2\pi k r_1}\int_0^\infty \frac{\sinh(\lambda z)+h\lambda\cosh(\lambda z)}{\cosh(\lambda a)+h\lambda\sinh(\lambda a)}\sin(\lambda r_1)J_0(\lambda r)\frac{d\lambda}{\lambda}. \qquad (42)$$

If we denote by V_a the potential at the disk electrode, we have

$$V_a=\frac{S}{2\pi k r_1}\int_0^\infty \frac{\sinh(\lambda a)+h\lambda\cosh(\lambda a)}{\cosh(\lambda a)+h\lambda\sinh(\lambda a)}\sin(\lambda r_1)J_0(\lambda r)\frac{d\lambda}{\lambda},$$

and if the area of the electrode be very small

$$V_a=\frac{S}{2\pi k}\int_0^\infty \frac{\sinh(\lambda a)+h\lambda\cosh(\lambda a)}{\cosh(\lambda a)+h\lambda\sinh(\lambda a)}J_0(\lambda r)\,d\lambda. \qquad (43)$$

This is the difference of potential between the electrodes, that is, the disk and the metal plate. Comparing it with the difference of potential for the same flow through the stratum of the conductor without the plate, that is with half the total difference of potential given by (23) for the two electrodes at distance $2a$, which is

$$\frac{S}{2\pi k}\int_0^\infty \tanh(\lambda a) J_0(\lambda r)\, d\lambda,$$

we see that it exceeds the latter by

$$\frac{Sh}{2\pi k}\int_0^\infty \frac{\lambda J_0(\lambda r)\, d\lambda}{\cosh(\lambda a)\{\cosh(\lambda a)+h\lambda \sinh(\lambda a)\}}.$$

The resistance of the compound stratum now considered is therefore, approximately,

$$R=\frac{1}{4kr_1}-\frac{1}{2}\frac{\log 2}{\pi ka}+\frac{h}{2\pi k}\int_0^\infty \frac{\lambda J_0(\lambda r)\, d\lambda}{\cosh(\lambda a)\{\cosh(\lambda a)+h\lambda \sinh(\lambda a)\}}. \quad (44)$$

Since the resistance is between the plate and the electrode, which is taken as of very small radius, $J_0(\lambda r)=J_0(0)$ nearly, and so we put unity for $J_0(\lambda r)$ in the expansion just found. The last term is the resistance of the film between the plate and the conductor, and in the case of a liquid in a voltaic cell, kept from complete contact with the plate by the disengagement of gas, is the apparent resistance of polarization. Its approximate value, if a/h is capable of being taken as infinitely small, is

$$\frac{1}{2\pi ka}\log\frac{h}{a}.$$

The value of V in (42) can, when the electrode is so small that we can assume $\sin(\lambda r_1)/(\lambda r_1)=1$, be expanded in a trigonometrical series so as to enable comparisons of the value of V to be made for different values of r. For, if $\mu=a\lambda$,

$$V=\frac{S}{2\pi ka}\int_0^\infty \frac{\sinh\left(\mu\frac{z}{a}\right)+\frac{h}{a}\mu\cosh\left(\mu\frac{z}{a}\right)}{\cosh\mu+\frac{h}{a}\mu\sinh\mu} J_0\left(\frac{\mu r}{a}\right) d\mu.$$

If now we take the integral

$$\int \frac{\sinh\left(\mu\frac{z}{a}\right)+\frac{h}{a}\mu\cosh\left(\mu\frac{z}{a}\right)}{\cosh\mu+\frac{h}{a}\mu\sinh\mu} G_0\left(\frac{\mu r}{a}\right) d\mu.$$

round the contour employed in § 3, we find that

$$V=\frac{S}{\pi ka}\sum\frac{\sin\left(\mu\frac{z}{a}\right)+\frac{h}{a}\mu\cos\left(\mu\frac{z}{a}\right)}{\sin\mu+\frac{h}{a}\sin\mu+\frac{h}{a}\mu\cos\mu}K_0\left(\frac{\mu r}{a}\right),$$

where the summation extends to all the positive roots of the transcendental equation

$$\cot\mu=\mu\frac{h}{a}. \tag{45}$$

Hence, by means of (45), we obtain

$$V=\frac{S}{\pi ka}\sum\frac{a^2+h^2\mu^2}{a^2+ha+h^2\mu^2}\cos\left(\mu\frac{z-a}{a}\right)K_0\left(\frac{\mu r}{a}\right), \tag{46}$$

which converges when $r>0$.

The first root of (45) is smaller the greater h is, the second root is always greater than π. Thus, if r be fairly great, the first term of the series just written down will suffice for V. Hence, for $z=a$, V has a considerable value at a distance from the axis.

Cylinder of Finite Radius. The solution can be modified by a like process to that used in § 4 to suit the case of a cylinder of finite radius c. We have to add to V in this case a function V' which fulfils the conditions

$$\frac{\partial V'}{\partial z}=0,\text{ for } z=a,\quad h\frac{\partial V'}{\partial z}=V',\text{ for } z=0,$$

$$\frac{\partial V}{\partial r}+\frac{\partial V'}{\partial r}=0,\text{ for } r=c,$$

and satisfies the general differential equation. The reader may verify that

$$V+V'=\frac{S}{\pi ka}\Sigma\frac{a^2+h^2\mu^2}{a^2+ha+h^2\mu^2}\frac{K_0\left(\frac{\mu r}{a}\right)I_1\left(\frac{\mu c}{a}\right)+I_0\left(\frac{\mu r}{a}\right)K_1\left(\frac{\mu c}{a}\right)}{I_1\left(\frac{\mu c}{a}\right)}$$
$$\times\cos\left(\mu\frac{z-a}{a}\right). \tag{47}$$

§ 6. Finite Cylindrical Conductor with Electrodes on the same Generating Line. As a final and very instructive example of the use of Fourier-Bessel expansions we take the problem of the flow of electricity in a right cylindrical conductor when the electrodes are placed on the same generating line of the cylindrical surface, at equal distances from the middle cross-section of the cylinder. We shall merely sketch the solution, leaving the reader to fill in the details of calculation.

The differential equation to be satisfied by the potential in this case is

$$\frac{\partial^2 V}{\partial r^2}+\frac{1}{r}\frac{\partial V}{\partial r}+\frac{1}{r^2}\frac{\partial^2 V}{\partial \theta^2}+\frac{\partial^2 V}{\partial z^2}=0. \tag{48}$$

If the electrodes be supposed to be small equal rectangular disks, having their sides parallel to generating lines and ends of the cylinder, and the radius be unity, the surface conditions to be satisfied are summed up in the equations

$$\frac{\partial V}{\partial z}=0, \text{ for } z=\pm a, \quad \frac{\partial V}{\partial r}=\Phi,$$

where

$$\Phi=\pm c, \text{ for } \begin{cases} -\phi<\theta<+\phi, \\ +\beta<z<\beta+\delta, \\ -\beta>z>-(\beta+\delta); \end{cases}$$

$$\Phi=0, \text{ for all other points.}$$

The distances of the centres of the electrodes from the central cross-section are here $\pm(\beta+\frac{1}{2}\delta)$ and the angle subtended at the axis by their breadth is 2ϕ, while the height of the cylinder is $2a$.

We have first to find an expression for Φ which fulfils these conditions. This can be obtained by Fourier's method and the result is

$$\Phi=\frac{4c}{\pi^2}\left\{\phi+2\sum_1^\infty\frac{1}{n}\sin n\phi\cos n\theta\right\}\sum_0^\infty\frac{1}{2m+1}$$
$$\left\{\cos\frac{(2m+1)\pi}{2a}\beta-\cos\frac{(2m+1)\pi}{2a}(\beta+\delta)\right\}\sin\frac{(2m+1)\pi}{2a}z.$$

Now assume

$$V=\sum_m\sum_n A_{m,n}\psi(r)\sin\frac{(2m+1)\pi z}{2a}\cos n\theta, \tag{49}$$

and the differential equation (48) will be satisfied if $\psi(r)$ be a function of r which satisfies the equation

$$\frac{\partial^2 u}{\partial r^2}+\frac{1}{r}\frac{\partial u}{\partial r}-\left\{\frac{n^2}{r^2}+\left(\frac{2m+1}{2a}\pi\right)^2\right\}u=0.$$

Hence we put

$$\psi(r)=I_n\left(\frac{2m+1}{2a}\pi r\right)=I_n(x). \tag{50}$$

To complete the solution the constant $A_{m,n}$ must be chosen so as to ensure the fulfilment of the surface condition. This clearly is done by writing

$$A_{m,n}=\frac{4c}{\pi^2}\frac{1}{2m+1}\frac{2\sin n\phi}{n\psi'(1)}\left\{\cos\frac{(2m+1)\pi}{2a}\beta-\cos\frac{(2m+1)\pi}{2a}(\beta+\delta)\right\},$$

in which when $n=0$, ϕ is to be put instead of $2\sin n\phi/n$.

To find the effect of making the electrodes very small we substitute

$$2\sin\frac{(2m+1)\pi}{2a}(\beta+\tfrac{1}{2}\delta)\sin\frac{(2m+1)\pi}{4a}\delta$$

for the cosines in the value $A_{m,n}$, and $\phi\delta$ for

$$\frac{\sin n\phi}{n}\frac{\sin\{(2m+1)\pi\delta/(4a)\}}{(2m+1)\pi/(4a)}.$$

Remembering that $c\phi\delta$ is finite, and therefore putting

$$4c\phi\delta/\pi^2=1,$$

we get the solution

$$V=\frac{\pi}{2a}\sum_{n=0}^{\infty}\sum_{m=0}^{\infty}\epsilon_n\frac{\psi(r)}{\psi'(1)}\cos n\theta\sin\frac{(2m+1)\pi\beta}{2a}\sin\frac{(2m+1)\pi z}{2a}, \qquad (51)$$

where $\epsilon_0=1, \quad \epsilon_1=\epsilon_2=\epsilon_3=\ldots=\epsilon_n=\ldots=2.$

For an infinitely long cylinder we can obtain the solution by putting in (51)

$$\frac{\pi}{a}=d\lambda, \qquad \frac{(2m+1)\pi}{2a}=\lambda,$$

and replacing summation by integration. Thus we obtain

$$V=\tfrac{1}{2}\sum_{0}^{\infty}\epsilon_n\cos n\theta\int_0^{\infty}\frac{I_n(\lambda r)}{\lambda I_n'(\lambda)}\sin(\lambda\beta)\sin(\lambda z)\,d\lambda, \qquad (52)$$

ϵ_0 as before being 1, and all the others 2.

The reader may verify as another example that if the electrodes be applied at the central cross-section at points for which $\theta=\pm\alpha$, the potential is given by

$$V=\sum_{1}^{\infty}\frac{r^n}{n}\sin n\alpha\sin n\theta+2\frac{a}{\pi}\sum_{1}^{\infty}\sum_{1}^{\infty}\frac{I_n\left(\frac{m\pi}{a}r\right)}{I_n'\left(\frac{m\pi}{a}\right)}\frac{1}{m}\sin n\alpha\sin n\theta\cos\frac{m\pi z}{a}.$$

If a be infinitely small the second part of this expression vanishes and the first term can be written

$$V = \frac{1}{4} \log \frac{1 - 2r\cos(a+\theta) + r^2}{1 - 2r\cos(a-\theta) + r^2},$$

which agrees with an expression given by Kirchhoff (*Pogg. Ann.* Bd. 64, 1845) for the potential at any part of a circular disk with a source and a sink in its circumference.

The reader may refer to another paper by Weber (*Crelle*, Bd. 76, 1873) for the solution of some more complicated problems of electric flow, for example a conducting cylinder covered with a coaxial shell of relatively badly conducting fluid, the two electrodes being in the fluid and core respectively; and a cylindrical core covered with a coaxial cylinder of material of conductivity comparable with that of the core.

CHAPTER XIII.

PROPAGATION OF ELECTROMAGNETIC WAVES ALONG WIRES.

§ 1. **Equations of the Electromagnetic Field.** The equations of the electromagnetic field were first given by Maxwell in 1865.* They have since been used in a somewhat modified form with great effect by Hertz and by Heaviside in their researches on the propagation of electromagnetic waves. The modification used by these writers is important as showing the reciprocal relation which exists between the electric and the magnetic force, and enables the auxiliary function called the vector-potential to be dispensed with in most investigations of this nature.

If P, Q, R, α, β, γ denote the components of electric and magnetic forces in a medium of conductivity k, electric inductive capacity κ, and magnetic inductive capacity μ, the equations referred to are

$$\left.\begin{aligned}\left(k+\frac{\kappa}{4\pi}\frac{\partial}{\partial t}\right)P&=\frac{1}{4\pi}\left(\frac{\partial\gamma}{\partial y}-\frac{\partial\beta}{\partial z}\right),\\ \left(k+\frac{\kappa}{4\pi}\frac{\partial}{\partial t}\right)Q&=\frac{1}{4\pi}\left(\frac{\partial\alpha}{\partial z}-\frac{\partial\gamma}{\partial x}\right),\\ \left(k+\frac{\kappa}{4\pi}\frac{\partial}{\partial t}\right)R&=\frac{1}{4\pi}\left(\frac{\partial\beta}{\partial x}-\frac{\partial\alpha}{\partial y}\right),\end{aligned}\right\}\qquad(1)$$

and

$$\left.\begin{aligned}\frac{\mu}{4\pi}\frac{\partial\alpha}{\partial t}&=-\frac{1}{4\pi}\left(\frac{\partial R}{\partial y}-\frac{\partial Q}{\partial z}\right),\\ \frac{\mu}{4\pi}\frac{\partial\beta}{\partial t}&=-\frac{1}{4\pi}\left(\frac{\partial P}{\partial z}-\frac{\partial R}{\partial x}\right),\\ \frac{\mu}{4\pi}\frac{\partial\gamma}{\partial t}&=-\frac{1}{4\pi}\left(\frac{\partial Q}{\partial x}-\frac{\partial P}{\partial y}\right).\end{aligned}\right\}\qquad(2)$$

* "On the Electromagnetic Field," *Phil. Trans.* 1865; *Electricity and Magnetism*, Vol. II. Chap. XX.

Putting λ for the operator $k+\frac{\kappa}{4\pi}\frac{\partial}{\partial t}$, we derive the equations

$$\frac{\partial(\lambda P)}{\partial x}+\frac{\partial(\lambda Q)}{\partial y}+\frac{\partial(\lambda R)}{\partial z}=0, \tag{3}$$

$$\frac{\partial \alpha}{\partial x}+\frac{\partial \beta}{\partial y}+\frac{\partial \gamma}{\partial z}=0. \tag{4}$$

The first of these expresses that the total current—conduction current plus displacement current—is solenoidal, and the second that the magnetic force, being purely inductive, fulfils the solenoidal condition at every point, except of course at the origin of the disturbance.

At the surface of separation between two media the normal components of the magnetic induction, and the tangential components of the magnetic force, are continuous. The tangential components of electric force are also continuous.

From the equations given above the equations of propagation of an electromagnetic wave can be at once derived. Eliminating Q and R by means of the first of (2), the second and the third of (1), and (4), we get

$$4\pi\mu k\frac{\partial \alpha}{\partial t}+\kappa\mu\frac{\partial^2 \alpha}{\partial t^2}=\nabla^2\alpha, \tag{5}$$

and similarly two equations of the same form for β and γ. These are the equations of propagation of magnetic force.

By a like process we obtain the equations of propagation of electric force

$$\left.\begin{aligned}4\pi\mu k\frac{\partial P}{\partial t}+\kappa\mu\frac{\partial^2 P}{\partial t^2}&=\nabla^2 P,\\ \&c. \qquad \&c.\end{aligned}\right\} \tag{6}$$

§ 2. **Waves Guided by a Straight Wire.** Now for the case of propagation with a straight wire as guide in an isotropic medium, we suppose that the electric field is symmetrical round the wire at every instant. This amounts to saying that there is no component of electric force at right angles to a plane coinciding with the axis. From this it follows by the equations connecting the forces, that the magnetic force at any point in a plane coinciding with the axis is at right angles to that plane. The lines of magnetic force are therefore circles round the wire as axis.

Thus we may choose the axis of x as the axis of symmetry, and consider only two components of electric force, one P, parallel to the axis, and another R, from the axis in a plane passing through it. We shall denote the distance of the point considered from the origin along the axis by x, and its distance from the axis by ρ, and shall use for the magnetic force at the same point the symbol H, which will thus correspond to the γ of equations (1) and (2). [R here is not the R of (1).]

From (1) and (2) we get for our special case the equations

$$4\pi kP+\kappa\frac{\partial P}{\partial t}=\frac{1}{\rho}\frac{\partial}{\partial\rho}(\rho H), \tag{7}$$

$$4\pi kR+\kappa\frac{\partial R}{\partial t}=-\frac{\partial H}{\partial x}, \tag{8}$$

$$\mu\frac{\partial H}{\partial t}=\frac{\partial P}{\partial\rho}-\frac{\partial R}{\partial x}, \tag{9}$$

while (3) becomes $$\frac{\partial P}{\partial x}+\frac{1}{\rho}\frac{\partial}{\partial\rho}(\rho R)=0.$$

Eliminating first H and R from these equations we find for the differential equation satisfied by P,

$$4\pi\mu k\frac{\partial P}{\partial t}+\kappa\mu\frac{\partial^2 P}{\partial t^2}=\frac{\partial^2 P}{\partial x^2}+\frac{\partial^2 P}{\partial\rho^2}+\frac{1}{\rho}\frac{\partial P}{\partial\rho}. \tag{10}$$

Eliminating H and P we see that R must be taken so as to satisfy a slightly different equation, namely,

$$4\pi\mu k\frac{\partial R}{\partial t}+\kappa\mu\frac{\partial^2 R}{\partial t^2}=\frac{\partial^2 R}{\partial x^2}+\frac{\partial^2 R}{\partial\rho^2}+\frac{1}{\rho}\frac{\partial R}{\partial\rho}-\frac{1}{\rho^2}R. \tag{11}$$

Finally, we easily find in the same way that H satisfies a differential equation precisely the same as (11).

In dealing with the problem we shall suppose at first that the wire has a certain finite radius, and is surrounded at a distance by a coaxial conducting tube which may be supposed to extend to infinity in the radial direction. There will therefore be three regions of the field to be considered, the wire, the outside conducting tube, and the space between them. The differential equations found above are perfectly general and apply, with proper values of the quantities k, μ, κ, to each region.

Taking first the space between the two conductors we shall suppose it filled with a perfectly insulating isotropic substance. The appropriate differential equations are therefore obtained by putting $k=0$, in (10) and (11).

If the electric and magnetic forces be simply periodic with respect to x and t, each will be of the form

$$f(\rho)\,e^{(nt-mx)i}.$$

Let
$$P = ue^{(nt-mx)i},$$

$$R = ve^{(nt-mx)i},$$

where u, v denote the values of $f(\rho)$ for these two quantities. Substituting in (10), remembering that $k=0$, we find

$$\frac{\partial^2 u}{\partial \rho^2} + \frac{1}{\rho}\frac{\partial u}{\partial \rho} - (m^2 - \kappa\mu n^2)u = 0. \qquad (12)$$

The quantity $m^2 - \kappa\mu n^2$ is in general complex since mi includes a real factor which gives the alteration of amplitude with distance travelled by the wave along the wire. On the other hand n is essentially real, being 2π times the frequency of the vibration.

If the wave were not controlled by the wire we should have in the dielectric $m^2 - \kappa\mu n^2 = 0$. The velocity of propagation of an electromagnetic disturbance in a medium of inductivities κ, μ is according to theory $\sqrt{(1/\kappa\mu)}$; and this velocity has, for air at least, been proved to be that of light.

If we denote $m^2 - \kappa\mu n^2$ by p^2 and write ξ for $p\rho$, (12) becomes

$$\frac{\partial^2 u}{\partial \xi^2} + \frac{1}{\xi}\frac{\partial u}{\partial \xi} - u = 0, \qquad (13)$$

which is the differential equation of the modified Bessel function of zero order $I_0(\xi)$.

In precisely the same way we get from (11) the equation

$$\frac{\partial^2 v}{\partial \xi^2} + \frac{1}{\xi}\frac{\partial v}{\partial \xi} - \left(1 + \frac{1}{\xi^2}\right)v = 0, \qquad (14)$$

the differential equation of the modified Bessel function of order 1, namely $I_1(\xi)$.

An equation of the same form as (14) is obtained in a similar manner for H.

Turning now to the conductors, we suppose that in them κ is small in comparison with k. In ordinary conductors κ/k is about 10^{-17} in order of magnitude, so that we may neglect the displacement currents represented by the second terms on the left in equations (1). We thus obtain the proper differential equations by substituting $m^2+4\pi k\mu ni$ for p^2. We shall denote this by q^2 and write the equations

$$\frac{\partial^2 u}{\partial \eta^2}+\frac{1}{\eta}\frac{\partial u}{\partial \eta}-u=0, \tag{15}$$

$$\frac{\partial^2 v}{\partial \eta^2}+\frac{1}{\eta}\frac{\partial v}{\partial \eta}-\left(1+\frac{1}{\eta^2}\right)v=0, \tag{16}$$

where $\eta=q\rho=\rho\surd(m^2+4\pi k\mu ni)$.

Two values of q will be required, one for the wire and the other for the outer conductor; we shall denote these by q_1 and q_2 respectively.

The general solution of (13) is

$$u=aI_0(\xi)+bK_0(\xi), \tag{17}$$

where a and b are arbitrary constants to be determined to suit the conditions of the problem. The solution of (15) has of course the same form, with η substituted for ξ.

For the outer conductor the coefficient of $I_0(\eta)$ must be zero, since u tends to zero as $\eta\to\infty$; while for the inner conductor the coefficient of $K_0(\eta)$ must be zero, since u is finite when $\eta=0$.

We thus get for the value of P in the three regions, the wire, the dielectric, and the outer conductor, the equations

$$P_1=AI_0(\eta)e^{(nt-mx)i}, \tag{18}$$

$$P_2=\{BI_0(\xi)+CK_0(\xi)\}e^{(nt-mx)i}, \tag{19}$$

$$P_3=DK_0(\eta)e^{(nt-mx)i}, \tag{20}$$

in which A, B, C, D are constants to be determined by means of the conditions which hold at the surfaces of separation between the adjacent regions.

For long high-frequency waves m is small and n large, and for any ordinary length of conductor it may be assumed that $m=0$. Then, if $l=\surd(4\pi k\mu n)$, $q=l\surd i$; and

$$\begin{aligned}P_1&=AI_0(l\rho\surd i)\,e^{nti}\\&=A\{\operatorname{ber}(l\rho)+i\operatorname{bei}(l\rho)\}e^{nti}.\end{aligned}$$

We shall not, however, develop the theory on these lines (for which see the references given at the end of Chapter III. § 6), but in what follows it will be assumed that the value of m must be taken into account.

From the value of P we can easily obtain the component R at right angles to the axis. Since all the quantities are periodic (8) and (9) may be written in the form

$$(4\pi k+\kappa ni)\,R=miH,$$

$$\mu niH=miR+\frac{\partial P}{\partial\rho}.$$

Eliminating first H, then R, between these equations we obtain

$$R=\frac{mi}{m^2-\mu\kappa n^2+4\pi k\mu ni}\,\frac{\partial P}{\partial\rho}, \tag{21}$$

$$H=\frac{4\pi k+\kappa ni}{m^2+4\pi\mu kni-\mu\kappa n^2}\,\frac{\partial P}{\partial\rho}. \tag{22}$$

Thus, if in the dielectric we put $k=0$, and write p^2 for $m^2-\mu\kappa n^2$, we get from (19), remembering that $p\rho=\xi$,

$$R_2=\frac{mi}{p}\,\frac{\partial P_2}{\partial\xi}=\frac{mi}{p}\{BI_0'(\xi)+CK_0'(\xi)\}e^{(nt-mx)i}, \tag{23}$$

$$H_2=\frac{\kappa ni}{p}\,\frac{\partial P_2}{\partial\xi}$$

$$=\frac{\kappa ni}{p}\{BI_0'(\xi)+CK_0'(\xi)\}e^{(nt-mx)i}. \tag{24}$$

In the wire, on the other hand, where

$$q_1\rho=\eta,\quad [q^2=m^2+4\pi\mu kni],$$

we have
$$R_1=\frac{mi}{q_1}\,\frac{\partial P_1}{\partial\eta}=\frac{mi}{q_1}\,AI_0'(\eta)e^{(nt-mx)i}, \tag{25}$$

$$H_1=\frac{4\pi k_1}{q_1}\,\frac{\partial P_1}{\partial\eta}=\frac{4\pi k_1}{q_1}\,AI_0'(\eta)\,e^{(nt-mx)i}. \tag{26}$$

Lastly, in the outer conductor we have

$$R_3=\frac{mi}{q_2}\,\frac{\partial P_3}{\partial\eta}=\frac{mi}{q_2}\,DK_0'(\eta)e^{(nt-mx)i}, \tag{27}$$

$$H_3=\frac{4\pi k_2}{q_2}\,\frac{\partial P_3}{\partial\eta}=\frac{4\pi k_2}{q_2}\,DK_0'(\eta)e^{(nt-mx)i}. \tag{28}$$

We now introduce the boundary conditions, namely that the tangential electric force and the tangential magnetic force are continuous. From the latter condition it follows that the lines of magnetic force, being circles round the axis of the wire in the dielectric, are so also in the wire and also in the outer conductor.

These conditions expressed for the surface of the wire, where $=a_1$ and where we assume $\xi=\xi_1$, $\eta=\eta_1$, give

$$\left.\begin{aligned} BI_0(\xi_1)+CK_0(\xi_1)&=AI_0(\eta_1),\\ \frac{\kappa ni}{p}\{BI_0'(\xi_1)+CK_0'(\xi_1)\}&=\frac{4\pi k_1}{q_1}AI_0'(\eta_1),\end{aligned}\right\} \tag{29}$$

nd for $\rho=a_2$, where $\xi=\xi_2$, $\eta=\eta_2$,

$$\left.\begin{aligned} BI_0(\xi_2)+CK_0(\xi_2)&=DK_0(\eta_2),\\ \frac{\kappa ni}{p}\{BI_0'(\xi_2)+CK_0'(\xi_2)\}&=\frac{4\pi k_2}{q_2}DK_0'(\eta_2).\end{aligned}\right\} \tag{30}$$

If now the four constants A, B, C, D are eliminated by means f equations (29) and (30), it is found that

$$\frac{4\pi k_1 pI_0(\xi_1)I_0'(\eta_1)-\kappa niq_1I_0'(\xi_1)I_0(\eta_1)}{4\pi k_2pI_0(\xi_2)K_0'(\eta_2)-\kappa niq_2I_0'(\xi_2)K_0(\eta_2)}$$
$$=\frac{4\pi k_1pK_0(\xi_1)I_0'(\eta_1)-\kappa niq_1K_0'(\xi_1)I_0(\eta_1)}{4\pi k_2pK_0(\xi_2)K_0'(\eta_2)-\kappa niq_2K_0'(\xi_2)K_0(\eta_2)}. \tag{31}$$

Long Waves of Low Frequency. Considering first long aves of low frequency and remembering that $\kappa\mu$ is $1/V^2$, here V is the velocity of light in the dielectric, we see that reduces to m nearly, and the real part of m is $2\pi/\lambda$, where λ the wave-length. Thus, if a_1 is not large, pa_1 is very small. lso if a_2, the radius of the insulating cylinder, is moderately nall, pa_2 is also small.

Now when a_1, a_2 are small the approximate values of the inctions at the cylindrical boundaries are

$$I_0(\xi)=1,\quad I_0(\eta)=1,\quad K_0(\xi)=-\log\xi,\quad K_0(\eta)=-\log\left(\frac{e^{\gamma}\eta}{2}\right),$$
$$I_0'(\xi)=\frac{1}{2}\xi,\quad I_0'(\eta)=\frac{1}{2}\eta,\quad K_0'(\xi)=-\frac{1}{\xi},\qquad K_0'(\eta)=-\frac{1}{\eta}.$$

Using these values for $I_0(\xi)$, $I_0'(\xi)$, $K_0(\xi)$, $K_0'(\xi)$, in (31), putting or brevity ϕ, χ, for the ratios $I_0(\eta_1)/I_0'(\eta_1)$, $K_0(\eta_2)/K_0'(\eta_2)$, and $_1$, a_2 for $4\pi k_1$, $4\pi k_2$, and neglecting terms involving the factors a_2, $a_1a_2^2$ in comparison with others involving the factor a_1a_2, e find after a little reduction that

$$p^2=\frac{\kappa n}{\log\left(\frac{a_2}{a_1}\right)}\left\{\frac{iq_2}{a_2a_2}\chi-\frac{iq_1}{a_1a_1}\phi+\frac{1}{2}\frac{\kappa nq_1q_2}{a_1a_2a_1a_2}(a_1^2-a_2^2)\phi\chi\right\}. \tag{32}$$

In all cases which occur in practice it may be assumed th $|q^2|$ is approximately $4\pi\mu kn$. Further $\kappa n = n/(\mu V^2)$, so that th last term within the brackets in the preceding expression is

$$\frac{i}{8\pi}\frac{n^2}{\mu V^2}\sqrt{\left(\frac{\mu_1\mu_2}{k_1k_2}\right)}\frac{a_1^2-a_2^2}{a_1a_2}\phi\chi.$$

The second of the other two terms within the brackets is

$$-\frac{i\sqrt{(4\pi\mu_1k_1ni)}}{4\pi k_1a_1}\phi = -\frac{1-i}{\sqrt{2}}\frac{\sqrt{(\mu_1 n)}\phi}{\sqrt{(4\pi k_1)}a_1}.$$

Hence the modulus of the second term, unless the frequenc $n/2\pi$, of the vibrations is very great, is large in comparison wit that of the third term. The same thing can be proved of th first term and the third. Hence the third term, on the suppos tion of low frequency and small values of a_1, a_2, may b neglected in comparison with the first and second. Equatio (32) thus reduces to

$$p^2 = \frac{n^{\frac{3}{2}}}{\mu V^2}\frac{1-i}{\sqrt{(8\pi)}}\left(\frac{\sqrt{\mu_1}}{\sqrt{k_1}}\frac{\phi}{a_1} - \frac{\sqrt{\mu_2}}{\sqrt{k_2}}\frac{\chi}{a_2}\right)\frac{1}{\log\frac{a_2}{a_1}}. \qquad (3$$

Let now the frequency be so small that q_1a_1 is very sma Then we have

$$\phi = \frac{I_0(\eta_1)}{I_0'(\eta_1)} = \frac{2}{q_1a_1}$$

and

$$\chi = \frac{K_0(\eta_2)}{K_0'(\eta_2)} = q_2a_2\log\left(\frac{e^\gamma q_2a_2}{2}\right),$$

and it is clear that the second term of (33) bears to the first onl a very small ratio unless a_2 be very great indeed. In this cas then we may neglect the second term in comparison with th first, and we get

$$p^2 = \frac{-ni}{\mu V^2}\frac{1}{2\pi a_1^2k_1}\frac{1}{\log\frac{a_2}{a_1}}, \qquad (3$$

or, since $p^2 = m^2 - \kappa\mu n^2 = m^2 - n^2/V^2$,

$$m^2 = \frac{n^2}{V^2}\left(1 - \frac{i}{2\pi\mu k_1na_1^2}\frac{1}{\log\frac{a_2}{a_1}}\right). \qquad (3$$

The modulus of the second term in the brackets is great i comparison with unity, and hence if we take only the imaginar part of m^2 as given by (35) we shall get a value of m, the re art of which is great in comparison with that which we should btain if we used only the real part, that is we shall make the rst approximation to m which (35) affords. Thus we write nstead of (35)

$$m^2 = \frac{n}{V^2}\frac{-i}{2\pi\mu k_1 a_1^2}\frac{1}{\log\frac{a_2}{a_1}}. \tag{36}$$

But if r be the resistance of the wire, and c the capacity of the able, each taken per unit of length,

$$r = 1/(\pi a_1^2 k_1), \quad c = \kappa/(2\log(a_2/a_1))$$

where κ is taken in electromagnetic units), and we have

$$m = \frac{1-i}{\sqrt{2}}\sqrt{(nrc)}, \tag{36'}$$

aking the positive sign.

This corresponds to a wave travelling with velocity $\sqrt{2n}/\sqrt{rc}$, nd having its amplitude damped down to $1/e$ of its initial amount n travelling a distance $\sqrt{2}/\sqrt{nrc}$.

The other root of m^2 would give a wave travelling with the same speed but in the opposite direction, and with increasing amplitude. It is therefore left out of account.

We have thus fallen upon the ordinary case of slow signalling along a submarine or telephone cable, in which the electromagnetic induction may be neglected, and the result agrees with that found by a direct solution of this simple case of the general problem.

The velocity of phase propagation being proportional to the square root of the frequency of vibration, the higher notes of a piece of music would be transmitted faster than the lower, and the harmony might, if the distance were great enough, be disturbed from this cause. Further, these higher notes are more rapidly damped out with distance travelled than the lower, and hence the relative strengths of the notes of the piece would be altered, the higher notes being weakened relatively to the lower.

The Electric and Magnetic Forces. We can now find the electric and magnetic forces. The electromotive intensity in the wire is given by

$$P_1 = AI_0(\eta)e^{(nt-mx)i},$$

where $\eta = q_1\rho$, the suffix denoting that ρ is less than the radius of the wire. But if the wire is, as we here suppose it to be, very thin, $I_0(\eta)=1$, and the value of P_1 is the same over any cross section of the wire. Hence, if γ_0 denote the total current in the wire at the plane $x=0$, when $t=0$, we have

$$AI_0(\eta)=\gamma_0 r,$$

and therefore
$$P_1=\gamma_0 r e^{(nt-mx)i}. \tag{37}$$

Hence realizing we obtain

$$P_1=\gamma_0 r e^{-\sqrt{\left(\frac{nrc}{2}\right)}x}\cos\left(\sqrt{\left(\frac{nrc}{2}\right)}x-nt\right). \tag{38}$$

The radial electromotive intensity in the wire is given by (25) and is

$$R_1=\frac{mi}{q_1}AI_0'(\eta)e^{(nt-mx)i}.$$

But
$$\frac{mi}{q_1}AI_0'(\eta)=\frac{mi}{q_1}\gamma_0 r\tfrac{1}{2}\eta$$
$$=\gamma_0\frac{1+i}{2\sqrt{2}}\rho r\sqrt{(nrc)},$$

so that
$$R_1=\frac{1+i}{2\sqrt{2}}\gamma_0 r\rho\sqrt{(nrc)}e^{(nt-mx)i}. \tag{39}$$

Again realizing we find that

$$R_1=\tfrac{1}{2}\gamma_0 r\rho\sqrt{(nrc)}e^{-\sqrt{\left(\frac{nrc}{2}\right)}x}\cos\left(\sqrt{\left(\frac{nrc}{2}\right)}x-nt-\frac{\pi}{4}\right). \tag{40}$$

R_1 therefore vanishes at the axis of the wire, and the electromotive intensity is there along the axis. Elsewhere R_1 is sensible, and at the surface the ratio of its amplitude to that of P_1 is $\frac{1}{2}a_1\sqrt{(nrc)}$.

The magnetic force in the wire is given by the equation [(26) above]

$$H_1=\frac{4\pi k_1}{q_1}AI_0'(\eta)e^{(nt-mx)i},$$

which by what has gone before reduces to

$$H_1=\frac{2}{a_1^2}\gamma_0\rho e^{(nt-mx)i}. \tag{41}$$

The realized form of this is

$$H_1=\frac{2}{a_1^2}\gamma_0\rho e^{-\sqrt{\left(\frac{nrc}{2}\right)}x}\cos\left(\sqrt{\left(\frac{nrc}{2}\right)}x-nt\right). \tag{42}$$

By a well-known theorem we ought to have numerically

$$2\pi\rho H_1 = 4\pi\frac{\rho^2}{a_1^2}\gamma,$$

where γ is the total current at any cross-section. For γ we have here the equation

$$\gamma = \gamma_0 e^{(nt-mx)i}, \tag{43}$$

which when compared with (41) obviously fulfils the required relation numerically. Hence the results are so far verified.

We shall now calculate the forces in the dielectric. Putting $P_{0\rho}$ for the electromotive intensity at distance ρ from the axis in the plane $x=0$, and at time $t=0$, we find, by the approximate values of the functions given at p. 163 above,

$$B - C\log(p\rho) = P_{0\rho}.$$

But at the surface of the wire $P_{0\rho} = \gamma_0 r$, where r denotes as before the resistance of the wire per unit length. Thus

$$B - C\log(pa_1) = \gamma_0 r.$$

Hence, subtracting the former equation, we find

$$P_{0\rho} = \gamma_0 r - C\log\frac{\rho}{a_1}.$$

C can be found from (29) by putting, since $I_0(\eta_1) \doteqdot 1$, $A = \gamma_0 r$ and eliminating B. Thus we obtain

$$C = 2\gamma_0 \mu c r V^2$$

very approximately. Hence

$$P_2 = \gamma_0 r\left(1 - 2\mu c V^2 \log\frac{\rho}{a_1}\right)e^{(nt-mx)i}, \tag{44}$$

of which the realized form is

$$P_2 = \gamma_0 r\left(1 - 2\mu c V^2 \log\frac{\rho}{a_1}\right)e^{-\sqrt{\left(\frac{nrc}{2}\right)}x}\cos\left(\sqrt{\left(\frac{nrc}{2}\right)}x - nt\right). \tag{45}$$

From (23), (44), and (36′), since $p = m$ nearly, we get

$$R_2 = (1-i)\mu V^2 \gamma_0 \sqrt{\left(\frac{2rc}{n}\right)}\frac{1}{\rho}e^{(nt-mx)i}, \tag{46}$$

or retaining only the real part

$$R_2 = 2\mu V^2 \gamma_0 \sqrt{\left(\frac{rc}{n}\right)}\frac{1}{\rho}e^{-\sqrt{\left(\frac{nrc}{2}\right)}x}\cos\left\{\sqrt{\left(\frac{nrc}{2}\right)}x - nt + \frac{\pi}{4}\right\}. \tag{47}$$

Finally, from (24) and (36) we have

$$H_2 = 2\frac{\gamma_0}{\rho} e^{(nt-mx)i}, \tag{48}$$

or

$$H_2 = 2\frac{\gamma_0}{\rho} e^{-\sqrt{\left(\frac{nrc}{2}\right)}x} \cos\left(\sqrt{\left(\frac{nrc}{2}\right)}x - nt\right). \tag{49}$$

Thus the solution is completed for slow vibrations in a cable of small radius.

So far we have followed with certain modifications the analysis of Sir J. J. Thomson, as set forth in his *Recent Researches in Electricity and Magnetism* (the Supplementary Volume to his Edition of Maxwell's *Electricity and Magnetism*). To that work the reader may refer for details of other applications to Electrical Oscillations. Reference should also be made to Mr. Oliver Heaviside's important memoirs on the same subject, *Electrical Papers*, Vols. I., II. and III. *passim*.

Bare Overhead Wires. The last term on the right of (33) in the case of bare overhead wires depends on a large value of a_2. But when x is large it follows from the asymptotic expansion of $K_n(x)$ that

$$\chi = \frac{K_0(x)}{K_0'(x)} = -\frac{K_0(x)}{K_1(x)} \doteq -1.$$

Hence

$$\sqrt{\left(\frac{\mu_2}{k_2}\right)}\frac{\chi}{a_2} \doteq -\sqrt{\left(\frac{\mu_2}{k_2}\right)}\frac{1}{a_2}.$$

This is small in comparison with the first term unless k_2 be very small. Supposing the latter not to be the case, we have the same solution as before.

Rapid Oscillations. As a further illustration the reader may work out the case of oscillations so rapid that both q_1a_1 and q_2a_2 are very large. From the asymptotic expansions for $I_n(x)$ it follows that

$$\phi = \frac{I_0(\nu_1)}{I_0'(\nu_1)} = \frac{I_0(\nu_1)}{I_1(\nu_1)} \doteq 1,$$

while χ as before is approximately equal to -1. Therefore, by (33),

$$\mu p^2 = \frac{n^2}{V^2}\left(\frac{\mu_1}{q_1a_1} + \frac{\mu_2}{q_2a_2}\right)\frac{1}{\log\left(\frac{a_2}{a_1}\right)}.$$

Thus $m^2 = p^2 + \dfrac{n^2}{V^2} = \dfrac{n^2}{V^2}\left\{1 + \left(\dfrac{\mu_1}{q_1a_1} + \dfrac{\mu^2}{q_2a_2}\right)\dfrac{1}{\mu\log\left(\dfrac{a_2}{a_1}\right)}\right\},$

and approximately

$$m=\frac{n}{V}\left\{1-\frac{i}{\sqrt{(32\pi n)}}\left(\sqrt{\left(\frac{\mu_1}{a_1^2k_1}\right)}+\sqrt{\left(\frac{\mu_2}{a_2^2k_2}\right)}\right)\frac{1}{\mu\log\left(\frac{a_2}{a_1}\right)}\right\}. \quad (50)$$

The velocity of propagation is thus V, and the distance travelled, while the amplitude is diminishing to the fraction $1/e$ of its original value, is the product of V/n by the reciprocal of the coefficient of $-i$ within the brackets. The damping in this case is slow, since the imaginary part of m is of much smaller modulus than the real part. Here, if $a_2^2k_2$ be small compared with $a_1^2k_1$, as in the case of a cable surrounded by sea water, the outside conductor will mainly control the damping, and nothing will be gained as regards damping by using copper in preference to an inferior metal.

§ 3. **Diffusion of Electric Current.** We shall now obtain an expansion of $xJ_0(x)/J_0'(x)$ in ascending powers of x which will be of use in the discussion of the effective resistance and self-inductance in the case of a cable carrying rapidly alternating currents, and which is also useful in other applications when pa_1 q_1a_1, q_2a_2 are not very small.

Denoting the function $xJ_0(x)/J_0'(x)$ (or, for brevity, xJ_0/J_0') by u, we have

$$u=x\frac{J_0}{J_0'}=-x\frac{J_0}{J_1}\left(=-2+x\frac{J_2}{J_1}\right). \quad (51)$$

Hence

$$\frac{1}{u}\frac{du}{dx}=\frac{1}{x}+\frac{J_0'}{J_0}-\frac{J_1'}{J_1}$$

$$=\frac{1}{x}-\frac{J_1}{J_0}+\frac{1}{J_1}\left(\frac{1}{x}J_1-J_0\right)$$

$$=\frac{2}{x}-\frac{J_0}{J_1}-\frac{J_1}{J_0}=\frac{2}{x}+\frac{u}{x}+\frac{x}{u}.$$

Therefore

$$x\frac{du}{dx}=u(u+2)+x^2. \quad (52)$$

Now, guided by the value in brackets in (51), we assume that

$$u=-2+\frac{x^2}{4}+a_4x^4+a_6x^6+\ldots.$$

Then, by (52),

$$x\left(\frac{x}{2}+4a_4x^3+6a_6x^5+\ldots\right)=x^2+\left(\frac{x^2}{4}+a_4x^4+\ldots\right)\left(-2+\frac{x^2}{4}+\ldots\right).$$

Multiplying these expressions out and equating coefficients, we find

$$\begin{aligned} 4a_4 &= -2a_4 + \tfrac{1}{16}, \\ 6a_6 &= -2a_6 + \tfrac{1}{2}a_4, \\ 8a_8 &= -2a_8 + \tfrac{1}{2}a_6 + a_4^2, \\ 10a_{10} &= -2a_{10} + \tfrac{1}{2}a_8 + 2a_4a_6, \\ &\dots\dots\dots\dots \end{aligned}$$

Hence

$$a_4 = \frac{1}{2^5 . 3}, \quad a_6 = \frac{1}{2^9 . 3}, \quad a_8 = \frac{1}{2^9 . 3^2 . 5}, \quad a_{10} = \frac{13}{2^{15} . 3^3 . 5}, \dots$$

Thus we have

$$x\frac{J_0(x)}{J_0'(x)} = -2 + \frac{x^2}{4} + \frac{x^4}{2^5 . 3} + \frac{x^6}{2^9 . 3} + \frac{x^8}{2^9 . 3^2 . 5} + \frac{13x^{10}}{2^{15} . 3^3 . 5} + \dots, \quad (53)$$

or

$$x\frac{I_0(x)}{I_0'(x)} = 2 + \frac{x^2}{4} - \frac{x^4}{2^5 . 3} + \frac{x^6}{2^9 . 3} - \frac{x^8}{2^9 . 3^2 . 5} + \frac{13x^{10}}{2^{15} . 3^3 . 5} - \dots. \quad (53')$$

This expansion may be converted into a continued fraction, the successive convergents of which will give the value of the function to any desired degree of accuracy. The result, which may be verified by the reader, is

$$x\frac{J_0(x)}{J_0'(x)} = -2 + \frac{x^2}{4-}\,\frac{x^2}{6-}\,\frac{x^2}{8-}\dots. \quad (54)$$

Using (53′) we obtain

$$q_1a_1\frac{I_0(q_1a_1)}{I_0'(q_1a_1)} = 2 + \frac{q_1^2a_1^2}{4} - \frac{q_1^4a_1^4}{2^5 . 3} + \frac{q_1^6a_1^6}{2^9 . 3} - \dots.$$

Now, approximately, $q_1^2 = 4\pi\mu_1k_1ni$, so that

$$q_1a_1\frac{I_0(q_1a_1)}{I_0'(q_1a_1)} = \left\{2 + \frac{(4\pi\mu_1k_1na_1^2)^2}{2^5 . 3} - \frac{(4\pi\mu_1k_1na_1^2)^4}{2^9 . 3^2 . 5} + \dots\right\}$$
$$+ i\left\{\frac{4\pi\mu_1k_1na_1^2}{4} - \frac{(4\pi\mu_1k_1na_1^2)^3}{2^9 . 3} + \dots\right\}. \quad (55)$$

The following table of values is given by Prof. J. J. Thomson

$4\pi\mu_1na_1^2k_1$	$q_1a_1I_0(q_1a_1)/I_0'(q_1a_1)$
·5	$2{\cdot}002 + {\cdot}124i$
1	$2{\cdot}010 + {\cdot}250i$
1·5	$2{\cdot}024 + {\cdot}372i$
2	$2{\cdot}042 + {\cdot}50i$
2·5	$2{\cdot}064 + {\cdot}62i$
3	$2{\cdot}090 + {\cdot}74i$

This table shows that for values of $4\pi\mu_1 na_1^2 k_1$ up to unity 2 may still be taken as an approximation to $\eta I_0(\eta)/I_0'(\eta)$ as above, p. 163. Thus the first term on the right of (33) is the same as before.

Current Density. We shall now calculate the current density at different distances from the axis in a wire carrying a simply periodic current, and the effective resistance and self-inductance of a given length l of the conductor. Everything is supposed symmetrical about the axis of the wire.

By (18) we have for the axially directed electromotive intensity at a point in the wire distant ρ $(=\eta/q)$ from the axis

$$P_1 = AI_0(\eta)e^{(nt-mx)i}. \tag{56}$$

This multiplied by k_1, the conductivity of the wire, gives an expression for the current density parallel to the axis of the wire at distance ρ from the axis.

If the value of P_1 at the surface of the wire be denoted by P_{a_1},

$$P_{a_1} = AI_0(\eta_1)e^{(nt-mx)i} \tag{57}$$

$(\rho = a_1)$.

The magnetic force at the surface is

$$H_{a_1} = \frac{4\pi k_1}{q_1} AI_0'(\eta_1)\, e^{(nt-mx)i}$$

$(\rho = a_1)$. Therefore, if Γ be the total current in the wire, we have $4\pi\Gamma = 2\pi a_1 H_{a_1}$, and so

$$\Gamma = \frac{2\pi k_1 a_1}{q_1} AI_0'(\eta_1)e^{(nt-mx)i}. \tag{58}$$

The electromotive intensity P is the resultant parallel to the axis of the impressed and induced electromotive intensities. To solve the problem proposed we must separate the part impressed by subtracting from P the induced part. Now the impressed electromotive force is the same all over any cross-section of the wire at a given instant, and will therefore be determined if we find it for the surface. But since the induced electromotive intensity due to any part of the current is directly proportional to its time-rate of variation, the induced electromotive intensity at the surface must be directly proportional to the time-rate of variation of the whole current in the wire. Hence, by (57), if E denote the impressed electromotive intensity

$$E - A'\dot{\Gamma} = P_{a_1},$$

where $A'\dot{\Gamma}$ (A' = a constant) is put for the induced intensity parallel to the axis at the surface. Thus

$$E = A\left\{I_0(\eta_1) + ni\frac{2\pi k_1 a_1}{q_1}A' I_0'(\eta_1)\right\} e^{(nt-mx)i}$$

$$= \left\{\frac{q_1 a_1}{2\pi k_1 a_1^2}\frac{I_0(\eta_1)}{I_0'(\eta_1)} + niA'\right\}\Gamma. \tag{59}$$

Putting r for the resistance $(=1/(\pi a_1^2 k_1))$ of unit length of the wire and using the expansion above, we get, since $q_1^2 = 4\pi\mu_1 k_1 ni$,

$$E = r\left(1 + \frac{1}{12}\frac{\mu_1^2 n^2}{r^2} - \frac{1}{180}\frac{\mu_1^4 n^4}{r^4} + \ldots\right)\Gamma$$

$$+ in\left\{A' + \mu_1\left(\frac{1}{2} - \frac{1}{48}\frac{\mu_1^2 n^2}{r^2} + \frac{13}{8640}\frac{\mu_1^4 n^4}{r^4} - \ldots\right)\right\}\Gamma. \tag{60}$$

Or taking the impressed difference of potential V between the two ends of a length l of the wire the resistance of which is R we have

$$V = R\left(1 + \frac{1}{12}\frac{\mu_1^2 n^2 l^2}{R^2} - \frac{1}{180}\frac{\mu_1^4 n^4 l^4}{R^4} + \ldots\right)\Gamma$$

$$+ in\left\{lA' + \mu_1\left(\frac{l}{2} - \frac{1}{48}\frac{\mu_1^2 n^2 l^3}{R^2} + \frac{13}{8640}\frac{\mu_1^4 n^4 l^5}{R^4} - \ldots\right)\right\}\Gamma. \tag{61}$$

If we denote the series in brackets in the first and second terms respectively by R', L' we get

$$V = R'\Gamma + L'\dot{\Gamma}. \tag{62}$$

Thus R' and L' are the effective resistance and self-inductance of the length l of the wire.

It remains to determine the constant A'. If there be no displacement current in the dielectric comparable with the current in the wire, a supposition sufficiently nearly in accordance with the fact for all practical purposes, and the return current be capable of being regarded as in a highly conducting skin on the outside of the dielectric, so that there is no magnetic force outside, we can find A' in the following manner. The inductive electromotive force per unit length in the conductor at any point is then equal to the rate of variation of the surface integral of magnetic force taken per unit length in the dielectric at that place. Now, if there is no displacement current, H will be in circles round the axis of the wire, and will be inversely as the radius of the circle at any point, since

$$2\pi\rho H = 4\pi\Gamma.$$

Thus, if H_ρ be the magnetic force at distance ρ from the axis of the wire,

$$\dot{H}_\rho = \frac{4\pi k_1 ni}{q_1} A I_0'(\eta_1) \frac{a_1}{\rho} e^{(nt-mx)i}$$

and

$$\int_{a_1}^{a_2} \dot{H}_\rho d\rho = \frac{4\pi k_1 n i a_1}{q_1} A I_0'(\eta_1) \log \frac{a_2}{a_1} e^{(nt-mx)i}. \tag{63}$$

But this last expression by what has been stated above is $A'\dot{\Gamma}$, and $\dot{\Gamma}$ is given by (58).

Thus we obtain

$$A' = 2 \log \frac{a_2}{a_1}$$

and

$$L' = 2l \log \frac{a_2}{a_1} + l\mu_1\left(\frac{1}{2} - \frac{1}{48}\frac{\mu_1^2 n^2 l^2}{R^2} + \frac{13}{8640}\frac{\mu_1^4 n^4 l^4}{R^4} - \dots\right). \tag{64}$$

Since $I_0(x\sqrt{i}) = \text{ber}\, x + i \,\text{bei}\, x$, it can easily be deduced from (59) that, for $x = 2\sqrt{(\mu_1 n/r)}$,

$$R' = \frac{x}{2} \frac{\text{ber}\, x \,\text{bei}' x - \text{bei}\, x \,\text{ber}' x}{\text{ber}'^2 x + \text{bei}'^2 x} R \tag{65}$$

and

$$L' = 2l \log\left(\frac{a_2}{a_1}\right) + \frac{xlr}{2n} \frac{\text{ber}\, x \,\text{ber}' x + \text{bei}\, x \,\text{bei}' x}{\text{ber}'^2 x + \text{bei}'^2 x}, \tag{66}$$

a form in which the values of R' and L' are easily calculated for any given values of x and n from the Table of $I_0(x\sqrt{i})$ given at the end of the book.

Equation (61) shows the effect of μ_1 on R' and L' at different frequencies. If however the frequency be very great, we must put in (59) $I_0(\eta_1)/I_0'(\eta_1) = 1$. We find for this case

$$R' = \sqrt{\tfrac{1}{2}\mu_1 n l R}, \quad L' = \sqrt{\frac{\mu_1 R l}{2n}} + lA' \dots. \tag{67}$$

Thus in the limit R' is indefinitely great, and L' reduces to the constant term lA'. The current is now insensible except in an infinitely thin stratum at the surface of the wire.

§ 4. **Hertz's Investigations.** The problem of electrical oscillations has been treated somewhat differently by Hertz in his various memoirs written in connection with his very remarkable experimental researches.* He discussed first the propagation, in an unlimited dielectric medium, of electric and magnetic disturbances from a vibrator consisting of two equal plates or balls connected

* See Hertz's *Untersuchungen über die Ausbreitung der elektrischen Kraft*, J. A. Barth, Leipzig, 1892; or *Electric Waves* (the English Translation of the same work, by Mr. D. E. Jones), Macmillan & Co., London, 1893.

by a straight wire with a spark-gap in the middle, and, secondly, the propagation in the same medium of disturbances generated by such a vibrator guided by a long straight wire. The action of the vibrator simply consisted in a flow of electricity alternately from one plate or ball to the other, set up by an initially impressed difference of potential between the two conductors.

Taking the simple case first as an introduction to the second, which we wish to give some account of here, we may take the vibrator as an electric doublet, that is as consisting electrically of two equal and opposite point-charges at an infinitesimal distance apart, and having the line joining them along the axis of x, and the origin midway between them. It is clear in this case that everything is symmetrical about the axis of x, that the electric forces lie in planes through the axis, and that the lines of magnetic force are circles round the wire. The medium is here an insulator.

The equations of motion are those given on p. 157 above. By symmetry the component α of magnetic force in the medium is zero, and by (4) the equation

$$\frac{\partial \beta}{\partial y}+\frac{\partial \gamma}{\partial z}=0$$

holds, connecting the other two components. This shows that $\beta\, dz-\gamma\, dy$ is a complete differential of some function of y, z. In Hertz's notation we take this function as $-\partial \Pi/\partial t$, so that

$$\beta=-\frac{\partial^2 \Pi}{\partial z\, \partial t}, \quad \gamma=\frac{\partial^2 \Pi}{\partial y\, \partial t}. \tag{68}$$

The equations of motion become then

$$\kappa \frac{\partial P}{\partial t}= \frac{\partial}{\partial t}\left(\frac{\partial^2 \Pi}{\partial y^2}+\frac{\partial^2 \Pi}{\partial z^2}\right),$$

$$\kappa \frac{\partial Q}{\partial t}=-\frac{\partial^3 \Pi}{\partial t\, \partial x\, \partial y},$$

$$\kappa \frac{\partial R}{\partial t}=-\frac{\partial^3 \Pi}{\partial t\, \partial x\, \partial z},$$

which declare that the quantities

$$\kappa P-\left(\frac{\partial^2 \Pi}{\partial y^2}+\frac{\partial^2 \Pi}{\partial z^2}\right), \quad \kappa Q+\frac{\partial^2 \Pi}{\partial x\, \partial y}, \quad \kappa R+\frac{\partial^2 \Pi}{\partial x\, \partial z},$$

are independent of t. The propagation of waves in the medium therefore will not be affected if we suppose each of these uantities to have the value zero. Thus we assume as the undamental equations

$$\kappa P = \left(\frac{\partial^2\Pi}{\partial y^2}+\frac{\partial^2\Pi}{\partial z^2}\right),$$

$$\kappa Q = -\frac{\partial^2\Pi}{\partial x\,\partial y},$$

$$\kappa R = -\frac{\partial^2\Pi}{\partial x\,\partial z}.$$

Using these in the equations of magnetic force (2), we obtain

$$\frac{\partial}{\partial z}\left(\frac{\partial^2\Pi}{\partial t^2}-\frac{1}{\kappa\mu}\nabla^2\Pi\right)=0,$$

$$\frac{\partial}{\partial y}\left(\frac{\partial^2\Pi}{\partial t^2}-\frac{1}{\kappa\mu}\nabla^2\Pi\right)=0,$$

vhich show that the quantity in brackets is a function of x and t only. Thus we write

$$\frac{\partial^2\Pi}{\partial t^2}-\frac{1}{\kappa\mu}\nabla^2\Pi=f(x,\,t).$$

It is easy to see that we may put $f(x, t)=0$ without affecting the electric and magnetic fields, and the equation of propagation is

$$\frac{\partial^2\Pi}{\partial t^2}=\frac{1}{\kappa\mu}\nabla^2\Pi. \tag{69}$$

A solution adapted to the vibrator we have supposed is

$$\Pi=\frac{\Phi}{r}\sin(mr-nt), \tag{70}$$

vhere r is the distance of the point considered from the origin, and Φ is the maximum moment of the electric doublet.

From this solution the electric and magnetic forces are found by differentiation. In cylindrical coordinates x, ρ, θ the equation becomes

$$\frac{\partial^2\Pi}{\partial t^2}=\frac{1}{\kappa\mu}\left(\frac{\partial^2\Pi}{\partial x^2}+\frac{\partial^2\Pi}{\partial \rho^2}+\frac{1}{\rho}\frac{\partial\Pi}{\partial\rho}\right), \tag{71}$$

since Π is independent of θ. Here $\rho^2=y^2+z^2$, and hence if we put now P and R for the axial and radial components of electric force, we must in calculating them from Π use the formulae

$$\left.\begin{aligned}\kappa P &= \frac{1}{\rho}\frac{\partial}{\partial\rho}\left(\rho\frac{\partial\Pi}{\partial\rho}\right),\\ \kappa R &= -\frac{\partial^2\Pi}{\partial x\,\partial\rho}.\end{aligned}\right\} \tag{72}$$

We take the meridian plane as plane of x, y, so that the magnetic force H which is at right angles to the meridian plane is identical with γ. Thus

$$H=\frac{\partial^2\Pi}{\partial t\,\partial\rho}. \qquad (73)$$

The fully worked out results of this solution are very interesting but, as they do not involve any applications of Bessel functions, we do not consider them in detail. We have referred to them inasmuch as the case of the propagation of waves along a wire, for the solution of which the use of Bessel functions is requisite, may be very instructively compared with this simple case, from which it may be regarded as built up.

In the problem of the wire we have Π at each point of the medium close to the surface of the conductor a simple harmonic function of the distance of the point from a chosen origin. We shall suppose that the wire is very thin and lies along the axis of x, and is infinitely extended in at least one way, so that there is no reflection to be taken into account.

Hence, at any point just outside the surface,

$$\Pi=A\sin(mx-nt+\epsilon).$$

If we exclude any damping out of the wave or change of form we see that A cannot involve x or t; it is therefore a function of ρ. Thus

$$\Pi=f(\rho)\sin(mx-nt+\epsilon). \qquad (74)$$

Substitution in the differential equation which holds for the medium gives for f the equation

$$\frac{\partial^2 f}{\partial\rho^2}+\frac{1}{\rho}\frac{\partial f}{\partial\rho}-(m^2-n^2\kappa\mu)f=0. \qquad (75)$$

Here n^2/m^2 is the square of the velocity of propagation. We shall denote $m^2-n^2\kappa\mu$ by p^2 and suppose that p^2 is positive, that is that the velocity of propagation is less than that of free propagation in the dielectric. We have therefore, instead of (75),

$$\frac{\partial^2 f}{\partial\rho^2}+\frac{1}{\rho}\frac{\partial f}{\partial\rho}-p^2 f=0.$$

This is satisfied by $I_0(p\rho)$ and by $K_0(p\rho)$, where $p\rho$ is real. The latter solution only is applicable outside the wire, as f must be zero at infinity. We have therefore in the insulating medium

$$\Pi=2CK_0(p\rho)\sin(mx-nt+\epsilon), \qquad (76)$$

where C and ϵ are constants.

Now, by v. (36) above, this solution may be written

$$\Pi = 2C\left\{\int_0^\infty \cos(p\rho\sinh\phi)\,d\phi\right\}\sin(mx - nt + \epsilon).$$

Putting $\rho\sinh\phi = \xi$, we get

$$\Pi = 2C\int_0^\infty \frac{\cos p\xi}{\sqrt{\rho^2+\xi^2}}\,d\xi\,.\sin(mx - nt + \epsilon),$$

or

$$\Pi = C\int_{-\infty}^{+\infty} \frac{\cos p\xi}{\sqrt{\rho^2+\xi^2}}\,d\xi\,.\sin(mx - nt + \epsilon). \qquad (77)$$

This result may be compared with that obtained above (70), p. 175, from which it is of course capable of being derived.

When $p\rho$ is small, we have

$$K_0(p\rho) = -\left(\gamma + \log\frac{p\rho}{2}\right).$$

Hence at the surface of the wire

$$\Pi = -2C\left(\gamma + \log\frac{p\rho}{2}\right)\sin(mx - nt + \epsilon). \qquad (78)$$

If $p = 0$, that is if the velocity of propagation is that of light, the solution is

$$\Pi = C'\log\rho\sin(mx - nt + \epsilon), \qquad (79)$$

as may easily be verified by solving directly for this particular case.

In all cases the wave at any instant in the wire may be divided up into half wave-lengths, such that for each lines of force start out from the wire and return in closed curves which do not intersect, and are symmetrically arranged round the wire. The direction of the force in the curves is reversed for each successive half-wave.

When $p = 0$ the electric force, as may very easily be seen, is normal to the wire, and each curve then consists of a pair of parallel lines, one passing out straight to infinity, the other returning to the wire.

CHAPTER XIV.

DIFFRACTION.

I. *Case of Symmetry round an Axis.*

§1. **Intensity (on a Screen at Right Angles to the Axis) expressed by Bessel Functions.** The problem here considered is the diffraction produced by a small circular opening in a screen on which falls light propagated in spherical waves from a point source. We take as the axis of symmetry the line drawn from the source to the centre of the opening; and it is required to find the intensity of illumination at any point P of a plane screen parallel to the plane of the opening, and at a fixed distance from the latter.

Let the distance of any point of the edge of the orifice from the source be a, and consider the portion of the wave-front of radius a which fills the orifice. If the angular polar distance of an element of this part of the wave-front be θ, and its longitude be ϕ, the area of the element may be written $a^2 \sin\theta\, d\theta\, d\phi$. Putting ξ for the distance of this element from the point P of the screen at which the illumination is to be found, regarding the element as a secondary source of light, and using the ordinary fundamental formula, we obtain for the disturbance (displacement or velocity of an ether particle) produced at P by this source the expression

$$\frac{a \sin\theta\, d\theta\, d\phi}{\lambda\xi} \sin(m\xi - nt),$$

where $m = 2\pi/\lambda$, $n = 2\pi/T$, λ and T being the length and period of the wave.

Thus, if the angular polar distance of the edge of the orifice be θ_1, the whole disturbance at P is

$$\frac{a}{\lambda}\int_0^{2\pi}\int_0^{\theta_1} \frac{1}{\xi} \sin\theta \sin(m\xi - nt)\, d\theta\, d\phi.$$

Let ζ be the distance of P from the axis of symmetry, and b the distance of the screen from the nearest point or pole of the spherical wave of radius a, so that the axial distance of the screen from the element is $a(1-\cos\theta)+b$. Because of the symmetry of the illumination we may suppose without loss of generality that the longitude of the point P is zero. Then the distance ξ from the element to P is given by

$$\xi^2=\{b+a(1-\cos\theta)\}^2+(a\sin\theta-\zeta\cos\phi)^2+\zeta^2\sin^2\phi.$$

This reduces to

$$\xi^2=b^2+4a(a+b)\sin^2\frac{\theta}{2}-2a\zeta\sin\theta\cos\phi+\zeta^2,$$

or, since θ and ζ are small,

$$\xi=b+\frac{2a(a+b)}{b}\sin^2\frac{\theta}{2}-\frac{a\zeta}{b}\sin\theta\cos\phi+\frac{\zeta^2}{2b}.$$

If now we write ρ for $a\sin\theta$, or $a\theta$, we have approximately $\sin^2\frac{1}{2}\theta=\rho^2/(4a^2)$, so that

$$\xi=b+\frac{\zeta^2}{2b}-\frac{\zeta\rho}{b}\cos\phi+\frac{a+b}{2ab}\rho^2.$$

Hence, finally, if the opening be of so small radius r, and P be so near the axis that we may substitute $1/b$ for the factor $1/\xi$, we obtain for the total disturbance the expression

$$\frac{1}{ab\lambda}\int_0^{2\pi}\int_0^r\sin\left\{m\left(b+\frac{\zeta^2}{2b}-\frac{\zeta\rho}{b}\cos\phi+\frac{a+b}{2ab}\rho^2\right)-nt\right\}\rho\,d\rho\,d\phi.$$

Separating now those terms of the argument within the large brackets which do not depend upon ρ from the others, and denoting them by ϖ, so that

$$\varpi=m\left(b+\frac{\zeta^2}{2b}\right)-nt,$$

we may write the expression in the form

$$\frac{1}{ab\lambda}\int_0^{2\pi}\int_0^r\sin(\varpi+\chi)\rho\,d\rho\,d\phi,$$

or

$$\frac{1}{ab\lambda}(C\sin\varpi+S\cos\varpi),$$

where

$$C=\int_0^{2\pi}\int_0^r\cos\frac{2\pi}{\lambda}\left(\frac{a+b}{2ab}\rho^2-\frac{\zeta}{b}\rho\cos\phi\right)\rho\,d\rho\,d\phi,$$

$$S=\int_0^{2\pi}\int_0^r\sin\frac{2\pi}{\lambda}\left(\frac{a+b}{2ab}\rho^2-\frac{\zeta}{b}\rho\cos\phi\right)\rho\,d\rho\,d\phi.$$

The intensity of illumination at P is thus proportional to

$$\frac{1}{a^2b^2\lambda^2}(C^2+S^2),$$

and it only remains to calculate the integrals C and S. This can be done by the following process due to Lommel,* depending upon the properties of Bessel Functions.

Changing the order of integration in C, we have

$$C=\int_0^r\left\{\int_0^{2\pi}\cos\frac{2\pi}{\lambda}\left(\frac{a+b}{2ab}\rho^2-\frac{\zeta}{b}\rho\cos\phi\right)d\phi\right\}\rho\,d\rho.$$

Now, considering the inner integral, and writing

$$\frac{2\pi}{\lambda}\frac{a+b}{2ab}\rho^2=\tfrac{1}{2}\psi,\quad \frac{2\pi}{\lambda}\frac{\zeta}{b}\rho=x,$$

we have $$\int_0^{2\pi}\cos\frac{2\pi}{\lambda}\left(\frac{a+b}{2ab}\rho^2-\frac{\zeta}{b}\rho\cos\phi\right)d\phi$$

$$=\int_0^{2\pi}\cos\left(\tfrac{1}{2}\psi-x\cos\phi\right)d\phi$$

$$=\cos\tfrac{1}{2}\psi\int_0^{2\pi}\cos\left(x\cos\phi\right)d\phi,$$

since $$\sin\tfrac{1}{2}\psi\int_0^{2\pi}\sin\left(x\cos\phi\right)d\phi=0.$$

But

$$\cos\tfrac{1}{2}\psi\int_0^{2\pi}\cos\left(x\cos\phi\right)d\phi=2\cos\tfrac{1}{2}\psi\int_0^{\pi}\cos\left(x\cos\phi\right)d\phi$$
$$=2\pi\cos\tfrac{1}{2}\psi\,.\,J_0(x),$$

by (V. 3) above.

Hence $$C=\frac{b^2\lambda^2}{2\pi\zeta^2}\int_0^z\cos\tfrac{1}{2}\psi\,.\,xJ_0(x)\,dx, \qquad (1$$

where z denotes the value of x when $\rho=r$, and is equal to $\frac{2\pi}{\lambda}\frac{\zeta}{b}r$.

Similarly we can show that

$$S=\frac{b^2\lambda^2}{2\pi\zeta^2}\int_0^z\sin\tfrac{1}{2}\psi\,.\,xJ_0(x)\,dx. \qquad (2$$

These integrals can be expanded in series of Bessel Functions in the following manner. First, by (II. 25), we have

$$\int_0^x x^nJ_{n-1}(x)\,dx=x^nJ_n(x).$$

Integrating by parts and using this result we get

$$\int_0^x\cos\tfrac{1}{2}\psi\,.\,xJ_0(x)\,dx=\cos\tfrac{1}{2}\psi\,.\,xJ_1(x)$$
$$+\frac{\lambda}{2\pi}\frac{a+b}{ab}\frac{b^2}{\zeta^2}\int_0^x\sin\tfrac{1}{2}\psi\,.\,x^2J_1(x)\,dx.$$

* *Abh. d. k. Bayer. Akad. d. Wissensch.* XV. 1886.

The same process may now be repeated on the integral of the second term on the right and so on. Thus, putting $\frac{1}{2}y$ for the value of $\frac{1}{2}\psi$ when $x=z$, so that $y=\frac{4\pi}{\lambda}\frac{a+b}{2ab}r^2$, and writing

$$\left.\begin{aligned} U_1&=\frac{y}{z}J_1(z)-\left(\frac{y}{z}\right)^3 J_3(z)+\ldots=\Sigma(-1)^n\left(\frac{y}{z}\right)^{2n+1}J_{2n+1}(z),\\ U_2&=\left(\frac{y}{z}\right)^2 J_2(z)-\left(\frac{y}{z}\right)^4 J_4(z)+\ldots=\Sigma(-1)^n\left(\frac{y}{z}\right)^{2n+2}J_{2n+2}(z),\end{aligned}\right\} \quad (3)$$

we obtain finally, putting $4\pi^2\zeta^2r^2/(b^2\lambda^2)$ for z^2,

$$C=\pi r^2\left\{\frac{\cos\frac{1}{2}y}{\frac{1}{2}y}U_1+\frac{\sin\frac{1}{2}y}{\frac{1}{2}y}U_2\right\}, \quad (4)$$

$$S=\pi r^2\left\{\frac{\sin\frac{1}{2}y}{\frac{1}{2}y}U_1-\frac{\cos\frac{1}{2}y}{\frac{1}{2}y}U_2\right\}. \quad (5)$$

The values of C and S can thus be found by evaluating the series U_1, U_2 for the given value of z. This can be done easily by the numerical tables of Bessel Functions given at the end of this volume.

The series U_1, U_2 proceed by ascending powers of y/z. Series proceeding by ascending powers of z/y can easily be found by a process similar to that used above. We begin by performing the partial integration first upon $\cos\frac{1}{2}\psi\,.\,x\,dx$, and then continuing the process, making use of the equation (II. 24)

$$\frac{\partial}{\partial x}(x^{-n}J_n(x))=-x^{-n}J_{n+1}(x).$$

Thus remembering that

$$\tfrac{1}{2}\psi=\frac{\lambda}{2\pi}\frac{b^2}{\zeta^2}\frac{a+b}{2ab}x^2=\mu x^2, \text{ say,}$$

we have as the first step in the process

$$\begin{aligned} C&=\frac{b^2\lambda^2}{2\pi\zeta^2}\int_0^z J_0(x)\cos\mu x^2\,.\,x\,dx\\ &=\frac{b^2\lambda^2}{2\pi\zeta^2}\left\{\frac{1}{2\mu}\sin\mu z^2\,.\,J_0(z)+\frac{1}{2\mu}\int_0^z\frac{1}{x}J_1(x)\sin\mu x^2\,.\,x\,dx\right\}\\ &=\frac{b^2\lambda^2}{2\pi\zeta^2}\left\{\frac{1}{2\mu}\sin\mu z^2\,.\,J_0(z)-\frac{1}{4\mu^2}\frac{1}{z}J_1(z)\cos\mu z^2\right.\\ &\qquad\left.+\frac{1}{4\mu^2}\frac{1}{2}-\frac{1}{4\mu^2}\int_0^z\frac{1}{x^2}J_2(x)\cos\mu x^2.\,x\,dx\right\}.\end{aligned}$$

Proceeding in this way we obtain

$$C=\pi r^2\left[\frac{\sin\frac{1}{2}y}{\frac{1}{2}y}\left\{J_0(z)-\left(\frac{z}{y}\right)^2 J_2(z)+\dots\right\}\right.$$
$$-\frac{\cos\frac{1}{2}y}{\frac{1}{2}y}\left\{\frac{z}{y}J_1(z)-\left(\frac{z}{y}\right)^3 J_3(z)+\dots\right\}$$
$$\left.+\frac{2}{y}\left\{\frac{z^2}{2y}-\frac{1}{3!}\left(\frac{z^2}{2y}\right)^3+\dots\right\}\right]$$
$$=\pi r^2\left\{\frac{2}{y}\sin\frac{z^2}{2y}+\frac{\sin\frac{1}{2}y}{\frac{1}{2}y}V_0-\frac{\cos\frac{1}{2}y}{\frac{1}{2}y}V_1\right\}, \tag{6}$$

where

$$\left.\begin{aligned} V_0&=J_0(z)-\left(\frac{z}{y}\right)^2 J_2(z)+\dots=\Sigma(-1)^n\left(\frac{z}{y}\right)^{2n}J_{2n}(z),\\ V_1&=\frac{z}{y}J_1(z)-\left(\frac{z}{y}\right)^3 J_3(z)+\dots=\Sigma(-1)^n\left(\frac{z}{y}\right)^{2n+1}J_{2n+1}(z).\end{aligned}\right\} \tag{7}$$

Similarly we obtain

$$S=\pi r^2\left\{\frac{2}{y}\cos\frac{z^2}{2y}-\frac{\cos\frac{1}{2}y}{\frac{1}{2}y}V_0-\frac{\sin\frac{1}{2}y}{\frac{1}{2}y}V_1\right\}. \tag{8}$$

Comparing (4) and (5) with (6) and (8) we get

$$U_1\cos\tfrac{1}{2}y+U_2\sin\tfrac{1}{2}y=\sin\frac{z^2}{2y}+V_0\sin\tfrac{1}{2}y-V_1\cos\tfrac{1}{2}y,$$

$$U_1\sin\tfrac{1}{2}y-U_2\cos\tfrac{1}{2}y=\cos\frac{z^2}{2y}-V_0\cos\tfrac{1}{2}y-V_1\sin\tfrac{1}{2}y,$$

which give

$$\left.\begin{aligned} U_1+V_1&=\sin\tfrac{1}{2}\left(y+\frac{z^2}{y}\right),\\ -U_2+V_0&=\cos\tfrac{1}{2}\left(y+\frac{z^2}{y}\right).\end{aligned}\right\} \tag{9}$$

Squaring (4) and (5) and (6) and (8) we obtain equivalent expressions for the intensity of illumination at the point P on the screen; thus, if $\pi r^2=1$,

$$\frac{1}{a^2b^2\lambda^2}(C^2+S^2)=\frac{1}{a^2b^2\lambda^2}\left(\frac{2}{y}\right)^2(U_1^2+U_2^2)$$
$$=\frac{1}{a^2b^2\lambda^2}\left(\frac{2}{y}\right)^2\left\{1+V_0^2+V_1^2-2V_0\cos\tfrac{1}{2}\left(y+\frac{z^2}{y}\right)\right.$$
$$\left.-2V_1\sin\tfrac{1}{2}\left(y+\frac{z^2}{y}\right)\right\}. \tag{10}$$

§ 2. **Discussion of the Series (U, V) of Bessel Functions which express the Intensity.** The calculation of these U and V functions by means of tables of Bessel Functions will be facilitated by taking advantage of certain properties which they possess. We follow Lommel in the following short discussion of these properties, adopting however a somewhat different analysis.

Consider the more general functions

$$U_n=\left(\frac{y}{z}\right)^n J_n(z)-\left(\frac{y}{z}\right)^{n+2} J_{n+2}(z)+\dots$$

$$=\Sigma(-1)^p\left(\frac{y}{z}\right)^{n+2p} J_{n+2p}(z), \qquad (11)$$

$$V_n=\left(\frac{z}{y}\right)^n J_n(z)-\left(\frac{z}{y}\right)^{n+2} J_{n+2}(z)+\dots$$

$$=\Sigma(-1)^p\left(\frac{z}{y}\right)^{n+2p} J_{n+2p}(z), \qquad (12)$$

where n may be any positive or negative integer.

First of all it is clear that the series are convergent for all values of y and z. Now, if in Chapter IV., example 12, we put $x=z$, we have

$$1=J_0^2(z)+2J_1^2(z)+2J_2^2(z)+\dots .$$

Hence we see that since, by IV. (9), $|J_0(z)|<1$ each of the other Bessel Functions must be numerically less than $1/\sqrt{2}$. It follows that if $y/z<1$ the series for U_n is more convergent than the geometric series

$$\Sigma\left(\frac{y}{z}\right)^{n+2p},$$

and if $z/y<1$, V_n is more convergent than the geometric series

$$\Sigma\left(\frac{z}{y}\right)^{n+2p}.$$

It is therefore more convenient in the former case to use U_n, in the latter to use V_n for purposes of calculation.

If $y=z$,

$$U_0=V_0=J_0-J_2+J_4-\dots ,$$

$$U_1=V_1=J_1-J_3+J_5-\dots .$$

But, putting, in IV. (7) and IV. (8), $\phi=0$, $x=z$, we find

$$\cos z= J_0(z)-2J_2(z)+2J_4(z)-\dots ;$$

$$\sin z=2J_1(z)-2J_3(z)+2J_5(z)-\dots$$

Therefore, when $z=y$,

$$U_0=V_0=\tfrac{1}{2}\{J_0(z)+\cos z\},$$

$$U_1=V_1=\tfrac{1}{2}\sin z,$$

$$U_2=V_2=\tfrac{1}{2}\{J_0(z)-\cos z\},$$

and generally

$$\left.\begin{aligned} U_{2n} &= V_{2n} = \frac{(-1)^n}{2}\{J_0(z)+\cos z\} - \sum_{p=0}^{p=n-1}(-1)^{n+p}J_{2p}(z), \\ U_{2n+1} &= V_{2n+1} = \frac{(-1)^n}{2}\sin z - \sum_{p=0}^{p=n-1}(-1)^{n+p}J_{2p+1}(z). \end{aligned}\right\} \quad (13)$$

Returning now to (11) and (12) we easily find

$$\left.\begin{aligned} U_n + U_{n+2} &= \left(\frac{y}{z}\right)^n J_n(z), \\ V_n + V_{n+2} &= \left(\frac{z}{y}\right)^n J_n(z), \end{aligned}\right\} \quad (14)$$

and therefore $\quad z^{2n}(U_n+U_{n+2}) = y^{2n}(V_n+V_{n+2}).$ (15)

Also, since $J_{-n}(z)=(-1)^nJ_n(z)$, we find, putting $-n$ for n in the second and first of (14) successively, and also $z=y$,

$$U_n+U_{n+2}=(-1)^n(V_{-n}+V_{-n+2}),$$
$$V_n+V_{n+2}=(-1)^n(U_{-n}+U_{-n+2}).$$

Differentiating (11), we find

$$\frac{\partial U_n}{\partial z} = -\frac{n}{z}\left(\frac{y}{z}\right)^n J_n(z) + \frac{n+2}{z}\left(\frac{y}{z}\right)^{n+2} J_{n+2}(z) - \ldots$$
$$+\left(\frac{y}{z}\right)^n J_n'(z) - \left(\frac{y}{z}\right)^{n+2} J_{n+2}'(z) + \ldots.$$

Using in the second line of this result the relation (II. 20)

$$J_n'(z) = \frac{n}{z}J_n(z) - J_{n+1}(z),$$

we get

$$\frac{\partial U_n}{\partial z} = -\left(\frac{y}{z}\right)^n J_{n+1}(z) + \left(\frac{y}{z}\right)^{n+2} J_{n+3}(z) - \ldots = -\frac{z}{y}U_{n+1}. \quad (16)$$

This gives, by successive differentiation, the equation

$$\frac{\partial^m U_n}{\partial z^m} = -\frac{m-1}{y}\frac{\partial^{m-2}}{\partial z^{m-2}}U_{n+1} - \frac{z}{y}\frac{\partial^{m-1}}{\partial z^{m-1}}U_{n+1}. \quad (17)$$

Similarly we obtain, by differentiating (12) and using the relation (II. 21)

$$J_n'(z) = J_{n-1}(z) - \frac{n}{z}J_n(z),$$

$$\frac{\partial V_n}{\partial z} = \frac{z}{y}V_{n-1}, \quad (18)$$

and therefore

$$\frac{\partial^m V_n}{\partial z^m} = \frac{m-1}{y}\frac{\partial^{m-2}}{\partial z^{m-2}}V_{n-1} + \frac{z}{y}\frac{\partial^{m-1}}{\partial z^{m-1}}V_{n-1}. \quad (19)$$

Again, differentiating the first of (9), we get

$$\frac{\partial U_1}{\partial z}+\frac{\partial V_1}{\partial z}=\frac{z}{y}\cos\frac{1}{2}\left(y+\frac{z^2}{y}\right).$$

But, by (16) and (18), this becomes

$$-U_2+V_0=\cos\frac{1}{2}\left(y+\frac{z^2}{y}\right).$$

Differentiating again we obtain

$$-\frac{\partial U_2}{\partial z}+\frac{\partial V_0}{\partial z}=-\frac{z}{y}\sin\frac{1}{2}\left(y+\frac{z^2}{y}\right),$$

or, by (16) and (18),

$$U_3+V_{-1}=-\sin\frac{1}{2}\left(y+\frac{z^2}{y}\right).$$

By repeating this process it is clear that we shall obtain

$$\left.\begin{aligned} U_{2n+1}+V_{-2n+1}&=(-1)^n\sin\frac{1}{2}\left(y+\frac{z^2}{y}\right),\\ -U_{2n+2}+V_{-2n}&=(-1)^n\cos\frac{1}{2}\left(y+\frac{z^2}{y}\right).\end{aligned}\right\} \qquad (20)$$

If in these equations we put $n=0$, we fall back upon (9). Putting in (9) the values of the functions as given in the defining equations (11) and (12), and using (14), we obtain the theorems

$$\left.\begin{aligned} \Sigma(-1)^p\left\{\left(\frac{y}{z}\right)^{2p+1}+\left(\frac{z}{y}\right)^{2p+1}\right\}J_{2p+1}(z)&=\sin\frac{1}{2}\left(y+\frac{z^2}{y}\right),\\ \Sigma(-1)^p\left\{\left(\frac{y}{z}\right)^{2p+2}+\left(\frac{z}{y}\right)^{2p+2}\right\}J_{2p+2}(z)&=J_0(z)-\cos\frac{1}{2}\left(y+\frac{z^2}{y}\right),\end{aligned}\right\} \qquad (21)$$

which include, as particular cases, those namely for which $y=z$, the equations

$$\sin z=2J_1(z)-2J_3(z)+2J_5(z)-\dots,$$
$$\cos z=J_0(z)-2J_2(z)+2J_4(z)-\dots,$$

used above.

By Taylor's theorem we have

$$U_n(y,z+h)=U_n+h\frac{\partial U_n}{\partial z}+\frac{h^2}{2!}\frac{\partial^2 U_n}{\partial z^2}+\dots.$$

Calculating the successive differential coefficients by means of (16), and rearranging the terms, we obtain

$$\begin{aligned} U_n(y,z+h)&=U_n-\frac{h(2z+h)}{2y}U_{n+1}+\frac{1}{2!}\frac{h^2(2z+h)^2}{(2y)^2}U_{n+2}-\dots\\ &=\Sigma(-1)^p\frac{h^p(2z+h)^p}{p!\,(2y)^p}U_{n+p}. \end{aligned} \qquad (22)$$

Similarly we can prove that

$$V_n(y, z+h)=\Sigma\frac{h^p(2z+h)^p}{p!(2y)^p}V_{n-p}. \tag{23}$$

These expansions are highly convergent and permit of easy calculation of $U_n(y, z+h)$, $V_n(y, z+h)$. The functions U_{n+1}, U_{n+2}, $U_{n+3}, \ldots$, V_{n-1}, $V_{n-2}, \ldots$ can be found from U_n, V_n, by using (16) and (18) to calculate U_{n+1}, V_{n-1}, and then deducing the others by successive applications of (16) and (18).

Differentiating (11) and (12) with respect to y, and using in the resulting expressions the relation (II. 26)

$$nJ_n(z)=\tfrac{1}{2}zJ_{n-1}(z)+\tfrac{1}{2}zJ_{n+1}(z),$$

we find

$$\left.\begin{aligned}\tfrac{1}{2}z^2U_{n+1}&=y^2\frac{\partial U_n}{\partial y}-\tfrac{1}{2}y^2U_{n-1},\\ \tfrac{1}{2}z^2V_{n-1}&=-y^2\frac{\partial V_n}{\partial y}-\tfrac{1}{2}y^2V_{n+1}.\end{aligned}\right\} \tag{24}$$

Now, if u be a function of y, we have

$$\frac{\partial^m(y^2u)}{\partial y^m}=(m-1)m\frac{\partial^{m-2}u}{\partial y^{m-2}}+2my\frac{\partial^{m-1}u}{\partial y^{m-1}}+y^2\frac{\partial^m u}{\partial y^m}.$$

Using this theorem we find by successive differentiation of (24)

$$\begin{aligned}\tfrac{1}{2}z^2\frac{\partial^m U_{n+1}}{\partial y^m}=y^2&\left(\frac{\partial^{m+1}U_n}{\partial y^{m+1}}-\frac{1}{2}\frac{\partial^m U_{n-1}}{\partial y^m}\right)\\ &+2my\left(\frac{\partial^m U_n}{\partial y^m}-\frac{1}{2}\frac{\partial^{m-1}U_{n-1}}{\partial y^{m-1}}\right)\\ &+(m-1)m\left(\frac{\partial^{m-1}U_n}{\partial y^{m-1}}-\frac{1}{2}\frac{\partial^{m-2}U_{n-1}}{\partial y^{m-2}}\right),\end{aligned} \tag{25}$$

$$\begin{aligned}-\tfrac{1}{2}z^2\frac{\partial^m V_{n-1}}{\partial y^m}=y^2&\left(\frac{\partial^{m+1}V_n}{\partial y^{m+1}}+\frac{1}{2}\frac{\partial^m V_{n+1}}{\partial y^m}\right)\\ &+2my\left(\frac{\partial^m V_n}{\partial y^m}+\frac{1}{2}\frac{\partial^{m-1}V_{n+1}}{\partial y^{m-1}}\right)\\ &+(m-1)m\left(\frac{\partial^{m-1}V_n}{\partial y^{m-1}}+\frac{1}{2}\frac{\partial^{m-2}V_{n+1}}{\partial y^{m-2}}\right).\end{aligned} \tag{26}$$

If we consider y as a function of z, then

$$\frac{dU_n}{dz}=\frac{\partial U_n}{\partial z}+\frac{\partial U_n}{\partial y}\frac{dy}{dz}.$$

If $y=cz$,

$$\frac{dU_n}{dz}=\tfrac{1}{2}\left(cU_{n-1}-\frac{1}{c}U_{n+1}\right),$$

by (16) and (24) above. By successive differentiation, and application of this result, we obtain

$$\frac{d^2 U_n}{dz^2} = \tfrac{1}{4}\left(c^2 U_{n-2} - 2U_n + \frac{1}{c^2} U_{n+2}\right),$$

and generally

$$\frac{d^m U_n}{dz^m} = \frac{1}{2^m} \Sigma (-1)^p \frac{m(m-1)\dots(m-p+1)}{p!} c^{m-2p} U_{n-m+2p}. \quad (27)$$

Similarly it can be shown that

$$\frac{d^m V_n}{dz^m} = \frac{1}{2^m} \Sigma (-1)^p \frac{m(m-1)\dots(m-p+1)}{p!} c^{-m+2p} V_{n-m+2p}. \quad (28)$$

The calculation of the differential coefficients can be carried out by these formulae with the assistance of (14), which now become

$$\left.\begin{aligned} U_n + U_{n+2} &= c^n J_n(z), \\ V_n + V_{n+2} &= \frac{1}{c^n} J_n(z). \end{aligned}\right\} \quad (29)$$

§ 3. **Bessel Function Integrals expressed in Terms of *U* and *V* Functions.** We conclude this analytical discussion with some theorems in which definite integrals involving Bessel Functions are expressed in terms of the *U* and *V* functions.

By (1) above we have

$$C = \frac{b^2 \lambda^2}{2\pi \zeta^2} \int_0^z \cos \tfrac{1}{2}\psi \, . \, x J_0(x)\, dx.$$

Now let $x = zu$, then

$$\tfrac{1}{2}\psi = \tfrac{1}{2} y \frac{x^2}{z^2} = \tfrac{1}{2} y u^2;$$

therefore, since $z^2 = 4\pi^2 \zeta^2 r^2 / (\lambda^2 b^2)$,

$$C = 2\pi r^2 \int_0^1 \cos(\tfrac{1}{2} y u^2) \, . \, u J_0(zu)\, du. \quad (30)$$

Similarly we obtain

$$S = 2\pi r^2 \int_0^1 \sin(\tfrac{1}{2} y u^2) \, . \, u J_0(zu)\, du. \quad (31)$$

But equations (4) and (5) give

$$C \cos \tfrac{1}{2} y + S \sin \tfrac{1}{2} y = \frac{\pi r^2}{\tfrac{1}{2} y} U_1,$$

$$C \sin \tfrac{1}{2} y - S \cos \tfrac{1}{2} y = \frac{\pi r^2}{\tfrac{1}{2} y} U_2,$$

and these, by (30) and (31), give the equations

$$\left.\begin{aligned}\int_0^1 J_0(zu)\,.\cos\{\tfrac{1}{2}y(1-u^2)\}\,.\,u\,du &= \frac{1}{y}U_1,\\ \int_0^1 J_0(zu)\,.\sin\{\tfrac{1}{2}y(1-u^2)\}\,.\,u\,du &= \frac{1}{y}U_2.\end{aligned}\right\} \tag{32}$$

Differentiating with respect to z we get, since

$$J_0'(z) = -J_1(z),$$

$$\int_0^1 J_1(zu)\cos\{\tfrac{1}{2}y(1-u^2)\}\,.\,u^2du = -\frac{1}{y}\frac{\partial U_1}{\partial z}$$

$$= \frac{z}{y^2}U_2, \text{ by (16)};$$

and similarly

$$\int_0^1 J_1(zu)\sin\{\tfrac{1}{2}y(1-u^2)\}\,.\,u^2du = \frac{z}{y^2}U_3.$$

Now, if we assume

$$\int_0^1 J_{n-1}(zu)\,.\cos\{\tfrac{1}{2}y(1-u^2)\}\,.\,u^n du = \frac{1}{y}\left(\frac{z}{y}\right)^{n-1}U_n \tag{33}$$

and differentiate, making use of the relation (II. 20)

$$J'_{n-1}(zu) = \frac{n-1}{zu}J_{n-1}(zu) - J_n(zu),$$

we easily obtain

$$\int_0^1 J_n(zu)\cos\{\tfrac{1}{2}y(1-u^2)\}\,.\,u^{n+1}du = \frac{1}{y}\left(\frac{z}{y}\right)^n U_{n+1}.$$

Thus, if the theorem (33) hold for any integral value of n it holds for $n+1$. But as we have seen above it holds for $n=1$; it therefore holds for all integral values of n.

Similarly we obtain

$$\int_0^1 J_{n-2}(zu)\sin\{\tfrac{1}{2}y(1-u^2)\}\,u^{n-1}du = \frac{1}{y}\left(\frac{z}{y}\right)^{n-2}U_n. \tag{34}$$

The values of C in (6) and (30) give

$$\int_0^1 \cos\tfrac{1}{2}yu^2\,.\,uJ_0(zu)\,du = \frac{1}{y}\sin\frac{z^2}{2y} + \frac{\sin\frac{1}{2}y}{y}V_0 - \frac{\cos\frac{1}{2}y}{y}V_1. \tag{35}$$

Similarly those of S in (8) and (31) give

$$\int_0^1 \sin\tfrac{1}{2}yu^2\,.\,uJ_0(zu)\,du = \frac{1}{y}\cos\frac{z^2}{2y} - \frac{\cos\frac{1}{2}y}{y}V_0 - \frac{\sin\frac{1}{2}y}{y}V. \tag{36}$$

If instead of u we use the variable $\rho(=ur)$, where r is the radius of the orifice, and write $y=kr^2$, $z=lr$, so that

$$k=\frac{2\pi}{\lambda}\cdot\frac{a+b}{ab}, \quad l=\frac{2\pi}{\lambda}\cdot\frac{\zeta}{b},$$

we have instead of (35), (36)

$$\int_0^r J_0(l\rho)\cos(\tfrac{1}{2}k\rho^2)\,.\,\rho\,d\rho=\frac{1}{k}\sin\frac{l^2}{2k}+\frac{1}{k}\sin(\tfrac{1}{2}kr^2)\,V_0-\frac{1}{k}\cos(\tfrac{1}{2}kr^2)\,V_1,$$

$$\int_0^r J_0(l\rho)\sin(\tfrac{1}{2}k\rho^2)\,.\,\rho\,d\rho=\frac{1}{k}\cos\frac{l^2}{2k}-\frac{1}{k}\cos(\tfrac{1}{2}kr^2)\,V_0-\frac{1}{k}\sin(\tfrac{1}{2}kr^2)\,V_1.$$

If now r be made infinite while l and k do not vanish, V_0 and V_1 vanish, and we have

$$\left.\begin{aligned}\int_0^\infty J_0(l\rho)\cos(\tfrac{1}{2}k\rho^2)\,.\,\rho\,d\rho&=\frac{1}{k}\sin\frac{l^2}{2k},\\ \int_0^\infty J_0(l\rho)\sin(\tfrac{1}{2}k\rho^2)\,.\,\rho\,d\rho&=\frac{1}{k}\cos\frac{l^2}{2k},\end{aligned}\right\}\qquad(37)$$

formulae which will be found useful in what follows [see also (51) below]. They are special cases of more general theorems which can easily be obtained by successive differentiation.

§ 4. **Two Cases of Diffraction: Case (1), $y=0$.** We come now to the application of these results to the problem stated above. Of this problem there are two cases which may be distinguished, (1) that in which $y=0$, (2) that in which y does not vanish. The first case is that of Fraunhofer's diffraction phenomena, and has received much attention. We shall consider it specially here, and afterwards pass on to the more general case (2).

When $y=0$, either $a=\infty$ and $b=\infty$, or $a=-b$. In the former case the wave incident on the orifice is plane, and the parallel screen on which the light from the orifice falls is at a very great distance from the orifice. This arrangement, as Lommel points out, is realised when the interference phenomena are observed with a spectrometer, the telescope and collimator of which are adjusted for parallel rays. The orifice is placed between the collimator and the telescope at right angles to the parallel beam produced by the former.

When $a=-b$, a may be either positive or negative. When a is negative the orifice is to be supposed illuminated by light converging *to* the point-source, and the screen is there situated with its plane at right angles to the axis of symmetry.

This can be realised at once by producing a converging beam of light by means of a convex lens, and then introducing the orifice between the lens and the screen, which now coincides with the focal plane of the lens.

When a is positive, and therefore b negative, the light-wave falls on the orifice, with its front convex towards the direction of propagation. The interference is then to be considered as produced on a screen passing through the source, and at right angles to the line joining the source with the centre of the orifice. This case can be virtually realised by receiving the light from the opening by an eye focused on the source. The diffraction pattern is then produced on the retina. Or, a convex lens may be placed at a greater distance from the source than the principal focal distance of the lens, so as to receive the light after having passed the orifice, and the screen in the focal plane of the lens.

The screen may be examined by the naked eye or through a magnifying lens. If a magnifying lens is used the arrangement is equivalent to a telescope focused upon the point-source, with the opening in front of the object-glass. This is Fraunhofer's arrangement; and we shall obtain the theory of the phenomena observed by him if we put $y=0$ in the above theoretical investigation.

Putting $y=0$ in (3), we have

$$\frac{2}{y}U_1=\frac{2}{z}J_1(z), \quad \frac{2}{y}U_2=0,$$

so that, writing M^2 for C^2+S^2, we obtain, with $\pi r^2=1$,

$$M^2=\left\{\frac{2}{z}J_1(z)\right\}^2. \tag{38}$$

Airy gave* for the same quantity the expression, in the present notation,

$$\left\{1-\frac{z^2}{2.4}+\frac{z^4}{2.4.4.6}-\frac{z^6}{2.4.4.6.6.8}+\dots\right\}^2,$$

which is simply the quantity on the right of (38).

By means of Tables of Bessel Functions the value of M can be found with the greatest ease, by simply doubling the value of J_1 for any given argument, and dividing the result by the argument. The result is shown graphically in Fig. 7.

* *Camb. Phil. Trans.* p. 283, 1834.

The maxima of light intensity are at those points for which $J_1(z)/z$ is a maximum or a minimum. The minima are those points for which $J_1(z)=0$. Now when $J_1(z)/z$ is a maximum or a minimum,

$$\frac{\partial}{\partial z}\left\{\frac{1}{z}J_1(z)\right\}=0.$$

But

$$\frac{1}{z}J_1'(z)-\frac{J_1(z)}{z^2}=-\frac{1}{z}J_2(z),$$

so that the condition becomes

$$J_2(z)=0,$$

which (II. 26) is equivalent to

$$\frac{2}{z}J_1(z)-J_0(z)=0.$$

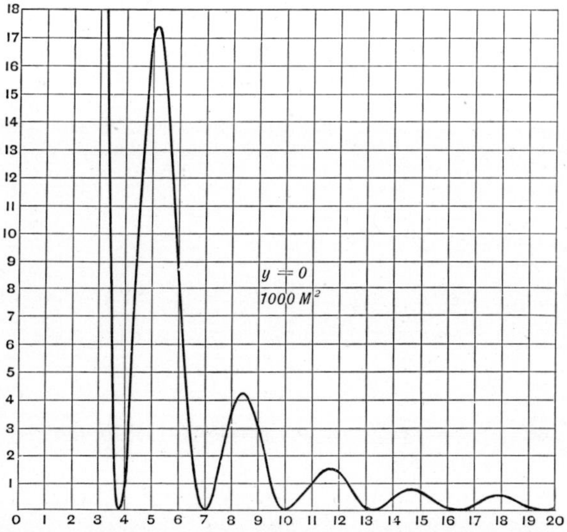

FIG. 7.

Thus when the maxima and minima values of $2J_1(z)/z$ have been calculated, their accuracy may be checked by observing whether they are also the values of $J_0(z)$ given in the Table for the same arguments. Or the arguments, which are the roots of $J_2(z)=0$, having been obtained, the corresponding values of $2J_1(z)/z$ are given by the Table of $J_0(z)$ either directly or by interpolation.

Places of maximum intensity alternate with places at which the intensity is zero, the light being supposed of definite wave-length, and therefore monochromatic. The roots of $J_1(z)=0$, which are the values of z for which the intensity is zero, can be calculated by the formula given at p. 87 above (Chap. VII.). It is there shown that the approximate value of the large roots of $J_1(z)=0$ is $(m+\frac{1}{4})\pi$, and of $J_2(z)=0$ is $(m+\frac{3}{4})\pi$, where m is the number of the root. Hence for great values of z the difference between the values of z for successive maxima or minima is approximately π, and the difference for a zero and the next following maximum is $\frac{1}{2}\pi$. The rings are thus ultimately equidistant.

The difference of path of the rays from opposite extremities of a diameter of the orifice to the point P is $2r\tan^{-1}\zeta/b$, that is $2r\zeta/b$ or $\lambda z/\pi$. The distance in wave-lengths is therefore z/π.

The following Table gives the values of z corresponding to maximum and zero values of $2z^{-1}J_1(z)$, which are contained in col. 2. Col. 3 contains the corresponding values of M^2.

z (roots of $J_2(z)=0$ and of $z^{-1}J_1(z)=0$)	$2z^{-1}J_1(z)$	M^2
0	+1	1
3·831706	0	0
5·135630	− 0·132279	0·017498
7·015587	0	0
8·417236	+ 0·064482	0·004158
10·173468	0	0
11·619857	− 0·040008	0·001601
13·323692	0	0
14·795938	+ 0·027919	0·000779
16·470630	0	0
17·959820	− 0·020905	0·000437
19·615859	0	0

For large values of z the asymptotic expansion of $J_1(z)$ (p. 57 above) is available. As z increases this expansion gives more and more approximately

$$\frac{2}{z}J_1(z)=\frac{2}{z}\sqrt{\frac{2}{z\pi}}\sin(z-\tfrac{1}{4}\pi),$$

and therefore

$$M^2 = \frac{8}{\pi z^3} \sin^2 (z - \tfrac{1}{4}\pi).$$

As the value of z approaches $(m + \frac{3}{4})\pi$, that of $\sin^2(z - \frac{1}{4}\pi)$ approaches 1, and so the ultimate maximum value of $M^2 z^3$ is $8/\pi$.

The whole light received within a circle of radius ζ is proportional to

$$\int_0^z M^2 z\, dz = 4 \int_0^z z^{-1} J_1^2(z)\, dz.$$

But
$$\frac{J_1^2(z)}{z} = \{J_0(z) - J_1'(z)\} J_1(z)$$
$$= -J_0(z) J_0'(z) - J_1(z) J_1'(z).$$

Hence
$$\int_0^z M^2 z\, dz = 2\{1 - J_0^2(z) - J_1^2(z)\}. \tag{39}$$

If z is made infinite the expression in the brackets becomes 1. Hence, as has been pointed out by Lord Rayleigh*, the fraction of the total illumination outside any value of z is $J_0^2(z) + J_1^2(z)$. But at a dark ring $J_1(z) = 0$, so that the fraction of the whole light outside any dark ring is $J_0^2(z)$. The values of this fraction for the successive roots of $J_1(z) = 0$ are approximately ·162, ·090, ·062 ·048, ..., so that more than $\frac{9}{10}$ of the whole light is received within the second dark ring.

§ 5. **Case (2), y not zero.** In the more general case of diffraction, contemplated by Fresnel, y is not zero, and we have $(\pi r^2 = 1)$

$$M^2 = \left(\frac{2}{y}\right)^2 (U_1^2 + U_2^2), \tag{40}$$

and U_1, U_2 can be calculated by the formulae given above from the Tables of Bessel Functions at the end of the present volume, equation (3) being used if $z > y$, and (9), with the expansions of V_0 and V_1, if $z < y$.

The maximum and minimum values of M^2 are given in the Table below for the values of y $(y < z)$ stated. We also give here some diagrams showing the forms of the intensity curve for the same values of y. The curves are drawn with values of z as abscissae, and of M^2 as ordinates.

* *Phil. Mag.*, March, 1881; or 'Wave Theory of Light,' *Encyc. Brit.*, 9th Edition, p. 433; *Collected Papers*, I., p. 513.

$y=\pi$.

z	$\frac{2}{y}U_1$	$\frac{2}{y}U_2$	M^2	
3·831706	−0·122609	+0·106159	0·026305	Min.
4·715350	−0·178789	0	0·031966	Max.
7·015587	+0·013239	−0·040631	0·001826	Min.
8·306007	+0·074093	0	0·005490	Max.
10·173467	−0·002313	+0·016225	0·000269	Min.
11·578479	−0·043104	0	0·001858	Max.

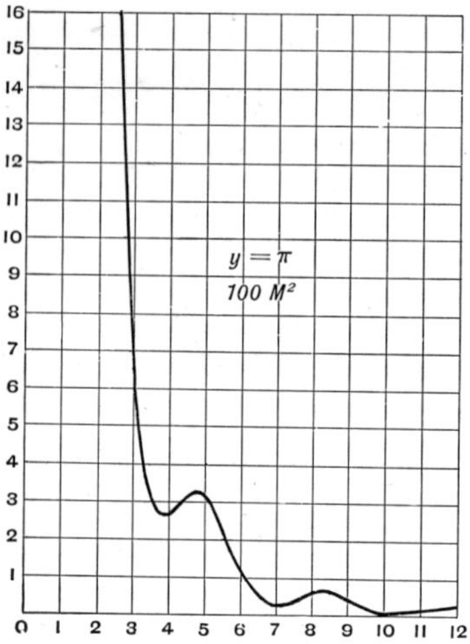

FIG. 8.

$y=5\pi$.

z	$\frac{2}{y}U_1$	$\frac{2}{y}U_2$	M^2	
3·030827	+0·114161	0	0·013033	Min.
3·625773	+0·114593	0	0·013132	Max.
3·831706	+0·114492	+0·004496	0·013128	Min.
7·015587	−0·002099	+0·173617	0·030147	Max.
9·440724	−0·134688	0	0·018141	Min.
10·173467	−0·118330	−0·067421	0·018548	Max.

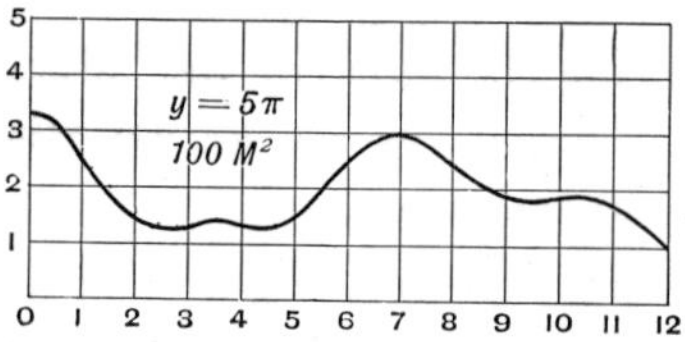

FIG. 9.

$y = 9\pi$.

z	$\frac{2}{y}U_1$	$\frac{2}{y}U_2$	M^2	
2·649454	+0·067178	0	0·004513	Min.
3·831706	+0·068485	−0·010782	0·004806	Max.
4·431978	+0·068964	0	0·004756	Min.
7·015587	+0·045384	+0·076624	0·007931	Max.
10·173467	−0·017711	+0·048204	0·002637	Min.

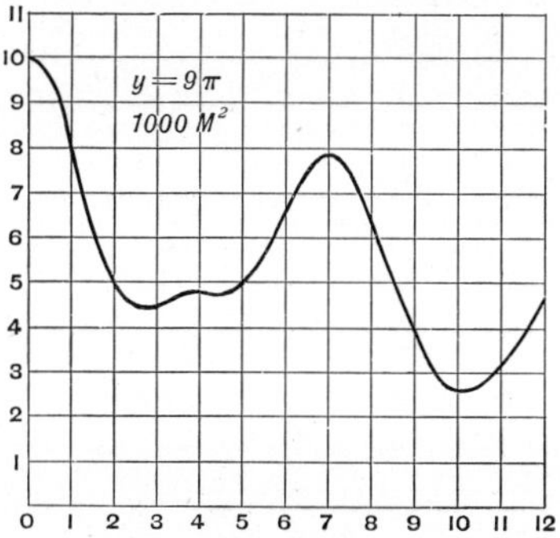

FIG. 10.

The maximum and minimum values of M^2 are those for which

$$\frac{\partial M^2}{\partial z} = 0.$$

But, by (16) and (14),

$$\begin{aligned}\frac{\partial M^2}{\partial z} &= 2\left(\frac{2}{y}\right)^2\left(U_1\frac{\partial U_1}{\partial z} + U_2\frac{\partial U_2}{\partial z}\right)\\ &= -\left(\frac{2}{y}\right)^2\frac{2z}{y}U_2(U_1+U_3)\\ &= -2\left(\frac{2}{y}\right)^2 J_1(z)U_2.\end{aligned} \qquad (41)$$

Hence a maximum or a minimum is obtained when either

$$\left.\begin{aligned} &J_1(z)[=-J_0'(z)]=0\\ \text{or}\quad &U_2 = -\frac{y}{z}\frac{\partial U_1}{\partial z} = 0.\end{aligned}\right\} \qquad (42)$$

Thus a value of z which gives a maximum or minimum of $J_0(z)$ or of $U_1(z)$ gives either a maximum or minimum of M^2. The roots of $J_1(z)=0$ are given at the end of this treatise, and are values of z which give a maximum or minimum of illumination. The values of $2U_1/y$, $2U_2/y$ which correspond to these values of z, are obtained by interpolation from those of U_1, U_2 or V_0, V_1 for the values of z for which Tables of Bessel Functions are available. The formulae of interpolation are (22), (23) above.

The maxima and minima which arise through the vanishing of U_2 are found in a similar manner. Supposing it is required to find the roots of U_2, the tabular value of $U_2(z)$ nearest to a zero value is taken, and the value of $z+h$ which causes U_2 to vanish is found by means of the expression on the right of (22) equated to zero, with 2 put for n, that is from the equation

$$U_2(z)-\frac{h(2z+h)}{2y}U_3(z)+\frac{1}{2!}\frac{h^2(2z+h)^2}{(2y)^2}U_4(z)-\ldots=0. \qquad (43)$$

Since the series is very convergent only a few terms need be retained; and the value of $h(2z+h)/2y$ found, and therefore that of h.

Values of z which render $U_2=0$, being thus found, those of $2U_1/y$ for the same arguments are calculated. The squares of these are the values of M^2 which correspond to the roots of $U_2=0$. Elaborate Tables, each accompanied by a graphical representation of the results, are given by Lommel in his memoir. The short Tables with illustrative diagrams given above will serve as a specimen. These diagrams are not minutely accurate.

§ 6. **Graphical Method of finding Situations of Maxima and Minima.** We conclude the discussion of this case of diffraction with an account of Lommel's graphical method of finding, for different values of y, the values of z which give maxima or minima. This is shown in the next diagram (Fig. 11). The axis of ordinates is that of y, and the axis of abscissae that of z. Lines parallel to the axis of y are drawn for the values of z which satisfy $J_1(z)=0$. These are called the lines $J_1(z)=0$. On the same diagram are drawn the curves $U_2/y^2=0$. These are transcendental curves having double points on the axis $z=0$, as will be seen from the short discussion below.

Let now the edge of a sheet of paper be kept parallel to the axis of z and be moved along the diagram from bottom to top. It will intersect all the curves. The distances from the axis of y along the edge of the paper in any of its positions to the points of intersection are values of z, for the value of y for that position, which satisfy (41); and are therefore values of z which with that value of y give maximum or minimum values of M^2.

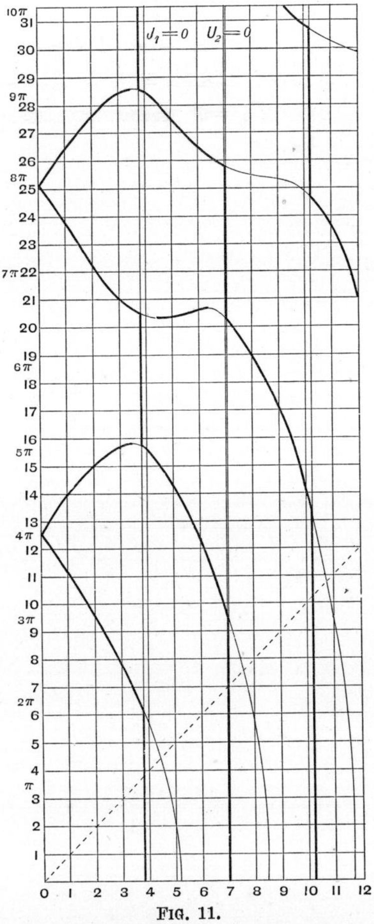

FIG. 11.

The equation of the curve $U_2=0$ differentiated gives

$$\frac{\partial U_2}{\partial z}+\frac{\partial U_2}{\partial y}\frac{dy}{dz}=0,$$

that is, since by (16) and (24) above,

$$\partial U_2/\partial z=-U_3\,.\,z/y,$$
$$\partial U_2/\partial y=\tfrac{1}{2}U_1+\tfrac{1}{2}U_3\,.\,(z/y)^2;$$

$$\frac{dy}{dz}=2\frac{z}{y}\frac{U_3}{U_1+\left(\frac{z}{y}\right)^2 U_3}. \tag{44}$$

When $z=0$, that is where the curve meets the axis of y, $V_0=1$, $V_1=0$, so that by (9),

$$U_1=\sin\tfrac{1}{2}y,$$
$$U_2=1-\cos\tfrac{1}{2}y.$$

Thus $U_2=0$, whenever $\cos\frac{1}{2}y=1$, that is when $\frac{1}{2}y=2m\pi$, or $y=4m\pi$. The curve $U_2=0$ therefore meets the axis of y at every multiple of 4π.

But this value of y makes U_1 and likewise

$$U_3 \,.\, z/y \;\;\{=J_1(z)-U_1 \,.\, z/y\}$$

zero, so that

$$\frac{\partial U_2}{\partial z}=0, \quad \frac{\partial U_2}{\partial y}=0.$$

The value of dy/dz is therefore indeterminate at the points on the axis of y, that is each point in which the curve meets the axis of y is a double point.

If y', z' be current coordinates the equation of the pair of tangents at a double point is

$$z'^2\frac{\partial^2 U_2}{\partial z^2}+2z'(y'-y)\frac{\partial^2 U_2}{\partial y\,\partial z}+(y'-y)^2\frac{\partial^2 U_2}{\partial y^2}=0. \qquad (45)$$

It is very easy to verify by differentiation and use of the properties of the functions that when $z=0$ and $y=4m\pi$,

$$\frac{\partial^2 U_2}{\partial z^2}=-\tfrac{1}{2}, \quad \frac{\partial^2 U_2}{\partial y\,\partial z}=0, \quad \frac{\partial^2 U_2}{\partial y^2}=\tfrac{1}{4},$$

so that the equation of the tangents reduces to

$$(y'-4m\pi)^2=2z'^2.$$

Thus the equations of the tangents are

$$y'-4m\pi=\sqrt{2}z', \quad y'-4m\pi=-\sqrt{2}z',$$

and their inclinations to the axis of z are given by

$$\tan\phi=\pm\sqrt{2},$$

that is

$$\phi=\pm 54^\circ\, 44'\, 8''{\cdot}2.$$

Where the curve meets the axis of z we may regard $U_2=0$ as equivalent to the two equations $y^2=0$, $U_2/y^2=0$, so that the curve $U_2=0$ splits into two straight lines coincident with the axis of z, and the curve represented by

$$\frac{1}{y^2}U_2=0.$$

We have, by (3),

$$\frac{\partial}{\partial y}\left(\frac{1}{y^2}U_2\right)=-2\frac{y}{z^4}J_4(z)+4\frac{y^3}{z^6}J_6(z)-\ldots$$

Hence for the last curve

$$\frac{dy}{dz} = -\frac{\dfrac{\partial}{\partial z}\left(\dfrac{1}{y^2}U_2\right)}{\dfrac{\partial}{\partial y}\left(\dfrac{1}{y^2}U_2\right)} = \frac{\dfrac{z}{y^3}U_3}{0} = \infty,$$

when $y=0$. Thus the branches of the curve $U_2/y^2=0$ cut the axis of abscissae at right angles, as shown in Fig. 11. We shall see below that this intersection takes place at points satisfying the equation $J_2(z)=0$. Thus the curves U_2/y^2, when $y=0$, touch the curves $J_2(z)=0$.

It will be seen from the curves in the diagram that the value of dy/dz is negative so long at least as $y<z$, that is, as we shall see, within the region of the curve corresponding to the geometrical shadow. But at points along a line $J_1(z)=0$,

$$\frac{dy}{dz} = -\frac{2\dfrac{z}{y}}{1-\left(\dfrac{z}{y}\right)^2},$$

and is positive so long as $z>y$, that is also within the region of the geometrical shadow. Hence no intersection of a line $J_1(z)=0$ with the other curves can exist in the region of the diagram corresponding to the geometrical shadow.

To settle where the maxima and minima are we have to calculate $\partial^2 M^2/\partial z^2$. Now

$$\frac{\partial^2 M^2}{\partial z^2} = -2\left(\frac{2}{y}\right)^2 \frac{\partial}{\partial z}(J_1 U_2)$$

$$= 2\left(\frac{2}{y}\right)^2 \left\{\frac{1}{z}J_1 U_2 - J_0 U_2 + J_1\left(J_1 - \frac{z}{y}U_1\right)\right\}. \qquad (46)$$

Thus considering first points upon the lines $J_1=0$, we have a maximum or a minimum according as $J_0 U_2$ is positive or negative.

On the other hand, when $U_2=0$ the points on the curves $U_2=0$ are maxima or minima according as $J_1 U_3 z/y$ $\{=J_1(J_1-U_1 z/y)\}$ is negative or positive, or as

$$J_1^2 < \text{ or } > \frac{z}{y}U_1 J_1.$$

Calculating $\partial^3 M^2/\partial z^3$ we see that this does not vanish for points satisfying the equations $J_1(z)=0$, $U_2=0$, that is wherever a line $J_1(z)=0$ and a curve $U_2=0$ intersect there is a point of inflexion of the curve of intensity, drawn with M^2 as ordinates and values of z as abscissae.

It follows by the statement above as to the inclination of the curve within the region corresponding to the geometrical shadow, that within that region there can be no point of inflexion on the intensity-curve.

Also, as can easily be verified, there are points of inflexion of the intensity-curve, wherever the curve $U_2/y^2=0$ has a maximum or minimum ordinate.

Referring now to Fig. 11, we can see how to indicate the points where there are maxima and minima. For pass along a line $J_1=0$ until a branch of the curve $U_2/y^2=0$ is crossed. Here clearly U_2 changes sign, while $J_0(z)$ does not. Thus $J_0(z)U_2$ changes sign, and so all points of a portion of a curve $J_1(z)=0$, intercepted between branches of the other curve, give maxima, or give minima, according to the number of branches of the latter which have been crossed to reach that portion by proceeding along $J_1(z)=0$ from the axis of z. $J_0(z)U_2$ is negative for the first portion, positive for the second, and so on, the number of crossings being 0, 1, 2, ...

If we pass along a curve $U_2/y^2=0$ and cross $J_1(z)=0$, then $J_1(z)$ changes sign, but not so U_3; for by (14) when $J_1(z)=0$, $U_3=-U_1$, and U_1 is a maximum or a minimum, since $U_2=0$. But it must be further noticed that when for a branch of the curve $U_2/y^2=0$ the value of dy/dz is zero, that is when $U_3z/y=0$, U_3 changes sign while $J_1(z)$ does not; also for $U_3=0$,

$$J_1(z)=\frac{z}{y}U_1,$$

and because of $U_2=0$, $\partial U_1/\partial z=0$, so that U_1 is a maximum or a minimum. At these points therefore $\partial^2 M^2/\partial z^2$ changes sign, and hence they also separate regions of the curve $U_2/y^2=0$ which give maxima from those which give minima, when the process described above of using the diagram is carried out.

The first three successive differential coefficients of M^2 all vanish when $z=0$ and $y=4m\pi$, that is at the double points, and as there, as the reader may verify,

$$\frac{\partial^4 M^2}{\partial z^4}=\frac{3}{2}\frac{1}{4m^2\pi^2},$$

the double points are places of minimum (zero) value of M^2.

The regions of the curves $U_2/y^2=0$ can now, starting from the double points, be easily identified as regions which give maxima or minima when the diagram is used in the manner described above. To mark regions which give minima they are ruled heavy in the diagram; the other regions, which give maxima, are ruled light.

Thus the first regions from the double points to a maximum or minimum of the curve, or to a point of crossing of $J_1(z)=0$, whichever comes first, are ruled heavy, then the region from that point to the next point at which U_3 changes sign is ruled light, and so on.

The lower regions of the curves $J_1(z)=0$, from the axis of z to the points of meeting with $U_2/y^2=0$, are ruled heavy; the next regions, from the first points of crossing to the second, light, and so on alternately. Thus the whole diagram is filled in.

As we have seen,

$$U_2=V_0-\cos\left(\tfrac{1}{2}y+\frac{z^2}{2y}\right)=J_0(z)-\left(\frac{z}{y}\right)^2 J_2(z)+\ldots-\cos\left(\tfrac{1}{2}y+\frac{z^2}{2y}\right).$$

Hence as y increases in comparison with z, the equation

$$U_2=J_0(z)-\cos\tfrac{1}{2}y$$

more and more nearly holds. The reader may verify that the curve $J_0(z)-\cos\frac{1}{2}y=0$ meets the axis of y at the same points as the exact curve, and has there the same double tangents.

On the other hand, if y be made smaller in comparison with z, then by (3) we have more and more nearly

$$\frac{2}{y}U_1=\frac{2}{z}J_1(z),\quad \frac{2}{y}U_2=2\frac{y}{z^2}J_2(z),$$

so that the branches of $U_2/y^2=0$ approach more and more nearly to the lines $J_2(z)=0$. Thus we verify the statement made at p. 199 above.

The value of M^2, namely

$$\left(\frac{2}{y}\right)^2(U_1^2+U_2^2),$$

with increasing z and stationary y, that is with increasing obliquity of the rays, approaches zero. Hence at a great distance from the geometrical image of the orifice the illumination is practically zero.

Consider a line drawn in the diagram to fulfil the equation $y=cz$. A line making the same angle with the axis of y would have the equation $y=\frac{1}{c}z$. Let us consider the intensities for points on these two lines.

Since $y/z=c$ for the first, (3) and (9) give for any point on that line

$$\left.\begin{aligned}U_1&=cJ_1-c^3J_3+\ldots\\&=\sin\left\{\tfrac{1}{2}z\left(c+\frac{1}{c}\right)\right\}-\left(\frac{1}{c}J_1-\frac{1}{c^3}J_3+\frac{1}{c^5}J_5-\ldots\right),\\U_2&=c^2J_2-c^4J_4+\ldots\\&=-\cos\left\{\tfrac{1}{2}z\left(c+\frac{1}{c}\right)\right\}+J_0-\frac{1}{c^2}J_2+\frac{1}{c^4}J_4-\ldots.\end{aligned}\right\}\quad(47)$$

For the other line we have, accenting the functions for distinction,

$$\left.\begin{aligned}U_1'&=\frac{1}{c}J_1-\frac{1}{c^3}J_3+\ldots\\&=\sin\left\{\tfrac{1}{2}z\left(c+\frac{1}{c}\right)\right\}-(cJ_1-c^3J_3+c^5J_5-\ldots),\\U_2'&=\frac{1}{c^2}J_2-\frac{1}{c^4}J_4+\ldots\\&=-\cos\left\{\tfrac{1}{2}z\left(c+\frac{1}{c}\right)\right\}+J_0-c^2J_2+c^4J_4-\ldots.\end{aligned}\right\}\quad(47')$$

Therefore
$$\left.\begin{aligned}U_1+U_1'&=\sin\left\{\tfrac{1}{2}z\left(c+\frac{1}{c}\right)\right\},\\U_2+U_2'&=J_0(z)-\cos\left\{\tfrac{1}{2}z\left(c+\frac{1}{c}\right)\right\}.\end{aligned}\right\}\quad(48)$$

Now if the radius of the geometrical shadow be ζ_0, then

$$\zeta_0=(a+b)r/a,$$

and
$$\frac{y}{z}=\frac{\zeta_0}{\zeta}=c.$$

If ζ' be the distance of a point of the illuminated area upon the other line $y=z/c$, we have evidently

$$\zeta\zeta'=\zeta_0^2.$$

As special cases of these lines we have $z=0$, or the axis of y, $y=0$ or the axis of z, and $y=z$. The last is dotted in the diagram, and by the result just stated corresponds to the edge of the geometrical shadow.

The intensities for points along the first line are the intensities at the axis of symmetry for different radii of the orifice, or with constant radius for different values of b, the distance of the screen from the orifice. Those for points along the second line are the intensities for the case of Fraunhofer, already fully considered.

In the first case we have, by (20), since $z=0$,

$$U_1=\sin\tfrac{1}{2}y,\quad U_2=2\sin^2\tfrac{1}{4}y,$$

so that

$$M^2=\left(\frac{2}{y}\right)^2(U_1^2+U_2^2)$$

$$=\left(\frac{\sin\frac{1}{4}y}{\frac{1}{4}y}\right)^2. \tag{49}$$

This is the expression for the intensity at a point of a screen, produced by diffraction through a narrow slit, $\frac{1}{4}y$ in that case denoting $2\pi a\xi/(\lambda f)$, where a is the half breadth of the slit, f the distance of the illuminated point from the slit, and ξ the distance of the point from the geometrical image of the slit on the screen. Thus Tables, which have been prepared for the calculation of the brightness in the latter case, are available also for calculating the brightness at the centre of the geometrical image of the circular orifice.

The intensity is zero when $\frac{1}{4}y=m\pi$ (m being any whole number, zero excluded), that is when the difference of path between the extreme and central rays is a whole number of wave-lengths. It is a maximum when $\tan\frac{1}{4}y=\frac{1}{4}y$, or

$$\tan\left(\frac{\pi}{\lambda}\frac{a+b}{2ab}r^2\right)=\frac{\pi}{\lambda}\frac{a+b}{2ab}r^2.$$

Some values are given in the following Table:

$z=0$.

$\frac{1}{4}y$	$M^2=\left(\frac{\sin\frac{1}{4}y}{\frac{1}{4}y}\right)^2$
0·000000	1·000000
4·493409	0·047190
7·725252	0·016480
10·904120	0·008340
14·066194	0·005029
17·220753	0·003361
20·371302	0·002404
23·519446	0·001805
26·666054	0·001404

As y increases these values of $\frac{1}{4}y$ are given approximately by the equations

$$\tfrac{1}{4}y=\frac{2m+1}{2}\pi,$$

or
$$\left(\frac{1}{a}+\frac{1}{b}\right)\frac{r^2}{2}=\frac{2m+1}{2}\lambda,$$

that is the difference of path between the extreme and central rays is an odd number of half wave-lengths. The maximum intensity is then $16/y^2$, that is (as will be shown presently) four times the intensity at the screen due to the uninterrupted wave.

For the line $y=z$ in the diagram which corresponds to the edge of the geometrical shadow, we have, by (13), since z is small,

$$U_1=\frac{1}{2}\sin z,$$

$$U_2=\frac{1}{2}(J_0(z)-\cos z),$$

so that
$$M^2=\frac{1}{z^2}\{\sin^2 z+(J_0(z)-\cos z)^2\}. \qquad (50)$$

Clearly M^2 cannot vanish unless $\sin z$ and $J_0(z)-\cos z$ vanish separately, that is unless $J_0(z)=1$, which is impossible unless $z=0$.

§ 7. **Case when Orifice is replaced by an Opaque Disk.** It remains finally to find the illumination at a point on the screen when the orifice is replaced by an opaque disk, all the rest of the wave being allowed to pass unimpeded. Going back to the original expressions, obtained at p. 180 above for the intensity, we see that for the total effect of the uninterrupted wave we have, by (1) and (2),

$$\left.\begin{aligned} C_\infty&=2\pi\int_0^\infty J_0(l\rho)\cos(\tfrac{1}{2}k\rho^2)\,\rho\,d\rho=\pi\frac{2}{k}\sin\frac{l^2}{2k},\\ S_\infty&=2\pi\int_0^\infty J_0(l\rho)\sin(\tfrac{1}{2}k\rho^2)\,\rho\,d\rho=\pi\frac{2}{k}\cos\frac{l^2}{2k},\end{aligned}\right\} \qquad (51)$$

as in (37).

Thus we get
$$M^2=\pi^2\left(\frac{2}{k}\right)^2=\pi r^2\left(\frac{2}{kr}\right)^2=\left(\frac{2}{y}\right)^2, \qquad (52)$$

if, as at p. 182 above, πr^2 be taken as unity. This is as it ought to be, as it leads to the expression $1/(a+b)^2$ for the intensity at the point in which the axis meets the screen. We thus verify the statement, made on the last page, that the maximum illumination at the centre of the geometrical image of the orifice is four times that due to the uninterrupted wave.

It might be objected that the original expressions obtained, which are here extended to the whole wave-front, had reference only to a small part of the wave-front, namely that filling the orifice. It is to be observed however that the effects of those elements of the wave-front, which lie at a distance from the axis, are very small compared with those of the elements near the axis, and so the integrals can be extended as above without error.

To find the illumination with the opaque disk we have simply to subtract from the values of C_∞, S_∞ the values of C_r, S_r, given on p. 182 for the orifice. Thus denoting the differences by C_1, S_1, we get $(\pi r^2=1)$

$$\left.\begin{aligned} C_1 &= C_\infty - C_r = -\frac{2}{y}(V_0 \sin \tfrac{1}{2}y - V_1 \cos \tfrac{1}{2}y), \\ S_1 &= S_\infty - S_r = \frac{2}{y}(V_0 \cos \tfrac{1}{2}y + V_1 \sin \tfrac{1}{2}y), \end{aligned}\right\} \tag{53}$$

and

$$M_1^2 = \left(\frac{2}{y}\right)^2 (V_0^2 + V_1^2), \tag{54}$$

or

$$M_1^2 = \left(\frac{2}{y}\right)\left\{1 + U_1^2 + U_2^2 - 2U_1 \sin \tfrac{1}{2}\left(y + \frac{z^2}{y}\right) + 2U_2 \cos \tfrac{1}{2}\left(y + \frac{z^2}{y}\right)\right\}. \tag{55}$$

Comparing these with the expressions on p. 182 for M^2, we see that they are the same except that now U_1 is replaced by V_1 and U_2 by $-V_0$.

If $z=0$, that is if the point considered be at the centre of the geometrical shadow, $V_0=1$, $V_1=0$, and

$$M_1^2 = \left(\frac{2}{y}\right)^2, \tag{56}$$

that is the brightness there is always the same, exactly, as if the opaque disk did not exist. This is the well-known theoretical result first pointed out by Poisson, and since verified by experiment.

For any given values of y and z the value of M_1^2 is easily calculated from those of U_1, U_2 by the equations (9)

$$V_0 = \cos \tfrac{1}{2}\left(y + \frac{z^2}{y}\right) + U_2,$$

$$V_1 = \sin \tfrac{1}{2}\left(y + \frac{z^2}{y}\right) - U_1.$$

A valuable set of numerical Tables of M_1^2 all fully illustrated by curves will be found in Lommel's memoir.

When z is continually increased in value the equations

$$V_0 = \cos \tfrac{1}{2}\left(y + \frac{z^2}{y}\right),$$

$$V_1 = \sin \tfrac{1}{2}\left(y + \frac{z^2}{y}\right)$$

more and more nearly hold, since, by (11), U_2 and U_1 continually approach zero. The value of M_1^2 thus becomes $4/y^2$ at a great distance from the shadow, as in the uninterrupted wave.

As before, we can find the conditions for a maximum or minimum. Differentiating, and reducing by (18) and (14), we obtain

$$\frac{\partial M_1^2}{\partial z} = -2\left(\frac{2}{y}\right)^2 J_1(z) V_0. \qquad (57)$$

The maxima and minima have place therefore when

$$J_1(z) = 0 \quad \text{or} \quad V_0 = 0.$$

The roots of these equations are the values of z which satisfy

$$\frac{\partial J_0(z)}{\partial z} = 0, \quad \frac{y}{z}\frac{\partial V_1}{\partial z} = 0,$$

and are, therefore, values of z which make $J_0(z)$ and V_1 a maximum or minimum. The roots of $J_1(z)=0$ are given at the end of this book; those of $V_0=0$ can be found by a formula of interpolation similar to, and obtained in the same way as, (43) above.

The tangent of the inclination of the curves $V_0=0$ to the axis of z is given according to (24) by

$$\frac{dy}{dz} = \frac{2\frac{z}{y}V_{-1}}{V_1 + \left(\frac{z}{y}\right)^2 V_{-1}}. \qquad (58)$$

By using in this the values

$$V_1 = \frac{z}{y}J_1 - \left(\frac{z}{y}\right)^3 J_3 + \dots,$$

$$\left(\frac{z}{y}\right)^2 V_{-1} = -\frac{z}{y}J_1 - \left(\frac{z}{y}\right)^3 J_1 + \left(\frac{z}{y}\right)^5 J_3 - \dots,$$

we see that if $y = \infty$, $\frac{dy}{dz} = \infty$, that is the curves are for great values of y parallel to the axis of y. Also, since

$$V_0 = J_0 - \left(\frac{z}{y}\right)^2 J_2 + \dots,$$

the asymptotes of these curves are the lines

$$J_0(z)=0,$$

drawn parallel to the axis of y. A table of the roots of this equation is given at the end of this book, and as has been seen above (p. 86) their large values are given approximately by the formula

$$(m+\tfrac{3}{4})\pi.$$

Writing now

$$V_0=\cos\tfrac{1}{2}\left(y+\frac{z^2}{y}\right)+U_2$$

$$=\cos\tfrac{1}{2}\left(y+\frac{z^2}{y}\right)+\left(\frac{y}{z}\right)^2 J_2-\left(\frac{y}{z}\right)^4 J_4+\ldots=0,$$

and making the values of y, z small, the terms after the first on the right all disappear, and we are left with

$$\cos\tfrac{1}{2}\left(y+\frac{z^2}{y}\right)=0,$$

that is

$$y^2+z^2=(2m+1)\,\pi y. \tag{59}$$

This equation represents a circle passing through the origin. We infer that the branches of the curve $V_0=0$ become near the origin arcs of circles all touching the axis of z at the origin.

The curves $V_0=0$ are shown in Fig. 12, p. 208, and give the maxima and minima of the intensity curve by the process already described for the diagram at p. 197.

In this case, calculating from (57),

$$\frac{\partial^2 M_1^2}{\partial z^2}=2\left(\frac{2}{y}\right)^2\left\{J_1^2+\frac{z}{y}J_1V_1+\left(\frac{1}{z}J_1-J_0\right)V_0\right\}, \tag{60}$$

so that points in which a line drawn parallel to the axis of z across the diagram cuts the lines $J_1(z)=0$, $V_0=0$, correspond to maxima or minima according as the quantity on the right is negative or positive. Hence, along the line $J_1(z)=0$, the intensity is a maximum or a minimum according as J_0V_0 is positive or negative. On the other hand, where $V_0=0$, the points correspond to maxima or minima according as

$$J_1^2(z)+\frac{z}{y}J_1(z)V_1 \quad \text{or} \quad -\frac{z}{y}J_1(z)V_{-1}$$

is negative or positive.

Where both $J_1(z)=0$ and $V_0=0$, the value of $\dfrac{\partial M_1^2}{\partial z^2}$ vanishes, but not so that of $\dfrac{\partial^3 M_1^2}{\partial z^3}$. Hence at such points the curves of intensity have points of inflexion, but there are no others.

As in the other case, points of inflexion of the intensity curve can only exist outside the shadow region of the diagram. For since $J_1(z)=0$, $V_{-1}=-V_1$, (58) becomes

$$\frac{dy}{dz}=-2\frac{\frac{z}{y}}{1-\left(\frac{z}{y}\right)^2},$$

which is positive if $y<z$, negative if $y>z$. But by the diagram $\frac{dy}{dz}$ is positive everywhere. Hence there can be no intersection of the line $J_1(z)=0$ with $V_0=0$, except when $y<z$. Thus the statement just made is proved.

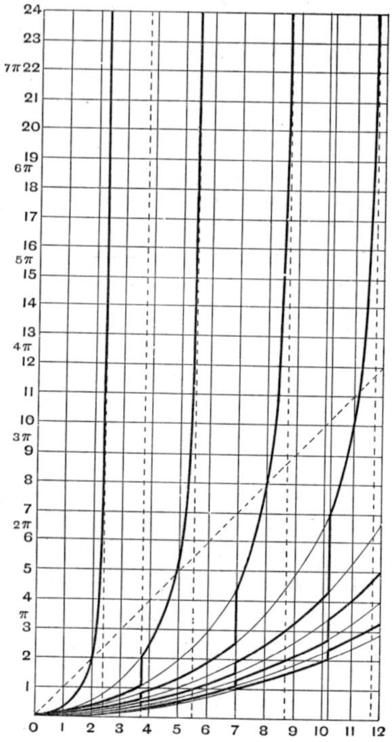

FIG. 12.

Lastly, for the sake of comparing further the case of the disk with that of the orifice, let us contrast the intensity along a line $y=cz$ with that along the line $y=z/c$. Accenting the quantities for the second line, we can easily prove that

$$V_0^2+V_1^2+V_0'^2+V_1'^2=U_1^2+U_2^2+U_1'^2+U_2'^2+2J_0(z)\cos\frac{1}{2}z\left(c+\frac{1}{c}\right). \quad (61)$$

Now we have for the orifice

$$M^2 = \frac{1}{c^2}\left(\frac{2}{z}\right)^2 (U_1^2 + U_2^2),$$

$$M'^2 = c^2\left(\frac{2}{z}\right)^2 (U_1'^2 + U_2'^2),$$

and for the disk
$$M_1^2 = \frac{1}{c^2}\left(\frac{2}{z}\right)^2 (V_0^2 + V_1^2),$$

$$M_1'^2 = c^2\left(\frac{2}{z}\right)^2 (V_0'^2 + V_1'^2).$$

Thus, by (61),

$$c^2(M_1^2 - M^2) + \frac{1}{c^2}(M_1'^2 - M'^2) = \frac{8}{z^2} J_0(z) \cos \frac{1}{2} z\left(c + \frac{1}{c}\right). \qquad (62)$$

The shadow region is that for which $y > z$, and is bounded therefore by the line $y = z$. On this line $M = M'$, $M_1 = M_1'$ and $c = 1$, so that (62) becomes

$$2(M_1^2 - M^2)_{y=z} = \frac{8}{z^2} J_0(z) \cos z.$$

It is clear from the diagram that as y increases the number of dark rings which fall within the shadow also increases.

The reader must refer for further information on these cases of diffraction to Lommel's paper, which contains, as we have indicated, a wealth of numerical and graphical results of great value. The discussion given above is in great part an account of this memoir, with deviations here and there from the original in the proofs of various theorems, and making use of the properties of Bessel functions established in the earlier chapters of this book.

§ 8. **Source of Light a Linear Arrangement of Point-Sources. Struve's Function.** The same volume of the *Abhandlungen der Königl. Bayer. Akademie der Wissenschaften* contains another most elaborate memoir by Lommel on the diffraction of a screen bounded by straight edges, in which the analysis is in many respects similar to that used in the first paper, and given above We can only here find space for some particular applications therein made of Bessel functions to the calculation of Fresnel's integrals, and a few other results.

From the result obtained above for Fraunhofer's interference phenomena, namely that the intensity of illumination is proportional to $\frac{4}{z^2}J_1^2(z)$, the source of light being a point, we can find the intensity at any point of the screen when the source is a uniform straight line arrangement of independent point-sources.

Let the circular orifice be the opening of the object-glass of the telescope which in Fraunhofer's experiments is supposed focused on the source of light. If the source is at a great distance from the telescope we may suppose with sufficient accuracy that the plane of the orifice is at right angles to the ray coming from any point of the linear source.

Let rectangular axes of ξ, η be drawn on the screen, and let the line of sources be parallel to the axis of η and in the plane $\xi=0$. A little consideration shows that the illumination at any point of the screen must depend upon ξ and (constant factors omitted) be represented by

$$\int_0^\infty \frac{J_1^2(z)}{z^2}\,d\eta.$$

But if r be the radius of the object-glass, and ζ the distance of the point considered from the axis of the telescope,

$$z=\frac{2\pi r}{b\lambda}\zeta=\mu\zeta, \text{ say,}$$

and

$$\eta^2=\zeta^2-\xi^2=\frac{z^2}{\mu^2}-\xi^2.$$

Hence

$$d\eta=\frac{z}{\mu^2}\frac{dz}{\eta}=\frac{z}{\mu}\frac{dz}{\sqrt{z^2-v^2}},$$

if $v^2=\mu^2\xi^2$. The integral is therefore

$$\frac{1}{\mu}\int_v^\infty \frac{J_1^2(z)\,dz}{z\sqrt{z^2-v^2}}.$$

This integral may be transformed in various ways into a form suitable for numerical calculation. The process here adopted depends on the properties of Bessel functions, and is due to Dr. H. Struve.* Another method of obtaining the same result will be found in Lord Rayleigh's *Wave Theory of Light*.†

Struve's analysis depends on three lemmas, which we shall prove in the first place.

* *Wied. Ann.* 16 (1882), p. 1008.

† *Encyc. Brit.*, 9th Ed. p. 433.

The first is a theorem of Neumann's, and is expressed by the equation

$$J_n^2(z)=\frac{2}{\pi}\int_0^{\frac{\pi}{2}}J_{2n}(2z\sin\alpha)\,d\alpha. \qquad (63)$$

By IV. (33) above, we have

$$J_0\left(2c\sin\frac{\alpha}{2}\right)=J_0^2(c)+2J_1^2(c)\cos\alpha+2J_2^2(c)\cos 2\alpha+\dots.$$

But $J_0\left(2c\sin\frac{\alpha}{2}\right)=\frac{1}{\pi}\int_0^\pi\cos\left(2c\sin\frac{\alpha}{2}\sin\phi\right)d\phi$

$$=\frac{1}{\pi}\int_0^\pi\{J_0(2c\sin\phi)+2J_2(2c\sin\phi)\cos\alpha + 2J_4(2c\sin\phi)\cos 2\alpha+\dots\}\,d\phi,$$

by IV. (4) above. Identifying terms in the two equations, we obtain

$$J_n^2(c)=\frac{1}{\pi}\int_0^\pi J_{2n}(2c\sin\phi)\,d\phi$$

or

$$J_n^2(z)=\frac{2}{\pi}\int_0^{\frac{1}{2}\pi}J_{2n}(2z\sin\alpha)\,d\alpha,$$

if we write z for c and α for ϕ. Thus the first lemma is established.

The second lemma is the equation

$$J_0(vx)=\frac{2}{\pi}\int_v^\infty\frac{\sin(xz)}{\sqrt{z^2-v^2}}\,dz, \qquad (64)$$

$v\geqq 0$.

From V. (29) we obtain

$$G_0(x)=K_0(-ix)=\int_1^\infty\frac{e^{ix\xi}\,d\xi}{\sqrt{(\xi^2-1)}}.$$

But the imaginary part of $G_0(x)$ is $\frac{i}{2}\pi J_0(x)$. Hence, equating imaginary parts, we get

$$\frac{1}{2}\pi J_0(x)=\int_1^\infty\frac{\sin(x\xi)\,d\xi}{\sqrt{(\xi^2-1)}}, \qquad (65)$$

which is the theorem stated in (64) in a slightly different form.

The third lemma is expressed by the equation

$$\int_0^{\frac{1}{2}\pi}J_0(z\sin\alpha)\sin\alpha\,d\alpha=\frac{\sin z}{z}. \qquad (66)$$

Using the general definition (p. 14 above) of a Bessel function of integral order, we get

$$\int_0^{\frac{1}{2}\pi} J_0(z\sin\alpha)\sin\alpha\,d\alpha=\sum_0^\infty\frac{(-)^s}{(\Pi s)^2}\left(\frac{z}{2}\right)^{2s}\int_0^{\frac{1}{2}\pi}\sin^{2s+1}\alpha\,d\alpha$$

$$=\sum\frac{(-)^s}{(\Pi s)^2}\left(\frac{z}{2}\right)^{2s}\frac{2^{2s}(\Pi s)^2}{\Pi(2s+1)}$$

$$=\sum\frac{(-)^s z^{2s}}{\Pi(2s+1)}=\frac{\sin z}{z},$$

which was to be proved.

Returning now to the integral

$$\int_v^\infty\frac{J_1^2(z)\,dz}{z\sqrt{z^2-v^2}},$$

let us denote it by Z. We have by the first lemma

$$Z=\frac{2}{\pi}\int_v^\infty\frac{dz}{z\sqrt{z^2-v^2}}\int_0^{\frac{1}{2}\pi}J_2(2z\sin\alpha)\,d\alpha.$$

But by II. (26),

$$J_2(2z\sin\alpha)=\frac{z\sin\alpha}{2}\{J_1(2z\sin\alpha)+J_3(2z\sin\alpha)\},$$

and by IV. (9),

$$J_1(2z\sin\alpha)=\frac{1}{\pi}\int_0^\pi\sin(2z\sin\alpha\sin\beta)\sin\beta\,d\beta,$$

$$J_3(2z\sin\alpha)=\frac{1}{\pi}\int_0^\pi\sin(2z\sin\alpha\sin\beta)\sin3\beta\,d\beta,$$

so that

$$Z=\frac{1}{\pi^2}\int_0^{\frac{1}{2}\pi}\sin\alpha\,d\alpha\int_0^\pi(\sin\beta+\sin3\beta)\,d\beta\int_v^\infty\frac{\sin(2z\sin\alpha\sin\beta)\,dz}{\sqrt{z^2-v^2}}.$$

But if we put $2\sin\alpha\sin\beta=x$ we get, by the second lemma,

$$\int_v^\infty\frac{\sin(2z\sin\alpha\sin\beta)\,dz}{\sqrt{z^2-v^2}}=\frac{\pi}{2}J_0(vx).$$

Hence

$$Z=\frac{1}{2\pi}\int_0^\pi(\sin\beta+\sin3\beta)\,d\beta\int_0^{\frac{1}{2}\pi}J_0(2v\sin\alpha\sin\beta)\sin\alpha\,d\alpha,$$

which by the third lemma becomes

$$Z=\frac{1}{\pi}\int_0^{\frac{1}{2}\pi}(\sin\beta+\sin3\beta)\frac{\sin(2v\sin\beta)}{2v\sin\beta}\,d\beta$$

$$=\frac{2}{\pi v}\int_0^{\frac{1}{2}\pi}\sin(2v\sin\beta)\cos^2\beta\,d\beta. \qquad (67)$$

Let now $H_0(z)$ be a function defined by the equation

$$H_0(z)=\frac{2}{\pi}\int_0^{\frac{1}{2}\pi}\sin(z\sin\theta)\,d\theta. \tag{68}$$

Expanding $\sin(z\sin\theta)$ and integrating, we obtain

$$H_0(z)=\frac{2}{\pi}\left\{z-\frac{z^3}{1^2.3^2}+\frac{z^5}{1^2.3^2.5^2}-\ldots\right\}. \tag{69}$$

Now let $H_1(z)$ be another function defined by

$$H_1(z)=\int_0^z H_0(z)z\,dz\,;$$

then, by the series in (69),

$$H_1(z)=\frac{2}{\pi}\left\{\frac{z^3}{1^2.3}-\frac{z^5}{1^2.3^2.5}+\frac{z^7}{1^2.3^2.5^2.7}-\ldots\right\}. \tag{70}$$

We shall now prove that

$$H_1(z)=\frac{2z^2}{\pi}\int_0^{\frac{1}{2}\pi}\sin(z\sin\theta)\cos^2\theta\,d\theta. \tag{71}$$

It can be verified by differentiating that

$$\frac{1}{z}\frac{d}{dz}\left(z\frac{d}{dz}\right)H_0(z)=\frac{2}{\pi z}-H_0(z). \tag{72}$$

Multiplying by $z\,dz$ and integrating, we find

$$H_1(z)=\frac{2z}{\pi}-z\frac{dH_0(z)}{dz}. \tag{73}$$

Now, by (68),

$$z\frac{dH_0(z)}{dz}=\frac{2z}{\pi}\int_0^{\frac{1}{2}\pi}\cos(z\sin\theta)\sin\theta\,d\theta.$$

Hence
$$H_1(z)=\frac{2z}{\pi}\left\{1-\int_0^{\frac{1}{2}\pi}\cos(z\sin\theta)\sin\theta\,d\theta\right\}$$
$$=\frac{2z}{\pi}\int_0^{\frac{1}{2}\pi}\{1-\cos(z\sin\theta)\}\sin\theta\,d\theta$$
$$=\frac{4z}{\pi}\int_0^{\frac{1}{2}\pi}\sin^2(\tfrac{1}{2}z\sin\theta)\sin\theta\,d\theta. \tag{74}$$

It may be noted that every element of this integral is positive. It is clear from the form of $H_1(z)$ given in the first of the three equations just written that $H_1(z)$ approximates when z is large to $2z/\pi$.

Integrating (74) by parts, we obtain

$$H_1(z)=\frac{2z^2}{\pi}\int_0^{\frac{1}{2}\pi}\sin(z\sin\theta)\cos^2\theta\,d\theta,$$

since the integrated term vanishes at both limits.

If we write $2v$ for z and β for θ, the equation becomes

$$H_1(2v) = 2\frac{(2v)^2}{\pi}\int_0^{\frac{1}{2}\pi} \sin(2v\sin\beta)\cos^2\beta\,d\beta. \tag{75}$$

Hence
$$\frac{H_1(2v)}{4v^3} = \frac{2}{\pi v}\int_0^{\frac{1}{2}\pi} \sin(2v\sin\beta)\cos^2\beta\,d\beta = Z,$$
by (67).

It is to be observed that the functions here denoted by $H_0(z)$, $H_1(z)$ are the same as Lord Rayleigh's $K(z)$, $K_1(z)$ discussed in the *Theory of Sound*, § 302, to which the reader is referred for further details. The function $H_1(z)$ differs, however, from the functions $H_1(z)$ used by Struve. If we denote the latter by $\mathfrak{H}_1(z)$, the relation between the two functions is

$$H_1(z) = z\mathfrak{H}_1(z).$$

The value of $H_1(z)$ can be calculated when z is not too great by the series in (70), but when z is large this series is not convenient. We must then have recourse to an asymptotic series, similar to that established in Chap. V. above for the Bessel functions. The series can be found easily by the method employed in that chapter. The following is a brief outline of the process.*

By the definitions of the functions we have

$$J_0(z) - iH_0(z) = \frac{2}{\pi}\int_0^{\frac{1}{2}\pi} e^{-iz\sin\theta}\,d\theta$$
$$= \frac{2}{\pi}\int_0^1 \frac{e^{-ivz}}{\sqrt{1-v^2}}\,dv.$$

Now take the integral $\int \frac{e^{-zw}\,dw}{\sqrt{1+w^2}}$ (in which $w = u + iv$) round the rectangle, the angular points of which are 0, h, $h+i$, i, where h is real and positive. This integral is zero, and if $h \to \infty$ it gives, after some reduction,

$$\int_0^1 \frac{e^{-izv}}{\sqrt{1-v^2}}\,dv = -\frac{i}{z}\int_0^\infty e^{-\beta}\left(1+\frac{\beta^2}{z^2}\right)^{-\frac{1}{2}} d\beta$$
$$+ \frac{e^{-i(z-\frac{1}{4}\pi)}}{\sqrt{2z}}\int_0^\infty e^{-\beta}\beta^{-\frac{1}{2}}\left(1-\frac{i\beta}{2z}\right)^{-\frac{1}{2}} d\beta.$$

Expanding the binomials and integrating, making use of the theorem

$$\int_0^\infty e^{-\beta}\beta^{q-\frac{1}{2}}\,d\beta = \Pi\left(q-\tfrac{1}{2}\right),$$

* See *Theory of Sound*, § 302.

and equating the real part of the result to $\frac{1}{2}\pi J_0(z)$ and the imaginary part to $-\frac{1}{2}i\pi H_0(z)$, we get the expansions required namely $J_0(z)$ as in Chap. V., and

$$H_0(z)=\frac{2}{\pi}(z^{-1}-z^{-3}+1^2.3^2z^{-5}-1^2.3^2.5^2z^{-7}+\ldots)$$
$$+\sqrt{\frac{2}{\pi z}}\{P\sin(z-\tfrac{1}{4}\pi)-Q\cos(z-\tfrac{1}{4}\pi)\}, \qquad (76)$$

where $$P=1-\frac{1^2.3^2}{2!(8z)^2}+\frac{1^2.3^2.5^2.7^2}{4!(8z)^4}-\ldots,$$

and $$Q=\frac{1}{8z}-\frac{1^2.3^2.5^2}{3!(8z)^3}+\frac{1^2.3^2.5^2.7^2.9^2}{5!(8z)^5}-\ldots.$$

Similarly, by using the equation

$$zJ_1(z)-iH_1(z)=\frac{2z^2}{\pi}\int_0^1 e^{-ivz}\sqrt{(1-v^2)}\,dv,$$

it can be shown that the asymptotic expansion of $H_1(z)$ is

$$H_1(z)=\frac{2}{\pi}(z+z^{-1}-3z^{-3}+1^2.3^2.5z^{-5}-\ldots)$$
$$-\sqrt{\frac{2z}{\pi}}\cos(z-\tfrac{1}{4}\pi)\left\{1-\frac{(1^2-4)(3^2-4)}{1.2.(8z)^2}\right.$$
$$\left.+\frac{(1^2-4)(3^2-4)(5^2-4)(7^2-4)}{1.2.3.4.(8z)^4}-\ldots\right\}$$
$$-\sqrt{\frac{2z}{\pi}}\sin(z-\tfrac{1}{4}\pi)\left\{\frac{1^2-4}{1.8z}\right.$$
$$\left.-\frac{(1^2-4)(3^2-4)(5^2-4)}{1.2.3.(8z)^3}+\ldots\right\}. \qquad (77)$$

It is to be noticed that, by (74), $H_1(2v)$ is nowhere zero, and that $H_1(2v)/v^3$ has maxima and minima values at points satisfying the equation

$$\frac{d}{dv}\frac{H_1(2v)}{v^3}=\frac{4v^2H_0(2v)-3H_1(2v)}{v^4}=0. \qquad (78)$$

The corresponding values of v are therefore the roots of

$$4v^2H_0(2v)-3H_1(2v)=0.$$

Now let there be two parallel and equally luminous line-sources, whose images in the focal plane are at a distance apart $v/\mu=\pi/\mu$, say. It is of great importance to compare the intensity at the image of either line with the intensity halfway between them. In this way can be determined the minimum distance apart at which the luminous lines may be placed and still be separated by the telescope. We shall take the image of one as corresponding to $v=0$, and that of the other as corresponding to $v=\pi$. Thus the intensity at any distance corresponding to v is proportional to $\frac{H_1(2v)}{4v^3}$. Putting

$$L(v)=\frac{\pi}{2}\frac{H_1(2v)}{(2v)^3},$$

we have, by (70),

$$L(v)=\frac{1}{1^2.3}-\frac{2^2v^2}{1^2.3^2.5}+\frac{2^4v^4}{1^2.3^2.5^2.7}-\dots.$$

The ratio of the intensity of illumination midway between the two lines to that at either is therefore

$$\frac{2L(\frac{1}{2}\pi)}{L(0)+L(\pi)}.$$

This has been calculated by Lord Rayleigh (to whom this comparison is due) with the following results:

$$L(0)=\cdot 3333,\quad L(\pi)=\cdot 0164,\quad L(\tfrac{1}{2}\pi)=\cdot 1671,$$

so that

$$\frac{2L(\frac{1}{2}\pi)}{L(0)+L(\pi)}=\cdot 955. \qquad (79)$$

The intensity is therefore, for the distance stated, only about $4\frac{1}{2}$ per cent. less than at the image of either line.

Now

$$v=\frac{2\pi r}{\lambda b}\xi=\pi,$$

which gives

$$\frac{\xi}{b}=\frac{\lambda}{2r}.$$

Since b is the focal length of the object-glass, the two lines are, by this result, at an angular distance apart equal to that subtended by the wave-length of light at a distance equal to the diameter of the object-glass. Two lines unless at a greater angular distance could therefore hardly be separated.

This result shows that the resolving (or as it is sometimes called the space-penetrating) power of a telescope is directly proportional to the diameter of the object-glass.

By multiplying

$$\frac{2}{\pi}\frac{H_1(2v)}{(2v)^3}$$

by $\mu\, d\xi$, that is by dv, and integrating from $\xi=-\infty$ to $\xi=+\infty$

we get an expression which, to a constant factor, represents the whole illumination received by the screen from a single luminous point the image of which is at the centre of the focal plane. Or, by the mode in which $H_1(2v)/v^3$ was obtained, it plainly may be regarded as the illumination received by the latter point from an infinite uniformly illuminated area in front of the object-glass.

If the integral is taken from ξ to $+\infty$ it will represent, on the same scale, the illumination received by the same point from an area bounded by the straight line parallel to η corresponding to the constant value of ξ. The point will be at a distance ξ from the edge of the geometrical shadow, and will be inside or outside the shadow according as ξ is positive or negative.

We have, by (71),

$$\int_0^\infty \frac{H_1(2v)}{(2v)^3}\,dv = \frac{1}{\pi}\int_0^{\frac{1}{2}\pi}\cos^2\beta\,d\beta\int_0^\infty \frac{\sin(2v\sin\beta)}{v}\,dv$$

$$=\tfrac{1}{2}\int_0^{\frac{1}{2}\pi}\cos^2\beta\,d\beta=\frac{\pi}{8}.$$

Now $$\int_v^\infty \frac{H_1(2v)}{(2v)^3}\,dv = \int_0^\infty \frac{H_1(2v)}{(2v)^3}\,dv - \int_0^v \frac{H_1(2v)}{(2v)^3}\,dv.$$

The second term on the right can be calculated by means of the ascending series (70). Hence we get

$$\int_v^\infty \frac{H_1(2v)}{(2v)^3}\,dv = \frac{\pi}{8} - \frac{2}{\pi}\left\{\frac{v}{1^2.3} - \frac{2^2v^3}{1^2.3^2.3.5} + \frac{2^4v^5}{1^2.3^2.5^2.5.7} - \dots\right\}. \qquad (80)$$

This multiplied by $4/\pi$ is the expression given by Struve for the intensity produced by a uniform plane source, the image of which extends from v to $+\infty$. For the sake of agreement with Struve's result we write when v is positive

$$I(+v) = \tfrac{1}{2} - \frac{4}{\pi^2}\left\{\frac{2v}{1^2.3} - \frac{(2v)^3}{1^2.3^2.3.5} + \dots\right\}. \qquad (81)$$

Hence, if I be the illumination when the plane source extends from $-\infty$ to $+\infty$, we have

$$I(+v)+I(-v)=I=1.$$

This states that the intensities at two points equally distant from the edge of the geometrical shadow, but on opposite sides of it, are together equal to the full intensity. The intensity at the edge of the shadow is therefore half the full intensity.

The reader may verify that when v is great the asymptotic series gives approximately

$$I(v)=\frac{2}{\pi^2}\left(\frac{1}{v}+\frac{1}{12v^3}\right)-\frac{1}{2\pi^{\frac{3}{2}}}\frac{\cos(2v+\frac{1}{4}\pi)}{v^{\frac{5}{2}}}.$$

The following Table (abridged from Struve's paper) gives the intensity within the geometrical shadow at a distance $\xi=b\lambda v/(2\pi r)$ from the edge, and therefore enables the enlargement of the image produced by the diffraction of the object-glass to be estimated:

$$v=\frac{2\pi r}{b\lambda}\xi.$$

$$I(-v)=1-I(+v).$$

v	$I(+v)$	v	$I(+v)$	v	$I(+v)$
0·0	·5000	2	·1073	7	·0293
0·5	·3678	3	·0630	9	·0222
1·0	·2521	4	·0528	11	·0186
1·5	·1642	5	·0410	15	·0135

II. *Case of a Slit.*

§ 9. **Diffraction produced by a Narrow Slit bounded by Parallel Edges. Fresnel's Integrals.** We shall now consider very briefly the theory of diffraction of light passing through a narrow slit bounded by parallel edges. We shall suppose that the diffraction may be taken as the same in every plane at right angles to the slit, so that the problem is one in only two dimensions. Let a then be the radius of a circular wave that has just reached the gap, and consider an element of the wave-front in the gap. Let also b be the distance of P from the pole so that its distance from the source is $a+b$, ds the length of the element of the wave and δ the retardation of the secondary wave (that is the difference between the distances of P from the element and from the pole). The disturbance at P produced will be proportional to

$$\cos 2\pi\left(\frac{t}{T}-\frac{\delta}{\lambda}\right)ds.$$

If the distance of the element from the pole be s, and s be small in comparison with b, then it is very easy to show that

$$\delta=\frac{a+b}{2ab}s^2.$$

Writing as usual $\frac{1}{2}\pi v^2$ for $2\pi\delta/\lambda$, we get

$$\frac{2\pi\delta}{\lambda}=\tfrac{1}{2}\pi v^2=\frac{\pi(a+b)s^2}{ab\lambda}.$$

The disturbance at P is therefore

$$\cos 2\pi\left(\frac{t}{T}-\frac{v^2}{4}\right)=\cos\tfrac{1}{2}\pi v^2\cos\left(2\pi\frac{t}{T}\right)+\sin\tfrac{1}{2}\pi v^2\sin\left(2\pi\frac{t}{T}\right).$$

The intensity of illumination due to the element is therefore constant, being proportional to

$$\cos^2\tfrac{1}{2}\pi v^2+\sin^2\tfrac{1}{2}\pi v^2,$$

where

$$v^2=\frac{2(a+b)}{ab\lambda}s^2.$$

The whole intensity is thus proportional to

$$\left\{\int\cos\tfrac{1}{2}\pi v^2 \,.\, dv\right\}^2+\left\{\int\sin\tfrac{1}{2}\pi v^2 \,.\, dv\right\}^2,$$

the integrals being taken over the whole arc of the wave at the slit.

The problem is thus reduced to quadratures, and it remains to evaluate the integrals. We shall write

$$C=\int_0^v\cos\tfrac{1}{2}\pi v^2 dv,\quad S=\int_0^v\sin\tfrac{1}{2}\pi v^2 dv.$$

C and S are known as Fresnel's integrals.

Various methods of calculating these integrals have been devised; but the simplest of all for purposes of numerical calculation is by means of Bessel functions, when Tables are available.

Let $\frac{1}{2}\pi v^2=z$; then

$$C=\tfrac{1}{2}\int_0^z\sqrt{\frac{2}{\pi z}}\cos z\,dz=\tfrac{1}{2}\int_0^z J_{-\frac{1}{2}}(z)\,dz, \qquad (82)$$

$$S=\tfrac{1}{2}\int_0^z\sqrt{\frac{2}{\pi z}}\sin z\,dz=\tfrac{1}{2}\int_0^z J_{\frac{1}{2}}(z)\,dz. \qquad (83)$$

Let us now consider the Bessel function integrals on the right. Using the relation

$$J_n'(z)=\tfrac{1}{2}(J_{n-1}(z)-J_{n+1}(z)),$$

we have

$$\begin{aligned}J_{-\frac{1}{2}}(z)&=2J_{\frac{1}{2}}'(z)+J_{\frac{3}{2}}(z)\\&=2J_{\frac{1}{2}}'(z)+2J_{\frac{5}{2}}'(z)+\ldots+2J_{\frac{4n+1}{2}}'(z)+J_{\frac{4n+3}{2}}(z).\end{aligned}$$

Thus we obtain

$$\frac{1}{2}\int_0^z J_{-\frac{1}{2}}(z)dz = J_{\frac{1}{2}}(z) + J_{\frac{5}{2}}(z) + \ldots + J_{\frac{4n+1}{2}}(z) + \frac{1}{2}\int_0^z J_{\frac{4n+3}{2}}(z)dz. \quad (84)$$

By taking $(4n+3)/2$ sufficiently great the integral on the right of (84) may be made as small as we please. Thus we get

$$C = \frac{1}{2}\int_0^z J_{-\frac{1}{2}}(z)\,dz = J_{\frac{1}{2}}(z) + J_{\frac{5}{2}}(z) + J_{\frac{9}{2}}(z) + \ldots. \quad (85)$$

Similarly we find

$$S = \frac{1}{2}\int_0^z J_{\frac{1}{2}}(z)\,dz = J_{\frac{3}{2}}(z) + J_{\frac{7}{2}}(z) + J_{\frac{11}{2}}(z) + \ldots. \quad (86)$$

These series are convergent, and give the numerical value of the integrals to any degree of accuracy from Tables of Bessel functions of order $(2n+1)/2$, by simple addition of the values of the successive alternate functions for the given argument. The series are apparently due to Lommel, and are stated in the second memoir referred to above, p. 209. He gives also the series

$$C = \frac{1}{2}\int_0^z J_{-\frac{1}{2}}(z)\,dz = \sqrt{2}(P\cos\tfrac{1}{2}z + Q\sin\tfrac{1}{2}z), \quad (87)$$

$$S = \frac{1}{2}\int_0^z J_{\frac{1}{2}}(z)\,dz = \sqrt{2}(P\sin\tfrac{1}{2}z - Q\cos\tfrac{1}{2}z), \quad (88)$$

where

$$P = J_{\frac{1}{2}}(\tfrac{1}{2}z) - J_{\frac{5}{2}}(\tfrac{1}{2}z) + J_{\frac{9}{2}}(\tfrac{1}{2}z) - \ldots,$$

$$Q = J_{\frac{3}{2}}(\tfrac{1}{2}z) - J_{\frac{7}{2}}(\tfrac{1}{2}z) + J_{\frac{11}{2}}(\tfrac{1}{2}z) - \ldots.$$

The proof is left to the reader.

C and S were expressed long ago in series of ascending powers of v by Knochenhauer, and in terms of definite integrals by Gilbert. From the latter asymptotic series suitable for use when v is large are obtainable by a process similar to that sketched at p. 214 above. It is not necessary however to pursue the matter here.

The very elegant construction shown in the diagram, which is known as Cornu's spiral, shows graphically how the value of C^2+S^2 varies.

The abscissae of the curve are values of C and the ordinates values of S.

It can be shown that the distance along the curve from the origin to any point is the value of v for that point, that the inclination of the tangent to the axis of abscissae is $\frac{1}{2}\pi v^2$, and that the curvature there is πv.

As v varies from 0 to ∞ and from 0 to $-\infty$ the curve is wrapped more and more closely round the poles A and B.

The origin of the curve corresponds to the pole of the point considered, so that if v_1, v_2 correspond to the distances from the pole to the edges of the slit, we have only to mark the two

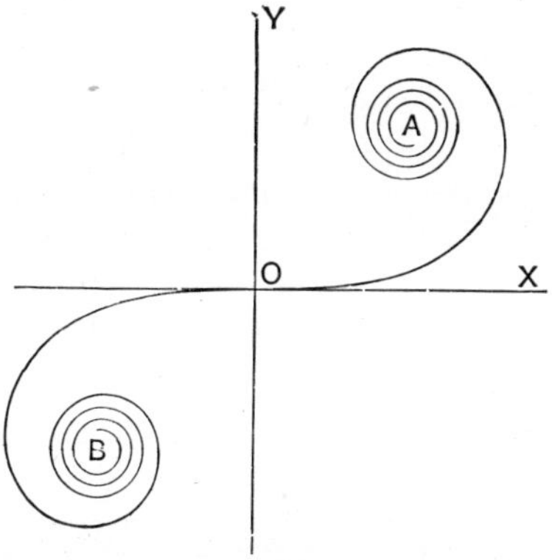

FIG. 13.

points v_1, v_2 on the spiral and draw the chord. The square of the length of this chord will represent the intensity of illumination at the point. The square of the length of the chord from the origin to any point v is the value of C^2+S^2, that is of

$$\frac{1}{4}\left\{\int_0^z J_{-\frac{1}{2}}(z)\,dz\right\}^2+\frac{1}{4}\left\{\int_0^z J_{\frac{1}{2}}(z)\,dz\right\}^2.$$

As v varies it will be seen that the value of this sum oscillates more and more rapidly while approaching more and more nearly to the value $\frac{1}{2}$.

CHAPTER XV.

EQUILIBRIUM OF AN ISOTROPIC ELASTIC ROD OF CIRCULAR SECTION.

In his writings on the equilibrium of isotropic elastic bodies, Dr. John Dougall has made frequent use of the properties of Bessel Functions. In this chapter an example of his methods as applied to the isotropic elastic circular cylinder (*Roy. Soc. Edin. Trans.*, Vol. XLIX., 1914) will be given. In another paper (*Roy. Soc. Edin., Trans.*, Vol. XLI., 1904) he has discussed the equilibrium of an isotropic elastic plate.

§ 1. **Solutions of the Equations of Equilibrium in Terms of Harmonic Functions.** The equations of equilibrium of a homogeneous isotropic elastic solid in rectangular coordinates are

$$\left.\begin{aligned}\frac{\partial \widehat{xx}}{\partial x}+\frac{\partial \widehat{xy}}{\partial y}+\frac{\partial \widehat{xz}}{\partial z}+X=0,\\ \frac{\partial \widehat{xy}}{\partial x}+\frac{\partial \widehat{yy}}{\partial y}+\frac{\partial \widehat{yz}}{\partial z}+Y=0,\\ \frac{\partial \widehat{xz}}{\partial x}+\frac{\partial \widehat{yz}}{\partial y}+\frac{\partial \widehat{zz}}{\partial z}+Z=0,\end{aligned}\right\} \qquad (1)$$

where X, Y, Z are the components of the body-force per unit volume; and $\widehat{xx}$, $\widehat{yy}$, $\widehat{zz}$, $\widehat{xy}$, $\widehat{xz}$, $\widehat{yz}$ are the components of stress, these being given in terms of the displacements u_x, u_y, u_z, by three pairs of equations of the type

$$\widehat{xx}=\lambda\Delta+2\mu e_{xx}, \quad \widehat{yz}=\mu e_{yz}. \qquad (2)$$

Here
$$\Delta=\frac{\partial u_x}{\partial x}+\frac{\partial u_y}{\partial y}+\frac{\partial u_z}{\partial z},$$

$$e_{xx}=\frac{\partial u_x}{\partial x}, \quad e_{xy}=\frac{\partial u_y}{\partial x}+\frac{\partial u_x}{\partial y}, \text{ etc.}$$

μ denotes the rigidity modulus; and, if E denote Young's modulus, k the modulus of compression, and σ Poisson's Ratio, then

$$E=\frac{\mu(3\lambda+2\mu)}{\lambda+\mu}, \quad k=\lambda+\tfrac{2}{3}\mu, \quad \sigma=\frac{\lambda}{2(\lambda+\mu)}.$$

Δ is called the dilatation, and $e_{xx}, \ldots, e_{yz}$ the components of strain.

In cylindrical coordinates ρ, ω, z, the displacements are u_ρ, u_ω, u_z; the strains are*

$$\left.\begin{aligned} &e_{\rho\rho}=\frac{\partial u_\rho}{\partial \rho}, \quad e_{\omega\omega}=\frac{1}{\rho}\frac{\partial u_\omega}{\partial \omega}+\frac{u_\rho}{\rho}, \quad e_{zz}=\frac{\partial u_z}{\partial z}, \\ &e_{\omega z}=\frac{1}{\rho}\frac{\partial u_z}{\partial \omega}+\frac{\partial u_\omega}{\partial z}, \quad e_{\rho z}=\frac{\partial u_\rho}{\partial z}+\frac{\partial u_z}{\partial \rho}, \\ &e_{\rho\omega}=\frac{\partial u_\omega}{\partial \rho}-\frac{u_\omega}{\rho}+\frac{1}{\rho}\frac{\partial u_\rho}{\partial \omega}, \\ \text{so that} \quad &\Delta=\frac{\partial u_\rho}{\partial \rho}+\frac{1}{\rho}\frac{\partial u_\omega}{\partial \omega}+\frac{u_\rho}{\rho}+\frac{\partial u_z}{\partial z}. \end{aligned}\right\} \qquad (3)$$

The stresses are therefore

$$\left.\begin{aligned} &\widehat{\rho\rho}=\lambda\Delta+2\mu\frac{\partial u_\rho}{\partial \rho}, \quad \widehat{\rho\omega}=\mu\left(\frac{\partial u_\omega}{\partial \rho}-\frac{u_\omega}{\rho}+\frac{1}{\rho}\frac{\partial u_\rho}{\partial \omega}\right), \\ &\widehat{\rho z}=\mu\left(\frac{\partial u_\rho}{\partial z}+\frac{\partial u_z}{\partial \rho}\right), \quad \widehat{zz}=\lambda\Delta+2\mu\frac{\partial u_z}{\partial z}, \\ &\widehat{\omega z}=\mu\left(\frac{1}{\rho}\frac{\partial u_z}{\partial \omega}+\frac{\partial u_\omega}{\partial z}\right), \quad \widehat{\omega\omega}=\lambda\Delta+2\mu\left(\frac{1}{\rho}\frac{\partial u_\omega}{\partial \omega}+\frac{u_\rho}{\rho}\right). \end{aligned}\right\} \qquad (4)$$

If the expressions (2) are substituted in (1), three equations of equilibrium in terms of displacements are obtained. In what follows the body-forces X, Y, Z are taken to be zero, and these equations of equilibrium are written in the compact form

$$\mu\nabla^2(u_x, u_y, u_z,)+(\lambda+\mu)\left(\frac{\partial\Delta}{\partial x}, \frac{\partial\Delta}{\partial y}, \frac{\partial\Delta}{\partial z}\right)=0. \qquad (5)$$

The following three solutions of equations (5) can easily be verified:

$$\left.\begin{aligned} &u_x=x\frac{\partial^2\phi}{\partial z^2}, \quad u_y=y\frac{\partial^2\phi}{\partial z^2}, \\ &u_z=-x\frac{\partial^2\phi}{\partial x\,\partial z}-y\frac{\partial^2\phi}{\partial y\,\partial z}-\frac{2(\lambda+2\mu)}{\lambda+\mu}\frac{\partial\phi}{\partial z}; \end{aligned}\right\} \qquad (6)$$

$$u_x=\frac{\partial\theta}{\partial x}, \quad u_y=\frac{\partial\theta}{\partial y}, \quad u_z=\frac{\partial\theta}{\partial z}; \qquad (7)$$

$$u_x=\frac{\partial\psi}{\partial y}, \quad u_y=-\frac{\partial\psi}{\partial x}, \quad u_z=0; \qquad (8)$$

* Love's *Elasticity*, 2nd Edit., §§ 20, 22.

where ϕ, θ, ψ are harmonic functions, that is to say, solutions of Laplace's equation.

If $$\nu = 2(\lambda+2\mu)/(\lambda+\mu) = 4(1-\sigma),$$

then in (6) $\Delta = (2-\nu)\dfrac{\partial^2\phi}{\partial z^2}$, and in (7) and (8) $\Delta = 0$.

From (6), (7), and (8) the displacements in cylindrical coordinates can be found; they are

$$\left.\begin{aligned} u_\rho &= \rho\frac{\partial^2\phi}{\partial z^2} + \frac{\partial\theta}{\partial\rho} + \frac{1}{\rho}\frac{\partial\psi}{\partial\omega}, \\ u_\omega &= \frac{1}{\rho}\frac{\partial\theta}{\partial\omega} - \frac{\partial\psi}{\partial\rho}, \\ u_z &= -\rho\frac{\partial^2\phi}{\partial\rho\,\partial z} - \nu\frac{\partial\phi}{\partial z} + \frac{\partial\theta}{\partial z}. \end{aligned}\right\} \quad (9)$$

These give by (4)

$$\left.\begin{aligned} \frac{\widehat{\rho\rho}}{\mu} &= (\nu-2)\frac{\partial^2\phi}{\partial z^2} + 2\rho\frac{\partial^3\phi}{\partial\rho\,\partial z^2} + 2\frac{\partial^2\theta}{\partial\rho^2} + \frac{2}{\rho}\frac{\partial^2\psi}{\partial\rho\,\partial\omega} - \frac{2}{\rho^2}\frac{\partial\psi}{\partial\omega}, \\ \frac{\widehat{\rho\omega}}{\mu} &= \frac{\partial^3\phi}{\partial\omega\,\partial z^2} + \frac{2}{\rho}\frac{\partial^2\theta}{\partial\rho\partial\omega} - \frac{2}{\rho^2}\frac{\partial\theta}{\partial\omega} - \frac{\partial^2\psi}{\partial\rho^2} + \frac{1}{\rho}\frac{\partial\psi}{\partial\rho} + \frac{1}{\rho^2}\frac{\partial^2\psi}{\partial\omega^2}, \\ \frac{\widehat{\rho z}}{\mu} &= 2\rho\frac{\partial^3\phi}{\partial z^3} - \nu\frac{\partial^2\phi}{\partial\rho\,\partial z} + \frac{1}{\rho}\frac{\partial^3\phi}{\partial\omega^2\,\partial z} + 2\frac{\partial^2\theta}{\partial\rho\,\partial z} + \frac{1}{\rho}\frac{\partial^2\psi}{\partial\omega\,\partial z}. \end{aligned}\right\} \quad (10)$$

§ 2. **The General Problem of Surface Traction for a Circular Cylinder.** Let the cylinder be bounded by the surface $\rho = a$. It is required to find values of ϕ, θ, ψ, which shall give, in accordance with (10), at $\rho = a$,

$$\left.\begin{aligned} &\text{the normal traction } \widehat{\rho\rho} = N(\omega, z), \\ &\text{the transverse traction } \widehat{\rho\omega} = T(\omega, z), \\ &\text{the longitudinal traction } \widehat{\rho z} = L(\omega, z), \end{aligned}\right\} \quad (11)$$

where N, T, L are given functions, which we shall suppose to vanish at all points outside a certain finite portion of the cylinder lying between two cross-sections $z = z_1$ and $z = z_2$ $(z_2 > z_1)$.

The functions N, T, L can be expressed in forms suitable for analytical treatment by means of Fourier's series and Fourier's integral. For example,

$$N(\omega, z) = \frac{1}{\pi}\Sigma'\int_0^{2\pi} N(\omega', z)\cos m(\omega-\omega')\,d\omega',$$

$$N(\omega', z) = \frac{1}{\pi}\int_0^\infty d\kappa\int_{z_1}^{z_2} N(\omega', z')\cos\kappa(z-z')\,dz,$$

so that

$$N(\omega, z) = \frac{1}{\pi^2}\Sigma'\int_0^{2\pi} d\omega' \int_0^{\infty} d\kappa \int_{z_1}^{z_2} N(\omega', z') \cos\kappa(z-z') \cos m(\omega-\omega')\, dz'. \quad (12)$$

This expansion suggests the possibility of deducing solutions for the three general problems of (11) from solutions of the three simplified problems in which N, T, L in (11) are replaced by $\cos\kappa(z-z')\cos m(\omega-\omega')$.

Normal Traction. For the simplified problem of normal traction assume

$$\phi = A\, J_m(i\kappa\rho) \cos\kappa(z-z') \cos m(\omega-\omega'),$$
$$\theta = B\, J_m(i\kappa\rho) \cos\kappa(z-z') \cos m(\omega-\omega'),$$
$$\psi = C\, J_m(i\kappa\rho) \cos\kappa(z-z') \sin m(\omega-\omega'),$$

or, in a useful compact notation,

$$\begin{pmatrix}\phi, \theta, \\ \psi\end{pmatrix} = \begin{pmatrix}A, B, \\ C\end{pmatrix} J_m(i\kappa\rho) \cos\kappa(z-z') \begin{matrix}\cos\\ \sin\end{matrix}\, m(\omega-\omega'). \quad (13)$$

These values of ϕ, θ, ψ give, at $\rho = a$, from (10),

$$\left.\begin{aligned} \widehat{\rho\rho}\,\frac{a^2}{\mu} &= (Aa_{1,m} + Bb_{1,m} + Cc_{1,m}) \cos\kappa(z-z') \cos m(\omega-\omega'), \\ \widehat{\rho\omega}\,\frac{a^2}{\mu} &= (Aa_{2,m} + Bb_{2,m} + Cc_{2,m}) \cos\kappa(z-z') \sin m(\omega-\omega'), \\ \widehat{\rho z}\,\frac{a}{\mu\kappa} &= (Aa_{3,m} + Bb_{3,m} + Cc_{3,m}) \sin\kappa(z-z') \cos m(\omega-\omega'), \end{aligned}\right\} \quad (14)$$

where $a_{1,m} = (2-\nu)\kappa^2a^2J - 2i\kappa^3a^3J'$,

$$b_{1,m} = -2\kappa^2a^2J'', \quad c_{1,m} = -2m(J - i\kappa aJ'),$$
$$a_{2,m} = m\kappa^2a^2J, \quad b_{2,m} = -c_{1,m}, \quad c_{2,m} = \kappa^2a^2J'' + i\kappa aJ' - m^2J,$$
$$a_{3,m} = 2\kappa^2a^2J + \nu i\kappa aJ' + m^2J, \quad b_{3,m} = -2i\kappa aJ', \quad c_{3,m} = -mJ,$$

and J, J', J'' are written instead of $J_m(i\kappa a)$, $J_m'(i\kappa a)$, $J_m''(i\kappa a)$.

For the problem of normal traction $\cos\kappa(z-z')\cos m(\omega-\omega')$,

$$\left.\begin{aligned} Aa_{1,m} + Bb_{1,m} + Cc_{1,m} &= \frac{a^2}{\mu}, \\ Aa_{2,m} + Bb_{2,m} + Cc_{2,m} &= 0, \\ Aa_{3,m} + Bb_{3,m} + Cc_{3,m} &= 0, \end{aligned}\right\} \quad (15)$$

which give

$$A = \frac{a^2}{\mu} A_{1,m}/D_m, \quad B = \frac{a^2}{\mu} B_{1,m}/D_m, \quad C = \frac{a^2}{\mu} C_{1,m}/D_m, \quad (16)$$

where
$$D_m \equiv \begin{vmatrix} a_{1,m}, & b_{1,m} & c_{1,m} \\ a_{2,m}, & b_{2,m} & c_{2,m} \\ a_{3,m}, & b_{3,m} & c_{3,m} \end{vmatrix},$$

and $A_{1,m}, B_{1,m}, \ldots$ are the co-factors of $a_{1,m}, b_{1,m}, \ldots$ in D_m.

In order to obtain a general solution of the problem of normal traction, it is natural, in view of (12), to try the result of multiplying the values of ϕ, θ, ψ just obtained by $N(\omega', z')$ and taking

$$\frac{1}{\pi^2}\sum_m{}' \int_0^{2\pi} d\omega' \int_0^\infty d\kappa \int_{z_1}^{z_2} N(\omega', z') \begin{pmatrix} \phi, \theta, \\ \psi \end{pmatrix} dz'$$

as the required values of ϕ, θ, ψ. It will be found that, owing to the presence of negative powers of κ, the integrations with regard to κ cannot be carried out. As, however, these terms contribute nothing to the surface traction at $\rho=a$, since this traction is finite, and as they are of the form $H_1/\kappa^4 + H_2/\kappa^2$ where H_1 and H_2 are rational integral harmonic functions of x, y, z, all that is necessary is to subtract them. The tentative solution for normal traction $N(\omega, z)$ is now

$$\begin{pmatrix} \phi, \theta, \\ \psi \end{pmatrix} = \frac{1}{\pi^2}\sum_m{}' \int_0^{2\pi} d\omega' \int_0^\infty d\kappa \int_{z_1}^{z_2} N(\omega', z') V\, dz', \tag{17}$$

where

$$V = \left\{ \begin{pmatrix} A, B, \\ C \end{pmatrix} J_m(i\kappa\rho) \cos\kappa(z-z') \begin{matrix}\cos\\ \sin\end{matrix}\, m(\omega-\omega') - \begin{pmatrix} \phi_m, \theta_m, \\ \psi_m \end{pmatrix} \right\}$$

and

$$\left.\begin{array}{l} \begin{pmatrix} \phi_m, \theta_m, \\ \psi_m \end{pmatrix} \text{ are the terms of negative degree in } \kappa \text{ in the ascending power} \\ \quad \text{expansions of } \begin{pmatrix} A, B, \\ C \end{pmatrix} J_m(i\kappa\rho) \cos\kappa(z-z') \begin{matrix}\cos\\ \sin\end{matrix}\, m(\omega-\omega'). \end{array}\right\} \tag{18}$$

Hence

$$\begin{pmatrix} \phi, \theta, \\ \psi \end{pmatrix} = \frac{1}{\pi^2} \int_0^{2\pi} d\omega' \int_{z_1}^{z_2} N(\omega', z')\, dz' \sum_m{}' \int_0^\infty V\, d\kappa.$$

Now suppose that $N(\omega, z)$ vanishes except over a small area σ_0 which encloses the point (a, ω', z'), and let it be constant and equal to N_0 over this area. Let σ_0 diminish and N_0 increase without limit while $N_0\sigma_0$ remains equal to unity. The limiting form of (17) is then

$$\begin{pmatrix} \phi, \theta, \\ \psi \end{pmatrix} = \frac{1}{\pi^2 a}\sum_m{}' \int_0^\infty d\kappa \left\{ \begin{pmatrix} A, B, \\ C \end{pmatrix} J_m(i\kappa\rho) \cos\kappa(z-z') \begin{matrix}\cos\\ \sin\end{matrix}\, m(\omega-\omega') - \begin{pmatrix} \phi_m, \theta_m, \\ \psi_m \end{pmatrix} \right\}. \tag{19}$$

This is the solution for a *unit element* of normal traction at (a, ω', z').

To simplify matters we confine our attention in the first place to the part of (19) depending on a simple integer m; this is

$$\begin{pmatrix}\phi, \theta, \\ \psi\end{pmatrix} = \frac{\epsilon_m}{\pi^2 a}\int_0^\infty d\kappa \left\{\frac{a^2}{\mu D_m}\begin{pmatrix}A_{1,m}, B_{1,m}, \\ C_{1,m}\end{pmatrix} J_m(i\kappa\rho)\cos\kappa(z-z') \times \begin{matrix}\cos \\ \sin\end{matrix}\, m(\omega-\omega') - \begin{pmatrix}\phi_m, \theta_m, \\ \psi_m\end{pmatrix}\right\}, \tag{20}$$

where $\epsilon_0 = \frac{1}{2}$, $\epsilon_1 = \epsilon_2 = \epsilon_3 = \ldots = 1$.

Expression of the solution in series. In each of these three integrals (20) the integrand is a uniform even function of κ of the form

$$V(\kappa) \equiv E(\kappa)\cos\kappa(z-z') - E_m(\kappa),$$

where $E_m(\kappa)$ stands for the terms of negative degree in the expansion of $E(\kappa)\cos\kappa(z-z')$ in ascending powers of κ.

Now, if
$$I = \int_0^\infty V(\kappa)\, d\kappa,$$
then
$$I = \tfrac{1}{2}\int_{-\infty}^\infty V(\kappa)\, d\kappa = \tfrac{1}{2}\int_C V(\kappa)\, d\kappa,$$

where C is a contour consisting of the real axis from $-\infty$ to $-\epsilon$, a semicircle with the origin as centre and ϵ as radius below the real axis, and the real axis from ϵ to ∞. But, since

$$E_m(\kappa) = H_4/\kappa^4 + H_2/\kappa^2,$$

the integral of $E_m(\kappa)$ along this contour has the value zero: hence

$$I = \tfrac{1}{2}\int_C E(\kappa)\cos\kappa(z-z')\, d\kappa$$
$$= \tfrac{1}{4}\int_C E(\kappa)e^{-i\kappa(z-z')}\, d\kappa + \tfrac{1}{4}\int_C E(\kappa)e^{i\kappa(z-z')}\, d\kappa.$$

In the latter integral change the sign of κ; then it becomes

$$\tfrac{1}{4}\int_{C'} E(\kappa)e^{-i\kappa(z-z')}\, d\kappa,$$

where the contour C' is the same as C, except that the semicircle lies above the real axis. Thus

$$I = \tfrac{1}{2}\int_C E(\kappa)e^{-i\kappa(z-z')}\, d\kappa - \tfrac{1}{4}\int_c E(\kappa)e^{-i\kappa(z-z')}\, d\kappa,$$

c being a circle about the origin described positively. In this equation change the variable from κ to β, where $\beta = i\kappa a$. Then, if $E(\kappa)$ becomes $E(\beta)$,

$$I = \frac{1}{2ia}\int_{C_1} E(\beta) e^{-\frac{\beta(z-z')}{a}} d\beta - \frac{1}{4ia}\int_{c_1} E(\beta) e^{-\frac{\beta(z-z')}{a}} d\beta,$$

where C_1 denotes the imaginary axis from $-\infty i$ to ∞i, with a semicircle to the right of the origin, and c_1 is a circle about the origin. Thus

$$\begin{pmatrix}\phi, \theta, \\ \psi\end{pmatrix} = \frac{\epsilon_m}{2\pi^2 i\mu}\int_{C_1} V(\beta)\, d\beta - \frac{\epsilon_m}{4\pi^2 i\mu}\int_{c_1} V(\beta)\, d\beta,$$

where

$$V(\beta) \equiv \frac{1}{D_m}\begin{Bmatrix} A_{1,m}, B_{1,m}, \\ C_{1,m} \end{Bmatrix} J_m\left(\frac{\beta\rho}{a}\right) e^{-\beta\left(\frac{z-z'}{a}\right)} \begin{matrix}\cos \\ \sin\end{matrix}\, m(\omega - \omega'). \quad (21)$$

If $\rho < a$ and $z > z'$, the contour C_1 can be deformed into a closed contour consisting of C_1 and an infinite semicircle to the right of the imaginary axis. Then, by the theory of residues,

$$\begin{pmatrix}\phi, \theta, \\ \psi\end{pmatrix} = -\frac{\epsilon_m}{\pi\mu}\sum_\beta \frac{1}{\frac{dD_m}{d\beta}} \begin{Bmatrix} A_{1,m}, B_{1,m}, \\ C_{1,m} \end{Bmatrix} J_m\left(\frac{\beta\rho}{a}\right) e^{-\frac{\beta(z-z')}{a}} \begin{matrix}\cos \\ \sin\end{matrix}\, m(\omega - \omega')$$

$$-\frac{\epsilon_m}{2\pi\mu} \times \text{coefficient of } \frac{1}{\beta} \text{ in}$$

$$\frac{1}{D_m}\begin{Bmatrix} A_{1,m}, B_{1,m}, \\ C_{1,m} \end{Bmatrix} J_m\left(\frac{\beta\rho}{a}\right) e^{-\frac{\beta(z-z')}{a}} \begin{matrix}\cos \\ \sin\end{matrix}\, m(\omega - \omega'), \quad (22)$$

where $\sum_\beta$ denotes that the series is taken over the zeros of D_m which lie to the right of the imaginary axis arranged in non-descending order of magnitude of their moduli.

The general solution for unit element of normal traction can now be obtained by summing with regard to m, and the solution for the general problem can be deduced by integration.

If $z < z'$, the corresponding results are found most simply by interchanging z and z', retaining the meaning of $\sum_\beta$ unchanged.

The transverse and longitudinal tractions can also be expanded in series by the same method.

For the solutions for forces at internal points, and for the physical applications of these results, the reader is referred to Dr. Dougall's papers.

CHAPTER XVI.

MISCELLANEOUS APPLICATIONS.

In this concluding chapter we propose to give a short account of some special applications of the Bessel functions which, although not so difficult as those already considered, appear too important or too interesting to be passed over entirely or simply placed in the collection of examples.

§1. **Variable Flow of Heat in a Solid Sphere.** We will begin with the equation

$$\frac{\partial u}{\partial t}=a^2\nabla^2 u, \tag{1}$$

which occurs in various physical problems, such as the small vibrations of a gas, or the variable flow of heat in a solid sphere.

In polar coordinates, u is a function of t, r, θ, ϕ, such that

$$\frac{\partial u}{\partial t}=\frac{a^2}{r^2}\left\{r^2\frac{\partial^2 u}{\partial r^2}+2r\frac{\partial u}{\partial r}+\frac{1}{\sin\theta}\frac{\partial}{\partial\theta}\left(\sin\theta\frac{\partial u}{\partial\theta}\right)+\frac{1}{\sin^2\theta}\frac{\partial^2 u}{\partial\phi^2}\right\}. \tag{2}$$

Assume, as a particular solution,

$$u=e^{-\kappa^2 a^2 t}vS_n,$$

where v is a function of r only, and S_n is a surface spherical harmonic of order n, so that

$$\frac{1}{\sin\theta}\frac{\partial}{\partial\theta}\left(\sin\theta\frac{\partial S_n}{\partial\theta}\right)+\frac{1}{\sin^2\theta}\frac{\partial^2 S_n}{\partial\phi^2}+n(n+1)S_n=0.$$

Then, after substitution for u in (2), it appears that v must satisfy the equation

$$\frac{d^2v}{dr^2}+\frac{2}{r}\frac{dv}{dr}+\left\{\kappa^2-\frac{n(n+1)}{r^2}\right\}v=0;$$

and now if we put $\qquad v=r^{-\frac{1}{2}}w,$

we find that w satisfies the equation

$$\frac{d^2w}{dr^2}+\frac{1}{r}\frac{dw}{dr}+\left\{\kappa^2-\frac{(n+\frac{1}{2})^2}{r^2}\right\}w=0.$$

Hence $$w = AJ_{n+\frac{1}{2}}(\kappa r) + BJ_{-n-\frac{1}{2}}(\kappa r),$$

and finally $$u = e^{-\kappa^2 a^2 t}\{AJ_{n+\frac{1}{2}}(\kappa r) + BJ_{-n-\frac{1}{2}}(\kappa r)\}\frac{S_n}{\sqrt{r}} \qquad (3)$$

is a particular solution of the equation (1) or (2). In practice n is a whole number, and by a proper determination of the constants n, κ, A, B, the function

$$U = \sum_{n,\,\kappa} e^{-\kappa^2 a^2 t}\{AJ_{n+\frac{1}{2}}(\kappa r) + BJ_{-n-\frac{1}{2}}(\kappa r)\}\frac{S_n}{\sqrt{r}} \qquad (4)$$

is adapted in the usual way to suit the particular conditions of the problem.

(See Riemann's *Partielle Differentialgleichungen*, pp. 176-189, and Rayleigh's *Theory of Sound*, Chap. XVII.)

If in the above we suppose $n=0$, the function S_n reduces to a constant, and

$$J_{n+\frac{1}{2}}(\kappa r) = \sqrt{\frac{2}{\pi\kappa r}}\sin\kappa r$$

(see p. 17); thus, with a simplified notation, we have a solution

$$U = \sum_{\kappa} A_\kappa \frac{\sin\kappa r}{r} e^{-\kappa^2 a^2 t}, \qquad (5)$$

which may be adapted to the following problem (Math. Tripos, 1886):

"A uniform homogeneous sphere of radius b is at uniform temperature V_0, and is surrounded by a spherical shell of the same substance of thickness b at temperature zero. The whole is left to cool in a medium at temperature zero. Prove that, after time t, the temperature at a point distant r from the centre is

$$V = V_0 \Sigma \frac{4}{\kappa} \frac{\sin\kappa b - \kappa b\cos\kappa b}{4\kappa b - \sin 4\kappa b} \frac{\sin\kappa r}{r} e^{-\kappa^2 a^2 t}, \qquad (6)$$

where the values of κ are given by the equation

$$\tan 2\kappa b = \frac{2\kappa b}{1-2hb}, \qquad (7)$$

h being the ratio of the 'surface conductivity' to the internal conductivity."

Here the conditions to be satisfied are

$$V = V_0 \text{ from } r=0 \text{ to } r=b,$$
$$V = 0 \quad \text{,,} \quad r=b \quad \text{,,} \quad r=2b,$$

when $t=0$; and $$\frac{\partial V}{\partial r} + hV = 0,$$

when $r=2b$, for all values of t.

Now, assuming a solution of the form

$$V=\Sigma A_\kappa \frac{\sin \kappa r}{r} e^{-\kappa^2 a^2 t},$$

we find the last condition satisfied if

$$\frac{\partial}{\partial r}\left(\frac{\sin \kappa r}{r}\right)+\frac{h \sin \kappa r}{r}=0,$$

when $r=2b$: that is, if

$$\frac{\kappa \cos 2\kappa b}{2b}-\frac{\sin 2\kappa b}{4b^2}+\frac{h \sin 2\kappa b}{2b}=0,$$

leading to

$$\tan 2\kappa b=\frac{2\kappa b}{1-2hb},$$

as above stated.

Proceeding as in Chap. VIII. above, we infer that

$$A_\kappa \int_0^{2b} \sin^2 \kappa r \, dr=\int_0^{2b} Vr \sin \kappa r \, dr,$$

that is,

$$A_\kappa\left(b-\frac{\sin 4\kappa b}{4\kappa}\right)=V_0 \int_0^b r \sin \kappa r \, dr$$

$$=V_0\left(\frac{\sin \kappa b}{\kappa^2}-\frac{b \cos \kappa b}{\kappa}\right),$$

and hence

$$A_\kappa=\frac{4}{\kappa} \cdot \frac{\sin \kappa b-\kappa b \cos \kappa b}{4\kappa b-\sin 4\kappa b} V_0,$$

which agrees with the result above given.

Returning to the solution given by equation (4) above, we may observe that when a^2 is real and positive, the solution is applicable to cases when there is a "damping" of the phenomenon considered, as in the problem just discussed. When there is a forced vibration imposed on the system, as when a spherical bell vibrates in air, we must take a^2 to be a pure imaginary $\pm ia/\kappa$, so as to obtain a time-periodic solution. The period is then $2\pi/(\kappa a)$. An illustration of this will be found at the end of the book.

§ 2. **Stability of a Vertical Cylindrical Rod.** We will now proceed to consider two problems suggested by the theory of elasticity.

The first is that of the stability of an isotropic circular cylinder of small cross-section held in a vertical position with its lower end clamped and upper end free.

It is a matter of common observation that a comparatively short piece of steel wire, such as a knitting-needle, is stable when placed vertically with its lower end clamped in a vice; whereas it would be impossible to keep vertical in the same way a very long piece of the same wire.

To find the greatest length consistent with stability, we consider the possibility of a position of equilibrium which only deviates *slightly* from the vertical.

Let w be the weight of the wire per unit length, β its flexural rigidity. Then if x is the height of any point on the wire above the clamped end, and y its horizontal displacement from the vertical through that end, we obtain by taking moments for the part of the wire above (x, y)

$$\beta \frac{d^2y}{dx^2} = \int_x^l w(y' - y)\, dx', \tag{8}$$

l being the whole length of the wire.

Differentiate with respect to x; then

$$\beta \frac{d^3y}{dx^3} = \int_x^l w\left(-\frac{dy}{dx}\right) dx = -w(l-x)\frac{dy}{dx},$$

or, with $p = \dfrac{dy}{dx}$, $\qquad \dfrac{d^2p}{dx^2} + \dfrac{w}{\beta}(l-x)p = 0.$

If we put $\zeta = w(l-x)^3/9\beta$, this equation becomes

$$\zeta \frac{d^2p}{d\zeta^2} + \frac{2}{3}\frac{dp}{d\zeta} + p = 0, \tag{8'}$$

with the solution, III. (59), $\quad p = BF_{-\frac{1}{3}}(\zeta)$. $\hfill (8'')$

For the reduction of the differential equation to the Bessel form, put

$$l - x = r^{\frac{2}{3}}; \tag{9}$$

then $\qquad \dfrac{dp}{dx} = -\dfrac{3}{2} r^{\frac{1}{3}} \dfrac{dp}{dr}, \quad \dfrac{d^2p}{dx^2} = \dfrac{9}{4}\left\{ r^{\frac{2}{3}} \dfrac{d^2p}{dr^2} + \dfrac{1}{3} r^{-\frac{1}{3}} \dfrac{dp}{dr} \right\},$

and the transformed equation is

$$\frac{d^2p}{dr^2} + \frac{1}{3r}\frac{dp}{dr} + \frac{4w}{9\beta}p = 0;$$

and now, if we put

$$p = r^{\frac{1}{3}} z, \tag{10}$$

it will be found that

$$\frac{d^2z}{dr^2} + \frac{1}{r}\frac{dz}{dr} + \left(\frac{4w}{9\beta} - \frac{1}{9r^2}\right) z = 0. \tag{11}$$

Hence, if
$$\kappa^2=\frac{4w}{9\beta},$$
it follows that
$$z=AJ_{\frac{1}{3}}(\kappa r)+BJ_{-\frac{1}{3}}(\kappa r). \tag{12}$$
When $x=l$, that is, when $r=0$, we must have
$$\frac{dp}{dx}=0,$$
whence
$$r^{\frac{1}{3}}\frac{dp}{dr}=0,$$
where $r=0$; that is,
$$r^{\frac{1}{3}}\left\{r^{\frac{1}{3}}\frac{dz}{dr}+\frac{1}{3}r^{-\frac{2}{3}}z\right\}=0,$$
or
$$\frac{3r\dfrac{dz}{dr}+z}{3r^{\frac{1}{3}}}=0.$$

Now the initial terms of $J_{\frac{1}{3}}(\kappa r)$ and $J_{-\frac{1}{3}}(\kappa r)$ are of the forms
$$J_{\frac{1}{3}}(\kappa r)=ar^{\frac{1}{3}}+\beta r^{\frac{7}{3}}+\dots,$$
$$J_{-\frac{1}{3}}(\kappa r)=a'r^{-\frac{1}{3}}+\beta' r^{\frac{5}{3}}+\dots,$$
and it is only the second of these that satisfies
$$r^{-\frac{1}{3}}\left(3r\frac{dz}{dr}+z\right)=0,$$
when $r=0$. Therefore $A=0$. This solution agrees with (8″).

Again, when $x=0$, that is, when $r=l^{\frac{3}{2}}$, p, and therefore z, must be zero. Hence, in order that the assumed form of equilibrium may be possible,
$$J_{-\frac{1}{3}}(\kappa l^{\frac{3}{2}})=0. \tag{13}$$

The least value of l obtained from this equation gives the critical length of the wire when it first shows signs of instability in the vertical position; and if l is less than this, the vertical position will be stable.

It is found that the least root of
$$J_{-\frac{1}{3}}(x)=0$$
is approximately 1·866: so that the critical length is about
$$\left(\frac{1\cdot 866}{\kappa}\right)^{\frac{2}{3}},$$
or
$$1\cdot 986\sqrt[3]{(\beta/w)},$$
approximately.

To the degree of approximation adopted we may put

$$l = 2\sqrt[3]{(\beta/w)}, \qquad (14)$$

or in terms of β and W, the whole weight of the wire,

$$l = \sqrt{(7\cdot83\beta/W)} = 2\cdot8\sqrt{(\beta/W)}. \qquad (15)$$

Of the two formulae given the first is the proper one for determining the critical length for a given kind of wire; the second is convenient if we wish to know whether a given piece of wire will be stable if placed in a vertical position with its lower end clamped.

(See Greenhill, *Proc. Camb. Phil. Soc.* IV. 1881, and Love, *Math. Theory of Elasticity*, 2nd Ed. p. 405.)

In connection with the reduction of the differential equation at p. 232, it may be pointed out here, that, if $yr^{-\lambda}$ be substituted for u, and $x^{\frac{1}{\mu}}\kappa^{-1}$ for r, the differential equation of the form

$$\frac{d^2u}{dr^2} + (2\lambda+1)\frac{1}{r}\frac{du}{dr} + (\kappa^{2\mu}\mu^2 r^{2\mu} + \lambda^2 - \mu^2 n^2)\frac{1}{r^2}u = 0, \qquad (16)$$

can be reduced to the standard form

$$\frac{d^2y}{dx^2} + \frac{1}{x}\frac{dy}{dx} + \left(1 - \frac{n^2}{x^2}\right)y = 0,$$

so that it is integrable by Bessel functions.

This gives a general rule for the transformation in cases in which it is not so obvious as in the case considered above. In that case

$$u = p, \quad \lambda = -\tfrac{1}{3}, \quad n = \pm\tfrac{1}{3}, \quad \mu = 1, \quad \kappa^2 = 4w/9\beta.$$

(See pp. 246, 247 below for other examples.)

Again, the substitution $u = yr^{-\lambda+\mu n}$ reduces (16) to

$$r^2\frac{d^2y}{dr^2} + (1+2\mu n)r\frac{dy}{dr} + \kappa^{2\mu}\mu^2 r^{2\mu}y = 0.$$

Now let $x = (\kappa r)^{2\mu}/4$, then the differential equation becomes

$$x\frac{d^2y}{dx^2} + (n+1)\frac{dy}{dx} + y = 0,$$

which is III. (59).

§ 3. **Torsional Vibration of a Solid Circular Cylinder.** As another simple illustration derived from the theory of elasticity, we will give, after Pochhammer and Love (*l.c.* p. 275), a short discussion of the torsional vibration of an isotropic solid circular cylinder of radius c.

If (r, θ, z) are the coordinates of any point of the cylinder, and u, v, w the corresponding displacements, the equations of motion for small vibrations are

$$\left.\begin{aligned}\rho\frac{\partial^2 u}{\partial t^2}&=(\lambda+2\mu)\frac{\partial\Delta}{\partial r}-\frac{2\mu}{r}\frac{\partial\varpi_3}{\partial\theta}+2\mu\frac{\partial\varpi_2}{dz},\\ \rho\frac{\partial^2 v}{\partial t^2}&=(\lambda+2\mu)\frac{1}{r}\frac{\partial\Delta}{\partial\theta}-2\mu\frac{\partial\varpi_1}{\partial z}+2\mu\frac{\partial\varpi_3}{\partial r},\\ \rho\frac{\partial^2 w}{\partial t^2}&=(\lambda+2\mu)\frac{\partial\Delta}{\partial z}-\frac{2\mu}{r}\frac{\partial}{\partial r}(r\varpi_2)+\frac{2\mu}{r}\frac{\partial\varpi_1}{\partial\theta},\end{aligned}\right\}\qquad(17)$$

where

$$\left.\begin{aligned}\Delta&=\frac{1}{r}\frac{\partial(ru)}{\partial r}+\frac{1}{r}\frac{\partial v}{\partial\theta}+\frac{\partial w}{\partial z},\\ 2\varpi_1&=\frac{1}{r}\left(\frac{\partial w}{\partial\theta}-\frac{\partial(rv)}{\partial z}\right),\\ 2\varpi_2&=\frac{\partial u}{\partial z}-\frac{\partial w}{\partial r},\\ 2\varpi_3&=\frac{1}{r}\left(\frac{\partial(rv)}{\partial r}-\frac{\partial u}{\partial\theta}\right).\end{aligned}\right\}\qquad(18)$$

The stresses across a cylindrical surface $r=$constant are

$$\left.\begin{aligned}P_{rr}&=\lambda\Delta+2\mu\frac{\partial u}{\partial r},\\ P_{\theta r}&=\mu\left\{\frac{1}{r}\frac{\partial u}{\partial\theta}+r\frac{\partial}{\partial r}\left(\frac{v}{r}\right)\right\},\\ P_{zr}&=\mu\left(\frac{\partial u}{\partial z}+\frac{\partial w}{\partial r}\right).\end{aligned}\right\}\qquad(19)$$

We proceed to construct a particular solution of the type

$$u=0,\quad w=0,\quad v=Ve^{i(\gamma z+pt)},\qquad(20)$$

where V is a function of r only, and γ, p are constants. In order to obtain a periodic vibration with no damping, we suppose that p is real. The torsional character of the oscillation is clear from the form of u, v, w.

If we put, for the moment,

$$e^{i(\gamma z+pt)}=Z,$$

we have

$$\begin{aligned}\Delta&=0,\\ 2\varpi_1&=-i\gamma VZ,\\ 2\varpi_2&=0,\\ 2\varpi_3&=\frac{Z}{r}\frac{\partial(rV)}{\partial r},\end{aligned}$$

and the equations of motion reduce to two identities and

$$-\rho p^2 VZ = -\mu\gamma^2 VZ + \mu Z \frac{d}{dr}\left(\frac{1}{r}\frac{d}{dr}(rV)\right).$$

Thus V must satisfy the equation

$$\frac{d^2V}{dr^2} + \frac{1}{r}\frac{dV}{dr} + \left\{\frac{\rho p^2 - \mu\gamma^2}{\mu} - \frac{1}{r^2}\right\} V = 0,$$

and since V must be finite when $r=0$, the proper solution is

$$V = AJ_1(\kappa r), \tag{21}$$

where
$$\kappa^2 = \frac{\rho}{\mu}p^2 - \gamma^2.$$

If the curved surface of the cylinder is free, then the stresses P_{rr}, $P_{\theta r}$, P_{zr} must vanish when $r=c$. Now P_{rr} and P_{zr} vanish identically; $P_{\theta r}$ will vanish if

$$\frac{d}{dr}\left\{\frac{J_1(\kappa r)}{r}\right\} = 0,$$

when $r=c$: that is, if

$$\kappa c J_1'(\kappa c) - J_1(\kappa c) = 0,$$

or, which is the same thing, if (II. 20)

$$\kappa c J_2(\kappa c) = 0.$$

If $\kappa = 0$, the differential equation to find V is

$$\frac{d^2V}{dr^2} + \frac{1}{r}\frac{dV}{dr} - \frac{1}{r^2}V = 0,$$

of which the solution is $V = Ar + \dfrac{B}{r}$,

or, for our present purpose,

$$V = Ar.$$

This leads to a solution of the original problem in the shape

$$u=0, \quad w=0,$$
$$v = Are^{i(\gamma z + pt)},$$

with
$$\rho p^2 - \mu\gamma^2 = 0;$$

and in particular we have as a special case

$$v = r\sum_n {\cos \atop \sin}\frac{n\pi z}{l}\left(A_n \cos\frac{n\pi t}{l}\sqrt{\frac{\mu}{\rho}} + B_n \sin\frac{n\pi t}{l}\sqrt{\frac{\mu}{\rho}}\right), \tag{22}$$

when $n=0, 1, 2, \ldots$, and l is a constant.

MISCELLANEOUS EXAMPLES.

1. Show that

$$\text{(i)}\quad J_{n+2}J_{-n} - J_{-(n+2)}J_n = \frac{4(n+1)\sin(n+1)\pi}{\pi x^2};$$

$$\text{(ii)}\quad J_{n+2}Y_n - Y_{n+2}J_n = \frac{2(n+1)}{x^2}.$$

2. Prove that

$$\text{(i)}\quad (n+1)J_{n+1}\{J_{n+1}+J_{n-1}\} = nJ_n\{J_n+J_{n+2}\};$$

$$\text{(ii)}\quad J_1^2 = 2(J_0J_2 + J_1J_3 + J_2J_4 + \ldots);$$

$$\text{(iii)}\quad 2J_1J_3 - J_2^2 = 2(J_0J_4 + J_1J_5 + J_2J_6 + \ldots).$$

3. Verify the following expansions:

$$\text{(i)}\quad e^{nx} = J_0(x) + \sum_1^\infty\{(n+\sqrt{n^2+1})^s + (n-\sqrt{n^2+1})^s\}J_s(x).$$

$$\text{(ii)}\quad \cosh nx = J_0(x) + 2\Sigma\cosh s\phi J_s(x), \qquad [s=2,\ 4,\ \ldots]$$

$$\sinh nx = 2\Sigma\sinh s\phi\, J_s(x), \qquad [s=1,\ 3,\ \ldots]$$

where $\phi = \sinh^{-1}n.$

$$\text{(iii)}\quad \cos nx = J_0(x) + 2\Sigma(-)^{\frac{1}{2}s}\cosh s\phi\, J_s(x), \qquad [s=2,\ 4,\ \ldots]$$

$$\sin nx = 2\Sigma(-)^{\frac{1}{2}(s-1)}\cosh s\phi\, J_s(x), \qquad [s=1,\ 3,\ \ldots]$$

where $\phi = \cosh^{-1}n$, n being supposed greater than 1. [See page 35.]

4. Show that

$$bcJ_1\{\sqrt{(b^2+c^2)}\} = 2\sqrt{(b^2+c^2)}\{J_1(b)J_1(c) - 3J_3(b)J_3(c) + 5J_5(b)J_5(c) - \ldots\}.$$

5. Prove that

$$J_n(z) + \frac{z}{2}J_{n+1}(z) + \frac{z^2}{2\,.\,4}J_{n+2}(z) + \ldots = \frac{z^n}{2^n\Pi(n)}.$$

[Show by means of (V. 40) that the sum of the series is

$$\frac{1}{2\pi i}z^n\int_{C'} e^{\frac{1}{2}\zeta}\,\zeta^{-n-1}\,d\zeta,$$

and apply App. I. (8′).]

6. If n is real, prove that, between two successive positive zeros of $J_n(x)$ there lies one and only one zero of $J_{n+2}(x)$, and that this zero is greater than the zero of $J_{n+1}(x)$ which lies in the interval in question. (M. Bôcher, *Bull. of the Amer. Math. Soc.*, 2nd Ser., Vol. III. No. 6, p. 207.)

7. If $x>|n|$, show that between two successive zeros of $J_n(x)$ there lies one and only one zero of $J''_n(x)$, and that this zero is greater than the zero of $J'_n(x)$ which lies in the interval in question.

(M. Bôcher, *ibid.*)

8. Prove that

$$\text{(i)}\quad \overline{Y}_0 = -\frac{4}{\pi}\int_0^\infty \cos(x\cosh\theta)\,d\theta\,;$$

$$\text{(ii)}\quad \int_0^\infty e^{-a^2x^2}\overline{Y}_0(bx)\,dx = -\frac{1}{a\sqrt{\pi}}\,e^{-\frac{b^2}{8a^2}}K_0\left(\frac{b^2}{8a^2}\right);$$

$$\text{(iii)}\quad \int_0^\infty e^{-a^2x^2}K_0(bx)\,dx = \frac{\sqrt{\pi}}{4a}\,e^{\frac{b^2}{8a^2}}K_0\left(\frac{b^2}{8a^2}\right).$$ (Basset.)

[From (v. 35),

$$G_0(x) = K_0(-ix) = \int_x^\infty \frac{\cos\xi\,d\xi}{\sqrt{(\xi^2-x^2)}} + i\int_0^x \frac{\cos\xi\,d\xi}{\sqrt{(x^2-\xi^2)}}.$$

Equate real parts to obtain (i). For (ii), substitute from (i), change the order of integration, and apply (v. 34). For (iii) substitute for $K_0(bx)$ from (v. 36).]

9. If

$$Q_n^m(\zeta) = \frac{e^{m\pi i}}{2^{n+1}}\,\frac{\sqrt{\pi}\,\Pi(n+m)}{\Pi(n+\frac{1}{2})}\,\frac{(\zeta^2-1)^{\frac{1}{2}m}}{\zeta^{n+m+1}}$$
$$\times F\left(\frac{n+m+2}{2},\ \frac{n+m+1}{2},\ n+\frac{3}{2},\ \frac{1}{\zeta^2}\right),$$

and x is real and positive, show that

$$I_n(x) = \frac{x^m}{2\pi i}\sqrt{\left(\frac{2}{\pi}\right)}e^{(m-\frac{1}{2})\pi i}\int_C e^{x\zeta}(\zeta^2-1)^{\frac{1}{2}(m-\frac{1}{2})}Q_{n-\frac{1}{2}}^{\frac{1}{2}-m}(\zeta)\,d\zeta,$$

where the contour C commences at $-\infty$ on the real axis, passes positively round $\zeta=1$, and returns to $-\infty$; the initial value of amp (ζ^2-1) is -2π.

10. If κ_q is a positive zero of $J_0(x)$, and m is a positive integer, show that

(i) $\displaystyle\sum_{q=1}^{\infty}\frac{1}{\kappa_q^{2m+1}J_1(\kappa_q)}$ is equal to the coefficient of x^{2m} in the expansion of $1/\phi(x)$, where

$$\phi(x) = 1 - \left(\frac{x}{2}\right)\frac{1}{(1\,!)^2} + \left(\frac{x}{2}\right)^2\frac{1}{(2\,!)^2} - \left(\frac{x}{2}\right)^3\frac{1}{(3\,!)^2} + \dots;$$

(ii) $m\sum_{q=1}^{\infty}\frac{1}{\kappa_q^{2m+2}J_1^2(\kappa_q)}$ is equal to the coefficient of x^{2m} in the expansion of $1/\{\phi(x)\}^2$.

(A. R. Forsyth, *Mess. of Maths.*, No. 597, Vol. I. 1921.)

11. Prove that

$$\int_1^{\infty}\frac{e^{-\epsilon\lambda}\sin(\lambda x)}{\sqrt{(\lambda^2-1)}}\,d\lambda=\int_0^{\infty}e^{-\epsilon\lambda}\sin(\lambda x)\,d\lambda\int_0^{\infty}\sin(\lambda r)J_0(r)\,dr.$$

Hence show, by integrating first with respect to λ on the right and having regard to (VI. 7), that

$$J_0(x)=\frac{2}{\pi}\int_1^{\infty}\frac{\sin(\lambda x)}{\sqrt{(\lambda^2-1)}}\,d\lambda,$$

and therefore $$\int_0^1\frac{\sin(\lambda x)}{\sqrt{(1-\lambda^2)}}\,d\lambda=\int_1^{\infty}\frac{\sin(\lambda x)}{\sqrt{(\lambda^2-1)}}\,d\lambda.$$

Deduce that $$J_0(x)=\frac{2}{\pi}\int_0^{\infty}\sin(x\cosh u)\,du.$$

12. Prove that $$\int_0^{\infty}\log x\,J_0(x)\,dx=-(\gamma+\log 2).$$

[See Ch. VI. ex. 12, and App. I. (31).]

13. Prove that, subject to suitable restrictions on the form of the function $\phi(x)$, if

$$f(x)=\int_0^{\infty}\lambda\phi(\lambda)J_n(x\lambda)\,d\lambda,$$

then $$\phi(x)=\int_0^{\infty}\lambda f(\lambda)J_n(x\lambda)\,d\lambda.$$ (Hankel.)

14. Show that the functions $e^{\pm ikr}/r$, $J_m\{\rho\sqrt{(h^2+k^2)}\}e^{\pm hz}\cos m(\phi-\phi_0)$, $G_m\{\rho\sqrt{(h^2+k^2)}\}e^{\pm hz}\cos m(\phi-\phi_0)$, are all solutions of the equation

$$\frac{\partial^2 u}{\partial\rho^2}+\frac{1}{\rho}\frac{\partial u}{\partial\rho}+\frac{1}{\rho^2}\frac{\partial^2 u}{\partial\phi^2}+\frac{\partial^2 u}{\partial z^2}+k^2u=0,$$

where $r^2=\rho^2+z^2$.

15. Prove that

$$\frac{1}{r}e^{ikr}=\int_0^{\infty}e^{-z\sqrt{(\lambda^2-k^2)}}J_0(\lambda\rho)\frac{\lambda\,d\lambda}{\sqrt{(\lambda^2-k^2)}}.$$

[From the previous example it follows that, if $z>0$,

$$\int J_0\{\rho\sqrt{(h^2+k^2)}\}e^{-hz}\,dh=\frac{1}{r}(Ae^{ikr}+Be^{-ikr}).$$

Put $h^2+k^2=\lambda^2$; then

$$\int_0^{\infty}e^{-z\sqrt{(\lambda^2-k^2)}}J_0(\lambda\rho)\frac{\lambda\,d\lambda}{\sqrt{(\lambda^2-k^2)}}=\frac{Ae^{ikr}+Be^{-ikr}}{r},$$

where $\operatorname{amp}(\lambda^2-k^2)=0$ for $\lambda>k$. Now put $\rho=0$, and get $A=1$, $B=0$.]

(Lamb, *Phil. Trans.*, A., 203, p. 5, (1904).)

16. Show that

$$\text{(i)} \int_0^\infty J_0(\lambda\rho)e^{ikr}\frac{\rho\, d\rho}{r} = \frac{e^{-|z|\sqrt{(\lambda^2-k^2)}}}{\sqrt{(\lambda^2-k^2)}} \text{ if } \lambda^2 > k^2$$

$$= \frac{ie^{i|z|\sqrt{(k^2-\lambda^2)}}}{\sqrt{(k^2-\lambda^2)}} \text{ if } k^2 > \lambda^2;$$

$$\text{(ii)} \frac{1}{2}\int_{-\infty}^\infty \frac{e^{ikR}}{R}\cos\lambda(a-b)\, da = K_0\{\rho\sqrt{(\lambda^2-k^2)}\}\cos\lambda(z-b),$$

where $\lambda^2 > k^2$, $R^2 = \rho^2 + (z-a)^2$.

(H. Lamb, *Proc. Lond. Math. Soc.*, Ser. 2, Vol. 7 (1909).)

17. Show that, if the transformation

$$x = r\sin\theta\cos\phi, \quad y = r\sin\theta\sin\phi, \quad z = r\cos\theta,$$

is applied to the equation $\nabla^2 u + k^2 u = 0$,

it becomes

$$\frac{\partial^2 u}{\partial r^2} + \frac{2}{r}\frac{\partial u}{\partial r} + \frac{1}{r^2\sin\theta}\frac{\partial}{\partial\theta}\left(\sin\theta\frac{\partial u}{\partial\theta}\right) + \frac{1}{r^2\sin^2\theta}\frac{\partial^2 u}{\partial\phi^2} + k^2 u = 0,$$

and is satisfied by $u = R\Theta\Phi$, where

$$R = r^{-\frac{1}{2}}J_{n+\frac{1}{2}}(kr) \quad \text{or} \quad r^{-\frac{1}{2}}G_{n+\frac{1}{2}}(kr),$$

$$\Theta = P_n^m(\cos\theta) \quad \text{or} \quad Q_n^m(\cos\theta),$$

$$\Phi = \sin m\phi \quad \text{or} \quad \cos m\phi.$$

18. Show that the complete solution of

$$\frac{d^2y}{dx^2} - \left\{\frac{\phi''(x)}{\phi'(x)} + (2m-1)\frac{\phi'(x)}{\phi(x)}\right\}\frac{dy}{dx} + [m^2 - n^2 + \{\phi(x)\}^2]\left\{\frac{\phi'(x)}{\phi(x)}\right\}^2 y = 0$$

is
$$y = \{\phi(x)\}^m[AJ_n\{\phi(x)\} + BG_n\{\phi(x)\}].$$

19. Show that the equation

$$\frac{d^2y}{dx^2} + \frac{k}{x}\frac{dy}{dx} + \left(1 - \frac{k}{x^2}\right)y = 0$$

is satisfied by
$$y = x^{\frac{1-k}{2}}\{AJ_{\frac{k+1}{2}}(x) + BJ_{-\frac{k+1}{2}}(x)\}.$$

20. Prove that if u is a function of x and y which satisfies the equation

$$\frac{\partial^2 u}{\partial x^2} + \frac{\partial^2 u}{\partial y^2} + \kappa^2 u = 0,$$

and which, as well as its derivatives $\frac{\partial u}{\partial x}$, $\frac{\partial u}{\partial y}$, is finite and continuous for all points within and upon the circle

$$x^2 + y^2 - r^2 = 0,$$

then
$$\int_0^{2\pi} u\, d\phi = 2\pi u_0 J_0(\kappa r),$$

when the integral is taken along the circumference of the circle, and u_0 is the value of u at the origin. (Weber, *Math. Ann.*, i. p. 9.)

21. If n is not a negative integer, show that

$$\left(\frac{z}{2}\right)^n = n^2 \sum_{s=0}^{\infty} \frac{\Gamma(n+s)}{s!\,(n+2s)^{n+1}} J_{n+2s}\{(n+2s)z\},$$

provided that $|z| < a$, where a is the positive root of the equation

$$\frac{x}{2} e^{1+\frac{x^2}{4}} = 1 \quad [a = \cdot 659\ldots].$$

(W. Kapteyn, *Ann. de l'École Normale Supérieure*, Vol. X. 1893.)

22. Prove that

$$\text{(i)} \sum_{s=1}^{\infty} \frac{J_{2s}(2sx)}{s^2} = \tfrac{1}{2}x^2; \qquad \text{(ii)} \sum_{s=1}^{\infty} \frac{\{J_s(sx)\}^2}{s^2} = \tfrac{1}{4}x^2.$$

23. Prove that if

$$V = 2\pi^{-1} \int_0^{\infty} d\mu \int_0^c e^{-\mu z} \cos \lambda v \cos \mu v J_0(\mu\varpi)\, dv,$$

then $\qquad V = J_0(\lambda\varpi)$ when $z = 0$ and $\varpi < c$,

and $\qquad \dfrac{\partial V}{\partial z} = 0 \qquad$ when $z = 0$ and $\varpi > c$.

Show also that if

$$V = 2\pi^{-1} \int_0^{\infty} d\mu \int_0^c e^{-\mu z} \sin \lambda v \sin \mu v J_1(\mu\varpi)\, dv,$$

then $\qquad V = J_1(\lambda\varpi)$ when $z = 0$ and $\varpi < c$,

$\qquad \dfrac{\partial V}{\partial z} = 0 \qquad$ when $z = 0$ and $\varpi > c$.

(Basset, *Hydrodynamics*, II. p. 33.)

24. If $\qquad x^4 - b^4 = \Sigma L_n J_0(nx),$

the summation extending to all values of n given by $J_0(nb) = 0$, then

$$L_n = \frac{2}{b^2\{J_1(nb)\}^2} \int_0^b (x^4 - b^4)\, x J_0(nx)\, dx$$

$$= \frac{8b}{n^3} \frac{2J_3(nb) - nbJ_2(nb)}{\{J_1(nb)\}^2} = \frac{32}{b} \frac{4 - n^2b^2}{n^5 J_1(nb)}.$$

25. Prove that $\qquad \dfrac{\sin 2x}{\pi} = J_{\frac{1}{2}}^2 - 3J_{\frac{3}{2}}^2 + 5J_{\frac{5}{2}}^2 - \ldots.$ $\qquad$ (Lommel.)

26. Prove that if D denote $\dfrac{d}{dx}$, then

$$D^m\{x^{-\frac{1}{2}n} J_n(\surd x)\} = (-\tfrac{1}{2})^m x^{-\frac{1}{2}(n+m)} J_{n+m}(\surd x),$$

$$D^m\{x^{\frac{1}{2}n} J_n(\surd x)\} = (\tfrac{1}{2})^m x^{\frac{1}{2}(n-m)} J_{n-m}(\surd x).$$

(Lommel).

27. Prove that the equation

$$\frac{\partial^2 V}{\partial x^2}+\frac{\partial^2 V}{\partial y^2}+V=0$$

is satisfied by

$$V=(A_m \cos m\phi + B_m \sin m\phi)(-2\rho)^m \frac{d^m J_0(\rho)}{d(\rho^2)^m},$$

where $x=\rho\cos\phi$, $y=\rho\sin\phi$.

Show also that

$$\left\{P_0(\mu)+\frac{1}{2!}P_2(\mu)+\frac{1}{4!}P_4(\mu)+\dots\right\}^2$$

$$-\left\{P_1(\mu)+\frac{1}{3!}P_3(\mu)+\frac{1}{5!}P_5(\mu)+\dots\right\}^2=\{J_0(\sqrt{1-\mu^2})\}^2,$$

and obtain a corresponding expression for $\{J_m(\sqrt{1-\mu^2})\}^2$.

28. Show that the equation

$$\frac{d^2R}{dx^2}+\frac{2}{x}\frac{dR}{dx}+R=\frac{n(n+1)}{x^2}R$$

is satisfied by either of the series

$$u_n=\frac{(-1)^n x^n}{1.3\dots(2n+1)}\left\{1-\frac{1}{1.(2n+3)}\frac{x^2}{2}+\frac{1}{1.2.(2n+3)(2n+5)}\frac{x^4}{4}-\dots\right\},$$

$$v_n=\frac{(-1)^n 1.3\dots(2n-1)}{x^{n+1}}\left\{1+\frac{1}{1.(2n-1)}\frac{x^2}{2}+\frac{1}{1.2.(2n-1)(2n-3)}\frac{x^4}{4}+\dots\right\}.$$

Express u_n as a Bessel function; and show that

$$u_n u_{-(n+1)}=v_n v_{-(n+1)}.$$

29. Verify the following solutions of differential equations by means of Bessel functions:

(i) If
$$\frac{d^2y}{dx^2}-\frac{2n-1}{x}\frac{dy}{dx}+y=0,$$
then
$$y=x^n[AJ_n(x)+BJ_{-n}(x)].$$

(ii) If
$$x^2\frac{d^2y}{dx^2}-(2n\beta-1)x\frac{dy}{dx}+\beta^2\gamma^2x^{2\beta}y=0,$$
then
$$y=x^{\beta n}[AJ_n(\gamma x^\beta)+BJ_{-n}(\gamma x^\beta)].$$

(iii) If
$$x^2\frac{d^2y}{dx^2}+(2\alpha-2\beta n+1)x\frac{dy}{dx}+\{\alpha(\alpha-2\beta n)+\beta^2\gamma^2x^{2\beta}\}y=0,$$
then
$$y=x^{\beta n-\alpha}[AJ_n(\gamma x^\beta)+BJ_{-n}(\gamma x^\beta)].$$

(iv) Deduce from (iii) that if

$$\frac{d^2y}{dx^2}+x^{2\beta-2}y=0$$

(a form of Riccati's equation),

$$y=\sqrt{x}\left[AJ_{\frac{1}{2\beta}}\left(\frac{x^\beta}{\beta}\right)+BJ_{-\frac{1}{2\beta}}\left(\frac{x^\beta}{\beta}\right)\right].$$

and solve $$\frac{d^2y}{dx^2}-x^{2\beta-2}y=0.$$ (Lommel.)

30. Prove that if u is any integral of

$$\frac{d^2u}{dx^2}+Xu=0,$$

where X is a function of x, and if

$$\psi=a\int\frac{dx}{u^2}+b,$$

where a, b are constants, then the complete integral of

$$\frac{d^2y}{dx^2}+\left\{X+\frac{a^2}{u^4}[1-(n^2-\tfrac{1}{4})\psi^{-2}]\right\}y=0$$

is $$y=u\sqrt{\psi}\{AJ_n(\psi)+BJ_{-n}(\psi)\}.$$ (Lommel.)

31. Prove that the solution of Riccati's equation

$$x\frac{dy}{dx}-ay+by^2=cx^p$$

can be made to depend upon the solution of Bessel's equation

$$r^2\frac{d^2w}{dr^2}+r\frac{dw}{dr}+(k^2r^2-n^2)w=0,$$

where $n=a/p$.

32. If a bead of mass M be attached to the lower end of a uniform flexible chain hanging vertically, then the displacement at a point of the chain distant s from the fixed end is, for the small oscillations about the vertical,

$$\sum_n(A_n\cos nt+B_n\sin nt)V_n,$$

where

$$V_n=\{n\sqrt{M}Y_0(n\beta\sqrt{M})-\sqrt{mg}Y_1(n\beta\sqrt{M})\}J_0(n\beta\sqrt{\mu-ms})$$
$$-\{n\sqrt{M}J_0(n\beta\sqrt{M})-\sqrt{mg}J_1(n\beta\sqrt{M})\}Y_0(n\beta\sqrt{\mu-ms}),$$

μ being the total mass of the chain and bead, and β denoting $2/\sqrt{mg}$, where m is the mass of unit length of the chain. How are the values of n to be determined?

33. Assuming that $J_0(x)$ vanishes when $x=2{\cdot}4$, show that in a V-shaped estuary 53 fathoms ($10{,}000\div32{\cdot}2$ ft.) deep, which communicates with the ocean, there will be no semi-diurnal tide at about 300 miles from the end of the estuary. (See p. 238 *et seq.*)

34. The initial temperature of a homogeneous solid sphere of radius a is given by

$$v_0 = Ar^{-2}\cos\theta\,(\sin mr - mr\cos mr):$$

prove that at time t its temperature is

$$u = v_0 e^{-m^2kt},$$

provided that m is a root of the equation

$$(ah - 2k)(ma\cot ma - 1) = m^2a^2k,$$

k, h being the internal and surface conductivities, and the surrounding medium being at zero temperature. (Weber.)

35. A spherical bell of radius c is vibrating in such a manner that the normal component of the velocity at any point of its surface is $S_n \cos kat$, where S_n is a spherical surface harmonic of degree n, and a is the velocity of transmission of vibrations through the surrounding air. Prove that the velocity potential at any point outside the bell at a distance r from the centre, due to the disturbance propagated in the air outwards, is the real part of the expression

$$-\frac{c^2}{r}e^{ik(at-r+c)}\frac{f_n(ikr)\,S_n}{(1+ikc)f_n(ikc) - ikcf'(ikc)},$$

where
$$f_n(x) = (-)^n xe^x P_n\left(\frac{d}{dx}\right)\frac{e^{-x}}{x},$$

P_n denoting the zonal harmonic of degree n.

Show that the resultant pressure of the air on the bell is zero except when $n = 1$.

A sphere is vibrating in a given manner as a rigid body about a position of equilibrium which is at a given distance from a large perfectly rigid obstacle whose surface is plane; determine the motion at any point in the air.

36. A sector of an infinitely long circular cylinder is bounded by two rigid planes inclined at an angle 2α, and is closed at one end by a flexible membrane which is forced to perform small normal oscillations, so that the velocity at any point, whose coordinates, referred to the centre as origin and the bisector of the angle of the sector as initial line, are r, θ, is $qr^p\cos p\theta\cos nct$, where $p\alpha = i\pi$, i being an integer and c the velocity of propagation of plane waves in air. Prove that, at time t, the velocity potential at any point (r, θ, z) of the air in the cylinder is

$$2qpa^p\cos p\theta\,\Sigma\frac{1}{k}\frac{J_p(n'r)}{(n'^2a^2-p^2)J_p(n'a)}\cos nct\{e^{-kz} \text{ or } \sin kz\},$$

where $J_p'(n'a) = 0$ gives the requisite values of n', a being the radius of the cylinder, and where k is a real quantity given by the equation

$n'^2 = n^2 \pm k^2$, the upper and lower sign before k^2 corresponding to the first and second term in the bracket respectively.

37. A given mass of air is at rest in a circular cylinder of radius c under the action of a constant force to the axis. Show that if the force suddenly cease to act, then the velocity function at any subsequent time varies as

$$\Sigma \frac{1}{k^2} \frac{J_0(kr)}{J_0(kc)} \sin kat,$$

where a is the velocity of sound in air, the summation extends to all values of k satisfying $J_1(kc) = 0$, and the square of the condensation is neglected.

38. A right circular cylinder of radius a is filled with viscous liquid, which is initially at rest, and made to rotate with uniform angular velocity ω about its axis. Prove that the velocity of the liquid at time t is

$$2\omega \Sigma \frac{e^{-\lambda^2 \nu t} J_1(\lambda r)}{\lambda J_1'(\lambda a)} + \omega r,$$

where the different values of λ are the roots of the equation $J_1(\lambda a) = 0$.

Show also that if the cylinder were surrounded by viscous liquid the solution of the problem might be obtained from the definite integral

$$\int_0^\infty d\lambda \int_0^a e^{-\lambda^2 \nu t} \lambda u \phi(u) J_1(\lambda u) J_1(\lambda r)\, du,$$

by properly determining $\phi(u)$ so as to satisfy the boundary conditions.

39. In two-dimensional motion of a viscous fluid, symmetrical with respect to the axis $r = 0$, a general form of the current function is

$$\psi = A\left(t + \frac{\rho r^2}{4\mu}\right) + \Sigma A_n e^{nt} J_0\left(r\sqrt{\frac{-n\rho}{\mu}}\right),$$

where A_n, n are arbitrary complex quantities. (Cf. p. 133.)

40. A right circular cylindrical cavity whose radius is a is made in an infinite conductor; prove that the frequency p of the electrical oscillations about the distribution of electricity where the surface density is proportional to $\cos s\theta$, is given by the equation

$$J_s'(pa/v) = 0,$$

where v is the velocity of propagation of electromagnetic action through the dielectric inside the cavity.

41. Prove that the current function due to a fine circular vortex, of radius c and strength m, may be expressed in the form

$$mra \int_0^\infty e^{\pm\lambda(z-z')} J_1(\lambda r) J_1(\lambda c)\, d\lambda,$$

the upper or lower sign being taken according as $z - z'$ is negative or positive.

42. A magnetic pole of strength m is placed in front of an iron plate of magnetic permeability μ and thickness c: if m be the origin of rectangular coordinates x, y, and x be perpendicular and y parallel to the plate, show that Ω, the potential behind the plate, is given by the equation

$$\Omega = m(1-\rho^2)\int_0^\infty \frac{e^{-xt}J_0(yt)\,dt}{1-\rho^2 e^{-2ct}},$$

where

$$\rho = \frac{\mu - 1}{\mu + 1}.$$

43. A right circular cylinder of radius a containing air, moving forwards with velocity V at right angles to its axis, is suddenly stopped; prove that ψ, the velocity potential inside the cylinder at a point distant r from the axis, and where the radius makes an angle θ with the direction in which the cylinder was moving, is given by the equation

$$\psi = -\Sigma V \cos\theta \frac{J_1(\kappa r)}{J_1''(\kappa a)} \cos \kappa \alpha t,$$

where α is the velocity of sound in air, and the summation is taken for all values of κ which satisfy the equation $J_1'(\kappa a) = 0$.

44. Prove that if the opening of the object-glass of the telescope in the diffraction problem considered at p. 189 above be ring-shaped, the intensity of illumination produced by a single point-source at any point of the focal plane is proportional to

$$\frac{4}{(1-p^2)^2}\frac{\{J_1(z) - pJ_1(pz)\}^2}{z^2},$$

if $z = 2\pi Rr/(\lambda f)$, where R is the outer radius, pR the inner radius of the opening, r the distance of the point illuminated from the geometrical image of the source, and f the focal length of the object-glass.

45. Prove that the integral of the expression in the preceding example taken for a line-source involves the evaluation of an integral of the form

$$\int_0^\infty \frac{J_1(ax)\,J_1(bx)}{x\sqrt{x^2-\xi^2}}\,dx.$$

46. Show that

$$J_n(ax)\,J_n(bx) = \frac{x^n a^n b^n}{2^n\sqrt{\pi}\,\Pi(n-\frac{1}{2})}\int_0^\pi \frac{J_n(x\sqrt{a^2+b^2-2ab\cos\phi})}{(a^2+b^2-2ab\cos\phi)^{n/2}}\sin^{2n}\phi\,d\phi.$$

47. Hence prove that

$$\int_z^\infty \frac{J_1(ax)J_1(bx)}{x\sqrt{x^2-\xi^2}}\,dx = \frac{ab}{\pi z}\int_0^\pi \frac{\sin(\xi\sqrt{a^2+b^2-2ab\cos\phi})}{a^2+b^2-2ab\cos\phi}\sin^2\phi\,d\phi.$$

(Struve.)

48. A solid isotropic sphere is strained symmetrically in the radial direction and is then left to perform radial oscillations: show that if u

be the radial displacement at distance r from the centre, k and n the bulk and rigidity moduli, and ρ the density, the equation of motion is

$$\frac{\partial^2 u}{\partial t^2} = \frac{k+\frac{4}{3}n}{\rho}\left(\frac{\partial^2 u}{\partial r^2} + \frac{4}{r}\frac{\partial u}{\partial r}\right),$$

with the surface condition

$$(k+\tfrac{4}{3}n)\frac{\partial u}{\partial r} + 3k\frac{u}{r} = 0.$$

Prove that the complete solution subject to the condition stated is

$$u = \Sigma \frac{1}{\eta_p^{\frac{3}{2}}} J_{\frac{3}{2}}(\eta_p)\{A_p \sin c_p t + A_p' \cos c_p t\}$$

$$+ \Sigma \frac{1}{\eta_p^{-\frac{3}{2}}} J_{-\frac{3}{2}}(\eta_p)\left\{\frac{1}{r^3}(B_p \sin c_p t + B_p' \cos c_p t)\right\},$$

where
$$\eta_p^2 = c^2 \frac{\rho}{k+\frac{4}{3}n} r^2,$$

c_p being the pth root of the equation

$$(k+\tfrac{4}{3}n) a \frac{\partial}{\partial a}\left\{\frac{1}{\eta^{\frac{3}{2}}} J_{\frac{3}{2}}(\eta)\right\} + 3k \frac{1}{\eta^{\frac{3}{2}}} J_{\frac{3}{2}}(\eta) = 0$$

[$\eta^2 = c^2\rho a^2/(k+\frac{4}{3}n)$], which holds at the surface $r=a$ of the sphere.

Show that for the motion specified $B_p = B_p' = 0$; and [using (23), p. 69 above] prove that, if the initial values of ru, $r\dot{u}$ be $\phi(r)$, $\psi(r)$,

$$A_p = \frac{\int_0^a \eta_p^{\frac{3}{2}} J_{\frac{3}{2}}(\eta_p)\psi(r)\,dr}{c_p\int_0^a \{J_{\frac{3}{2}}(\eta_p)\}^2 r\,dr}, \quad A_p' = \frac{\int_0^a \eta_p^{\frac{3}{2}} J_{\frac{3}{2}}(\eta_p)\phi(r)\,dr}{\int_0^a \{J_{\frac{3}{2}}(\eta_p)\}^2 r\,dr}.$$

49. Obtain the equation of motion of a simple pendulum of variable length in the form

$$l\frac{d^2\theta}{dt^2} + 2\frac{dl}{dt}\frac{d\theta}{dt} + g\sin\theta = 0,$$

and show that if $l = a + bt$, where a and b are constants, the equation of motion for the small oscillations may be written

$$x\frac{d^2u}{dx^2} + u = 0,$$

where
$$u = l\theta, \quad x = gl/b^2.$$

Solve the equation in u by means of Bessel functions, and prove that when $b/\sqrt{ga}$ is small, we have approximately

$$\theta = \rho\left(1 - \frac{3bt}{4a}\right)\sin\left(\sqrt{\frac{g}{a}}t - \omega\right) + \frac{b\rho}{8\sqrt{ga}}\left(1 - \frac{2gt^2}{a}\right)\cos\left(\sqrt{\frac{g}{a}}t - \omega\right),$$

ρ and ω being arbitrary constants.

(See Lecornu, *C.R.*, Jan. 15, 1894. The problem is suggested by the swaying of a heavy body let down by a crane.)

50. A quantity Q of heat per unit length is instantaneously generated along the axis of an infinitely long circular cylinder at the time $t=0$. The temperature v was everywhere previously zero, and the temperature at the boundary $r=a$ is maintained at zero. Prove that at any subsequent instant

$$v=\frac{Q}{\pi ca^2}\sum_s \frac{J_0(m_s r)}{\{J_1(m_s a)\}^2} e^{-\kappa m_s^2 t},$$

where κ is the thermometric conductivity, c the specific heat per unit volume, and the quantities m_s are the zeros of $J_0(m_s a)$.

Prove that when a is made infinite the above expression assumes the form

$$v=\frac{Q}{2\pi c}\int_0^\infty J_0(ru)ue^{-\kappa u^2 t}\,du,$$

and by comparison with an independent solution of the problem, evaluate the definite integral.

51. Prove that if $n>m>-1$,

$$\int_0^\infty J_m(bx)J_n(ax)x^{m-n+1}dx=\frac{b^m}{a^n}\frac{(a^2-b^2)^{n-m-1}}{2^{n-m-1}\Pi(n-m-1)},$$

if $a>b$; and that the value of the integral is zero if $a<b$. (Sonine.)

52. If $m>-\frac{1}{2}$,

$$\int_0^\infty J_m(ax)J_m(bx)J_m(cx)x^{1-m}dx$$

$$=\frac{[(a+b+c)(a+b-c)(b+c-a)(c+a-b)]^{m-\frac{1}{2}}}{\sqrt{\pi}\,.\,2^{3m-1}\Pi(m-\frac{1}{2})\,.\,a^m b^m c^m},$$

provided that $b+c-a$, $c+a-b$, $a+b-c$ are all positive; and that if this is not the case the value of the integral is zero. (Sonine.)

[Cf. J. Dougall, *Proc. Edin. Math. Soc.*, XXXVII.]

53. Prove that $$J_0(r)=\frac{2}{\pi}\int_0^\infty \frac{\sin(u+r)}{u+r}J_0(u)du,$$

$$\overline{Y}_0(r)=4\int_0^\infty \frac{\cos(u+r)}{u+r}J_0(u)du.$$

(Sonine and Hobson.)

54. Verify the following expansions:

(i) $$e^{r\cos\theta}J_0(r\sin\theta)=\sum_0^\infty \frac{r^n}{n!}P_n(\cos\theta),$$

(ii) $$J_0(r\sin\theta)=\sqrt{\frac{2\pi}{r}}\sum_0^\infty \frac{(2n+\frac{1}{2})(2n)!}{2^{2n+1}n!\,n!}P_{2n}(\cos\theta)J_{2n+\frac{1}{2}}(r),$$

(iii) $$\frac{J_{\frac{1}{2}}(r\sin\theta)}{(r\sin\theta)^{\frac{1}{2}}}=\frac{2\sqrt{2}}{\pi r}\sum_0^\infty C_{2s}^{1}(\cos\theta)J_{2s+1}(r),$$

with the notation of page 35. (Hobson, *Proc. L.M.S.*, xxv).

55. Prove that:

(i) $$\sqrt{\frac{2}{\pi}}\int_0^{\frac{1}{2}\pi} J_n(r\sin\theta)\sin^{n+1}\theta\,d\theta = \frac{J_{n+\frac{1}{2}}(r)}{\sqrt{r}};$$

(ii) $$\int_0^\infty e^{-\lambda z}\overline{Y}_0(\lambda\rho)d\lambda = \frac{-2}{\sqrt{z^2+\rho^2}}\log\frac{z+\sqrt{z^2+\rho^2}}{\rho}.$$ (*Ibid.*)

56. If $R^2 = x^2 - 2x\rho\cos\theta + \rho^2$, apply (VI. 54) to show that

$$\int_0^a \rho\,d\rho\int_0^{2\pi}\frac{d\theta}{\sqrt{(R^2+z^2)}} = 2\pi a\int_0^\infty e^{-\lambda z}J_0(\lambda x)\,J_1(\lambda a)\,\frac{d\lambda}{\lambda}.$$

57. By integrating $\zeta G_n(\zeta)\,J_n(\zeta x)\,J_n(\zeta r)/J_n(\zeta)$ round a contour similar to that employed in Chapter VIII. § 2, prove that

$$\Sigma A_s J_n(\lambda_s r) = \tfrac{1}{2}\{f(r+0)+f(r-0)\},$$

where λ_s is a positive zero of $J_n(x)$ and

$$A_s = 2\int_0^1 xf(x)\,J_n(\lambda_s x)\,dx/\{J_n'(\lambda_s)\}^2.$$

58. By integrating

$$\frac{\zeta\{A\zeta G_n'(\zeta)+BG_n(\zeta)\}\,J_n(\zeta x)\,J_n(\zeta r)}{A\zeta J_n'(\zeta)+BJ_n(\zeta)},$$

prove that $$\Sigma A_s J_n(\lambda_s r) = \tfrac{1}{2}\{f(r+0)+f(r-0)\},$$

where λ_s is a positive zero of $AxJ_n'(x)+BJ_n(x)$ and

$$A_s = \frac{A^2\lambda_s^2}{\{B^2+A^2(\lambda_s^2-n^2)\}\,J_n^2(\lambda_s)}\int_0^1 xf(x)\,J_n(\lambda_s x)\,dx.$$

59. By means of Cauchy's Formula,

$$\int_{-\frac{1}{2}\pi}^{\frac{1}{2}\pi}(\cos\theta)^{m+n-2}\,e^{i\theta(m-n)}\,d\theta = \frac{\pi\Gamma(m+n-1)}{2^{m+n-2}\,\Gamma(m)\,\Gamma(n)},$$

where $R(m+n)>1$, prove that

$$\frac{J_m(x)\,J_n(y)}{x^m\,y^n}$$

$$=\frac{1}{\pi}\int_{-\frac{1}{2}\pi}^{\frac{1}{2}\pi} e^{i\theta(m-n)}\left(\frac{2\cos\theta}{x^2e^{i\theta}+y^2e^{-i\theta}}\right)^{\frac{m+n}{2}} J_{m+n}[\sqrt{\{2\cos\theta\,(x^2e^{i\theta}+y^2e^{-i\theta})\}}]\,d\theta,$$

where $R(m+n)>-1$. (MacRobert, *Proc.* E.M.S., Ser. 2, II.)

APPENDIX I.

FORMULAE FOR THE GAMMA FUNCTION AND THE HYPERGEOMETRIC FUNCTION.

$$\Gamma(z) = \operatorname*{Lim}_{n\to\infty} \frac{n!\,n^z}{z(z+1)\ldots(z+n)}. \tag{1}$$

$$\frac{1}{\Gamma(z)} = e^{\gamma z} z \prod_1^\infty \left\{\left(1+\frac{z}{n}\right)e^{-\frac{z}{n}}\right\}, \tag{2}$$

where γ is Euler's Constant. [It may be noted that, to twenty-two places

$$\gamma = \cdot 57721\ 56649\ 01532\ 86060\ 65\ldots.]$$

$$\Gamma(z+1) = z\Gamma(z). \tag{3}$$

If n is a positive integer, $\Gamma(n+1) = n!$. (4)

$$\Gamma(1) = 1. \tag{4'}$$

$$\Gamma(\tfrac{1}{2}) = \sqrt{\pi}. \tag{5}$$

$$\Gamma(z)\Gamma(1-z) = \frac{\pi}{\sin \pi z}. \tag{6}$$

$$\Gamma(2z) = \frac{1}{\sqrt{\pi}}\Gamma(z)\Gamma(z+\tfrac{1}{2})2^{2z-1}. \tag{7}$$

$$(e^{2\pi z i}-1)\Gamma(z) = \int_C e^{-\zeta}\zeta^{z-1}\,d\zeta, \tag{8}$$

where C is the contour of Fig. 5, p. 52.

$$\frac{1}{\Gamma(z)} = \frac{1}{2\pi i}\int_{C'} e^{\zeta}\zeta^{-z}\,d\zeta, \tag{8'}$$

where C' is the contour of Fig. 6, p. 53, and amp $\zeta = -\pi$ initially.

If $R(z) > 0$, $\quad \Gamma(z) = \int_0^\infty e^{-t}t^{z-1}\,dt.$ (9)

Stirling's Formula is

$$\operatorname*{Lim}_{n\to\infty} \Gamma(n+1) \Big/ \left\{\sqrt{(2\pi n)}\left(\frac{n}{e}\right)^n\right\} = 1, \tag{10}$$

where $-\pi < \operatorname{amp} n < \pi$.

If $0 < R(z) < 1$,

$$\int_0^\infty \cos t \,.\, t^{z-1}\, dt = \Gamma(z) \cos(\tfrac{1}{2}\pi z). \qquad (11)$$

The Beta function is $B(p, q) = \dfrac{\Gamma(p)\Gamma(q)}{\Gamma(p+q)}$. (12)

If $R(p) > 0$, $R(q) > 0$,

$$\int_0^1 x^{p-1}(1-x)^{q-1}\, dx = B(p, q). \qquad (13)$$

If $R(m) > 0$, $R(n) > 0$,

$$2\int_0^{\frac{\pi}{2}} \cos^{2m-1}\theta \sin^{2n-1}\theta \, d\theta = B(m, n). \qquad (14)$$

$$\int^{(1+,\,0+,\,1-,\,0-)} z^{p-1}(1-z)^{q-1}\, dz = (1 - e^{2p\pi i})(1 - e^{2q\pi i}) B(p, q), \qquad (15)$$

where the initial point lies on the real axis between 0 and 1, and the original amplitude of the integrand is zero.

If p is zero or a positive integer,

$$\int^{(-1+,\,+1-)} z^p (z^2-1)^n\, dz = 0 \quad \text{or} \quad = 2i \sin(n\pi) B\left(n+1, \frac{p+1}{2}\right), \qquad (16)$$

according as p is odd or even.

$$\Pi(z) = \Gamma(z+1). \qquad (17)$$

$$\Pi(z) = z\Pi(z-1). \qquad (18)$$

If n is a positive integer, $\Pi(n) = n!$; $\Pi(0) = 1$. (19)

$$\Pi(\tfrac{1}{2}) = \tfrac{1}{2}\sqrt{\pi}. \qquad (20)$$

If n is a positive integer, $\dfrac{1}{\Pi(-n)} = 0$. (21)

$$\Pi(-z)\Pi(z-1) = \frac{\pi}{\sin \pi z}. \qquad (22)$$

$$\Pi(2z) = \frac{1}{\sqrt{\pi}} \Pi(z)\Pi(z-\tfrac{1}{2}) 2^{2z}. \qquad (23)$$

$$\psi(z) = \frac{d}{dz} \log \Gamma(z+1) = \frac{d}{dz} \log \Pi(z). \qquad (24)$$

If n is a positive integer,

$$\psi(z+n) = \psi(z) + \sum_{r=1}^{n} \frac{1}{z+r}. \qquad (25)$$

If n is a positive integer,

$$\psi(n) = \phi(n) - \gamma, \qquad (26)$$

where
$$\left.\begin{aligned}\phi(n)&=1+\frac{1}{2}+\frac{1}{3}+\ldots+\frac{1}{n},\\ \phi(0)&=0.\end{aligned}\right\}\tag{27}$$
and

$$\psi(0)=-\gamma.\tag{28}$$

$$\psi(-z-1)=\psi(z)+\pi\cot\pi z.\tag{29}$$

$$2\psi(2z)=\psi(z)+\psi(z-\tfrac{1}{2})+2\log 2.\tag{30}$$

$$\psi(-\tfrac{1}{2})=-\gamma-2\log 2.\tag{31}$$

The Hypergeometric Function is defined by the equation

$$F(\alpha,\beta,\gamma,z)=1+\frac{\alpha\,.\,\beta}{1!\,\gamma}z+\frac{\alpha(\alpha+1)\beta(\beta+1)}{2!\,\gamma(\gamma+1)}z^2+\frac{\alpha(\alpha+1)(\alpha+2)\beta(\beta+1)(\beta+2)}{3!\,\gamma(\gamma+1)(\gamma+2)}z^3+\ldots.\tag{32}$$

$$F(\alpha,\beta,\gamma,z)=(1-z)^{-\alpha}F\left(\alpha,\gamma-\beta,\gamma,\frac{z}{z-1}\right).\tag{33}$$

$$=(1-z)^{\gamma-\alpha-\beta}F(\gamma-\alpha,\gamma-\beta,\gamma,z).\tag{33'}$$

Gauss's Theorem is

$$F(\alpha,\beta,\gamma,1)=\frac{\Gamma(\gamma)\Gamma(\gamma-\alpha-\beta)}{\Gamma(\gamma-\alpha)\Gamma(\gamma-\beta)},\tag{34}$$

provided that $R(\gamma)>0$, $R(\gamma-\alpha-\beta)>0$.

If $|z|<1$,

$$F(n,n+\tfrac{1}{2},2n,z)=\frac{1}{\sqrt{(1-z)}}\left\{\frac{2}{1+\sqrt{(1-z)}}\right\}^{2n-1};\tag{35}$$

$$F\left(\frac{1+n}{2},\frac{1-n}{2},\frac{3}{2},z^2\right)=\frac{\sin(n\sin^{-1}z)}{nz};\tag{36}$$

$$F\left(1+\frac{n}{2},1-\frac{n}{2},\frac{3}{2},z^2\right)=\frac{\sin(n\sin^{-1}z)}{nz\sqrt{(1-z^2)}};\tag{37}$$

$$F\left(\frac{n}{2},-\frac{n}{2},\frac{1}{2},z^2\right)=\cos(n\sin^{-1}z);\tag{38}$$

$$F\left(\frac{1+n}{2},\frac{1-n}{2},\frac{1}{2},z^2\right)=\frac{\cos(n\sin^{-1}z)}{\sqrt{(1-z^2)}}.\tag{39}$$

APPENDIX II.

STOKES'S METHOD* OF OBTAINING THE ASYMPTOTIC EXPANSIONS OF THE BESSEL FUNCTIONS.

In Bessel's differential equation put $J_n(x) = ux^{-\frac{1}{2}}$; then it will be found that u is a solution of

$$\frac{d^2u}{dx^2} + \left(1 - \frac{n^2 - \frac{1}{4}}{x^2}\right)u = 0. \qquad (1)$$

Now when x is large compared with n, the value of $(n^2 - \frac{1}{4})/x^2$ is small; and if, after the analogy of the process employed in the expansion of an implicit function defined by an algebraical equation $f(u, x) = 0$, we omit the term $(n^2 - \frac{1}{4})u/x^2$ in the differential equation, we obtain

$$\frac{d^2u}{dx^2} + u = 0,$$

of which the complete solution is

$$u = u_1 = A \sin x + B \cos x,$$

where A and B are constants.

Let us now try to obtain a closer approximation by putting

$$u = u_2 = \left(A_0 + \frac{A_1}{x}\right) \sin x + \left(B_0 + \frac{B_1}{x}\right) \cos x,$$

where A_0, A_1, B_0, B_1 are constants. This value of u gives

$$\frac{d^2u}{dx^2} + \left(1 - \frac{n^2 - \frac{1}{4}}{x^2}\right)u = \left\{\frac{2B_1 - (n^2 - \frac{1}{4}) A_0}{x^2} - \frac{(n^2 - \frac{9}{4}) A_1}{x^3}\right\} \sin x$$
$$- \left\{\frac{2A_1 + (n^2 - \frac{1}{4}) B_0}{x^2} + \frac{(n^2 - \frac{9}{4}) B_1}{x^3}\right\} \cos x.$$

The expression on the right becomes comparable with x^{-3}, if we assume

$$2A_1 = -(n^2 - \tfrac{1}{4}) B_0,$$
$$2B_1 = (n^2 - \tfrac{1}{4}) A_0.$$

* "On the Numerical Calculation of a Class of Definite Integrals and Infinite Series" (*Camb. Phil. Trans.*, IX. (1856; read March 11, 1850), p. 166; or *Collected Papers*, II. p. 329).

"On the Effect of the Internal Friction of Fluids on the Motion of Pendulums" (*Camb. Phil. Trans.*, IX. (1856; read Dec. 9, 1850), p. [8].)

The value of u_2 thus becomes

$$u_2 = A_0\left\{\sin x + \frac{n^2-\frac{1}{4}}{2x}\cos x\right\} + B_0\left\{\cos x - \frac{n^2-\frac{1}{4}}{2x}\sin x\right\},$$

and we have

$$\frac{d^2u_2}{dx^2} + \left(1 - \frac{n^2-\frac{1}{4}}{x^2}\right)u_2 = \frac{(n^2-\frac{1}{4})(n^2-\frac{9}{4})}{2x^3}(-A_0\cos x + B_0\sin x).$$

It will be observed that we have thus obtained the exact solutions when $n = \pm\frac{1}{2}$, or $\pm\frac{3}{2}$.

Let us now assume

$$u = u_2 + \frac{A_2\sin x + B_2\cos x}{x^2};$$

then it will be found that

$$\begin{aligned}\frac{d^2u}{dx^2} + \left(1 - \frac{n^2-\frac{1}{4}}{x^2}\right)u = &-\left\{\frac{(n^2-\frac{1}{4})(n^2-\frac{9}{4})}{2}A_0 + 4A_2\right\}\frac{\cos x}{x^3}\\ &+\left\{\frac{(n^2-\frac{1}{4})(n^2-\frac{9}{4})}{2}B_0 + 4B_2\right\}\frac{\sin x}{x^3}\\ &-\frac{(n^2-\frac{25}{4})}{x^4}(A_2\sin x + B_2\cos x).\end{aligned}$$

If, then, we put

$$A_2 = -\frac{(n^2-\frac{1}{4})(n^2-\frac{9}{4})}{2\,.\,4}A_0,$$

$$B_2 = -\frac{(n^2-\frac{1}{4})(n^2-\frac{9}{4})}{2\,.\,4}B_0,$$

the value of u becomes

$$\begin{aligned}u = u_3 = A_0&\left\{\sin x + \frac{(n^2-\frac{1}{4})}{2x}\cos x - \frac{(n^2-\frac{1}{4})(n^2-\frac{9}{4})}{2\,.\,4x^2}\sin x\right\}\\ &+ B_0\left\{\cos x - \frac{(n^2-\frac{1}{4})}{2x}\sin x - \frac{(n^2-\frac{1}{4})(n^2-\frac{9}{4})}{2\,.\,4x^2}\cos x\right\},\end{aligned}$$

and we have

$$\frac{d^2u_3}{dx^2} + \left(1 - \frac{n^2-\frac{1}{4}}{x^2}\right)u_3 = \frac{(n^2-\frac{1}{4})(n^2-\frac{9}{4})(n^2-\frac{25}{4})}{2\,.\,4x^4}(A_0\sin x + B_0\cos x).$$

Proceeding in this way, we find by induction that, if we put

$$u_r = A_0U_r + B_0V_r, \tag{2}$$

where

$$\begin{aligned}U_r = \sin x &+ \frac{n^2-\frac{1}{4}}{2x}\cos x - \frac{(n^2-\frac{1}{4})(n^2-\frac{9}{4})}{2\,.\,4x^2}\sin x - \ldots\\ &+ \frac{(n^2-\frac{1}{4})(n^2-\frac{9}{4})\ldots\{n^2-(r-\frac{3}{2})^2\}}{2\,.\,4\,.\,6\ldots(2r-2)x^{r-1}}\sin\left(x + \frac{r-1}{2}\pi\right),\end{aligned} \tag{3}$$

$$\begin{aligned}V_r = \cos x &- \frac{n^2-\frac{1}{4}}{2x}\sin x - \frac{(n^2-\frac{1}{4})(n^2-\frac{9}{4})}{2\,.\,4x^2}\cos x + \ldots\\ &+ \frac{(n^2-\frac{1}{4})(n^2-\frac{9}{4})\ldots\{n^2-(r-\frac{3}{2})^2\}}{2\,.\,4\,.\,6\ldots(2r-2)\,x^{r-1}}\cos\left(x + \frac{r-1}{2}\pi\right),\end{aligned} \tag{4}$$

then $$\frac{d^2u_r}{dx^2}+\left(1-\frac{n^2-\frac{1}{4}}{x^2}\right)u_r=-\frac{(n^2-\frac{1}{4})(n^2-\frac{9}{4})\dots\{n^2-(r-\frac{1}{2})^2\}}{2.4.6\dots(2r-2)x^{r+1}}$$
$$\times\left\{A_0\sin\left(x+\frac{r-1}{2}\pi\right)+B_0\cos\left(x+\frac{r-1}{2}\pi\right)\right\}. \quad (5)$$

Thus, when $n=\pm\frac{1}{2}, \pm\frac{3}{2}, \dots, \pm(r-\frac{1}{2})$, u_r is an exact solution of (1). Stokes assumes that when x is so large that the expression on the right-hand side of (5) is very small in comparison with u_r, then u_r is an approximate solution of (1).

It is convenient to alter the notation by putting

$$\left.\begin{aligned}A_0\sin x+B_0\cos x&=C\cos(\alpha-x),\\ A_0\cos x-B_0\sin x&=C\sin(\alpha-x),\end{aligned}\right\} \quad (6)$$

C and α being new constants: this is legitimate, because $C^2=A_0^2+B_0^2$, which is independent of x. Then we have

$$u_r=C\{P_r\cos(\alpha-x)+Q_r\sin(\alpha-x)\}, \quad (7)$$

where $$P_r=1-\frac{(4n^2-1)(4n^2-9)}{1.2(8x)^2}$$
$$+\frac{(4n^2-1)(4n^2-9)(4n^2-25)(4n^2-49)}{1.2.3.4(8x)^4}-\dots, \quad (8)$$

$$Q_r=\frac{4n^2-1}{8x}-\frac{(4n^2-1)(4n^2-9)(4n^2-25)}{1.2.3(8x)^3}+\dots, \quad (9)$$

and P_r, Q_r between them contain r terms, involving $x^0, x^{-1}, x^{-2}, \dots, x^{-r+1}$ respectively.

The values of C and α for the various Bessel Functions are given in Chapter V. § 3, where the asymptotic expansions are fully treated by a different method.

APPENDIX III.

FORMULAE FOR CALCULATION OF THE ZEROS OF BESSEL FUNCTIONS.

IN a paper* entitled "On the Roots of the Bessel and certain related Functions," Professor J. M'Mahon obtains the following important results, the first of which has already been given in part.

(i) The sth root, in order of magnitude, of the equation

$$J_n(x) = 0$$

is
$$x_n^{(s)} = \beta - \frac{m-1}{8\beta} - \frac{4(m-1)(7m-31)}{3(8\beta)^3}$$
$$- \frac{32(m-1)(83m^2-982m+3779)}{15(8\beta)^5}$$
$$- \frac{64(m-1)(6949m^3-153855m^2+1585743m-6277237)}{105(8\beta)^7}$$
$$- \dots,$$

where
$$\beta = \tfrac{1}{4}\pi(2n+4s-1), \quad m = 4n^2.$$

(ii) The sth root, in order of magnitude, of the equation

$$J_n'(x) = 0$$

is
$$x_n^{(s)} = \gamma - \frac{m+3}{8\gamma} - \frac{4(7m^2+82m-9)}{3(8\gamma)^3}$$
$$- \frac{32(83m^3+2075m^2-3039m+3537)}{15(8\gamma)^3} - \dots,$$

where
$$\gamma = \tfrac{1}{4}\pi(2n+4s+1), \quad m = 4n^2.$$

(iii) The sth root, in order of magnitude, of the equation

$$\frac{d}{dx}\{x^{-\frac{1}{2}}J_n(x)\} = 0$$

is
$$x_n^{(s)} = \gamma - \frac{m+7}{8\gamma} - \frac{4(7m^2+154m+95)}{3(8\gamma)^3}$$
$$- \frac{32(83m^3+3535m^2+3561m+6133)}{15(8\gamma)^5} - \dots,$$

where, as above,
$$\gamma = \tfrac{1}{4}\pi(2n+4s+1), \quad m = 4n^2.$$

* *Annals of Mathematics*, Vol. 9, p. 23, 1894-95.

(iv) The sth root, in order of magnitude, of the equation

$RG_n(x)$[*i.e.*, the real part of $G_n(x) = -Y_n(x) - (\gamma - \log 2)J_n(x)$] $= 0$

is given by the series for $x_n^{(s)}$ in (i) if $\beta - \frac{1}{2}\pi$ be therein substituted for β.

(v) The sth root, in order of magnitude, of the equation

$$\frac{d}{dx}\{RG_n(x)\} = 0$$

is given by the series for $x_n^{(s)}$ in (ii) if $\gamma - \frac{1}{2}\pi$ be therein substituted for γ. [The γ in the expression here differentiated is of course Euler's constant, and is not to be confounded with the γ in the expression for the root.]

(vi) The sth root, in order of magnitude, of the equation

$$\frac{G_n(x)}{J_n(x)} - \frac{G_n(\rho x)}{J_n(\rho x)} = 0, \quad \rho > 1,$$

or, which is the same,

$$\frac{Y_n(x)}{J_n(x)} - \frac{Y_n(\rho x)}{J_n(\rho x)} = 0,$$

is

$$x_n^{(s)} = \delta + \frac{p}{\delta} + \frac{q - p^2}{\delta^3} + \frac{r - 4pq + 2p^3}{\delta^5} + \dots,$$

where
$$\delta = \frac{s\pi}{\rho - 1}, \quad p = \frac{m-1}{8\rho}, \quad q = \frac{4(m-1)(m-25)(\rho^3 - 1)}{3(8\rho)^3(\rho - 1)},$$

$$r = \frac{32(m-1)(m^2 - 114m + 1073)(\rho^5 - 1)}{5(8\rho)^5(\rho - 1)}, \quad m = 4n^2.$$

(vii) The sth root, in order of magnitude, of the equation

$$\frac{Y_n'(x)}{J_n'(x)} - \frac{Y_n'(\rho x)}{J_n'(\rho x)} = 0, \quad \rho > 1,$$

is given by the same formula as in (vi), but with

$$p = \frac{m+3}{8\rho}, \quad q = \frac{4(m^2 + 46m - 63)(\rho^3 - 1)}{3(8\rho)^3(\rho - 1)},$$

$$r = \frac{32(m^3 + 185m^2 - 2053m + 1899)(\rho^5 - 1)}{5(8\rho)^5(\rho - 1)}.$$

[Of course here also the G functions may be used instead of the Y functions, without altering the equation.]

(viii) The sth root, in order of magnitude, of the equation

$$\frac{\dfrac{d}{dx}\{x^{-\frac{1}{2}}Y_n(x)\}}{\dfrac{d}{dx}\{x^{-\frac{1}{2}}J_n(x)\}} - \frac{\dfrac{d}{dx}\{(\rho x)^{-\frac{1}{2}}Y_n(\rho x)\}}{\dfrac{d}{dx}\{(\rho x)^{-\frac{1}{2}}J_n(\rho x)\}} = 0, \quad \rho > 1,$$

is also given by the formula in (vi), but with

$$p=\frac{m+7}{8\rho},\quad q=\frac{4(m^2+70m-199)(\rho^3-1)}{3(8\rho)^3(\rho-1)},$$

$$r=\frac{32(m^3+245m^2-3693m+4471)(\rho^5-1)}{5(8\rho)^5(\rho-1)}.$$

[As before, the G functions may here replace the Y functions.]

The following notes on these equations may be useful:

1. Examples of the equation in (i) are found in all kinds of physical applications, see pp. 93, 113, 191, and elsewhere above.

When $n=\frac{3}{2}$ the equation is equivalent to

$$\tan x = x,$$

which occurs in many problems (see p. 203 above). The roots of this equation can therefore be calculated by the formula in (i).

2. The equation of which the roots are given in (ii) is also of great importance for physical applications; for example it gives the wave lengths of the vibrations of a fluid within a right cylindrical envelope. It expresses the condition that there is no motion of the gas across the cylindrical boundary. [See Lord Rayleigh's *Theory of Sound*, 2nd edit., Vol. II., pp. 297-301.]

When $n=\frac{1}{2}$, the equation is equivalent to

$$\tan x = 2x,$$

and when $n=\frac{3}{2}$, it is equivalent to

$$\tan x=\frac{3x}{3-2x^2},$$

and other equivalent equations can be obtained by means of the Table on p. 17 above.

3. The roots of the equation given in (iii) are required for the problem of waves in a fluid contained within a rigid spherical envelope. The equation is the expression of the surface condition which the motion must fulfil, and $x=\kappa a$, where a is the radius. The roots therefore give the possible values of κ. (See Lord Rayleigh's *Theory of Sound*, 2nd edit., Vol. II., p. 264 *et seq.*)

When $n=\frac{1}{2}$, the equation is equivalent to

$$\tan x = x,$$

given also by the equation in (i) when $n=\frac{3}{2}$. Again when $n=\frac{3}{2}$ the equation is equivalent to

$$\tan x=\frac{2x}{2-x^2},$$

which gives the spherical nodes of a gas vibrating within a spherical envelope.

4. The roots of the equation in (vi) are required for many physical problems, for example the problem of the cooling of a body bounded by two coaxial right cylindrical surfaces, or the vibrations of an annular membrane. (See p. 116 above.) The values of x and ρx are those of κa, κb, where a, b are the internal and external radii. The roots of the equation thus give the possible values of κ for the problem.

5. The roots of the equation in (vii) are required for the determination of the wave lengths of the vibrations of a fluid contained between two coaxial right cylindrical surfaces. It is the proper extension of (iii) for this annular space. As before, x and ρx are the values of κa, κb, where a, b are the internal and external radii.

6. In (viii) the equation given is derived from the conditions which must hold at the internal and external surfaces of a fluid vibrating in the space between two concentric and fixed spherical surfaces. The values of x and ρx are as before those of κa, κb, where a, b are the internal and external radii. The roots thus give the possible values of κ for the problem.

7. If for low values of s the formulae for the roots are any of them not very convergent, it may be preferable to interpolate the values from Tables of the numerical values of the functions, if these are available.

EXPLANATION OF THE TABLES.

TABLE I. is a reprint of Dr. Meissel's "Tafel der Bessel'schen Functionen I_k^0 und I_k^1," originally published in the Berlin *Abhandlungen* for 1888. We are indebted to Dr. Meissel and the Berlin Academy of Sciences for permission to include this table in the present work. The only change that has been made is to write $J_0(x)$ and $J_1(x)$ instead of I_k^0 and I_k^1. Three obvious misprints in the column of arguments have been corrected; and the value of $J_0(1{\cdot}71)$ has been altered from ·3932... to ·3922... in accordance with a communication from Dr. Meissel.

Table II. is derived from an unpublished MS. very kindly placed at our disposal by its author, Dr. Meissel. It gives, for positive integral values of n and x, all the values of $J_n(x)$, from $x=1$ to $x=24$, which are not less than 10^{-18}. The table may be used, among other purposes, for the calculation of $J_n(x)$ when x is not integral. Thus, if x lies between two consecutive integers, y, $y+1$, we may put $x=y+h$, and then

$$J_n(x)=J_n(y)+hJ'_n(y)+\frac{h^2}{2!}J''_n(y)+\ldots$$

$$=J_n(y)+h\left\{\frac{n}{y}J_n(y)-J_{n+1}(y)\right\}$$

$$+\frac{h^2}{2}\left\{\left(\frac{n(n-1)}{y^2}-1\right)J_n(y)+\frac{1}{y}J_{n+1}(y)\right\}+\ldots.$$

We take this opportunity of referring to two papers on the Bessel functions by Dr. Meissel contained in the annual reports on the Ober-Realschule at Kiel for the years 1889-90 and 1891-2. It is there shown, among other things, that, when x is given, there is a special value of n for which the function $J_n(x)$ changes sign for the last time from negative to positive; that the function then increases to its absolute maximum, and then diminishes as n increases, with ever increasing rapidity.

Table III. was given by R. W. Willson and B. O. Peirce in the *Bulletin of the American Mathematical Society*, Vol. 3, 1897. The first ten roots were incorporated from a table by Meissel. Table IV., which is taken from the first of the papers referred to in the previous paragraph, gives the first 50 roots of the equation $J_1(x)=0$, with the corresponding values of $J_0(x)$, which are, of course, maximum or minimum values of $J_0(x)$ according as they are positive or negative.

Table V. is due to J. Bourget, *Ann. de l'École Normale*, Vol. III., 1866.

Tables VI., VII., VIII. and IX. are extracted from the Reports of the British Association for the years 1889, 1893 and 1896. The Association tables corresponding to VII. and VIII. were thought too long to reprint, so the tabular difference has been taken to be ·01 instead of ·001. These tables do not require any special explanation: the functions I_n are the same as those denoted by that symbol in the present work.

Tables X. and XI. were given by W. S. Aldis in the *Proceedings of the Royal Society*, Vol. LXIV., 1898, and XII. by J. G. Isherwood in the *Memoirs of the Manchester Philosophical Society*, Vol. XLVIII., 1904.

Table XIII. is taken from a paper by J. R. Airey in the *Phil. Mag.*, Vol. XLI., 1921.

As the Committee of the British Association on the Calculation of Mathematical Tables has announced its intention to publish at an early date a volume of fairly complete Tables of Bessel and other functions, it has been thought unnecessary to reproduce here all the available tables. The following references may, however, be found useful by those who require other tables:

"Tables of Zeros of Neumann and Bessel Functions," by J. R. Airey (*Proc. Phys. Soc.*, Vol. XXIII., 1911, p. 219).

"Tables for calculating Phase and Amplitude," by A. Lodge (*Brit. Ass. Rep.*, 1907, p. 94, 1909, p. 33).

"Tables of Y_0, Y_1, RG_0, RG_1," by J. R. Airey (*Brit. Ass. Rep.*, 1913, p. 116).

"Tables of Y_0, Y_1," by B. A. Smith (*Mess. of Maths.* Vol. XXVI. 1897, p. 98).

"Tables of Bessel and Neumann Functions," by B. A. Smith (*Phil. Mag.*, Vol. XLV., 1898, p. 122).

"Tables of RG_0, RG_1, ber, bei, etc.," by W. S. Aldis (*Proc. Roy. Soc.*, Vol. LXVI., 1900, p. 32).

"Tables of ber, bei, ber′, bei′," by A. G. Webster (*Brit. Ass. Rep.*, 1912, p. 57).

"Tables of J_n, RG_0, RG_1, Y_n" (*Brit. Ass. Rep.*, 1915, p. 29).

"Tables of ker, kei, ker′, kei′," by H. G. Savidge, (*Brit. Ass. Rep.*, 1915, p. 36).

"Tables of ber, bei, ker, etc.," by Russell and Savidge (*Phil. Mag.*, April 1909, Jan. 1910).

"Tables of Zeros of $J_n(x)Y_n(kx) - J_n(kx)Y_n(x)$," by A. Kalähne (*Zeitsch. f. Math. u. Phys.*, Vol. LIV., 1907, p. 68). These tables are reproduced in full in Jahnke and Emde's *Funktionentafeln*, a useful work which contains a large number of tables of Bessel functions.

Tables of Bessel and Neumann Functions of Equal Order and Argument, that is, of $J_\alpha(\alpha)$, $J_{\alpha-1}(\alpha)$, $G_\alpha(\alpha)$, $G_{\alpha-1}(\alpha)$ [functions which, for distinction from the G functions of the present edition, would be denoted by $RG(\alpha)$, etc.], $-Y_\alpha(\alpha)$, $-Y_{\alpha-1}(\alpha)$, are given in the *B.A. Report*, 1916.

Tables of the functions $S_n(x)$, $C_n(x)$, which are connected with the "Bessel Functions of Half-Integral Order" by the equations

$$S_n(x) = \sqrt{\tfrac{1}{2}\pi x}\, J_{n+\frac{1}{2}}(x), \quad C_n(x) = (-1)^n \sqrt{\tfrac{1}{2}\pi x}\, J_{-n-\frac{1}{2}}(x),$$

are also given in *B.A. Report*, 1916.

Tables of $J_{\pm\frac{1}{3}}(x)$, and of the functions $U_n(x)$, $V_n(x)$ defined by the equations

$$J_m(x) = U_m(x)\cos(x - \tfrac{1}{2}m\pi - \tfrac{1}{4}\pi) - V_m(x)\sin(x - \tfrac{1}{2}m\pi - \tfrac{1}{4}\pi),$$
$$J_{-m}(x) = U_m(x)\cos(x + \tfrac{1}{2}m\pi - \tfrac{1}{4}\pi) - V_m(x)\sin(x + \tfrac{1}{2}m\pi - \tfrac{1}{4}\pi),$$

are given in a paper by Dr. G. N. Watson "On the Zeros of Bessel Functions," *Proc. R.S.*, A. XCIV. (1918).

A table of the values of the zeros of Bessel Functions of small fractional order is given in the *Phil. Mag.* for February 1921, in a paper by Dr. J. R. Airey. A selection of these values and of some others is given in the Table XIII. below, on account of the importance of these zeros for problems of elastic stability.

Reference may also be made to a short paper on the zeros of Bessel functions of fractional order, by Professor Akinamasa Ono, *Phil. Mag.* Dec. 1921.

x	$J_0(x)$	$-J_1(x)$	x	$J_0(x)$	$-J_1(x)$
0·00	1·000000 000000	0·000000 000000	0·40	0·960398 226660	−0·196026 577955
0·01	0·999975 000156	−0·004999 937500	0·41	0·958414 468885	−0·200722 502946
0·02	0·999900 002500	−0·009999 500008	0·42	0·956383 826663	−0·205403 409375
0·03	0·999775 012656	−0·014998 312563	0·43	0·954306 451921	−0·210068 948818
0·04	0·999600 039998	−0·019996 000267	0·44	0·952182 500067	−0·214718 774133
0·05	0·999375 097649	−0·024992 188314	0·45	0·950012 129972	−0·219352 539483
0·06	0·999100 202480	−0·029986 502025	0·46	0·947795 503959	−0·223969 900370
0·07	0·998775 375105	−0·034978 566876	0·47	0·945532 787790	−0·228570 513659
0·08	0·998400 639886	−0·039968 008532	0·48	0·943224 150650	−0·233154 037611
0·09	0·997976 024926	−0·044954 452875	0·49	0·940869 765137	−0·237720 131905
0·10	0·997501 562066	−0·049937 526036	0·50	0·938469 807241	−0·242268 457675
0·11	0·996977 286887	−0·054916 854430	0·51	0·936024 456336	−0·246798 677529
0·12	0·996403 238704	−0·059892 064781	0·52	0·933533 895163	−0·251310 455583
0·13	0·995779 460562	−0·064862 784157	0·53	0·930998 309812	−0·255803 457487
0·14	0·995105 999233	−0·069828 640001	0·54	0·928417 889710	−0·260277 350453
0·15	0·994382 905214	−0·074789 260161	0·55	0·925792 827604	−0·264731 803281
0·16	0·993610 232721	−0·079744 272921	0·56	0·923123 319544	−0·269166 486388
0·17	0·992788 039685	−0·084693 307032	0·57	0·920409 564868	−0·273581 071836
0·18	0·991916 387745	−0·089635 991743	0·58	0·917651 766187	−0·277975 233357
0·19	0·990995 342249	−0·094571 956833	0·59	0·914850 129363	−0·282348 646381
0·20	0·990024 972240	−0·099500 832639	0·60	0·912004 863497	−0·286700 988064
0·21	0·989005 350457	−0·104422 250091	0·61	0·909116 180910	−0·291031 937312
0·22	0·987936 553327	−0·109335 840739	0·62	0·905184 297124	−0·295341 174811
0·23	0·986818 660958	−0·114241 236785	0·63	0·903209 430845	−0·299628 383050
0·24	0·985651 757131	−0·119138 071113	0·64	0·900191 803946	−0·303893 246349
0·25	0·984435 929296	−0·124025 977323	0·65	0·897131 641447	−0·308135 450885
0·26	0·983171 268563	−0·128904 589754	0·66	0·894029 171498	−0·312354 684718
0·27	0·981857 869696	−0·133773 543525	0·67	0·890884 625356	−0·316550 637815
0·28	0·980495 831102	−0·138632 474553	0·68	0·887698 237371	−0·320723 002080
0·29	0·979085 254825	−0·143481 019596	0·69	0·884470 244964	−0·324871 471373
0·30	0·977626 246538	−0·148318 816273	0·70	0·881200 888607	−0·328995 741540
0·31	0·976118 915533	−0·153145 503099	0·71	0·877890 411804	−0·333095 510438
0·32	0·974563 374711	−0·157960 719516	0·72	0·874539 061070	−0·337170 477956
0·33	0·972959 740576	−0·162764 105918	0·73	0·871147 085910	−0·341220 346045
0·34	0·971308 133222	−0·167555 303687	0·74	0·867714 738801	−0·345244 818737
0·35	0·969608 676323	−0·172333 955219	0·75	0·864242 275167	−0·349243 602175
0·36	0·967861 497127	−0·177099 703954	0·76	0·860729 953361	−0·353216 404632
0·37	0·966066 726439	−0·181852 194406	0·77	0·857178 034643	−0·357162 936538
0·38	0·964224 498614	−0·186591 072196	0·78	0·853586 783157	−0·361082 910503
0·39	0·962334 951548	−0·191315 984074	0·79	0·849956 465910	−0·364976 041342
0·40	0·960398 226660	−0·196026 577955	0·80	0·846287 352750	−0·368842 046094

x	$J_0(x)$	$-J_1(x)$	x	$J_0(x)$	$-J_1(x)$
0·80	0·846287 352750	−0·368842 046094	1·20	0·671132 744264	−0·498289 05756
0·81	0·842579 716344	−0·372680 644052	1·21	0·666137 120084	−0·500829 67264
0·82	0·838833 832154	−0·376491 556779	1·22	0·661116 273214	−0·503333 56702
0·83	0·835049 978414	−0·380274 508136	1·23	0·656070 571706	−0·505800 57262
0·84	0·831228 436109	−0·384029 224303	1·24	0·651000 385275	−0·508230 52439
0·85	0·827369 488950	−0·387755 433798	1·25	0·645906 085271	−0·510623 26032
0·86	0·823473 423352	−0·391452 867506	1·26	0·640788 044651	−0·512978 62146
0·87	0·819540 528409	−0·395121 258696	1·27	0·635646 637944	−0·515296 45197
0·88	0·815571 095868	−0·398760 343044	1·28	0·630482 241224	−0·517576 59906
0·89	0·811565 420110	−0·402369 858653	1·29	0·625295 232074	−0·519818 91306
0·90	0·807523 798123	−0·405949 546079	1·30	0·620085 989562	−0·522023 24741
0·91	0·803446 529473	−0·409499 148347	1·31	0·614854 894203	−0·524189 45868
0·92	0·799333 916288	−0·413018 410976	1·32	0·609602 327933	−0·526317 40655
0·93	0·795186 263226	−0·416507 081996	1·33	0·604328 674074	−0·528406 95388
0·94	0·791003 877452	−0·419964 911971	1·34	0·599034 317304	−0·530457 96666
0·95	0·786787 068613	−0·423391 654020	1·35	0·593719 643626	−0·532470 31406
0·96	0·782536 148813	−0·426787 063833	1·36	0·588385 040333	−0·534443 86841
0·97	0·778251 432583	−0·430150 899695	1·37	0·583030 895983	−0·536378 50525
0·98	0·773933 236862	−0·433482 922506	1·38	0·577657 600358	−0·538274 10330
0·99	0·769581 880965	−0·436782 895795	1·39	0·572265 544440	−0·540130 544481
1·00	0·765197 686558	−0·440050 585745	1·40	0·566855 120374	−0·541947 713931
1·01	0·760780 977632	−0·443285 761209	1·41	0·561426 721439	−0·543725 500014
1·02	0·756332 080477	−0·446488 193730	1·42	0·555980 742014	−0·545463 794323
1·03	0·751851 323654	−0·449657 657556	1·43	0·550517 577543	−0·547162 491686
1·04	0·747339 037965	−0·452793 929666	1·44	0·545037 624510	−0·548821 490179
1·05	0·742795 556434	−0·455896 789778	1·45	0·539541 280398	−0·550440 691132
1·06	0·738221 214269	−0·458966 020374	1·46	0·534028 943664	−0·552019 999133
1·07	0·733616 348841	−0·462001 406715	1·47	0·528501 013700	−0·553559 322039
1·08	0·728981 299655	−0·465002 736858	1·48	0·522957 890804	−0·555058 570983
1·09	0·724316 408322	−0·467969 801675	1·49	0·517399 976146	−0·556517 660374
1·10	0·719622 018528	−0·470902 394866	1·50	0·511827 671736	−0·557936 507910
1·11	0·714898 476008	−0·473800 312980	1·51	0·506241 380391	−0·559315 034582
1·12	0·710146 128520	−0·476663 355426	1·52	0·500641 505700	−0·560653 164677
1·13	0·705365 325811	−0·479491 324496	1·53	0·495028 451994	−0·561950 825786
1·14	0·700556 419592	−0·482284 025373	1·54	0·489402 624312	−0·563207 948806
1·15	0·695719 763505	−0·485041 266154	1·55	0·483764 428365	−0·564424 467949
1·16	0·690855 713099	−0·487762 857858	1·56	0·478114 270507	−0·565600 320742
1·17	0·685964 625798	−0·490448 614448	1·57	0·472452 557702	−0·566735 448033
1·18	0·681046 860871	−0·493098 352841	1·58	0·466779 697485	−0·567829 793994
1·19	0·676102 779403	−0·495711 892924	1·59	0·461096 097935	−0·568883 306126
1·20	0·671132 744264	−0·498289 057567	1·60	0·455402 167639	−0·569895 935262

x	$J_0(x)$	$-J_1(x)$	x	$J_0(x)$	$-J_1(x)$
1·60	0·455402 167639	−0·569895 935262	2·00	0·223890 779141	−0·576724 807757
1·61	0·449698 315660	−0·570867 635566	2·01	0·218126 821326	−0·576060 090955
1·62	0·443984 951500	−0·571798 364542	2·02	0·212369 710458	−0·575355 433450
1·63	0·438262 485071	−0·572688 083032	2·03	0·206619 845483	−0·574610 928248
1·64	0·432531 326660	−0·573536 755217	2·04	0·200877 624399	−0·573826 671543
1·65	0·426791 886896	−0·574344 348624	2·05	0·195143 444226	−0·573002 762707
1·66	0·421044 576715	−0·575110 834122	2·06	0·189417 700977	−0·572139 304279
1·67	0·415289 807326	−0·575836 185927	2·07	0·183700 789621	−0·571236 401957
1·68	0·409527 990183	−0·576520 381599	2·08	0·177993 104055	−0·570294 164587
1·69	0·403759 536945	−0·577163 402048	2·09	0·172295 037073	−0·569312 704151
1·70	0·397984 859446	−0·577765 231529	2·10	0·166606 980332	−0·568292 135757
1·71	0·392204 369660	−0·578325 857645	2·11	0·160929 324324	−0·567232 577628
1·72	0·386418 479668	−0·578845 271345	2·12	0·155262 458341	−0·566134 151091
1·73	0·380627 601627	−0·579323 466925	2·13	0·149606 770449	−0·564996 980564
1·74	0·374832 147732	−0·579760 442028	2·14	0·143962 647452	−0·563821 193544
1·75	0·369032 530185	−0·580156 197639	2·15	0·138330 474865	−0·562606 920596
1·76	0·363229 161163	−0·580510 738087	2·16	0·132710 636881	−0·561354 295339
1·77	0·357422 452782	−0·580824 071043	2·17	0·127103 516344	−0·560063 454436
1·78	0·351612 817064	−0·581096 207515	2·18	0·121509 494713	−0·558734 537577
1·79	0·345800 665906	−0·581327 161851	2·19	0·115928 952037	−0·557367 687469
1·80	0·339986 411043	−0·581516 951731	2·20	0·110362 266922	−0·555963 049819
1·81	0·334170 464016	−0·581665 598167	2·21	0·104809 816503	−0·554520 773326
1·82	0·328353 236143	−0·581773 125501	2·22	0·099271 976413	−0·553041 009659
1·83	0·322535 138478	−0·581839 561397	2·23	0·093749 120752	−0·551523 913451
1·84	0·316716 581784	−0·581864 936842	2·24	0·088241 622061	−0·549969 642278
1·85	0·310897 976496	−0·581849 286141	2·25	0·082749 851289	−0·548378 356647
1·86	0·305079 732690	−0·581792 646910	2·26	0·077274 177765	−0·546750 219981
1·87	0·299262 260050	−0·581695 060074	2·27	0·071814 969172	−0·545085 398603
1·88	0·293445 967833	−0·581556 569863	2·28	0·066372 591512	−0·543384 061721
1·89	0·287631 264839	−0·581377 223803	2·29	0·060947 409082	−0·541646 381412
1·90	0·281818 559374	−0·581157 072713	2·30	0·055539 784446	−0·539872 532604
1·91	0·276008 259222	−0·580896 170703	2·31	0·050150 078400	−0·538062 693065
1·92	0·270200 771606	−0·580594 575158	3·32	0·044778 649952	−0·536217 043381
1·93	0·264396 503162	−0·580252 346743	2·33	0·039425 856288	−0·534335 766941
1·94	0·258595 859901	−0·579869 549389	2·34	0·034092 052749	−0·532419 049921
1·95	0·252799 247180	−0·579446 250290	2·35	0·028777 592796	−0·530467 081267
1·96	0·247007 069667	−0·578982 519892	2·36	0·023482 827990	−0·528480 052675
1·97	0·241219 731308	−0·578478 431892	2·37	0·018208 107961	−0·526458 158577
1·98	0·235437 635298	−0·577934 063221	2·38	0·012953 780380	−0·524401 596119
1·99	0·229661 184046	−0·577349 494047	2·39	0·007720 190934	−0·522310 565146
2·00	0·223890 779141	−0·576724 807757	2·40	0·002507 683297	−0·520185 268182

x	$J_0(x)$	$-J_1(x)$	x	$J_0(x)$	$-J_1(x)$
2·40	+0·002507 683297	−0·520185 268182	2·80	−0·185036 033364	−0·409709 24685
2·41	−0·002683 400894	−0·518025 910413	2·81	−0·189116 518066	−0·406383 73306
2·42	−0·007852 722067	−0·515832 699667	2·82	−0·193163 629309	−0·403034 60445
2·43	−0·012999 942745	−0·513605 846395	2·83	−0·197177 132431	−0·399662 15846
2·44	−0·018124 727564	−0·511345 563651	2·84	−0·201156 795751	−0·396266 69423
2·45	−0·023226 743305	−0·509052 067073	2·85	−0·205102 390590	−0·392848 51255
2·46	−0·028305 658919	−0·506725 574866	2·86	−0·209013 691285	−0·389407 91582
2·47	−0·033361 145552	−0·504366 307779	2·87	−0·212890 475203	−0·385945 20805
2·48	−0·038392 876569	−0·501974 489084	2·88	−0·216732 522761	−0·382460 69479
2·49	−0·043400 527581	−0·499550 344558	2·89	−0·220539 617438	−0·378954 68317
2·50	−0·048383 776468	−0·497094 102464	2·90	−0·224311 545792	−0·375427 48181
2·51	−0·053342 303407	−0·494605 993526	2·91	−0·228048 097475	−0·371879 40082
2·52	−0·058275 790893	−0·492086 250909	2·92	−0·231749 065248	−0·368310 75179
2·53	−0·063183 923765	−0·489535 110203	2·93	−0·235414 244994	−0·364721 84771
2·54	−0·068066 389230	−0·486952 809393	2·94	−0·239043 435734	−0·361113 00300
2·55	−0·072922 876886	−0·484339 588844	2·95	−0·242636 439638	−0·357484 53344
2·56	−0·077753 078750	−0·481695 691279	2·96	−0·246193 062043	−0·353836 75618
2·57	−0·082556 689272	−0·479021 361753	2·97	−0·249713 111464	−0·350169 98968
2·58	−0·087333 405369	−0·476316 847635	2·98	−0·253196 399605	−0·346484 55368
2·59	−0·092082 926441	−0·473582 398581	2·99	−0·256642 741376	−0·342780 76921
2·60	−0·096804 954397	−0·470818 266518	3·00	−0·260051 954902	−0·339058 95852
2·61	−0·101499 193675	−0·468024 705615	3·01	−0·263423 861537	−0·335319 44508
2·62	−0·106165 351268	−0·465201 972264	3·02	−0·266758 285876	−0·331562 553524
2·63	−0·110803 136741	−0·462350 325057	3·03	−0·270055 055766	−0·327788 60965
2·64	−0·115412 262258	−0·459470 024758	3·04	−0·273314 002318	−0·323997 94038
2·65	−0·119992 442602	−0·456561 334286	3·05	−0·276534 959916	−0·320190 873724
2·66	−0·124543 395193	−0·453624 518688	3·06	−0·279717 766231	−0·316367 738762
2·67	−0·129064 840115	−0·450659 845115	3·07	−0·282862 262330	−0·312528 865600
2·68	−0·133556 500133	−0·447667 582797	3·08	−0·285968 292186	−0·308674 585389
2·69	−0·138018 100713	−0·444648 003025	3·09	−0·289035 703688	−0·304805 230202
2·70	−0·142449 370046	−0·441601 379118	3·10	−0·292064 347651	−0·300921 133101
2·71	−0·146850 039066	−0·438527 986406	3·11	−0·295054 078324	−0·297022 628058
2·72	−0·151219 841469	−0·435428 102199	3·12	−0·298004 753302	−0·293110 049938
2·73	−0·155558 513735	−0·432302 005768	3·13	−0·300916 233531	−0·289183 734465
2·74	−0·159865 795147	−0·429149 978317	3·14	−0·303788 383321	−0·285244 018200
2·75	−0·164141 427809	−0·425972 302958	3·15	−0·306621 070350	−0·281291 238504
2·76	−0·168385 156663	−0·422769 264686	3·16	−0·309414 165674	−0·277325 733514
2·77	−0·172596 729515	−0·419541 150353	3·17	−0·312167 543732	−0·273347 842110
2·78	−0·176775 897046	−0·416288 248646	3·18	−0·314881 082360	−0·269357 903890
2·79	−0·180922 412832	−0·413010 850055	3·19	−0·317554 662788	−0·265356 259134
2·80	−0·185036 033364	−0·409709 246852	3·20	−0·320188 169657	−0·261343 248781

	$J_0(x)$	$-J_1(x)$	x	$J_0(x)$	$-J_1(x)$
0	−0·320188 169657	−0·261343 248781	3·60	−0·391768 983701	−0·095465 547178
1	−0·322781 491017	−0·257319 214392	3·61	−0·392702 729637	−0·091284 136789
2	−0·325334 518339	−0·253284 498129	3·62	−0·393594 676939	−0·087105 877039
3	−0·327847 146516	−0·249239 442719	3·63	−0·394444 858817	−0·082931 108843
4	−0·330319 273873	−0·245184 391424	3·64	−0·395253 311888	−0·078760 172463
5	−0·332750 802171	−0·241119 688015	3·65	−0·396020 076171	−0·074593 407483
6	−0·335141 636607	−0·237045 676741	3·66	−0·396745 195072	−0·070431 152776
7	−0·337491 685828	−0·232962 702298	3·67	−0·397428 715388	−0·066273 746480
8	−0·339800 861926	−0·228871 109797	3·68	−0·398070 687288	−0·062121 525964
9	−0·342069 080449	−0·224771 244740	3·69	−0·398671 164315	−0·057974 827802
0	−0·344296 260399	−0·220663 452985	3·70	−0·399230 203371	−0·053833 987745
1	−0·346482 324240	−0·216548 080719	3·71	−0·399747 864713	−0·049699 340694
2	−0·348627 197900	−0·212425 474424	3·72	−0·400224 211942	−0·045571 220667
3	−0·350730 810771	−0·208295 980854	3·73	−0·400659 311994	−0·041449 960775
4	−0·352793 095716	−0·204159 946997	3·74	−0·401053 235132	−0·037335 893193
5	−0·354813 989067	−0·200017 720051	3·75	−0·401406 054936	−0·033229 349130
6	−0·356793 430631	−0·195869 647392	3·76	−0·401717 848294	−0·029130 658803
7	−0·358731 363688	−0·191716 076543	3·77	−0·401988 695389	−0·025040 151411
8	−0·360627 734994	−0·187557 355145	3·78	−0·402218 679692	−0·020958 155102
9	−0·362482 494781	−0·183393 830929	3·79	−0·402407 887951	−0·016884 996950
.0	−0·364295 596762	−0·179225 851682	3·80	−0·402556 410179	−0·012821 002927
.1	−0·366066 998124	−0·175053 765218	3·81	−0·402664 339640	−0·008766 497873
.2	−0·367796 659535	−0·170877 919353	3·82	−0·402731 772845	−0·004721 805471
.3	−0·369484 545139	−0·166698 661869	3·83	−0·402758 809533	−0·000687 248221
.4	−0·371130 622559	−0·162516 340485	3·84	−0·402745 552664	+0·003336 852592
5	−0·372734 862895	−0·158331 302831	3·85	−0·402692 108403	+0·007350 176918
6	−0·374297 240720	−0·154143 896414	3·86	−0·402598 586110	+0·011352 405975
7	−0·375817 734085	−0·149954 468592	3·87	−0·402465 098327	+0·015343 222272
8	−0·377296 324511	−0·145763 366540	3·88	−0·402291 760761	+0·019322 309635
9	−0·378732 996992	−0·141570 937221	3·89	−0·402078 692280	+0·023289 353237
50	−0·380127 739987	−0·137377 527362	3·90	−0·401826 014888	+0·027244 039621
51	−0·381480 545425	−0·133183 483416	3·91	−0·401533 853719	+0·031186 056727
52	−0·382791 408696	−0·128989 151538	3·92	−0·401202 337020	+0·035115 093918
53	−0·384060 328649	−0·124794 877553	3·93	−0·400831 596137	+0·039030 842006
54	−0·385287 307591	−0·120601 006927	3·94	−0·400421 765502	+0·042932 993278
55	−0·386472 351282	−0·116407 884739	3·95	−0·399972 982615	+0·046821 241521
56	−0·387615 468930	−0·112215 855647	3·96	−0·399485 388031	+0·050695 282047
57	−0·388716 673186	−0·108025 263865	3·97	−0·398959 125344	+0·054554 811719
58	−0·389775 980144	−0·103836 453128	3·98	−0·398394 341172	+0·058399 528975
59	−0·390793 409330	−0·099649 766668	3·99	−0·397791 185139	+0·062229 133855
60	−0·391768 983701	−0·095465 547178	4·00	−0·397149 809864	+0·066043 328024

x	$J_0(x)$	$-J_1(x)$	x	$J_0(x)$	$-J_1(x)$
4·00	−0·397149 809864	+0·066043 328024	4·40	−0·342256 790004	+0·202775 52
4·01	−0·396470 370937	+0·069841 814795	4·41	−0·340214 269569	+0·205724 22
4·02	−0·395753 026909	+0·073624 299158	4·42	−0·338142 392830	+0·208646 74
4·03	−0·394997 939273	+0·077390 487802	4·43	−0·336041 422538	+0·211542 89
4·04	−0·394205 272445	+0·081140 089137	4·44	−0·333911 623508	+0·214412 46
4·05	−0·393375 193748	+0·084872 813321	4·45	−0·331753 262593	+0·217255 24
4·06	−0·392507 873396	+0·088588 372282	4·46	−0·329566 608658	+0·220071 03
4·07	−0·391603 484474	+0·092286 479742	4·47	−0·327351 932553	+0·222859 64
4·08	−0·390662 202921	+0·095966 851242	4·48	−0·325109 507090	+0·225620 871
4·09	−0·389684 207511	+0·099629 204162	4·49	−0·322839 607016	+0·228354 531
4·10	−0·388669 679836	+0·103273 257747	4·50	−0·320542 508985	+0·231060 431
4·11	−0·387618 804284	+0·106898 733130	4·51	−0·318218 491534	+0·233738 385
4·12	−0·386531 768024	+0·110505 353352	4·52	−0·315867 835056	+0·236388 206
4·13	−0·385408 760984	+0·114092 843385	4·53	−0·313490 821772	+0·239009 716
4·14	−0·384249 975834	+0·117660 930159	4·54	−0·311087 735706	+0·241602 733
4·15	−0·383055 607963	+0·121209 342578	4·55	−0·308658 862659	+0·244167 083
4·16	−0·381825 855461	+0·124737 811545	4·56	−0·306204 490179	+0·246702 591
4·17	−0·380560 919100	+0·128246 069984	4·57	−0·303724 907535	+0·249209 087
4·18	−0·379261 002313	+0·131733 852860	4·58	−0·301220 405692	+0·251686 403
4·19	−0·377926 311172	+0·135200 897203	4·59	−0·298691 277281	+0·254134 373
4·20	−0·376557 054368	+0·138646 942126	4·60	−0·296137 816574	+0·256552 836
4·21	−0·375153 443190	+0·142071 728849	4·61	−0·293560 319453	+0·258941 630
4·22	−0·373715 691507	+0·145475 000717	4·62	−0·290959 083385	+0·261300 599
4·23	−0·372244 015741	+0·148856 503224	4·63	−0·288334 407392	+0·263629 589
4·24	−0·370738 634848	+0·152215 984028	4·64	−0·285686 592028	+0·265928 448
4·25	−0·369199 770300	+0·155553 192978	4·65	−0·283015 939344	+0·268197 029
4·26	−0·367627 646055	+0·158867 882130	4·66	−0·280322 752864	+0·270435 184
4·27	−0·366022 488543	+0·162159 805765	4·67	−0·277607 337557	+0·272642 770
4·28	−0·364384 526637	+0·165428 720414	4·68	−0·274869 999807	+0·274819 649
4·29	−0·362713 991635	+0·168674 384873	4·69	−0·272111 047384	+0·276965 682
4·30	−0·361011 117237	+0·171896 560222	4·70	−0·269330 789420	+0·279080 735
4·31	−0·359276 139517	+0·175095 009847	4·71	−0·266529 536373	+0·281164 6774
4·32	−0·357509 296907	+0·178269 499458	4·72	−0·263707 600004	+0·283217 378
4·33	−0·355710 830168	+0·181419 797104	4·73	−0·260865 293347	+0·285238 7144
4·34	−0·353880 982370	+0·184545 673196	4·74	−0·258002 930679	+0·287228 5609
4·35	−0·352019 998867	+0·187646 900522	4·75	−0·255120 827491	+0·289186 7986
4·36	−0·350128 127272	+0·190723 254265	4·76	−0·252219 300460	+0·291113 3103
4·37	−0·348205 617435	+0·193774 512024	4·77	−0·249298 667418	+0·293007 9819
4·38	−0·346252 721418	+0·196800 453825	4·78	−0·246359 247327	+0·294870 7021
4·39	−0·344269 693470	+0·199800 862145	4·79	−0·243401 360242	+0·296701 3626
4·40	−0·342256 790004	+0·202775 521923	4·80	−0·240425 327291	+0·298499 8581

x	$J_0(x)$	$-J_1(x)$	x	$J_0(x)$	$-J_1(x)$
4·80	−0·240425 327291	+0·298499 858100	5·20	−0·110290 439791	+0·343223 005872
4·81	−0·237431 470639	+0·300266 086117	5·21	−0·106856 051931	+0·343648 917051
4·82	−0·234420 113459	+0·301999 947217	5·22	−0·103417 574396	+0·344040 944641
4·83	−0·231391 579906	+0·303701 344899	5·23	−0·099975 345904	+0·344399 112424
4·84	−0·228346 195084	+0·305370 185627	5·24	−0·096529 704924	+0·344723 447160
4·85	−0·225284 285019	+0·307006 378837	5·25	−0·093080 989639	+0·345013 978579
4·86	−0·222206 176625	+0·308609 836942	5·26	−0·089629 537922	+0·345270 739379
4·87	−0·219112 197679	+0·310180 475336	5·27	−0·086175 687302	+0·345493 765217
4·88	−0·216002 676790	+0·311718 212399	5·28	−0·082719 774939	+0·345683 094703
4·89	−0·212877 943365	+0·313222 969504	5·29	−0·079262 137591	+0·345838 769398
4·90	−0·209738 327585	+0·314694 671015	5·30	−0·075803 111586	+0·345960 833801
4·91	−0·206584 160372	+0·316133 244299	5·31	−0·072343 032791	+0·346049 335349
4·92	−0·203415 773359	+0·317538 619723	5·32	−0·068882 236587	+0·346104 324405
4·93	−0·200233 498860	+0·318910 730662	5·33	−0·065421 057834	+0·346125 854251
4·94	−0·197037 669840	+0·320249 513497	5·34	−0·061959 830846	+0·346113 981085
4·95	−0·193828 619886	+0·321554 907624	5·35	−0·058498 889359	+0·346068 764007
4·96	−0·190606 683176	+0·322826 855452	5·36	−0·055038 566506	+0·345990 265014
4·97	−0·187372 194447	+0·324065 302408	5·37	−0·051579 194783	+0·345878 548995
4·98	−0·184125 488969	+0·325270 196936	5·38	−0·048121 106024	+0·345733 683714
4·99	−0·180866 902512	+0·326441 490501	5·39	−0·044664 631371	+0·345555 739809
5·00	−0·177596 771314	+0·327579 137591	5·40	−0·041210 101245	+0·345344 790780
5·01	−0·174315 432057	+0·328683 095718	5·41	−0·037757 845318	+0·345100 912978
5·02	−0·171023 221828	+0·329753 325415	5·42	−0·034308 192484	+0·344824 185600
5·03	−0·167720 478098	+0·330789 790243	5·43	−0·030861 470832	+0·344514 690673
5·04	−0·164407 538685	+0·331792 456787	5·44	−0·027418 007614	+0·344172 513049
5·05	−0·161084 741725	+0·332761 294658	5·45	−0·023978 129221	+0·343797 740393
5·06	−0·157752 425645	+0·333696 276491	5·46	−0·020542 161155	+0·343390 463171
5·07	−0·154410 929130	+0·334597 377947	5·47	−0·017110 427996	+0·342950 774642
5·08	−0·151060 591092	+0·335464 577712	5·48	−0·013683 253380	+0·342478 770844
5·09	−0·147701 750643	+0·336297 857492	5·49	−0·010260 959967	+0·341974 550584
5·10	−0·144334 747061	+0·337097 202018	5·50	−0·006843 869418	+0·341438 215429
5·11	−0·140959 919761	+0·337862 599041	5·51	−0·003432 302361	+0·340869 869689
5·12	−0·137577 608269	+0·338594 039331	5·52	−0·000026 578369	+0·340269 620408
5·13	−0·134188 152185	+0·339291 516672	5·53	+0·003372 984068	+0·339637 577354
5·14	−0·130791 891157	+0·339955 027866	5·54	+0·006766 067573	+0·338973 853000
5·15	−0·127389 164849	+0·340584 572725	5·55	+0·010152 355907	+0·338278 562520
5·16	−0·123980 312914	+0·341180 154069	5·56	+0·013531 533995	+0·337551 823766
5·17	−0·120565 674960	+0·341741 777728	5·57	+0·016903 287956	+0·336793 757265
5·18	−0·117145 590523	+0·342269 452530	5·58	+0·020267 305125	+0·336004 486197
5·19	−0·113720 399033	+0·342763 190303	5·59	+0·023623 274084	+0·335184 136388
5·20	−0·110290 439791	+0·343223 005872	5·60	+0·026970 884685	+0·334332 836291

x	$J_0(x)$	$-J_1(x)$	x	$J_0(x)$	$-J_1(x)$
5·60	+0·026970 84685	+0·334332 836291	6·00	+0·150645 257251	+0·276683 858128
5·61	+0·030309 828079	+0·333450 716975	6·01	+0·153402 218596	+0·274704 492725
5·62	+0·033639 796739	+0·332537 912108	6·02	+0·156139 269116	+0·272701 730538
5·63	+0·036960 484490	+0·331594 557948	6·03	+0·158856 175969	+0·270675 796964
5·64	+0·040271 586530	+0·330620 793320	6·04	+0·161552 708575	+0·268626 919220
5·65	+0·043572 799459	+0·329616 759609	6·05	+0·164228 638636	+0·266555 326316
5·66	+0·046863 821304	+0·328582 600738	6·06	+0·166883 740153	+0·264461 249036
5·67	+0·050144 351544	+0·327518 463159	6·07	+0·169517 789443	+0·262344 919911
5·68	+0·053414 091135	+0·326424 495830	6·08	+0·172130 565159	+0·260206 573201
5·69	+0·056672 742533	+0·325300 850207	6·09	+0·174721 848302	+0·258046 444869
5·70	+0·059920 009724	+0·324147 680223	6·10	+0·177291 422243	+0·255864 772558
5·71	+0·063155 598244	+0·322965 142271	6·11	+0·179839 072737	+0·253661 795571
5·72	+0·066379 215205	+0·321753 395193	6·12	+0·182364 587942	+0·251437 754842
5·73	+0·069590 569321	+0·320512 600255	6·13	+0·184867 758430	+0·249192 892918
5·74	+0·072789 370930	+0·319242 921139	6·14	+0·187348 377209	+0·246927 453930
5·75	+0·075975 332017	+0·317944 523919	6·15	+0·189806 239737	+0·244641 683576
5·76	+0·079148 166242	+0·316617 577048	6·16	+0·192241 143934	+0·242335 829091
5·77	+0·082307 588961	+0·315262 251336	6·17	+0·194652 890201	+0·240010 139225
5·78	+0·085453 317250	+0·313878 719939	6·18	+0·197041 281434	+0·237664 864220
5·79	+0·088585 069926	+0·312467 158333	6·19	+0·199406 123040	+0·235300 255786
5·80	+0·091702 567575	+0·311027 744304	6·20	+0·201747 222949	+0·232916 567073
5·81	+0·094805 532571	+0·309560 657922	6·21	+0·204064 391629	+0·230514 052652
5·82	+0·097893 689100	+0·308066 081529	6·22	+0·206357 442103	+0·228092 968487
5·83	+0·100966 763183	+0·306544 199716	6·23	+0·208626 189957	+0·225653 571908
5·84	+0·104024 482698	+0·304995 199305	6·24	+0·210870 453362	+0·223196 121594
5·85	+0·107066 577404	+0·303419 269333	6·25	+0·213090 053077	+0·220720 877539
5·86	+0·110092 778957	+0·301816 601028	6·26	+0·215284 812471	+0·218228 101034
5·87	+0·113102 820941	+0·300187 387793	6·27	+0·217454 557531	+0·215718 054638
5·88	+0·116096 438881	+0·298531 825185	6·28	+0·219599 116876	+0·213191 002155
5·89	+0·119073 370272	+0·296850 110895	6·29	+0·221718 321770	+0·210647 208606
5·90	+0·122033 354593	+0·295142 444729	6·30	+0·223812 006132	+0·208086 940207
5·91	+0·124976 133333	+0·293409 028587	6·31	+0·225880 006549	+0·205510 464342
5·92	+0·127901 450011	+0·291650 066443	6·32	+0·227922 162289	+0·202918 049537
5·93	+0·130809 050195	+0·289865 764324	6·33	+0·229938 315309	+0·200309 965435
5·94	+0·133698 681524	+0·288056 330291	6·34	+0·231928 310269	+0·197686 482769
5·95	+0·136570 093728	+0·286221 974417	6·35	+0·233891 994542	+0·195047 873339
5·96	+0·139423 038646	+0·284362 908764	6·36	+0·235829 218223	+0·192394 409984
5·97	+0·142257 270250	+0·282479 347366	6·37	+0·237739 834141	+0·189726 366557
5·98	+0·145072 544661	+0·280571 506204	6·38	+0·239623 697870	+0·187044 017898
5·99	+0·147868 620168	+0·278639 603186	6·39	+0·241480 667734	+0·184347 639808
6·00	+0·150645 257251	+0·276683 858128	6·40	+0·243310 604823	+0·181637 509024

	$J_0(x)$	$-J_1(x)$	x	$J_0(x)$	$-J_1(x)$
40	+0·243310 604823	+0·181637 509024	6·80	+0·293095 603104	+0·065218 663402
41	+0·245113 372998	+0·178913 903193	6·81	+0·293732 652315	+0·062190 881458
42	+0·246888 838899	+0·176177 100845	6·82	+0·294339 415275	+0·059161 461866
43	+0·248636 871957	+0·173427 381364	6·83	+0·294915 877066	+0·056130 696324
44	+0·250357 344403	+0·170665 024967	6·84	+0·295462 025686	+0·053098 876291
45	+0·252050 131270	+0·167890 312675	6·85	+0·295977 852047	+0·050066 292954
46	+0·253715 110409	+0·165103 526284	6·86	+0·296463 349971	+0·047033 237205
47	+0·255352 162491	+0·162304 948344	6·87	+0·296918 516185	+0·043999 999614
48	+0·256961 171015	+0·159494 862126	6·88	+0·297343 350324	+0·040966 870403
49	+0·258542 022319	+0·156673 551601	6·89	+0·297737 854921	+0·037934 139418
50	+0·260094 605582	+0·153841 301410	6·90	+0·298102 035405	+0·034902 096105
51	+0·261618 812832	+0·150998 396839	6·91	+0·298435 900099	+0·031871 029480
52	+0·263114 538957	+0·148145 123790	6·92	+0·298739 460212	+0·028841 228107
53	+0·264581 681702	+0·145281 768758	6·93	+0·299012 729839	+0·025812 980070
54	+0·266020 141682	+0·142408 618801	6·94	+0·299255 725950	+0·022786 572947
55	+0·267429 822386	+0·139525 961513	6·95	+0·299468 468391	+0·019762 293785
56	+0·268810 630181	+0·136634 085000	6·96	+0·299650 979874	+0·016740 429070
57	+0·270162 474318	+0·133733 277851	6·97	+0·299803 285973	+0·013721 264707
58	+0·271485 266933	+0·130823 829111	6·98	+0·299925 415120	+0·010705 085992
59	+0·272778 923059	+0·127906 028255	6·99	+0·300017 398594	+0·007692 177584
60	+0·274043 360624	+0·124980 165161	7·00	+0·300079 270520	+0·004682 823482
61	+0·275278 500456	+0·122046 530081	7·01	+0·300111 067856	+0·001677 306999
62	+0·276484 266288	+0·119105 413617	7·02	+0·300112 830394	−0·001324 089265
63	+0·277660 584760	+0·116157 106694	7·03	+0·300084 600744	−0·004321 083446
64	+0·278807 385424	+0·113201 900529	7·04	+0·300026 424335	−0·007313 394442
65	+0·279924 600745	+0·110240 086609	7·05	+0·299938 349401	−0·010300 741939
66	+0·281012 166103	+0·107271 956661	7·06	+0·299820 426973	−0·013282 846438
67	+0·282070 019798	+0·104297 802626	7·07	+0·299672 710878	−0·016259 429273
68	+0·283098 103049	+0·101317 916630	7·08	+0·299495 257720	−0·019230 212645
69	+0·284096 359998	+0·098332 590962	7·09	+0·299288 126879	−0·022194 919639
70	+0·285064 737711	+0·095342 118041	7·10	+0·299051 380502	−0·025153 274254
71	+0·286003 186176	+0·092346 790394	7·11	+0·298785 083486	−0·028105 001425
72	+0·286911 658311	+0·089346 900625	7·12	+0·298489 303478	−0·031049 827049
73	+0·287790 109957	+0·086342 741391	7·13	+0·298164 110861	−0·033987 478007
74	+0·288638 499883	+0·083334 605375	7·14	+0·297809 578741	−0·036917 682190
75	+0·289456 789785	+0·080322 785255	7·15	+0·297425 782943	−0·039840 168524
6	+0·290244 944284	+0·077307 573684	7·16	+0·297012 801997	−0·042754 666991
7	+0·291002 930929	+0·074289 263257	7·17	+0·296570 717126	−0·045660 908657
8	+0·291730 720194	+0·071268 146488	7·18	+0·296099 612239	−0·048558 625692
9	+0·292428 285479	+0·068244 515780	7·19	+0·295599 573917	−0·051447 551397
80	+0·293095 603104	+0·065218 663402	7·20	+0·295070 691401	−0·054327 420222

x	$J_0(x)$	$-J_1(x)$	x	$J_0(x)$	$-J_1(x)$
7·20	+0·295070 691401	−0·054327 420222	7·60	+0·251601 833850	−0·159213 768
7·21	+0·294513 056583	−0·057197 967799	7·61	+0·249998 194750	−0·161510 921
7·22	+0·293926 763993	−0·060058 930954	7·62	+0·248371 678346	−0·163789 196
7·23	+0·293311 910786	−0·062910 047738	7·63	+0·246722 474402	−0·166048 397
7·24	+0·292668 596729	−0·065751 057450	7·64	+0·245050 774627	−0·168288 330
7·25	+0·291996 924192	−0·068581 700653	7·65	+0·243356 772660	−0·170508 803
7·26	+0·291296 998131	−0·071401 719205	7·66	+0·241640 664046	−0·172709 628
7·27	+0·290568 926079	−0·074210 856276	7·67	+0·239902 646217	−0·174890 616
7·28	+0·289812 818129	−0·077008 856374	7·68	+0·238142 918467	−0·177051 581
7·29	+0·289028 786922	−0·079795 465364	7·69	+0·236361 681936	−0·179192 341
7·30	+0·288216 947635	−0·082570 430493	7·70	+0·234559 139586	−0·181312 715
7·31	+0·287377 417963	−0·085333 500412	7·71	+0·232735 496182	−0·183412 523
7·32	+0·286510 318111	−0·088084 425194	7·72	+0·230890 958266	−0·185491 588
7·33	+0·285615 770772	−0·090822 956363	7·73	+0·229025 734139	−0·187549 736
7·34	+0·284693 901119	−0·093548 846906	7·74	+0·227140 033840	−0·189586 794
7·35	+0·283744 836788	−0·096261 851305	7·75	+0·225234 069120	−0·191602 592
7·36	+0·282768 707860	−0·098961 725549	7·76	+0·223308 053424	−0·193596 961
7·37	+0·281765 646852	−0·101648 227162	7·77	+0·221362 201866	−0·195569 737
7·38	+0·280735 788696	−0·104321 115218	7·78	+0·219396 731209	−0·197520 754
7·39	+0·279679 270724	−0·106980 150367	7·79	+0·217411 859839	−0·199449 852
7·40	+0·278596 232657	−0·109625 094854	7·80	+0·215407 807746	−0·201356 872
7·41	+0·277486 816584	−0·112255 712538	7·81	+0·213384 796501	−0·203241 657
7·42	+0·276351 166945	−0·114871 768912	7·82	+0·211343 049230	−0·205104 052
7·43	+0·275189 430519	−0·117473 031128	7·83	+0·209282 790594	−0·206943 905
7·44	+0·274001 756407	−0·120059 268011	7·84	+0·207204 246765	−0·208761 066
7·45	+0·272788 296009	−0·122630 250080	7·85	+0·205107 645402	−0·210555 387
7·46	+0·271549 203014	−0·125185 749572	7·86	+0·202993 215628	−0·212326 724
7·47	+0·270284 633379	−0·127725 540456	7·87	+0·200861 188009	0·214014 933
7·48	+0·268994 745315	−0·130249 398456	7·88	+0·198711 794526	−0·215799 873
7·49	+0·267679 699262	−0·132757 101068	7·89	+0·196545 268555	−0·217501 407
7·50	+0·266339 657880	−0·135248 427580	7·90	+0·194361 844841	−0·219179 399
7·51	+0·264974 786027	−0·137723 159089	7·91	+0·192161 759476	−0·220833 716
7·52	+0·263585 250739	−0·140181 078522	7·92	+0·189945 249872	−0·222464 225
7·53	+0·262171 221215	−0·142621 970654	7·93	+0·187712 554741	−0·224070 800
7·54	+0·260732 868795	−0·145045 622124	7·94	+0·185463 914068	−0·225653 313
7·55	+0·259270 366946	−0·147451 821455	7·95	+0·183199 569087	−0·227211 641
7·56	+0·257783 891239	−0·149840 359071	7·96	+0·180919 762257	−0·228745 663
7·57	+0·256273 619329	−0·152211 027316	7·97	+0·178624 737238	−0·230255 259
7·58	+0·254739 730943	−0·154563 620468	7·98	+0·176314 738866	−0·231740 314
7·59	+0·253182 407850	−0·156897 934760	7·99	+0·173990 013218	−0·233200 714
7·60	+0·251601 833850	−0·159213 768396	8·00	+0·171650 807138	−0·234636 346

	$J_0(x)$	$-J_1(x)$	x	$J_0(x)$	$-J_1(x)$
00	+0·171650 807138	−0·234636 346854	8·40	+0·069157 261657	−0·270786 268277
01	+0·169297 369111	−0·236047 103631	8·41	+0·066447 598160	−0·271141 908453
02	+0·166929 948339	−0·237432 878137	8·42	+0·063734 513946	−0·271470 411269
03	+0·164548 795169	−0·238793 566425	8·43	+0·061018 280395	−0·271771 776141
04	+0·162154 160970	−0·240129 067056	8·44	+0·058299 168877	−0·272046 005084
05	+0·159746 298117	−0·241439 281101	8·45	+0·055577 450731	−0·272293 102707
06	+0·157325 459958	−0·242724 112158	8·46	+0·052853 397237	−0·272513 076214
07	+0·154891 900797	−0·243983 466348	8·47	+0·050127 279588	−0·272705 935396
08	+0·152445 875859	−0·245217 252327	8·48	+0·047399 368869	−0·272871 692631
09	+0·149987 641274	−0·246425 381291	8·49	+0·044669 936026	−0·273010 362878
10	+0·147517 454044	−0·247607 766982	8·50	+0·041939 251843	−0·273121 963674
11	+0·145035 572024	−0·248764 325692	8·51	+0·039207 586917	−0·273206 515132
12	+0·142542 253891	−0·249894 976273	8·52	+0·036475 211629	−0·273264 039934
13	+0·140037 759122	−0·250999 640134	8·53	+0·033742 396123	−0·273294 563325
14	+0·137522 347965	−0·252078 241253	8·54	+0·031009 410275	−0·273298 113112
15	+0·134996 281417	−0·253130 706180	8·55	+0·028276 523672	−0·273274 719657
16	+0·132459 821198	−0·254156 964039	8·56	+0·025544 005583	−0·273224 415870
17	+0·129913 229721	−0·255156 946534	8·57	+0·022812 124938	−0·273147 237207
18	+0·127356 770071	−0·256130 587952	8·58	+0·020081 150296	−0·273043 221660
19	+0·124790 705977	−0·257077 825169	8·59	+0·017351 349826	−0·272912 409756
20	+0·122215 301784	−0·257998 597649	8·60	+0·014622 991279	−0·272754 844546
21	+0·119630 822433	−0·258892 847451	8·61	+0·011896 341961	−0·272570 571599
22	+0·117037 533429	−0·259760 519231	8·62	+0·009171 668713	−0·272359 639000
23	+0·114435 700818	−0·260601 560243	8·63	+0·006449 237878	−0·272122 097337
24	+0·111825 591161	−0·261415 920344	8·64	+0·003729 315286	−0·271857 999697
25	+0·109207 471506	−0·262203 551993	8·65	+0·001012 166219	−0·271567 401658
26	+0·106581 609366	−0·262964 410256	8·66	−0·001701 944606	−0·271250 361281
27	+0·103948 272687	−0·263698 452805	8·67	−0·004412 753067	−0·270906 939104
28	+0·101307 729828	−0·264405 639923	8·68	−0·007119 995658	−0·270537 198130
29	+0·098660 249531	−0·265085 934502	8·69	−0·009823 409518	−0·270141 203821
30	+0·096006 100895	−0·265739 302042	8·70	−0·012522 732450	−0·269719 024092
31	+0·093345 553353	−0·266365 710658	8·71	−0·015217 702949	−0·269270 729296
32	+0·090678 876643	−0·266965 131077	8·72	−0·017908 060228	−0·268796 392222
33	+0·088006 340781	−0·267537 536636	8·73	−0·020593 544236	−0·268296 088078
34	+0·085328 216040	−0·268082 903285	8·74	−0·023273 895691	−0·267769 894490
35	+0·082644 772917	−0·268601 209586	8·75	−0·025948 856095	−0·267217 891486
36	+0·079956 282113	−0·269092 436712	8·76	−0·028618 167764	−0·266640 161489
37	+0·077263 014501	−0·269556 568447	8·77	−0·031281 573850	−0·266036 789304
38	+0·074565 241107	−0·269993 591184	8·78	−0·033938 818366	−0·265407 862113
39	+0·071863 233078	−0·270403 493925	8·79	−0·036589 646207	−0·264753 469460
40	+0·069157 261657	−0·270786 268277	8·80	−0·039233 803177	−0·264073 703240

x	$J_0(x)$	$-J_1(x)$	x	$J_0(x)$	$-J_1(x)$
8·80	−0·039233 803177	−0·264073 703240	9·20	−0·136748 370765	−0·217408 6549
8·81	−0·041871 036007	−0·263368 657691	9·21	−0·138914 405500	−0·215795 0167
8·82	−0·044501 092388	−0·262638 429381	9·22	−0·141064 205893	−0·214161 8163
8·83	−0·047123 720982	−0·261883 117196	9·23	−0·143197 577219	−0·212509 2337
8·84	−0·049738 671456	−0·261102 822332	9·24	−0·145314 326565	−0·210837 4506
8·85	−0·052345 694498	−0·260297 648278	9·25	−0·147414 262841	−0·209146 6504
8·86	−0·054944 541843	−0·259467 700807	9·26	−0·149497 196801	−0·207437 0183
8·87	−0·057534 966296	−0·258613 087962	9·27	−0·151562 941057	−0·205708 7409
8·88	−0·060116 721752	−0·257733 920049	9·28	−0·153611 310096	−0·203962 0065
8·89	−0·062689 563221	−0·256830 309615	9·29	−0·155642 120296	−0·202197 0049
8·90	−0·065253 246851	−0·255902 371444	9·30	−0·157655 189943	−0·200413 9278
8·91	−0·067807 529947	−0·254950 222539	9·31	−0·159650 339244	−0·198612 9680
8·92	−0·070352 170997	−0·253973 982110	9·32	−0·161627 390345	−0·196794 3202
8·93	−0·072886 929689	−0·252973 771561	9·33	−0·163586 167343	−0·194958 1804
8·94	−0·075411 566939	−0·251949 714476	9·34	−0·165526 496306	−0·193104 7462
8·95	−0·077925 844909	−0·250901 936605	9·35	−0·167448 205283	−0·191234 2166
8·96	−0·080429 527028	−0·249830 565850	9·36	−0·169351 124322	−0·189346 7920
8·97	−0·082922 378016	−0·248735 732253	9·37	−0·171235 085481	−0·187442 6745
8·98	−0·085404 163904	−0·247617 567976	9·38	−0·173099 922846	−0·185522 0672
8·99	−0·087874 652054	−0·246476 207294	9·39	−0·174945 472543	−0·183585 1750
9·00	−0·090333 611183	−0·245311 786573	9·40	−0·176771 572752	−0·181632 2040
9·01	−0·092780 811380	−0·244124 444261	9·41	−0·178578 063718	−0·179663 3614
9·02	−0·095216 024131	−0·242914 320868	9·42	−0·180364 787772	−0·177678 8562
9·03	−0·097639 022336	−0·241681 558953	9·43	−0·182131 589336	−0·175678 8984
9·04	−0·100049 580330	−0·240426 303111	9·44	−0·183878 314938	−0·173663 6994
9·05	−0·102447 473906	−0·239148 699952	9·45	−0·185604 813228	−0·171633 4717
9·06	−0·104832 480333	−0·237848 898088	9·46	−0·187310 934989	−0·169588 4292
9·07	−0·107204 378374	−0·236527 048119	9·47	−0·188996 533147	−0·167528 7869
9·08	−0·109562 948310	−0·235183 302612	9·48	−0·190661 462784	−0·165454 7613
9·09	−0·111907 971956	−0·233817 816088	9·49	−0·192305 581154	−0·163366 5697
9·10	−0·114239 232683	−0·232430 745006	9·50	−0·193928 747687	−0·161264 4307
9·11	−0·116556 515436	−0·231022 247743	9·51	−0·195530 824010	−0·159148 5641
9·12	−0·118859 606752	−0·229592 484581	9·52	−0·197111 673948	−0·157019 1907
9·13	−0·121148 294781	−0·228141 617686	9·53	−0·198671 163543	−0·154876 5325
9·14	−0·123422 369306	−0·226669 811094	9·54	−0·200209 161060	−0·152720 8125
9·15	−0·125681 621757	−0·225177 230692	9·55	−0·201725 537001	−0·150552 2548
9·16	−0·127925 845233	−0·223664 044201	9·56	−0·203220 164114	−0·148371 0843
9·17	−0·130154 834519	−0·222130 421159	9·57	−0·204692 917400	−0·146177 5272
9·18	−0·132368 386105	−0·220576 532901	9·58	−0·206143 674127	−0·143971 8106
9·19	−0·134566 298203	−0·219002 552542	9·59	−0·207572 313841	−0·141754 1625
9·20	−0·136748 370765	−0·217408 654960	9·60	−0·208978 718369	−0·139524 8117

x	$J_0(x)$	$-J_1(x)$	x	$J_0(x)$	$-J_1(x)$
9·60	−0·208978 718369	−0·139524 811741	10·00	−0·245935 764451	−0·043472 746169
9·61	−0·210362 771833	−0·137283 988215	10·01	−0·246357 974862	−0·040969 056455
9·62	−0·211724 360660	−0·135031 922668	10·02	−0·246755 140400	−0·038463 812722
9·63	−0·213063 373585	−0·132768 846695	10·03	−0·247127 246760	−0·035957 261846
9·64	−0·214379 701667	−0·130494 992737	10·04	−0·247474 282103	−0·033449 650599
9·65	−0·215673 238291	−0·128210 594048	10·05	−0·247796 237059	−0·030941 225625
9·66	−0·216943 879179	−0·125915 884679	10·06	−0·248093 104724	−0·028432 233416
9·67	−0·218191 522398	−0·123611 099451	10·07	−0·248364 880658	−0·025922 920290
9·68	−0·219416 068367	−0·121296 473933	10·08	−0·248611 562881	−0·023413 532364
9·69	−0·220617 419863	−0·118972 244417	10·09	−0·248833 151876	−0·020904 315537
9·70	−0·221795 482032	−0·116638 647900	10·10	−0·249029 650581	−0·018395 515458
9·71	−0·222950 162390	−0·114295 922054	10·11	−0·249201 064392	−0·015887 377509
9·72	−0·224081 370836	−0·111944 305207	10·12	−0·249347 401155	−0·013380 146780
9·73	−0·225189 019654	−0·109584 036317	10·13	−0·249468 671167	−0·010874 068044
9·74	−0·226273 023521	−0·107215 354950	10·14	−0·249564 887171	−0·008369 385737
9·75	−0·227333 299512	−0·104838 501258	10·15	−0·249636 064351	−0·005866 343931
9·76	−0·228369 767107	−0·102453 715952	10·16	−0·249682 220330	−0·003365 186314
9·77	−0·229382 348196	−0·100061 240280	10·17	−0·249703 375168	−0·000866 156165
9·78	−0·230370 967084	−0·097661 316004	10·18	−0·249699 551355	+0·001630 503669
9·79	−0·231335 550495	−0·095254 185376	10·19	−0·249670 773804	+0·004124 550795
9·80	−0·232276 027579	−0·092840 091113	10·20	−0·249617 069854	+0·006615 743298
9·81	−0·233192 329916	−0·090419 276375	10·21	−0·249538 469258	+0·009103 839761
9·82	−0·234084 391517	−0·087991 984743	10·22	−0·249435 004182	+0·011588 599292
9·83	−0·234952 148834	−0·085558 460188	10·23	−0·249306 709197	+0·014069 781546
9·84	−0·235795 540759	−0·083118 947058	10·24	−0·249153 621275	+0·016547 146743
9·85	−0·236614 508629	−0·080673 690044	10·25	−0·248975 779783	+0·019020 455697
9·86	−0·237408 996230	−0·078222 934162	10·26	−0·248773 226477	+0·021489 469834
9·87	−0·238178 949800	−0·075766 924729	10·27	−0·248546 005495	+0·023953 951217
9·88	−0·238924 318032	−0·073305 907338	10·28	−0·248294 163353	+0·026413 662567
9·89	−0·239645 052073	−0·070840 127831	10·29	−0·248017 748933	+0·028868 367285
9·90	−0·240341 105535	−0·068369 832284	10·30	−0·247716 813482	+0·031317 829476
9·91	−0·241012 434487	−0·065895 266972	10·31	−0·247391 410602	+0·033761 813968
9·92	−0·241658 997463	−0·063416 678354	10·32	−0·247041 596243	+0·036200 086339
9·93	−0·242280 755465	−0·060934 313045	10·33	−0·246667 428695	+0·038632 412933
9·94	−0·242877 671958	−0·058448 417794	10·34	−0·246268 968580	+0·041058 560885
9·95	−0·243449 712877	−0·055959 239457	10·35	−0·245846 278846	+0·043478 298146
9·96	−0·243996 846626	−0·053467 024979	10·36	−0·245399 424757	+0·045891 393496
9·97	−0·244519 044079	−0·050972 021363	10·37	−0·244928 473884	+0·048297 616575
9·98	−0·245016 278580	−0·048474 475654	10·38	−0·244433 496098	+0·050696 737897
9·99	−0·245488 525942	−0·045974 634906	10·39	−0·243914 563561	+0·053088 528877
10·00	−0·245935 764451	−0·043472 746169	10·40	−0·243371 750714	+0·055472 761849

x	$J_0(x)$	$-J_1(x)$	x	$J_0(x)$	$-J_1(x)$
10·40	−0·243371 750714	+0·055472 761849	10·80	−0·203201 967112	+0·142166 568299
10·41	−0·242805 134273	+0·057849 210087	10·81	−0·201770 826005	+0·144058 996415
10·42	−0·242214 793214	+0·060217 647828	10·82	−0·200320 840603	+0·145935 398812
10·43	−0·241600 808767	+0·062577 850293	10·83	−0·198852 172014	+0·147795 605727
10·44	−0·240963 264405	+0·064929 593703	10·84	−0·197364 983034	+0·149639 449122
10·45	−0·240302 245833	+0·067272 655308	10·85	−0·195859 438131	+0·151466 762702
10·46	−0·239617 840978	+0·069606 813400	10·86	−0·194335 703428	+0·153277 381926
10·47	−0·238910 139979	+0·071931 847339	10·87	−0·192793 946683	+0·155071 144022
10·48	−0·238179 235177	+0·074247 537568	10·88	−0·191234 337275	+0·156847 888004
10·49	−0·237425 221101	+0·076553 665638	10·89	−0·189657 046181	+0·158607 454682
10·50	−0·236648 194462	+0·078850 014227	10·90	−0·188062 245963	+0·160349 686681
10·51	−0·235848 254136	+0·081136 367158	10·91	−0·186450 110748	+0·162074 428448
10·52	−0·235025 501155	+0·083412 509421	10·92	−0·184820 816208	+0·163781 526274
10·53	−0·234180 038696	+0·085678 227191	10·93	−0·183174 539542	+0·165470 828298
10·54	−0·233311 972068	+0·087933 307849	10·94	−0·181511 459461	+0·167142 184528
10·55	−0·232421 408701	+0·090177 540002	10·95	−0·179831 756165	+0·168795 446850
10·56	−0·231508 458131	+0·092410 713500	10·96	−0·178135 611325	+0·170430 469041
10·57	−0·230573 231989	+0·094632 619458	10·97	−0·176423 208066	+0·172047 106783
10·58	−0·229615 843992	+0·096843 050272	10·98	−0·174694 730946	+0·173645 217675
10·59	−0·228636 409922	+0·099041 799642	10·99	−0·172950 365937	+0·175224 661243
10·60	−0·227635 047621	+0·101228 662586	11·00	−0·171190 300407	+0·176785 298957
10·61	−0·226611 876971	+0·103403 435462	11·01	−0·169414 723099	+0·178326 994235
10·62	−0·225567 019886	+0·105565 915987	11·02	−0·167623 824113	+0·179849 612465
10·63	−0·224500 600296	+0·107715 903254	11·03	−0·165817 794883	+0·181353 021005
10·64	−0·223412 744130	+0·109853 197747	11·04	−0·163996 828161	+0·182837 089204
10·65	−0·222303 579310	+0·111977 601366	11·05	−0·162161 117996	+0·184301 688406
10·66	−0·221173 235728	+0·114088 917441	11·06	−0·160310 859712	+0·185746 691967
10·67	−0·220021 845238	+0·116186 950748	11·07	−0·158446 249891	+0·187171 975260
10·68	−0·218849 541635	+0·118271 507531	11·08	−0·156567 486350	+0·188577 415689
10·69	−0·217656 460650	+0·120342 395515	11·09	−0·154674 768122	+0·189962 892696
10·70	−0·216442 739924	+0·122399 423927	11·10	−0·152768 295436	+0·191328 287775
10·71	−0·215208 519001	+0·124442 403513	11·11	−0·150848 269694	+0·192673 484480
10·72	−0·213953 939309	+0·126471 146550	11·12	−0·148914 893455	+0·193998 368432
10·73	−0·212679 144146	+0·128485 466871	11·13	−0·146968 370410	+0·195302 827334
10·74	−0·211384 278663	+0·130485 179874	11·14	−0·145008 905360	+0·196586 750976
10·75	−0·210069 489850	+0·132470 102543	11·15	−0·143036 704202	+0·197850 031243
10·76	−0·208734 926518	+0·134440 053463	11·16	−0·141051 973900	+0·199092 562127
10·77	−0·207380 739286	+0·136394 852837	11·17	−0·139054 922470	+0·200314 239736
10·78	−0·206007 080560	+0·138334 322500	11·18	−0·137045 758956	+0·201514 962299
10·79	−0·204614 104523	+0·140258 285937	11·19	−0·135024 693407	+0·202694 630176
10·80	−0·203201 967112	+0·142166 568299	11·20	−0·132991 936860	+0·203853 145865

	$J_0(x)$	$-J_1(x)$	x	$J_0(x)$	$-J_1(x)$
20	−0·132991 936860	+0·203853 145865	11·60	−0·044615 674094	+0·232000 474620
21	−0·130947 701315	+0·204990 414012	11·61	−0·042294 477301	+0·232235 010376
22	−0·128892 199715	+0·206106 341416	11·62	−0·039971 051364	+0·232446 303109
23	−0·126825 645926	+0·207200 837037	11·63	−0·037645 628720	+0·232634 351719
24	−0·124748 254710	+0·208273 812006	11·64	−0·035318 441806	+0·232799 157379
25	−0·122660 241711	+0·209325 179625	11·65	−0·032989 723038	+0·232940 723529
26	−0·120561 823424	+0·210354 855380	11·66	−0·030659 704782	+0·233059 055883
27	−0·118453 217184	+0·211362 756947	11·67	−0·028328 619340	+0·233154 162418
28	−0·116334 641133	+0·212348 804193	11·68	−0·025996 698919	+0·233226 053376
29	−0·114206 314208	+0·213312 919188	11·69	−0·023664 175616	+0·233274 741260
30	−0·112068 456110	+0·214255 026208	11·70	−0·021331 281388	+0·233300 240831
31	−0·109921 287289	+0·215175 051739	11·71	−0·018998 248037	+0·233302 569105
32	−0·107765 028918	+0·216072 924488	11·72	−0·016665 307180	+0·233281 745349
33	−0·105599 902872	+0·216948 575381	11·73	−0·014332 690232	+0·233237 791079
34	−0·103426 131706	+0·217801 937572	11·74	−0·012000 628381	+0·233170 730054
35	−0·101243 938632	+0·218632 946448	11·75	−0·009669 352567	+0·233080 588274
36	−0·099053 547496	+0·219441 539632	11·76	−0·007339 093458	+0·232967 393973
37	−0·096855 182759	+0·220227 656988	11·77	−0·005010 081428	+0·232831 177619
38	−0·094649 069469	+0·220991 240623	11·78	−0·002682 546537	+0·232671 971904
39	−0·092435 433245	+0·221732 234896	11·79	−0·000356 718505	+0·232489 811743
40	−0·090214 500248	+0·222450 586415	11·80	+0·001967 173307	+0·232284 734267
41	−0·087986 497163	+0·223146 244045	11·81	+0·004288 899920	+0·232056 778820
42	−0·085751 651176	+0·223819 158911	11·82	+0·006608 232761	+0·231805 986948
43	−0·083510 189950	+0·224469 284397	11·83	+0·008924 943683	+0·231532 402401
44	−0·081262 341601	+0·225096 576153	11·84	+0·011238 804987	+0·231236 071121
45	−0·079008 334679	+0·225700 992096	11·85	+0·013549 589443	+0·230917 041237
46	−0·076748 398145	+0·226282 492413	11·86	+0·015857 070317	+0·230575 363062
47	−0·074482 761342	+0·226841 039560	11·87	+0·018161 021385	+0·230211 089083
48	−0·072211 653982	+0·227376 598268	11·88	+0·020461 216961	+0·229824 273953
49	−0·069935 306115	+0·227889 135543	11·89	+0·022757 431916	+0·229414 974489
50	−0·067653 948112	+0·228378 620665	11·90	+0·025049 441700	+0·228983 249662
51	−0·065367 810637	+0·228845 025194	11·91	+0·027337 022362	+0·228529 160587
52	−0·063077 124631	+0·229288 322968	11·92	+0·029619 950574	+0·228052 770520
53	−0·060782 121280	+0·229708 490101	11·93	+0·031898 003653	+0·227554 144849
54	−0·058483 032003	+0·230105 504990	11·94	+0·034170 959578	+0·227033 351083
55	−0·056180 088419	+0·230479 348310	11·95	+0·036438 597013	+0·226490 458847
56	−0·053873 522332	+0·230830 003018	11·96	+0·038700 695332	+0·225925 539874
57	−0·051563 565704	+0·231157 454348	11·97	+0·040957 034634	+0·225338 667993
58	−0·049250 450632	+0·231461 689817	11·98	+0·043207 395768	+0·224729 919124
59	−0·046934 409328	+0·231742 699216	11·99	+0·045451 560353	+0·224099 371266
60	−0·044615 674094	+0·232000 474620	12·00	+0·047689 310797	+0·223447 104491

x	$J_0(x)$	$-J_1(x)$	x	$J_0(x)$	$-J_1(x)$
12·00	+0·047689 310797	+0·223447 104491	12·40	+0·129561 026518	+0·180710 246
12·01	+0·049920 430320	+0·222773 200930	12·41	+0·131360 894344	+0·179260 532
12·02	+0·052144 702973	+0·222077 744768	12·42	+0·133146 181728	+0·177794 184
12·03	+0·054361 913660	+0·221360 822234	12·43	+0·134916 723111	+0·176311 359
12·04	+0·056571 848157	+0·220622 521586	12·44	+0·136672 354521	+0·174812 216
12·05	+0·058774 293132	+0·219862 933107	12·45	+0·138412 913587	+0·173296 917
12·06	+0·060969 036167	+0·219082 149091	12·46	+0·140138 239554	+0·171765 624
12·07	+0·063155 865777	+0·218280 263834	12·47	+0·141848 173298	+0·170218 500
12·08	+0·065334 571427	+0·217457 373624	12·48	+0·143542 557339	+0·168655 711
12·09	+0·067504 943560	+0·216613 576726	12·49	+0·145221 235856	+0·167077 423
12·10	+0·069666 773607	+0·215748 973377	12·50	+0·146884 054700	+0·165483 804
12·11	+0·071819 854013	+0·214863 665770	12·51	+0·148530 861410	+0·163875 024
12·12	+0·073963 978255	+0·213957 758045	12·52	+0·150161 505225	+0·162251 254
12·13	+0·076098 940860	+0·213031 356277	12·53	+0·151775 837096	+0·160612 664
12·14	+0·078224 537427	+0·212084 568463	12·54	+0·153373 709704	+0·158959 430
12·15	+0·080340 564642	+0·211117 504511	12·55	+0·154954 977468	+0·157291 725
12·16	+0·082446 820302	+0·210130 276228	12·56	+0·156519 496560	+0·155609 725
12·17	+0·084543 103331	+0·209122 997309	12·57	+0·158067 124921	+0·153913 608
12·18	+0·086629 213798	+0·208095 783320	12·58	+0·159597 722266	+0·152203 552
12·19	+0·088704 952938	+0·207048 751691	12·59	+0·161111 150104	+0·150479 737
12·20	+0·090770 123171	+0·205982 021700	12·60	+0·162607 271746	+0·148742 343
12·21	+0·092824 528115	+0·204895 714458	12·61	+0·164085 952318	+0·146991 553
12·22	+0·094867 972612	+0·203789 952902	12·62	+0·165547 058774	+0·145227 550
12·23	+0·096900 262741	+0·202664 861776	12·63	+0·166990 459905	+0·143450 519
12·24	+0·098921 205837	+0·201520 567620	12·64	+0·168416 026353	+0·141660 645
12·25	+0·100930 610511	+0·200357 198756	12·65	+0·169823 630622	+0·139858 114
12·26	+0·102928 286663	+0·199174 885273	12·66	+0·171213 147086	+0·138043 115
12·27	+0·104914 045507	+0·197973 759015	12·67	+0·172584 452006	+0·136215 837
12·28	+0·106887 699579	+0·196753 953565	12·68	+0·173937 423535	+0·134376 469
12·29	+0·108849 062765	+0·195515 604234	12·69	+0·175271 941729	+0·132525 202
12·30	+0·110797 950308	+0·194258 848041	12·70	+0·176587 888562	+0·130662 229
12·31	+0·112734 178832	+0·192983 823702	12·71	+0·177885 147930	+0·128787 741
12·32	+0·114657 566356	+0·191690 671617	12·72	+0·179163 605667	+0·126901 935
12·33	+0·116567 932311	+0·190379 533851	12·73	+0·180423 149549	+0·125005 003
12·34	+0·118465 097559	+0·189050 554121	12·74	+0·181663 669309	+0·123097 143
12·35	+0·120348 884405	+0·187703 877780	12·75	+0·182885 056640	+0·121178 550
12·36	+0·122219 116616	+0·186339 651802	12·76	+0·184087 205211	+0·119249 424
12·37	+0·124075 619437	+0·184958 024768	12·77	+0·185270 010670	+0·117309 961
12·38	+0·125918 219608	+0·183559 146848	12·78	+0·186433 370658	+0·115360 363
12·39	+0·127746 745377	+0·182143 169785	12·79	+0·187577 184813	+0·113400 828
12·40	+0·129561 026518	+0·180710 246883	12·80	+0·188701 354781	+0·111431 559

x	$J_0(x)$	$-J_1(x)$	x	$J_0(x)$	$-J_1(x)$
12·80	+0·188701 354781	+0·111431 559278	13·20	+0·216685 922259	+0·027066 702765
12·81	+0·189805 784222	+0·109452 757129	13·21	+0·216945 650832	+0·024878 857605
12·82	+0·190890 378823	+0·107464 624869	13·22	+0·217183 496687	+0·022690 195350
12·83	+0·191955 046298	+0·105467 365986	13·23	+0·217399 452738	+0·020500 932874
12·84	+0·192999 696401	+0·103461 184712	13·24	+0·217593 514066	+0·018311 286951
12·85	+0·194024 240934	+0·101446 286001	13·25	+0·217765 677921	+0·016121 474234
12·86	+0·195028 593748	+0·099422 875508	13·26	+0·217915 943717	+0·013931 711237
12·87	+0·196012 670759	+0·097391 159571	13·27	+0·218044 313033	+0·011742 214308
12·88	+0·196976 389945	+0·095351 345187	13·28	+0·218150 789610	+0·009553 199615
12·89	+0·197919 671360	+0·093303 639994	13·29	+0·218235 379352	+0·007364 883118
12·90	+0·198842 437136	+0·091248 252250	13·30	+0·218298 090319	+0·005177 480555
12·91	+0·199744 611493	+0·089185 390809	13·31	+0·218338 932728	+0·002991 207414
12·92	+0·200626 120738	+0·087115 265106	13·32	+0·218357 918950	+0·000806 278917
12·93	+0·201486 893280	+0·085038 085131	13·33	+0·218355 063505	−0·001377 090000
12·94	+0·202326 859628	+0·082954 061409	13·34	+0·218330 383064	−0·003558 684713
12·95	+0·203145 952399	+0·080863 404982	13·35	+0·218283 896439	−0·005738 290927
12·96	+0·203944 106324	+0·078766 327385	13·36	+0·218215 624587	−0·007915 694697
12·97	+0·204721 258250	+0·076663 040627	13·37	+0·218125 590599	−0·010090 682449
12·98	+0·205477 347147	+0·074553 757168	13·38	+0·218013 819702	−0·012263 041002
12·99	+0·206212 314114	+0·072438 689899	13·39	+0·217880 339252	−0·014432 557586
13·00	+0·206926 102377	+0·070318 052122	13·40	+0·217725 178732	−0·016599 019864
13·01	+0·207618 657300	+0·068192 057526	13·41	+0·217548 369742	−0·018762 215954
13·02	+0·208289 926385	+0·066060 920168	13·42	+0·217349 946004	−0·020921 934445
13·03	+0·208939 859276	+0·063924 854454	13·43	+0·217129 943348	−0·023077 964423
13·04	+0·209568 407762	+0·061784 075111	13·44	+0·216888 399712	−0·025230 095486
13·05	+0·210175 525783	+0·059638 797173	13·45	+0·216625 355135	−0·027378 117768
13·06	+0·210761 169428	+0·057489 235957	13·46	+0·216340 851750	−0·029521 821957
13·07	+0·211325 296943	+0·055335 607039	13·47	+0·216034 933785	−0·031660 999316
13·08	+0·211867 868729	+0·053178 126239	13·48	+0·215707 647547	−0·033795 441703
13·09	+0·212388 847348	+0·051017 009592	13·49	+0·215359 041426	−0·035924 941590
13·10	+0·212888 197522	+0·048852 473334	13·50	+0·214989 165880	−0·038049 292086
13·11	+0·213365 886137	+0·046684 733877	13·51	+0·214598 073436	−0·040168 286951
13·12	+0·213821 882244	+0·044514 007788	13·52	+0·214185 818679	−0·042281 720622
13·13	+0·214256 157060	+0·042340 511767	13·53	+0·213752 458244	−0·044389 388228
13·14	+0·214668 683969	+0·040164 462629	13·54	+0·213298 050815	+0·046491 085613
13·15	+0·215059 438525	+0·037986 077278	13·55	+0·212822 657111	−0·048586 609352
13·16	+0·215428 398451	+0·035805 572692	13·56	+0·212326 339882	−0·050675 756773
13·17	+0·215775 543638	+0·033623 165893	13·57	+0·211809 163903	−0·052758 325976
13·18	+0·216100 856151	+0·031439 073935	13·58	+0·211271 195961	−0·054834 115851
13·19	+0·216404 320223	+0·029253 513878	13·59	+0·210712 504851	−0·056902 926099
13·20	+0·216685 922259	+0·027066 702765	13·60	+0·210133 161369	−0·058964 557249

x	$J_0(x)$	$-J_1(x)$	x	$J_0(x)$	$-J_1(x)$
13·60	+0·210133 161369	−0·058964 557249	14·00	+0·171073 476110	−0·133375 154699
13·61	+0·209533 238299	−0·061018 810678	14·01	+0·169731 671331	−0·134983 384921
13·62	+0·208912 810407	−0·063065 488629	14·02	+0·168373 856986	−0·136577 042971
13·63	+0·208271 954434	−0·065104 394233	14·03	+0·167000 179537	−0·138155 981458
13·64	+0·207610 749084	−0·067135 331522	14·04	+0·165610 786908	−0·139720 054543
13·65	+0·206929 275015	−0·069158 105453	14·05	+0·164205 828478	−0·141269 117950
13·66	+0·206227 614833	−0·071172 521923	14·06	+0·162785 455058	−0·142803 028980
13·67	+0·205505 853079	−0·073178 387788	14·07	+0·161349 818877	−0·144321 646527
13·68	+0·204764 076220	−0·075175 510884	14·08	+0·159899 073571	−0·145824 831084
13·69	+0·204002 372641	−0·077163 700040	14·09	+0·158433 374159	−0·147312 444762
13·70	+0·203220 832633	−0·079142 765100	14·10	+0·156952 877033	−0·148784 351297
13·71	+0·202419 548383	−0·081112 516941	14·11	+0·155457 739939	−0·150240 416070
13·72	+0·201598 613965	−0·083072 767489	14·12	+0·153948 121961	−0·151680 506109
13·73	+0·200758 125328	−0·085023 329736	14·13	+0·152424 183503	−0·153104 490110
13·74	+0·199898 180285	−0·086964 017760	14·14	+0·150886 086277	−0·154512 238442
13·75	+0·199018 878503	−0·088894 646742	14·15	+0·149333 993280	−0·155903 623164
13·76	+0·198120 321493	−0·090815 032981	14·16	+0·147768 068780	−0·157278 518033
13·77	+0·197202 612595	−0·092724 993914	14·17	+0·146188 478301	−0·158636 798515
13·78	+0·196265 856970	−0·094624 348132	14·18	+0·144595 388601	−0·159978 341800
13·79	+0·195310 161589	−0·096512 915397	14·19	+0·142988 967659	−0·161303 026807
13·80	+0·194335 635216	−0·098390 516658	14·20	+0·141369 384657	−0·162610 734200
13·81	+0·193342 388402	−0·100256 974070	14·21	+0·139736 809960	−0·163901 346396
13·82	+0·192330 533469	−0·102112 111008	14·22	+0·138091 415099	−0·165174 747575
13·83	+0·191300 184501	−0·103955 752084	14·23	+0·136433 372759	−0·166430 823692
13·84	+0·190251 457328	−0·105787 723166	14·24	+0·134762 856750	−0·167669 462485
13·85	+0·189184 469514	−0·107607 851391	14·25	+0·133080 042002	−0·168890 553486
13·86	+0·188099 340348	−0·109415 965181	14·26	+0·131385 104536	−0·170093 988031
13·87	+0·186996 190826	−0·111211 894262	14·27	+0·129678 221452	−0·171279 659270
13·88	+0·185875 143642	−0·112995 469678	14·28	+0·127959 570912	−0·172447 462171
13·89	+0·184736 323171	−0·114766 523805	14·29	+0·126229 332114	−0·173597 293538
13·90	+0·183579 855458	−0·116524 890369	14·30	+0·124487 685284	−0·174729 052013
13·91	+0·182405 868205	−0·118270 404461	14·31	+0·122734 811649	−0·175842 638087
13·92	+0·181214 490755	−0·120002 902550	14·32	+0·120970 893423	−0·176937 954108
13·93	+0·180005 854081	−0·121722 222501	14·33	+0·119196 113786	−0·178014 904291
13·94	+0·178780 090769	−0·123428 203590	14·34	+0·117410 656869	−0·179073 394724
13·95	+0·177537 335004	−0·125120 686515	14·35	+0·115614 707731	−0·180113 333378
13·96	+0·176277 722558	−0·126799 513414	14·36	+0·113808 452342	−0·181134 630112
13·97	+0·175001 390777	−0·128464 527879	14·37	+0·111992 077563	−0·182137 196684
13·98	+0·173708 478559	−0·130115 574971	14·38	+0·110165 771130	−0·183120 946756
13·99	+0·172399 126347	−0·131752 501232	14·39	+0·108329 721631	−0·184085 795902
14·00	+0·171073 476110	−0·133375 154699	14·40	+0·106484 118490	−0·185031 661615

x	$J_0(x)$	$-J_1(x)$	x	$J_0(x)$	$-J_1(x)$
14·40	+0·106484 118490	−0·185031 661615	14·80	+0·027082 314586	−0·206595 567180
14·41	+0·104629 151946	−0·185958 463314	14·81	+0·025015 737179	−0·206716 471994
14·42	+0·102765 013033	−0·186866 122350	14·82	+0·022948 053986	−0·206816 724913
14·43	+0·100891 893564	−0·187754 562014	14·83	+0·020879 471508	−0·206896 329814
14·44	+0·099009 986107	−0·188623 707542	14·84	+0·018810 196197	−0·206955 292607
14·45	+0·097119 483970	−0·189473 486119	14·85	+0·016740 434436	−0·206993 621235
14·46	+0·095220 581177	−0·190303 826889	14·86	+0·014670 392520	−0·207011 325670
14·47	+0·093313 472454	−0·191114 660960	14·87	+0·012600 276630	−0·207008 417910
14·48	+0·091398 353204	−0·191905 921406	14·88	+0·010530 292822	−0·206984 911980
14·49	+0·089475 419488	−0·192677 543276	14·89	+0·008460 646998	−0·206940 823925
14·50	+0·087544 868010	−0·193429 463596	14·90	+0·006391 544891	−0·206876 171810
14·51	+0·085606 896092	−0·194161 621377	14·91	+0·004323 192042	−0·206790 975716
14·52	+0·083661 701655	−0·194873 957618	14·92	+0·002255 793783	−0·206685 257736
14·53	+0·081709 483202	−0·195566 415311	14·93	+0·000189 555214	−0·206559 041974
14·54	+0·079750 439794	−0·196238 939443	14·94	−0·001875 318817	−0·206412 354539
14·55	+0·077784 771035	−0·196891 477005	14·95	−0·003938 623732	−0·206245 223541
14·56	+0·075812 677046	−0·197523 976991	14·96	−0·006000 155243	−0·206057 679091
14·57	+0·073834 358450	−0·198136 390405	14·97	−0·008059 709376	−0·205849 753289
14·58	+0·071850 016350	−0·198728 670261	14·98	−0·010117 082484	−0·205621 480228
14·59	+0·069859 852307	−0·199300 771592	14·99	−0·012172 071276	−0·205372 895984
14·60	+0·067864 068323	−0·199852 651447	15·00	−0·014224 472827	−0·205104 038614
14·61	+0·065862 866820	−0·200384 268898	15·01	−0·016274 084604	−0·204814 948148
14·62	+0·063856 450617	−0·200895 585039	15·02	−0·018320 704486	−0·204505 666588
14·63	+0·061845 022913	−0·201386 562994	15·03	−0·020364 130779	−0·204176 237900
14·64	+0·059828 787267	−0·201857 167913	15·04	−0·022404 162240	−0·203826 708006
14·65	+0·057807 947575	−0·202307 366980	15·05	−0·024440 598094	−0·203457 124785
14·66	+0·055782 708050	−0·202737 129411	15·06	−0·026473 238057	−0·203067 538060
14·67	+0·053753 273205	−0·203146 426455	15·07	−0·028501 882349	−0·202657 999596
14·68	+0·051719 847828	−0·203535 231400	15·08	−0·030526 331722	−0·202228 563094
14·69	+0·049682 636966	−0·203903 519571	15·09	−0·032546 387470	−0·201779 284182
14·70	+0·047641 845902	−0·204251 268330	15·10	−0·034561 851456	−0·201310 220408
14·71	+0·045597 680133	−0·204578 457081	15·11	−0·036572 526126	−0·200821 431239
14·72	+0·043550 345355	−0·204885 067267	15·12	−0·038578 214533	−0·200312 978045
14·73	+0·041500 047438	−0·205171 082373	15·13	−0·040578 720351	−0·199784 924098
14·74	+0·039446 992407	−0·205436 487924	15·14	−0·042573 847897	−0·199237 334565
14·75	+0·037391 386420	−0·205681 271486	15·15	−0·044563 402147	−0·198670 276496
14·76	+0·035333 435752	−0·205905 422669	15·16	−0·046547 188761	−0·198083 818818
14·77	+0·033273 346769	−0·206108 933120	15·17	−0·048525 014094	−0·197478 032331
14·78	+0·031211 325913	−0·206291 796530	15·18	−0·050496 685220	−0·196852 989694
14·79	+0·029147 579677	−0·206454 008627	15·19	−0·052462 009949	−0·196208 765420
14·80	+0·027082 314586	−0·206595 567180	15·20	−0·054420 796844	−0·195545 435866

x	$J_0(x)$	$-J_1(x)$	x	$J_0(x)$	$-J_1(x)$
15·20	−0·054420 796844	−0·195545 435866	15·35	−0·082890 403582	−0·183360 322017
15·21	−0·056372 855242	−0·194863 079227	15·36	−0·084719 235661	−0·182403 162448
15·22	−0·058317 995271	−0·194161 775523	15·37	−0·086538 408385	−0·181428 468883
15·23	−0·060256 027869	−0·193441 606594	15·38	−0·088347 746952	−0·180436 349242
15·24	−0·062186 764798	−0·192702 656088	15·39	−0·090147 077648	−0·179426 913096
15·25	−0·064110 018670	−0·191945 009455	15·40	−0·091936 227862	−0·178400 271655
15·26	−0·066025 602957	−0·191168 753932	15·41	−0·093715 026106	−0·177356 537757
15·27	−0·067933 332015	−0·190373 978539	15·42	−0·095483 302024	−0·176295 825856
15·28	−0·069833 021097	−0·189560 774066	15·43	−0·097240 886416	−0·175218 252010
15·29	−0·071724 486374	−0·188729 233063	15·44	−0·098987 611250	−0·174123 933866
15·30	−0·073607 544951	−0·187879 449832	15·45	−0·100723 309676	−0·173012 990652
15·31	−0·075482 014884	−0·187011 520415	15·46	−0·102447 816048	−0·171885 543160
15·32	−0·077347 715198	−0·186125 542581	15·47	−0·104160 965933	−0·170741 713736
15·33	−0·079204 465905	−0·185221 615823	15·48	−0·105862 596129	−0·169581 626266
15·34	−0·081052 088022	−0·184299 841336	15·49	−0·107552 544683	−0·168405 406163
15·35	−0·082890 403582	−0·183360 322017	15·50	−0·109230 650900	−0·167213 180352

TABLE II.

n	$J_n(1)$
0	+0·76519 76865 57966 551
1	+0·44005 05857 44933 516
2	+0·11490 34849 31900 480
3	+0·01956 33539 82668 406
4	+0·00247 66389 64109 955
5	+0·00024 97577 30211 234
6	+0·00002 09383 38002 389
7	15023 25817 437
8	00942 23441 726
9	00052 49250 180
10	+0· 00002 63061 512
11	11980 067
12	00499 972
13	00019 256
14	689
15	023
16	001

n	$J_n(2)$
0	+0·22389 07791 41235 668
1	+0·57672 48077 56873 387
2	+0·35283 40286 15637 719
3	+0·12894 32494 74402 051
4	+0·03399 57198 07568 434
5	+0·00703 96297 55871 685
6	+0·00120 24289 71789 993
7	+0·00017 49440 74868 274
8	+0·00002 21795 52287 926
9	24923 43435 133
10	+0· 02515 38628 272
11	00230 42847 584
12	00019 32695 149
13	00001 49494 201
14	10729 463
15	00718 302
16	00045 060
17	00002 659
18	148
19	008

n	$J_n(3)$
0	−0·26005 19549 01933 438
1	+0·33905 89585 25936 459
2	+0·48609 12605 85891 077
3	+0·30906 27222 55251 644
4	+0·13203 41839 24612 210
5	+0·04302 84348 77047 584
6	+0·01139 39323 32213 069
7	+0·00254 72944 51804 694
8	+0·00049 34417 76208 835
9	+0·00008 43950 21309 092
10	+0·00001 29283 51645 716
11	17939 89662 347
12	02275 72544 832
13	00265 90696 309
14	00028 80156 513
15	00002 90764 476
16	27488 250
17	02443 521
18	00204 983
19	00016 280
20	+0· 00001 228
21	088
22	006

n	$J_n(4)$
0	−0·39714 98098 63847 372
1	−0·06604 33280 23549 136
2	+0·36412 81458 52072 804
3	+0·43017 14738 75621 940
4	+0·28112 90649 61360 106
5	+0·13208 66560 47098 272
6	+0·04908 75751 56385 574
7	+0·01517 60694 22058 451
8	+0·00402 86678 20819 004
9	+0·00093 86018 61217 564
10	+0·00019 50405 54660 035
11	+0·00003 66009 12082 608
12	62644 61794 312
13	09858 58683 265
14	01436 19646 909
15	00194 78845 096
16	00024 71691 311
17	00002 94685 392
18	33134 523
19	03525 313
20	+0· 00355 951
21	00034 199
22	00003 134
23	275
24	023
25	002

n	$J_n(5)$
0	−0·17759 67713 14338 304
1	−0·32757 91375 91465 222
2	+0·04656 51162 77752 216
3	+0·36483 12306 13666 994
4	+0·39123 26304 58648 178
5	+0·26114 05461 20170 090
6	+0·13104 87317 81692 002
7	+0·05337 64101 55890 715
8	+0·01840 52166 54802 001
9	+0·00552 02831 39475 688
10	+0·00146 78026 47310 474
11	+0·00035 09274 49766 209
12	+0·00007 62781 31660 846
13	+0·00001 52075 82205 849
14	28012 95809 572
15	04796 74327 752
16	00767 50156 939
17	00115 26676 659
18	00016 31244 339
19	00002 18282 584
20	+0· 27703 301
21	03343 820
22	00384 787
23	00042 309
24	00004 454
25	450
26	044
27	004

n	$J_n(6)$
0	+0·15064 52572 50996 932
1	−0·27668 38581 27565 608
2	−0·24287 32099 60185 468
3	+0·11476 83848 20775 296
4	+0·35764 15947 80960 764
5	+0·36208 70748 87172 389
6	+0·24583 68633 64326 551
7	+0·12958 66518 41480 713
8	+0·05653 19909 32461 779
9	+0·02116 53239 78417 365
10	+0·00696 39810 02790 316
11	+0·00204 79460 30883 689
12	+0·00054 51544 43783 211
13	+0·00013 26717 44249 154
14	+0·00002 97564 47963 121
15	61916 79578 746
16	12019 49930 610
17	02187 20051 176
18	00374 63692 719
19	00060 62105 141
20	+0· 00009 29639 841
21	00001 35493 798
22	18816 747
23	02496 677
24	00316 779
25	00038 554
26	00004 415
27	507
28	055
29	006
30	+0· 001

n	$J_n(7)$
0	+0·30007 92705 19555 597
1	−0·00468 28234 82345 833
2	−0·30141 72200 85940 120
3	−0·16755 55879 95334 236
4	+0·15779 81446 61367 918
5	+0·34789 63247 51183 285
6	+0·33919 66049 83179 632
7	+0·23358 35695 05696 084
8	+0·12797 05340 28212 537
9	+0·05892 05082 73075 428
10	+0·02353 93443 88267 135
11	+0·00833 47614 07687 815
12	+0·00265 56200 35894 568
13	+0·00077 02215 72522 133
14	+0·00020 52029 47759 069
15	+0·00005 05902 18514 143
16	+0·00001 16122 74444 403
17	24944 64660 269
18	05036 96762 619
19	00959 75833 201
20	+0· 00173 14903 330
21	00029 66471 543
22	00004 83925 930
23	75348 588
24	11221 932
25	01601 804
26	00219 522
27	00028 933
28	00003 673
29	450
30	+0· 053
31	006
32	001

n	$J_n(8)$
0	+0·17165 08071 37553 906
1	+0·23463 63468 53914 624
2	−0·11299 17204 24075 250
3	−0·29113 22070 65952 249
4	−0·10535 74348 75388 937
5	+0·18577 47721 90563 312
6	+0·33757 59001 13593 077
7	+0·32058 90779 79826 304
8	+0·22345 49863 51102 954
9	+0·12632 08947 22379 605
10	+0·06076 70267 74251 156
11	+0·02559 66722 13248 286
12	+0·00962 38218 12181 630
13	+0·00327 47932 23296 605
14	+0·00101 92561 63532 336
15	+0·00029 26033 49066 572
16	+0·00007 80063 95467 308
17	+0·00001 94222 32802 661
18	45380 93944 002
19	09991 89945 347
20	+0· 02080 58296 397
21	00411 01536 639
22	00077 24770 956
23	00013 84703 619
24	00002 37274 853
25	38945 500
26	06134 520
27	00928 879
28	00135 416
29	00019 034
30	+0· 00002 583
31	339
32	043
33	005
34	001

n	$J_n(9)$
0	−0·09033 36111 82876 134
1	+0·24531 17865 73325 272
2	+0·14484 73415 32503 973
3	−0·18093 51903 36656 840
4	−0·26547 08017 56941 866
5	−0·05503 88556 69513 708
6	+0·20431 65176 79704 413
7	+0·32746 08792 42452 925
8	+0·30506 70722 53000 137
9	+0·21488 05825 40658 430
10	+0·12469 40928 28316 722
11	+0·06221 74015 22267 619
12	+0·02739 28886 70559 681
13	+0·01083 03015 99224 863
14	+0·00389 46492 82756 591
15	+0·00128 63850 58240 087
16	+0·00039 33009 11377 031
17	+0·00011 20181 82211 578
18	+0·00002 98788 88088 932
19	74973 70144 148
20	+0· 17766 74741 915
21	03989 62042 141
22	00851 48121 408
23	00173 17662 520
24	00033 64375 918
25	00006 25675 712
26	00001 11600 257
27	19125 771
28	03154 368
29	00501 407
30	+0· 00076 922
31	00011 403
32	00001 636
33	227
34	031
35	004

n	$J_n(10)$
0	−0·24593 57644 51348 335
1	+0·04347 27461 68861 437
2	+0·25463 03136 85120 623
3	+0·05837 93793 05186 812
4	−0·21960 26861 02008 535
5	−0·23406 15281 86793 640
6	−0·01445 88420 84785 105
7	+0·21671 09176 85051 514
8	+0·31785 41268 43857 225
9	+0·29185 56852 65120 046
10	+0·20748 61066 33358 858
11	+0·12311 65280 01597 669
12	+0·06337 02549 70156 015
13	+0·02897 20839 26776 767
14	+0·01195 71632 39463 579
15	+0·00450 79731 43721 253
16	+0·00156 67561 91700 181
17	+0·00050 56466 69719 325
18	+0·00015 24424 85345 524
19	+0·00004 31462 77524 563
20	+0·00001 15133 69247 813
21	29071 99466 691
22	06968 68512 289
23	01590 21987 380
24	00346 32629 661
25	00072 14634 990
26	00014 40545 292
27	00002 76200 527
28	50937 552
29	09049 767
30	+0· 01551 096
31	00256 809
32	00041 123
33	00006 376
34	958
35	140
36	020
37	003

n	$J_n(11)$
0	−0·17119 03004 07196 088
1	−0·17678 52989 56721 501
2	+0·13904 75187 78701 270
3	+0·22734 80330 58067 417
4	−0·01503 95007 47028 133
5	−0·23828 58517 83178 787
6	−0·20158 40008 74043 491
7	+0·01837 60326 47858 615
8	+0·22497 16787 89499 910
9	+0·30885 55001 36868 527
10	+0·28042 82305 25375 862
11	+0·20101 40099 09269 403
12	+0·12159 97892 93162 945
13	+0·06429 46212 75813 386
14	+0·03036 93155 40577 785
15	+0·01300 90910 09293 703
16	+0·00511 00235 75677 768
17	+0·00185 64321 19950 713
18	+0·00062 80393 40533 526
19	+0·00019 89693 58159 009
20	+0·00005 93093 51288 506
21	+0·00001 67010 10162 830
22	44581 42060 481
23	11315 58079 093
24	02738 28088 453
25	00633 28125 065
26	00140 27025 479
27	00029 81449 927
28	00006 09183 254
29	00001 19846 638
30	+0· 22735 384
31	04164 546
32	00737 509
33	00126 418
34	00020 997
35	00003 383
36	529
37	080
38	012
39	002

n	$J_n(12)$
0	+0·04768 93107 96833 537
1	−0·22344 71044 90627 612
2	−0·08493 04948 78604 805
3	+0·19513 69395 31092 677
4	+0·18249 89646 44151 144
5	−0·07347 09631 01658 581
6	−0·24372 47672 28866 628
7	−0·17025 38041 27208 047
8	+0·04509 53290 80457 240
9	+0·23038 09095 67817 701
10	+0·30047 60352 71269 311
11	+0·27041 24825 50964 484
12	+0·19528 01827 38832 243
13	+0·12014 78829 26700 003
14	+0·06504 02302 69017 762
15	+0·03161 26543 67674 776
16	+0·01399 14056 50169 178
17	+0·00569 77606 99443 032
18	+0·00215 22496 64919 412
19	+0·00075 89882 95315 204
20	+0·00025 12132 70245 400
21	+0·00007 83892 72169 462
22	+0·00002 31491 82347 716
23	64910 63105 497
24	17332 26223 355
25	04418 41787 923
26	01077 81226 324
27	00252 10192 815
28	00056 64641 343
29	00012 24800 120
30	+0· 00002 55225 904
31	51329 401
32	09976 003
33	01875 946
34	00341 699
35	00060 351
36	00010 346
37	00001 723
38	279
39	044
40	+0· 007
41	001

n	$J_n(13)$
0	+0·20692 61023 77067 811
1	−0·07031 80521 21778 371
2	−0·21774 42642 41956 791
3	+0·00331 98169 70407 051
4	+0·21927 64874 59067 738
5	+0·13161 95599 27480 788
6	−0·11803 06721 30236 362
7	−0·24057 09495 86160 507
8	−0·14104 57351 16398 030
9	+0·06697 61986 73670 624
10	+0·23378 20102 03018 894
11	+0·29268 84324 07896 905
12	+0·26153 68754 10345 099
13	+0·19014 88760 41970 970
14	+0·11876 08766 73596 841
15	+0·06564 37814 08852 996
16	+0·03272 47727 31448 533
17	+0·01490 95053 14712 625
18	+0·00626 93180 91646 024
19	+0·00245 16832 46768 672
20	+0·00089 71406 29677 786
21	+0·00030 87494 59932 207
22	+0·00010 03576 25487 806
23	+0·00003 09225 03257 290
24	90604 62961 066
25	25315 13829 722
26	06761 28691 713
27	01730 00937 128
28	00424 90585 590
29	00100 35431 567
30	+0· 00022 82878 324
31	00005 00929 928
32	00001 06172 104
33	21763 505
34	04319 539
35	00831 008
36	00155 121
37	00028 122
38	00004 956
39	850
40	+0· 142
41	023
42	004
43	001

n	$J_n(14)$
0	+0·17107 34761 10458 659
1	+0·13337 51546 98793 253
2	−0·15201 98825 82059 623
3	−0·17680 94068 65096 003
4	+0·07624 44224 97018 479
5	+0·22037 76482 91963 705
6	+0·08116 81834 25812 739
7	−0·15080 49196 41267 072
8	−0·23197 31030 67079 810
9	−0·11430 71981 49681 283
10	+0·08500 67054 46061 018
11	+0·23574 53487 86911 308
12	+0·28545 02712 19085 324
13	+0·25359 79733 02949 247
14	+0·18551 73934 86391 849
15	+0·11743 68136 69834 451
16	+0·06613 29215 20396 260
17	+0·03372 41498 05357 001
18	+0·01576 85851 49756 457
19	+0·00682 36405 79731 031
20	+0·00275 27249 95227 770
21	+0·00104 12879 78062 597
22	+0·00037 11389 38960 020
23	+0·00012 51486 87240 324
24	+0·00004 00638 90543 902
25	+0·00001 22132 23195 912
26	35547 63727 213
27	09901 84933 738
28	02645 21017 203
29	00678 99135 075
30	+0· 00167 75399 538
31	00039 95434 356
32	00009 18666 897
33	00002 04185 745
34	43923 044
35	09154 753
36	01850 722
37	00363 244
38	00069 281
39	00012 851
40	+0· 00002 320
41	408
42	070
43	012
44	002

n	$J_n(15)$
0	−0·01422 44728 26780 773
1	+0·20510 40386 13522 761
2	+0·04157 16779 75250 475
3	−0·19401 82578 20122 635
4	−0·11917 89811 03299 529
5	+0·13045 61345 65029 553
6	+0·20614 97374 79985 897
7	+0·03446 36554 18959 165
8	−0·17398 36590 88957 343
9	−0·22004 62251 13846 998
10	−0·09007 18110 47659 054
11	+0·09995 04770 50301 592
12	+0·23666 58440 54768 056
13	+0·27871 48734 37327 297
14	+0·24643 99365 69932 593
15	+0·18130 63414 93213 542
16	+0·11617 27464 16494 492
17	+0·06652 88508 61974 707
18	+0·03462 59822 03981 511
19	+0·01657 35064 27580 920
20	+0·00736 02340 79223 485
21	+0·00305 37844 50348 374
22	+0·00119 03623 81751 963
23	+0·00043 79452 02790 717
24	+0·00015 26695 73472 902
25	+0·00005 05974 32322 570
26	+0·00001 59885 34268 998
27	48294 86476 623
28	13976 17046 846
29	03882 83831 601
30	+0· 01037 47102 011
31	00267 04576 442
32	00066 31813 951
33	00015 91163 081
34	00003 69303 606
35	83013 267
36	18091 639
37	03826 599
38	00786 251
39	00157 074
40	+0· 00030 535
41	00005 781
42	00001 067
43	192
44	034
45	006
46	001

n	$J_n(16)$
0	−0·17489 90739 83629 185
1	+0·09039 71756 61304 186
2	+0·18619 87209 41292 208
3	−0·04384 74954 25981 134
4	−0·20264 15317 26035 133
5	−0·05747 32704 37036 433
6	+0·16672 07377 02887 363
7	+0·18251 38237 14201 955
8	−0·00702 11419 52960 653
9	−0·18953 49656 67162 607
10	−0·20620 56944 22597 281
11	−0·06822 21523 61083 994
12	+0·11240 02349 26106 790
13	+0·23682 25047 50244 178
14	+0·27243 63352 93040 000
15	+0·23994 10820 12575 821
16	+0·17745 31934 80539 665
17	+0·11496 53049 48503 509
18	+0·06684 80795 35030 292
19	+0·03544 28740 05314 648
20	+0·01732 87462 27591 996
21	+0·00787 89915 63665 343
22	+0·00335 36066 27029 529
23	+0·00134 34266 60665 861
24	+0·00050 87450 22384 822
25	+0·00018 28084 06488 605
26	+0·00006 25312 47892 069
27	+0·00002 04181 49160 619
28	63800 05525 020
29	19118 70176 952
30	+0· 05505 23866 431
31	01525 49322 163
32	00407 79131 952
33	00105 22205 645
34	00026 24966 335
35	00006 33901 280
36	00001 48351 763
37	33681 654
38	07425 886
39	01591 305
40	+0· 00331 726
41	00067 325
42	00013 313
43	00002 567
44	483
45	089
46	016
47	003

n	$J_n(17)$
0	−0·16985 42521 51183 548
1	−0·09766 84927 57780 650
2	+0·15836 38412 38503 471
3	+0·13493 05730 49193 232
4	−0·11074 12860 44670 566
5	−0·18704 41194 23155 851
6	+0·00071 53334 42814 183
7	+0·18754 90606 76907 039
8	+0·15373 68341 73462 202
9	−0·04285 55696 90119 084
10	−0·19911 33197 27705 938
11	−0·19139 53946 95417 314
12	−0·04857 48381 13422 350
13	+0·12281 91526 52938 702
14	+0·23641 58951 12034 482
15	+0·26657 17334 13941 622
16	+0·23400 48109 12568 380
17	+0·17390 79106 56775 329
18	+0·11381 10104 00982 277
19	+0·06710 36407 80598 906
20	+0·03618 53631 08591 747
21	+0·01803 83900 63146 381
22	+0·00838 00711 65064 018
23	+0·00365 12058 93489 902
24	+0·00149 96624 29085 127
25	+0·00058 31350 82750 457
26	+0·00021 54407 55475 041
27	+0·00007 58601 69290 845
28	+0·00002 55268 41095 878
29	82282 48436 754
30	+0· 25460 06511 871
31	07576 56899 262
32	02172 12767 790
33	00600 85285 358
34	00160 59516 541
35	00041 52780 805
36	00010 40169 125
37	00002 52641 372
38	59563 905
39	13644 321
40	+0· 03039 452
41	00658 981
42	00139 163
43	+0·00000 00000 00028 646
44	00005 752
45	00001 127
46	216
47	040
48	007
49	001

n	$J_n(18)$
0	−0·01335 58057 21984 111
1	−0·18799 48854 88069 594
2	−0·00753 25148 87801 400
3	+0·18632 09932 90780 394
4	+0·06963 95126 51394 864
5	−0·15537 00987 79049 343
6	−0·15595 62341 95311 166
7	+0·05139 92759 82175 233
8	+0·19593 34488 48114 125
9	+0·12276 37896 60592 878
10	−0·07316 96591 87521 246
11	−0·20406 34109 80060 930
12	−0·17624 11764 54775 446
13	−0·03092 48243 92972 998
14	+0·13157 19858 09370 005
15	+0·23559 23577 74215 227
16	+0·26108 19438 14322 041
17	+0·22855 33201 17912 845
18	+0·17062 98830 75068 889
19	+0·11270 64460 32224 933
20	+0·06730 59474 37405 969
21	+0·03686 23260 50899 443
22	+0·01870 61466 81359 398
23	+0·00886 38102 81312 419
24	+0·00394 58129 26439 006
25	+0·00165 83575 22524 930
26	+0·00066 07357 47241 354
27	+0·00025 04346 36172 316
28	+0·00009 05681 61275 594
29	+0·00003 13329 76685 088

n	$J_n(18)$
30	+0·00001 03936 52487 466
31	33125 31606 465
32	10161 78601 469
33	03005 47865 425
34	00858 30238 423
35	00236 99701 950
36	00063 35269 160
37	00016 41374 689
38	00004 12604 562
39	00001 00733 463
40	+0· 23907 111
41	05520 363
42	01241 210
43	00271 949
44	00058 104
45	00012 114
46	00002 466
47	490
48	095
49	018
50	+0· 003

n	$J_n(19)$
0	+0·14662 94396 59651 204
1	−0·10570 14311 42409 267
2	−0·15775 59060 95694 285
3	+0·07248 96614 38052 575
4	+0·18064 73781 28763 519
5	+0·00357 23925 10900 486
6	−0·17876 71715 44079 053
7	−0·11647 79745 38739 888
8	+0·09294 12955 68165 452
9	+0·19474 43287 01405 531
10	+0·09155 33316 22639 788
11	−0·09837 24006 77574 175
12	−0·20545 82166 17725 675
13	−0·16115 37676 81658 257
14	−0·01506 79917 88754 044
15	+0·13894 83060 98231 244
16	+0·23446 00540 49119 166
17	+0·25593 17849 31864 194
18	+0·22352 31400 39479 918
19	+0·16758 57435 63992 493
20	+0·11164 83470 88505 067
21	+0·06746 34082 01281 333
22	+0·03748 12920 93274 722
23	+0·01933 53734 88407 496
24	+0·00933 06647 73396 058
25	+0·00423 68322 54908 861
26	+0·00181 88937 92153 576
27	+0·00074 11928 60458 822
28	+0·00028 76543 37571 496
29	+0·00010 66304 50278 219
30	+0·00003 78491 42225 174
31	+0·00001 28931 56748 644
32	42232 64007 245
33	13325 74644 181
34	04056 79493 594
35	01193 30911 839
36	00339 60707 917
37	00093 62297 110
38	00025 02975 563
39	00006 49605 144
40	+0· 00001 63824 500
41	40182 226
42	09593 529
43	02231 272
44	00505 913
45	00111 905
46	00024 163
47	00005 096
48	00001 051
49	212
50	+0· 042
51	008
52	002

n	$J_n(20)$
0	+0·16702 46643 40583 155
1	+0·06683 31241 75850 046
2	−0·16034 13519 22998 150
3	−0·09890 13945 60449 676
4	+0·13067 09335 54863 247
5	+0·15116 97679 82394 975
6	−0·05508 60495 63665 760
7	−0·18422 13977 20594 431
8	−0·07386 89288 40750 341
9	+0·12512 62546 47994 158
10	+0·18648 25580 23945 083
11	+0·06135 63033 75950 926
12	−0·11899 06243 10399 065
13	−0·20414 50525 48429 804
14	−0·14639 79440 02559 680
15	−0·00081 20690 55153 748
16	+0·14517 98404 19829 058
17	+0·23309 98137 26880 240
18	+0·25108 98429 15867 351
19	+0·21886 19035 21680 991
20	+0·16474 77737 75326 532
21	+0·11063 36440 28972 073
22	+0·06758 28786 85514 822
23	+0·03804 86890 79160 535
24	+0·01992 91061 96554 408
25	+0·00978 11657 92570 045
26	+0·00452 38082 84870 704
27	+0·00198 07357 48093 786
28	+0·00082 41782 34982 517
29	+0·00032 69633 09857 262
30	+0·00012 40153 63603 543
31	+0·00004 50827 80953 368
32	+0·00001 57412 57351 896
33	52892 42572 701
34	17132 43138 017
35	05357 84096 556
36	01620 01199 928
37	00474 20223 186
38	00134 53625 859
39	00037 03555 077
40	+0· 00009 90238 941
41	00002 57400 689
42	65103 882
43	16035 615
44	03849 264
45	00901 145
46	+0·00000 00000 00205 887
47	00045 937
48	00010 015
49	00002 135
50	+0· 445
51	091
52	018
53	004
54	001

n	$J_n(21)$
0	+0·03657 90710 00862 743
1	+0·17112 02727 63900 104
2	−0·02028 19021 66205 590
3	−0·17498 34922 24129 740
4	−0·02971 33813 26402 907
5	+0·16366 41088 61690 537
6	+0·10764 86712 60541 258
7	−0·10215 05824 27095 533
8	−0·17574 90595 45271 613
9	−0·03175 34629 40730 458
10	+0·14853 18055 96074 078
11	+0·17321 23254 13181 961
12	+0·03292 87257 89164 167
13	−0·13557 94959 39851 484
14	−0·20078 90540 95646 957
15	−0·13213 92428 54344 458
16	+0·01201 87071 60869 159
17	+0·15045 34632 89954 606
18	+0·23157 26143 56200 203
19	+0·24652 81613 20674 313
20	+0·21452 59632 71686 649
21	+0·16209 27211 01585 971
22	+0·10965 94789 31485 294
23	+0·06766 99966 59621 310
24	+0·03857 00375 61018 529
25	+0·02049 00891 94135 328
26	+0·01021 58890 91684 632
27	+0·00480 63980 80512 332
28	+0·00214 34202 58204 222
29	+0·00090 93892 74698 928

n	$J_n(21)$
30	+0·00036 82263 10011 863
31	+0·00014 26858 96763 539
32	+0·00005 30368 13766 205
33	+0·00001 89501 07095 370
34	65206 65676 388
35	21644 29380 552
36	06940 98925 453
37	02153 38363 859
38	00647 12451 956
39	00188 59081 313
40	+0· 00053 35564 351
41	00014 66878 120
42	00003 92245 451
43	00001 02103 682
44	25893 439
45	06402 159
46	01544 385
47	00363 716
48	00083 679
49	00018 818
50	+0· 00004 139
51	891
52	188
53	039
54	008
55	002

n	$J_n(22)$
0	−0·12065 14757 04867 180
1	+0·11717 77896 43851 701
2	+0·13130 40020 36126 426
3	−0·09330 43347 28192 351
4	−0·15675 06387 80178 885
5	+0·03630 41024 44490 938
6	+0·17325 25035 27674 766
7	+0·05819 72631 16058 934
8	−0·13621 78815 44728 171
9	−0·15726 48133 30406 695
10	+0·00754 66706 38031 784
11	+0·16412 54230 01344 681

n	$J_n(22)$
12	+0·15657 87523 63312 897
13	+0·00668 77613 94996 661
14	−0·14867 50343 51044 115
15	−0·19591 05323 87234 626
16	−0·11847 56916 31548 557
17	+0·02358 22536 50436 726
18	+0·15492 09927 27678 042
19	+0·22992 48253 58490 979
20	+0·24222 18874 36988 195
21	+0·21047 86063 45123 920
22	+0·15960 09064 94612 017
23	+0·10872 32066 44100 114
24	+0·06772 94346 70324 584
25	+0·03905 01053 63880 797
26	+0·02102 08047 93040 864
27	+0·01063 54332 37852 155
28	+0·00508 43495 18050 788
29	+0·00230 65473 53549 852
30	+0·00099 65480 50398 821
31	+0·00041 13109 65719 660
32	+0·00016 26010 34811 129
33	+0·00006 17102 26458 170
34	+0·00002 25296 44563 381
35	79268 56737 734
36	26921 72329 410
37	08838 89067 607
38	02809 09079 813
39	00865 24117 203
40	+0· 00258 58244 815
41	00075 05863 943
42	00021 18157 153
43	00005 81645 187
44	00001 55546 760
45	40541 854
46	10306 278
47	02557 128
48	00619 634
49	00146 728
50	+0· 00033 973
51	00007 696
52	00001 706
53	370
54	079
55	016
56	003
57	001

n	$J_n(23)$
0	−0·16241 27813 13486 542
1	−0·03951 93218 83701 511
2	+0·15897 63185 40990 759
3	+0·06716 73772 82134 687
4	−0·14145 43940 32607 797
5	−0·11636 89056 41302 616
6	+0·09085 92176 66824 051
7	+0·16377 37148 58776 034
8	+0·00882 91305 08083 100
9	−0·15763 17110 27066 051
10	−0·13219 30782 68395 662
11	+0·04268 12081 84982 867
12	+0·17301 85817 49683 622
13	+0·13785 99205 97295 695
14	−0·01717 69323 78827 619
15	−0·15877 09687 10651 057
16	−0·18991 56355 04630 281
17	−0·10545 94806 87095 422
18	+0·03401 90118 80228 354
19	+0·15870 66297 17018 062
20	+0·22819 19415 65279 749
21	+0·23814 89208 31294 545
22	+0·20668 86964 74475 507
23	+0·15725 55419 89441 207
24	+0·10782 23875 04406 908
25	+0·06776 50928 02364 513
26	+0·03949 30316 31168 121
27	+0·02152 35004 50711 239
28	+0·01104 04042 09632 179
29	+0·00535 74837 11871 458
30	+0·00246 97721 07261 064
31	+0·00108 54000 46200 881
32	+0·00045 60888 86845 660
33	+0·00018 37168 56326 172
34	+0·00007 10986 13916 400
35	+0·00002 64877 41339 705
36	95162 51030 530
37	33022 61886 301
38	11084 17647 134
39	03603 35556 401
40	+0· 01135 89891 967
41	00347 59720 006
42	00103 36066 315
43	00029 89391 752
44	00008 41659 366
45	00002 30870 169
46	61745 644
47	16112 408
48	04105 067
49	01021 783
50	+0· 00248 619
51	00059 168
52	00013 780
53	00003 142
54	702
55	154
56	034
57	007
58	001

n	$J_n(24)$
0	−0·05623 02741 66859 267
1	−0·15403 80651 83121 221
2	+0·04339 37687 34932 499
3	+0·16127 03599 72276 638
4	−0·00307 61787 41863 339
5	−0·16229 57528 86231 084
6	−0·06454 70516 27399 613
7	+0·13002 22270 72531 278
8	+0·14039 33507 53042 858
9	−0·03642 66599 03836 039
10	−0·16771 33456 80919 887
11	−0·10333 44614 96930 534
12	+0·07299 00893 08733 565
13	+0·17632 45508 05664 098
14	+0·11802 81740 64069 208
15	−0·03862 50143 97583 355
16	−0·16630 94420 61048 403
17	−0·18312 09083 50481 181
18	−0·09311 18447 68799 938
19	+0·04345 31411 97281 275
20	+0·16191 26516 64495 289
21	+0·22640 12782 43544 208
22	+0·23428 95852 61707 074
23	+0·20312 96280 69585 428
24	+0·15504 22018 71664 996
25	+0·10695 47756 73744 565
26	+0·06778 02474 48636 180
27	+0·03990 24271 31633 826
28	+0·02200 02135 97539 927
29	+0·01143 14045 95959 338

n	$J_n(24)$
30	+0·00562 56808 42695 140
31	+0·00263 27975 10778 513
32	+0·00117 57127 26816 017
33	+0·00050 24364 27397 533
34	+0·00020 59874 48527 199
35	+0·00008 11946 76762 864
36	+0·00003 08303 58697 822
37	+0·00001 12963 99330 601
38	40002 05904 866
39	13709 19368 140
40	+0· 04552 82041 591
41	01466 87437 162
42	00459 00035 379
43	00139 62686 664
44	00041 32925 168
45	00011 91372 284
46	00003 34720 896
47	91724 484
48	24533 335
49	06408 854
50	+0· 01636 153
51	00408 451
52	00099 762
53	00023 852
54	00005 585
55	00001 281
56	288
57	064
58	014
59	003
60	+0· 001

The first forty roots of $J_0(x)=0$, with the corresponding values of $J_1(x)$.

No. of zero (n)	Value of zero (x_n)	$J_1(x_n)$	No. of zero (n)	Value of zero (x_n)	$J_1(x_n)$
1	2·40482 55577	+0·51914 750	21	65·18996 48002	+0·09882 255
2	5·52007 81103	−0·34026 481	22	68·33146 93299	−0·09652 404
3	8·65372 79129	+0·27145 230	23	71·47298 16036	+0·09437 879
4	11·79153 44391	−0·23245 983	24	74·61450 06437	−0·09237 051
5	14·93091 77086	+0·20654 642	25	77·75602 56304	+0·09048 519
6	18·07106 39679	−0·18772 880	26	80·89755 58711	−0·08871 080
7	21·21163 66299	+0·17326 589	27	84·03909 07769	+0·08703 686
8	24·35247 15308	−0·16170 155	28	87·18062 98436	−0·08545 424
9	27·49347 91320	+0·15218 121	29	90·32217 26372	+0·08395 493
10	30·63460 64684	−0·14416 598	30	93·46371 87819	−0·08253 186
11	33·77582 02136	+0·13729 694	31	96·60526 79510	+0·08117 879
12	36·91709 83537	−0·13132 463	32	99·74681 98587	−0·07989 015
13	40·05842 57646	+0·12606 950	33	102·88837 42542	+0·07866 100
14	43·19979 17132	−0·12139 863	34	106·02993 09165	−0·07748 689
15	46·34118 83717	+0·11721 120	35	109·17148 96498	+0·07635 913
16	49·48260 98974	−0·11342 918	36	112·31305 02805	−0·07528 823
17	52·62405 18411	+0·10999 114	37	115·45461 26537	+0·07425 684
18	55·76551 07550	−0·10684 789	38	118·59617 66309	−0·07326 670
19	58·90698 39261	+0·10395 957	39	121·73774 20880	+0·07231 515
20	62·04846 91902	−0·10129 350	40	124·87930 89132	−0·07139 973

The first fifty roots of $J_1(x)=0$, with the corresponding maximum or minimum values of $J_0(x)$.

No. of root (n)	Value of root (x_n)	$J_0(x_n)=\frac{\text{Min.}}{\text{Max.}}$	No. of root (n)	Value of root (x_n)	$J_0(x_n)=\frac{\text{Max.}}{\text{Min.}}$
1	3·8317 0597 0207 5123	−0·4027 5939 5702 5547	26	82·4622 5991 4373 5565	+0·0878 6187 6039 4105
2	7·0155 8666 9815 6188	+0·3001 1575 2526 1326	27	85·6040 1943 6350 2310	−0·0862 3466 3413 2884
3	10·1734 6813 5062 7221	−0·2497 0487 7057 8259	28	88·7457 6714 4926 3069	+0·0846 9463 4803 7192
4	13·3236 9193 6314 2231	+0·2183 5940 7247 8730	29	91·8875 0425 1694 9853	−0·0832 3427 2981 9746
5	16·4706 3005 0877 6328	−0·1964 6537 1468 6572	30	95·0292 3180 8044 6953	+0·0818 4693 7926 4857
6	19·6158 5851 0468 2420	+0·1800 6337 5344 3156	31	98·1709 5073 0790 7820	−0·0805 2673 9448 4029
7	22·7600 8438 0592 7719	−0·1671 8460 0473 8180	32	101·3126 6182 3038 7301	+0·0792 6843 1724 5187
8	25·9036 7208 7618 3826	+0·1567 2498 6252 8622	33	104·4543 6579 1282 7601	−0·0780 6732 5407 9485
9	29·0468 2853 4016 8551	−0·1480 1110 9972 7775	34	107·5960 6325 9509 1722	+0·0769 1921 3961 3909
10	32·1896 7991 0974 4036	+0·1406 0579 8193 1148	35	110·7377 5478 0899 2151	−0·0758 2031 1569 1671
11	35·3323 0755 0083 8651	−0·1342 1124 0310 0007	36	113·8794 4084 7594 9981	+0·0747 6720 0537 0746
12	38·4747 6623 4771 6151	+0·1286 1662 2072 0700	37	117·0211 2189 8892 4250	−0·0737 5678 6512 8573
13	41·6170 9421 2814 4509	−0·1236 6796 0769 8371	38	120·1627 9832 8149 0038	+0·0727 8626 0189 2388
14	44·7593 1899 7652 8217	+0·1192 4981 2010 6895	39	123·3044 7048 8635 7180	−0·0718 5306 4408 8573
15	47·9014 6088 7185 4471	−0·1152 7369 4120 1680	40	126·4461 3869 8516 5957	+0·0709 5486 5793 0974
16	51·0435 3518 3571 5095	+0·1116 7049 6859 2113	41	129·5878 0324 5103 9968	−0·0700 8953 0177 2614
17	54·1855 5364 1061 3205	−0·1083 8534 8943 6825	42	132·7294 6438 8509 6159	+0·0692 5510 1263 7661
18	57·3275 2543 7901 0107	+0·1053 7405 5395 2352	43	135·8711 2236 4789 0006	−0·0684 4978 2005 1879
19	60·4694 5784 5347 4916	−0·1026 0056 7103 3972	44	139·0127 7738 8659 7042	+0·0676 7191 8315 5457
20	63·6113 5669 8481 2326	+0·1000 3514 6811 5233	45	142·1544 2965 5859 0290	−0·0669 1998 4772 3973
21	66·7532 2673 4098 4934	−0·0976 5301 5783 1733	46	145·2960 7934 5195 9072	+0·0661 9257 2028 7533
22	69·8950 7183 7495 7740	+0·0954 3333 9020 5353	47	148·4377 2662 0342 2304	−0·0654 8837 5698 2572
23	73·0368 9522 5573 8348	−0·0933 5845 3290 4550	48	151·5793 7163 1401 4280	+0·0648 0618 6514 0981
24	76·1786 9958 4641 4576	+0·0914 1327 2155 9213	49	154·7210 1451 6285 9535	−0·0641 4488 1592 6670
25	79·3204 8717 5476 2994	−0·0895 8482 1964 8557	50	157·8626 5540 1930 2978	+0·0635 0341 6658 3216

TABLE V.—The smallest roots of $J_n(x_s)=0$.

s	$n=0$	$n=1$	$n=2$	$n=3$	$n=4$	$n=5$
1	2·405	3·832	5·135	6·379	7·586	8·780
2	5·520	7·016	8·417	9·760	11·064	12·339
3	8·654	10·173	11·620	13·017	14·373	15·700
4	11·792	13·323	14·796	16·224	17·616	18·982
5	14·931	16·470	17·960	19·410	20·827	22·220
6	18·071	19·616	21·117	22·583	24·018	25·431
7	21·212	22·760	24·270	25·749	27·200	28·628
8	24·353	25·903	27·421	28·909	30·371	31·813
9	27·494	29·047	30·571	32·050	33·512	34·983

TABLE VI.

x	$I_0(x\sqrt{i}) = \text{ber } x + i \text{ bei } x$	
	ber x	bei x
0·0	+1·00000 0000	Nil
0·2	+0·99997 5000	+0·00999 9972
0·4	+0·99960 0004	+0·03999 8222
0·6	+0·99797 5114	+0·08997 9750
0·8	+0·99360 1138	+0·15988 6230
1·0	+0·98438 1781	+0·24956 6040
1·2	+0·96762 9156	+0·35870 4420
1·4	+0·94007 5057	+0·48673 3934
1·6	+0·89789 1139	+0·63272 5677
1·8	+0·83672 1794	+0·79526 1955
2·0	+0·75173 4183	+0·97229 1627
2·2	+0·63769 0457	+1·16096 9944
2·4	+0·48904 7772	+1·35748 5476
2·6	+0·30009 2090	+1·55687 7774
2·8	+0·06511 2108	+1·75285 0564
3·0	−0·22138 0250	+1·93758 6785
3·2	−0·56437 6430	+2·10157 3388
3·4	−0·96803 8995	+2·23344 5750
3·6	−1·43530 5322	+2·31986 3655
3·8	−1·96742 3273	+2·34543 3061
4·0	−2·56341 6557	+2·29269 0323
4·2	−3·21947 9832	+2·14216 7987
4·4	−3·92830 6622	+1·87256 3796
4·6	−4·67835 6937	+1·46103 6836
4·8	−5·45307 6175	+0·88365 6854
5·0	−6·23008 2479	+0·11603 4382
5·2	−6·98034 6403	−0·86583 9727
5·4	−7·66739 4351	−2·08451 6693
5·6	−8·24657 5962	−3·55974 6593
5·8	−8·66444 5263	−5·30684 4640
6·0	−8·85831 5966	−7·33474 6541

x	$I_0(x)$	x	$I_0(x)$	x	$I_0(x)$	x	$I_0(x)$
·00	1·00000 0000	·45	1·05126 9338	·90	1·21298 5166	1·35	1·51022 7098
·01	1·00002 5000	·46	1·05360 3728	·91	1·21798 9524	1·36	1·51868 0615
·02	1·00010 0003	·47	1·05599 2145	·92	1·22306 0325	1·37	1·52722 3514
·03	1·00022 5013	·48	1·05843 4768	·93	1·22819 7952	1·38	1·53585 6452
·04	1·00040 0040	·49	1·06093 1780	·94	1·23340 2796	1·39	1·54458 0090
·05	1·00062 5098	·50	1·06348 3371	·95	1·23867 5250	1·40	1·55339 5100
·06	1·00090 0203	·51	1·06608 9731	·96	1·24401 5716	1·41	1·56230 2157
·07	1·00122 5375	·52	1·06875 1057	·97	1·24942 4599	1·42	1·57130 1946
·08	1·00160 0640	·53	1·07146 7550	·98	1·25490 2308	1·43	1·58039 5160
·09	1·00202 6025	·54	1·07423 9413	·99	1·26044 9261	1·44	1·58958 2496
·10	1·00250 1563	·55	1·07706 6856	1·00	1·26606 5878	1·45	1·59886 4661
·11	1·00302 7288	·56	1·07995 0092	1·01	1·27175 2586	1·46	1·60824 2371
·12	1·00360 3241	·57	1·08288 9337	1·02	1·27750 9817	1·47	1·61771 6345
·13	1·00422 9465	·58	1·08588 4813	1·03	1·28333 8010	1·48	1·62728 7314
·14	1·00490 6006	·59	1·08893 6745	1·04	1·28923 7606	1·49	1·63695 6014
·15	1·00563 2915	·60	1·09204 5364	1·05	1·29520 9055	1·50	1·64672 3190
·16	1·00641 0247	·61	1·09521 0904	1·06	1·30125 2811	1·51	1·65658 9594
·17	1·00723 8061	·62	1·09843 3604	1·07	1·30736 9333	1·52	1·66655 5988
·18	1·00811 6417	·63	1·10171 3706	1·08	1·31355 9088	1·53	1·67662 3139
·19	1·00904 5383	·64	1·10505 1458	1·09	1·31982 2545	1·54	1·68679 1823
·20	1·01002 5028	·65	1·10844 7111	1·10	1·32616 0184	1·55	1·69706 2826
·21	1·01105 5425	·66	1·11190 0922	1·11	1·33257 2485	1·56	1·70743 6939
·22	1·01213 6652	·67	1·11541 3151	1·12	1·33905 9938	1·57	1·71791 4964
·23	1·01326 8789	·68	1·11898 4063	1·13	1·34562 3036	1·58	1·72849 7709
·24	1·01445 1923	·69	1·12261 3927	1·14	1·35226 2281	1·59	1·73918 5993
·25	1·01568 6141	·70	1·12630 3018	1·15	1·35897 8177	1·60	1·74998 0640
·26	1·01697 1537	·71	1·13005 1614	1·16	1·36577 1239	1·61	1·76088 2485
·27	1·01830 8206	·72	1·13385 9999	1·17	1·37264 1983	1·62	1·77189 2371
·28	1·01969 6249	·73	1·13772 8458	1·18	1·37959 0934	1·63	1·78301 1150
·29	1·02113 5771	·74	1·14165 7286	1·19	1·38661 8622	1·64	1·79423 9681
·30	1·02262 6879	·75	1·14564 6778	1·20	1·39372 5584	1·65	1·80557 8834
·31	1·02416 9686	·76	1·14969 7236	1·21	1·40091 2363	1·66	1·81702 9487
·32	1·02576 4307	·77	1·15380 8967	1·22	1·40817 9507	1·67	1·82859 2525
·33	1·02741 0862	·78	1·15798 2280	1·23	1·41552 7572	1·68	1·84026 8846
·34	1·02910 9474	·79	1·16221 7492	1·24	1·42295 7120	1·69	1·85205 9354
·35	1·03086 0272	·80	1·16651 4923	1·25	1·43046 8718	1·70	1·86396 4962
·36	1·03266 3387	·81	1·17087 4897	1·26	1·43806 2941	1·71	1·87598 6594
·37	1·03451 8954	·82	1·17529 7745	1·27	1·44574 0369	1·72	1·88812 5183
·38	1·03642 7112	·83	1·17978 3802	1·28	1·45350 1591	1·73	1·90038 1670
·39	1·03838 8006	·84	1·18433 3406	1·29	1·46134 7201	1·74	1·91275 7007
·40	1·04040 1782	·85	1·18894 6902	1·30	1·46927 7798	1·75	1·92525 2154
·41	1·04246 8592	·86	1·19362 4640	1·31	1·47729 3991	1·76	1·93786 8082
·42	1·04458 8591	·87	1·19836 6974	1·32	1·48539 6393	1·77	1·95060 5771
·43	1·04676 1939	·88	1·20317 4262	1·33	1·49358 5625	1·78	1·96346 6212
·44	1·04898 8799	·89	1·20804 6870	1·34	1·50186 2315	1·79	1·97645 0404

x	$I_0(x)$	x	$I_0(x)$	x	$I_0(x)$	x	$I_0(x)$
1·80	1·98955 9357	2·25	2·72707 8307	2·70	3·84165 0977	3·15	5·51574 963
1·81	2·00279 4090	2·26	2·74721 0068	2·71	3·87194 8687	3·16	5·56121 041
1·82	2·01615 5635	2·27	2·76752 7063	2·72	3·90252 1288	3·17	5·60708 279
1·83	2·02964 5030	2·28	2·78803 0900	2·73	3·93337 1236	3·18	5·65337 053
1·84	2·04326 3327	2·29	2·80872 3200	2·74	3·96450 1009	3·19	5·70007 739
1·85	2·05701 1587	2·30	2·82960 5601	2·75	3·99591 3107	3·20	5·74720 718
1·86	2·07089 0880	2·31	2·85067 9754	2·76	4·02761 0057	3·21	5·79476 375
1·87	2·08490 2289	2·32	2·87194 7330	2·77	4·05959 4407	3·22	5·84275 099
1·88	2·09904 6908	2·33	2·89341 0011	2·78	4·09186 8729	3·23	5·89117 279
1·89	2·11332 5838	2·34	2·91506 9500	2·79	4·12443 5621	3·24	5·94003 313
1·90	2·12774 0194	2·35	2·93692 7511	2·80	4·15729 7704	3·25	5·98933 599
1·91	2·14229 1102	2·36	2·95898 5780	2·81	4·19045 7623	3·26	6·03908 541
1·92	2·15697 9698	2·37	2·98124 6054	2·82	4·22391 8051	3·27	6·08928 543
1·93	2·17180 7129	2·38	3·00371 0100	2·83	4·25768 1683	3·28	6·13994 018
1·94	2·18677 4554	2·39	3·02637 9702	2·84	4·29175 1240	3·29	6·19105 380
1·95	2·20188 3143	2·40	3·04925 6658	2·85	4·32612 9469	3·30	6·24263 046
1·96	2·21713 4077	2·41	3·07234 2786	2·86	4·36081 9143	3·31	6·29467 439
1·97	2·23252 8550	2·42	3·09563 9921	2·87	4·39582 3061	3·32	6·34718 985
1·98	2·24806 7765	2·43	3·11914 9913	2·88	4·43114 4048	3·33	6·40018 113
1·99	2·26375 2940	2·44	3·14287 4633	2·89	4·46678 4955	3·34	6·45365 2594
2·00	2·27958 5302	2·45	3·16681 5966	2·90	4·50274 8661	3·35	6·50760 8601
2·01	2·29556 6092	2·46	3·19097 5818	2·91	4·53903 8072	3·36	6·56205 3582
2·02	2·31169 6562	2·47	3·21535 6111	2·92	4·57565 6120	3·37	6·61699 2002
2·03	2·32797 7977	2·48	3·23995 8787	2·93	4·61260 5766	3·38	6·67242 8365
2·04	2·34441 1612	2·49	3·26478 5806	2·94	4·64988 9997	3·39	6·72836 7221
2·05	2·36099 8757	2·50	3·28983 9144	2·95	4·68751 1830	3·40	6·78481 3160
2·06	2·37774 0714	2·51	3·31512 0799	2·96	4·72547 4310	3·41	6·84177 0817
2·07	2·39463 8796	2·52	3·34063 2787	2·97	4·76378 0509	3·42	6·89924 4868
2·08	2·41169 4331	2·53	3·36637 7142	2·98	4·80243 3529	3·43	6·95724 0035
2·09	2·42890 8658	2·54	3·39235 5918	2·99	4·84143 6501	3·44	7·01576 1083
2·10	2·44628 3129	2·55	3·41857 1188	3·00	4·88079 2586	3·45	7·07481 2823
2·11	2·46381 9111	2·56	3·44502 5046	3·01	4·92050 4974	3·46	7·13440 0110
2·12	2·48151 7983	2·57	3·47171 9603	3·02	4·96057 6884	3·47	7·19452 7844
2·13	2·49938 1135	2·58	3·49865 6994	3·03	5·00101 1567	3·48	7·25520 0972
2·14	2·51740 9974	2·59	3·52583 9370	3·04	5·04181 2305	3·49	7·31642 4489
2·15	2·53560 5920	2·60	3·55326 8904	3·05	5·08298 2407	3·50	7·37820 3432
2·16	2·55397 0404	2·61	3·58094 7791	3·06	5·12452 5217	3·51	7·44054 2891
2·17	2·57250 4872	2·62	3·60887 8245	3·07	5·16644 4109	3·52	7·50344 7999
2·18	2·59121 0787	2·63	3·63706 2500	3·08	5·20874 2488	3·53	7·56692 3940
2·19	2·61008 9621	2·64	3·66550 2814	3·09	5·25142 3791	3·54	7·63097 5945
2·20	2·62914 2864	2·65	3·69420 1463	3·10	5·29449 1490	3·55	7·69560 9296
2·21	2·64837 2017	2·66	3·72316 0747	3·11	5·33794 9085	3·56	7·76082 9322
2·22	2·66777 8599	2·67	3·75238 2987	3·12	5·38180 0112	3·57	7·82664 1404
2·23	2·68736 4142	2·68	3·78187 0525	3·13	5·42604 8139	3·58	7·89305 0972
2·24	2·70713 0191	2·69	3·81162 5726	3·14	5·47069 6769	3·59	7·96006 3509

x	$I_0(x)$	x	$I_0(x)$	x	$I_0(x)$	x	$I_0(x)$
3·60	8·02768 4547	4·00	11·30192 1952	4·40	16·01043 5525	4·80	22·79367 7993
3·61	8·09591 9671	4·01	11·39996 1069	4·41	16·15154 0625	4·81	22·99713 7940
3·62	8·16477 4519	4·02	11·49889 4589	4·42	16·29393 9460	4·82	23·20247 2677
3·63	8·23425 4781	4·03	11·59873 0783	4·43	16·43764 4056	4·83	23·40969 9714
3·64	8·30436 6201	4·04	11·69947 7998	4·44	16·58266 6554	4·84	23·61883 6721
3·65	8·37511 4576	4·05	11·80114 4658	4·45	16·72991 9208	4·85	23·82990 1540
3·66	8·44650 5757	4·06	11·90373 9268	4·46	16·87671 4387	4·86	24·04291 2178
3·67	8·51854 5653	4·07	12·00727 0413	4·47	17·02576 4578	4·87	24·25788 6813
3·68	8·59124 0224	4·08	12·11174 6758	4·48	17·17618 2385	4·88	24·47484 3797
3·69	8·66459 5490	4·09	12·21717 7049	4·49	17·32798 0530	4·89	24·69380 1651
3·70	8·73861 7524	4·10	12·32357 0116	4·50	17·48117 1856	4·90	24·91477 9076
3·71	8·81331 2459	4·11	12·43093 4870	4·51	17·63576 9326	4·91	25·13779 4945
3·72	8·88868 6484	4·12	12·53928 0308	4·52	17·79178 6027	4·92	25·36286 8313
3·73	8·96474 5845	4·13	12·64861 5508	4·53	17·94923 5168	4·93	25·59001 8412
3·74	9·04149 6849	4·14	12·75894 9638	4·54	18·10813 0082	4·94	25·81926 4659
3·75	9·11894 5861	4·15	12·87029 1948	4·55	18·26848 4229	4·95	26·05062 6651
3·76	9·19709 9305	4·16	12·98265 1778	4·56	18·43031 1194	4·96	26·28412 4173
3·77	9·27596 3667	4·17	13·09603 8555	4·57	18·59362 4693	4·97	26·51977 7196
3·78	9·35554 5493	4·18	13·21046 1793	4·58	18·75843 8569	4·98	26·75760 5880
3·79	9·43585 1389	4·19	13·32593 1097	4·59	18·92476 6796	4·99	26·99763 0575
3·80	9·51688 8026	4·20	13·44245 6163	4·60	19·09262 3480	5·00	27·23987 1824
3·81	9·59866 2135	4·21	13·56004 6777	4·61	19·26202 2859	5·01	27·48435 0363
3·82	9·68118 0512	4·22	13·67871 2818	4·62	19·43297 9309	5·02	27·73108 7126
3·83	9·76445 0016	4·23	13·79846 4257	4·63	19·60550 7336	5·03	27·98010 3243
3·84	9·84847 7569	4·24	13·91931 1158	4·64	19·77962 1587	5·04	28·23142 0046
3·85	9·93327 0161	4·25	14·04126 3683	4·65	19·95533 6846	5·05	28·48505 9067
3·86	10·01883 4845	4·26	14·16433 2086	4·66	20·13266 8036	5·06	28·74104 2042
3·87	10·10517 8741	4·27	14·28852 6720	4·67	20·31163 0221	5·07	28·99939 0912
3·88	10·19230 9038	4·28	14·41385 8034	4·68	20·49223 8607	5·08	29·26012 7828
3·89	10·28023 2989	4·29	14·54033 6575	4·69	20·67450 8544	5·09	29·52327 5147
3·90	10·36895 7917	4·30	14·66797 2992	4·70	20·85845 5527	5·10	29·78885 5440
3·91	10·45849 1213	4·31	14·79677 8030	4·71	21·04409 5195		
3·92	10·54884 0339	4·32	14·92676 2540	4·72	21·23144 3338		
3·93	10·64001 2826	4·33	15·05793 7470	4·73	21·42051 5893		
3·94	10·73201 6274	4·34	15·19031 3876	4·74	21·61132 8947		
3·95	10·82485 8358	4·35	15·32390 2914	4·75	21·80389 8741		
3·96	10·91854 6823	4·36	15·45871 5847	4·76	21·99824 1666		
3·97	11·01308 9486	4·37	15·59476 4045	4·77	22·19437 4271		
3·98	11·10849 4239	4·38	15·73205 8983	4·78	22·39231 3260		
3·99	11·20476 9048	4·39	15·87061 2245	4·79	22·59207 5494		

x	$I_1(x)$	x	$I_1(x)$	x	$I_1(x)$	x	$I_1(x)$
·00	*Nil*	·45	0·23074 3570	·90	0·49712 6448	1·35	0·84090 4230
·01	0·00500 0063	·46	0·23613 7373	·91	0·50375 1599	1·36	0·84980 9949
·02	0·01000 0500	·47	0·24154 8938	·92	0·51041 4946	1·37	0·85878 0872
·03	0·01500 1687	·48	0·24697 8674	·93	0·51711 7001	1·38	0·86781 7710
·04	0·02000 4000	·49	0·25242 6993	·94	0·52385 8282	1·39	0·87692 1172
·05	0·02500 7814	·50	0·25789 4304	·95	0·53063 9310	1·40	0·88609 1981
·06	0·03001 3502	·51	0·26338 1026	·96	0·53746 0608	1·41	0·89533 0860
·07	0·03502 1441	·52	0·26888 7571	·97	0·54432 2705	1·42	0·90463 8540
·08	0·04003 2009	·53	0·27441 4358	·98	0·55122 6129	1·43	0·91401 5758
·09	0·04504 5577	·54	0·27996 1803	·99	0·55817 1417	1·44	0·92346 3255
·10	0·05006 2526	·55	0·28553 0329	1·00	0·56515 9104	1·45	0·93298 1780
·11	0·05508 3230	·56	0·29112 0360	1·01	0·57218 9733	1·46	0·94257 2087
·12	0·06010 8065	·57	0·29673 2318	1·02	0·57926 3847	1·47	0·95223 4935
·13	0·06513 7410	·58	0·30236 6629	1·03	0·58638 1997	1·48	0·96197 1092
·14	0·07017 1639	·59	0·30802 3722	1·04	0·59354 4734	1·49	0·97178 1330
·15	0·07521 1135	·60	0·31370 4026	1·05	0·60075 2614	1·50	0·98166 6428
·16	0·08025 6272	·61	0·31940 7973	1·06	0·60800 6196	1·51	0·99162 7170
·17	0·08530 7432	·62	0·32513 5997	1·07	0·61530 6043	1·52	1·00166 4351
·18	0·09036 4993	·63	0·33088 8532	1·08	0·62265 2724	1·53	1·01177 8765
·19	0·09542 9332	·64	0·33666 6018	1·09	0·63004 6810	1·54	1·02197 1216
·20	0·10050 0834	·65	0·34246 8895	1·10	0·63748 8876	1·55	1·03224 2518
·21	0·10557 9878	·66	0·34829 7605	1·11	0·64497 9503	1·56	1·04259 3488
·22	0·11066 6843	·67	0·35415 2590	1·12	0·65251 9270	1·57	1·05302 4951
·23	0·11576 2116	·68	0·36003 4297	1·13	0·66010 8769	1·58	1·06353 7735
·24	0·12086 6075	·69	0·36594 3176	1·14	0·66774 8588	1·59	1·07413 2681
·25	0·12597 9109	·70	0·37187 9677	1·15	0·67543 9326	1·60	1·08481 0635
·26	0·13110 1599	·71	0·37784 4255	1·16	0·68318 1582	1·61	1·09557 2447
·27	0·13623 3930	·72	0·38383 7364	1·17	0·69097 5960	1·62	1·10641 8977
·28	0·14137 6489	·73	0·38985 9461	1·18	0·69882 3068	1·63	1·11735 1091
·29	0·14652 9663	·74	0·39591 1007	1·19	0·70672 3524	1·64	1·12836 9664
·30	0·15169 3840	·75	0·40199 2463	1·20	0·71467 7942	1·65	1·13947 5574
·31	0·15686 9409	·76	0·40810 4296	1·21	0·72268 6944	1·66	1·15066 9712
·32	0·16205 6756	·77	0·41424 6975	1·22	0·73075 1160	1·67	1·16195 2973
·33	0·16725 6278	·78	0·42042 0971	1·23	0·73887 1219	1·68	1·17332 6261
·34	0·17246 8361	·79	0·42662 6755	1·24	0·74704 7758	1·69	1·18479 0486
·35	0·17769 3400	·80	0·43286 4802	1·25	0·75528 1420	1·70	1·19634 6565
·36	0·18293 1789	·81	0·43913 5593	1·26	0·76357 2846	1·71	1·20799 5429
·37	0·18818 3922	·82	0·44543 9607	1·27	0·77192 2691	1·72	1·21973 8009
·38	0·19345 0196	·83	0·45177 7329	1·28	0·78033 1610	1·73	1·23157 5249
·39	0·19873 1008	·84	0·45814 9245	1·29	0·78880 0263	1·74	1·24350 8096
·40	0·20402 6756	·85	0·46455 5845	1·30	0·79732 9314	1·75	1·25553 7513
·41	0·20933 7840	·86	0·47099 7619	1·31	0·80591 9438	1·76	1·26766 4463
·42	0·21466 4660	·87	0·47747 5069	1·32	0·81457 1307	1·77	1·27988 9923
·43	0·22000 7618	·88	0·48398 8688	1·33	0·82328 5603	1·78	1·29221 4874
·44	0·22536 7121	·89	0·49053 8979	1·34	0·83206 3015	1·79	1·30464 0310

x	$I_1(x)$	x	$I_1(x)$	x	$I_1(x)$	x	$I_1(x)$
1·80	1·31716 7230	2·25	2·00396 7457	2·70	3·01610 7694	3·15	4·52562 0649
1·81	1·32979 6644	2·26	2·02241 1151	2·71	3·04347 4850	3·16	4·56659 6009
1·82	1·34252 9568	2·27	2·04101 4722	2·72	3·07108 6362	3·17	4·60794 3508
1·83	1·35536 7027	2·28	2·05977 9695	2·73	3·09894 4528	3·18	4·64966 6635
1·84	1·36831 0061	2·29	2·07870 7611	2·74	3·12705 1673	3·19	4·69176 8912
1·85	1·38135 9709	2·30	2·09780 0028	2·75	3·15541 0139	3·20	4·73425 3895
1·86	1·39451 7026	2·31	2·11705 8510	2·76	3·18402 2290	3·21	4·77712 5171
1·87	1·40778 3076	2·32	2·13648 4642	2·77	3·21289 0513	3·22	4·82038 6363
1·88	1·42115 8927	2·33	2·15608 0021	2·78	3·24201 7219	3·23	4·86404 1126
1·89	1·43464 5663	2·34	2·17584 6257	2·79	3·27140 4837	3·24	4·90809 3153
1·90	1·44824 4373	2·35	2·19578 4977	2·80	3·30105 5823	3·25	4·95254 6165
1·91	1·46195 6157	2·36	2·21589 7825	2·81	3·33097 2651	3·26	4·99740 3925
1·92	1·47578 2125	2·37	2·23618 6453	2·82	3·36115 7821	3·27	5·04267 0227
1·93	1·48972 3395	2·38	2·25665 2534	2·83	3·39161 3857	3·28	5·08834 8897
1·94	1·50378 1096	2·39	2·27729 7753	2·84	3·42234 3306	3·29	5·13444 3807
1·95	1·51795 6370	2·40	2·29812 3813	2·85	3·45334 8735	3·30	5·18095 8856
1·96	1·53225 0362	2·41	2·31913 2429	2·86	3·48463 2737	3·31	5·22789 7983
1·97	1·54666 4233	2·42	2·34032 5336	2·87	3·51619 7933	3·32	5·27526 5168
1·98	1·56119 9148	2·43	2·36170 4281	2·88	3·54804 6962	3·33	5·32306 4420
1·99	1·57585 6293	2·44	2·38327 1029	2·89	3·58018 2492	3·34	5·37129 9790
2·00	1·59063 6855	2·45	2·40502 7363	2·90	3·61260 7212	3·35	5·41997 5369
2·01	1·60554 2033	2·46	2·42697 5075	2·91	3·64532 3840	3·36	5·46909 5281
2·02	1·62057 3039	2·47	2·44911 5981	2·92	3·67833 5120	3·37	5·51866 3697
2·03	1·63573 1095	2·48	2·47145 1912	2·93	3·71164 3814	3·38	5·56868 4817
2·04	1·65101 7434	2·49	2·49398 4712	2·94	3·74525 2718	3·39	5·61916 2888
2·05	1·66643 3299	2·50	2·51671 6246	2·95	3·77916 4648	3·40	5·67010 2192
2·06	1·68197 9944	2·51	2·53964 8394	2·96	3·81338 2452	3·41	5·72150 7056
2·07	1·69765 8635	2·52	2·56278 3055	2·97	3·84790 8999	3·42	5·77338 1845
2·08	1·71347 0648	2·53	2·58612 2143	2·98	3·88274 7188	3·43	5·82573 0963
2·09	1·72941 7273	2·54	2·60966 7592	2·99	3·91789 9943	3·44	5·87855 8859
2·10	1·74549 9810	2·55	2·63342 1351	3·00	3·95337 0217	3·45	5·93187 0019
2·11	1·76171 9567	2·56	2·65738 5389	3·01	3·98916 0991	3·46	5·98566 8980
2·12	1·77807 7871	2·57	2·68156 1694	3·02	4·02527 5271	3·47	6·03996 0312
2·13	1·79457 6055	2·58	2·70595 2269	3·03	4·06171 6094	3·48	6·09474 8632
2·14	1·81121 5465	2·59	2·73055 9137	3·04	4·09848 6520	3·49	6·15003 8601
2·15	1·82799 7461	2·60	2·75538 4341	3·05	4·13558 9648	3·50	6·20583 4922
2·16	1·84492 3415	2·61	2·78042 9941	3·06	4·17302 8594	3·51	6·26214 2346
2·17	1·86199 4709	2·62	2·80569 8017	3·07	4·21080 6510	3·52	6·31896 5664
2·18	1·87921 2738	2·63	2·83119 0666	3·08	4·24892 6577	3·53	6·37630 9712
2·19	1·89657 8912	2·64	2·85691 0009	3·09	4·28739 2003	3·54	6·43417 9377
2·20	1·91409 4651	2·65	2·88285 8180	3·10	4·32620 6027	3·55	6·49257 9585
2·21	1·93176 1388	2·66	2·90903 7340	3·11	4·36537 1921	3·56	6·55151 5315
2·22	1·94958 0572	2·67	2·93544 9665	3·12	4·40489 2984	3·57	6·61099 1589
2·23	1·96755 3660	2·68	2·96209 7349	3·13	4·44477 2545	3·58	6·67101 3473
2·24	1·98568 2127	2·69	2·98898 2613	3·14	4·48501 3970	3·59	6·73158 6089

x	$I_1(x)$	x	$I_1(x)$	x	$I_1(x)$	x	$I_1(x)$
3·60	6·79271 4601	4·00	9·75946 5154	4·40	14·04622 1338	4·80	20·25283 4600
3·61	6·85440 4223	4·01	9·84849 4681	4·41	14·17499 7247	4·81	20·43944 3796
3·62	6·91666 0219	4·02	9·93834 7267	4·42	14·30497 0189	4·82	20·62779 5525
3·63	6·97948 7901	4·03	10·02903 0650	4·43	14·43615 1440	4·83	20·81790 6249
3·64	7·04289 2632	4·04	10·12055 2634	4·44	14·56855 2384	4·84	21·00979 2573
3·65	7·10687 9825	4·05	10·21292 1103	4·45	14·70218 4510	4·85	21·20347 1276
3·66	7·17145 4946	4·06	10·30614 4016	4·46	14·83705 9420	4·86	21·39885 9282
3·67	7·23662 3510	4·07	10·40022 9397	4·47	14·97318 8822	4·87	21·59627 3684
3·68	7·30239 1084	4·08	10·49518 5359	4·48	15·11058 4538	4·88	21·79543 1735
3·69	7·36876 3288	4·09	10·59102 0085	4·49	15·24925 8499	4·89	21·99645 0853
3·70	7·43574 5797	4·10	10·68774 1837	4·50	15·38922 2754	4·90	22·19934 8620
3·71	7·50334 4337	4·11	10·78535 8956	4·51	15·53048 9464	4·91	22·40414 2793
3·72	7·57156 4687	4·12	10·88387 9856	4·52	15·67307 0904	4·92	22·61085 1286
3·73	7·64041 2684	4·13	10·98331 3038	4·53	15·81697 9464	4·93	22·81949 2189
3·74	7·70989 4216	4·14	11·08366 7081	4·54	15·96222 7657	4·94	23·03008 3764
3·75	7·78001 5230	4·15	11·18495 0646	4·55	16·10882 8111	4·95	23·24264 4448
3·76	7·85078 1728	4·16	11·28717 2471	4·56	16·25679 3575	4·96	23·45719 2854
3·77	7·92219 9767	4·17	11·39034 1384	4·57	16·40613 6918	4·97	23·67374 7769
3·78	7·99427 5465	4·18	11·49446 6292	4·58	16·55687 1133	4·98	23·89232 8160
3·79	8·06701 4991	4·19	11·59955 6184	4·59	16·70900 9334	4·99	24·11295 3174
3·80	8·14042 4579	4·20	11·70562 0143	4·60	16·86256 4762	5·00	24·33564 2142
3·81	8·21451 0518	4·21	11·81266 7328	4·61	17·01755 0780	5·01	24·56041 4578
3·82	8·28927 9159	4·22	11·92070 6992	4·62	17·17398 0885	5·02	24·78729 0180
3·83	8·36473 6907	4·23	12·02974 8470	4·63	17·33186 8690	5·03	25·01628 8837
3·84	8·44089 0236	4·24	12·13980 1191	4·64	17·49122 7953	5·04	25·24743 0624
3·85	8·51774 5677	4·25	12·25087 4666	4·65	17·65207 2549	5·05	25·48073 5808
3·86	8·59530 9818	4·26	12·36297 8507	4·66	17·81441 6491	5·06	25·71622 4854
3·87	8·67358 9318	4·27	12·47612 2406	4·67	17·97827 3926	5·07	25·95391 8413
3·88	8·75259 0893	4·28	12·59031 6150	4·68	18·14365 9128	5·08	26·19383 7336
3·89	8·83232 1322	4·29	12·70556 9622	4·69	18·31058 6520	5·09	26·43600 2675
3·90	8·91278 7451	4·30	12·82189 2796	4·70	18·47907 0647	5·10	26·68043 5680
3·91	8·99399 6193	4·31	12·93929 5743	4·71	18·64912 6207		
3·92	9·07595 4517	4·32	13·05778 8626	4·72	18·82076 8025		
3·93	9·15866 9467	4·33	13·17738 1705	4·73	18·99401 1070		
3·94	9·24214 8147	4·34	13·29808 5340	4·74	19·16887 0460		
3·95	9·32639 7737	4·35	13·41990 9985	4·75	19·34536 1448		
3·96	9·41142 5473	4·36	13·54286 6196	4·76	19·52349 9439		
3·97	9·49723 8668	4·37	13·66696 4630	4·77	19·70329 9977		
3·98	9·58384 4704	4·38	13·79221 6043	4·78	19·88477 8763		
3·99	9·67125 1025	4·39	13·91863 1291	4·79	20·06795 1638		

x	$I_0(x)$	$I_1(x)$	$I_2(x)$
0·0	1·00000000000	Nil	Nil
0·2	1·01002502780	·100500834028	$\cdot 0^2 501668751391$
0·4	1·04040178223	·204026755734	·0202680035615
0·6	1·09204536432	·313704025606	·0463652789678
0·8	1·16651492287	·432864802620	·0843529163180
1·0	1·26606587775	·565159103990	·135747669767
1·2	1·39372558413	·714677941552	·202595681546
1·4	1·55339509973	·886091981415	·287549411997
1·6	1·74998063974	1·08481063513	·393967345826
1·8	1·98955935662	1·31716723040	·526040211741
2·0	2·27958530233	1·59063685463	·688948447698
2·2	2·62914286357	1·91409465059	·889056817580
2·4	3·04925665799	2·29812381254	1·13415348087
2·6	3·55326890424	2·75538434051	1·43374248847
2·8	4·15729770350	3·30105582264	1·79940068733
3·0	4·88079258586	3·95337021738	2·24521244092
3·2	5·74720718718	4·73425389471	2·78829850299
3·4	6·78481316043	5·67010219264	3·44945892947
3·6	8·02768454705	6·79271460136	4·25395421296
3·8	9·51688802610	8·14042457894	5·23245403722
4·0	11·3019219521	9·75946515371	6·42218937528
4·2	13·4424561633	11·7056201430	7·86835133327
4·4	16·0104355250	14·0462213375	9·62578946244
4·6	19·0926234795	16·8625647618	11·7610735829
4·8	22·7936779931	20·2528346003	14·3549969097
5·0	27·2398718236	24·3356421424	17·5056149666
5·2	32·5835927106	29·2543098818	21·3319350638
5·4	39·0087877856	35·1820585061	25·9783957463
5·6	46·7375512926	42·3282880326	31·6203055668
5·8	56·0380968926	50·9461849787	38·4704468999
6·0	67·2344069764	61·3419367775	46·7870947172

x	$I_3(x)$	$I_4(x)$	$I_5(x)$
0·0	Nil	Nil	Nil
0·2	$\cdot0^{3}167083750232$	$\cdot0^{5}417500694777$	$\cdot0^{7}834723214702$
0·4	$\cdot0^{2}134672011869$	$\cdot0^{4}672017811684$	$\cdot0^{5}268449532285$
0·6	$\cdot0^{2}460216582095$	$\cdot0^{3}343620758320$	$\cdot0^{4}205557100196$
0·8	·0111002210296	$\cdot0^{2}110125859602$	$\cdot0^{4}876350693866$
1·0	·0221684249243	$\cdot0^{2}273712022104$	$\cdot0^{3}271463155956$
1·2	·0393590030648	$\cdot0^{2}580066622187$	$\cdot0^{3}687894919051$
1·4	·0645222328531	·0110255569122	$\cdot0^{2}151905049781$
1·6	·0998922705633	·0193713312135	$\cdot0^{2}303561449592$
1·8	·148188982086	·0320769381221	$\cdot0^{2}562481265409$
2·0	·212739959240	·0507285699791	$\cdot0^{2}982567932312$
2·2	·297627709533	·0773448824914	·0163735913822
2·4	·407868011092	·114483453137	·0262565006355
2·6	·549626665935	·165373259392	·0407858678054
2·8	·730483412160	·234079089848	·0616860125932
3·0	·959753629490	·325705181936	·0912064776610
3·2	1·24888076598	·446647066782	·132263099020
3·4	1·61191521679	·604902664549	·188614829615
3·6	2·06609880918	·810456197666	·265085036586
3·8	2·63257822397	1·07575157832	·367838059088
4·0	3·33727577842	1·41627570765	·504724363113
4·2	4·21195220660	1·85127675241	·685710773430
4·4	5·29550364442	2·40464812914	·923416136884
4·6	6·63554425495	3·10601585905	1·23377754356
4·8	8·29033717554	3·99207544030	1·63687810838
5·0	10·3311501691	5·10823476364	2·15797454732
5·2	12·8451290635	6·51063229818	2·82877168171
5·4	15·9388023977	8·26861530445	3·68900194663
5·6	19·7423554848	10·4677818331	4·78838143757
5·8	24·4148422891	13·2137134973	6·18903056865
6·0	30·1505402994	16·6365544178	7·96846774238

x	$I_6(x)$	$I_7(x)$	$I_8(x)$
0·0	Nil	Nil	Nil
0·2	$\cdot 0^{8}139087425642$	$\cdot 0^{10}198660852119$	$\cdot 0^{12}248291584037$
0·4	$\cdot 0^{7}893980971214$	$\cdot 0^{8}255240920874$	$\cdot 0^{10}637748154995$
0·6	$\cdot 0^{5}102559132723$	$\cdot 0^{7}438834749717$	$\cdot 0^{8}164357788982$
0·8	$\cdot 0^{5}582022868887$	$\cdot 0^{6}331639053615$	$\cdot 0^{7}165452506106$
1·0	$\cdot 0^{4}224886614771$	$\cdot 0^{5}159921823120$	$\cdot 0^{7}996062403333$
1·2	$\cdot 0^{4}682085631142$	$\cdot 0^{5}580928790861$	$\cdot 0^{6}433537513798$
1·4	$\cdot 0^{3}175196213558$	$\cdot 0^{4}173686673046$	$\cdot 0^{5}150954051219$
1·6	$\cdot 0^{3}398740613950$	$\cdot 0^{4}450598913012$	$\cdot 0^{5}446656506452$
1·8	$\cdot 0^{3}827978932673$	$\cdot 0^{3}104953102941$	$\cdot 0^{4}116770209099$
2·0	$\cdot 0^{2}160017336352$	$\cdot 0^{3}224639142001$	$\cdot 0^{4}276993695123$
2·2	$\cdot 0^{2}291946711786$	$\cdot 0^{3}449225284743$	$\cdot 0^{4}607607604085$
2·4	$\cdot 0^{2}508136715570$	$\cdot 0^{3}849664857007$	$\cdot 0^{3}124988823159$
2·6	$\cdot 0^{2}850453706344$	$\cdot 0^{2}153415828186$	$\cdot 0^{3}243684776533$
2·8	·0137719020155	$\cdot 0^{2}266357538382$	$\cdot 0^{3}454025096400$
3·0	·0216835897328	$\cdot 0^{2}447211872992$	$\cdot 0^{3}813702326455$
3·2	·0333248823452	$\cdot 0^{2}729479022559$	$\cdot 0^{2}141017510822$
3·4	·0501531656813	·0116036566222	$\cdot 0^{2}237340311951$
3·6	·0741088738166	·0180554571973	$\cdot 0^{2}389320693838$
3·8	·107756685981	·0275537875687	$\cdot 0^{2}624273178058$
4·0	·154464799871	·0413299635012	$\cdot 0^{2}980992761666$
4·2	·218632053769	·0610477626605	·0151395115677
4·4	·305975090770	·0889386166028	·0229885833970
4·6	·423890764347	·127975549614	·0343999611745
4·8	·581912714514	·182096322090	·0507984417519
5·0	·792285668997	·256488941728	·0741166321596
5·2	1·07068675643	·357956089960	·106958821921
5·4	1·43713021810	·495379239735	·152813670643
5·6	1·91710069457	·680308520630	·216329392995
5·8	2·54297113760	·927710973612	·303668787505
6·0	3·35577484714	1·25691804811	·422966068203

x	$I_9(x)$	$I_{10}(x)$	$I_{11}(x)$
0·0	Nil	Nil	Nil
0·2	$\cdot 0^{14}275848890728$	$\cdot 0^{16}275823817735$	$\cdot 0^{18}25072993174$
0·4	$\cdot 0^{11}141658875600$	$\cdot 0^{13}283214795193$	$\cdot 0^{15}514780037287$
0·6	$\cdot 0^{10}547312431307$	$\cdot 0^{11}164059590224$	$\cdot 0^{13}447130560011$
0·8	$\cdot 0^{9}734041402172$	$\cdot 0^{10}293190617555$	$\cdot 0^{11}106485828421$
1·0	$\cdot 0^{8}551838586274$	$\cdot 0^{9}275294803983$	$\cdot 0^{10}124897830849$
1·2	$\cdot 0^{7}287877246335$	$\cdot 0^{8}172164429560$	$\cdot 0^{10}9365304020$
1·4	$\cdot 0^{6}116775736690$	$\cdot 0^{8}813818331745$	$\cdot 0^{9}51597501248$
1·6	$\cdot 0^{6}394240656000$	$\cdot 0^{7}313576845153$	$\cdot 0^{8}22695995590$
1·8	$\cdot 0^{5}115736151949$	$\cdot 0^{6}103405714922$	$\cdot 0^{8}84091314720$
2·0	$\cdot 0^{5}304418590271$	$\cdot 0^{6}301696387935$	$\cdot 0^{7}272220233597$
2·2	$\cdot 0^{5}732884540826$	$\cdot 0^{6}797479795484$	$\cdot 0^{7}79029085679$
2·4	$\cdot 0^{4}164060359505$	$\cdot 0^{5}194355352977$	$\cdot 0^{6}20975653574$
2·6	$\cdot 0^{4}345596570386$	$\cdot 0^{5}442561241924$	$\cdot 0^{6}51648458289$
2·8	$\cdot 0^{4}691462615510$	$\cdot 0^{5}951341501153$	$\cdot 0^{5}11932971830$
3·0	$\cdot 0^{3}132372988831$	$\cdot 0^{4}194643934705$	$\cdot 0^{5}26103656940$
3·2	$\cdot 0^{3}243914684482$	$\cdot 0^{4}381550080109$	$\cdot 0^{5}544588441373$
3·4	$\cdot 0^{3}434700765661$	$\cdot 0^{4}720461248306$	$\cdot 0^{4}109000313633$
3·6	$\cdot 0^{3}752315248879$	$\cdot 0^{3}131630693989$	$\cdot 0^{4}210336156069$
3·8	$\cdot 0^{2}126860112417$	$\cdot 0^{3}233568560836$	$\cdot 0^{4}39292909243$
4·0	$\cdot 0^{2}209025303452$	$\cdot 0^{3}403788961327$	$\cdot 0^{4}713082278832$
4·2	$\cdot 0^{2}337343287863$	$\cdot 0^{3}681942087915$	$\cdot 0^{3}126089602839$
4·4	$\cdot 0^{2}534376788633$	$\cdot 0^{2}112771477116$	$\cdot 0^{3}217791653765$
4·6	$\cdot 0^{2}832351074598$	$\cdot 0^{2}182970173372$	$\cdot 0^{3}36828581676$
4·8	·0127681829170	$\cdot 0^{2}291775581322$	$\cdot 0^{3}61086702855$
5·0	·0193157188168	$\cdot 0^{2}458004441917$	$\cdot 0^{3}995541140110$
5·2	·0288520225117	$\cdot 0^{2}708643630312$	$\cdot 0^{2}159649826893$
5·4	·0425979933861	·0108203593556	$\cdot 0^{2}252258836536$
5·6	·0622245406441	·0163219409248	$\cdot 0^{2}393189448412$
5·8	·0900039735967	·0243461108260	$\cdot 0^{2}605186730033$
6·0	·129008532906	·0359404694846	$\cdot 0^{2}920696795753$

x	$K_0(x)$	$K_1(x)$	x
0·1	2·4270690 2470201 6612519	9·8538447 8087060 6134849	0·1
0·2	1·7527038 5552814 5906617	4·7759725 4322047 2248750	0·2
0·3	1·3724600 6054429 7376645	3·0559920 3345732 4978851	0·3
0·4	1·1145291 3452443 4406170	2·1843544 2473268 7379723	0·4
0·5	0·9244190 7122766 5861782	1·6564411 2000330 0893696	0·5
0·6	0·7775220 9190472 9289468	1·3028349 3976350 2176671	0·6
0·7	0·6605198 5991510 1548740	1·0502835 3531291 7951430	0·7
0·8	0·5653471 0526589 5668369	0·8617816 3447218 0346690	0·8
0·9	0·4867303 0816290 0521582	0·7165335 7877601 9074786	0·9
1·0	0·4210244 3824070 8333336	0·6019072 3019723 4574738	1·0
1·1	0·3656023 9154318 5880566	0·5097600 2716702 7048822	1·1
1·2	0·3185082 2028659 3615118	0·4345923 9106071 5038502	1·2
1·3	0·2782476 4630002 6999011	0·3725474 9563196 2166173	1·3
1·4	0·2436550 6118154 1893927	0·3208359 0222987 5750946	1·4
1·5	0·2138055 6264752 5736722	0·2773878 0045684 3816085	1·5
1·6	0·1879547 5196933 2325059	0·2406339 1135761 1855164	1·6
1·7	0·1654963 1805699 6539364	0·2093624 8820408 2474675	1·7
1·8	0·1459314 0048982 7981234	0·1826230 9980174 6979604	1·8
1·9	0·1288459 7927604 7479856	0·1596601 5303266 7610382	1·9
2·0	0·1138938 7274953 3435653	0·1398658 8181652 2427285	2·0
2·1	0·1007837 4088996 6945812	0·1227464 1153350 7910608	2·1
2·2	0·0892690 0567160 1745130	0·1078968 1011908 7275030	2·2
2·3	0·0791399 3300209 3626828	0·0949824 4384536 2636833	2·3
2·4	0·0702173 4154341 5895531	0·0837248 3875483 2182453	2·4
2·5	0·0623475 5320036 6186029	0·0738908 1634774 7063649	2·5
2·6	0·0553983 0328632 1951484	0·0652840 4505853 1495000	2·6
2·7	0·0492554 0091581 7592455	0·0577383 9895652 5947419	2·7
2·8	0·0438199 8197549 8528903	0·0511126 8560727 2438995	2·8
2·9	0·0390062 3456622 3424101	0·0452864 2329836 1443561	2·9
3·0	0·0347395 0438627 9248072	0·0401564 3112819 4184377	3·0
3·1	0·0309547 0803804 1442502	0·0356340 5494961 7493670	3·1
3·2	0·0275949 9767510 0610315	0·0316428 9521139 8770897	3·2
3·3	0·0246106 3214583 9314335	0·0281169 3427271 6612255	3·3
3·4	0·0219580 1880680 8280394	0·0249989 8412318 6272784	3·4
3·5	0·0195988 9717036 8489108	0·0222393 9292592 3833739	3·5
3·6	0·0174996 4101814 6603343	0·0197949 6201972 0617134	3·6
3·7	0·0156306 5992162 6661612	0·0176280 3510222 3266688	3·7
3·8	0·0139658 8453424 5617659	0·0157057 2907847 3492808	3·8
3·9	0·0124823 2275724 9775684	0·0139992 8208227 4828044	3·9
4·0	0·0111596 7608585 3024270	0·0124834 9888726 8431470	4·0

x	$K_0(x)$	$K_1(x)$	x
4·1	0·0099800 0722784 0242646	0·0111362 7763347 9931554	4·1
4·2	0·0089274 5154154 2371598	0·0099382 0473591 7087547	4·2
4·3	0·0079879 6603176 4522372	0·0088722 0718859 1397612	4·3
4·4	0·0071491 1062330 7253932	0·0079232 5336144 5598749	4·4
4·5	0·0063998 5724323 3975046	0·0070780 9490896 8089693	4·5
4·6	0·0057304 2291729 2834887	0·0063250 4364426 4015020	4·6
4·7	0·0051321 2364845 4615086	0·0056537 7824003 0826704	4·7
4·8	0·0045972 4631672 4657899	0·0050551 7644405 6299816	4·8
4·9	0·0041189 3623551 5888790	0·0045211 6917729 9838509	4·9
5·0	0·0036910 9833404 2594275	0·0040446 1344545 2164208	5·0
5·1	0·0033083 1021801 7464327	0·0036191 8146231 7798328	5·1
5·2	0·0029657 4560102 9581462	0·0032392 6377308 9456376	5·2
5·3	0·0026591 0680338 9557342	0·0028998 8449169 0688906	5·3
5·4	0·0023845 6518972 4900197	0·0025966 2704017 7797776	5·4
5·5	0·0021387 0856595 0287432	0·0023255 6900884 9005155	5·5
5·6	0·0019184 9468435 6577228	0·0020832 2495060 9789166	5·6
5·7	0·0017212 1011572 3315288	0·0018664 9608831 1830924	5·7
5·8	0·0015444 3384228 1102204	0·0016726 2605414 1651512	5·8
5·9	0·0013860 0500730 4947106	0·0014991 6189972 2485306	5·9
6·0	0·0012439 9432801 3123085	0·0013439 1971773 5509006	6·0
7·0	0·0004247 9574186 9231	0·0004541 8248688 4898	7·0
8·0	0·0001464 7070522 2804	0·0001553 6921180 4984	8·0
9·0	0·0000508 8131295 6458	0·0000536 3701637 9453	9·0
10·0	0·0000177 8006231 6066	0·0000186 4877345 3874	10·0
11·0	0·0000062 4302054 7653	0·0000065 2086067 4582	11·0

x	$K_0(x)$	$K_1(x)$	x	x	$K_0(x)$	$K_1(x)$	x
6·1	0·001116 6787	0·001204 9543	6·1	9·1	0·000045 791979 331	0·000048 245426 023	9·1
6·2	0·001002 5189	0·001080 5324	6·2	9·2	0·000041 214069 631	0·000043 398790 454	9·2
6·3	0·000900 1392	0·000969 1088	6·3	9·3	0·000037 095910 423	0·000039 041668 525	9·3
6·4	0·000808 3099	0·000869 3058	6·4	9·4	0·000033 391083 017	0·000035 124303 368	9·4
6·5	0·000725 9318	0·000779 8944	6·5	9·5	0·000030 057884 958	0·000031 602034 110	9·5
6·6	0·000652 02137	0·000699 77768	6·6	9·6	0·000027 058847 266	0·000028 434769 224	9·6
6·7	0·000585 69916	0·000627 97668	6·7	9·7	0·000024 360301 507	0·000025 586514 844	9·7
6·8	0·000526 17809	0·000563 61716	6·8	9·8	0·000021 931991 556	0·000023 024952 359	9·8
6·9	0·000472 75379	0·000505 91831	6·9	9·9	0·000019 746725 314	0·000020 721059 930	9·9
7·0	0·000424 79574	0·000454 18249	7·0	10·0	0·000017 780062 316	0·000018 648773 4539	10·0
7·1	0·000381 739385	0·000407 786222	7·1	10·1	0·000016 010033 412	0·000016 784682 675	10·1
7·2	0·000343 079156	0·000366 172174	7·2	10·2	0·000014 416889 253	0·000015 107758 866	10·2
7·3	0·000308 362213	0·000328 841997	7·3	10·3	0·000012 982874 576	0·000013 599110 702	10·3
7·4	0·000277 182870	0·000295 349978	7·4	10·4	0·000011 692025 596	0·000012 241765 367	10·4
7·5	0·000249 177617	0·000265 297390	7·5	10·5	0·000010 529988 143	0·000011 020472 310	10·5
7·6	0·000224 020678	0·000238 327458	7·6	10·6	0·000009 483854 408	0·000009 921527 234	10·6
7·7	0·000201 420050	0·000214 120873	7·7	10·7	0·000008 542016 3447	0·000008 932614 226	10·7
7·8	0·000181 113953	0·000192 391797	7·8	10·8	0·000007 694034 0412	0·000008 042664 1317	10·8
7·9	0·000162 867668	0·000172 884307	7·9	10·9	0·000006 930517 5175	0·000007 241727 5238	10·9
8·0	0·000146 470705 2	0·000155 369211 8	8·0	11·0	0·000006 243020 5476	0·000006 520860 6746	11·0
8·1	0·000131 734278 6	0·000139 641228 9	8·1	11·1	0·000005 623945 3026	0·000005 872023 2610	11·1
8·2	0·000118 489040 5	0·000125 516451 2	8·2	11·2	0·000005 066456 6819	0·000005 287986 5395	11·2
8·3	0·000106 583060 1	0·000112 830094 0	8·3	11·3	0·000004 564405 3501	0·000004 762250 9296	11·3
8·4	0·000095 880013 8	0·000101 434481 3	8·4	11·4	0·000004 112258 5922	0·000004 288972 0217	11·4
8·5	0·000086 257566 3	0·000091 197247 7	8·5	11·5	0·000003 705038 1654	0·000003 862894 1453	11·5
8·6	0·000077 605920 7	0·000081 999731 8	8·6	11·6	0·000003 338264 4751	0·000003 479290 7324	11·6
8·7	0·000069 826521 36	0·000073 735540 60	8·7	11·7	0·000003 007906 3800	0·000003 133910 7412	11·7
8·8	0·000062 830892 86	0·000066 309267 33	8·8	11·8	0·000002 710336 0930	0·000002 822930 5593	11·8
8·9	0·000056 539599 34	0·000059 635344 08	8·9	11·9	0·000002 442288 6370	0·000002 542910 7952	11·9
9·0	0·000050 881312 956	0·000053 637016 382	9·0	12·0	0·000002 200825 397302	0·000002 290757 464767	12·0

x	$K_2(x)$	$K_3(x)$	$K_4(x)$	$K_5(x)$	$K_6(x)$	$K_7(x)$	$K_8(x)$	$K_9(x)$	$K_{10}(x)$	x
·2	49·512	995·02	29900·	11970×10^2	59880×10^3	35940×10^5	25164×10^7	20135×10^9	18124×10^{11}	·2
·4	12·036	122·55	1850·2	37127·0	93003×10	27938×10^3	97876×10^4	39178×10^6	17640×10^8	·4
·6	5·1203	35·438	359·50	4828·8	80839·0	16216×10^2	37918×10^3	10128×10^5	30422×10^6	·6
·8	2·7198	14·461	111·17	1126·2	14189·0	21396×10	37585×10^2	75383×10^3	16999×10^5	·8
1·0	1·6248	7·10126	44·232	360·96	3653·8	44207·0	62255×10	10005×10^3	18071×10^4	1·0
1·2	1·0428	3·9106	20·596	141·22	1197·4	12115·0	14254×10	19126×10^2	28832×10^3	1·2
1·4	·70199	2·3265	10·673	63·314	462·92	4031·2	40775·0	47002×10	60839×10^2	1·4
1·6	·48874	1·4625	5·9731	31·328	201·77	1544·6	13717·0	13872×10	15743×10^2	1·6
1·8	·34884	·95783	3·5416	16·698	96·310	658·77	5220·0	47059·0	47581×10	1·8
2·0	·25376	·64738	2·1959	9·4310	49·351	305·54	2188·1	17810·0	16248×10	2·0
2·2	·18736	·44854	1·4106	5·5782	26·766	151·57	991·33	7361·2	61219·0	2·2
2·4	·13999	·31704	·93258	3·4256	15·206	79·456	478·70	3270·8	25009·0	2·4
2·6	·10562	·22777	·63124	2·1700	8·9775	43·605	243·77	1543·7	10931·0	2·6
2·8	·080328	·16587	·43575	1·4108	5·4742	24·872	129·83	766·78	5059·1	2·8
3·0	·061510	·12217	·30585	·93776	3·4317	14·664	71·866	397·95	2459·5	3·0
3·2	·047371	·090856	·21773	·63517	2·2026	8·8950	41·118	214·49	1247·6	3·2
3·4	·036663	·068131	·15689	·43729	1·4430	5·5302	24·214	119·48	656·75	3·4
3·6	·028496	·051456	·11425	·30536	·96246	3·5135	14·626	68·519	357·22	3·6
3·8	·022232	·039107	·083980	·21591	·65215	2·2753	9·0350	40·317	200·01	3·8
4·0	·017401	·029884	·062227	·15434	·44807	1·4985	5·6930	24·271	114·91	4·0
4·2	·013659	·022947	·046440	·11140	·31169	1·0019	3·6515	14·912	67·561	4·2
4·4	·010750	·017696	·034881	·081116	·21923	·67903	2·3798	9·3127	40·477	4·4
4·6	·0084800	·013699	·026348	·059521	·15574	·46580	1·5734	5·9385	24·811	4·6
4·8	·0067030	·010641	·020004	·043981	·11163	·32306	1·0539	3·8360	15·439	4·8
5·0	·0053090	·0082910	·015258	·032704	·080666	·22630	·71409	2·5114	9·7550	5·0

The first two positive zeros ρ_1 and ρ_2 of $J_n(x)$ when n is small.

n	ρ_1	ρ_2	n	ρ_1	ρ_2
$-\frac{1}{2}$	1·5708	4·7124	$\frac{1}{4}$	2·7809	5·9061
$-\frac{19}{40}$	1·6167	4·7541	$\frac{11}{40}$	2·8175	5·9442
$-\frac{9}{20}$	1·6620	4·7958	$\frac{3}{10}$	2·8541	5·9822
$-\frac{17}{40}$	1·7068	4·8372	$\frac{13}{40}$	2·8905	6·0201
$-\frac{2}{5}$	1·7509	4·8785	$\frac{7}{20}$	2·9267	6·0579
$-\frac{3}{8}$	1·7946	4·9196	$\frac{3}{8}$	2·9628	6·0957
$-\frac{7}{20}$	1·8378	4·9606	$\frac{2}{5}$	2·9988	6·1333
$-\frac{13}{40}$	1·8805	5·0014	$\frac{17}{40}$	3·0347	6·1709
$-\frac{3}{10}$	1·9228	5·0421	$\frac{9}{20}$	3·0704	6·2084
$-\frac{11}{40}$	1·9647	5·0826	$\frac{19}{40}$	3·1061	6·2458
$-\frac{1}{4}$	2·0063	5·1230	$\frac{1}{2}$	3·1416	6·2832
$-\frac{9}{40}$	2·0475	5·1633	$\frac{21}{40}$	3·1770	6·3204
$-\frac{1}{5}$	2·0883	5·2034	$\frac{11}{20}$	3·2123	6·3576
$-\frac{7}{40}$	2·1288	5·2434	$\frac{23}{40}$	3·2474	6·3947
$-\frac{3}{20}$	2·1690	5·2833	$\frac{3}{5}$	3·2825	6·4318
$-\frac{1}{8}$	2·2090	5·3231	$\frac{5}{8}$	3·3175	6·4688
$-\frac{1}{10}$	2·2486	5·3627	$\frac{13}{20}$	3·3524	6·5057
$-\frac{3}{40}$	2·2880	5·4022	$\frac{27}{40}$	3·3872	6·5425
$-\frac{1}{20}$	2·3272	5·4416	$\frac{7}{10}$	3·4219	6·5793
$-\frac{1}{40}$	2·3661	5·4809	$\frac{29}{40}$	3·4565	6·6160
0	2·4048	5·5200	$\frac{3}{4}$	3·4910	6·6526
$\frac{1}{40}$	2·4433	5·5591	$\frac{31}{40}$	3·5254	6·6892
$\frac{1}{20}$	2·4815	5·5981	$\frac{4}{5}$	3·5597	6·7257
$\frac{3}{40}$	2·5196	5·6369	$\frac{33}{40}$	3·5940	6·7621
$\frac{1}{10}$	2·5574	5·6757	$\frac{17}{20}$	3·6282	6·7985
$\frac{1}{8}$	2·5951	5·7143	$\frac{7}{8}$	3·6623	6·8348
$\frac{3}{20}$	2·6326	5·7529	$\frac{9}{10}$	3·6963	6·8711
$\frac{7}{40}$	2·6699	5·7913	$\frac{37}{40}$	3·7302	6·9073
$\frac{1}{5}$	2·7070	5·8297	$\frac{19}{20}$	3·7641	6·9435
$\frac{9}{40}$	2·7440	5·8679	$\frac{39}{40}$	3·7979	6·9795
$-\frac{1}{3}$	1·8663		$\frac{1}{6}$	2·6575	
$-\frac{1}{6}$	2·1423		$\frac{1}{3}$	2·9026	

BIBLIOGRAPHY.

(Other references will be found in the text.)

I. TREATISES.

RIEMANN. Partielle Differentialgleichungen.

NEUMANN (C.). Theorie der Bessel'schen Functionen.

,, Ueber die nach Kreis-, Kugel-, und Cylinderfunctionen fortschreitenden Entwickelungen.

LOMMEL (E.). Studien über die Bessel'schen Functionen.

HEINE (E.). Handbuch der Kugelfunctionen.

TODHUNTER (I.). Treatise on Laplace's, Lamé's, and Bessel's Functions.

BYERLEY. Treatise on Fourier Series and Spherical, Cylindrical, and Ellipsoidal Harmonics.

FOURIER. Théorie Analytique de la Chaleur.

RAYLEIGH. Theory of Sound.

BASSET. Treatise on Hydrodynamics, Vol. II.

NIELSEN (N.). Handbuch der Theorie der Cylinder Funktionen.

GRAF UND GUBLER. Einleitung in die Theorie der Besselschen Funktionen.

SCHAFHEITLIN (P.). Die Theorie der Besselschen Funktionen.

WHITTAKER AND WATSON. Modern Analysis.

JAHNKE UND EMDE. Funktionentafeln mit Formeln und Kurven.

JORDAN. Cours d'Analyse, Vol. III.

LAMB. Hydrodynamics.

LOVE. The Mathematical Theory of Elasticity.

GRAY (A.). Absolute Measurements in Electricity and Magnetism.

RUSSELL (A.). Alternating Currents, Vol. I.

MACDONALD (H. M.). Electric Waves.

BATEMAN (H.). Electrical and Optical Wave-Motion.

CARSLAW. Fourier's Series and Integrals.

SCHOTT (G. A.). Electromagnetic Radiation.

II. MEMOIRS.

BERNOULLI (Dan.). Theoremata de oscillationibus corporum filo flexili connexorum, etc. (Comm. Ac. Petrop. VI. 108.)

BERNOULLI (Dan.). Demonstratio theorematum, etc. (ibid. VII. 162).

EULER. (Ibid. VII. 99 and Acta Acad. Petrop. V. pt. I. pp. 157, 178.)

POISSON. Sur la distribution de la Chaleur dans les corps solides (Journ. de l'École Polyt. cap. 19).

BESSEL. Untersuchung des Theils der planetarischen Störungen, etc. (Berlin Abh. 1824).

JACOBI. Formula transformationis integralium definitorum, etc. (Crelle XV. 13).

HANSEN. Ermittelung der absoluten Störungen in Ellipsen, etc. pt. I. (Schriften der Sternwarte Seeburg (Gotha, 1843)).

HAMILTON (W. R.). On Fluctuating Functions (Irish Acad. Trans. XIX. (1843), p. 264).

HARGREAVES. On a general method of Integration, etc. (Phil. Trans. 1848).

ANGER. Untersuchungen über die Function I_k^h, etc. (Danzig, 1855).

SCHLÖMILCH. Ueber die Bessel'sche Function (Zeitsch. d. Math. u. Phys. II. 137).

RIEMANN. Ueber die Nobili'schen Farbenringe (Pogg. Ann. XCV.).

LIPSCHITZ. Ueber die Bessel'sche Transcendente I. (Crelle LVI.).

WEBER (H.). Ueber einige bestimmte Integrale (Crelle LXIX.).

" Ueber die Bessel'schen Functionen u. ihre Anwendung, etc. (ibid. LXXV.).

" Ueber eine Darstellung willkürlicher Functionen durch Bessel'sche Functionen (Math. Ann. VI.).

" Ueber die stationären Strömungen der Elektricität in Cylindern (Crelle LXXVI.).

HEINE (E.). Die Fourier-Bessel'sche Function (Crelle LXIX.).

HANKEL (H.). Die Cylinderfunctionen erster u. zweiter Art (Math. Ann. I.).

" Bestimmte Integrale mit Cylinderfunctionen (ibid. VIII.).

" Die Fourier'schen Reihen u. Integrale für Cylinderfunctionen (ibid. VIII.).

NEUMANN (C.). Entwickelung einer Function nach Quadraten u. Produkten der Fourier-Bessel'schen Functionen (Leipzig Ber. 1869).

LOMMEL. Integration der Gleichung

$$x^{m+\frac{1}{2}}\frac{d^{2m+1}y}{dx^{2m+1}}\mp y=0$$

durch Bessel'sche Functionen (Math. Ann. II.).

" Zur Theorie der Bessel'schen Functionen (ibid. III., IV.).

LOMMEL. Ueber eine mit den Bessel'schen Functionen verwandet Function (ibid. IX.).
,, Zur Theorie der Bessel'schen Functionen (ibid. XIV., XVI.).
,, Ueber die Anwendung der Bessel'schen Functionen in der Theorie der Beugung (Zeitsch. d. Math. u. Phys. XV.).
,, Die Beugungserscheinungen einer kreisrunden Oeffnung, etc. Abh. d. k. Bayer. Akad. d. Wissensch. XV. 1866.
,, Die Beugungserscheinungen geradliniger begrenzter Schirme (ibid.).

SCHLÄFLI. Einige Bemerkungen zu Herrn Neumann's Untersuchungen über die Bessel'schen Functionen (Math. Ann. III.).
,, Ueber die Convergenz der Entwickelung einer arbiträren Function zweier Variabeln nach den Bessel'schen Functionen, etc. (Math. Ann. X.).
,, Sopra un Teorema di Jacobi, etc. (Brioschi Ann. (2) V.).
,, Sull' uso delle linee lungo le quali il valore assoluto di una funzione è costante (Ann. di Mat. (2) VI.).

DU BOIS-REYMOND (P.). Die Fourier'schen Integrale u. Formeln (Math. Ann. IV.).

MEHLER. Ueber die Darstellung einer willkürlichen Function zweier Variabeln durch Cylinderfunctionen (Math. Ann. V.).
,, Notiz über die Functionen $P_n(\cos\theta)$ und $J(x)$ (ibid.).

SONINE (N.). Recherches sur les fonctions cylindriques, etc. (Math. Ann. XVI.).

GEGENBAUER (L.). Various papers in the Wiener Berichte, Vols. LXV., LXVI., LXIX., LXXII., LXXIV., XCV.

STRUTT [Lord Rayleigh]. Notes on Bessel Functions (Phil. Mag. 1872).

RAYLEIGH. On the relation between the functions of Laplace and Bessel (Proc. L. M. S. IX.).
,, The Problem of the Whispering Gallery (Phil. Mag. Ser. 6, XX. 1910).

POCHHAMMER. Ueber die Fortpflanzungsgeschwindigkeit kleiner Schwingungen, etc. (Crelle LXXXI.).

GLAISHER (J. W. L.). On Riccati's Equation (Phil. Trans. 1881).

GREENHILL. On Riccati's Equation and Bessel's Equation (Quart. Journ. of Math. XVI.).
,, On Height consistent with Stability (Camb. Phil. Soc. Proc. IV. 1881).
,, The Bessel-Clifford Function, and its Applications (Phil. Mag. Ser. 6, XXXVIII.).
,, The Fourier and Bessel Function Contrasted (Comp. rend. du Congrès Internat., Strasburg, 1920).

BRYAN. Stability of a Plane Plate, etc. (Proc. L. M. S. XXII.).

CHREE. The Equations of an Isotropic Elastic Solid in Polar and Cylindrical Coordinates (Proc. Camb. Phil. Soc. XIV. p. 250).

HOBSON. Systems of Spherical Harmonics (Proc. L. M. S. XXII. p. 431).

,, On Bessel's Functions, and relations connecting them with Hyperspherical and Spherical Harmonics (ibid. XXV. p. 49).

,, On the Representation of a Function by Series of Bessel Functions (ibid. Ser. 2, VII.).

THOMSON (J. J.). Electrical Oscillations in Cylindrical Conductors (Proc. L. M. S. XVII. p. 310).

MCMAHON (J.). On the Roots of the Bessel and Certain Related Functions (Annals of Math., Jan. 1895).

MACDONALD (H. M.). Zeroes of the Bessel Functions (Proc. L. M. S. XXIX.).

,, ,, Note on Bessel Functions (ibid. XXIX.).

,, ,, On the Addition-Theorem for the Bessel Functions (ibid. XXXII.).

,, ,, On Some Applications of Fourier's Theorem (ibid. XXXV.).

,, ,, Note on the Evaluation of a Certain Integral Containing Bessel's Functions (ibid. Ser. 2, VII.).

YOUNG (W. H.). On Series of Bessel Functions (Proc. L. M. S. Ser. 2, XVIII.).

WHITTAKER. On a New Connexion of Bessel Functions with Legendre Functions (Proc. L. M. S. XXXV.).

DOUGALL (J.). The Determination of Green's Function by means of Cylindrical or Spherical Harmonics (Proc. E. M. S. XVIII.).

,, A Theorem of Sonine in Bessel Functions, with two Extensions to Spherical Harmonics (ibid. XXXVII.).

,, An Analytical Theory of the Equilibrium of an Isotropic Elastic Plate (Trans. Roy. Soc. Edin. XLI.).

,, An Analytical Theory of the Equilibrium of an Isotropic Elastic Rod of Circular Section (ibid. XLIX.).

,, The Method of Permanent and Transitory Modes of Equilibrium in the Theory of Thin Elastic Bodies (Fifth Internat. Cong. of Math., Camb. 1912).

GIBSON (G. A.). A Proof of the Binomial Theorem, with Some Applications (Proc. E. M. S. XXXVIII.).

MACROBERT (T. M.). The Modified Bessel Function $K_n(z)$ (Proc. E. M. S. XXXVIII.).

MacRobert (T. M.). Asymptotic Expressions for the Bessel Functions, and the Fourier-Bessel Expansions (ibid. xxxix.).

Gray (A.). Notes on Electric and Magnetic Field Constants (Phil. Mag. Ser. 6, xxxviii.).

Green (G.). On Ship-Waves, and on Waves in Deep Water due to the Motion of Submerged Bodies (Phil. Mag. xxxvi. 1918).

Forsyth (A. R.). The Expression of Bessel Functions of Positive Order as Products, and of their Inverse Powers as Sums of Rational Functions (Mess. of Math. Vol. i. 1921).

Nagaoka (H.). On the Potential and Lines of Force of a Circular Current (Phil. Mag. Ser. 6, vi. 1903).

Watson (G. N.). Bessel Functions and Kapteyn Series (Proc. L. M. S. Ser. 2, xvi. 1917).

" " The Zeros of Bessel Functions (Proc. R. S., A. xciv. 1918).

Bôcher (M.). On Certain Methods of Sturm and their Applications to the Roots of Bessel Functions (Bull. Amer. Math. Soc. 2nd Ser. iii.).

Hardy (G. H.). Some Multiple Integrals (Q. J. M. xxxix.).

Nicholson (J. W.). Notes on Bessel Functions (Q. J. M. xlii.).

Sommerfeld. Mathematische Theorie der Diffraction (Math. Ann. xlvii.).

Carson (J. R.). Wave Propagation over Parallel Wires: The Proximity Effect (Phil. Mag. xli. 1921).

Airey (J. R.). The Lommel-Weber Function and its Application to Electric Waves on an Anchor Ring (Proc. R. S., A. xciv. 1918).

Bateman (H.). Some Equations of Mixed Differences occurring in the Theory of Probability and the Related Expansions in Series of Bessel's Functions.

See also the references on pages 264, 265, 266.

An extensive bibliography of the literature of the Bessel functions is given by Nielsen in his Handbuch, pages 389-404.

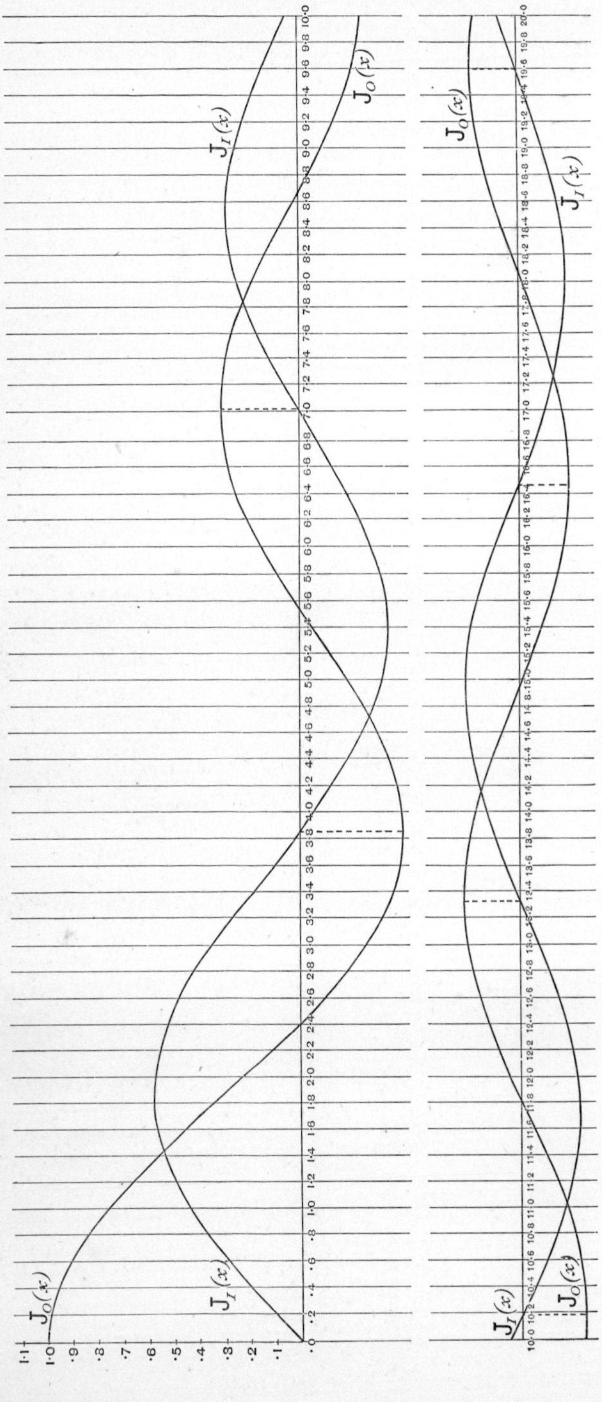

FIG. 14.

GRAPH OF $J_0(x)$ AND $J_1(x)$.

The abscissae represent arguments and the ordinates values of the functions on the scales indicated by the numbers on the graph.

INDEX

The numbers refer to the pages.

PRINTED IN GREAT BRITAIN BY ROBERT MACLEHOSE AND CO. LTD.
THE UNIVERSITY PRESS, GLASGOW.